TWO CENTURIES OF VALOR

THE STORY OF THE 5TH INFANTRY REGIMENT

SAMUEL MARTIN KIER

PARK PLACE PUBLICATIONS
PACIFIC GROVE, CALIFORNIA

TWO CENTURIES OF VALOR
The Story of the 5th Infantry Regiment

Samuel Martin Kier

© 2010 Samuel Martin Kier

ISBN 978-1-935530-15-2

Library of Congress Control Number: 2010927938

Printed in the U.S.A.

First Edition
July 2010
Revised Edition
September 2015

All rights reserved. No part of this book may be reproduced
by any means whatsoever without written permission from the author,
except brief portions quoted for purpose of review.

Published by
Park Place Publications
P.O. Box 722
Pacific Grove, CA 93950
www.parkplacepublications.com

Available on Amazon, Barnes & Nobel, and other on-line retailers

Contents

Preface and Acknowledgements vii
Introduction ix
Maps xi
Photos xxvii

One	WAR OF 1812	3
Two	TAMING THE NORTHWEST	22
Three	WAR WITH MEXICO	34
Four	RETURN TO THE FRONTIER	53
Five	CIVIL WAR IN NEW MEXICO	62
Six	THE RED RIVER WAR	72
Seven	FORT KEOGH, MONTANA	83
Eight	CUBAN OCCUPATION AND PHILIPPINE INSURRECTION	116
Nine	WORLD WAR I AND THE GREAT DEPRESSION	130
Ten	WITH THE 71ST DIVISION IN WORLD WAR II	140
Eleven	KOREA: THE FLUID WAR	177
Twelve	KOREA: THE BATTLE FOR THE RIDGES	244
Thirteen	THE COLD WAR	302
Fourteen	VIETNAM	314
Fifteen	GUARDIAN OF THE PACIFIC	377
Sixteen	GLOBAL WAR ON TERRORISM	398

Appendices 444
Notes 464
Selected Bibliography 482
Index of Persons 486
Index of Subjects 497
Index of Military Units 510

PREFACE AND ACKNOWLEDGEMENTS

I reported to Service Company of the 5th Infantry Regiment at North Ft. Lewis, Washington on a drizzly Saturday in 1954 with three dozen other draftees. We had just completed basic and advanced individual training at the "soldier factory" at Fort Ord, California. As we formed a line outside the company orderly room, we wondered if that moist part of the world and those coal smoke-stained World War I-era barracks were going to be our home for the next eighteen months and, if so, how we would spend our time until we had satisfied the active duty requirement of the Manpower Training Act of 1951 and could once again be civilians.

We wouldn't know our assignments until the Personnel Office opened on Monday morning but some enterprising clerk had already tagged some of us for guard duty that evening and KP at the company mess hall on Sunday. The 5th Regimental Combat Team had returned from Korea the previous week and the enlisted ranks were thin. They were glad to see us.

After a short stint typing purchase orders at the motor pool, I had the good fortune to be assigned to the Troop Information and Education Office, part of the Regimental S-3 Section. One of my first tasks was to up-date the regimental history in preparation for the 147th anniversary of the 5th Infantry's inception.

Due to a period of inactivity in the late 1940's and a period of frenzied activity from 1950-1953, the document had not been amended for ten years. I scanned the few available after-action reports and monthly command reports and promptly knocked out a two-page summary of the 5th Regimental Combat Team's service during the Korean War. The job was completed just in time for the April 12, 1955 Organization Day ceremony.

Years later I obtained a copy of the regimental history from the U. S. Army History Institute at Carlisle Barracks and noted, with chagrin, the sketchy tale of the 5th Infantry's Korean War service written by a 22-year-old at Ft. Lewis in 1955. It was little more than a sterile outline. There was no description of the chaos at Bloody Gulch and Death Valley, the tough fighting to secure Waegwan, the hardy little band of Able Company riflemen and Dog Company gunners that defeated a Chinese regiment at Outpost Harry, nor any of the other remarkable moments that added to the record of the 5th Regimental Combat Team, the unit that drew more than its share of dirty jobs in Korea.

So, some may ask, is Two Centuries of Valor nothing more than the author's atonement for a lackadaisical effort made fifty-four years ago? I hope that it is much more than that. Both veterans and active duty members of the 5th Infantry Regiment can use this story of men long gone and men who are currently serving their country to gauge their own contributions to the proud record of the regiment. Knowledge of the regimental history can also contribute to unit pride and engender a connection between the generations. Both the 5th Infantry Regiment Association and the Fifth RCT Association have been tremendously supportive of the young active-duty 5th Infantry "Bobcats" and their families. At a recent reunion at Schofield Barracks, 5th Infantry veterans were reminded to thank the young active-duty soldiers for serving their country and, invariably, the young men beat their elders to the punch, thanking them for paving the way and passing on a proud tradition.

It is expected that there will be varied reactions to this book from living veterans who served with the 5th Infantry. They will range from "You spent more time on that guy's battle than mine" to "That's not the way it happened." Historical research is not an exact science. This book is a composite of the information that was available to me. The U.S. Army has done a better job of maintaining war time records than peace time documents. The chapters devoted to the Cold War era and the post-Vietnam period were based largely upon anecdotal

PREFACE AND ACKNOWLEDGEMENTS

information from men who served during those years. Furthermore, they represent the unique perspectives of men who were willing to respond to my questions. Many others, who were contacted, did not reply to my e-mail and letters.

I am especially grateful to those individuals who helped me fill in the blanks for that relatively peaceful thirty-year period between the Vietnam War and our military incursions into Afghanistan and Iraq. Harrison Sarles, Director of Army Public Affairs in New York City, introduced me to important contacts throughout the Western Hemisphere. Two former commanders of Company C, LTC RET Alexander Von Plinsky, Columbia, South Carolina, and COL Dan Baggio, Public Affairs Officer at Fort McNair, Virginia, shared much information about the 1980's at Schofield Barracks and the 1990's in Korea. In each case, they patched me through to other former members of 1st Battalion. Adam Elia, 25th ID Historian, Schofield Barracks and COL RET William Alexander and SGT Gary Johnson of the 2nd ID Museum near Uijongbu, Korea were of tremendous help. Throughout the project, Vietnam veteran and editor of the Bobcat Bulletin, Fred Deverse was a constant source of encouragement and information. A special thank you to all of these men and to the many others who responded to my queries.

Earlier this month, the 1st Battalion, 5th Infantry Regiment returned from its second tour of combat in a frustrating war that has lasted for six years and offers no quick, and perhaps, no really satisfactory resolution. But, as members of the highly respected, third oldest regiment in the United States Army, they distinguished themselves as did their predecessors from Cook's Mills, Canada to Ben Cui, Vietnam. This is their heritage. This is their story.

I'll try, sir.
Sam Kier
Pacific Grove, CA
September 27, 2009

INTRODUCTION

At the close of the Revolutionary War, Congress disbanded the Continental Army and approved the formation of one 700-man unit, the United States Infantry Regiment. It was composed of eight infantry and two artillery companies. The authorization was for one year. The citizenry shared Congress' lack of enthusiasm for a standing army. Only two hundred men, primarily Revolutionary War veterans, enlisted. Most were assigned to Fort Pitt, at the confluence of the Allegheny and Monongahela Rivers. There was a small artillery detachment at West Point.

In April of 1785, New York, Pennsylvania, New Jersey and Connecticut were asked to recruit another 700 men for the U.S. Infantry Regiment for three-year enlistments. Despite urging from War Secretary Henry Knox, the states failed to fill their quotas. Dropping the term of enlistment to one year did very little to improve recruitment. Secretary Knox reported to Congress that the army had only 518 men in its ranks.

The inauguration of George Washington, in April 1789, as the country's first president and commander-in-chief, led to modest improvements. During his four-year term, Congress agreed to slight pay raises, increased the size of companies and increased terms of enlistment to three years.

In 1791, a second infantry regiment was authorized. The U.S Infantry Regiment was re-designated the 1st Regiment of Infantry and the new one became the 2nd Regiment. A six dollar recruiting bonus helped to swell the ranks. These two infantry regiments and an artillery battalion constituted the federal army.

The following year, Congress voted to increase the regular army to 5,120 men. This action provided more troops for the two infantry regiments and the artillery battalion and authorized the formation of three more infantry regiments and four troops of dragoons (cavalry). Pay and ration allowances were increased. This action by Congress had the potential for giving birth to the 5th Regiment of Infantry but recruiting fell far short of the mark.

President Washington took this opportunity to organize the larger force by creating the Legion of the United States. He appointed former Major General Anthony Wayne as commander. There were sufficient troops to form four sub-legions commanded by brigadiers. A sub-legion was the forerunner of the modern combat team. It was composed of two battalions (four companies each) of infantry, armed with muskets, one battalion of riflemen for sniping, a company of mounted dragoons and a company of horse-drawn artillery.

In November, 1796, the army was reorganized into four separate regiments of infantry and two companies of light dragoons. Support for these units came from the Corps of Artillerists and Engineers that had been formed two years earlier. The infantry of the 1st Sub-legion became the 1st Infantry Regiment, the 2nd Sub-legion, the 2nd infantry Regiment, etc.

Disputes with the French over territory bordering on the United States led Congress to believe that war with France was imminent. On 16 July 1798, Congress increased the strength of the four infantry regiments and authorized the formation of twelve new infantry regiments and six more troops of light dragoons. Some earlier 5th Infantry historians have pointed to this congressional action as the inception of the first 5th Infantry Regiment. It did authorize a fifth infantry regiment but there is no evidence that one was ever formed.

As the threat of war with France subsided, plans for the expansion of the army were dropped in 1800. In 1802 the federal army was limited to two companies of dismounted dragoons, two regiments of artillerists and engineers and the four regiments of infantry. Although 5,438 slots were authorized, rosters showed that only 248 officers, 9 cadets and 3,794 enlisted men were on duty.

MAPS

Eastern half of the Northern Theater, War of 1812 xiii

Northwest Territory, 1815–1845 xiv

Taylor's Northern Campaign and Scott's March to Mexico City, 1846–1848 xv

Southwest Frontier Forts, 1848–1876 xvi

Department of New Mexico during the Civil War, 1862 xvii

Department of Missouri at the time of the
Red River War, 1874–1875 xviii

Department of the Dakota,
Indian Wars in the West, 1876-1888 xix

Luzon, The Philippine Insurrection, 1900–1903 xx

5th Infantry in Central Europe, Spring 1945 xxi

Korean Peninsula; The Fluid War, July, 1950 – May, 1951 xxii

Area of Operations; 5th Regimental Combat Team,
May, 1952 – August, 1953 xxiii

War Zone C, III Corps Tactical Zone,
South Vietnam, 1965 – 1971 xxiv

Oruzgan Province, Central Afghanistan,
April, 2004 – June, 2005 xxv

Ninevah Province, Iraq, October, 2004 – September, 2009 xxvi

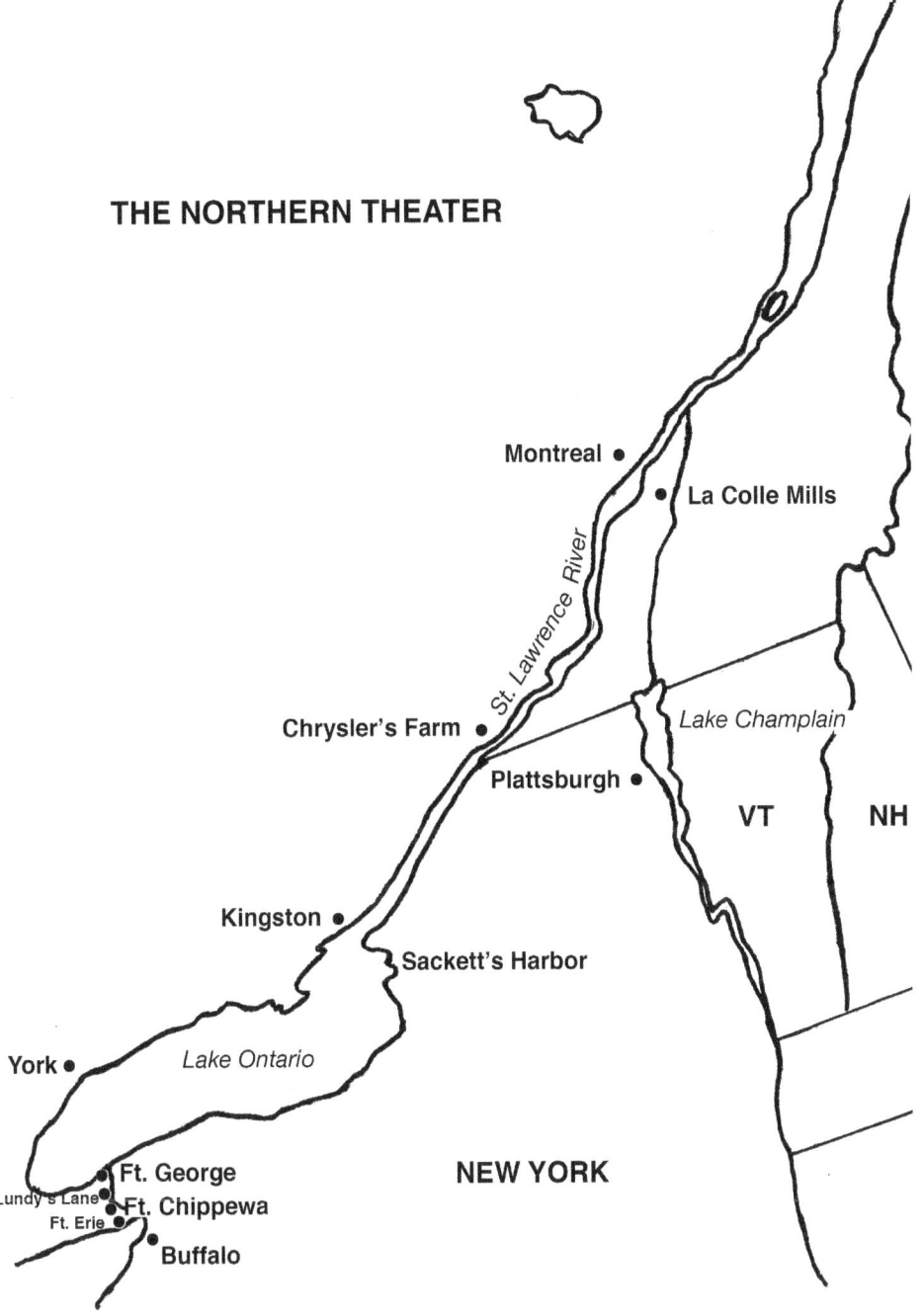

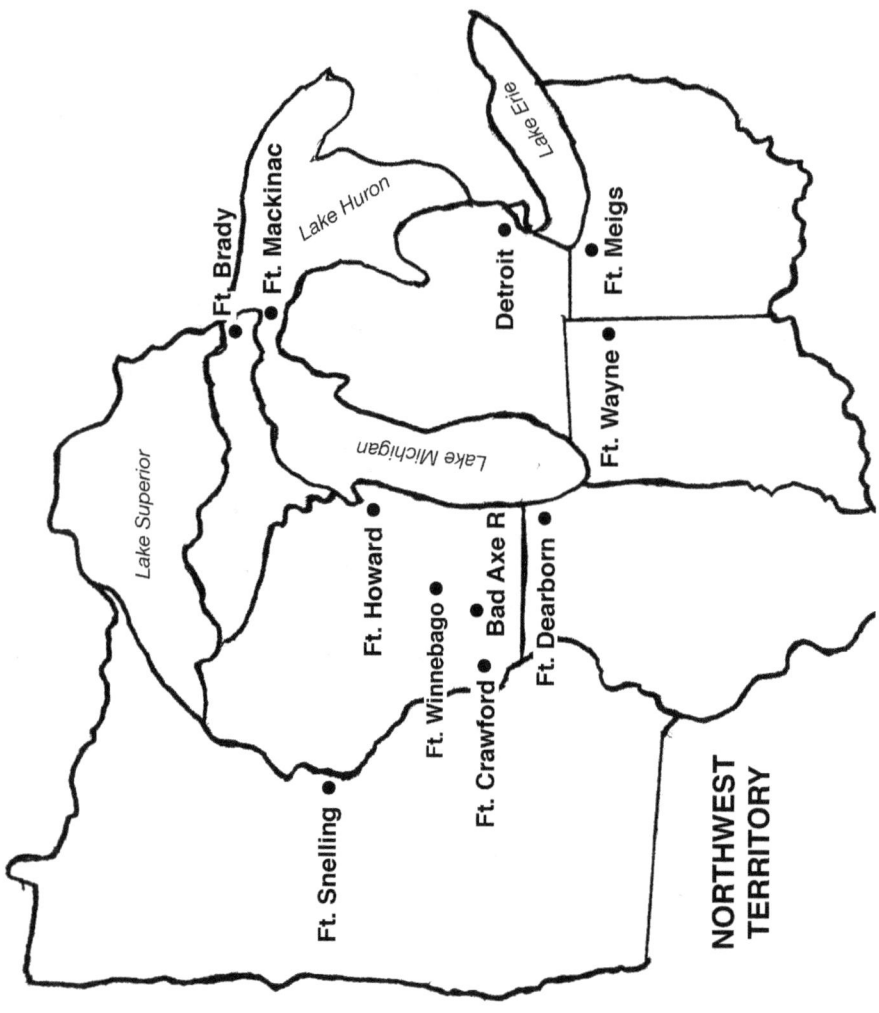

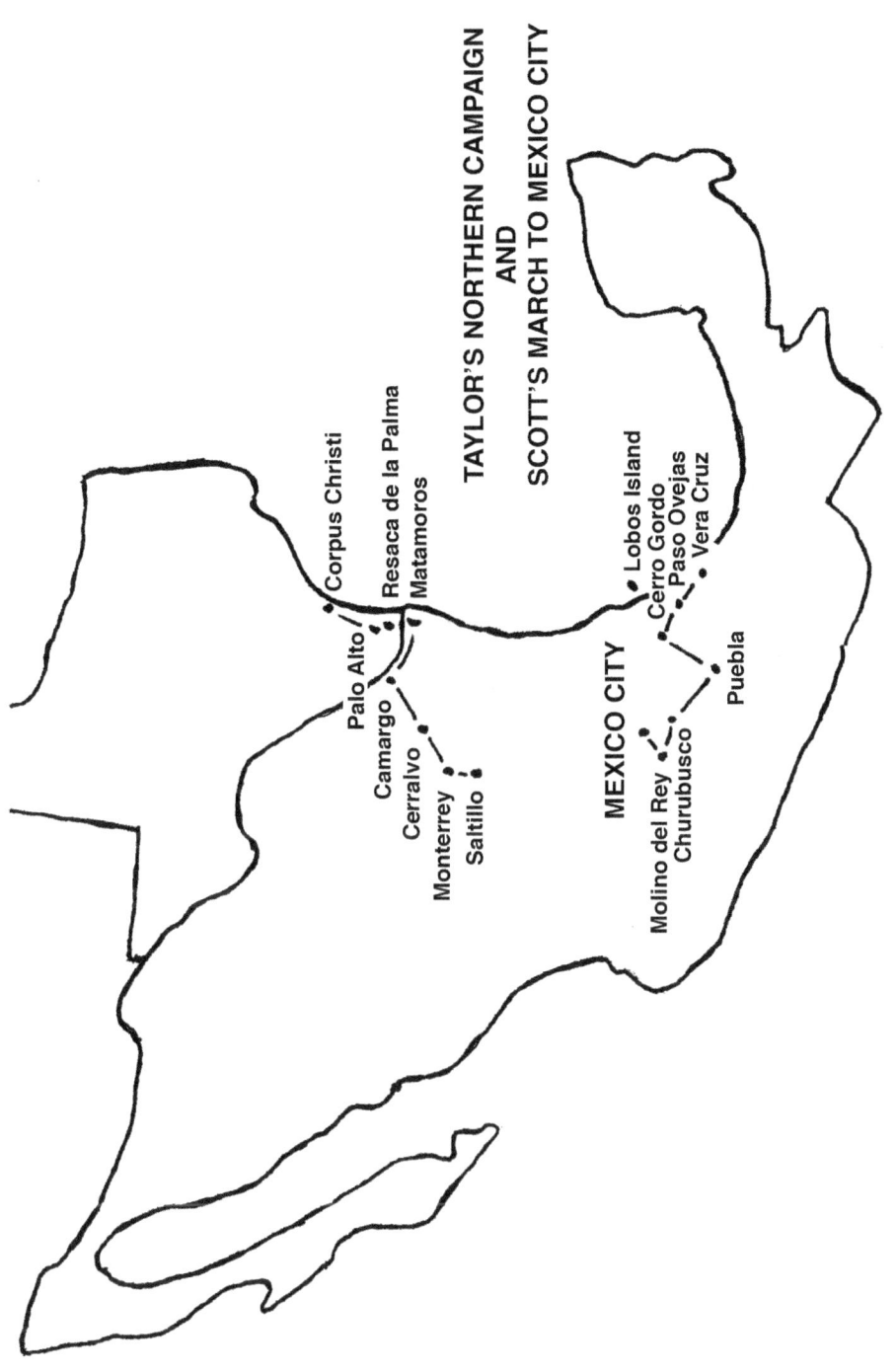

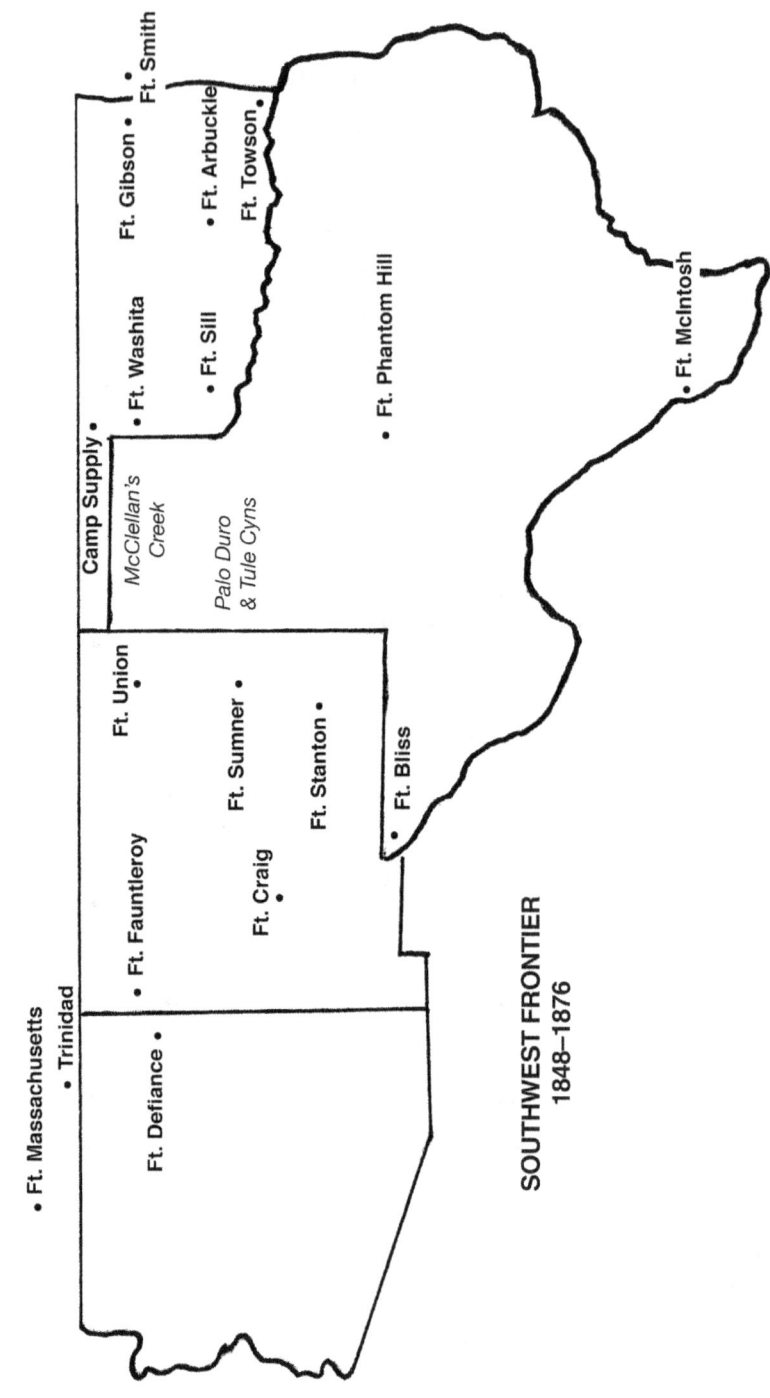

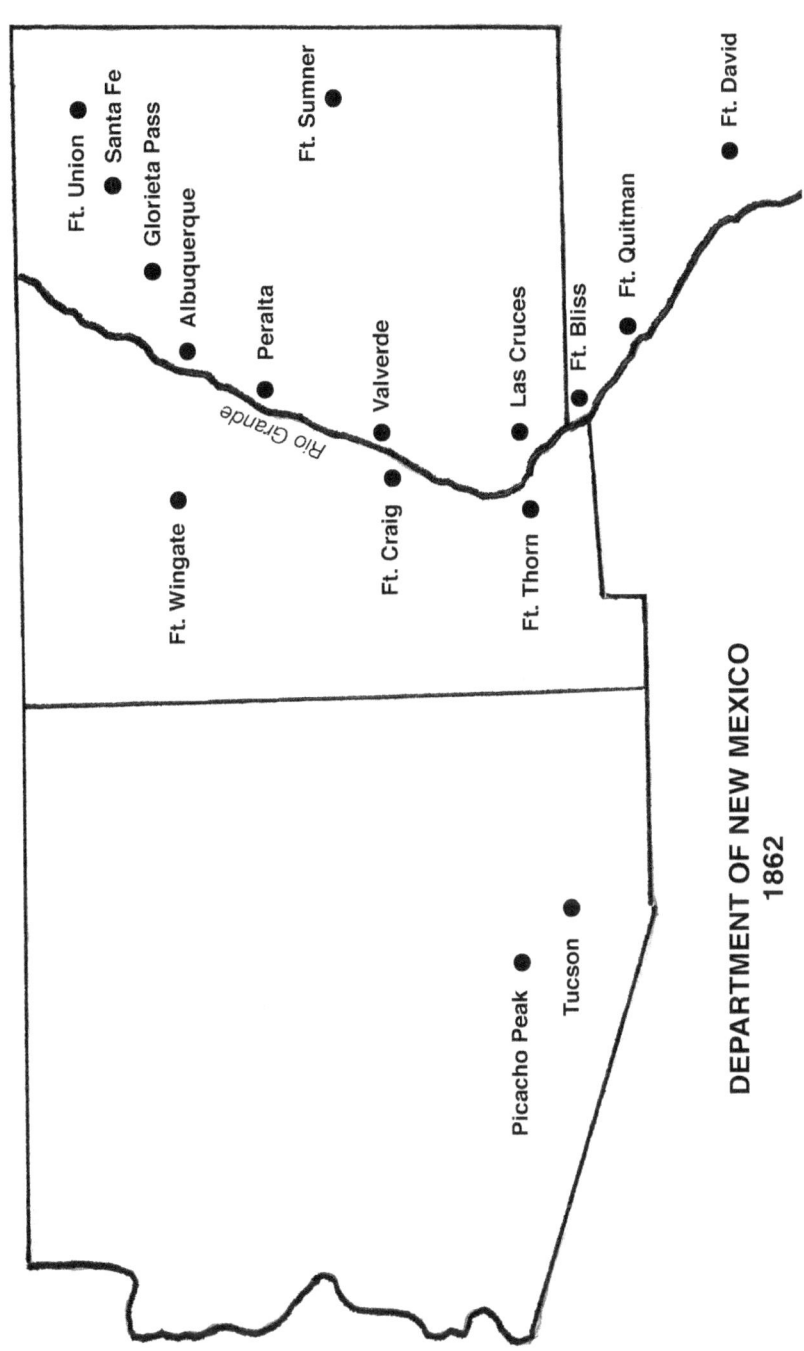

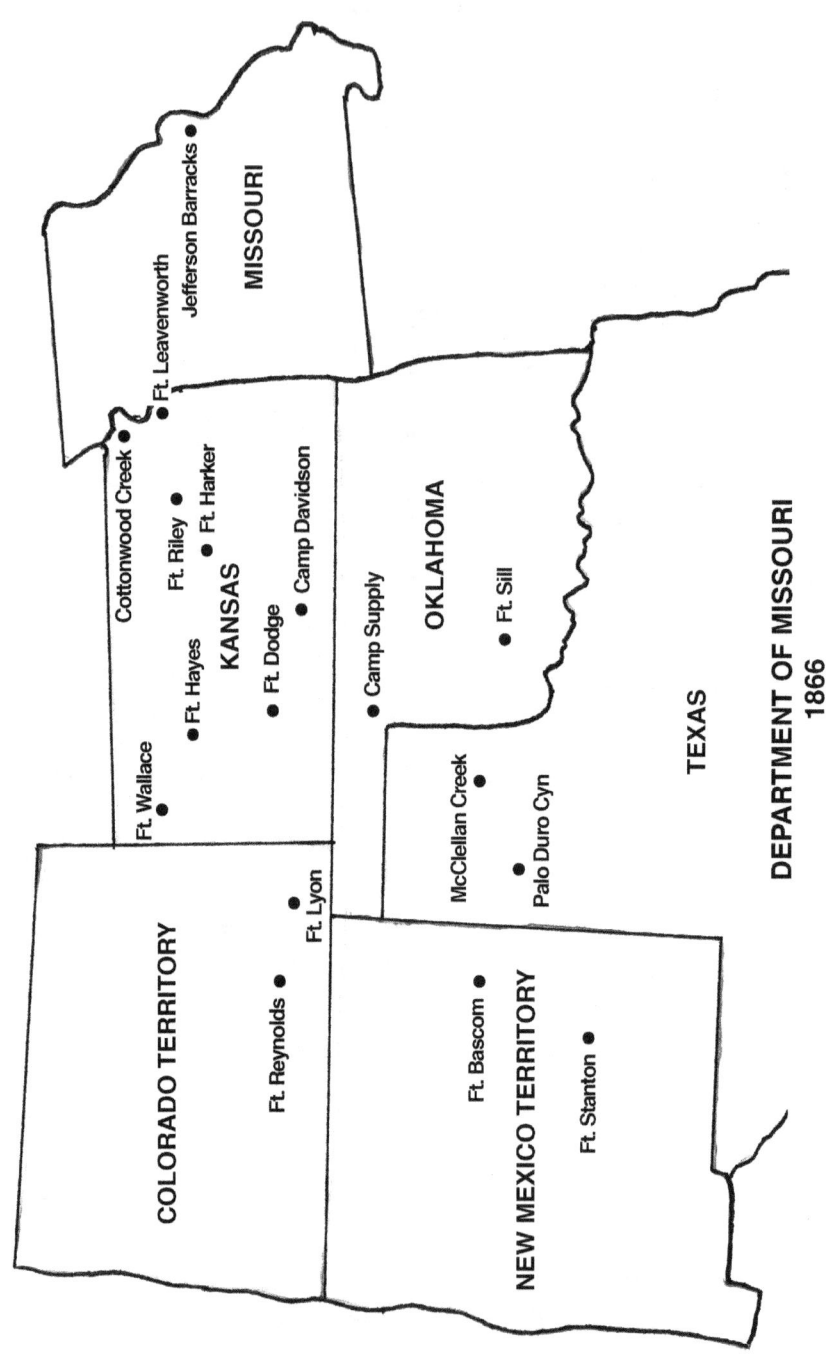

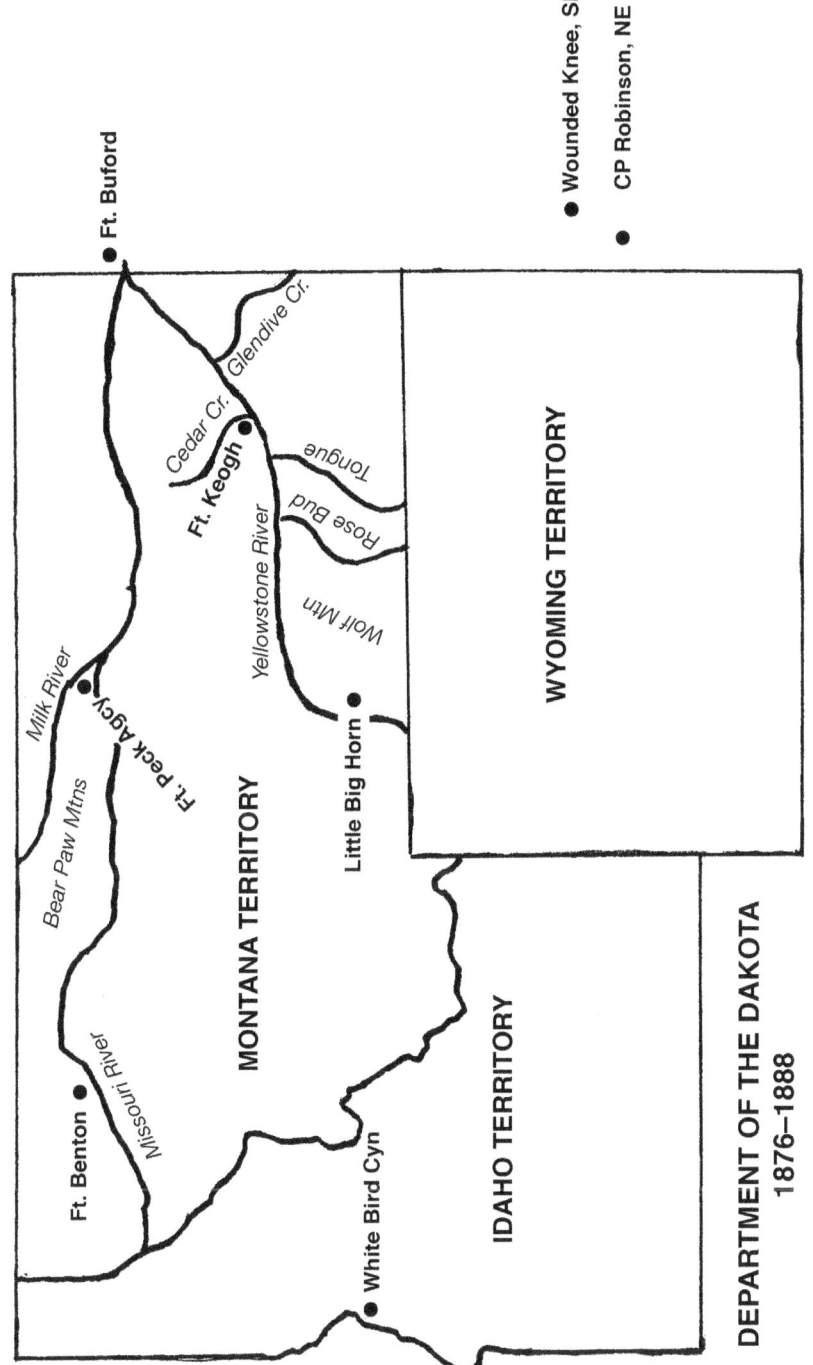

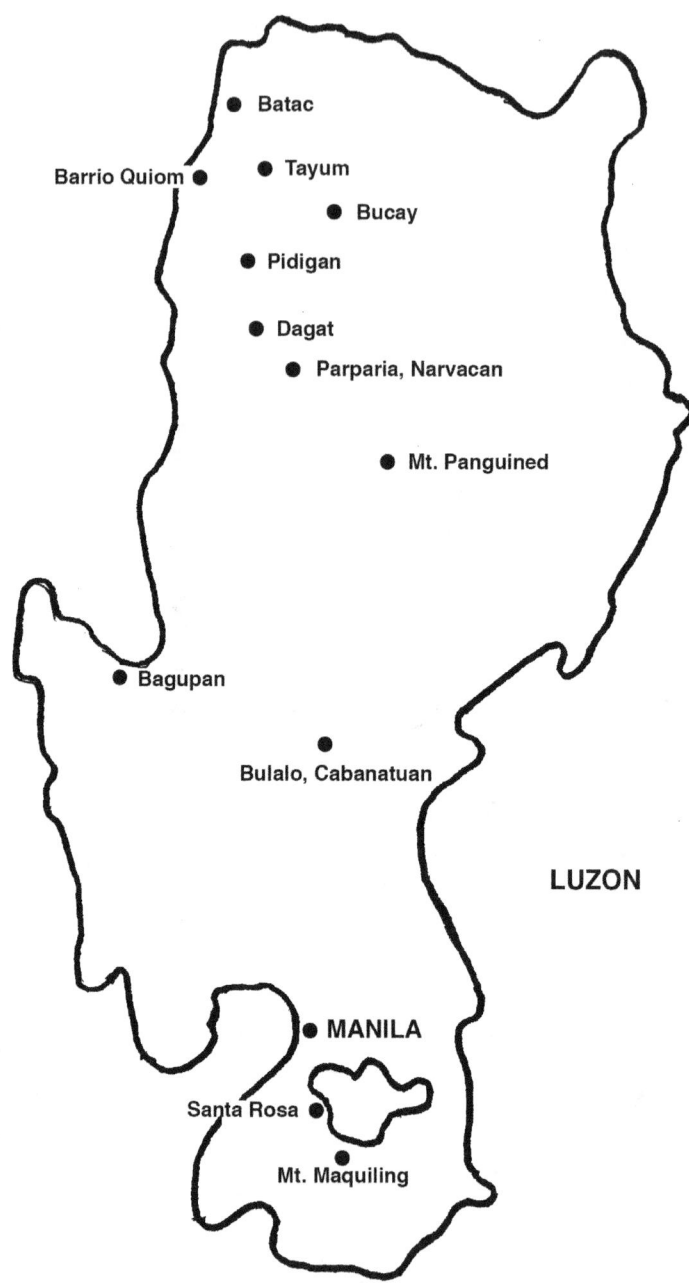

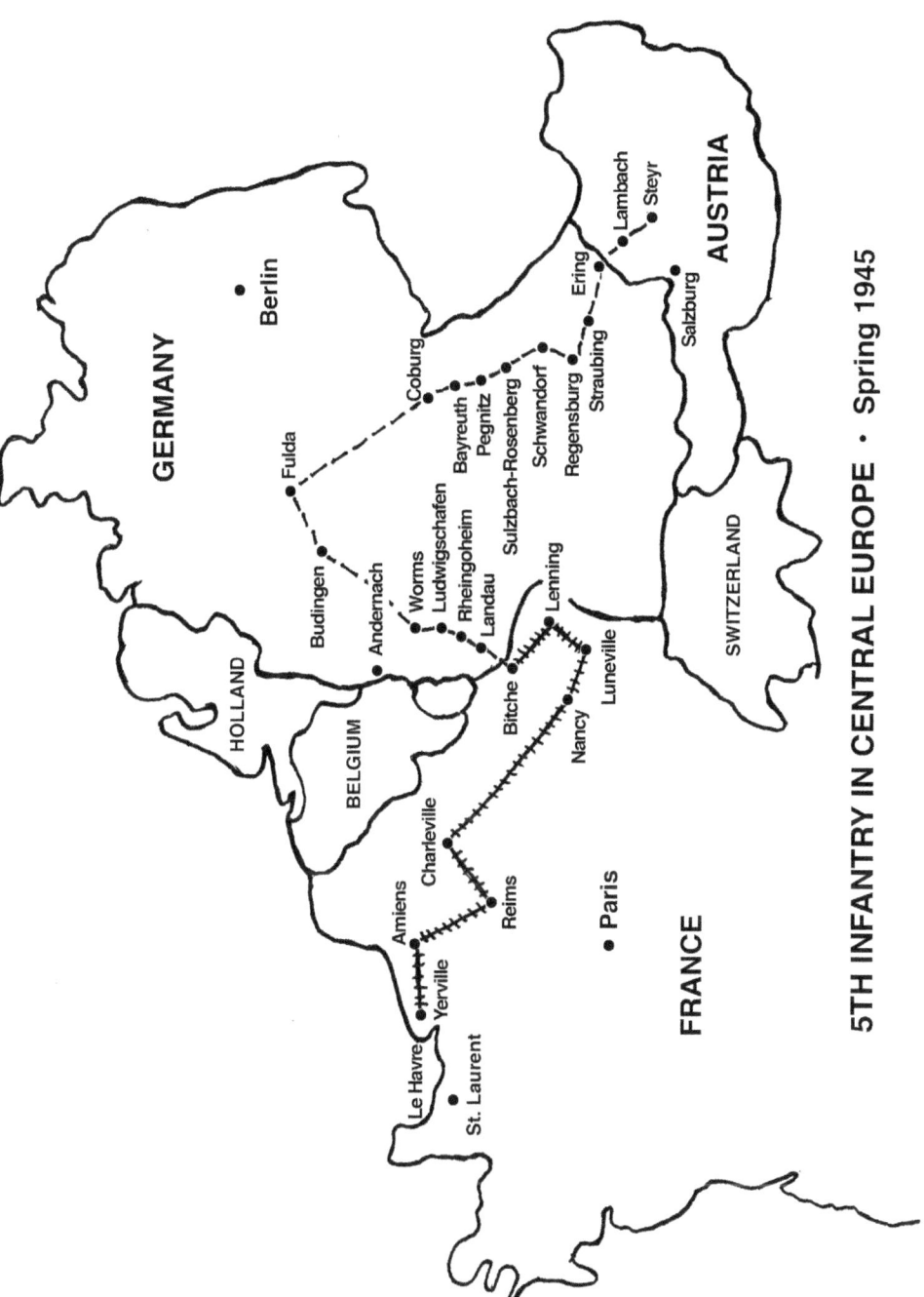

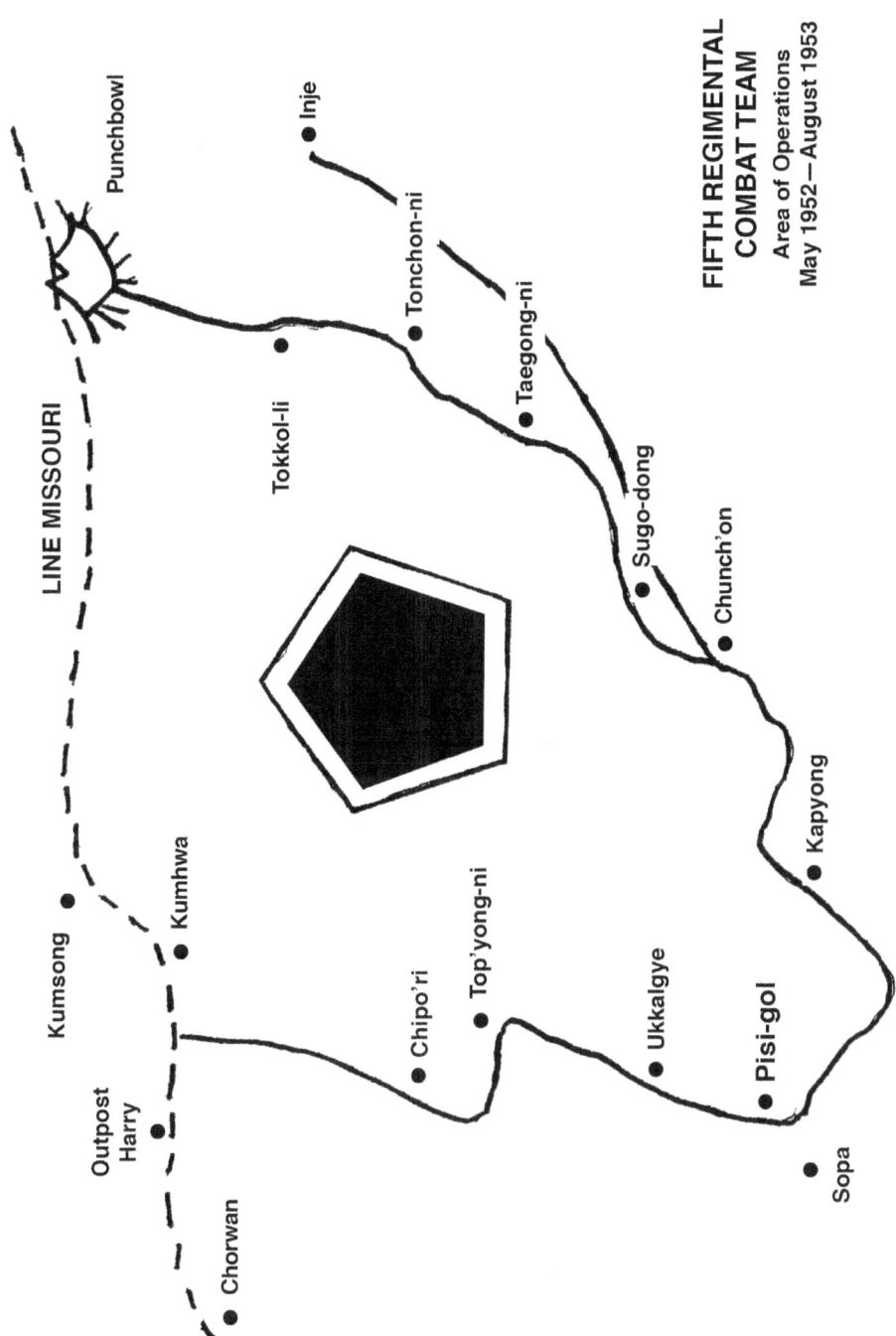

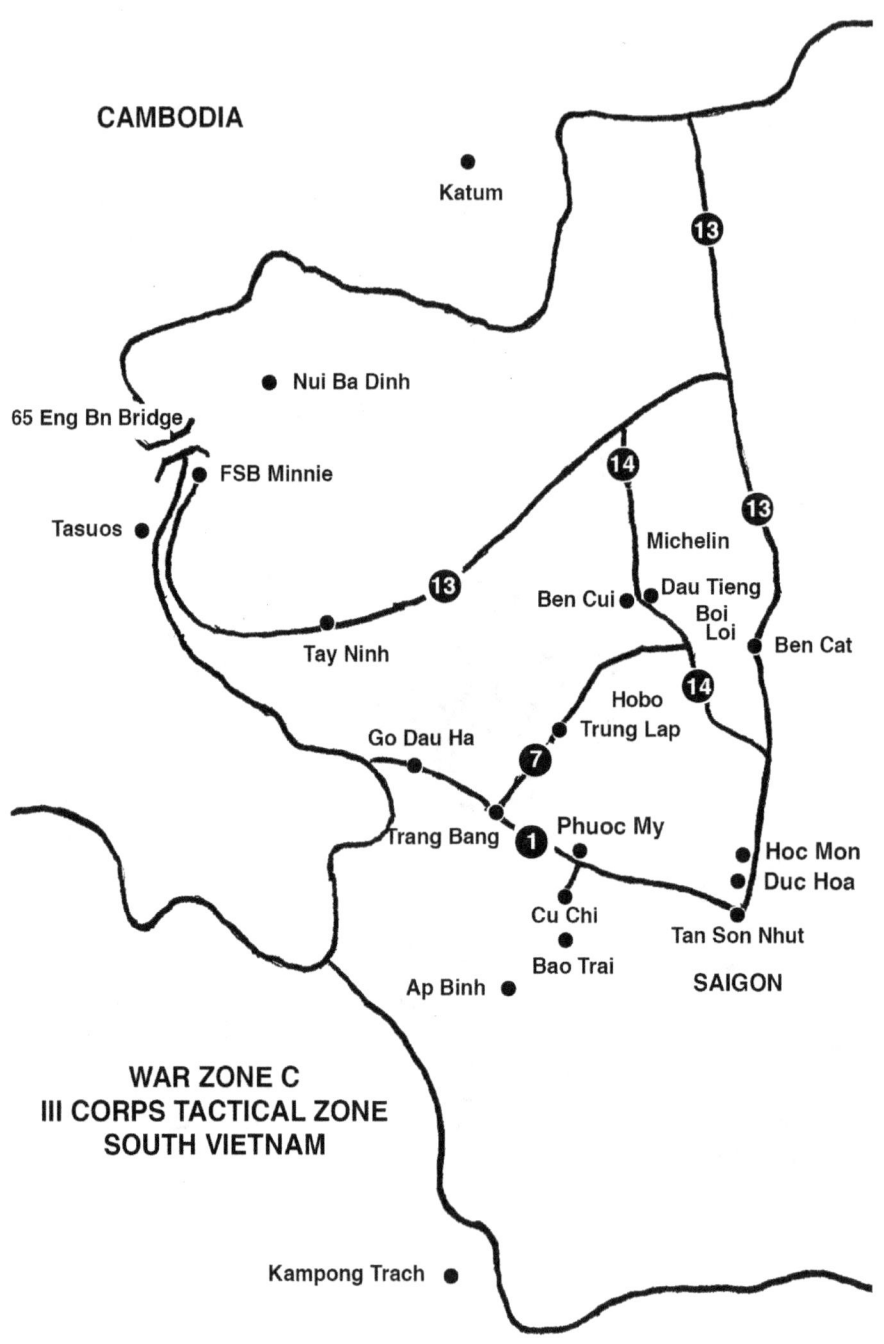

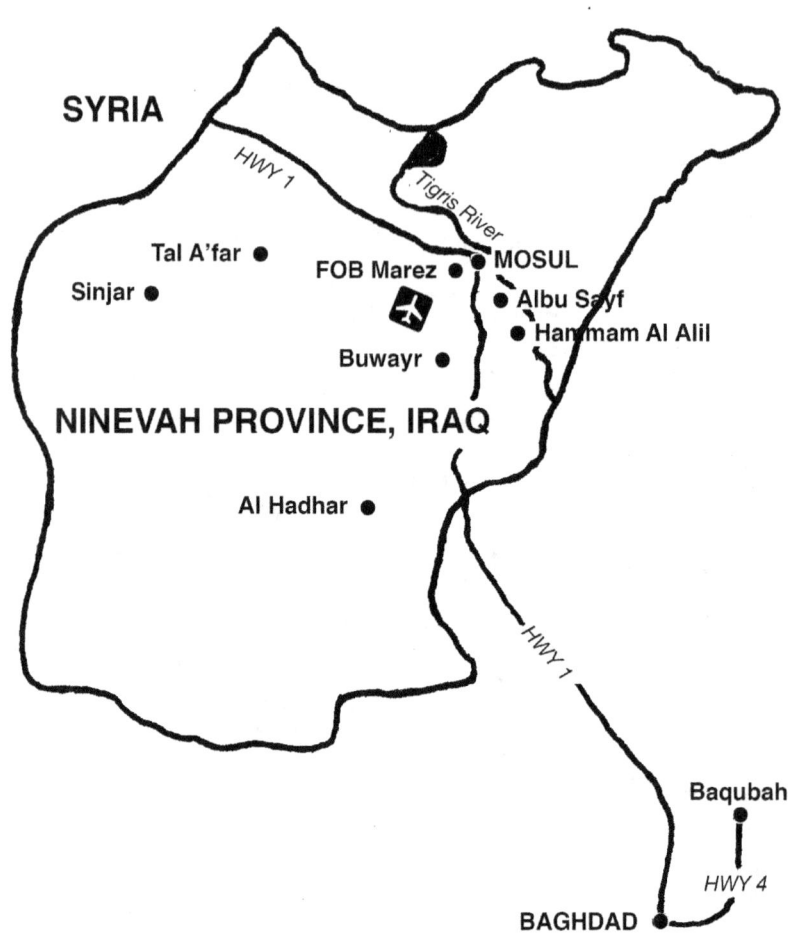

PHOTO GALLERY

Fort Snelling at the confluence of the Mississippi and Minnesota Rivers. (NARA)

Tongue River Cantonment, winter, 1876. (NARA)

5th Infantry command prior to fighting Crazy Horse at Wolf Mountain. L-R: LT Oscar Long, Dr. Henry Tilton, LT J.W. Poppe, COL N.A. Miles, LT F.D. Baldwin, LT Charles Hargous, LT Hobart Bailey. (NARA)

Company H at Fort Keogh, Montana, in 1889. (NARA)

*Nelson A. Miles, Commanding, 5th Infantry.
March 1869–December 1880. (NARA)*

Francis Dwight Baldwin, 5th Infantry, May 1869–1898. (NARA)

Three intact buildings and a dozen or so chimneys are all that remain of Ft. Belknap (Fort Phantom Hill), built by the 5th Infantry in 1851 on the Clear Fork of the Brazos River, Texas. (fortphantom.org)

Some remains of Ft. Craig, New Mexico. Selden's Battalion from the 5th Infantry departed here on 21 February 1862 to fight Sibley's Texans at the battle of Valverde. (USDOI-BLM photo)

Hunter Liggett served with the 5th Infantry from summer 1879 until June 1898. (NARA)

The Army Transport Ship, Kilpatrick, bringing the 1st and 3rd Battalions of the 5th Infantry home from the Philippines, docked at Weehawken, NJ on 12 September 1903. (historyNYC.com)

Preparing for inspection at Ft. Preble, Maine, in 1927. Maine Historical Society.

Soldiers of the 5th Infantry enter Bitche, France, on 22 March 1945 as they move north to the Siegfried Line. (NARA)

5th Infantry entering Steyr, Austria, May 1945. (NARA)

COL Wooten gives instructions to LTG von Rendulic after the fall of Steyr. (71st ID PRO)

LTC Throckmorton (right) confers with LTC Ward, 2nd Battalion CO, somewhere north of the 38th Parallel. (NARA)

2nd Battalion assaulting Hill 256 on 29 January 1951. (NARA)

An enemy round lands approximately 100 yards left of Company E's position on north rim of Punchbowl, 9 August 1952. (NARA)

View of OP Harry, in June 1953, as seen from OP Howe, 1900 yards south of Harry. Star Hill is the higher mound to the left. (Jim Jarboe)

Jack Salyers, Heavy Mortar and C Company, 1955-56. (Jack Salyers)

SGT Kirk Luykx, Company I, receiving flame thrower instructions at Ft. Lewis, 25 September 1955. (NARA)

PFC Irving Pearson, Commo Platoon, HQ Co, 1st Battle Group, 5th Infantry, works on a wire splice during FTX Saberhawk, Breitenbrunn, Germany, 11 February 1958. (NARA)

Kurt Mauer of HQ Company with "Charlie," mascot of Heavy Mortar Company at Monteith Barracks, Furth, Germany in 1957. (Bill Mawhinney)

Company C on search and destroy mission northwest of Dau Tieng, September 1968. (Gary Tippey)

Dust-off for casualty from Company C. 21 August 1968. (Gary Tippey)

Bravo Company's tracks assembled at Cu Chi Base Camp for resupply. (Ignacio Medina)

B Company machine gunner, Bob Galas, recons by fire while Track 12 escorts a convoy from the French Fort to Katum. Dec 1967. (Roger Smith)

Tito, an American Lynx from Northern Mexico, served as mascot for 1st Bn/ 5th Infantry. (Ignacio Medina)

Bill Adler, Alpha Company, with Bich, the company's "Kit Carson" scout, near Dau Tieng, August 1968. (Bill Adler)

TOP PHOTO:
Two men of the 5th Infantry at Camp Empire. Panama, 1915. (www.bobcat.ws)

CENTER PHOTO:
5th Infantry anti-tank truck, w/37mm gun, near Bajuco, Canal Zone, Panama, 13 April 1942. (NARA)

BOTTOM PHOTO:
Bravo Company, 3/5, boards landing craft at Jungle Operations Training School. Panama 1969. (M.C. Toyers)

Ken Krueger joins other members of 1/5 for flight to Brisbane, Australia, for PAC-BOND 4 exercise. (Krueger)

Charlie Company, 1985, enjoys a 9-mile march to the top of Mauna Kea on the Big Island. (Von Plinsky)

TOP PHOTO:
SGT Fred Moore
and Jeff Brodeur of
Company A during
ORIENT SHIELD,
1985. (Brodeur)

BOTTOM PHOTO:
LTC David Hunt, CO of
1/5, discusses the spirit
of the bayonet with
Rep. John Murtha in
September 1989.
(2 ID, Indianhead)

FOB Anaconda was home to Company A and Scout Platoon in Oruzgan Province, Afghanistan. (www.bobcat.ws)

Soldiers of Bravo Company off-load a CH-47 bearing relief supplies to a snowed-in village in the Baguchar Valley, February 25, 2005. (Task Force 2-5, Bobcats' Newsletter)

PFC Matt Baugh and PVT Josh Murray, Charlie Company, search vehicle occupants at a traffic control point near Hamman Al Alil, Iraq, 27 November 2004. (DOD photo)

Bobcats patrol the streets of Baqubah's Tahrir neighborhood in order to secure possible election sites. (www.bobcat.ws)

TWO CENTURIES OF VALOR

The Story of the 5th Infantry Regiment

CHAPTER ONE

THE WAR OF 1812

On June 22, 1807, the United States Navy frigate *Chesapeake* put to sea after a period of refitting at Hampton Roads, Virginia. Ten miles from shore, she was intercepted by the British ship *HMS Leopard*. A Royal Navy officer came aboard and demanded the return of deserters. Commodore James Barron of the *Chesapeake* refused his request. The American ship was then fired upon by the *Leopard*, twenty-one members of the crew were killed or wounded, and a full search was carried out. Four men, said to be British sailors, were carried off. Five years later, after one had been hanged and a second one had died, the two survivors were returned to the deck of the *Chesapeake*. The Americans, justifiably, considered this reparation too little and too late.

President Jefferson issued a proclamation listing grievances against Britain, describing the *Chesapeake* outrage, and banning all British armed vessels from the ports and harbors of the United States, including a demand for the total abolition of impressments of "deserters" from the decks of any ship flying the American flag. From that moment on, relations between the two countries deteriorated further.

Jefferson's government passed an embargo act that put an end to American exports but the law failed to keep American merchantmen in check. Their livelihood depended upon trade with England and France. Jefferson eventually repealed the embargo.

While the Americans were pre-occupied with England, a Shawnee war chief named Tecumseh decided that it would be an opportune time to pull together an alliance of Shawnee, Creek, Choctaw and Chickasaw warriors and drive the American settlers out of the Ohio Valley. British authorities in Canada encouraged him to do so. Tecumseh established a headquarters for his federation at Prophet's Town, a large Indian settlement at the junction of Tippecanoe Creek and the Wabash River, near the present Lafayette, Indiana.

President Jefferson, long opposed to establishing a regular army, finally acquiesced. On April 12, 1808, Congress authorized the creation of five regiments of infantry and one each of light dragoons, light artillery and riflemen (1). The units were designated the 3rd, 4th, 5th, 6th, and 7th Regiments of Infantry, 1st Regiment Light Artillery, the 1st Dragoons, and the 1st Rifle Regiment. The term of service was for five years unless discharged sooner.

Colonel Alexander Parker assumed command of the newly created 5th Infantry Regiment on May 3, 1808 (2). He had served as a captain in the 2nd Virginia Regiment of the Continental Army during the Revolutionary War. On that same day, another Virginian and future colonel of the regiment, George Mercer Brooke, was commissioned first lieutenant in the Fifth United States Infantry. He became a captain and company commander on May 1, 1810.

Early nineteenth century infantry regiments consisted of ten companies. Each regiment was commanded by a colonel. His staff included a lieutenant colonel, major, paymaster, surgeon, surgeon's mate and sergeant major. Each company was commanded by a captain, assisted by one first lieutenant, one second lieutenant, one ensign and two cadets. There were four sergeants, four corporals, two musicians (fifer and drummer) and sixty-eight privates.

On December 2, 1808, War Secretary Dearborn ordered BG James Wilkinson, Governor of Louisiana Territory, to take command of U. S. forces in New Orleans. The secretary directed the 3rd, 5th, and 7th Infantry Regiments, part of the 6th Infantry, the Rifle Regiment, Light Dragoons and several Light Artillery companies, including that of CPT Zachary Taylor, to assemble in New Orleans as soon as possible.

The history of the 5th Infantry Regiment, in its formative years,

THE WAR OF 1812

is rather convoluted because there were a number of unit mergers and reorganizations. The honors of a de-activated unit were retained in the oral history passed along by its re-assigned soldiers. It was not until 1861 that the War Department ruled that battle honors won by units that were dissolved to become a new unit would henceforth be credited to the new unit and would become part of its tradition. Therefore it's necessary to examine the military records of several regiments to discuss the lineage of the 5th Infantry. While doing so, we'll also follow the careers of several men who will eventually serve as colonels of the regiment.

Tippecanoe

By 1811, Tecumseh's insurgencies had become widespread. William Henry Harrison, Governor of Indiana Territory, was ordered to raise a brigade of volunteers and stamp out the Indian alliance. The 4th Infantry, which would ultimately become a component of the Fifth, was dispatched to Vincennes to form a nucleus for Harrison's force. Harrison mustered an additional one thousand recruits and, after long and careful preparation, set out for the heart of Tecumseh's territory in September.

On November 6, Harrison's troops arrived within sight of the Shawnee village and crossed to the north bank of the Wabash River and camped for the night. Just before dawn on the 7th, the Shawnees attacked. Night attacks by Indians were very uncommon but this one did not catch the 4th Infantry with its guard down.

The companies of Captains Barton, Snelling, Bean and Prescott stopped the charge with a disciplined blast of musketry. General Harrison's report of the battle, in which the 4th Infantry launched a victorious counterattack, was extravagant in its praise of the regiment (3). Tecumseh's defeat at Tippecanoe broke the back of his conspiracy and provided the regiment with one of the army's oldest battle honors.

The 4th Infantry then returned to Fort Vincennes and, in 1812, after a trying march through the forests of Ohio, joined the brigade of BG William Hull at Dayton. The 4th Infantry's Major James Miller, who figured prominently in the history of the 5th Infantry Regiment, was ill and missed the fight at Tippecanoe.

War with England

Within months of the Battle of Tippecanoe, war was declared against Great Britain. On 12 July 1812, General Hull crossed with his command into Canada and made camp at Sandwich (now Windsor) Ontario. Colonel James Miller and his men of the 4th Infantry grew restless and were delighted when a detachment from the regiment was given the mission of escorting a supply train to Camp Detroit. Previous escorts had been surprised and routed. As predicted, they were ambushed at Maguage, fourteen miles below Detroit, by an equal force of British, Canadians and Indians. Miller ordered a charge and the British withdrew leaving the Shawnees to fight it out with the Americans. Shawnee Chief Tecumseh was wounded and eventually he and his braves were forced to withdraw.

General Hull became increasingly nervous about his lines of communication during his invasion of Canada so he dispatched the rest of the 4th Infantry, under the command of Major Thomas Van Horne, south to re-open the lines to Detroit. Van Horne carried a communication from Hull outlining what the general viewed as his increasingly precarious position.

When Van Horne and his two hundred regulars stopped to obtain water at the house of a French settler, the Frenchman told him that a party of Indians was planning to ambush them outside the village of Brownstown, Michigan. Van Horne apparently did not believe him because he took no special precautions as he set out in that direction. Before reaching the town, Van Horne's men were fired upon by Tecumseh and about twenty-five of his warriors. Van Horne, fearing that he would be surrounded, ordered a retreat. In his panic, he left General Hull's mail, which was subsequently delivered to the British at Fort Malden.

Van Horne's detachment made it back to Detroit after losing 17 killed and several wounded. Their failure to open the lines out of Detroit further agitated an already anxious Hull. He summoned James Miller and his detachment, before they could follow up on the success at Maguage, and ordered them to return to Detroit.

Arriving there, Colonel Miller found that Hull had surrendered his entire force, including the 4th Infantry, to an inferior enemy without a fight. Hull was soon court-martialed for cowardice and neglect of duty and sentenced to die but President Monroe mitigated the death sentence, content with purging Hull from the rolls of the U.S. Army.

Shortly before Hull's shameful surrender, the general had been attending the Detroit wedding of Josiah Snelling and Abigail Hunt. Several minutes after the ceremony concluded, those gathered heard a long drum roll signaling the call to arms. As Snelling rushed for the door, General Hull laid his hand on the young officer's shoulder and said, "Snelling, you need not go. I will excuse you."

"By no means," the future 5th Infantry commander replied, "I feel more like doing my duty now than ever."

A short time later, as General Hull's aide was trying to place a white flag in position, he called, "Snelling, come and help me fix this flag."

"No, sir," Snelling replied. "I will not soil my hands with that flag."

After remaining several months in Canada as prisoners of war, the officers and men of the Fourth Infantry were paroled to Boston and given furloughs until they were exchanged for British prisoners of war. The exchange was completed early in 1813 and the regiment reassembled and recruited to strength.

Two Centuries of Valor

North to Ontario and Quebec

The Twenty-first Infantry, another forerunner of the Fifth, fared better than the 4th, during its first foray into Canada. The 21st, part of MG Henry Dearborn's U. S. Army of the North, was assigned to BG Zebulon Pike's Brigade. The brigade was given orders to capture the Canadian city of York (Toronto) and destroy its shipyards.

The U.S. Navy dropped the 1700 U.S. Army regulars off at York on the morning of 27 April 1813. The British commander, MG Roger Sheaffe, had no more than 800 men to repel the attack. When the invasion fleet came into view, he placed his regular troops behind earthworks constructed between the shoreline and the city and his Canadian militia in the city proper.

Pike's Brigade, assisted by naval gun fire, pushed the outnumbered British regulars back toward York. Their withdrawal alarmed many of the militia members, who quickly withdrew from the fight and looked for something else to do.

General Sheafe ordered the main powder magazine exploded rather than allow it to fall into the hands of the American troops. The resulting explosion killed two hundred U.S. soldiers. Zebulon Pike was struck on the back by a falling rock and lived just long enough to receive the British flag from his victorious troops. Officers of the Canadian militia negotiated the surrender of their city while Sheaffe hurried his remaining regulars out of town.

Infuriated by the loss of so many of their comrades in the explosion, bands of U.S. soldiers destroyed public buildings and property and vandalized private homes. General Dearborn, crippled by the loss of Pike, could not restrain his ill-disciplined troops. Fortunately, for the citizens of York, the Americans left town on May 8.

Three weeks later, the men of the 21st U.S. Infantry were recuperating at Sacket's Harbor, New York when they were attacked by a combined force of British troops and ships. Still festering from the experience of the powder explosion at York, Pike's former brigade proved, once again, to be inhospitable to the British, who were quickly repelled and sailed home licking their wounds.

Fort George was the principal British headquarters on the Niagara frontier as the war began in 1812. It was a log-and-palisade structure built on high ground on the Niagara River's west bank. The thousand-man garrison became General Dearborn's next target. His force of 2500 men included the 13th Infantry, another 5th Infantry predecessor. On 27 May 1813 the U.S. Army swarmed ashore from one hundred and eighty bateaux (the 1813 equivalent of the landing craft, infantry) and convinced the British to vacate the premises. Fort George remained in American hands until it was abandoned at the end of the year.

British Brigadier John Vincent, who had withdrawn his division from Fort George in the face of General Dearborn's overwhelming assault, established new positions, away from the river at Burlington Heights. When Dearborn heard that Vincent was about to be reinforced, he ordered newly promoted BG William Winder to defeat Vincent's troops before the reinforcements arrived. Winder's Brigade included the actual 5th Infantry, recently transferred from the U.S. Army of the South, as well as the 13th, 14th, and 16th Regiments.

When Winder reached Burlington Heights, he sent word to General Dearborn that he judged the British position too strong to be taken by his present force. He was soon joined by BG John Chandler's brigade, composed of the 9th, 23rd and 25th Regiments. The two brigades camped at Stoney Creek while Winder and Chandler planned their attack. Chandler, being senior, took command but failed to set proper security.

Before dawn, the British stormed the surprised camp with bayonets. During the melee, the Americans defended themselves fiercely and the British suffered heavy losses and withdrew, but not before capturing Brigadiers Winder and Chandler. Dragoon Colonel James Burn, the surviving senior American officer, fearful of another

British attack, ordered the brigades to withdraw before burying their dead or striking their tents. They returned to Fort George.

As the fall of 1813 approached, Secretary of War John Armstrong devised a plan to capture Montreal. General James Wilkinson's division of eight thousand regulars, including those Fifth Infantry forerunners, the 9th, 13th, and 21st Regiments, was to proceed down the St. Lawrence River in anything that floated, while another division, under Wade Hampton, would advance north from Lake Champlain.

There were several problems with this arrangement (4). Wilkinson had an unsavory reputation as a scoundrel and Hampton, who was no prize either, initially refused to serve in the same army as Wilkinson. Their troops lacked training and warm uniforms and there were too few experienced officers. More importantly, it appeared that neither force would be able to sustain itself once it reached Montreal. There could be no siege or prolonged operation.

On 21 October, Hampton started his troops down the Chateauguay River. When they approached the Canadian border, nearly all of the 1400 New York militiamen refused to cross. Hampton pressed on with his four thousand regulars, including the ill-fated Fourth Infantry.

Five days later, the column came upon a log roadblock defended by 1700 Canadians and a few Indians. The road was flanked by swampy woods that were impassable to Hampton's wagons and guns. Hampton sent a strong force across the river so it could move through the forest and gain the Canadians' rear. The sound of the flank attack the next morning would signal Hampton to begin his frontal assault.

Things went badly. The flanking force became lost in the marshy woods where they encountered a smaller but very determined bunch of Canadians. Hampton, mindful that things were going awry, decided to go ahead with his attack which turned into little more than a two-hour fire fight. After losing about four dozen men, Hampton called off the offensive and ignored Wilkinson's orders to continue on to Montreal. So, one prong of the last U.S. offensive of 1813 was blunted primarily

THE WAR OF 1812

by Hampton's mistrust of General Wilkinson and the Secretary of War rather than enemy action. Hampton resigned in March, 1814.

When Wilkinson's column made contact with the British on the morning of November 11, 1813 at Chrysler's Farm near Cornwall, Ontario, it was cold and raining. An outnumbered force of British regulars and Canadian militia beat off repeated attacks by American infantry and dragoons.

By 4:30 on the afternoon of the 12th, the American Army was retreating in great confusion. The crest-fallen men found their boats and crossed to the south bank of the St. Lawrence. The army went into winter quarters at French Mills and Plattsburgh, New York. Wilkinson's soldiers suffered through a hard winter made worse by their commander's neglect of their material needs. They were inadequately clothed and had not had a pay day in six months.

On March 30, 1814, when the spring thaw had turned the roads to mud, Wilkinson and his troops crossed once more into Canada. His force now included four regiments destined to merge into the 5th Infantry; the 4th, 9th, 13th, and 21st.

At about 3 o'clock that afternoon the Americans reached the south bank of La Colle Creek and found that British troops were occupying the stone mill building, a barn, and a block house on the north bank. Wilkinson ordered his men to begin firing their muskets at the stone walls of the mill when they came within 250 yards of the building. As the American riflemen carried out their futile fusillade, British reinforcements arrived and made several attempts to cross the creek and push back the four thousand Americans. The redcoats were unable to cross and retreated to the blockhouse. General Wilkinson eventually realized that musket balls were not going to damage the stone walls of La Colle Mill and decided to withdraw.

The defeat at La Colle Mill was Wilkinson's last hurrah. He would see no more combat in the War of 1812. He had been relieved from duty the week before the battle but the news had traveled slowly.

The future members of the 5th Infantry at La Colle Mill would have a chance to redeem their honor at their next encounter, the battle for Plattsburg, New York. LTC Thomas Aspinwall and the men of the 9th Infantry drew special mention for their courage during the otherwise dismal U.S. showing at Chrysler's Farm. Captain George Brooke, of the 9th, was promoted to major on May 1, 1814 and transferred to the 23rd Infantry.

Wilkinson, on the other hand, was summoned to a court of inquiry in Troy, New York and charged with neglect of duty, conduct unbecoming an officer, drunkenness and encouraging disobedience of orders. Surprisingly, he was acquitted on all counts. He returned to his plantation south of New Orleans.

Chippewa

At this point the focus of the fighting shifted back to the Niagara Peninsula. A winter offensive by the British had cleared the Americans from both sides of the Niagara River. The American response began on 3 July when the brigades of Winfield Scott and Eleazar Ripley, including the 9th and 21st Regiments, landed on the shore of Lake Erie and surrounded the small garrison at Fort Erie, taking 137 prisoners. The two brigades then marched north along the Niagara River, hoping to rendezvous with the small U.S. fleet on Lake Ontario and then march west and conquer all of Upper Canada.

The capture of Fort Erie triggered an immediate British reaction. The area commander, MG Phineas Riall, gathered 2000 troops to face the U.S. Army. For most of a hot July 4, small British patrols slowed the progress of Scott's Brigade. By nightfall Scott stopped his advance on the south bank of the Chippewa River. The British were strongly positioned on the north bank. Scott doubled back a mile and camped for the night.

Around 4:00 P.M. on the 5th, the British fixed bayonets and began a general advance. From his position near the Chippewa,

The War of 1812

General Riall saw Scott's Brigade on the march. He noticed that the soldiers were wearing non-standard grey coats rather than the blue uniforms prescribed for U.S. regulars. For a few brief moments he thought that his opposition was an inferior militia outfit. As Scott's soldiers, including the 9th Infantry, dressed their lines and marched steadily through the British artillery barrage, Riall changed his opinion, exclaiming, "Those are regulars, by God!"

The battle unfolded rapidly. The artillery of both sides inflicted heavy casualties. As the Americans pressed forward, Scott extended his lines to create a concave formation, a maneuver that apparently confused the British, who marched steadily forward. When the lines were no more than seventy yards apart, both sides stopped and delivered a volley of musketry.

Scott's concave formation caught the British in a cross fire and U.S. artillery destroyed a British caisson, leaving the Redcoats without any functioning artillery. Riall signaled retreat, using a reserve regiment to cover his troops as they scampered across the sole bridge over the Chippewa leaving 515 British casualties on the field. The Americans suffered 318 casualties.

Lundy's Lane

It is to the 21st Infantry that the present Fifth Infantry owes its motto and one of the proudest incidents in its long service. In the early evening of July 25, 1814, Major General Jacob Brown, commander of the U.S. Army of the North, received word that the British were on the move. According to the reports, General Phineas Riall's Redcoats were staging a two-pronged advance. A column from Queenstown Heights, New York was said to be advancing toward Brown's army while others were crossing the Niagara River in an attempt to take over the American supply depot at Fort Schlosser. Brown sent Winfield Scott's Brigade in the direction of Queenstown to intercept the British and get an idea of their numbers (5).

Two Centuries of Valor

Three miles into the march, Scott's men discovered that there was no British advance in progress. They spied the army of Phineas Riall perched on the high ground above Lundy's Lane, a spur from the main portage road along the Niagara River. A formidable cluster of British cannons glistened in the twilight beside a little church at the top of a knoll.

The rest of Riall's line stretched down both sides of the hill forming a crescent, similar to that deployed by the Americans at Chippewa. Scott's men soon found themselves partially surrounded. The Americans could hear bugles signal the arrival of eight hundred British reinforcements under the command of LTG Gordon Drummond. A cautious commander would have fallen back but Scott sent a dispatch to Brown. "Brigadier General Scott will engage the British. Send reinforcements."

The initial volleys from the cannons on the knoll decimated Scott's brigade as it moved from the forest into an open field. The American troops had nothing but muskets with which to respond. Scott sent the 25th U.S. Infantry to flank the British left. They were able to push the British and Canadian troops back and capture a seriously wounded General Riall, but the British rallied.

When General Brown arrived on the field, he sent Eleazar Ripley's brigade forward to help Scott. The brigade commanders soon concluded that they would have to take the British guns if they were to control the battle. Colonel James Miller, one of Ripley's regimental commanders, was asked to make a frontal assault. Colonel Miller modestly replied, "I'll try, sir."

Miller's three hundred members of the 21st Infantry Regiment relieved Scott's battered brigade and prepared for a direct attack up the south side of the hill. Militia private Alexander McMullen remembered moving forward and passing over "the dead and dying, who were literally in heaps (6)."

Darkness was falling but the British artillerymen continued to rain grapeshot and canister upon the steadily advancing 21st Infantry. When the Americans reached the moonlit hilltop, they advanced within twelve yards of the British cannons, dressed their line, and delivered a volley that swept away every member of the gun crews. Then, with rifle butts and bayonets, they cleared the hill.

The British returned in an equally furious counterattack but were halted by the fury of American musketry. The red-coated wave lapped the crest of the hill four times and receded before the stubborn ranks of blue. Baffled and beaten, the British withdrew, leaving their seven guns in the hands of Miller's exhausted troops. The hill was securely in American hands by 9:00 P.M.

Following the battle, Ripley wanted to hold the captured ground but General Brown ordered a withdrawal. The Americans had run out of ammunition and water. Scott's and Ripley's brigades returned to Chippewa, Ontario.

Hours later, Eleazar Ripley was admonished by General Brown for abandoning six of the seven captured field pieces. Ripley explained that no living horses could be found and that the men were simply too exhausted to physically pull the heavy guns all the way to Chippewa. Nevertheless, Brown ordered Ripley to march out in the morning, retake the battlefield, and collect the abandoned guns.

When he led his 1200-man brigade north at daybreak, Ripley found that a superior British force, commanded by LTG Drummond, had moved forward a mile and was in battle formation. Ripley and his fellow officers decided not to tangle with the British and Drummond, unsure of the size of the American force, made a similar decision. The six guns (three 24-pounders, two 6-pounders and one 5.5 inch howitzer) remained in British hands.

Back at Chippewa, the U.S. Army burned Riall's former fortifications north of the river as well as the Chippewa Bridge and then moved southward toward Fort Erie. There were so many casualties that Ripley ordered rations dumped in the river so that the carts could be used to transport the wounded.

The British eventually followed the Americans to Fort Erie and found them entrenched. General Brown's army had reinforced the fort and had regained its fighting spirit. General Drummond's troops laid siege to the fort on August 3 and tried for the better part of seven weeks to dislodge the Americans.

On September 17, General Brown ordered an attack against the British lines, with Brevet Brigadier General James Miller commanding the right column. Miller's attack, in combination with that of the left brigade, carried the whole line of British entrenchments and forced them to abandon the siege. Brevet LTC George M. Brooke, of the 23rd Infantry, also distinguished himself during the attack to relieve the siege and was promoted to brevet colonel.

For the first time in history, American regulars had faced seasoned veterans of Wellington's Peninsular War and had prevailed. The story of the 21st Infantry's gallant charge sent a thrill through the country and did much to counteract the disrepute into which a series of disastrous defeats had plunged the U.S. Army.

Plattsburgh, New York

During the summer of 1814 while the army was earning some respect along the Niagara River, not all regiments that would soon fold their flags to become part of the 5th Infantry were sharing in the glory. The British secretary of state for war and the colonies ordered Sir John Sherbrooke, Lieutenant Governor of Nova Scotia, to attack the small settlements along the coast of the Maine District of Massachusetts in order to seize territory that could be used for trade-offs during any peace negotiations with the United States.

On 11 July, Admiral Sir Thomas Hardy transported 1000 men commanded by LTC Andrew Pilkington to Moose Island where the 40th U.S. Infantry maintained an 85-man garrison at Fort Sullivan commanded by Major Purley Putnam. Understandably, no fight ensued. Admiral Hardy declared the area a part of Great Britain and it remained so until the Treaty of Ghent ended the war.

President Madison had been searching for a diplomatic resolution since the declaration of war in June, 1812. Finally, on August 8, 1814, delegations from the United States and Great Britain began deliberations in the Belgian city of Ghent. The British envoys opened with a demand for territory in Massachusetts and Minnesota and insisted on the creation of an Indian barrier state in the Great Lakes region. These territorial demands were completely unacceptable to the American delegation.

In late August, 1814, the British commander for Quebec and Montreal, Sir George Prevost, was ordered to march his 17,000 troops toward Plattsburgh, New York to increase territorial gains and move closer to their food supplies. A British fleet, moored on Lake Champlain, set sail to support the ground troops. It was anticipated that the invasion would be a cake-walk since the American Secretary of War, John Armstrong, had ordered MG George Izard, commander of U.S. forces at Plattsburgh, to move the bulk of his men, including COL John Bowyer's 5th Infantry, to Sacket's Harbor. BG Alexander Macomb was left to command the 3500 defenders of Plattsburgh. Macomb's brigade included the 13th and 4th Infantry Regiments.

The American troops had established defensive positions in the southern part of the town on a peninsula between the Saranac River and Lake Champlain. With water protecting three sides, the Americans constructed Forts Brown, Moreau, and Scott and two blockhouses to protect the open end of their position.

When he got wind of the British intentions, Macomb appealed to the governors of New York and Vermont for volunteers. Soon 2500 Vermonters and 800 New Yorkers were on their way to Plattsburg. They were joined on September 3 by LT Thomas Macdonough and his fleet of three frigates, the *Saratoga*, *Ticonderoga*, and *Preble*; the sloop *Eagle*, and ten gunboats.

Lord Prevost and his five brigades of Redcoats reached the outskirts of Plattsburgh on September 5. He split his troops into two columns and advanced on the town. Major John Wool and 300 regulars ambushed the inland column and Macdonough's gunboats harassed the group moving along the shore of Lake Champlain. However the British persevered and arrived in Plattsburgh after suffering 200 casualties. There they were held in check by the 4th Infantry and others who manned the inner defenses.

Prevost decided to await the arrival of the British fleet. He planned to launch a two-pronged ground attack on the American fortifications as soon as the British Navy arrived on Lake Champlain with its four frigates and twelve gunboats. The British entered the lake on September 11 and the opposing navies joined the fight at 9:00 A.M., punishing each other severely. Ninety minutes later, the British flagship, *Confiance*, struck her colors and the battle ended in a U.S. victory.

Prevost, feeling that he could not hold Plattsburgh without control of the lake, gave the order to withdraw. The British retreated into Canada after suffering the loss of two thousand men. The Americans had lost 150. Many years later Sir Winston Churchill would call the U.S. victory at Plattsburgh, "the most decisive engagement of the war (7)."

Cook's Mills

While the Left Division under Jacob Brown was having military success in the Fort Erie area, the Right Division, commanded by MG George Izard, had been involved in an arduous march from Plattsburgh to the Niagara frontier. On March 9, 1814, the 5th Infantry's COL Daniel Bissell had been promoted to brigadier and COL John Bowyer had assumed command of the regiment. Bowyer, from Augusta County, Virginia, entered the regular army in 1792. In 1813, while commanding the 2nd Infantry, he was stationed on the southern frontier and participated in the capture of Mobile from Spanish troops.

The War of 1812

On 17 October, General Izard dispatched Bissell's 900-man brigade, composed of the 5th, 14th, 15th and 16th Regiments, to Cook's Mills on Lyon's Creek, a tributary of the Chippewa River (8). Intelligence had been received that the British were storing a large quantity of grain at that location. Poor roads precluded artillery support, but the infantrymen arrived at Cook's Mills on the evening of 18 October.

A heavy skirmish between the American riflemen and the Glengarry Fencibles convinced Bissell that sizable enemy forces were in the vicinity. His suspicions were confirmed on 19 October when U.S. outposts across the creek were attacked by 750 British troops of LTC Christopher Myers' 100th Foot. As Bissell's riflemen and light troops disputed Myers' advance, the brigade deployed for an immediate counterattack.

The U.S. line surged across Lyon's Creek in the face of heavy fire from muskets, artillery and rockets. Holding the 15th and 16th Regiments in reserve, Bissell ordered the 14th Infantry to attack the enemy front while the Fifth Infantry, under MAJ Ninian Pinkney, turned the British left flank. Both movements were successful and Myers, perceiving himself outnumbered, withdrew from Cook's Mills in orderly fashion.

The victorious Americans sustained 12 killed and 55 wounded to a British loss of 1 killed and 35 wounded. The U.S. troops returned to the mill, burned 200 bushels of wheat, and returned to Fort Erie without further incident.

The battle at Cook's Mills was the last encounter between regular forces in Canada during the War of 1812. The victory, over veterans of Wellington's army, reflects credit upon the officers and senior non-coms of Bissel's brigade. They had provided their young recruits with a full summer of instruction and drill at Plattsburgh and their efforts had paid dividends.

In October, the Duke of Wellington, was asked to assume

command of a renewed military effort. Britain's old war horse agreed to take command but expressed his sincere opinion that further efforts to force the United States to relinquish territory would be futile. His bleak outlook helped break the deadlock at Ghent and negotiations resumed.

On November 3, 1814, Congress bestowed a gold medal on James Miller. It bore his likeness, his famous words, "I'll try, sir," and the names of the battles of Chippewa, Niagara and Fort Erie.

The final peace treaty was signed on Christmas Eve, 1814. Both nations agreed to evacuate territories belonging to the other. Confiscation of enemy property was forbidden and all prisoners were to be returned as soon as possible. Both parties agreed to make peace with the Indians and there was an additional pledge to cooperate in the suppression of the slave trade. Hostilities would cease when both countries had ratified the treaty.

The U.S. Senate ratified the Treaty of Ghent on 16 February 1815. The war officially ended the following day with the United States and Great Britain exchanging ratifications. During the next few months there were several clashes between American and British naval vessels but, for all practical purposes, the war of 1812 was concluded.

The "New" Fifth

The Army was reduced to a peace footing in 1815 and COL Bowyer was discharged. He became an Indian agent and took over an agency near Green Bay, Wisconsin. He was of Huguenot descent, spoke French, and made himself about as popular with the unwilling natives as any American Indian agent could. He died on the job in 1820.

On May 17, 1815, the 4th, 9th, 13th, 21st, 40th, and 46th Regiments were collapsed into a single regiment commanded by James Miller (9). Colonel Miller had returned to his permanent rank. Eight regiments were retained in service and renumbered according to the date of rank of their commanding officers. James Miller, being the fifth-ranking colonel, became commander of the 5th Infantry Regiment, the designation that the regiment has retained ever since. By absorbing the men, the honors and the flag of the 4th Infantry, this new 5th Infantry preserved its April 12, 1808 authorization date. The new 2nd Infantry preserved the same date by absorbing the 6th Infantry Regiment. Therefore the 5th and the 2nd Infantry Regiments share the distinction of being the third oldest infantry units in the Regular Army. The two regiments are junior, only, to the oldest Regular Army regiment, the 3rd, and the second oldest, the 1st. There are several infantry regiments in the Army National Guard that are older than these Regular Army units.

The men of the old 5th Infantry Regiment, originally authorized on April 12, 1808, who had served with Winder's brigade, joined with those of the 17th, 19th, and 28th Regiments to form the 3rd United States Infantry. They were commanded by COL John Miller, the third-ranking American colonel. The 3rd (Old Guard) Infantry traces its roots to 3 June 1784, making it our nation's oldest infantry unit. Members of the Old Guard are garrisoned in Washington, DC, where their duties are largely ceremonial (10).

CHAPTER TWO

TAMING THE NORTHWEST

Article IX of the Treaty of Ghent provided that the United States would make peace with the Indian tribes and restore the possessions, rights and privileges that they had enjoyed before hostilities began. President Madison appointed a commission to negotiate peace treaties with the tribes. The commission was successful in a few cases, but by and large, the warring tribes of the upper Mississippi and upper Missouri River were reluctant to negotiate (1).

The Chippewas, Menominees and Winnebagoes refused to send delegations and the Sacs of Rock River not only refused to attend, but showed their contempt by harassing the frontier settlements during the period of negotiations. The peace commission closed its report with the opinion that the exertion of the military power of the government would be necessary to secure the peace and safety of this country.

In order to implement this policy, the 5th Infantry Regiment was assigned to the northwest, establishing its headquarters in Detroit in December, 1815 (2). Seven of the regiment's ten companies were scattered among small posts along the Great Lakes including St. Peters, Prairie du Chien and Fort Armstrong.

In May of 1816, Secretary of War Crawford directed BG Alexander Macomb, of Plattsburgh fame, to begin construction of a 70-mile road from Detroit, Michigan to Fort Meigs, near Perrysburg, Ohio. The construction job was assigned to the 5th Infantry from Detroit and the 3rd Infantry from Fort Wayne, Indiana. The road took over two years to complete. Those soldiers involved in the project received extra pay of 15 cents a day and an extra whiskey ration.

On February 10, 1818, LTC Henry Leavenworth was assigned to the 5th Infantry. Six years earlier, the young New York attorney had raised a company of volunteers and was elected captain. He distinguished himself at the battles of Chippewa and Niagara Falls and was commissioned in the regular army following the war.

Fort Snelling

On the tenth of February, 1819, the Secretary of War ordered the 5th Infantry to concentrate at Detroit and prepare to be transported across Lake Huron and Lake Michigan, up the Fox River, and down the Wisconsin River to Prairie du Chien. There a complement would garrison Fort Crawford, a part would proceed to Fort Armstrong, and the remainder would ascend the Mississippi and erect a post near the Falls of St. Anthony which would be the headquarters of the regiment. The Falls of St. Anthony are located where the cities of St. Paul and Minneapolis now stand.

Colonel James Miller remained in command until he resigned in 1819 to become the governor of Arkansas Territory. On June 1, 1819, Josiah Snelling was appointed colonel of the 5th Infantry and ordered to St. Louis where he spent the winter. In the summer of 1820 he set out to join his new regiment on the frontier but was detained in Prairie du Chien in order to preside over a court martial. Due to Snelling's long absence, command devolved upon LTC Henry Leavenworth. Leavenworth was acting as Superintendent of Indian Affairs in Prairie de Chien when the order arrived to assemble the regiment in Detroit.

On May 14, 1819, the 5th Infantry departed for the Northwest frontier. Accompanied by the wives and children of its married members, the regiment left Detroit in schooners, crossed Lake Huron, the Straits of Mackinac, and Lake Michigan and debarked at Fort Howard, the present site of Green Bay, Wisconsin. There they found that CPT Whistler's company of the 3rd U.S. Infantry had prepared flat boats for the troops to use in their ascent of the Fox River.

The regiment began its flat boat journey on June 7th and, when it reached the outlet of Lake Winnebago, an Indian emissary approached them and explained that Chief Four Legs, CEO of a nearby village, had the custom of exacting tribute from travelers using the Fox-Wisconsin route. Four Legs sent the message, "The lake is locked." Upon hearing this, LTC Leavenworth raised his rifle above his head and replied, "You tell him that this is the key and I shall unlock it and go on." The regiment moved on, unmolested, and, on June 30th, moored near Fort Crawford and Prairie de Chien. Within an hour after the regiment's arrival at Fort Crawford, a daughter, Charlotte Ouisconsin Clark, was born to LT and Mrs. Nathan Clark, the first white child born in the western Wisconsin wilderness.

At Fort Crawford there was a frustrating wait. Provisions, ammunition and recruits were expected from St. Louis. On July 5, MAJ Thomas Forsyth, the nineteenth century equivalent of a civil affairs officer, joined the party. On July 31, Forsyth's journal entry was "no boats, no recruits, no news, nor anything else from St. Louis" and on August 2, he recorded "Thank God, a boat loaded with ordnance and stores of different kinds arrived today and they said that a provision boat would arrive tomorrow, but no news of the recruits." To make personnel matters worse, MAJ Marston and twenty-seven soldiers had left the previous day to garrison Fort Armstrong at Rock Island.

Leaving a detachment at Fort Crawford, LTC Leavenworth, MAJ Forsyth, a dozen company officers and ninety-eight enlisted men set off on August 8, 1819 in the direction of the confluence of the Mississippi and the St. Peters River, which was about three hundred miles to the north. For sixteen days, the boatmen poled their flatboats up the river. Occasionally fog and rain impeded their progress. On August 17, when they reached the lower end of Lake Pepin, they went ashore for several hours so the men could draw provisions from the supply boats and wash their dirty underwear. As they traveled north, Major Forsyth stopped at Indian villages to distribute gifts and to brief the natives on the Army's mission and the value they would derive from having a fort in their midst.

Taming the Northwest

On Tuesday morning, August 24, LTC Leavenworth arrived at the mouth of the Minnesota River, ahead of the troops, and spent the entire day choosing a camp site, a spot on the right bank of the Minnesota, just above its mouth. When the troops arrived they were immediately put to work constructing a loading ramp on the river bank and cutting down trees for lumber.

Colonel Leavenworth turned around and headed for Prairie du Chien to look for the badly needed supplies and reinforcements. On September 1, on Lake Pepin, he encountered two keel boats and a flat boat bearing one hundred and twenty new recruits. He gave them their orders and continued on to Prairie du Chien where he remained for awhile to urge on any other boats that might arrive. The new troops reached the regimental camp site on September 5.

Thanks to the increase in numbers of strong backs and hands, log cabins and a stockade were hastily erected on the low ground. In November the men were able to move off the boats and into the barracks. Looking forward to a pleasant winter, the name Cantonment New Hope was bestowed on the new garrison. The men of the 5th Infantry and the small group of wives and children were the first white settlers in Minnesota.

Snow came early that year and the encampment was barely finished in time for what became a cruel ordeal. The winter of 1819-1820 was one of the coldest on record (3). Surgeon Edward Purcell recorded twenty sub-zero mornings during January. The crude shelters were inadequate and most of the salt meat, flour and hard tack, so laboriously transported through the wilderness, was covered with mold. Toward the close of winter, scurvy and pneumonia took the lives of forty men of the regiment. There were days when work was suspended so that the few able-bodied members of the regiment could attend to the sick and bury the dead.

Late in the fall, a lieutenant named Oliver and a small detail of men had left Prairie du Chien with a keel boat loaded with supplies, but the river froze and the boat was unable to progress farther than the vicinity of Hastings, Minnesota. There they were obligated to remain on guard all winter to protect the food from Indians and wolves.

Thinking that much of the sickness was caused by the unhealthful location, Colonel Leavenworth, on May 5, moved the troops to a place on the west bank of the Mississippi, north of Minnesota, where there was a nice spring of cold water. Here the men, quartered in tents, named their community Camp Cold Water.

Colonel Snelling finally arrived and assumed his new command in August of 1820. When he found that construction was still proceeding at the site of the infamous winter camp and resembled a camp rather than a fort, he put a stop to it. Snelling chose a new site on a commanding bluff overlooking the confluence of the two rivers.

A saw mill was needed to make the lumber for furniture and for the interior of the buildings. The mill was erected at the Falls of St. Anthony and, during the winter of 1820-21, a party of soldiers was sent upstream and devoted full time to cutting logs and dragging them to the river bank. These soldiers received the extra 15 cents a day, raising a private's pay from $8.00 to $12.50 a month. Other men, not involved in the construction of the fort, spent many hours cultivating ninety acres of corn, potatoes, wheat and peas.

The fort was partially occupied in the fall of 1822 before the surrounding stone wall had been completed. Once finished, the ten foot wall was diamond shaped, one point being at the edge of the bluff where the valley of the Minnesota met that of the Mississippi. Two points rested on their respective river bluffs and the fourth was on the plateau approximately seven hundred feet from the first point. The final building, the Indian Council House, was completed in July, 1823 and consummated at the end of the month when Governor Cass of Michigan Territory used it to facilitate a peace agreement between the Sioux and the Chippewa. Colonel Snelling named the structure Fort St. Anthony.

Sometime in the early summer of 1824, General Winfield Scott inspected the new post. He was favorably impressed and, in his report to the Secretary of War, recommended that the fort be named Fort Snelling in honor of the energetic officer that oversaw its construction. A general order issued January 7, 1825 directed the name change and Fort Snelling began its career as guardian of the Northwest.

During the first years of its existence, while the buildings were being erected and the fort was making its place in the Indian life and the fur trade of the surrounding region, the frontier was comparatively quiet. The first rumbles occurred in 1826 in Illinois and Wisconsin, where the Winnebagoes were constantly butting heads with the lead miners around Galena. This prompted COL Snelling to reinforce the garrison at Fort Crawford with three companies of the 5th Infantry under the command of CPT Wilcox.

Soon thereafter the Secretary of War decided to abandon Fort Crawford. The Winnebagoes were delighted with that decision. On June 26th, the Winnebago chief, Red Bird, and three of his men were enraged by a rumor that two of their kinsmen had been killed by soldiers at the Fort Snelling stockade. The foursome attacked a farm house near Prairie du Chien and scalped a child. As they returned to their village, they spotted a keel boat, the *O. H. Perry* coming down the river. After rallying several more warriors, Red Bird's group attacked the boat. During a skirmish that lasted several hours, they killed two of the Perry's crew members and lost seven of their own warriors.

Major John Fowle and four companies of the 5th Infantry from Fort Snelling linked up with elements of the 6th Infantry from Jefferson Barracks and the 3rd Infantry from Fort Howard and descended upon Red Bird's home turf. Governor Lewis Cass proposed the convening of a council to prevent open warfare. The rapidity of the military movements impressed the Winnebagoes and they backed off. In September, a group of Red Bird's people approached the camp of the 3rd Infantry bearing a white flag of surrender and two American flags. They turned over two perpetrators of the June murder.

On the 9th of September a provisional treaty was ratified in which the United States promised to appoint a commission to look at Indian grievances. Following the treaty, the 6th and 3rd Infantry Regiments were sent home but, as a precaution, Major Fowle's battalion was directed to re-occupy Fort Crawford. The outpost was provisioned for a year.

Garrison Life

A soldier's life on the frontier was generally one of monotonous drills and tedious routine (4). Any pretext to make an incursion into Indian country would have been hailed with delight. No sooner was dawn visible over the Mississippi bluffs than the drummers and fifers of the post were summoned to the parade ground and five minutes later reveille was sounded. The officers and men arose and assembled in front of their quarters for roll call. They straightened up their quarters, swept the ground in front of the buildings and fed and watered the horses. At eight-thirty the sick were marched to the hospital and breakfast was served at nine, preceded by a second roll call. Then the various tasks of the day were performed under the direction of the officer of the day.

A party called the "general fatigue" swept the entire parade ground—unless there were enough prisoners in the guard house to perform this dusty duty. A guard mount furnished sentinels to watch over the prisoners, the colors, the colonel's quarters and the regimental armory. Other soldiers were posted at the front and rear of the fort. Several additional detachments were formed for reconnoitering, foraging, and agricultural duties.

At three o'clock in the afternoon the third roll call was followed by dinner. Then thirty minutes before sunset the musicians called out the regiment for dress parade, dismounted drill, a fourth roll call and the reading of orders. After the parade, the men retired to their quarters, placed their arms in the rifle racks and attended to the horses. After a fifth roll call, the bugler sounded tattoo. Following that the candles were extinguished and everyone was expected to be quiet for the night.

The monotony of the daily program was equaled only by the blandness of the meals. The regulation daily diet prescribed by Congress in 1802 consisted of a pound and a quarter of beef, or three-quarters of a pound of pork, eighteen ounces of bread or flour, and one gill (4 ounces) of rum, whiskey or brandy. For every hundred rations, two quarts of salt, four quarts of vinegar, four pounds of soap and a pound and a half of candles were supplied. In 1832, coffee and sugar replaced the liquor ration. The neighboring Indians made a good living selling freshly killed game to the hungry soldiers.

Given the daily routine and diet of the soldier, one can understand why desertions were prevalent and five roll calls a day were required in the 1820's. A War Department study of the problem yielded some numbers for the 5th Infantry for 1823-25 during COL Snelling's tenure.

In 1823, six of 251 soldiers deserted. In 1824 the percentage remained the same as eight of 335 soldiers took off. For some reason, in 1825, twenty-nine of 246 men went over the hill. Numbers for 1832, when the booze ration was replaced by coffee, were not readily available.

Certainly the location of Fort Snelling kept a lid on the desertion rate. It was scary out in those woods and the closest settlement was Prairie du Chien, a military town. A soldier named Dixon was captured by Indians who brought him back to Fort Snelling to collect a twenty dollar reward. Dixon received fifty lashes with a cat o' nine tails and was drummed out of the army. Four other deserters were killed by some of Red Bird's warriors and left on the shore of Lake Pepin, where they were devoured by birds.

Colonel Snelling served as regimental commander until the regiment was ordered to Fort Howard in 1828. On the way to Fort Howard, a detachment was dropped at Portage, Wisconsin to help the 3rd Infantry establish Fort Winnebago. In 1829 the regiment was split among Fort Dearborn, Fort Brady, Fort Mackinac and Fort Howard. Fort Dearborn was located in what is now the Chicago area and Fort Brady still stands at Sault Ste. Marie, Michigan where it is now the home of Lake Superior State University. Fort Mackinac is located on nearby Mackinac Island, Michigan.

Josiah Snelling died on August 20, 1828. He was an excellent soldier, but said to be a problem drinker and cruel disciplinarian, especially when he'd downed a few too many. Behind his back, the men referred to him as the "Prairie Hen" because of his flaming red hair and high forehead. When, as often happened, the regiment was paraded to witness the whipping of a transgressor, Snelling frequently wielded the lash himself. Nevertheless, he was respected and his sudden death in Washington, D.C. was genuinely regretted by many.

William Lawrence became the new colonel. He resigned in 1831, making way for George M. Brooke, who would command the regiment for the next thirteen years. Brooke had entered the service in 1808 as a lieutenant in the old 5th Infantry. On July 15, 1831, Brevet Brigadier Brooke was granted the permanent rank of colonel and given command of the regiment.

The Black Hawk War

In 1831, white settlers, who had moved into Illinois, used force to impose a "treaty" that compelled the Sac and Fox Indians to retire from their lands. In April, 1832, Black Hawk, a Sac leader, with some four hundred braves and their families, returned to Illinois. When one of the peaceful emissaries that he had sent to the white community was shot down in cold blood, the outraged Black Hawk successfully attacked a larger white force and then retired into Wisconsin.

The companies of the 5th Infantry scattered throughout Wisconsin on the trail of Chief Black Hawk. On August 2, Company F, commanded by CPT T. F. Hunt, was present at the battle of Bad Axe River, near Victory, Wisconsin, when a Sioux war party and a large force of volunteers commanded by General Henry Atkinson cornered Black Hawk and his band (6). Black Hawk displayed a white flag, but was ignored and almost all of his group, including women and children, were slain.

In 1833, Headquarters and Companies G, H, I, and K were posted at Fort Howard, C, D, E, and F at Fort Winnebago, and A and B at Fort Brady. During the year the latter two were shifted to Fort Dearborn. That summer the entire regiment was assembled at Fort Winnebago for its first concentration since 1819.

After leaving the 5th Infantry, COL Henry Leavenworth devoted several years to explorations and Indian duties along the west bank of the Missouri River. He established Fort Leavenworth in May of 1827. During a campaign against the Pawnee, who had been harassing traders along the Santa Fe Trail, Leavenworth contracted cholera. He died on July 21, 1834 in a hospital wagon at Cross Timbers in Indian Territory.

Return to Fort Snelling

In the autumn of 1837 there was another major reshuffling. Headquarters and Company K returned to Fort Howard while D, G, and H remained at Winnebago. Companies A, E, F and I were shifted to Fort Snelling and B and D returned to Fort Crawford. They remained at these posts until December, 1840.

When the four companies returned to Fort Snelling in 1837, CPT Joseph Plympton, who had served with the 5th Infantry since its 1815 reorganization, was named post commander. Most of his service had been as commander of Company E.

Plympton's nickname among the troops was "Old Ring", earned because of his method of meting out punishment. The guilty party was assigned to a wood chopping detail and was required to use an axe with a loose metal ring on its handle. Whenever the axe was raised, the heavy ring slid down the handle, sharply striking the hand of its wielder. CPT Plympton usually staged these sessions in front of his own quarters, where he could keep an eye on the victim to see that he worked steadily.

During the 5th Infantry's second tour at Fort Snelling, a trivial incident occurred which, while highly exciting in the humdrum life of the garrison might have been forgotten but for the subsequent fame of one of its principals (7). One afternoon CPT Plympton was attracted to the parade ground by a sudden uproar. There he discovered a badly frightened post quartermaster fleeing for his life with the Post Surgeon, Dr. John Emmerson, in hot pursuit. Emmerson was brandishing a pair of horse pistols and roaring at his prospective target to stand and take it like a man.

Plympton halted the chase and demanded an explanation. He was told that a few minutes earlier, Dr. Emmerson had encountered the quartermaster delivering sheet metal stoves to the quarters and he had requested one for his Negro man servant. The quartermaster quickly replied that he was all out of them and one word led to another, leading to the doctor calling the smaller man a liar. The quartermaster promptly punched Dr. Emmerson on the nose. The infuriated surgeon returned to his quarters, procured his pistols and went hunting for the now thoroughly alarmed supply officer.

The affair blew over after much excited talk of a duel and the departure of John Emmerson for his home in St. Louis. The black man, over whom the fight started, was Dred Scott, whose celebrated fight for freedom twenty years later was a contributing cause to the bitterness that precipitated the Civil War. Mr. Scott's plea was based upon his having resided in free territory at Fort Snelling while his master served with the 5th Infantry.

Joseph C. Plympton was transferred to the 2nd Infantry in September, 1840 when he was promoted to major. He was brevetted colonel of the 7th Infantry on April 18, 1847 for gallant and meritorious conduct during the battle of Cerro Gordo, Mexico. He died in New York in 1860.

Taming the Northwest

In 1842, there were widespread reports of large quantities of copper ore in upper Michigan, near the shore of Lake Superior. An influx of miners led the army to send Companies A and B of the 5th Infantry to the area, in March, 1844, to maintain order. These soldiers, under the command of CPT R.E. Clary, quickly built a permanent fortification, Fort Wilkins, near the present community of Copper Harbor (8).

On August 1, 1844, COL George M. Brooke was appointed to the command of Military Department #4 with responsibility for the states of Ohio, Indiana, Michigan, Wisconsin, Illinois, Iowa, and Missouri. He was relieved of his command of the 5th Infantry by LTC James Simmons McIntosh, one of four men who would lead the regiment during the war with Mexico.

McIntosh, a Georgian, had entered the army on November 13, 1812 as a second lieutenant with the 1st U.S. Rifle Regiment. Following the war he served on the frontier with the 4th and 7th Infantry Regiments and, upon being promoted to lieutenant colonel on July 1, 1839, was assigned to the staff of the 5th Infantry.

The frontier years were peaceful but far from easy. What would be the prosperous farm and manufacturing states of Minnesota, Wisconsin, Michigan and Illinois were a howling wilderness, covered with forests and peopled by fierce, unpredictable folks who were held in check only by constant vigilance. Living conditions were primitive and communications with the East Coast took a matter of months. The unmilitary duties of farming, hunting and wood cutting were more important to the regiment's mission than close order drill and maneuvers. Nevertheless, the small regular army clung, as best it could, to its military forms and social amenities. The 5th Infantry fought no major battles during this period but its contribution to the settlement of the mid-west was probably more valuable than a victory upon the battlefield.

CHAPTER THREE

WAR WITH MEXICO

James K. Polk became the nation's eleventh president in 1845. He had campaigned on the proposition that Texas should be "re-annexed" and that all of Oregon should be "re-occupied." He also favored acquiring California. His Whig opponent, Henry Clay, opposed Polk's expansionist views. The Whigs, the forerunners of today's Republicans, argued that the United States did not have a valid claim to Texas and California and suspected that the Democrats were bent on starting a war designed to spread slavery and increase the political power of the south. Clay came within a narrow margin of defeating Polk in the presidential campaign. Clay would not have authorized the Mexican War. Some believe he might even have been able to mediate the deeply rooted tensions that would soon lead to the Civil War (1).

Polk sent an envoy to offer Mexico up to $20 million for California and the New Mexico area. His envoy was turned away. Polk responded by sending Zachary Taylor to Corpus Christi, Texas to bring military pressure to bear. His forces were said to be an "army of observation."

In the spring of 1845 the 5th Infantry was ordered to pack up and march south. When the regiment reached Texas on the 11th of October, it was assigned to Persifor Frazer Smith's Brigade of General William Worth's Division. Worth was a 51-year-old veteran of the War of 1812 who had been severely wounded at Lundy's Lane. He and Smith had met during the Seminole War in 1840 when Smith was serving as colonel for a regiment of Louisiana volunteers. The 5th Infantry, as previously mentioned, was commanded by LTC James McIntosh.

In August, Taylor re-designated his force an "army of occupation

WAR WITH MEXICO

(2)." With the arrival of the 5th, 7th, and 8th Infantry Regiments the army grew to 3900 men. This represented half of the total strength of the regular army, leaving one regiment to watch the 2000 miles of border with Canada and three to protect the 1500 miles of Indian frontier.

Because of soft public support for going to war, especially among Americans in the northeast, President Polk decided to avoid large scale use of state militias. The War Department requested the raising of 50,000 volunteers by the governors of the more sympathetic states of Louisiana, Alabama, Mississippi, Tennessee and Kentucky. The regular army was authorized to double its size by recruiting enough men to bring its units to full strength.

When they reached Corpus Christi, the 5th Infantry and its sister regiments started extensive training programs. The elements of the 5th hadn't served together in nine years and junior officers had forgotten what they had learned of battalion drill and tactics. Drilling took place on a large field hacked out of the underbrush about a quarter of a mile from camp. The training was so incessant that one soldier complained that life had become "nothing but drill and parades, and your ears are filled all day with drumming and fifing." By mid-November, the regiment could mount a creditable review.

As the beautiful weather of early fall gave way to the miserable, wet, and unhealthy climate of winter, drill ceased, diarrhea and dysentery spread and discipline began to disappear. The men shivered in leaking tents around which they had banked earth to keep out the wind. At one point a fifth of the force was on the sick list and half of the others were scarcely able to perform their duties.

General Taylor received orders on February 3, 1846 to advance to the Rio Grande as soon as possible. The dragoons and Ringgold's Battery crossed the line of departure on Sunday morning, March 8 and the three infantry brigades followed on successive days. Their move south got the expected reaction from the Mexicans.

On April 11, Major General Pedro de Ampudia and his Mexican

Division of the North arrived in Matamoros on the south bank of the Rio Grande. He gave the American residents twenty-four hours to retire to Victoria, Texas and sent a letter to Taylor demanding that he pull his troops back across the Nueces River. Taylor refused on the grounds that his orders would not permit a withdrawal and ordered the mouth of the Rio Grande blockaded in order to cut Ampudia's supply line from New Orleans, the main source of the Mexican Army's supplies. General Ampudia made plans to cross the river, but put those on hold when he got word that he was being replaced by Major General Mariano Arista.

Arista reached Matamoros on April 24 and immediately notified Taylor that hostilities had commenced. Arista sent a 1600-man force of cavalry, sappers and light infantry across the Rio Grande to cut the Point Isabel road and isolate the American troops from their supply point.

Palo Alto, Texas

At 3 o'clock on the afternoon of the twenty-fourth, Taylor received a report that Mexicans were crossing south of his positions. He sent CPT Croghan Ker with a detachment of dragoons to investigate. They found nothing. A second report during the evening caused the American general to send CPT Seth B. Thornton with two squadrons to check the river crossings. The following morning, about twenty miles from camp, Thornton rode into an ambush. He tried to fight his way out but lost eleven men killed and six wounded. Most of the rest of his eighty men were captured, including CPT Thornton and his second-in-command CPT William J. Hardee. One injured captive returned to the American camp and related the story of the ambush. General Taylor dispatched the news of the clash to Washington and stated that "hostilities may now be considered as commenced."

Congress declared war and Taylor, with two of his brigades of regulars, advanced to Palo Alto, Texas, where the opening battle was fought on May 8. The first pitched battle between Taylor's column of 2300 and the 4000 Mexicans under General Arista was primarily an artillery duel in which the superior American batteries dealt the hardest punch. While the American barrage wreaked havoc among the closely packed Mexicans, the latter's copper projectiles flew so slowly that the Americans had time to open ranks and let them pass harmlessly through.

About 3:00 P.M., Arista dispatched his cavalry to strike the American right flank under cover of a prairie fire smoke screen. Taylor had placed the four hundred members of the 5th Infantry on his right. As the Mexican lancers exited the smoke, they were met by such a discharge of musketry that they fled, leaving men, horses, and unit guidons on the field.

The two sides paused to catch their breath. Arista tried another flank attack on Taylor's left, toward the U.S. Army's exposed wagon train, but his horsemen lost their nerve and fell back.

By late afternoon both armies were being blinded by the pungent smoke from the grass and chaparral. When the haze began to clear, Taylor sent a force of dragoons forward toward the Mexican wagon park. The wagons were well protected, however, and the American horsemen withdrew.

Arista's disheartened soldiers now demanded that the slaughter end. They were being killed unmercifully at long range. Many Mexican wounded, lying on the field, burned to death in the prairie fire. The two armies broke contact at 7:00 in the evening.

Resaca de la Palma

The next morning, at 6:00 A.M., Arista decided to retreat from the field of Palo Alto to a stronger position. Four hours later the Mexicans arrived at a place called Resaca de la Palma. It was a dry ravine that had once been a channel of the ever-changing Rio Grande.

Upon discovering that the Mexicans had withdrawn, General

Two Centuries of Valor

Taylor called a council of war to discuss the next move. Because of the size difference between the opposing armies, seven out of ten of Taylor's commanders suggested that they remain at Palo Alto until the volunteers, that Taylor had requested at an early date, arrived. LTC McIntosh of the 5th Infantry was one of the three that favored continuing the attack. "Old Zack" heard his officers out and then said, "Gentlemen, you will prepare your commands to move forward (3)."

Taylor's men hit the road. The 5th Infantry was deployed on the left of the main assault line, facing the best of Arista's artillery. At about 3:00 P.M. the regiment began receiving fire from the Mexican guns.

Taylor responded by calling forward May's squadron of dragoons and ordering it to assault the offending battery. May's men charged at a full gallop in a column of fours. The troopers cleared the gun line with little loss, but their momentum was so great that they overshot by a quarter mile and became exposed to heavy fire from their flanks. With no accompanying infantry the dragoons could not hold the guns. They returned with several prisoners in tow, including a brigade commander, General Romolo Diaz de la Vega.

A disgusted Taylor ordered the 5th Infantry and the newly arrived 8th Infantry to take the guns. It was a particularly bloody transaction in which both Lieutenant Colonels McIntosh of the 5th and Belknap of the 8th were wounded. The 5th Infantry suffered nine killed and twenty-four wounded during the fight. Nevertheless the infantrymen secured the guns and forced the Mexicans to abandon their positions east of the road. McIntosh was brevetted colonel for "gallant and distinguished service." Major Thomas Staniford, who assumed command when McIntosh fell and who led the winning assault, was promoted to brevet lieutenant colonel.

Following Resaca there was a long period of inactivity, during which Taylor's reinforcements arrived. Casualties and promotions necessitated several changes within the regiment at this time. Major

Staniford was promoted permanently to lieutenant colonel and transferred to the 8th Infantry. Captain Martin Scott was promoted to major and took over the 5th Regiment in the absence of Colonel McIntosh.

Monterrey

The next step in Taylor's plan was to capture the city of Monterrey in an effort to separate Northern and Southern Mexico. On Monday, July 6, three companies of the 7th Infantry embarked on the steamer *Enterprise* at Matamoros. Mechanical problems caused a three day delay at Reynosa forcing transfer of part of the command to another steamer but they managed to reach Ciudad Camargo on the morning of the 14th. The rest of the Seventh arrived the next day, followed shortly by General Worth and the 5th Infantry.

Worth's Division departed Ciudad Camargo on the 19th on a sixty-mile march to Cerralvo where they would establish a supply depot and wait for the rest of the army. It was an unpleasant hike. The road, scarcely more than a trail at times, had to be rebuilt as they headed south.

On August 25, the division reached the picturesque town of Cerralvo with its low stone houses and fruit trees. It was a pleasant change from their previous camp on the Rio Grande. Here Worth awaited the rest of the army. By September 9, the last division had arrived bringing the strength of the expedition to 6,640 officers and men. They left Cerralvo for Monterrey on September 15.

At about 9:00 A.M. on September 19, Taylor and his advance guard rode out onto the plain before Monterrey. Within the city, General Ampudia had assembled a strong defense. Taylor sent Worth's two thousand regulars on a wide sweep to the north and west of the town. Their mission was to cut Ampudia's communications and attack Monterrey from the rear.

Worth's column was detected and attacked by Mexican cavalry

who failed to halt the march. Reaching the highway, the Americans found the route guarded by two well-fortified hills. Independencia Hill barred the main road while across the San Juan River, to the south, Federación Ridge protected a branch road to Saltillo.

The fight for Monterrey lasted four days that began with Worth's Division assaulting Federación on September 20. The 5th Infantry, originally placed before Independencia was shifted across the river and assisted taking Federación with a flanking attack from the north. That night the regiment re-crossed the river and, after a miserable night spent huddled in the cold and rain, helped storm Independencia. Crawling quietly up the slope just before dawn, the Americans carried the crest with a short and sudden rush. The division spent the rest of that day and all of the 22nd preparing for a counterattack and making arrangements for an assault upon the city center.

On the morning of the 23rd an attack was launched east of the town to relieve the pressure on Worth's exposed position. Under cover of the diversion, Worth's men moved forward, carrying pick axes, crowbars and fused shells. Reaching the town, the column, with the 5th Infantry still in the thick of battle, fought its way from house to house, opening breaches in the adobe walls with tools, clearing interiors with its crude but effective grenades and pushing on to the next. By nightfall the battered and exhausted Americans were within a block of the central plaza.

Companies E, F, G, H, I and K participated in this series of engagements (4). The remainder of the regiment had been assigned to the division's rear guard. Among those cited for conspicuous gallantry was the interim regimental commander, Major Scott.

Negotiations for a cessation of hostilities began on the early morning of September 24, when COL Francisco Moreno, General Ampudia's aide-de-camp, was escorted to General Taylor's headquarters. Moreno laid down the audacious condition that Ampudia's troops be permitted to march off with all of their arms and equipment. After several attempts to reach an agreement, Taylor compromised. The Mexicans would retain one battery of cannons and twenty-one rounds of artillery shot and there would be an eight week armistice to allow Ampudia ample time to vacate the city. The surrender was duly signed by the army representatives during the early morning hours of September 25, 1846.

On September 28, Taylor designated William J. Worth to be the military governor of Monterrey and his division moved in. The men were grateful for the respite. The process of rebuilding and refitting the army would take awhile. Taylor estimated six weeks.

When news of Taylor's victory reached the White House on October 11, President Polk was incensed. He disapproved of the truce that Taylor had negotiated. "The enemy had been in his power," Polk claimed, "and Taylor should have made prisoners of them all, stripped them of their arms, put them on parole, and pushed on into the country." He was especially unhappy that Taylor had agreed to an eight-week cease fire.

Saltillo

While General Taylor was in Monterrey plotting his overland campaign to subdue the rest of Mexico, his civilian "betters" in Washington were in a hurry to accelerate the war. Polk decided that Winfield Scott would lead an amphibious assault that would land on Mexico's east coast at Vera Cruz. Taylor, on the other hand, decided to strike south to Saltillo. On November 8, he ordered Worth to depart for Saltillo in four days.

Along the route to Saltillo, the men of the 5th Infantry marched thirty miles up the Santa Catarina River, past a village of the same name, then southward into the gorge of Rinconada Pass, then upward once again, breaking out into a wide valley that led to Saltillo. Here in the higher altitudes the vegetation turned from citrus groves to wheat fields. A seventy-mile march had brought them from the tropics to a temperate zone.

Two Centuries of Valor

Along with the change in scenery, Worth's men could easily detect hostility in the attitude of the Mexican people. When they were within a dozen miles of Saltillo, they were met by a group of citizens bearing a protest from the governor of the state of Nuevo Leon. The protest was ignored and the division marched on to the Saltillo town plaza with drums beating and colors flying.

Despite the cold welcome they received, the men found Saltillo to be a fairly pleasant place with good streets and well-built houses. Flour was plentiful but fuel had to be brought in from miles away and a lack of firewood would mean a cold winter. The townspeople attempted to gouge the soldiers for forage for the division's animals but backed down when General Taylor threatened to seize what he wanted and set his own price.

General Scott planned to leave New York for the Rio Grande in late November. Before sailing he wrote a letter to Zachary Taylor informing him that he would soon leave for Mexico to conduct operations in a new area.

When Scott arrived in Texas, he notified Taylor that he would be stripping him of nine thousand officers and men, including his two regular infantry divisions. He advised Taylor to pull out of Saltillo and return to Monterrey until he was reinforced. Taylor was left with fewer than a thousand regulars and a volunteer force of new levies to hold a defensive line. A Mexican army of over twenty thousand was approaching from the south.

Zachary "Old Rough and Ready" Taylor was outraged by Scott's message. He responded by ignoring Scott and, leaving Worth's Division in Saltillo, pushed south toward San Luis Potosí with the newly-arrived Wool's Division. Thanks, once again, to the artillery, Taylor's army squeaked by in a fight with General Santa Anna at Buena Vista on February 22-23, 1847.

War With Mexico

Veracruz

In January 1847, the 5th Infantry and the rest of Worth's regulars were ordered to return to the mouth of the Rio Grande. From there they sailed to Lobos Island, sixty miles south of Tampico, to prepare for their transfer to General Scott's expedition.

Finally, on March 2, an invasion fleet large enough to transport seven regiments of regular infantry, ten regiments of volunteers, four artillery battalions, six companies of dragoons and engineer and ordnance personnel had been assembled. Scott gave the order to move out. The 5th Infantry spent the next seven days aboard the sailing ship *Huron*, commanded by CPT N. G. Weeks.

On the evening of March 9, the troops debarked. The 4th, 5th, 6th, and 8th Infantry Regiments were placed on the right flank of the invading force. Eight miles of sand dunes covered with thorny mimosa and prickly pear bushes lay between them and Veracruz. They were instructed to hack their way forward for a third of the distance and then stop. Scott had decided to reduce the city by siege despite protests from Worth and other impatient officers.

After two weeks of fruitless negotiations with Mexican General Juan Morales, the U.S. Navy proceeded to shell Veracruz. By March 25, Scott's four 24-pounders, ten 10-inch mortars, two 8-inch siege howitzers, three 32-pounders, and three long 8-inch Paixhans were emplaced and pounding the city and its walls.

That afternoon, the consuls of England, France and Prussia petitioned Scott to suspend the bombardment while the foreign nationals as well as the Mexican women and children vacated the city. Scott refused, so the foreign consuls went to work on General Morales, imploring him to surrender. Morales complained of a stomach ache and turned his command over to General J. J. Landero. The latter proposed that both sides appoint commissioners and arrange a "convention." Scott ordered a cease fire and the representatives met for the first time on the afternoon of the twenty-sixth.

At first the Mexicans demanded that their garrison of three thousand men be allowed to march out, without parole, carrying arms and accoutrements. That refused, they met again the next day with new instructions. When it became obvious that Scott was getting impatient and about ready to recommence the bombardment, the Mexicans signed the agreement. It was 9:00 P.M, March 27, 1847.

Cerro Gordo

Veracruz, while an important city and port, was only a base from which to advance to Mexico City. Scott decided to travel west by way of Jalapa, Perote and Puebla. When the general ordered Twigg's Division to take the point, Worth threw a fit; considering the decision a personal rejection.

Unfortunately, for General Scott, the one-year enlistment of his volunteer regiments expired in May, 1847. Very few of his citizen soldiers were interested in seeing any more of Mexico. The Tennessee Cavalry, the 3rd and 4th Illinois Infantry, the 1st and 2nd Tennessee Infantry and the infantry regiments from Georgia and Alabama packed their knapsacks. Leaving their tents and camp equipment, they headed east to Veracruz and home.

Scott was left with a little over 7000 men. Nevertheless, he instructed Worth to march toward Puebla and, as he passed by Perote, to garrison one regiment there.

On May 15th, General Worth met with commissioners from Puebla to work out the details of the occupation and, shortly before 10:00 A.M., 4200 American troops marched into the city. Puebla, population 80,000, was laid out in a rectangular grid. The city was noted for lovely women, large cotton mills and a beautiful twin-towered cathedral. Nearly as far above sea level as Mexico City, the new American position offered the occupation forces a bracing climate and a rich agricultural hinterland. The remainder of the U.S. Army closed on Puebla about a week behind Worth. Scott and his headquarters staff arrived on May 29. While resting at Puebla, Scott drilled his troops and waited for replacements, which arrived in driblets.

Colonel James McIntosh, still somewhat disabled by wounds suffered at Resaca de Palma, led a detachment of 700 raw recruits. They were serving as guards for a wagon train carrying ammunition and $350,000 to pay the army and buy supplies. They left Veracruz on June 4, but the reports of treasure in the train resulted in so many guerrilla attacks that McIntosh had to halt at Paso de Ovejas. The teamsters could not keep the column sufficiently compact to defend it effectively.

McIntosh sent word to BG George Cadwalader who was enroute with a sizable force of reinforcements that had been diverted from the Rio Grande. Cadwalader rushed forward with 500 men and linked up with McIntosh on June 8. Five days later the combined force drove the guerrillas from the Puente Nacional. When they reached Jalapa on July 16, they incorporated that garrison of 400 into their ranks. The Cadwalader column joined a larger group of reinforcements led by MG Gideon Pillow and finally reached the main body of the army at Puebla on August 8. They had been preceded, two days earlier, by a smaller group of 2500 men commanded by BG Franklin Pierce. Pierce's column was a composite of new recruits and COL Samuel E. Watson's Marine battalion.

By the eighth of August, the army was up to 10,500 effectives and ready to proceed. Scott could spare no men to keep his communications open with Veracruz. His army would have to live off the land.

Scott issued the order for the advance to Mexico City on August 5. General Twiggs formed his division on the seventh and the column began moving. The divisions of Worth, Quitman and Pillow followed at one-day intervals. By the 10th only a small garrison remained in Puebla to guard the supplies and care for the sick and wounded. The 5th Infantry was assigned to the column's rear guard.

Two Centuries of Valor

Churubusco

General Santa Anna's troops were centered at Churubusco on the northern rim of a large oval lava bed called the Pedregal. Scott ordered General Worth to attack along the San Antonio-Churubusco Road until he had linked up with General Pillow's Division. Then Worth was to pursue the retreating enemy.

Clarke's Brigade with the 5th Infantry on point, was sent through the Pedregal to turn Santa Anna's position. The brigade struggled over the tortuous volcanic rock, requiring two hours to cover less than three miles. Seeing the American maneuver, the Mexicans fell back and scrambled toward Churubusco.

Built at the crossing of a tiny river of the same name, Churubusco was a convent village whose fortress-like monastery had been converted into a strong position flanking a bridge. Where the river traversed the town, it had been straightened and widened into a twenty-foot irrigation canal, devoid of cover and holding about three feet of water.

Clarke's Brigade, in hot pursuit of the retreating Mexicans, hit the bridgehead and recoiled under the converging fire of the two flanking strongholds. Deploying to the right, with the 6th Infantry on the road and the 5th and 8th floundering in some tall corn and a maze of rivulets on the right of the highway, Clarke launched two confused attacks against the bridge. They were repulsed with bloody losses.

Rattled by the cut-up ground and the destructive enfilading fire, the troops became disorganized and, for a time, appeared to be on the verge of panic. Discipline and training held, however, and finally the badly intermingled 5th and 7th Regiments reached the river and waded across under a galling fire from the bridge. The bridge was captured by a bayonet charge and the convent, defended by the notorious San Patricio Battalion of Irish-American deserters was over-run.

Eight companies of the 5th Infantry were in the thick of the fight at Churubusco on August 20. Companies C and D, at that time, were

War With Mexico

still away on supply train escort duty. The regiment went into action with 14 officers and 370 men, losing two officers wounded and 49 men killed, wounded and missing (5).

Colonel McIntosh, commanding the Fifth, became brigade commander, in the midst of the action, when Colonel Clarke was wounded. Brevet LTC Martin Scott assumed command of the 5th Infantry. One of the five 5th Infantry officers brevetted for bravery was 2nd LT Frederick T. Dent. Dent, the commander of Company E, was the West Point roommate and brother-in-law of Ulysses S. Grant. He rose to star rank in the Civil War and Chief of Staff to his famous relative.

The truly inspired enemy resistance at Churubusco was the toughest that the 5th Infantry had experienced in the war. Eight members of the regiment were killed in action and 58 were wounded; eleven of them severely. The good defensive position at the Convento de Churubusco and the presence of the San Patricios combined to bring out the tenacity and courage of the Mexican soldiers. General Anaya stated in his after-action report that 35 members of the St. Patrick's Battalion were killed, 85 were taken prisoner and another 85 escaped with the retreating Mexican forces.

Among those captured was CPT John Riley, formerly PVT John Riley of Company K, 5th U.S. Infantry. Riley, who had enlisted in Michigan in September, 1845, deserted at Matamoros in April, 1846.

Following the engagement at Monterrey, where U.S. troops fired on innocent civilians taking refuge in Catholic churches, Irish desertions increased and the San Patricios increased their roster to eight hundred men. By the time of the battle of Churubusco, the strength of the fierce fighting battalion had dwindled and Riley had advanced to the rank of captain in the Mexican Army and commander of the battalion's 1st Company.

The fifty men who had deserted following the declaration of war were hanged. Those that left military service before the official declaration of war with Mexico, Riley among them, were sentenced to receive fifty lashes on their bare backs, to be branded with the letter "D" for deserter, and to wear iron yokes around their necks for the duration of the war (6).

In 1997, President Ernesto Zedillo commemorated the 150th anniversary of the execution of the San Patricios in Mexico City's San Jacinto Plaza, the site of the first twenty hangings. Both the Republic of Ireland and Mexico jointly issued commemorative postage stamps to mark this anniversary. To honor John Riley (Juan Reley, on his Mexican death certificate) the Mexican flag flies daily in the town center of his birthplace; Clifden, County Galway, Ireland.

Molino del Rey

Companies C and D of the 5th Infantry reached Jalapa on the day of the Churubusco fight. They had just finished a march of 14 days as part of the escort for a train from Veracruz. During their trek they had fought engagements at Paso Ovejas, the Puente Nacional, Cerro Gordo and Las Animas. Mexican guerrillas suspected that the train contained a large amount of cash.

Following the battle of Churubusco, the Mexicans requested an armistice to discuss terms of surrender. During the truce, the 5th Infantry bivouacked at Tacubaya, where Scott had his headquarters. It soon became obvious that Santa Anna was making full use of the respite to rebuild his force and fortify the city. That wasn't part of the agreement.

The truce ended on the afternoon of September 7, when Scott received word that a large body of Mexican troops had massed in the vicinity of Molino del Rey, within a mile and a third of his headquarters. Scott ordered Worth to capture and destroy Molino del Rey.

Worth's Division attacked, at first light on the following morning, without knowledge of the extremely strong defensive positions occupied there. The 5th, once more under Major Scott, was in the center of the line. As the attack moved forward, the regiment was struck front and flank by a concentrated sheet of fire that broke up the first assault. As they paused they could see Mexican defenders coming out of a stone fortress called the Casa Mata and murdering the American wounded. It was an expensive crime. The Americans would not forget it.

The Mexicans in the Casa Mata were in a hopeless position; without artillery and with walls crumbling. A little more softening with artillery would have led to their surrender. However, the impetuous Worth ordered McIntosh to attack again. McIntosh obeyed and quickly fell, as did his second and third in command. The brigade dropped back and sometime later, under the shells of Duncan's Battery, the garrison of the Casa Mata did flee, leaving it in Worth's hands.

By the time the 5th Infantry withdrew, its command had devolved upon CPT William Chapman. Chapman wrote, "Brevet Colonel McIntosh, temporarily in command of the brigade, was thrice wounded while gallantly engaged in urging on the command. He is happily still preserved to us. Brevet Lieutenant Colonel Scott, commanding the regiment, was very active, as he always was, in leading and urging the regiment to the charge. When within twenty yards of the enemy, he received a mortal wound and almost immediately expired. He left no better or more gallant soldier to lament his fall and met his fate with his face to the enemy at the head of his command (7)."

The cost to Worth's Division was frightful. There were 116 dead and 671 wounded. The 5th Infantry lost 3 officers and 27 men killed and 4 officers and 107 men wounded; 38% of its effective strength. Five men were missing in action. General Scott observed the capture of Molino de Rey on September 8, but had allowed Worth to conduct the misguided attack without interference. Major Dixon S. Miles replaced LTC Scott as commander of the 5th Infantry.

Chapultapec and Mexico City

The skies were deep blue on the morning of September 13, 1847. It promised to be a warm day. For Scott's troops it was a day of foreboding. The victory at Molino del Rey had come at great cost. Their army was greatly reduced and was facing an army of overwhelming numbers. Even General Worth had said privately, "We shall be defeated."

Chapultapec Castle stood on a hill about 200 feet above a marsh. It stood between the American troops and access to the Belem Causeway that would take them to the heart of Mexico City. The building could hold only 260 Mexican defenders, including a group of young military college cadets who, at their own insistence, had been allowed to remain. Santa Anna posted another six hundred riflemen outside the castle to defend the walls around the courtyard.

Scott's bombardment began at dawn and poured shot and shell into the castle until 7:30 A.M., at which time the muzzles were lowered to rake the defenders off the walls surrounding the grounds. After thirty minutes the firing stopped. It was time for the infantry assault.

The attack was a murderous and chaotic affair, but the Americans inched their way up the western slope, paying in blood for every forward step. At the critical moment, Clarke's Brigade was sent forward and the 5th Infantry joined the tangled wave of cheering men that poured over the parapet in a final rush.

By 9:30 A.M. Chapultapec was in American hands and the hand-to-hand slaughter throughout the castle began. Scott's troops, thirsting to avenge the cruel and needless slaughter of their wounded comrades at Molino del Rey, killed Mexicans unmercifully. General Nicolas Bravo survived to surrender his bejeweled sword, but not six of the young cadets who chose to die rather than surrender. One of the young boys met his doom by plunging off the wall with the Mexican flag clutched in his arms.

Pausing just long enough to reorganize, the army headed down the causeway toward the city gates. Worth's Division, reinforced by two brigades, advanced north and then east over the San Cosme road, arriving at the Mexico City gate at about 4:00 P.M. When grapeshot and canister began to rake the road, the troops took to the ditches. The men of the 5th Infantry remained in the drainage ditches until they reached the outskirts and began a house-to-house clean up, employing the tactics that they had used in Monterrey.

The advance was halted at six o'clock. The regiment had penetrated well within the city. Sporadic fighting would continue during the following morning but, by midday, September 14, 1847, Winfield Scott rode triumphantly through the city square amid the deafening cheers of what was left of his army. The city authorities capitulated and opened the gates for the tattered and powder-stained Americans, who limped into the heart of the capital and raised the Stars and Stripes above the beautiful palace from which Montezuma had once ruled a mighty empire.

Like COL McIntosh, Dr. William Roberts, Assistant Regimental Surgeon, the regiment's only doctor, had been severely wounded at Molino del Rey. Throughout the fall, the surviving medical staff of stewards and attendants struggled to keep the 5th Infantry's wounded from succumbing to their infected wounds. James McIntosh died on 27 September. His body was returned to Savannah, Georgia, where it rests in the Colonial Park Cemetery. Dr. Roberts lasted until October 13.

William Roberts had been assigned to the general hospital at Tacubaya but preferred to travel with the regiment so had been relieved of hospital duty. At Molino del Rey, he impulsively took command of a company that had lost all of its officers and was soon mortally wounded on the battlefield (8).

Following the capture of Mexico City, guerrilla activity persisted for many months. LTC Dixon Miles and his 1200 soldiers of the 5th Infantry provided escort for wagon trains bringing supplies from Veracruz to the capital. They were not always successful. They left Veracruz on January 3, 1848 with a 9-mile long train. The wagon train was too extended to protect adequately and its richness drew guerrillas like ants to a picnic. Near Santa Fe, Tlaxcala, the insurgents drove off more than 250 mules carrying civilian goods, but the column was able to proceed without further difficulties. Colonel William Goldsmith Belknap, a former brigade commander, relieved LTC Miles in March.

Worth's Division, the last American troops in Mexico City, formed in the Grand Plaza in the early morning of June 12, 1848 and watched the American flag come down. Then the 5th Infantry and its sister regiments un-stacked arms and began their march to the coast. The passage of the troops through Veracruz was said to have been rapid and well-handled. In order to protect the men from malaria and yellow fever, they were held in the high country at Jalapa until just before they were scheduled to embark.

The 5th Infantry completed its out-loading and sailed for home on July 15, 1848. The majority of the ships sailed to New Orleans or Pass Christian, Mississippi, where newly erected hospitals awaited the sick and wounded.

The tri-color flag of the Mexican Republic flew once more over the national palace. The Treaty of Guadalupe Hidalgo was ratified by both the U.S and Mexican Senates. Mexico ceded New Mexico and California to the United States for a payment of $15,000,000; five million less than President Polk had offered Mexico before the war. The United States had lost 12,876 of its sons and spent $73 million on the war, but it had saved five million bucks.

Soldiers, however, are neither politicians nor economists. They dedicate their lives to the defense of their nation's interests as defined by the federal government. Throughout the conflict with Mexico, the men of the 5th Infantry Regiment conducted themselves with conspicuous gallantry. They participated with distinction in nearly every major battle of the war resulting in a casualty list that was more than 75% of the regiment's original strength. Ten officers and thirty-nine enlisted men were brevetted or awarded certificates of merit. It was a proud chapter in the history of the regiment.

CHAPTER FOUR

RETURN TO THE FRONTIER

When Mexico ceded California and New Mexico to the United States after the Mexican War, the U.S. Army played a key role in bringing the new territory under national control as it subdued Native American tribes in the area, protected the waves of settlers that swept across the Great Plains, and explored, mapped, and surveyed the western frontier. Between the end of the Mexican War and the beginning of the Civil War, the army established more than eighty new posts in the west.

In 1849 the 1st Infantry Regiment built Fort McIntosh on the Rio Grande River near Laredo to honor the 5th Infantry's James McIntosh. Fort McIntosh was abandoned in 1858 but then rebuilt after the Civil War and used as an army post until 1946. Since 1947 it has been the home of Laredo Community College (1).

The 1st Infantry also built Fort Merrill on the Nueces River in Texas. Part of the frontier defense system, it honored CPT Moses Merrill, Company K, 5th Infantry who also died at Molino del Rey. It was abandoned in 1855.

Following their return to the United States, the companies of the 5th Infantry, commanded by Colonel Belknap, were parceled among Forts Gibson, Smith, Washita and Towson in the Arkansas and Indian Territories. The regimental headquarters was at Fort Gibson, Indian Territory (2). It remained there until July of 1850 when CPT William Chapman turned the post over to the 7th Infantry. The regimental mission was similar to the one it had before the war, but infinitely more strenuous in the face of difficult terrain and Indians who were not as easily intimidated as the Northwest tribes.

The discovery of gold in California and the subsequent stampede to the west brought serious problems to the under-strength army attempting to patrol the frontier. Soldiers deserted by platoons to join the gold rush, sometimes leaving officers without a private in the ranks of their companies. Constant escort duty not only taxed the shrinking units but exposed them to epidemics carried in the wagon trains. In the month of May, 1849, the 5th Infantry lost forty-six men to cholera, contracted from gold seekers in a passing wagon train (3).

In 1850, the War Department attempted to retain some of the soldiers with "gold fever" by promising double pay to those men serving in the west. However, the government retained half of the man's pay until he received an honorable discharge. Veterans of the Mexican War received an additional $2 a month and a five-year enlistment warranted a monthly bonus of $1(4).

Word reached the regiment in 1851 that COL James Miller, of "I'll try, sir" fame, had died at his farm in Temple, New Hampshire at the age of 75. Following his resignation from the army, Miller served as the first territorial governor of Arkansas and then became a duty collector for the port of Salem, Massachusetts.

A valuable service provided by the 5th Infantry during this period in history was the exploration of the southwest conducted by CPT Randolph Barnes Marcy and LT James Hervey Simpson. In the summer of 1849, Marcy and Simpson, accompanied by fifty-two members of the regiment and twenty-six men from F Troop, 1st Dragoons made a reconnaissance trip from Fort Smith, Arkansas to Santa Fe. In September, they returned to Arkansas by a different route, their mission being to find the shortest practical wagon road from the New Mexico border to Fort Smith (5).

Randolph Marcy had been a member of the 5th Infantry Regiment since graduating from the U. S. Military Academy in 1832. He saw action at Palo Alto and Resaca de la Palma but was then detached for recruiting duty. In the ensuing years, he would bring honor to the regiment more as an explorer than a warrior.

Return to the Frontier

In 1850, CPT Marcy supervised the construction of Fort Arbuckle near the Canadian River in Indian Territory (close to Purcell, Oklahoma) to protect travelers on the route to New Mexico and California (6). The fort was named in memory of General Matthew Arbuckle, who had died of cholera, a short time before, at Fort Smith.

The men of Company D, 5th Infantry did the construction work, living in their tents until they could move into rude cabin barracks in December. The main barracks was a long house, 200 by 25 feet, with built-in bunks. Four separate huts were built for the officers. One of the cabins was occupied by Captain Marcy and his wife, Mary.

The winter passed without many incidents of note. There was an abundance of game and the bill of fare included such items as bear meat, buffalo tongue, venison, wild turkey, goose, duck, quail and pigeon. A popular winter pastime was horse racing, using as steeds the half-wild ponies so plentiful on the plains.

One winter day, they were visited by a band of Indians and one of the chiefs took a fancy to Mrs. Marcy. He offered to trade one of his wives for her. Marcy was amused but turned him down.

The fort was relocated in April, 1851 to the site of a Kickapoo Indian village about five miles from the Washita River. At the time of the move, almost every officer and man in the company was ill with malaria and ready for a change. In 1861 Fort Arbuckle was taken over by Texas Confederate troops until it was re-occupied by the 6th Infantry and 10th Cavalry after the Civil War. When the army abandoned the post in 1870, the land reverted to the Chickasaw Nation.

On May 15, 1851, COL Gustavus Loomis took over the reins of the regiment so that BG Belknap could devote full time to his duties as post commander of Fort Gibson and the Seventh Military Department. Loomis had served with the 6th U.S. Infantry during the Mexican War.

In June 1851, the 5th Infantry was ordered to relieve the 7th Infantry in Texas on the Brazos River. Lieutenant Colonel John

Abercrombie arrived at the Clear Fork of the Brazos with Companies B, C, E, G, and K (7). He had been ordered to establish a new post near the confluence of the Brazos River and Elm Creek. The location had been recommended by CPT Marcy following his 1849 exploration of the area.

From the outset, the lack of water and the scarcity of timber challenged the garrison. It was necessary to haul both from great distances. Lieutenant Clinton Lear didn't think much of Marcy's recommendation. He described the Clear Fork Valley as beautiful and abundant with game but felt that it was never intended "for white men to occupy such a barren waste."

Colonel Belknap contracted typhoid in the fall of 1851 while checking on the construction of the new post. Hoping to reach his family at Fort Gibson, he died on November 11, somewhere between the Brazos and Fort Washita. He was buried immediately at Ft. Washita. In October, 1872 his remains were disinterred and reburied near the family home in Keokuk, Iowa. The veteran of the War of 1812, the Mexican War and many Indian skirmishes was 57 years old at the time of his death.

Despite the limitations of the Brazos site, construction continued to house a garrison of one hundred to two hundred and fifty soldiers, 11-14 commissioned officers, officers' wives, laundresses, scouts, Indian interpreters and guides. Although vulnerable to attacks, the post, currently referred to as Fort Phantom Hill, enjoyed peaceful relations with the Indians. Army records refer to the site as the "Post on the Clear Fork of the Brazos" or Fort Belknap.

During the summer of 1852, CPT Marcy, assisted by his future son-in-law, Lieutenant George B. McClellan, led a party from Fort Belknap, Texas to explore the headwaters of the Red River (8). During their thousand-mile journey across previously undocumented Texas and Oklahoma territory, they found both forks of the Red River and explored Palo Duro and Tule Canyons. In addition to discovering numerous mineral deposits they came upon twenty-five new species of mammals and ten new species of reptiles. While they were gone, it was reported that the one hundred and twenty men in the expedition had been ambushed and wiped out by Comanches. When they returned by way of Fort Arbuckle on July 28, they had the rare pleasure of reading their own obituaries.

Marcy's passionate interest in geology, zoology and botany enabled him to add a lot to our country's knowledge of the Southwest. His report entitled "Exploration of the Red River of Louisiana, In the Year 1852—With Reports on the Natural History of the Country" was published in 1853.

Brush Fires in Florida and Utah

The Brazos post was abandoned in 1854 when the 5th Infantry moved to Fort McIntosh. The regiment remained at McIntosh until the spring of 1857 when it was ordered to Florida to coax the Seminoles out of their stronghold. Companies C and K, supported by Battery M of the 4th Artillery, invaded the swamps.

LT Edmund Freeman and a small patrol were attacked by a Seminole war party near Bowleg's Town, Florida on March 5 (9). Freeman and three of his men were severely wounded and one man was killed. When the rest of the company, commanded by CPT Carter Stevenson, arrived on the scene, there was a brief skirmish and the Indians withdrew.

This indecisive two-month long campaign against the Seminoles ended on April 23, when the 5th Infantry was withdrawn. Failure to carry out this mission was no discredit to the regiment. The elusive Seminoles have never been conquered.

The campaign in Florida had been aborted because troubles were brewing in Utah. The Mormons were being accused of denying the sovereignty of the United States and of inciting the Indians to attack settlers who were encroaching on what they considered to be Mormon territory. A large scale military expedition assembled at Ft. Leavenworth, Kansas prior to marching to Utah. The troops, commanded by COL Albert Sydney Johnston of the 2nd Cavalry, consisted of the 5th and 10th Infantry Regiments, eight companies of the 2nd Cavalry and two batteries of artillery (10).

The column reached the Utah border in October, 1857, to find the Mormons up in arms and ready to oppose an invasion with force. The troops were forbidden to enter Utah and their animals and supply trains were attacked and destroyed. Wintering at Ft. Bridger, the command faced a severe shortage of supplies because of these depredations. Johnston decided to send a relief-seeking expedition across the Rocky Mountains to New Mexico. The regiment's respected explorer, CPT Randolph Marcy, drew the assignment.

Marcy and his band of sixty-five volunteers, left Fort Bridger on November 24, 1857. Fifty-one days later, they limped into Fort Massachusetts, New Mexico. They had covered 600 miles of trackless mountain wilderness in the dead of winter. The snow drifts often cut the marching distance to three miles a day. Pack mules died, luggage had to be abandoned, and the rations gave out ten days before reaching their destination. The men killed and ate their last few horses and mules and kept moving. They arrived at journey's end with one fatality and thirty-nine cases of frostbitten feet.

Marcy drew supplies at Fort Massachusetts and returned with a strong escort, since he had received word that the Mormons planned to ambush him on the way back. The party reached Fort Bridger safely, with its precious cargo, after a round-trip of 1300 miles and an absence of three months.

That spring, a greatly augmented column, totaling nearly 5500 regulars, moved into the valley of the Great Salt Lake. Confronted with superior numbers, the Mormon leaders concluded a peaceful agreement and asked for a withdrawal of the so-called Army of Utah.

Randolph Marcy was recalled to Washington to prepare a

semiofficial guidebook for the War Department. The result, *The Prairie Traveler*, was an excellent compendium of practical hints for travelers about essential equipment, the organization of a wagon train and techniques for avoiding Indian attacks. He included detailed notes on thirty-four of the most important overland trails. On August 22, 1859, Marcy was promoted to major and assigned as regimental paymaster.

Campaigning in the Southwest

When the 5th Infantry returned to New Mexico from Utah Territory, most of its companies were distributed among Forts Defiance, Fauntleroy, Stanton and Hatch's Ranch. Forts Defiance and Fauntleroy were constructed at Bear Springs, 15 miles south of Canyon de Chelly. Fort Stanton was located near Capitan, New Mexico and Hatch's Ranch was in the vicinity of Dilia. These small frontier forts were generally a group of barracks, stables and an orderly room built around a parade ground. There were no stockades or block houses.

In September 1858, CPT Earl Van Dorn departed Fort Belknap with four troops of the 2nd Cavalry and one company of the 5th Infantry in search of hostile Comanche and Kiowa Indians (11). On October 1, near the present Rush Springs, Oklahoma, they caught up with a band of Comanches led by a brave named Buffalo Hump. During the fighting 56 Comanche warriors and two women were killed. Van Dorn was wounded and five soldiers were killed. The troops burned 120 lodges and captured 300 horses.

Further west, on September 18, 1860, a detachment from Companies C, G, and H of the 5th Infantry had a brush with Apaches near Fort Fauntleroy, New Mexico. Between October 13 and 23, a large force including the 3rd Cavalry and Companies A, B, D, F, G and I of the 5th Infantry waged a fierce battle at the southern base of Black Rock, near Cold Springs.

Meanwhile, the Apaches' cousins, the Navajos, had been waging hostile actions against the U. S. Army and the ranchers of New Mexico. They frequently attacked isolated army posts, rustled government and privately-owned cattle, and ambushed government supply trains.

From September until November 1860, Colonel Edward Canby, 10th Infantry, led the expedition against the Navajos. His six hundred man force, gathered from Fort Defiance and other Arizona army posts included nine infantry companies drawn from the 5th, 7th, 8th, and 10th Regiments, six companies of mounted riflemen and the 2nd Cavalry. Companies B and G of the 5th participated in this campaign. After a month in the field and at least nine fire fights, Canby's task force prompted the Navajo tribal elders to initiate peace overtures.

The Navajo leaders met with Colonel Canby at Fort Fauntleroy on January 12, 1861. Having the upper hand, Canby agreed to a partial armistice. Peace would be granted to those Navajos living west of Fort Fauntleroy; a safe distance from New Mexican towns and ranches. Operations would still be conducted in the east, where Canby believed most of the hostiles resided (13). Canby's plan included establishing a Navajo reservation at Bosque Redondo, near the Gila River. He hoped that the truce with the Navajos would hold so that he could focus on the Apaches.

On September 18, 1860, a detachment from Companies C, G, and H of the 5th Infantry had a brush with Apaches near Fort Fauntleroy. Between October 13 and 23, a large force including the 3rd Cavalry and Companies A, B, D, F, G and I of the 5th Infantry waged a fierce battle at the southern base of Black Rock, near Cold Springs (12).

Company A, with two companies of the 7th Infantry, tangled with Apaches at Las Calitas on November 19th and again during the first week of January, 1861. On January 3, K Company got into a scrap in the Chusca Valley and, four days later, Company G joined A Company of the 10th Infantry to beat off another attack near Fort Fauntleroy, New Mexico.

In October, 1860, Apaches raided the ranch of John Ward near

Fort Buchanan, Arizona (14). They plundered Ward's house, ran off all of his stock and kidnapped his son, Mickey Free. Three months later, LTC Morrison, at Fort Buchanan, ordered young 2nd LT George N. Bascom, Company C, 7th Infantry to proceed to Apache Pass, 150 miles to the northeast, rescue the boy and reclaim the stock.

On February 3, while Bascom and his detail of fifty-four mounted infantrymen rested in Apache Canyon, Cochise, leader of the Chiricahua Apaches, and a small party of relatives and friends, entered the army's camp. The Apaches, who had come simply to greet their visitors, were invited into Bascom's tent. When the young lieutenant accused the Indians of taking Mickey Free, Cochise denied kidnapping the boy and offered to find out who did. Lieutenant Bascom didn't buy Cochise's story and informed the group that they were under arrest and would be held until the boy was returned.

Cochise produced a knife, slashed an escape hole in the tent and bounded up the side of the canyon, amid a volley of rifle fire from his surprised captors. The rest of his greeting committee failed to escape. During the next two weeks, several white civilians were captured and cruelly murdered. The U.S. Army responded by hanging Cochise's people. Another long bloody conflict ensued but it would soon have to compete for attention with some trouble brewing "back east."

CHAPTER FIVE

THE CIVIL WAR IN NEW MEXICO

The Civil War was a frustrating period of exile for a regiment whose colors had led the battle line so proudly from Resaca de la Palma to Chapultepec. While huge armies clashed in the east, the men of the Fifth Infantry looked longingly from the New Mexico-Texas border, as they stood guard at the back door of the Union.

As the southern states seceded, many officers from those states resigned their federal commissions or simply left their posts to return home. Nine officers of the 5th Infantry left the service of the United States to serve in the Confederate Army. Five of them attained star rank and three died fighting for the south. Captain Carter Stevenson, who had served with the regiment during the Mexican War, Seminole War and Utah Expedition, became a major general. Others to lay aside their 5th Infantry shoulder straps and join the Confederacy were Major Richard Gatlin, Lieutenant Colonel Gabriel Rains, Captain Daniel Ruggles, Lieutenant Archibald Gracie and Second Lieutenant Bryan Thomas. Gracie was killed near Petersburg, Virginia in 1864. Second Lieutenant Robert Hill became Colonel of the 4th North Carolina Infantry and died in 1863. Lieutenant Lucius Rich died while commanding the 1st Missouri Infantry at Shiloh (1).

Twenty-two former 5th Infantry officers went east to serve the Union. One was the renown regimental explorer, Randolph Marcy. Soon after war broke out, he was promoted to colonel and named inspector general of McClellan's Army of the Potomac. In March of 1865, he was brevetted brigadier general in the regular army for "faithful and meritorious service during the war."

When Texas seceded in 1861, the U.S. Army's commander of the

The Civil War in New Mexico

Department of Texas was Mexican War division commander General David E. Twiggs, a southerner and secession sympathizer. Twiggs immediately opened negotiations with the Confederate government for the surrender of the troops under his command (2). His department was composed of 102 officers and 2,328 enlisted men. He was partly foiled by the independent action of regiments and even companies that evacuated their posts and escaped piecemeal into New Mexico. Those remaining in Texas, following the bombardment of Fort Sumter, became prisoners of the Confederate Army.

Once across the New Mexico line, the twelve hundred refugees from Texas came under the energetic command of Colonel Edward Canby, senior officer in the district. Canby gathered the remnants of five regular regiments—about eighteen companies in all—to which he added enough New Mexico volunteers to raise his strength to about four thousand men. The War Department welcomed his efforts and confirmed Canby in command with the rank of brigadier general.

At the time of the bombardment of Fort Sumter, the 5th Infantry was still distributed among the New Mexico posts. During May and June, 1861, the regiment was assembled in Albuquerque and began preparations to depart for the east. However, Canby raised such a ruckus at the thought of losing more than half of his regular troops that the orders were revoked (3).

The Confederate government sent General Henry H. Sibley, a former cavalry officer with extensive service in the southwest, to Texas to recruit an army for the conquest of California. Sibley collected a volunteer force equivalent to Canby's and, in January, 1862, advanced to Fort Bliss to prepare for his invasion of New Mexico.

Aware that the Texans were close to the border, Canby hurried to reinforce Ft. Craig, a federal stronghold on the Santa Fe Trail about thirty miles south of Albuquerque. Canby's regulars at Fort Craig included Companies B, D, F, and I of the 5th Infantry, elements of the 7th and 10th Infantry Regiments, and companies from the 1st and 3rd Cavalry

Regiments. They were supported by eight artillery pieces manned by cavalrymen. His irregular troops included COL Kit Carson's 1st New Mexico Volunteer Infantry, seventeen other New Mexican volunteer companies and about a thousand New Mexico militia members.

Valverde

On February 16, 1862, Colonel Tom Green's party of Texans pulled within a mile and half of Fort Craig, hoping to lure the Union troops into a fight beyond reach of the fort's artillery. Canby positioned a large number of his own troops in a protective line in front of the fort and refused to take the bait, so Green returned to the Confederate camp four miles to the south.

Three days later, the Texans forded the Rio Grande seven miles south of Fort Craig and moved north along a rugged volcanic shelf above the river. They were within a thousand yards of the fort as they marched northward for the purpose of seizing the ford at Valverde.

Canby became aware of the Confederate threat to his rear late in the afternoon and immediately sent Colonel Benjamin Roberts with a small force of cavalry, infantry and artillery to block the enemy's northern movement. When this group reached Valverde, they discovered that the Texans had already arrived and had occupied a cottonwood grove on the east side of the river (4).

Roberts had the guns unlimber on the west bank and, supported by the infantry, open fire on the Confederates. The Texans were soon pinned down by the federals' heavier artillery and long-range rifled muskets. Their own light howitzers, shotguns, carbines and revolvers could not effectively reach Roberts' force on the opposite bank of the river. The federal infantry forded the river and drove the Texans from their positions behind the bank of an old river channel. Casualties mounted as the latter tried repeatedly to regain their lost ground.

News of what was happening at Valverde had been relayed to Canby. At 10:00 A.M. he sent reinforcements to Roberts; the battalion from the 5th Infantry commanded by CPT Henry Selden, a company of Colorado volunteers, and Kit Carson and his 1st New Mexico Volunteers.

Selden's troops had difficulty finding a ford. They finally got across by wading through cold, swift-flowing water up to four feet deep. On the eastern shore, the soldiers of the 5th, shivering in soaking-wet clothes, fixed bayonets, drove a force of dismounted Texans out of the copse of cottonwoods, and then regrouped. They were on the northern flank of the Union line.

When General Canby arrived on the scene, he rearranged his units in preparation for bringing a speedy end to the conflict. He decided to launch his principal attack against the enemy's left flank. The 5th Infantry, minus CPT David Brotherton's company, was moved to the center. Brotherton's company and a battery of two guns were placed on the right.

As the troops were getting into place, Colonel Green decided to silence the artillery that had been punishing the southerners and ordered attacks against the right and left flanks of the federal line. Seeing the Texans mass for the attack on the right, Major Thomas Duncan requested help for his dismounted cavalrymen. Canby ordered the 5th Infantry to shift to the right and help Duncan. Hit by withering fire from the 5th Infantry and Duncan's troopers, the attacking Texans broke and fled back toward the hills, with the mounted companies of New Mexicans and Duncan's regulars on their tail.

When Colonel Carson heard the commotion, he ordered his New Mexico Volunteers to follow the lead of the 5th Infantry. Soon there was a wide gap in the Union center that isolated those on the Union left. Seven hundred and fifty yelling Texans took advantage of the breach, charged through a storm of grapeshot, canister and minié balls and swarmed over McRae's six cannon battery. Selden sent his 5th Infantry battalion back to the left but his men were beaten back by Confederate reinforcements. Canby ordered a general withdrawal to the fort. Among the regular army casualties was Captain George N. Bascom, the young officer who had dealt with Cochise in such a clumsy fashion.

The 5th Infantry was asked to serve as rear guard and cover the retreat. General Canby wrote: "The movement of Selden's column in the immediate presence and under fire of the enemy was admirably executed, the command moving with deliberation, halting occasionally to allow the wounded to keep up with it, and many of the men picking up and carrying the arms (weapons) of their dead and wounded comrades (5)."

Flushed with victory, Sibley sent a delegation of his officers to Canby to demand the surrender of the fort and its supplies. Canby's angry refusal put Sibley in a precarious position. He still wasn't willing to attack the fort, but he now had only five days' rations left. Sibley decided to live off the land until he could capture the federal stores at Albuquerque. He started north again on February 23, leaving Canby and the fort isolated to his rear.

Given time, however, the small federal garrison at Albuquerque was able to load all available wagons with government supplies, set fire to the buildings that housed what they could not take with them and, on March 1, withdrew safely to Santa Fe. On March 4, they moved again, delivering the goods to Fort Union, eighty-five miles to the northeast. However, Sibley was confident of an easy victory at Fort Union and looked forward to acquiring its glut of supplies, which he would need for an invasion of Colorado.

Glorieta Pass

The War Department finally awakened to the seriousness of the situation in New Mexico. A brigade of California Volunteers and a battery of the 3rd U.S. Artillery, assembled at Fort Yuma, were ordered to march east to drive the Texans out of New Mexico (6). Colorado's governor, Lewis Weld, was ordered to "send all forces you can possibly spare to reinforce Colonel Canby." Weld immediately directed the 1st Colorado Volunteer Infantry commanded by Colonel John P. Slough, a Denver attorney, to march to New Mexico.

The 1st Colorado, organized in mining camps and frontier towns, was a tough, semi-disciplined outfit composed of adventurers, miners, and saloon brawlers. The men had become bored by inaction and the announcement, at Camp Weld, that they were to leave to fight the Texans in New Mexico was greeted by "deafening cheers" according to one of their number.

On February 22, the troops in Denver started south along the front range of the Rockies to rendezvous near the New Mexico border with the remainder of the regiment coming from Fort Wise. While trudging south through Colorado, they learned of the Union defeat at Valverde and stepped up their pace to forty miles a day, laboring at times through several inches of snow. They finally reached Fort Union on March 11. Only one of the companies had been mounted; the rest of the regiment's 950 men had walked more than four hundred miles in thirteen days.

Colonel Slough pulled seniority on post commander Colonel Gabriel Paul and stripped Fort Union of most of its fighting men. He proposed to march at once against the Confederates. His force of 1342 men included his own 1st Colorado, one battalion of the 5th Infantry, mounted troopers from the 1st and 3rd Cavalry Regiments, a company from the 4th New Mexico Volunteers and two four-gun artillery batteries.

After an overnight stop at Bernal Springs, Slough sent forward an advance guard of 418 infantry and cavalrymen under the command of Major John Chivington. Companies A and G of the 5th Infantry were part of Chivington's column. At Glorieta Pass, a high tip of the Sangre de Cristo Mountains, the two armies ran into each other on the afternoon of March 26.

Stripping themselves of knapsacks, canteens, overcoats and

extra clothing, Chivington's men moved forward on the double quick, entering a narrow valley at the western end of Glorieta Pass known as Apache Canyon. Rounding a bend in the road, they halted abruptly, face to face with the vanguard of Major Charles Pyron's Texans—two field guns and a company of mounted men carrying the Lone Star Flag. Chivington directed the infantry and some of the dismounted cavalry to climb the wooded slopes that bordered the road and flank the enemy. The rest of the infantrymen opened with frontal fire against the Confederates on the road.

The federals on the hillside gradually forced the Confederates back, threatening to flank their guns. Then a column of mounted infantrymen from Colorado galloped down the road toward the rebel position and were soon fighting hand to hand with their adversaries. They took many prisoners. The Texans fought on as they retreated slowly. As the sun set, Major Pyron ordered his men to break off the fight and withdraw. This skirmish in Apache Canyon was the first Union victory in New Mexico territory.

At dawn, on March 28, Chivington with 490 men, including Companies A and G of the 5th Infantry, left the federal camp with orders to climb the mountain and head directly west across the high wilderness south of Glorieta Pass. When they returned to camp at 10:00 P.M., they had quite a story to tell.

Guided by Lieutenant Colonel Manuel Chaves, they had crossed sixteen miles through the mountain wilderness south of Glorieta Pass to a two hundred foot high bluff directly above the western end of Apache Canyon where the Confederates had parked their supply trains. Rappelling the steep hill with ropes and leather straps, they had surprised and driven away the small guard, released some federal prisoners, destroyed all eighty of the Confederates' wagons, spiked a cannon and burned the rebel's stores—ammunition, food, saddles, forage, tents, clothing and medical supplies—everything the Texans would need to continue their campaign.

The Civil War in New Mexico

This exploit by Chivington and his men at Glorieta Pass—regarded eventually by New Mexicans as "the Gettysburg of the West"—brought Sibley's hopes of conquering the Southwest to an abrupt halt. With barely enough food, low on ammunition, and lacking blankets, tents and medical supplies, the dismayed Texans left their wounded at a nearby ranch and, mostly afoot, in torn, disheveled uniforms and shoes, retreated to Santa Fe.

On April 15, the retreating Confederate column moved into Peralta, New Mexico, hoping to get a breather. However, Canby's federal troops, through light skirmishing and bombardment, convinced the rebels to cross to the west bank of the Rio Grande. Companies B, D, E, F, G, I and K of the 5th Infantry were present at Peralta (7).

The Texans burned most of their personal possessions to lighten their loads and speed up their retreat down river. Their leaders now agreed that they lacked the ammunition to risk another battle or attempt to take Fort Craig. Packing their mules with seven days rations, blankets and cooking gear, they abandoned most of their remaining wagons and, leaving their sick and wounded to Canby's mercy, set off to circle around Fort Craig on the west and return to the Rio Grande south of the post.

When Sibley reached Fort Bliss, he received the news that Colonel James Carleton's brigade of California volunteers had finally left Yuma and was headed in his direction. As the Californian's moved east, they fought the western-most Civil War battle at Picacho Peak, west of Tucson, chased the Confederates out of the city of Tucson, fought several sharp engagements with bands of Chiricahua Apaches and, on July 4, 1862, arrived at the Rio Grande three miles above Fort Thorn, about eighty miles north of the Texas border. Four companies from the 5th Infantry Regiment linked up with the California column on August 10, 1862 (8).

Sibley withdrew to San Antonio, reorganized his brigade and gave the men sixty day furloughs to return to their homes and families.

Survivors continued to straggle in all through the summer, but, of the 3500 Texans who had set out, the previous year, to conquer California, more than 500 had died in combat or from disease and another five hundred were missing or in federal prison camps.

Carleton's Californians occupied Forts Bliss, Quitman and Davis in West Texas. For the rest of the war, West Texas and New Mexico Territory, including Arizona, remained under federal control. Canby went east for another assignment and Carleton took over command of the Department of New Mexico in September 1862.

One of Carleton's first tasks was to do something about a base of operations in western New Mexico. His predecessor had received clearance to erect a new garrison in west central New Mexico to replace defunct Forts Defiance and Fauntleroy.

Captain Henry Selden, who had commanded the Fort Craig battalion of the 5th Infantry at Valverde, chose the site in the Ojo del Gallo Valley for Fort Wingate. The fort was named for Selden's comrade Brevet Major Benjamin Wingate, 5th Infantry, who had died from wounds suffered at the battle of Valverde. Captain Selden, in command of Troops D and G of the 1st U.S. Cavalry, settled into the new fort in October 1862 (9).

By now the reader is probably as confused as the author regarding the top leadership of the 5th Infantry during the Civil War. The companies of the regiment were scattered in battalion-sized groups among garrisons in the Southwest. These battalions were usually commanded by a senior captain. Captain Henry Selden had commanded the Fort Craig battalion of Companies B, D, F, and I at the battle of Valverde. With his transfer to the cavalry in September, 1862, there was a shuffling of the companies in the battalions. Companies D, E, F, and G moved to Fort Sumner under Captain Henry B. Bristol while Companies A, B, I and K remained at Fort Craig under Captain Archer (10).

On June 1, 1863, Major General John F. Reynolds, U.S.

THE CIVIL WAR IN NEW MEXICO

Volunteers, was rewarded with an appointment to colonel in the regular army and assigned, on paper, to the 5th Infantry Regiment. Reynolds replaced COL Gustavus Loomis, who hadn't served with the regiment since 1857. When General Reynolds was killed a month later at Gettysburg, the paper colonelcy went to another prominent U.S. Volunteer, Daniel Butterfield. Butterfield retained the title "Colonel of the 5th Infantry Regiment" until his retirement from the Army on March 2, 1869. Heitman's listing suggests that Lieutenant Colonel Thomas Ludwell Alexander, who had distinguished himself at Churubusco, served as actual "hands-on" regimental commander until 16 October 1863 (11).

In 1865 Captain Bristol was brevetted lieutenant colonel for his service in New Mexico and could very well have taken over the day-to-day management of the regiment until the arrival of Colonel Nelson Miles in 1869. Bristol's citation read: "for untiring zeal and energy for controlling the Navajo tribe of Indians at the Bosque Redondo and for his praiseworthy efforts in advancing their condition from that of savages to that of civilized men."

The 5th Infantry Regiment remained quietly on the frontier until the close of the war, its boredom broken periodically by expeditions against the Navajo Indians. During the winter of 1863-64, the Navajos staged a series of raids that brought the troops into the field. On December 16, 1863 and again on January 6, 1864, D Company, commanded by Lieutenant Charles Newbold, was ordered from Fort Sumner in pursuit of marauding Navajos. Mounted on Indian ponies and government horses, Newbold's command caught the raiders on both occasions and inflicted severe punishment. Newbold was brevetted captain for his service on these two occasions. Sergeant Welch, Corporal Flynn and Private Fitzgerald of Company D were commended in Newbold's reports.

CHAPTER SIX

THE RED RIVER WAR

The Civil War was followed by a massive mustering out of the enormous army raised during the four years of battle. Once that was completed, the regular army units were redistributed. In 1866 the 5th Infantry was assigned to General Philip Sheridan's Department of Missouri, embracing the states of Missouri and Kansas and the Territories of Colorado and New Mexico.

Company A was quartered at Fort Sumner, New Mexico with two other companies of infantry and a troop of cavalry. According to Luke Cahill, a former private with the company, they were tasked with the responsibility of keeping 20,000 Navajos on the Fort Sumner Reservation (1). In August, 1867, a courier arrived at the fort with the message that the village of Trinidad, Colorado was surrounded by Ute Indians and that all the whites were about to be killed. Company A marched day and night, reached Trinidad in time and chased away the Utes. Taking advantage of the army's absence, the Navajos slipped away from the reservation and surrounded Fort Sumner. Company A, hearing of the siege, conducted another forced march home. They were joined by reinforcements from nearby Forts Bascom and Stanton. The troops saved the garrison but were unable to stem the mass exodus as thousands of Navajos left the reservation.

Company A left Fort Sumner in November and marched north to Ft. Lyon, Colorado. The men spent a cold winter dwelling in tents while the fort was under construction. Despite the cold weather, the Indians continued stopping wagon trains and mail coaches so the troops were kept busy providing security for winter travelers. Private Cahill complained that there was no firewood along the trail, requiring them to dig beneath the snow for buffalo chips to fuel their cooking fires.

The Red River War

On October 20, 1868, regimental headquarters was established at Ft. Riley, Kansas where two companies became part of the garrison. The other companies were distributed among Forts Wallace, Hays, Lyon, and Reynolds and Camps Davidson and Cottonwood Creek. All of these posts, with the exception of Ft. Lyon, were in Kansas. From these scattered outposts, columns pushed west into Arizona, Texas and Western Kansas where Indian marauders were waging constant war on the rising tide of settlers. The tribes had become bolder and stronger while the government had been preoccupied with the Civil War. Nine engagements with the Indians were fought by 5th Infantry detachments between January 1865 and June 1869, four in Arizona and five in various parts of Kansas.

There was only a handful of tribes that had the capability and willingness to resist the influx of settlers moving west. On the Great Plains these included the Sioux, Cheyenne, Arapaho, Comanche and Kiowa. In the Rocky Mountains there were the Nez Perce, Ute and Bannock. The Paiute and Modoc held out in the West and the Apache in the Southwest. Although there were no more than 100,000 Indians who were ready to actively oppose the Army as it moved back to the western frontier, it would take twenty-five years and thousands of determined soldiers to subdue them.

In the summer of 1868, a band of renegade Indians, drawn from several tribes, roamed the Saline and Solomon Valleys in Western Kansas. They killed a number of settlers, drove away livestock, and abducted two young white women. General Sheridan ordered one of his staff members, Colonel G. A. Forsythe to organize a company of fifty ex-soldiers, buffalo hunters and frontiersman and go after the culprits.

Forsythe's party followed the renegades' trail to the Arickaree Fork of the Republican River where they ran into seven hundred braves led by a Cheyenne chief named Roman Nose. The company of irregulars quickly moved to an island in the dry bed of Arickaree Creek and held off the attacking Indians for eight days until a column of 10th Cavalry Buffalo Soldiers and one hundred members of the 5th Infantry from Fort Wallace came to the rescue. The latter had been dispatched by Brevet LTC Bankhead, 5th Infantry. This provides further evidence that there was someone in charge of the regiment during the aftermath of the Civil War (2).

Nelson Miles

On March 3, 1869, the Fifth Infantry, retaining its own designation, was consolidated with one-half of the 37th Infantry. Seven captains and fifteen lieutenants of the former 5th Regiment remained with the new unit. The field grade officers were all new. Brevet Major General Nelson A. Miles became the colonel, Brevet Major General C. R. Woods, the lieutenant colonel, and Brevet Lieutenant Colonel George Gibson, the major.

Nelson Appleton Miles had entered the service in October, 1861 as a lieutenant in the 22nd Massachusetts Volunteers. During the Civil War, he advanced rapidly, achieving the rank of brevet major general by the end of the conflict. He was severely wounded at Chancellorsville and received the Medal of Honor for his actions there as a regimental commander. Following the war he received a colonel's commission in the regular army and, on April 21, 1869, reported to the 5th Infantry Regiment at Fort Hays, Kansas.

In June of 1868, Miles had married Mary Hoyt Sherman, niece of William Tecumseh Sherman. Sherman had temporarily resigned from the Army to serve in the U. S. Senate. As a married officer, Miles found accommodations at Fort Hays not to his liking and soon transferred his headquarters to Fort Harker, seventy miles east of Fort Hays and closer to the "confines of civilization." Miles took advantage of his relationship with his wife's influential uncle throughout much of his army career.

When Ulysses Grant became President in 1869, he offered

The Red River War

General Sherman a fourth star and the post of General of the Army.

The Red River War, a series of engagements fought between the United States Army and warriors of the Kiowa, Comanche, southern Cheyenne and southern Arapaho tribes from June of 1874 into the spring of 1875, began when the federal government defaulted on promises made to those tribes through the 1867 Treaty of Medicine Lodge (3). Rations to be issued the Indians fell short or failed entirely, gun running and liquor trafficking by white profiteers were not curtailed and white outlaws from Kansas and Texas, who stole Indian livestock, were neither pursued nor punished. Between 1872 and 1874, professional buffalo hunters, based in Dodge City, Kansas, wiped out the buffalo herds on the Cheyenne-Arapaho Reservation.

On June 27, 1874, a war party of 700 Comanche, Kiowa, Cheyenne and Arapahoe warriors attacked a buffalo hunters' camp at Adobe Walls in the Texas Panhandle. This was followed by numerous incidents in Texas, Kansas and Indian Territory. An appeal went out to the army and General-in-Chief William T. Sherman and Lieutenant General Philip Sheridan developed a plan.

Peaceful Indians were to be quickly registered at their agencies and confined to the reservation before the hostiles could return. Then, troop columns would enter the field from five different directions, force the warriors into their traditional refuges in the canyons of the Texas Panhandle, and there annihilate them or else force their surrender. This strategy was in force by July 25.

Colonel Miles' column left Fort Dodge, Kansas on August 11, 1874. It was comprised of eight companies of the 6th Cavalry, Companies C,D,E, and I of the 5th Infantry, one ten-pounder Parrott gun and two ten-barrel Gatling guns, a group of scouts, which included some of the buffalo hunters from Adobe Walls, and a few Delaware Indian trackers.

Miles had appointed Lieutenant Frank Dwight Baldwin, chief of scouts. Baldwin had entered regular service as a first lieutenant in

1866. He had served as a company commander with the 19th Michigan Volunteers during the Civil War and had received the Medal of Honor for his actions at the battle of Peach Tree, Georgia. In May, 1869, Frank Baldwin was assigned to the 5th Infantry.

On August 30, near Palo Duro Canyon, Texas, several hundred Cheyenne ambushed Baldwin's scouts, who repulsed the attack with a hail of gunfire. Mile's troops came forward, their ten-pound Parrott and Gatling guns providing covering fire.

"If any man is killed, I will make him a corporal!" shouted an excited Captain Adna Chaffee as his men swept forward. The Indians withdrew across the Red River, then a stagnant pool of alkali and gypsum. The men of the 5th Infantry scrambled up the sides of the canyon in vain pursuit. Casualties were limited. Fortunately no one qualified for corporal. One soldier and one civilian scout were wounded and three Indians were killed.

Further pursuit was made impossible by a lack of provisions and a tremendous thunderstorm that soon transformed the creek beds into raging torrents. Colonel Miles fired off petulant diatribes against the shortage of supplies and the lack of qualified company grade officers (4). Sheridan's report depicted this battle as a significant victory, but later sources indicate that the engagement was at best inconclusive because Miles outran his supply lines and left himself open to attack from the rear.

On the evening of September 6, Lieutenant Baldwin left the 5th Infantry encampment on the Red River for Camp Supply, Indian Territory, carrying dispatches from Colonel Miles to General John Pope, the officer in charge of two of the converging columns. Baldwin was accompanied by three civilian scouts armed with new long-range Spencer carbines. After riding all night, they stopped to camp at the head of a small creek. Baldwin sent one of the men to a nearby high point while the three unsaddled (5).

Within thirty minutes, according to a letter that Baldwin wrote to his wife, they were surrounded by a band of twenty-six Comanches. After an hour of exchanging fire, the lieutenant gave the order to saddle up, draw their pistols and break through the Indians' lines. They were followed but were able to keep their adversaries at bay with their long-range Spencer repeating rifles. On the morning of the 8th, as they neared the banks of the Washita River, they came upon an outpost for a Kiowa village where they captured a white boy that was serving as a picket.

On the evening of the 8th, they crossed the Canadian River west of Antelope Hills where they encountered a supply train led by Captain Wyllys Lyman, which was being desperately awaited by Colonel Miles. They were able to hand off their young white prisoner and exchange their horses for fresh mounts. The following evening they left for General Pope's headquarters at Camp Supply, covering the seventy-five mile leg by 10:00 A.M. on the 10th. Frank Baldwin's letter made the trip sound like just another week at the office.

Apparently the "Indianized" white boy had been a popular member of a band of Kiowas led by Chief Poor Buffalo. The band set out in search of the young white brave and, when they found him, they attacked the wagon train. Captain Lyman circled the wagons and deployed Company I, 5th Infantry to deliver defensive fire. The Indians attacked with reckless fury but finally broke before the disciplined steadiness of the soldiers' fire. After a three-day siege the Kiowas finally withdrew. Sergeant William De Armond was killed and Lieutenant Granville Lewis suffered a severe knee injury.

Seven members of Company I were decorated with the Medal of Honor for gallantry during the fight to protect the supply train (6). They were 1st Sergeant John Mitchell, Sergeants William Koeplin, Fred S. Hay, and William De Armond; Corporals John A. Knox, John Kelly and John James and Private Thomas Kelly. Many years later Sergeant Hay's medal was discovered for sale in a pawn shop and reclaimed by the War Department (7). The medal was returned to the regiment with instructions to hold it pending the discovery of a legitimate heir or claimant. It was still in the custody of the regiment in 1962 but apparently not at the time of this writing (2009)(8).

Earlier regimental historians attributed much of the hostile Indian action during the battles on the Red River to the leadership of Kiowa war chief Satanta. Satanta, a big-boned man, well over six feet tall, had been a thorn in the flesh of the U.S. government since the middle of the 1850's but, by 1874, he had lost his steam. He had been paroled from Huntsville Prison in October, 1873 after serving twenty-three months of a life sentence, and had resigned his office as war chief and passed on his medicine lance and shield to another warrior.

Nevertheless, on September 28, 1874, when the converging columns of Miles' 5th Infantry, John "Black Jack" Davidson's 10th Cavalry "Buffalo Soldiers", and Ranald Mackenzie's 4th Cavalry closed in on the Comanche and Kiowa raiders, Satanta was in the neighborhood doing a little consulting (9). Davidson captured Satanta and Mackenzie broke the power of the Kiowas at Palo Duro Canyon by burning five of their villages and destroying their horses. In the mopping up operations that followed, Lieutenant Baldwin distinguished himself once more.

In September of 1874, a Southern Cheyenne war party raided the Kansas homestead of the Germaine family. The warriors killed Mr. and Mrs. Germaine and three of their seven children. The four surviving Germaine children, all girls, were carried off by the war party.

In November, word reached Colonel Miles that two of the Germaine girls, Julia, 7, and Adelaide, 5, were being held at the Cheyenne village of Chief Grey Beard. The village was believed to be in the McClellan Creek area, currently a national grassland near Pampa, Texas. Miles sent Frank Baldwin with Company D, a detachment from D Troop, 6th Cavalry, a howitzer and a train of wagons to find the village and recover the girls.

The Red River War

Baldwin discovered the village on November 8. Fearing that the Indians might kill their captives before he could reach them by ordinary measures, he stripped the covers from the wagons and loaded them with the men of Company D. Down into the village swept the cavalry. They were followed closely by the "wagonized" infantry, bouncing and clattering, and firing their carbines and yelling. Grey Beard's startled warriors, rattled by the unorthodox assault, fled, leaving the two young captives. A scout, entering one of the lodges, found the two white youngsters hidden under a buffalo robe. Baldwin described the children as "nearly starved to death and naked." The children revealed that two older sisters, Catherine and Sophia, were still in captivity.

With the elder Germaine sisters in mind, Miles planned another winter campaign toward the head waters of the Red River. The endless pursuits and the numbing cold had rendered most of the southern plains people destitute. In late February, 1875, the Kiowa leaders surrendered. On March 6, the southern Cheyenne turned themselves in at the Cheyenne Indian Agency near Fort Sill. With them came Catherine and Sophia Germaine, barely alive after their long ordeal.

Colonel Miles was appointed guardian for the two younger girls. He found a home for them at Fort Leavenworth. Congress diverted five thousand dollars from Cheyenne annuities for their care and upbringing. Miles resigned his guardianship when he left Kansas, but continued to press the case for Catherine and Sophia. Finally, in 1879, Congress appropriated another five thousand dollars for the older girls. Frank Baldwin received his second Medal of Honor for the rescue of the Germaine sisters.

Following the Red River War, the Indian leaders were sentenced to imprisonment at Fort Marion, Florida. On April 6, 1875, while being shackled, a Cheyenne brave named Black Horse broke away and ran toward the camp of his people. He was pursued and finally killed. Some of the shots fired at him strayed into the Indian camp, wounding several persons. This caused a stampede of the Cheyenne and half of the tribe fled into the hills opposite the agency. Captain Bennett's H Company, 5th Infantry, and three troops of cavalry followed.

The Cheyenne were well armed, occupied some high ground and held out against the troops for several hours. By nightfall the troops had forced their way to a point just below the crest of the hill. However, the following morning it was found that the Indians had withdrawn during the night. The bodies of eleven Cheyenne warriors were found. Nineteen soldiers had been wounded. Troops from other posts were ordered to assist in the pursuit and eventually most of the escaped Indians gave themselves up. The Texas Panhandle was safe for white settlement.

The Noonan Affair

It is doubtful that there is a current or former soldier who has never heard the question, "How do I get out of this chicken shit outfit?" None has had a better reason to ask that question than PVT Patrick Noonan of G Company, 5th Infantry (10).

In 1875, Private Noonan was assigned as a teamster and watchman at the Fort Leavenworth stables. On the 23rd of January, an accidental fire erupted. While Noonan was busy leading the horses to safety, the fire destroyed his tent and extra clothing.

With the help of the company clerk, PVT Noonan submitted the following request:

Fort Leavenworth, Kansas

February 15, 1875

To Post Adjutant

    Sir: I have the honor to request that my clothing destroyed by fire on the morning of the 23rd of January 1875 when the post stables were burned, be replaced by a gratuitous issue. I worked getting public property out of these stables until it was removed and during the time that I was so employed my clothing in the tent used as a watchman's room was burned up in the tent.

As it was destroyed without my fault under the circumstances when I was doing my best to save public property I ask the government to replace it.

Very respectfully, your obedient servant.

Patrick (+) Noonan (his mark)
Private, Company G, 5th Infantry

The letter was first endorsed by Lieutenant F. H. Hathaway, Regimental Quartermaster, then by Captain Samuel Ovenshine, commander of Company G, and then by Colonel Nelson Miles. From there the request wound its way to the desk of R. Williams, Assistant Adjutant General and then to Brevet Major General Stewart Van Vliet, Assistant Quartermaster General, Department of Missouri. Van Vliet saw no evidence that a board of survey had been convened to consider Private Noonan's loss of property, so he bucked the request back to R. Williams at Fort Leavenworth.

Colonel Miles ordered Captain Ovenshine to convene a board of survey. Ovenshine met with 1st Lieutenant Mason Carter and 2nd Lieutenant George P. Borden and the three determined that Private Noonan was "duly detailed as a teamster and was required to occupy the tent where his clothing was destroyed. The nature of his duties made it necessary for him to keep his clothing in the tent. They recommended gratuitous replacement of: 2 blankets, wool, 1 great coat, mounted, 1 pair of trousers, 1 sack coat, lined, 1 forage cap, 2 pairs of drawers, 2 shirts, 1 pair of shoes, 2 pairs of stockings.

The board of survey's proceedings were then certified by P.H. Doty, Notary Public, and accompanied by a copy of the orders detailing Private Noonan to the Post Quartermaster as a teamster. The request received nine more endorsements before it, once again, left Fort Leavenworth.

When the request reached the Judge Advocate General in Washington, DC, nearly a year had elapsed since the stable fire. The JAG pointed out that army regulations permitted "gratuitous replacement" of clothing only in the event that it is damaged during combat. He recommended that William W. Belknap, Secretary of War, ask the Congress to pass a special or joint resolution to authorize the gratuitous issue of clothing. The secretary did so and, on January 12, 1876, Congress authorized new clothing for Patrick Noonan of G Company.

It is doubtful that Army red tape forced Private Noonan to live for a year in the same shirt and trousers that he wore on the day of the fire. There have always been informal ways to get things done in the army while the formal procedures move at a snail's pace. Experienced NCO's know how to take care of things and then cover their tracks, retroactively, with the proper paperwork.

CHAPTER SEVEN

FORT KEOGH, MONTANA

The Sioux and Northern Cheyenne tribes were outraged over the continued intrusion of whites into their sacred area in the Black Hills. In late 1875 they defiantly left their reservations and gathered in Montana with Chief Sitting Bull, intent on fighting for their lands. The War Department responded, the following June, by sending three columns of cavalry to force the Indians to return to their reservations. One column, the 7th U.S. Cavalry, was under the command of Lieutenant Colonel George Custer.

On June 25, 1876, Custer spotted a Sioux village beside the Rosebud River in the valley of the Little Big Horn. Without ascertaining the strength of the Indian war party and the features of the terrain, Custer attacked. Cheyenne and Hunkpapa Sioux crossed the river and slammed into Custer's 210-man squadron. Another force, largely Oglala Sioux led by Crazy Horse, moved downstream and then doubled back in a sweeping arc, catching the troopers in the open and enveloping them in a pincer move. In less than an hour Custer and his men died in one of the worst American military disasters ever.

The news of the Custer massacre aroused the whole nation. Reinforcements were gathered from the countryside and sent to Generals Terry and Crook. The 5th Infantry departed the Department of the Missouri and headed for the Department of the Dakota, where, after several long and punishing marches in search of elusive hostiles, it was sent to Montana to establish a garrison. General Alfred Terry, commander of the Department of the Dakota, assigned Colonel Miles and the 5th Infantry the task of patrolling the Yellowstone River to ensure that no hostile forces made their way into Canada.

Two companies, commanded by Lieutenant Colonel Joseph

Whistler, steamed up the Yellowstone in the summer of 1876 to select a location and begin construction of the new fort. Whistler selected a site in a stand of cottonwoods west of the mouth of the Tongue River and south of the Yellowstone River. A supply depot was established some distance away at the junction of Glendive Creek and the Yellowstone after it was determined that the river would be navigable to that point throughout most of the year.

Miles arrived on August 24, 1876 and christened the camp, naming it the Tongue River Cantonment. With most of the 5th Infantry and two companies of the 22nd Infantry, commanded by Lieutenant Colonel Elwell Otis, Miles began settling in for the winter.

There being a serious shortage of construction equipment, the troops threw up crude buildings of cottonwood logs chinked with mud. These were erected by digging ditches and then placing the logs vertically to form walls (1). Then the men worked frantically to procure heavy coats, masks, and buffalo moccasins. Woolen blankets were crafted into crude underclothing. Miles urgently requested regulation winter uniforms, pack animals, Sibley tents, mounted troops and more appropriate artillery pieces. The Napoleon guns attached to his regiment were too immobile for service against the Indians (2).

Throughout the coming campaigns, Miles was to be ably assisted by his chief scout, Luther S. "Yellowstone" Kelly. Kelly was a quiet, nature-loving New Yorker, who had traveled west to the valley of the Yellowstone after being discharged from the Union Army. When he received word of the massacre of Colonel Custer and the Seventh Cavalry, he rode to the Tongue River Cantonment and offered his services. His knowledge of the topography and nature of the upper Missouri and Yellowstone valleys would contribute greatly to the 5th Infantry's success.

With the onset of winter, ice and low water blocked the progress of supply boats on the Yellowstone River. A road from Fort Buford, at the confluence of the Yellowstone and Missouri Rivers was the only supply route. On October 16, 1876, Miles advised General Sherman, "Tonight I am somewhat concerned about a wagon train out from Glendive as it has been seven days enroute and should have come in today. I shall start down to meet it tomorrow morning if my scouts do not bring me word of it tonight (3)."

The Cedar Creek Campaign

Miles left the Tongue River Cantonment on the following day with most of the regiment. His concern was confirmed. In the early hours of October 11, several hundred Hunkpapas, Minneconjous and Sans Arcs had attacked the ninety-four-wagon supply train escorted by Captain Charles Miner and four infantry companies. The Indians captured forty-seven mules in the initial skirmish and forced Miner to retrace his steps to Glendive Creek.

Lieutenant Colonel Otis assumed command of the train, replaced the panicky civilian teamsters with soldiers, increased the escort to 185 men and added a battery of Gatling guns. The supply train set out again, but the Indians, well-armed with Spencer and Henry rifles, harassed it with long-range sniping.

Otis received a message from Sitting Bull, offering friendship, asking for food, and demanding that the bluecoats leave the Sioux hunting grounds, as they were frightening the buffalo. The lieutenant colonel couldn't meet such terms so the parley soon broke up. Miles reached the beleaguered supply train on October 18. Otis went on to the Tongue River Cantonment and the 5th Infantry picked up the Indians' trail to the northeast.

When Miles caught up with the Indian coalition two days later at Clear Creek, Sitting Bull, hungry and tired of war, requested further talks. He called for trade and an end to white trespass. He suggested that Miles and his men take a winter break from their Indian fighting duties. Having reached an impasse, the talks ended about sundown on the 20th. Miles then edged his command farther north along Cedar

Creek to cut off possible flight to Canada by the Indians.

The following day the principals met again. Miles demanded that Sitting Bull camp his people at some point on the Yellowstone River or go into some government agency. Though several chiefs seemed to waiver, Sitting Bull wasn't buying. Miles gave him fifteen minutes to make up his mind. Sitting Bull answered with a rifle shot.

"An engagement immediately followed," reported Miles matter-of-factly. The Indians, numbering between eight hundred and a thousand, seemed surprised by the stubborn advance of Mile's 398 infantrymen, who opened a steady fire with their single-shot Springfield rifles. A model 1861 artillery ordnance rifle, expertly handled by Captain Simon Snyder and crew, discouraged the Indians from advancing too closely. The Indians finally set the prairie afire and Miles halted the chase after overrunning their campsites and capturing a great deal of equipment and supplies.

Miles divided his command into three elements in an effort to corral the fleeing Indians (4). Lieutenant Frank Baldwin's battalion found Sitting Bull and forced him to sacrifice more equipment and some horses as he continued to flee north. Some of the smaller bands, who had thrown in with Sitting Bull the previous year, surrendered to Miles. As the winter of 1876 approached, the 5th Infantry continued to follow Sitting Bull northward toward the Fort Peck Indian Agency, 120 miles from the Tongue River Cantonment.

On Monday, November 6, reveille sounded at 0300 and, at 0430, the ten companies moved down and crossed the Yellowstone River. Colonel Miles and his staff followed at 0800. Lieutenant Baldwin recollected that it was a pleasant sunny day but the snow was 3" deep and made the trail slushy underfoot (5). It had been blustery and cold during the previous three days so Colonel Miles had delayed the start of the expedition. The column reached Sunday Creek at the end of the first day.

The infantrymen were accompanied by seven scouts, thirty-eight

FORT KEOGH, MONTANA

mule teams and two ambulances. The command had drawn rations for thirty days. The provender included slabs of bacon and beef on the hoof. The wagons carried full forage for thirty days for the animals and 250 rounds of ammunition per man.

A week later the early morning temperatures dropped to 10°. A cold wind blew from the northwest and the train moved slowly. The animals were nervous because of the myriad of ravines and washouts. Marches were delayed until there was sufficient daylight.

On the 13th, Companies D, H, and E left at 0900 to make a reconnaissance up the Yellowstone Valley. The scouts went as far as thirteen miles from camp. Signs of Indian camps were observed but they were old.

On November 15, the scouts sighted Indians to the front of the regiment. Baldwin rode to the top of the bluff and through his binoculars could distinctly see from one to two hundred Indians moving away from the regiment. Colonel Miles came forward and they soon discovered that they were chasing a group of reservation Indians along the north bank of the Missouri River. Lieutenant Baldwin lamented, "So our fond expectations of a good fight vanished."

Baldwin rode down to the river and encountered a company-sized patrol from the 6th Infantry out of Fort Peck. The company commander told him that there were about three thousand Yantonais living at the agency including some warriors that had ridden with Sitting Bull. Baldwin noted that the river was frozen in several places that would enable them to cross.

On November 19th, Miles proposed that Lieutenant Baldwin take Companies I, G, H, and E and an artillery piece and make a detour, crossing the Missouri at Fort Peck, then head west to the mouth of Squaw Creek and then south to Black Buttes where Sitting Bull's camp was believed to be. Baldwin agreed to do so.

Then Colonel Miles decide to expand the group with Companies A and B and join the expedition himself. He was probably worried that Frank Baldwin's venture might be successful and deprive him, Miles, of the glory. However, he assured Baldwin that the battalion-sized foray was his (Baldwin's) to command. The six companies were issued enough supplies for twenty-five days and crossed the river at 1:00 P.M.

Although the going was rough and five wagons were damaged by deep, muddy ruts in the trail, Baldwin's detachment covered between eighteen and twenty-five miles a day. Many antelope, buffalo, sage hens and prairie dogs checked out the bedraggled soldiers before diving for cover. On the 23rd, Baldwin admitted that he was "tired and aching with rheumatism." The surgeon issued him a quart of whiskey that evening.

Baldwin's group reached the north shore of the Missouri at noon on November 25th. They halted opposite the mouth of Squaw Creek and found that the river was almost free from ice but that it was about 500 feet wide at that point. They immediately began constructing an 80' by 12' raft using nothing more than a 1 ½ inch drill, hand saw, axes and rope. While the raft was under construction, Captain Bennett and B Company returned to the previous night's camp to bring the ammunition forward. They killed a couple of deer and enjoyed venison for dinner that night.

On the 26th, Miles, Baldwin and Lieutenant J.W. Pope with twelve men from E Company launched the raft, with a supply wagon aboard, and tried to cross to the south shore. They battled swift currents for awhile and finally caught on a snag in the middle of the river. Fashioning a small boat by wrapping wagon canvas around the bed of the wagon, they made several trips to take men back to the north shore but were unsuccessful in going in the opposite direction in order to stretch a rope from the raft to the south shore. After making five attempts, they gave up, cut the raft free from the snag, pulled it back to the north shore and went ashore to wait for the light of another day.

At 0630 on the 27th, Baldwin and twenty-two of the men went

about a half mile below camp and succeeded in reaching the south shore with the end of a rope. Then they brought the raft down and attached it to the north rope. They released it and the current carried the craft to the south bank. But when the men on the north shore attempted to draw it back, the rope broke and the raft drifted back to shore.

Large chunks of ice were flowing swiftly downstream. As Baldwin and three soldiers named Bellows, Montrose and Kelly attempted to return to the north shore, a large cake of ice hit the raft covering about a third of the deck. Fortunately all hands managed to stay aboard.

As he made his journal entry that evening, Frank Baldwin complained that, "The General (Miles insisted on being addressed by his Civil War brevet rank) has been very annoying today. . Just as we would get a thing all ready to operate and pretty sure of succeeding but before we could get time and complete the trial, he would want to do something else and in this way we have not as yet accomplished anything ...Tired, cold and wet tonight. Wonder how wife and baby are by this time."

Nelson Miles decided to build a raft of his own design and took the ropes from Baldwin's raft and set it adrift. The new raft was launched on the 29th and made two successful trips across the river but the floating ice still made the venture very dangerous. The battalion's supplies were dwindling and they were going to have to either risk a crossing or backtrack to a different route.

On December 1, the ice chunks were continuing to sweep down the Missouri. A frustrated Colonel Miles assembled Companies A and E, the gun, eight mounted men, seven six-mule teams and the ambulance and started for old Fort Hawley. There had been reports that the river was still frozen tight at that location. They would pick up Company B at Carroll, Montana, a small steamboat landing on the river. Baldwin was left with the 106 enlisted men and four officers of Companies G, H, and I. He was given orders to march to Fort Peck and then on to Fort Buford in Dakota Territory. By this time the snow was piled two feet deep.

At 5:40 the following morning, Baldwin's three companies began their return trip to Fort Peck. The sky was clear and there was still moonlight to help them find their way until the sun rose at about 8:30. They went into camp at three o'clock after covering twenty-three miles.

Baldwin's column arrived at Fort Peck at noon on December 6. The lieutenant immediately learned that Sitting Bull, with one hundred lodges, was camping on the Porcupine River about fifteen miles away. The news came from an Indian scout named John Brughiere. The scout mentioned that he would be leaving that evening with dispatches for Colonel Miles so that if Baldwin wanted the first crack at Sitting Bull, he would "have to shake a leg."

The three companies moved out at around 8:00 that evening and headed east for Sitting Bull's camp. When they were a few miles from Fort Peck they encountered a group of Indians that was heading for the fort. From them it was learned that Sitting Bull had left the Porcupine and moved to the near side of the Missouri River. Elated that their adversary was on their side of the river, Baldwin and his men sped down the trail.

At 4:30 on the morning of December 7, the three companies halted at the Milk River for breakfast. When they neared the Missouri, Baldwin spotted Indians on their right. One of them, who was subsequently identified as Sitting Bull's brother, Little Assiniboine, came within twenty yards of the battalion's rear guard. Baldwin had given strict orders not to fire at Indians on the north side of the river unless fired upon, so Little Assiniboine slipped away without being challenged.

Baldwin followed the Indians to the bank of the Missouri to a place where the trail crossed the river on the ice. He deployed his men in line of battle and sent three mounted troopers across the river on a reconnaissance. They no sooner reached the opposite bank when they spotted Indians and a brisk fire fight erupted.

Company H crossed the ice and drove the Indians out of the timber. The company's reception gave Baldwin a clearer picture of Sitting Bull's situation. The old chief had assembled no less than six hundred warriors. Reluctantly, Baldwin withdrew Company H. As they returned, three braves from the camp of Medicine Bear rode up. One of the Indians stated that he had been in Sitting Bull's camp that morning when the chief's brother returned from his recon and reported the location of Baldwin's column.

Sitting Bull immediately moved all of his lodges to Bark Creek and left his young men in the timber to await the army's approach. He intended to pull back into the hills and draw the soldiers on until he could catch them at a disadvantage. If the soldiers didn't attack, then he would follow them north and annihilate them. Baldwin moved slowly down the Yellowstone Valley to the mouth of the Porcupine River and camped on some high ground. One of Sitting Bull's scouts followed them and remained in sight for several hours.

Just prior to darkness a severe north wind began to blow and the temperature dropped to 30° below zero. Baldwin's men were short of rations and had one blanket each for warmth. So at 9:00 P.M. they headed for Fort Peck rather than freeze to death on the banks of the Porcupine.

At six o'clock on the morning of December 8, the freezing column was about seven miles from Fort Peck. Frank Baldwin rode ahead and sent three wagons back for his men. He then had the tents pitched so that they would be able to bed down as soon as they arrived. Twenty-five men reported to sick call that evening but the surgeon found that none had severe cold injuries. Baldwin sent dispatches to Colonel Miles.

While the men recovered, Baldwin and the fort's carpenter kept busy repairing an old howitzer, rebuilding a wheel and using an old wagon tongue to replace the gun's broken trail. His men were also in disrepair. They were badly in need of new clothing and many had wrapped their worn-out shoes in pieces of buffalo skin or old grain sacks.

The three companies left Fort Peck at 6:00 A.M. on the 12th. The icy wagon road thawed during the day making it a very difficult march. By the following day, the rations were nearly exhausted. Baldwin wrote "Everything moving along nicely. Officers growling. Men all right. Mules playing out due to lack of grain and needing to be shod. Broke the gun carriage today."

Then, on December 18, Baldwin was riding ahead of the column, east of Redwater Creek, when he spotted Sitting Bull's large village. He returned to the column, called them into line and drove forward, driving the Indians from their camp. The six hundred warriors jumped on their ponies and headed north. Companies G, H, and I captured most of the village's winter provisions, along with sixty horses, ponies and mules. Sitting Bull, however, slipped across the border into Canada.

The exhausted men of the 5th Infantry turned for home and reached the Tongue River Cantonment at 5:00 A.M. on December 22. Frank Baldwin received a brevet captaincy for his successful attack on Sitting Bull's camp.

Wolf Mountains

With Sitting Bull out of the country, Nelson Miles turned his attention to Crazy Horse. The timing was right. The Sioux chief was poorly equipped for winter fighting, hampered by his women and children, and short of ammunition. On the 29th of December, Colonel Miles with Companies A, C, D, E, and K of the 5th Infantry and Companies E and F of the 22nd Infantry; a column of 436 officers and men, supported by two artillery pieces, began a march up the Tongue River (6). Alerted to the approach of the bluecoats, the Indians abandoned their winter camps and fought two sharp skirmishes with the infantry on the 1st and 3rd of January.

Fort Keogh, Montana

Luther Barker of Company D recalled "We experienced much difficulty in crossing some rough ranges with our mile-long wagon train. The teams would often have to be taken from the wagons and a company of soldiers would have to lower the wagons by ropes, then a company on the opposite side of the gorge would draw them up…This was very laborious and when added to our tramping all day in the snow and being on picket guard quite often, with other duties incidental to campaign work, we truly felt we were earning our $13 a month (7)."

On the evening of January 7, 1877, the regimental scouts captured a young warrior and seven Cheyenne women and children. The prisoners proved to be relatives of one of the head men of the tribe. The Indian party, escorted by a brave named Big Horse had ventured out to locate Crazy Horse. Spying smoke, Big Horse ordered the small group to remain hidden while he went forward to investigate the fire. The women, however, disregarded his instructions and ventured out on their own, blundering into the army scouts.

Big Horse returned in time to see the scouts surrounding the women. Realizing that he was helpless to prevent their capture, he fled the scene in order to search out Crazy Horse's village and inform them of the army's presence. Near midnight he located the camp of the Lakota Sioux and Northern Cheyenne and entered it howling like a wolf to draw people out of their lodges to hear the news. The warriors painted their faces, grabbed their weapons, and rounded up their horses while Crazy Horse and other war leaders planned the attack.

The war party would follow the Tongue River to within a few miles of the army's camp. At that point the group would split. Half of the warriors, primarily Northern Cheyenne, would cross the river and use the terrain to conceal their movement as they approached the soldiers from the south. Crazy Horse would lead the remaining braves along the river and attack the soldiers from the west.

Dawn broke, on January 8, in cold grey hues with the sun illuminating the thickly packed clouds that hung low over the mountains surrounding the Tongue River Valley. A light snow was piling fresh powder on the already thick blanket that covered the ground to depths of nearly three feet in some places. On a flat in a horseshoe bend of the river, Nelson Miles' soldiers had responded to reveille at 4:00 A.M. and were busying themselves preparing for the day's activities (8).

The ruggedness of the valley facilitated the regiment's defense. Across the river, due north of the camp, a series of towering bluffs followed the course of the river for a quarter of a mile before sloping down into a wide floodplain that lay on both sides of the river. Southwest of camp sat a conical knoll that the soldiers would dub Battle Butte. A broad canyon ran southeast from the foot of Battle Butte toward thickly packed hills. It was a difficult but defensible site.

Miles placed Captain Ezra Ewers' E Company, 5th Infantry on top of Battle Butte where they had a panoramic view of the valley floor. Any frontal assault on the regiment's camp would have to pass through a quarter-mile-wide opening between Battle Butte and the bluffs north of the camp. K Company, commanded by Lieutenant Mason Carter, was positioned in a grove of cottonwood trees to cover the gap.

Meanwhile, in heavy falling snow, Crazy Horse and approximately four hundred warriors moved north along the river toward Mile's encampment. Near the mouth of Wall Creek, a few miles upstream from the soldiers' camp, the war party divided into two groups. Half the warriors crossed the Tongue River with Big Crow and began maneuvering through the valley's southern foothills. Crazy Horse and Medicine Bear continued down the northern bank of the frozen river making no attempt to conceal their advance.

Suddenly the scouts galloped into camp warning of approaching warriors. Colonel Miles joined E Company on top of the butte. Through his field glasses he was surprised to see that a great many of the warriors were, uncharacteristically, dismounting and forming firing lines a few hundred yards from K Company. Miles signaled Captain

Fort Keogh, Montana

James Casey to bring his A Company and Lieutenant Charles Hargous' detachment of mounted infantry to the top of the knoll. Those two units would support Lieutenant James Pope's two artillery pieces on the northwestern edge of the butte. Two other companies were brought into position near the cottonwood grove to support K Company. The colonel sent Companies E and F of the 22nd Infantry to cover the left flank on the opposite side of the river and placed Companies C and D of the 5th Infantry in reserve at the base of Battle Butte.

At about 7:00 A.M. Lakota Sioux and Northern Cheyenne braves charged K Company's lines. There was heavy skirmishing until the Indians were repulsed by the three companies posted along the river and a few well-placed artillery rounds from Pope. Throughout the morning, the Indians tried to collapse Lieutenant Carter's line but were eventually forced to retreat to the shelter of the hills.

As the fighting raged in the valley, Crazy Horse's column worked its way into the bluffs overlooking the army camp where they could provide covering fire to others who were attacking along the river. Medicine Bear led his group along the north bank of the Tongue and then across the frozen river and toward the hills south of Battle Butte. Captain Ezra Ewers shifted E Company to a line that extended from the center of the plateau to rock outcroppings on its extreme southwestern edge. Behind these natural breastworks, the company poured fire into Medicine Bear's warriors, as did Lieutenant Pope's gun crews.

Halfway across the open flood plain, Medicine Bear began waving a Northern Cheyenne talisman, called a Turner, above his head. Medicine Bear believed that the Turner would pull the bullets toward him and then render them harmless, thereby protecting his men as they crossed to the safety of the hills south of the army's position. Amazingly the warriors suffered no obvious casualties and managed to take up new positions on a small elevation a few hundred yards to the south of Company E. As Medicine Bear waved the Turner, a shell from one of Pope's artillery pieces struck his horses flank and horse and rider were knocked to the ground by its force. The shell failed to detonate and, moments later, Medicine Bear and his mount retreated safely.

With Indians now occupying the northwestern valley and the butte south of his position and with others crossing the river, Miles found himself nearly surrounded. A growing number of Northern Cheyenne and Lakota warriors were gathering on a series of three ridges about a quarter of a mile southeast of the plateau. These were the braves who had crossed the Tongue River with Big Crow before dawn and had maneuvered through the southern hills.

Miles decided to take the offensive. He ordered Captain James Casey to deploy Company A in a skirmish line and attack the ridges. Casey's riflemen took the first hill without taking any casualties. The attack on the other two ridges, however, soon stalled.

When Miles saw the assault grind to a stop, he sent Company D, 5th Infantry, to join Casey. Lieutenant Robert McDonald advanced his company across the valley floor and shifted them to the left of Company A so they could ascend the taller, steeper second hill. Company D met fierce resistance as they climbed the steep and slippery slope.

As they pushed the Indians back from the second summit, McDonald's men saw a warrior, dressed in bright red and wearing a war bonnet with a tail that reached the ground, begin to dance across the third ridge. Big Crow, a Northern Cheyenne medicine man, believed that he was impervious to soldiers' bullets and was deliberately exposing himself to danger in an attempt to rally the fighting spirit of his warriors.

Wooden Leg, a Northern Cheyenne veteran of the fight, remembered "He used up his cartridges and came back to us hidden behind the rocks to ask for more. Cheyenne and Sioux, here and there, each gave him one or two or three. He soon had enough to fill his belt. He went out again to walk along the ridge, to shoot at the soldiers and defy them in their efforts to hit him with a bullet. All of us kept behind the rocks, only peeping around at times to shoot. Crazy Horse, the Oglala chief, was near me (9)."

Incredibly, Big Crow traversed the ridge several times without being hit by any one of the nearly one hundred soldiers then positioned across from him. It was not until Sergeant Danny Burns and Corporal Byron Bronson of Company D fired from below the lip of the second summit, two hundred yards away, that Big Crow fell into the snow.

As Big Crow fell with a bullet in his abdomen, the resolve of many of the Northern Cheyenne was destroyed. He was regarded as a very brave and powerful medicine man. Several of his tribesmen moved forward to remove his body from the field. Others deserted the ranks, believing that Big Crow's death was a sign of impending disaster. However, many of the warriors facing Companies A and D were Crazy Horse's Lakota Sioux, who were less affected by the failure of Big Crow's medicine. The shrill sound of eagle-bone whistles filled the air as Crazy Horse rallied his three hundred men and advanced within fifty yards of Company D. Miles ordered Company C, his last reserve unit, commanded by Captain Edmund Butler, to reinforce the two hard pressed companies by attacking the third ridge.

Butler deployed his men in a skirmish line and moved them across the snow-covered valley floor at the quick step. As they approached the hills, Miles realized that Captain Butler was positioning to reinforce D Company at the second ridge. Miles dispatched Brevet Captain Frank Baldwin to redirect Butler.

Baldwin grabbed a half-empty crate of rifle cartridges and galloped across the valley. At the base of the second hill, he directed Butler around D Company. When they reached the base of the third hill, Butler gave the order to charge. As he began the ascent, his horse was shot out from under him, so he continued on foot to lead the left wing of C Company to the summit of the hill. Baldwin remained with the right wing and led an advance through a wide drainage channel that provided a direct line of assault. The Indians maintained a steady fire with their Winchester and Sharps rifles but their lack of experience with downhill plunging fire saved C Company from heavy loss.

Miles repositioned the Rodman gun and the Napoleon cannon and the gunners began lobbing shells over the heads of their comrades and into the Indian line. The Lakotas and Northern Cheyennes fell back slowly. Butler's and McDonald's troops chased the Indians for about a mile before heavy snow began to fall. Exhausted, running low on ammunition and seeing their enemy in full retreat, Butler ordered an end to the attack.

As the weather degenerated into blizzard conditions, the Indians engaging Miles' other troops also withdrew from the battlefield. The colonel gave the order to fix lunch but stay alert for another attack.

Tents were pitched on Battle Butte to shelter the wounded. Amazingly, given the staggering amount of ammunition discharged by the Indians, casualties were light. August Rathman was killed and eight others were wounded, including Privates John Diamond and William Daily of Company D and Privates Rodenburg and Dauha of A Company. Captain Baldwin had contracted pneumonia and the cold was taking its toll in frozen hands and feet. On the return march, Bernard McCann died of his wounds.

The return trip to the cantonment proved even more demanding than the trip out, owing to the increased depth of snow. Private Barker remembered that they were able to cover no more than several miles a day, but added "when we turned a point of timber and saw Old Glory flying, we cheered. I remember Sergeant Thomas Gray had prepared D Company a good dinner, but we would rather sleep than eat. When our first sergeant called out 'General Miles orders these men excused from duty for three days' my Irish bunky said, 'Bless Paddy Miles (10).'"

Captain James Casey, who held one brevet for gallantry during the Civil War, was brevetted lieutenant colonel and later awarded the

Medal of Honor for his leadership of Company A during the action. Captain Edmund Butler and 1st Lieutenant Robert McDonald also received the Medal of Honor for their part in the fight in the Wolf Mountains.

Nelson Miles also recommended that twenty-eight enlisted members of the 5th Infantry receive the Medal of Honor for gallant conduct during the winter of 1876-77 (11). The medals were conferred on 27 April 1877 during a visit by General Sherman. During the Civil War and Indian campaigns, the Medal of Honor was the only way of recognizing conduct that was beyond the simple discharge of duty. The Distinguished Service Cross was first awarded in 1918, the Silver Star in 1932, and the Bronze Star was created during World War II.

Constructing the Fort

From January through April, most of the command remained at the cantonment to participate in the construction of the new post. Colonel Miles chose a site, on higher ground, about one mile west of the old cantonment. The buildings were laid out with officers' quarters facing in toward a diamond-shaped parade ground and sets of enlisted barracks facing the same diamond from the northeast and southeast. The headquarters was constructed at the northern tip and the commander's quarters at the western tip (12).

All did not go according to schedule, tight money being the biggest reason. Anxious officers wanted the new quarters finished in a hurry so that their families could be transported up the river to join them. Some officers had their families join them and stay in the old log huts while others, on returning from the field and finding the new quarters not finished, used their own money to continue construction. These men requested that the government refund the $189.44 expended. The government started construction, in earnest, in December of 1877 after this request for a refund was made. An army quartermaster, Captain Charles Heintzelman arrived in June to superintend the project.

Two Centuries of Valor

Among the major buildings were two cavalry barracks to house six troops, two large four-company infantry barracks, several one-company barracks, the commander's quarters, thirteen officers' quarters built as duplexes and quadraplexes, stables for the cavalry and supply trains, a bake house and a granary. Captain Heintzelman reported a total cost of $183,300.43, approximately double the amount that had been authorized by Congress. Those buildings completed in 1877 were quickly occupied by anxious soldiers and families who were tired of living at the rundown cantonment. Companies F and K moved in in November 1877 but the other units had to wait until May of 1878.

Although she was pleased with the move to the newly-built fort, Alice Blackwood Baldwin noted in her memoirs that the cottonwood used in the fireplace burned quickly and gave off little heat. She had about the same luck with pine. The high foundations under the quarters allowed cold winds to billow the carpets and create a chill in the house. Banking the buildings with manure and dirt corrected this problem (13).

The enlisted dependents had much different living quarters. Their area was 490 feet southeast of the most easterly infantry barracks and was dubbed "Tub Town" since many of the wives of enlisted soldiers worked as company laundresses to augment the family income. Tub Town was composed of about sixty log buildings constructed like the old cantonment huts.

When Dominick O'Malley arrived at Fort Keogh in October, 1877, he recalled that his family spent the first winter in a 10 x 14 wall tent, which he remembered as being "comfortable." In the spring they moved into one of the log houses in Tub Town (14).

As the cantonment was being vacated, the quartermaster had some trouble keeping track of army property. Some of the neighbors were taking lumber from the cantonment huts. Floors, windows, and door frames disappeared.

Many of the filched building materials ended up directly across the Tongue River from the fort where civilian workers and camp followers established Miles City, Montana in order to take advantage of the security and commercial opportunities offered by proximity to a good-sized military installation. In addition to the merchants, bartenders, government officials, inn keepers and ladies of the night, the town accommodated many long-term employees at the fort including blacksmiths, carpenters, clerks, foragers, guides, herders, interpreters, masons, packers, saddlers, scouts, teamsters and wagon masters.

Initially there was ferry service between Miles City and the fort. During the 1880's a succession of wooden bridges were built but each one failed to survive the spring run-off. Much of the time, those going to and from Miles City had to rely on the ferry boat or a railroad bridge built in 1881. On numerous occasions drunken soldiers returning to the post fell the sixteen feet from the railroad bridge to the river or to its banks.

On November 8, 1878, officials in the War Department officially named the new garrison, Fort Keogh, in honor of Captain Myles Walter Keogh, a young Irish immigrant, who died while commanding Company I, Seventh Cavalry at the battle of Little Big Horn. The Indians, who knew the Yellowstone River as the Elk River, called Fort Keogh the Elk River Fort. During the early cantonment days, when the living conditions were extremely poor, the troops labeled the fort with some unprintable names.

The Campaigns Continue

Within weeks of the battle in the Wolf Mountains, the bonds that held the rebellious bands of Indians together began to dissolve. In late January the first of many messengers sent out from the Tongue River Cantonment and Camp Robinson, Nebraska arrived at the Lakota and Northern Cheyenne camps near the headwaters of the Big Horn River.

These messengers promised good treatment from the army. Tribal councils split over the question of continuing the fight. One by one the bands of Indians surrendered at Miles' post or on the Great Sioux Reservation until only Crazy Horse and his people held out. Finally on May 6, 1877, Crazy Horse led most of his tired and hungry band into Camp Robinson.

Colonel Miles learned from those who had surrendered in April that a band of renegades, chiefly Minneconjous led by Lame Deer, had broken off and gone westward. Miles went after them with a mixed command that included Companies E and H of the 5th Infantry, four troops of the 2nd Cavalry and four companies of the 22nd Infantry. At dawn on May 8, 1877, near Muddy Creek, Montana, the column surprised Lame Deer and captured his entire force after a running fight that covered eight miles from Lame Deer's village to the Rose Bud River.

The encounter nearly led to Miles' demise. Only the sudden rearing of the Colonel's horse caused Lame Deer to miss a point blank shot. Miles' orderly was killed by the bullet meant for his commander (15). Fourteen Indians, including Lame Deer, were killed. Four soldiers died in this engagement but none were members of the 5th Infantry. The Great Sioux War was over.

The capture of Lame Deer's band provided the 5th Infantry with a herd of 450 Indian horses, mules and ponies. Upon his return to the Tongue River garrison, Miles organized Companies B, F, G, I, and K into a mounted battalion and assigned them to a separate camp on the Miles City side of the river. At the time there were only ten regiments of cavalry on active duty, so the mounted battalion of the 5th Infantry called themselves the "11th Cavalry."

When word came in June of 1877 that rain and coyotes had disinterred some of the troopers that had died with Custer, Nelson Miles dispatched I Troop of the 7th Cavalry to rebury their comrades. Captain H. J. Nowlan and his men were replacements for Captain

Myles Keogh and his troopers who had died at the Little Big Horn.

The Nez Perce

The Nez Perce tribe in Washington and Idaho had been living peacefully with its white neighbors. In 1877, they balked when the U.S. government decided to move them to another reservation. When a group of white trappers and hunters trespassed on their hunting grounds, the Nez Perce killed the intruders. At that point the tribal leader, Chief Joseph, felt his only option was to round up his people and head east to link up with Sitting Bull.

Joseph was probably the best Native American tactician of his generation. His small band of three hundred warriors was well-trained, disciplined and were excellent rifle marksman. U. S. Army units from Fort Benton, Montana made several unsuccessful attempts to force the Nez Perce to return to their reservation but did serve to slow down their advance toward Canada.

Finally, when Chief Joseph entered the Yellowstone country, Colonel Miles decided that he would have to go after the Nez Perce himself. On September 17, 1877, his column, composed of six troops of cavalry, the five mounted infantry companies, two pieces of light artillery and detachments of white and Indian scouts crossed to the north bank of the Yellowstone River and rode in a northwest direction to intercept the Nez Perce tribe as it headed toward Canada (16).

On September 30, Joseph encountered the mounted elements of Miles' column in the Bear Paw Mountains, just thirty miles south of the Canadian border. The Nez Perce went into a defensive position at the base of a crescent-shaped cove on the east side of Snake Creek. The creek had carved several dry creek beds in the alluvial soil that served as natural trenches. Using knives, pans and captured bayonets, the Indians dug shelter pits for the old people, women and children and rifle pits for the fighters. An escort of warriors evacuated a large group of women and children.

Miles arranged his attack as follows: Initially Captain Owen Hale and his 7th Cavalry would assault the southern flank of the village. Then Captain Simon Snyder's battalion of 5th Infantry, supported by Lieutenant Marion Maus and his scouts would dismount and attack from the front. Lieutenant Edward McClernand and his 2nd Cavalry detachment were ordered to pursue the escaping group of women and children while the artillery crews unlimbered their two guns.

The squadron from the 7th Cavalry executed its movement on the southern flank with precision but, when the troopers came within range of the Indian rifles, they ran into a steep bank which their horses could not descend. The Indians opened fire on their exposed line, dropping many men and horses before they could fall back over the ridge and out of sight.

The Fifth (mounted) Infantry also encountered a steep bank to its front. Company I found a ravine that allowed them to descend toward the Indian camp but, with no friendly troops on their flanks, they were forced to return and find cover behind a nearby ridge.

During the initial attack, losses were staggering. Two officers and twenty-two men were killed. Forty-two more were wounded. A disappointed Nelson Miles was compelled to switch to siege tactics. When the wagon train arrived, the train guard distributed picks and shovels and the troops dug in so they would be able to hold their ground.

Prior to entrenching, former scout Louis Shambow recalled that he used his dead horse as a bulwark until the odor resulting from repeated hits forced him to wiggle into a new position behind a rock (17). There he was soon joined by "Yellowstone" Kelley and Corporal John Haddoo. They exchanged shots with the nearly invisible sharpshooters until the corporal, a Medal of Honor recipient from the Cedar Creek campaign, was mortally wounded. He died while they were carrying him away. Shambow described the Nez Perce as "the best shots I ever saw. I would put a small stone on the top of my rock

Fort Keogh, Montana

and they would get it every time."

The artillerymen experienced difficulty in placing their shots in the dry creek beds. Then they discovered that by sinking the trails in a shallow pit they were able to elevate the muzzles and thereby convert the cannons into mortars. Exploding shrapnel proved to be deadly as it ripped through Chief Joseph's rifle pits and tunnels. Miles had the Nez Perce corralled and their surrender was inevitable.

When he heard that Joseph had sent couriers north to enlist aid from Sitting Bull, Colonel Miles thought it prudent to send messages to his old Civil War mentor, General Oliver O. Howard, Commander of the Department of the Columbia, and to Colonel Samuel Sturgis of the 7th Cavalry informing them that he had Chief Joseph under siege and was requesting reinforcements.

Colonel Sturgis received Miles' request for help on October 2 and set out immediately in the direction of the Snake Creek battlefield. In all probability, Miles feared being reinforced more than he feared the possibility that Sitting Bull might lend a hand to the Nez Perce. He would not have wanted to share the victory with Sturgis, whom he considered a rival for the next brigadier general vacancy and to General Howard, being his superior in rank, would go the honor of and resulting publicity from negotiating the surrender. To forestall such a calamity, Miles began negotiating with Chief Joseph.

A parley was arranged and Joseph and a couple of his warriors went forward to meet Miles and several of his officers at a halfway point marked by a bison robe. Miles demanded that the Nez Perce surrender all firearms, but Joseph insisted that his people retain half of them to enable them to shoot game. This disagreement broke up the parley and, as they were parting, Miles took Joseph into custody, a move that didn't score many points with the younger Nez Perce warriors.

During the evening of October 4, General Howard reached the battlefield with an escort from the 7th Cavalry. He had been on Joseph's trail since June and wanted to be there for the surrender.

The following morning, Miles released Joseph in exchange for Lieutenant Lovell Jerome, who had been sent out to see if the Indians were stacking their arms. While doing so, Lieutenant Jerome drifted too close to the Nez Perce camp.

On the afternoon of October 5, Chief Joseph rode out from the coulees followed by several warriors on foot. Lieutenant C. E. Wood, General Howard's aide-de-camp, wrote (18):

"Joseph's hair hung in two braids on either side of his face. He wore a blanket and moccasin leggings. His rifle was across the pommel in front of him. When he dismounted he walked to General Howard and offered him the rifle. Howard waved him to Miles. He then walked to Miles and handed him the rifle. Then Chief Joseph stepped back and began his formal speech of surrender."

"Tell General Howard I know his heart. What he told me before I have in my heart." (Howard had previously tried to intervene with the U.S. Government on Chief Joseph's behalf; requesting that the Nez Perce be allowed to remain in their homeland, the Wallowa Valley, west of the Snake River in Washington Territory.)

"I am tired of fighting. Our chiefs are killed. Looking Glass is dead. The old men are all killed. It is the young men who say yes or no. He who led the young men is dead. It is cold and we have no blankets. The little children are freezing to death. My people, some of them, have run away to the hills and have no blankets, no food, no one knows where they are, perhaps freezing to death. I want to look for my children and see how many of them I can find. Maybe I shall find them among the dead. Hear me, my chiefs, I am tired; my heart is sick and sad. From where the sun now stands, I will fight no more forever."

There were so many wounded soldiers that the next two days were spent building stretchers. Colonel Miles was not able to leave the battlefield until October 7th. He wrote: "Our success was not without serious loss. Captain Hale and Lieutenant Biddle, with twenty soldiers, were killed; Captains Moyland and Godfrey, Lieutenant Romeyn and

Assistant Adjutant Baird and twenty-eight soldiers were wounded..."

The next five days were spent slogging through mud and snow until they reached the Missouri River. There they were able to load the wounded on steamers for transport to hospitals at Forts Buford and Lincoln in Dakota Territory. Their dressings had not been changed since the battle on September 30 and several died during their first night on the river.

Medals of Honor for the Nez Perce campaign were awarded to First Lieutenants George Baird, Mason Carter, Henry Romeyn and Second Lieutenant Oscar Long. The regimental surgeon, Major Henry Tilton, was similarly cited for "fearlessly risking his life and displaying great gallantry in rescuing and protecting the wounded men." First Sergeant Henry Hogan of Company G received his second award of the Medal of Honor for carrying severely wounded Lieutenant Romeyn to safety while under fire.

Following the capitulation, 87 Nez Perce men, 184 women and 147 children turned themselves in. Their baggage was loaded in the army wagons and they were issued coats and blankets. According to the surrender terms, they were to spend the rest of the winter at Fort Keogh before moving to the Lapwai Reservation in the Pacific Northwest.

However, the surrender terms were not punitive enough to satisfy Nelson Miles' superiors in Washington. In the spring of 1878, the Nez Perce were ushered aboard fourteen flatboats and transported to the Indian Territory. When Joseph learned that his people would be exiled, his only comment was, "When will the white man learn to tell the truth?"

Many of the Nez Perce became ill and perished during their stay in the Indian Territory. In 1885, those surviving were sent back to their beloved reservation in Idaho. Chief Joseph was the guest of Nelson Miles several times during the ensuing years. He respected Miles, knowing that he was the only man who had whipped him in an equal fight. However, Nelson Miles went on for the rest of his career arguing with General Howard about who should get the credit for capturing Chief Joseph.

The Bannock Uprising

In May of 1878 a party of Bannocks, Paiutes, and Shoshones arrived at their traditional root-digging area near Camas Prairie, Idaho and discovered that most of the roots had been eaten by hogs belonging to some white settlers. Some of the Indians returned to their reservations but about two hundred warriors, led by Buffalo Horn, a Bannock Indian, launched an offensive. Buffalo Horn was killed on a raid near Silver City, Idaho. The surviving Bannocks withdrew to the west and were joined by Paiute, Oyte and Egan warriors bringing their force to 450.

On August 29, 1878, Miles received word that a number of Bannock Indians were following the Nez Perce trail to Canada. Their intent was to join forces with Sitting Bull. Companies A, C, F, G, I and K, the mounted units of the regiment, along with seventy-five Crow warriors, moved quickly to block Yellowstone's eastern passes.

Lookouts spotted the Bannocks on September 3 near Clark's Fork, Montana. At daybreak, the following morning, the soldiers attacked, killing thirteen of the surprised Indians and capturing thirty-seven. Captain Andrew S. Bennett, an interpreter named "Rock", and a Crow guide died during the fight. One of the enlisted men was mortally wounded.

Andrew Bennett had enlisted in Company F of the 5th Wisconsin Infantry on July 12, 1861. He survived the murderous assault on Maryes Heights at Fredricksburg and was mustered out as a first lieutenant on August 3, 1864. He received a regular army appointment, at the same rank, in March, 1867 and was assigned to the 15th U.S. Infantry, where he soon advanced to the rank of captain. Bennett was assigned to the 5th Infantry in January, 1871 and served with the regiment until the time of his death (19).

Fort Keogh, Montana

Sitting Bull Surrenders

Although Sitting Bull was in exile in Canada, scattered bands of Sioux refused to surrender and kept up sporadic resistance. For the next several years, troops were employed in rounding up these small groups. Largest of these operations with the Milk River expedition of the summer of 1879, involving seven troops from the 2nd Cavalry and nine companies of infantry including A, B, C, G, H, I and K of the 5th. This expedition fought engagements at the Milk River on July 17th and at the Poplar River on August 14th.

That summer, 2nd Lieutenant Hunter Liggett joined the 5th Infantry following his graduation from West Point. Liggett embarked on a long career with the regiment, much of it as commander of Company D. He left the 5th Infantry in June of 1898 when he was promoted to major and became adjutant general of volunteer troops serving in Cuba (20).

On March 8, 1880 the men from the regiment fought two skirmishes. Lieutenant S. W. Miller, nine men from Company E and a party of Indian scouts were searching for stolen cattle near Porcupine Creek when they came upon the camp of the Indian rustlers. A hot firefight ensued in which the eight rustlers were killed and much of the stock recaptured. A civilian named Hawkings, presumably the owner of the cattle, was killed. Two of Lieutenant Miller's scouts died.

In hot pursuit, mounted Companies I and K, under the command of Captain Frank Baldwin, caught up with the band of surviving Indians near Rosebud Creek and took them in tow. During the chase, K Company had covered 120 miles in thirty hours; a pace seldom equaled by regular cavalry.

During the summer of 1880, small Indian bands were spotted all over the Yellowstone Valley. Some wanted to surrender; others wanted trouble. On August 1, Company E marched 125 miles to Willow Creek and returned with 140 prisoners.

Colonel Miles sent word that all hostile forces had until October 25, 1880 to surrender their guns and ponies. Sitting Bull moved his followers closer to the Fort Peck Indian Reservation, prepared to avoid conflict by moving north if Miles made a move.

It was the army that relieved Sitting Bull of his Nelson Miles problem. Colonel Miles was promoted to the permanent rank of brigadier general and, on December 15, 1880, bade farewell to the regiment he had led so successfully for eleven years. He was transferred to Vancouver Barracks, Washington Territory, where he assumed command of the Department of the Columbia. Lieutenant Colonel Joseph N. G. Whistler, long-time second-in-command, took over the helm of the 5th Infantry.

In the final weeks of 1880, Major Guido Ilges took a detachment from the 7th Cavalry and Companies A, B, C, F and G of the 5th Infantry into the field in pursuit of Sioux Chiefs Gall and Crow. The column of 180 officers and men marched 200 miles from Fort Keogh through deep snow and sub-zero temperatures. On January 2, 1881, they located their adversaries on the bank of the Missouri River. The Indians fled from their villages and took refuge in some timber. Major Ilges' column killed eight of the more assertive braves and took 324 prisoners. During its return to Fort Keogh, Ilges' command fought a similar action at the Poplar River, capturing another sixty-four Indian warriors. On February 12, they corralled another 185 at Redwater, Montana.

In early June, 1881, Major Ilges sent scout John Brughiere to a nearby Indian camp to convey an order. They were to break camp and move to a steamboat landing on the Yellowstone River, about a mile and a half east of Fort Keogh, and prepare to embark for Standing Rock. The Indians, not having been harassed by the army for six months, had become somewhat emboldened and sent back word that if the white chief wanted their tepees down to send some soldiers to take them down.

Ilges ordered the trumpeter to sound Boots and Saddles and, in twenty-five minutes, every mounted trooper in the fort was in the saddle awaiting orders. When the column arrived at a clearing in front of the Indian camp, the cavalrymen and mounted infantrymen formed a skirmish line and men from Company H, 5th Infantry rolled two revolving Hotchkiss guns into place. The Hotchkiss, a light-weight cannon, had five 37mm rifled barrels, was capable of firing 43 rounds per minute and was accurate at 2000 yards. The Indians had their tepees down and rolled in forty minutes.

The soldiers escorted the three thousand Indians to their boat landing campsite and two troops from the 2nd U.S. Cavalry remained there to guard them until five steamers finally arrived to take them to the reservation. Meanwhile, Company E of the 5th Infantry, commanded by Captain Ezra Ewers, drove the Indians' ponies overland to their new home.

Scattered by constant harassment and unable to get arms and sufficient ammunition, the insurgent Indians were no longer capable of serious resistance. On July 20, 1881, Sitting Bull, with the last of his followers, surrendered at Fort Buford. With the surrender of Sitting Bull, hostilities virtually ceased in Montana.

The army had won the peace. It now had the job of keeping it. This would not only involve preventing clashes between rival Indian tribes but dealing with white men who were robbing supply trains and attempting to usurp Indian lands. The 5th Infantry, however, would once again carry out its mission on foot. On October 31, 1881, the mounted elements of the regiment released their ponies and became officially dismounted. The "11th Cavalry" had been ordered to fold its flag.

Fort Keogh became easily accessible to the world in 1881 when the Northern Pacific Railroad was completed from Bismarck to the fort. Thanks to the troops, the track construction had made good progress through hostile Indian country (21).

A grateful Northern Pacific showed its appreciation. All officers, enlisted men and their families were given unlimited tickets at half-price to St. Paul from all places east of Walla Walla, Washington. The railroad brought recruits to Ft. Keogh. Troops were transported on the Northern Pacific when needed, as in a threatened Crow uprising in 1887 and in the eventual transfer of the Fifth Infantry from Fort Keogh to Texas.

During the Indian War period, telegraphic communication was essential to the life of an army post. In 1878, soldiers from the 5th Infantry ran a telegraph line from Fort Keogh to Bismarck. After the Indians were somewhat subdued, serious construction began on a communications network. Several companies of the regiment ran a line from Terry Point, a supply center at the mouth of the Big Horn River, to Fort Buford. In October 1878, Companies D and H constructed a line between Forts Keogh and Buford. Troop B, Second Cavalry, started a line from Fort Keogh to Deadwood in the same month. By the end of 1879, Fort Keogh was in telegraphic communication with Bismarck, Deadwood, Fort Custer, Fort Ellis, Helena, Fort Shaw, Fort Benton and Fort Assinniboine. The men from Fort Keogh had run 650 miles of line while erecting an average of twenty poles per mile.

In addition to telegraphic communication, Colonel Miles had the first telephone in Montana Territory. The line ran from his quarters to the post telegraph office. Five years later a telephone line was strung between Fort Keogh and Miles City.

Nelson Miles' subsequent career, while not part of the regiment's history, was certainly of interest to his old command. On April 2, 1886, Miles replaced a long-time rival, George Crook, as commander of the Department of Arizona. His headquarters were at Fort Bowie in the southern part of the state. He inherited General Crook's main assignment, that of capturing Geronimo and his Chiracahua Apaches so that they could be shipped to Fort Barrancas, Florida.

Miles' troopers tracked Geronimo for three thousand miles through the Sierra Madre Mountains without success. Finally, Lieutenant Charles Gatewood, 6th Cavalry, a former Indian agent, convinced Geronimo to surrender on September 4, 1886. Even those

Fort Keogh, Montana

Chiracahuas who had worked for the army were exiled to Florida, in violation of an earlier pledge that they had received from General Miles.

More than one historian claims that Nelson Miles assumed credit for the successful negotiations with Geronimo in an effort to earn a promotion. Lieutenant Gatewood became irate about his lack of recognition so Miles had him transferred to Dakota Territory.

When Major General Crook died in March of 1890, Nelson Miles lobbied Washington officials and finally received his second star. He was appointed commander of the Department of the Missouri with headquarters in Chicago. Then after serving as Chief of Staff during the Spanish American War, he was promoted to Lieutenant General and became General of the Army on October 5, 1895.

Miles retired in 1903 but then asked to be returned to active duty in 1918 so he could participate in World War I. President Woodrow Wilson turned down the 79-year-old's request because of his age. On May 16, 1925, while attending the Barnum and Bailey Circus in Washington, D.C. with his grandchildren, Nelson Appleton Miles suffered a massive heart attack which killed him instantly.

Following the departure of Nelson Miles from the 5th Infantry, two officers, Colonels Pinckney Lugenbeel and Daniel Huston were temporarily appointed as regimental commander while they awaited retirement. Neither man ever saw the regiment. Actual command of the regiment from December 1880 until June 1882 devolved upon the long-time second-in-command LTC Joseph N. G. Whistler. Whistler was a veteran of the Mexican, Civil and Indian Wars with a long record of citations for gallantry. He retired as colonel of the 15th Infantry in 1886.

Lieutenant Colonel John Darragh Wilkins of the 8th Infantry was promoted to colonel and assumed command of the 5th Infantry on June 22, 1882. Wilkins graduated from West Point just in time for the Mexican War and distinguished himself as a junior officer with the

3rd Infantry at Contreras and Churubusco. He remained with the 3rd Infantry during much of the Civil War.

Blessed with a sour disposition, Wilkins complained bitterly as he perceived his West Point classmates advancing through the ranks with ease. He received his captaincy fifteen years after entering the army and yet, as a captain, led his regiment with gallantry at the battle of Malvern Hill. He was brevetted a lieutenant colonel for his actions during the subsequent battles of Fredericksburg and Chancellorsville and, from then on, was frequently placed in very responsible positions without the accompanying permanent rank. He was finally promoted to major in April, 1865 and transferred to the 15th Infantry. He remained in the army after the war, serving tours with the 33rd Infantry and the 8th Infantry before assuming command of the Fifth.

Colonel George Gibson became the commanding officer of the 5th Infantry when Colonel Wilkins retired in August, 1886. Under Gibson's direction, the regiment served quietly at Fort Keogh until May, 1888, when orders were received transferring it to the Texas border. The troops moved by rail to Bismarck, North Dakota and then boarded the steamers *General Terry* and *Helena*. The regimental strength at the time was thirty-five officers and 418 enlisted men.

As it neared the end of the river passage to Omaha, Nebraska, the *General Terry* collided with the Union Pacific railroad bridge and sank thirty feet from shore. The troops spent the next twelve days recovering public and private property from the capsized hull (22).

Proceeding from Omaha by rail, the regiment arrived at Fort Bliss one month after leaving Fort Keogh. It had traveled 2200 miles. The command was promptly dispersed along the border. Headquarters and Companies B and E remained at Fort Bliss. Companies I and K went to Fort Davis, C and F to Fort McIntosh, A and G to Piña Station, D to Fort Brown and H to Fort Hancock. In July, A and G were shifted from Piña Station to Fort Ringgold.

Less than a month after arriving in Texas, the regiment lost

Fort Keogh, Montana

Colonel Gibson, who died suddenly on August 5, 1888 at Las Vegas, New Mexico. LTC Nathan W. Osborn, of the 6th Infantry, was immediately promoted to colonel to fill the 5th Infantry vacancy. During the Civil War, Osborn had been brevetted major for gallant and meritorious service during the siege of Vicksburg, Mississippi.

The regiment's second Texas tour was vastly different from their first one. Patrol duty along the border was routine. For the first time in nearly thirty years the troops spent more time loading their stomachs than loading their rifles. From September, 1890 through February, 1891, the re-enlistment rate was an enthusiastic 89%.

In November, 1889, K Company, quartered at Fort Davis, made a six-day practice march with full packs. They covered 126 miles in thirty-three hours of actual hiking, rivaling the company's record in the early 1880's when it was a mounted infantry unit.

While the 5th Infantry enjoyed good duty in Texas, its former commander, Major General Nelson Miles, Commander of the Department of the Missouri, was engaged in the wind-up of the Indian War. On the 15th of December, 1890, Sitting Bull got into an argument with the Indian agent at Standing Rock Reservation, South Dakota and was killed by an Indian policeman. Another Sioux chief, Big Foot, left that agency and led his Miniconjou band toward the Pine Ridge Reservation. They were pursued by the 7th Cavalry, caught, and escorted to Wounded Knee Creek, Montana.

During the process of disarming the Indians, a scuffle developed, leading to shots being fired. Soon two hundred Indians including Big Foot, and many women and children perished in a spray of Hotchkiss fire.

General Miles quickly dispatched 3500 troops to surround the Pine Ridge Reservation. The Sioux formally surrendered when Chief Kicking Bear gave Miles his rifle. The Pine Ridge affair, including the unfortunate massacre at Wounded Knee, was the last campaign of the Indian War.

CHAPTER EIGHT

THE CUBAN OCCUPATION AND PHILIPPINE INSURRECTION

In May, 1891, most of the regiment was shifted from Texas to stations in the southeast. Headquarters, Companies C, D, and E, and the regimental band were dispatched to St. Francis Barracks near St. Augustine, Florida while Companies B, H, I and K went to Mt. Vernon Barracks, Alabama. Companies A and F remained at Forts Ringgold and Davis in Texas. On the train trip to St. Augustine, there was a railroad accident in which Private Charles Carter was killed and Sergeant Otto Rehbease and Privates Reed and Wechter were injured. All were members of Company C (1).

Company F moved to Fort Sam Houston in San Antonio in July, 1891 and remained there for three years. During the Mexican revolution of 1891, Company A enjoyed a little excitement when detachments were sent to the Rio Grande to prevent revolutionaries from crossing the border. In October the company was ordered to Fort Leavenworth. A detachment from A Company took part in the Chicago World's Fair in 1893. Following that, the company rejoined the regiment.

Companies I and K were placed on inactive status in August, 1890 and were not re-activated until the Spanish-American War. The regimental strength remained the same, however, as the men were transferred to other companies. For eight years the two inactive companies were represented by three officers and three non-commissioned officers.

In addition to Hunter Liggett, there were a couple of other junior officers, who served with the 5th Infantry during the early 1890's, who would later attain distinction. Lutz Wahl, a lieutenant with the regiment, went on to serve as the U.S. Army's Adjutant General during

THE CUBAN OCCUPATION AND PHILIPPINE INSURRECTION

the 1920's. Another member of the 5th Infantry, Second Lieutenant Allyn Capron, became one of Roosevelt's Rough Riders. He was killed at the battle of Las Guasimas, Cuba and was the first American officer to fall in the Spanish-American War.

During the summer of 1894, a series of labor troubles disrupted service on the nation's railroads. There was some disorder and violence. The regular army was eventually called out to protect the mail and to insure the operation of interstate commerce. Company A left Fort Leavenworth early in July and spent several weeks in Chicago guarding mail trains and railroad stations.

In the fall of 1894, Company F was transferred from Fort Sam Houston to Fort McPherson, Georgia. By December of that year, the rest of the regiment was moved to Fort McPherson. At the time of the move, Colonel Osborn became gravely ill (2). He was replaced by Colonel William Kellogg. Captain Hunter Liggett was appointed Post Adjutant.

The Romeyn Scandal

Fort McPherson was a fine facility and considered a relatively pleasant duty station by the officers and men of the regiment but the garrison was kept on edge by the troubles of Medal of Honor recipient Captain Henry Romeyn, a hero of the clash with Chief Joseph at Bear Paw Mountain. Romeyn had been severely wounded in that fight and twenty years later continued to suffer frequent paroxysms of pain.

He was not eligible for retirement until June 1, 1897. The War Department was considering whether to place him on limited duty at three-quarters salary or, in deference to his exceptional and honorable service, place him on a year's leave at full pay (3).

Shortly after the regiment arrived at Ft. McPherson, Captain Romeyn's daughter became engaged to a young lieutenant named Bamford. That relationship soured soon after another young couple, Lieutenant and Mrs. O'Brien, arrived at the post. Mrs. O'Brien was quite a social gadfly and became popular with the officers. Lieutenant Bamford began spending a lot of time at the O'Brien quarters and neglecting Miss Romeyn.

Henry Romeyn upbraided young Bamford for neglecting his daughter and later was heard to say that the other officers would not allow their wives and daughters to visit the O'Brien home because of Mrs. O'Brien's reputation. Gossips quickly relayed that tidbit to Lieutenant O'Brien, at which point the lieutenant confronted Captain Romeyn on the parade ground and demanded that he retract his statement about his wife. When Romeyn refused to do so, the lieutenant denounced him as a "liar and a scoundrel." The old Indian fighter decked O'Brien with one punch.

Lieutenant O'Brien filed charges and, tragically, two months before retirement, Henry Romeyn faced a court-martial for "conduct unbecoming an officer and a gentleman (4)." After two trials, Romeyn was exonerated. Stories of Lieutenant O'Brien's previous drunken escapades in Japan, Lieutenant Bamford's philandering, and Captain Romeyn's chronic pain were taken into account by the officers of court (4). Henry Romeyn retired on June 1, 1897 and died in 1913 while a patient at Walter Reed Hospital.

Remember the Maine

The battleship *U.S.S. Maine* arrived in Havana harbor in January of 1898, ostensibly to protect the interests of Americans being brutalized by the Spanish governor. When the *Maine* developed mechanical problems and exploded on February 15, killing 260 crew members, American newspapers began beating their war drums. On March 9, Congress appropriated $50,000,000 for a military build-up. President William McKinley, a former Civil War quartermaster sergeant, delivered a rebuke to Spain and called for war. Congress made the declaration of war official on April 25, 1898.

On the eve of war with Spain, there was a gradual departure of

THE CUBAN OCCUPATION AND PHILIPPINE INSURRECTION

many company officers who had led the regiment on its Indian War campaigns. Captain Romeyn's contemporary, Captain Mason Carter, left in January, 1898. When the war came, Captain Frank Baldwin and most of the other officers were promoted and transferred to volunteer commands (5).

In April, 1898, Headquarters and Companies A, C, D, and F were sent to Picnic Island near Tampa, Florida. A number of the men contracted typhoid fever and were shipped back to the general hospital at Fort McPherson. One of them, First Lieutenant John Bradley, died on August 30 (6). Meanwhile, Company G at Fort Barrancas and Company H at Tybee Island, near Savannah, fared somewhat better.

The following month, someone in the War Department entertained himself by shipping Headquarters back to Fort McPherson, sending Companies A and C to Tortugas Island, Company F to Fort Point at Galveston, and D Company to Fort St. Phillip, Florida. Then Company H replaced D sending the latter to Land's End near Charleston.

On April 26, 1898, Congress approved a third battalion for regular infantry regiments. In June, this led to Companies I and K being reconstituted at Fort McPherson and Companies L and M being organized for the first time. Company strength was increased to 100 and the soldiers took off their traditional two-tone blue uniforms and donned the newly adopted khaki field uniforms. They exchanged their model 1873 single-shot Springfield carbines for the Norwegian-made .30 caliber Krag-Jorgensen rifle with its five-round magazine. This flurry of activity gave the men of the 5th Infantry a glimmer of hope that they would see action in Cuba. The hopes were heightened in July, when all of the companies gathered at Tampa, but faded as the war drew to a close on August 13, 1898.

One week later, the 5th Infantry boarded the transport ships *Saratoga* and *Knickerbocker* and set sail for Cuba and occupation duty. They reached Santiago in late August. They were badly equipped to battle the tropical heat and disease. The sick book was overloaded during the regiment's two-year stay in Cuba (7). Captain Thomas M. Woodruff, regimental adjutant, died of yellow fever on July 11, 1899. He was the only casualty of the war in Cuba, and its aftermath, among the 5th Infantry officers. Company M lost five more men to yellow fever in June and July of 1899.

In April, 1899, the regiment left Santiago and its companies were dispersed among a number of small Cuban villages. Companies I, K, L, and M served as a mounted infantry battalion.

In September, 3rd Battalion returned to the United States and proceeded to Fort Sheridan, Illinois, where its members became permanent party for the post, helping to process troops bound for the Philippines. It was during this period of preparation for involvement in the Philippine Insurrection that records first refer to the regiment as being composed of three battalions rather than merely a collection of companies.

The Philippine Insurrection

When the Spanish government surrendered to U. S. forces in August, 1898, the United States handed them a check for $20,000,000 for the Philippine Islands, Puerto Rico and Guam. Then the War Department shipped 13,000 volunteer and 2000 regular troops to the Philippines. These soldiers constituted the VIII Army Corps under the command of Major General Wesley Merritt.

Filipino nationalist Emilio Aguinaldo, who had previously been battling with Spanish troops for the independence of his country, surmised that it was America's intent to keep the Philippines under colonial rule. The 80,000 nationalists turned their guns on the U. S. Army of Occupation stationed on Luzon. Guerrilla units were particularly active in the northern half of the island.

General Merritt, a veteran of the Civil and Indian Wars, was 67 years old and in poor health. He was exasperated with President McKinley and Lieutenant General Nelson Miles, General of the

THE CUBAN OCCUPATION AND PHILIPPINE INSURRECTION

Army, for sending him to the Philippines without clear guidelines for engagement. Army Intelligence had furnished Merritt with nothing more than a copy of an encyclopedia article about the Philippine Islands. Following the takeover of Manila, the general asked to be relieved and his aide, Major General Elwell Otis, assumed temporary command of the VIII Corps.

Otis' plan for the pacification of Northern Luzon involved dividing the 30,000 square miles of jungles and mountains into three military districts (8). He had received instructions from Washington to treat the Filipino people with "benevolence and win their hearts." This would involve building roads and schools and providing medical care but Otis still had to do something about the guerrillas or Insurrectos. He requested reinforcements.

In July, 1900, 1st Battalion, 5th Infantry, composed of Companies A, B, C, and D, left for the Presidio of San Francisco to be processed for shipment to the Philippines. The 3rd Battalion, Companies I, K, L, and M, followed on August 21. Second Battalion remained at Fort Sheridan. While the first two battalions were in transit, Lieutenant General Arthur MacArthur, father of future General Douglas MacArthur, assumed the position of corps commander and military governor of the Philippines.

When they reached the Islands, both battalions were deployed near isolated villages in Military District 1, Northern Luzon. Regimental Commander Colonel Richard Comba and both battalions, less Company I, were located in Abra Province. Company I, along with the 36th U.S. Volunteer Infantry, and the 3rd U.S. Cavalry were placed in the more mountainous Lepanto Province (currently Mountain Province.) Troops B, G, H, and I of the 3rd Cavalry and Company I of the 5th Infantry had their first fight with the Insurrectos on October 6, 1900 (9).

Brigadier General Samuel Young, District 1 Commander, instructed Colonel Comba to "prosecute the war with utmost rigor and use the most severe measures known to the laws of war (10)." Comba had his troops conduct sweeps and local patrols in the neighborhood of suspected Insurrecto positions. First Battalion had its first clash with the insurgents on December 10, 1900 when Captain W. F. Martin and 48 men from Company C were ambushed at Pidigan (11). One Insurrecto was killed. Company C suffered no casualties. A short time later, Captain Burnham's Company L had a brush at Dagat. The regiment suffered its first death when Private Eugene R. Lyons of K Company was captured and died while being tortured. On December 30, Company K was involved in a firefight at Barrio Quiom. One member of Company K was killed in action.

Company M, commanded by Captain Lorenzo Davison, engaged in a skirmish with Filipinos on January 28 in the mountains east of Batac. The company survived the battle unscathed but lost Private Lon Stumon in September. He died of small pox at Pidigan (12).

February 2, 1901 was a relatively bloody day for 1st Battalion. A mounted detachment of twenty-one men, commanded by Lieutenant G. F. Baltzell was ambushed on a trail between Tayum and Bucay. Private Warner of A Company was killed and another man was wounded. A short distance away, Lieutenant Williams with D Company's pack train, heard the firing and hurried forward with twenty-seven men from the company. They were also bushwhacked. Corporals Moncrief and Campbell and Private Fleming were killed. Private Heaps died later from wounds suffered during the action. These four men were the last members of the regiment to die during the Philippine War. PVT James O'Brien received the Certificate of Merit, the forerunner of the Distinguished Service Cross, for his actions during this fight. First Battalion was involved in a similar action near Tayum on February 8.

Two other clashes with the guerrillas took place in February. Company C bumped into an enemy unit in the Parparia section of the City of Narvacan and Company K, after forming a task force with two troops from the 3rd Cavalry and Company H of the 20th Infantry, ranged as far south as the neighborhood of Parañaque in the city of

THE CUBAN OCCUPATION AND PHILIPPINE INSURRECTION

Manila where they engaged in a fire fight.

It was hoped that these isolated clashes between October 1900 and March 1901 would result in the capture of the Villamor brothers, commanders of the local Insurrectos. This was not the case, but the cumulative effect of these operations left the guerrillas harried, hungry, sick and exhausted.

In mid-March, Major William C. H. Bowen assumed command of the 5th Infantry in Abra Province. He was reinforced by a battalion from the 7th U.S. Infantry and five companies from the 48th U.S. Volunteers and told to intensify operations. Later on, Bowen stated that "during the insurrection the province suffered severely (13). Every man in the area was either an active Insurrecto or sympathizer. Whole villages were destroyed and the entire province was as devoid of food products as the Shenadoah Valley after Sheridan's raid."

The 3rd Battalion was in Abra Province on April 14, 1901, when guerrilla leader Juan Villamor surrendered his portion of the guerrilla force. Further south, in Laguna Province, Company D mopped up around Quimbong and Santa Rosa.

Second Battalion, 5th Infantry, commanded by Lieutenant Colonel George P. Borden, finally reached the Philippines in May of 1901. It provided a sixty-man expedition that engaged in three small skirmishes. There were no friendly casualties.

Colonel Charles L. Davis took over the regiment in October. Davis had served in the 82nd Pennsylvania Volunteers and as a captain in the Signal Corps during the Civil War. Following the war, he accepted a regular army commission as first lieutenant and served with the 10th, 6th, and 11th U.S. Infantry Regiments before transferring to the Fifth (14).

Following the successful pacification of Northern Luzon, the army's attention was directed to the southern end of the island. The new commander of the Department of the Philippines, Major General Adna Chaffee selected Brigadier General J. Franklin Bell to lead the effort.

Two Centuries of Valor

On January 1, 1902, Bell sent his American troops south in platoon-sized groups to kill Insurrectos and destroy supply caches. They were successful in destroying the linkage between the guerrillas in the field and the infrastructure in the towns. During the drive, Bell's brigade burned six thousand structures and fourteen hundred tons of rice and killed hundreds of water buffalos, cattle and horses. During the process, they killed 210 Insurrectos, wounded 139 and captured 899 along with 629 rifles.

Company I, as part of this thrust into Southern Luzon, was the last 5th Infantry unit to see action in the Philippines when they fought with a group of insurgents on Mt. Maquiling, in Laguna Province, on April 5, 1902. During the skirmish, the wily rebel commander, Colonel Hernandes, was captured. Three days later, Company I fought its final action of the war in the Bulalo neighborhood of Cabanatuan. It would be more than forty years before the rifles of the 5th Infantry would again fire a shot in anger (15).

On July 4, President Theodore Roosevelt announced the end of the Philippine Insurrection "except in the country inhabited by the Moro tribes." Battles with the Moro tribesman would bog down one-fifth of the U.S. Army well into 1913.

The first open Moro attack on U.S. troops occurred in the spring of 1902. While on patrol, on the south side of Lake Lanao, eighteen men from the 15th Cavalry were ambushed by 200 Moros. A soldier was killed and the troopers' horses were stolen.

On May 2, Colonel Frank D. Baldwin, having advanced to brigade command, led 1200 U.S. troops against the forts of the Sultan of Bayan and the Datu (Chief) of Binadayan. These medieval defenses had walls ten feet high and several feet thick, covered by dense, thorny growth and surrounded by trenches. Brass swivel cannons were mounted in the openings in the walls. Pitched battles resulted in the capture of the fortifications. Ten Americans were killed during the action and forty were wounded.

THE CUBAN OCCUPATION AND PHILIPPINE INSURRECTION

Only thirty of the more than three hundred Moro defenders survived.

Following the end of major hostilities, the ranks of the 5th Infantry grew to more than 2000 men, the largest muster experienced by the regiment up to that time. In February 1903, when Colonel Davis retired, the battalions of the regiment were stationed at Bagupan, Bagambang and Manila. Davis'successor, COL H. H. Adams remained in the United States to await the return of the regiment. The 1st and 3rd Battalions left for home in June of 1903 on the transport ship *Kilpatrick* leaving the 2nd Battalion behind at Camp Gregg.

During its three years of campaigning in the Philippines, the 5th Infantry was involved in thirty-eight skirmishes and minor engagements while various detachments marched an estimated distance of 15,426 miles. Eighty-six enlisted men were lost by death, six in battle and most of the rest from cholera (16).

More than 125,000 Americans fought in the Philippines. Forty-two hundred of them died and 2800 were wounded. The financial cost to our nation totaled more than $400,000,000 or twenty times the original purchase price for the islands. Somewhere between sixteen and twenty thousand Insurrectos were killed. Thirty-four thousand Filipinos died as a direct result of the war. It was certainly more than an insignificant skirmish for all those involved.

In 1900, Mark Twain echoed the sentiments of many Americans when he wrote (17):

"There is the case of the Philippines. I have tried hard, and yet I cannot, for the life of me, comprehend how we got into that mess. Perhaps we could not have avoided it—perhaps it was inevitable that we should come to be fighting the natives of those islands—but I cannot understand it and have never been able to get at the bottom of the origin of our antagonism to the natives. I thought we should act as their protector—and not try to get them under our heel. We were there to relieve them from Spanish tyranny, to enable them to set up a government of their own, and we were to stand by and see that it got a fair trial. It was not to be a government according to our ideas but a government that represented the feeling of the majority of Filipinos, a government according to Filipino ideas. That would have been a worthy mission for the United States. But now — why, we have got into a mess, a quagmire from which each fresh step renders the difficulty of extrication immensely greater. I sure wish I could see what we were getting out of it, and all it means to us as a nation."

Nevertheless, the 5th Infantry was leaving the quagmire and the journey home was unique in the annals of the army. It brought the regiment to New York by way of the Suez Canal, Mediterranean Sea and the Atlantic Ocean. The *Kilpatrick* docked at Singapore, Ceylon; Aden, Yemen; Suez and Port Said, Egypt, Malta and Gibraltar before sailing west to New York Harbor. It traveled 12,000 miles in 72 days. Counting the journey from Cuba to New York, Chicago to San Francisco and the Philippines as part of the same expedition, the 5th Infantry enjoys the distinction of being one of the few U.S. Army units to circumnavigate the globe.

Plattsburgh Barracks

The Kilpatrick pulled into the Lake Shore docks at Weehawken, New Jersey on the afternoon of September 12, 1903 with nearly four hundred officers and men from the 1st and 3rd Battalions. In the ship's hold were the bodies of 302 American soldiers who had died in the Philippines. After the happy band of surviving troops went ashore, the ship proceeded to Pier 12, East River to unload those who had made the supreme sacrifice. In addition, The Kilpatrick brought several tons of Philippine products to be displayed at the Louisiana Purchase Exhibition.

Those members of the regiment that were interviewed by the press had a more optimistic view of conditions in the Philippines than

THE CUBAN OCCUPATION AND PHILIPPINE INSURRECTION

that expressed three years earlier by Mark Twain. They were of the opinion that more U. S. troops could be withdrawn from the Philippines without effecting security there. They had utmost confidence in the soldiers of the regular Filipino Army, characterizing them as "well-disciplined, keen, good fighters," quite capable of protecting the country's citizens from the Moros and other insurgents. The Filipino troops were commanded by American officers (18).

Following their arrival at the Lake Shore docks, the men of the 5th Infantry entrained for Plattsburgh Barracks, New York, where they were greeted by their new commander, Colonel Adams. They were joined by the 2nd Battalion in November. The next three years were spent in routine garrison duties interspersed with occasional side trips. In August, 1904, the entire command went to Manassas, Virginia for maneuvers.

During this period the men received new olive drab uniforms, crossed-rifles collar insignia and russet-colored footgear. They also received chevrons that were reduced in size and which they applied to their sleeves with the points up rather than down, as had been customary since 1851. On June 23, the M-1903 Springfield rifle began its long army career (19). It represented a major improvement in range and accuracy over the Krag-Jorgensen.

On March 4, 1905, 2nd Battalion participated in the inaugural parade for re-elected President Theodore Roosevelt. Colonel Adams left the regiment the following month. He would later serve as a transportation officer in France during World War I. Lieutenant Colonel Borden once again filled in as interim commander until Colonel Calvin Duvall Cowles arrived in April.

Colonel Cowles began his military career in 1873 with the 23rd Infantry fighting Utes and Cheyennes in the Southwest. In March, 1889, Lieutenant Cowles was assigned to the War Records Office and spent the next six years compiling a very successful atlas of Civil War maps that included drawings of uniforms and unit flags. He dropped out of federal service for a year in the spring of 1898 to go to Cuba with the 1st North Carolina Volunteer Infantry and then re-entered regular service in August of 1899. He served with the 17th and 4th Infantry Regiments prior to reporting to the 5th Infantry on April 11, 1905 (20).

During the summer of 1905, 1st Battalion encamped with the Massachusetts National Guard for a few weeks and then proceeded to Fort Jay, New York where it remained until May. The 3rd Battalion pulled targets for the first national rifle matches held at Sea Girt, New Jersey in August and September. A detail of forty men from Company B escorted 120 prisoners from Fort Jay to the Disciplinary Barracks at Fort Leavenworth. In December of 1905, the men of the regiment received their first metal identification "dog tags."

The army sponsored an indoor athletic tournament at Madison Square Garden in April, 1906. Company A participated in that event. In July the entire regiment went on maneuvers at Camp Roosevelt near Mt. Gretna, Pennsylvania. Following that it was the 1st Battalion's turn to pull targets at the national rifle matches at Sea Girt.

During the summer, as the riflemen of Company L pulled targets for the men in Company M and vice versa, some of the men in the target pits marked fraudulently high scores for the men on the firing line. This practice resulted in pay increases of from $1 to $2 a month for those with the inflated scores. When Colonel Cowles got wind of the collusion on the rifle range, he recommended that the War Department rescind the pay raises and require the men to repay their ill-gotten gains.

While the rifle range scandal was being investigated, the political situation in Cuba had become so acute that the Cuban government requested American intervention. An expeditionary force, the Army of Cuban Occupation, including the 2nd and 3rd Battalions of the 5th Infantry, was shipped to Cuba. Upon arrival, Colonel Cowles' headquarters and the 3rd Battalion were posted at Cardensa and Companies E and

THE CUBAN OCCUPATION AND PHILIPPINE INSURRECTION

F were placed at Sagua La Grande. Companies G and H camped at Carbarien. This deployment complicated the investigation of the rifle range problem but, nevertheless, in January of 1907, nearly sixty men were ordered to return their pay raises to the government and an investigation of the entire 3rd Battalion was launched (21).

On December 8, 1906, Private Winchester McDowell of Company B was awarded a certificate of merit for conspicuous gallantry while attempting a rescue on the ice of Lake Champlain. He had greatly endangered his life during the attempt and his decoration was later upgraded to the Distinguished Service Cross.

The Cuban pacification, lasting until 1909, was a peaceful affair which offered the regiment valuable field training. While there, the regiment received its first machine guns. Twenty-one men from the 2nd Battalion were selected to become the regiment's first machine gun platoon.

The 2nd and 3rd Battalions returned from Cuba in February, 1909. They debarked at Newport News, Virginia and proceeded by rail to Plattsburgh. Colonel Cowles remained in command until he retired on June 26, 1913. He was replaced by Colonel Charles Morton. The men of the 5th Infantry performed their routine garrison duties at Plattsburgh Barracks until Europe exploded in 1914.

CHAPTER NINE

WORLD WAR I AND THE GREAT DEPRESSION

The outbreak of World War I caused so much apprehension over the security of the newly opened Panama Canal that the Panama garrison was heavily augmented. The 5th Infantry, commanded by Colonel Charles Morton, left Plattsburgh for New York City on November 14, 1914. The regiment sailed for Panama on the following day and arrived at Cristobal on the 25th.

Colonel Morton had been a battalion commander with the regiment in 1910 before leaving to assume a position with the Inspector General's Office. He returned to the 5th Infantry in June, 1913.

The contrast between the invigorating climate and settled surroundings of Plattsburgh, New York and that of the new station at Empire, on the west bank of the Isthmus of Panama, was a shock to the men of the regiment. Empire had been a construction town but was abandoned when the canal was finished. Most of its buildings were badly in need of repair.

The Canal Zone was still jungle-covered and scarred by the debris of canal building. The banks of the canal were choked with dense foliage and the country was infested with poisonous snakes, vivid tropical birds, and strange animals of every description. The weather, just reaching the climax of the rainy season, contributed to a long succession of dripping, mud-bespattered days.

Despite the discomforts of forbidding country, steamy climate and crude living conditions, the men pitched into the task of building their new home. This housekeeping, however, was secondary to the task of guarding the canal locks and other installations. Lock guarding became particularly critical after the United States entered the world

World War I and the Great Depression

conflict on April 6, 1917. When Colonel Morton was appointed commander of all U.S. troops in Panama, in September, 1916, Colonel Evan M. Johnson assumed command of the 5th Infantry.

In June, 1917, the regiment parted with 514 men who formed the nucleus of the newly organized 33rd Infantry Regiment (1). Colonel Johnson went with this contingent of troops. He was promoted to brigadier and quickly assumed command of the 77th Infantry Division. He took the division to France and served as its commander until May, 1918. One of the company commanders, Captain William D. Davis, was killed in action. Fort Davis, in the Canal Zone, bears his name.

Meanwhile, former regimental adjutant, and now Major General Hunter Liggett took command of the 41st Infantry Division at Camp Fremont, California in August, 1917 and deployed with the unit to France. When General Pershing formed I Corps in January, 1918, he was somewhat hesitant to appoint a 61-year-old, three hundred pound officer to its command, but he had no one else with Liggett's talent and experience. Apparently he wasn't disappointed with the old soldier because in October, 1918, Pershing relinquished command of the First Army to Lieutenant General Liggett.

Hunter Liggett relieved Pershing while the U.S. Army was bogged down in a costly fight in the Meuse-Argonne region of France. Several younger officers, who would go on to lead the 5th Infantry during the Great Depression, also participated in the Meuse-Argonne campaign. They included: Lucius Bennett, who commanded the 364th Infantry of the 91st "Wild West" Division and Charles A. Hunt, commander of the 18th Infantry, 1st Infantry Division. Wilson B. Burtt, who had first been assigned to the 5th Infantry in 1900 as a young first lieutenant served as chief of staff for V Corps. These three and Joseph W. Beacham, Jr., a veteran of the Spanish-American War, the Philippine Insurrection and World War I, would command the 5th Infantry from August, 1929 until December, 1939.

A great deal of credit for a successful end to the bloody Meuse-

Two Centuries of Valor

Argonne campaign must go to 5th Infantry alumnus Hunter Liggett (2). General Pershing had finally tired of ordering hundreds of thousands of Doughboys to launch futile bayonet assaults against German machine guns, artillery and mustard gas when he turned the First Army over to General Liggett. Liggett immediately visited the trenches, rounded up thousands of demoralized stragglers and rested and reorganized the front line units. He vowed that there would be no more mindless frontal assaults without regard to losses.

While the First Army caught its breath, Liggett and his operations chief, George C. Marshall, developed a plan emphasizing fire and maneuver and combined arms. Their tactical plan would employ one group of infantry firing to suppress an enemy emplacement while a second group maneuvered to destroy it. Riflemen would attack in coordination with supporting arms, including machine guns, mortars, tanks, artillery and even planes. The ideas weren't new but they had been terribly neglected because of Pershing's belief in the invincibility of the Springfield rifle and the bayonet. Liggett's plan went into effect when the American Expeditionary Force resumed its attack on November 1. On November 11, the Imperial German Army packed up and went home.

During the summer of 1918, the 5th Infantry returned from Panama to the United States. The regiment was sent to Camp Beauregard, Louisiana for further combat training prior to sailing for France. In Louisiana it was brigaded with the 29th Infantry as part of the newly organized 17th Division. Although half of its seasoned troops were transferred to the 83rd Infantry Regiment, replacements swelled the regimental strength to 3700 men. Most of the recruits were from Louisiana.

The world-wide plague of Spanish influenza struck Camp Beauregard in September carrying off four officers and 148 men of the regiment. Despite war time confusion and the ravages of the epidemic, intensive training continued for the men of the regiment whose chances of joining the fight in France were quickly diminishing.

World War I and the Great Depression

Deployment to Europe

As soon as Germany capitulated in the summer of 1919, the 5th Infantry moved to Camp Zachary Taylor, Kentucky where it remained for the next year spinning its wheels. Demobilization whittled its strength to 43 officers and 500 men and there were eight changes of the regimental commander. Lieutenant Colonel Robert Spence, a decorated veteran of the Spanish-American War, stepped in to run the skeleton regiment on three occasions. Finally, Colonel Edgar A. Fry assumed command on September 7, 1919, the day that the regiment entrained for Camp Meade, Maryland to process for overseas shipment.

At Camp Meade, Colonel Fry was told that the 5th Infantry would become part of a provisional brigade whose mission would be to occupy the Silesian area of Germany and keep the Germans and Poles from killing each other. A flood of new recruits brought the regimental strength up to eighty officers and 1582 men. These newcomers had to be equipped and trained in five weeks while the regiment prepared to sail for Europe.

The 5th Infantry left Camp Meade for Hoboken, New Jersey on October 16, 1919 and sailed for France at midnight on the following day. They arrived at Brest on October 30th and were brigaded with the 50th Infantry. Brigadier General William H. Sage was placed in command and told to operate in the Polish plebiscite region, east of the German border. Apparently these orders were changed because the new "Silesian Brigade" crossed France and was deployed around Andernach on the Rhine in western Germany, far from Silesia. Shortly thereafter, the misnomer "Silesian Brigade" was dropped and the 5th and the 50th became known as the 2nd Brigade, American Forces in Germany.

Lieutenant General Hunter Liggett returned to the United States and was given command of the IX Corps area with headquarters in San Francisco (3). He retired in March 1921 and was living in the Bay Area when he passed away on December 30, 1935. Six years later, the army established a training area, the Hunter Liggett Military Reservation, on 165,000 acres in South Monterey County that was previously the summer ranch of William Randolph Hearst.

The regiment's occupation deployment lasted nearly two and a half years. Hostilities had ceased but the war had not officially ended. Large scale maneuvers, range firing and periodic marches kept the men in excellent condition and ready for action at a moment's notice. The 5th Infantry attained and held a level of high efficiency and earned an enviable reputation, not only among its own army and allies, but with the German people as well.

During a competitive inspection of the brigade in the spring of 1920, the 5th Infantry captured trophies for the best company, battalion, and regiment in the contest. Company A received highest rating among the companies and 1st Battalion took honors in its class. Eight of the nine best companies in the army of occupation were from the 5th Infantry and Headquarters Company was rated best among the provisional units. The regimental commander at the time was Lieutenant Colonel Allen J. Greer who had relieved Colonel Edgar Fry on May 29, 1920.

An Allied Forces small arms competition at nearby Coblenz brought the regiment international honors. The 5th Infantry led American representatives to lopsided victories in every event except the machine gun problem, in which they placed second to the Belgians. The Americans swept the officers' and enlisted men's rifle and pistol matches and the automatic rifle competitions, winning the first five places in each event. Nineteen of the thirty-six American competitors were from the 5th Infantry (4).

Meanwhile the regiment continued to excel in athletic competition. In 1920 and 1921, the 5th Infantry baseball team won the championship of the American Forces in Germany. Third Battalion captured the basketball championship in 1921. A hexathalon competition held at Coblenz in 1922 was won by Company A. Blue

World War I and the Great Depression

ribbons at various inter-Allied horse shows were monopolized by the 5th Infantry.

In December, 1921, regimental headquarters, provisional units and the 1st Battalion were stationed at Andernach. The 2nd Battalion was posted at Mayen and the 3rd Battalion was garrisoned at historic Fortress Sherenbreitstein, picturesque "Gibraltar of the Rhine." Companies D, H and M were at Engers undergoing transformation from rifle to machine gun units. This was evidently the point in army history when the fourth company of each battalion became a "weapons" company.

On December 31, 1921, the 50th Infantry was disbanded and most of its members were absorbed into the 5th Infantry. Colonel Harry E. Knight assumed command of the expanded regiment. The consolidation provided the regiment with what is believed to have been the largest regimental band in the history of the army, an excellent musical organization of 94 pieces. This band distinguished itself repeatedly in concerts and parades.

Peacetime Soldiering

The 5th Infantry was alerted for shipment home in early March, 1922. On March 10th the battalions marched out of their garrisons and caught a train for Antwerp, Belgium. The demonstrations of sincere regret by the civilian population at having to say goodbye to the regiment, to say nothing of the large group of German brides accompanying their soldier husbands to a new country, spoke eloquently for the manner in which regulations against "fraternizing with the enemy" had been consistently ignored (5).

The 1st and 2nd Battalions sailed from Antwerp on the U. S. Army Transport *Cantigny*. They arrived at Portland, Maine on the morning of March 22, 1922, after an uncharacteristically calm Atlantic voyage. When the 3rd Battalion arrived in April, the companies were assigned at Forts Williams, Preble and McKinley in Portland Harbor. The regimental headquarters was established at Fort Williams. The 5th Infantry and the 13th Infantry composed the 18th Infantry Brigade.

New England and the Depression Years

During the summer of 1922, the regiment moved to Camp Devens, near Boston, to staff a one-month summer camp for ROTC, National Guard and Army Reserve personnel. The trainees arrived on August 1. This Citizens Military Training Camp was designed to be completed after four summers of training. Graduates became eligible to apply for Army Reserve commissions. The trek to Camp Devens was an annual event until 1925, when the summer camp was switched to Fort McKinley.

Although the winter of 1922-23 was too severe to permit use of the new equipment, the 5th Infantry enjoyed the distinction of being one of the first motorized infantry regiments in the army. In January, 1923, forty-five trucks, passenger cars, and motorcycles arrived at the regimental installations at Portland. Thereafter the regimental baggage rolled on rubber tires. The machine gun companies, however, didn't relinquish their mules until 1939.

The Regimental Crest

On July 25th, 1923, the 5th Infantry commemorated the victory at Lundy's Lane and held a belated celebration of Organization Day. Colonel Knight invited retired General Nelson A. Miles to be the regiment's guest of honor (6). The old Indian fighter was bursting with reminiscences of his days as commanding officer of the 5th and, despite his advanced age, was said to have run circles around a squad of youthful aides. General Miles presented the regiment with a regimental crest that he had designed by modifying his own family crest. The silver shield, embellished with seven cannons, a fist full of arrows and the I'll Try Sir motto, continues to be worn today by active-duty members and veterans of the 5th Infantry.

There was an element of sadness at this first Organization Day

World War I and the Great Depression

celebration in that General Miles' long-time lieutenant, Major General Francis Leonard Dwight Baldwin, had succumbed to cirrhosis of the liver on April 22 in Denver, Colorado. Frank Baldwin was eighty-one years old at the time of his death. He had been promoted to brigadier general in 1902, a month after his victory at Lake Lanao in the Philippines and retired from active duty on June 26, 1906. He came out of retirement during World War I to serve as Adjutant General for the state of Colorado.

Wholesale discharges among veterans of the Army of Occupation brought a vast change to the regiment. By the spring of 1924, fully 50 percent of the veterans had been discharged and the vacant slots were filled with recruits from New England. The Maine contingent continued to grow during the regiment's stay in Portland. As might be expected, the *Maine Stein Song* was chosen as the official regimental marching song.

Despite being loaded with raw recruits, the 5th Infantry continued to turn in notable records in small arms firing. In 1924, the rifle qualification rate was 99.4%, machine gun, 94.3%, and 100% of weapons platoon members qualified on mortars and the 37 mm cannon. Company D's pistol team placed fourth in the NRA pistol matches. The squad was third among service teams and highest in the United States. The other two army squads were from foreign countries. On December 1, the regimental band participated in the first radio show ever broadcast from Portland.

A brigade machine gun school was established in 1927 at the Fort Ethan Allen Artillery Reservation in Vermont. Annually, thereafter, the weapons companies devoted several weeks to training there prior to maneuvers. Soldiering became a little more comfortable as the men of the regiment traded in their service coats with the "choker" collar for a single-breasted sack coat of olive drab wool.

The 5th Infantry was alerted during the Montpelier flood of 1927, but the waters receded before the troops were called out. The alert came on Saturday night when most of the men were absent from barracks and scattered throughout Portland, but with the cooperation of the Portland radio station and police, the entire command was recalled and ready to move within four hours. Patrols had already reconnoitered routes into the flooded area when the waters began to recede and the need for military assistance passed.

The regiment's placid routine continued for the next few years. Corps maneuvers were held in the Alstead, New Hampshire area in 1929 and brigade maneuvers were conducted at Fort Ethan Allen in 1930 and 1936. Post activities, athletics, and Regimental Commander Joseph W. Beacham's skills as an educator, helped keep the members of the regiment out of trouble. Colonel Beacham had been Dwight Eisenhower's football coach at West Point.

As the Great Depression deepened, the army was called upon to organize, equip, and lead the Civilian Conservation Corps through its period of infancy. The 5th Infantry furnished officers and enlisted cadres for many camps in the New England area. In 1932, Congress reduced the pay of officers and enlisted men by 10% in an effort to balance the budget. (7)

On the evening of June 30, 1933, PFC Fritz O. Gaebler, Company D, was standing on the shore near Fort Preble when he heard cries for help. Plunging in, he swam through the darkness toward the frantic screaming. Suddenly he was seized by a severe cramp and barely made it back to shore. Gaebler found a plank and set out again. Meanwhile a rescue had been made. Nevertheless, PFC Gaebler was awarded the Soldier's Medal for his heroic effort, the first receipt of that medal by a member of the regiment. The medal had been authorized by Congress in 1926 for bravery in non-combat action.

In the late 1930's, the regiment continued to garner nationwide prestige through the exploits of two of its sharpshooting riflemen, Sergeant Wadie Giacobbe, Company K, and Sergeant Lloyd Jenkins, Company E. Giacobbe won the Leech Cup in 1938, took second in

World War I and the Great Depression

the Navy Cup match and had the third highest grand aggregate score for the entire program. A former Marine, he helped outshoot his old service in the 1939 matches, won the Farnsworth Trophy and took third place in the President's Match.

Sergeant Jenkins was a member of the All Infantry Squad from 1936 to 1939. In 1938 he captured the Marine Corps Cup and, like Giacobbe, won Distinguished Marksman's ranking. He was third in the 1939 Rumbold Trophy Shoot over a course of 600 to 1000 yards.

Early in August, 1939, the regiment moved by motor convoy to its old home in Plattsburgh, New York, where it participated with honors in large-scale First Army maneuvers. Several companies and individuals won distinction in these exercises. During the maneuvers, Company B captured a regimental commander and his entire staff.

While the U.S. Army was playing at war, the real thing flared up again in Europe. The German invasion of Poland focused attention upon America's defenses, particularly in the Caribbean area. The Panama Canal was critical to the strategic defense of the United States. On September 8, 1939, the 5th Infantry was ordered to return to the Canal Zone.

CHAPTER TEN

WITH THE 71ST DIVISION IN WORLD WAR II

There was just a handful of old timers in the regiment that could recall anything as furious as the activity that occupied the next few weeks. Relationships in Maine had grown deep. The period was too short and the parting tearful. A subdued crowd of many thousands from Portland and nearby communities crowded the pier when the transports pulled away.

The 5th Infantry landed in Panama in two echelons. The 3rd Battalion arrived in late October, 1939 and the remainder, a week later. The Canal Zone presented a far more civilized presence that it had twenty-five years earlier but, as far as the regiment's new camp site at Paraiso was concerned, it was the old Empire mess all over again.

Like Empire, Paraiso was an abandoned labor town. When the regiment marched in, hot and uncomfortable in the steaming rain, the camp was ankle deep in mud. There were no adequate drainage facilities and no screens on the doors and windows. There was only one passable road into the area (1).

The 5th Infantry had met this challenge numerous times in its history and promptly demonstrated that it hadn't lost the "I'll try, sir" touch. Every man pitched in, some even cheerfully, and by December, the camp was coming out of the mud and construction was far enough along to permit diverting some time to training.

The regiment participated in the Mobile Force Maneuvers of 1940 with a thoroughness that brought much favorable comment from the high command. Colonel Louis P. Ford, who had served with the 5th Infantry in Germany, relieved Colonel Charles A. Hunt and led the regiment through the maneuvers as well as the completion of the

WITH THE 71ST DIVISION IN WORLD WAR II

construction projects at Paraiso.

The world was again at war. Whether or not the conflict would involve the United States was anybody's guess. But, if the bugles blew, the 5th Infantry was ready to march, blessed with three 1939 innovations; the M-1, semi-automatic Garand rifle, the C-ration and the truck, ¼ ton (jeep).

Outposts were strengthened and the troops became more vigilant in defense of the ships transiting the canal. The Organization Day celebration in July, 1940 was rather grim. Training was intensified and was highlighted by maneuvers involving a face-off between the 5th and 33rd Infantry Regiments.

When Pearl Harbor was attacked on December 7, 1941, the regiment stepped up its activity on the Pacific side of the Canal Zone. Units were dispersed to Rio Hato, Pacora, Chorrera and Piña by hacking campsites out of the jungle. Defenses against air attack and submarines were maintained around the clock. Fortifications were established in the Campaña Mountain region, an area on the west flank of the canal that was most vulnerable to enemy landing craft.

During 1942, many men left the regiment to join the 158th Infantry which was receiving jungle training in Panama. In January, 1943, the 158th "Bushmasters" staged in Australia and then began island hopping in the New Guinea area, engaging and defeating Japanese units of division strength. The 158th fought with such distinction in the Philippines, it was selected to spearhead the final invasion of Japan. Japan's timely surrender saved the Bushmasters from what would have been a certain suicide mission (2).

About the time that the 158th left Panama, the members of the 5th Infantry boarded the *U.S.S Yarmouth* and set sail for New Orleans. They went first to Camp Jackson to turn in their tropical gear for equipment better befitting a cooler climate. From there the unit was transported to Camp Van Dorn at McComb, Mississippi.

This time the adversities of poor buildings, bad weather

and miserable surroundings caused a lot of grumbling. The new regimental commander, Colonel William Bigelow, sent the men home on furloughs. Many of these leaves were the first in three and a half years. When they returned, the cadre began to organize and train a new unit as a large number of replacements began to arrive.

The Seventy-first Infantry Division

In June, 1943, the regiment was transferred to Fort Carson, Colorado to become a part of the 71st Light Infantry Division, a mountain division of 9000 men and 1800 mules. The 71st was composed of the 66th, 14th and 5th Regiments and various support units. The 66th was formed by combining the 1st Battalion of the 14th, the 2nd Battalion of the 5th, some cadre from the 34th Infantry and a number of troops from the 89th Division. The first division commander was Brigadier General Robert L. Spragins. At the time of the division's organization, the commanding officer of the 5th was still Colonel William Bigelow. Lieutenant Colonel Sidney Wooten was Regimental Executive Officer (3).

Following the activation ceremony for the 71st Division on August 21, 1943, training resumed. The nearby mountain range offered a great opportunity for man and beast to get into shape. Training problems were conducted along the slopes without much pause between exercises. During a week-long, division-wide exercise in December, no fires were allowed, resulting in many cases of frostbite and a lot of runny noses.

Hunter Liggett Maneuvers

During the first week in February, 1944, elements of the 71st Division began to leave for the Hunter Liggett Military Reservation in California for a period of maneuvers. It would also offer an opportunity to evaluate new equipment and test the palatability of the new, "improved" C-rations. Before the first phase began, and while the Division waited for the mules and equipment to arrive, base camp areas were established at the foot of the Santa Lucia Mountains. Pup tents were pitched and the areas were organized with the usual military neatness.

At 0500, three weeks after settling into their base camps, the units were alerted to break camp and begin their 21-day battle with the 89th Division. By six o'clock the mules were brought to camp and loaded with equipment. Chow was served and by seven o'clock the units were ready to move.

The twenty-one days of maneuvers against the 89th Division at Hunter Liggett has been described as one of the worst periods in the history of the 71st Division. The wind and rain were incessant as the troops moved higher into the Santa Lucia Mountains that stand between the Salinas Valley and the Pacific Ocean. As they moved farther away from the main supply base at Camp Roberts, the logistics became more complicated and the food supply dwindled. Casualties from colds, poison oak and exhaustion began to mount. At one time, more than fifteen hundred men were hospitalized. A year later, when the 71st Division was in combat, a grumbling replacement might hear, "So, you think this is tough - - well, you should have been at Hunter Liggett."

When the troops returned to the base camp, a mobile PX arrived with beer, cigarettes and candy. Many of the men picked up three-day passes and hopped a train or a Greyhound bus for Los Angeles or San Francisco at nearby Camp Roberts. A USO show from Hollywood starring Carole Landis, Jack Benny, Pat O'Brien and a host of chorus girls toured the units to entertain those men who chose to stay in camp.

On the day after the maneuvers were terminated, those senior privates who had served with the three regiments before the activation of the 71st Division were transferred to the China-Burma-India Theater. The non-commissioned officers remained to train the newcomers that would fill the ranks of what would become a standard infantry division rather than a light mountain division. Much to the delight of many of the men, the mules were discharged from service and shipped to pastures in Nebraska. The pup tents were discarded in favor of six-man pyramidal tents and the 71st moved to a new base camp to await its next assignment.

Fort Benning, Georgia

Orders arrived in mid-May directing the division to move to Fort Benning. The depleted 5th Infantry Regiment left for Georgia on Saturday, May 20, 1944 with Colonel Sidney C. Wooten in command. The troop train took five days to cross the country from Camp Roberts, California to Columbus, Georgia.

In June, the 71st was reorganized as a regular triangular (three regiments of infantry) division. The regiments were authorized to grow from 2075 to 3350 men and the three artillery battalions, the 607th, 608th, and 609th, swapped their 75mm mountain howitzers for larger 105mm howitzers. The division also acquired the 564th FAB, equipped with 155mm guns. The 581st Anti-tank Battery was assigned to the 5th Infantry as its Anti-tank Company.

Fortunately, a cadre of top-notch NCOs formed the nucleus of the regiment and, with the arrival of new officers, training started to roll again. Large groups of replacements arrived, new training areas were built and, what had seemed to be a forgotten unit began to recover.

In addition to field training, there were morning calisthenics, running the obstacle course, KP duty once or twice a month, and scrubbing the barracks for Saturday morning inspection. Company inspections were held every afternoon at five. Replacements began to trickle in during July and August and, by the end of September, the 5th Infantry was approaching full strength.

The more adventurous troops spent their free time in Phenix City on the Alabama side of the Chattahoochie River. Phenix City, with its slat-boarded beer joints and its cohort of B-girls, who hustled for drinks and upstairs trade, was especially the place to go on Sundays when Georgia law closed down Columbus' gin mills. Atlanta was also accessible on a weekend pass.

The 71st Division was first alerted for overseas shipment on October 13, 1944. New equipment was requisitioned and new weapons were issued. Then, suddenly, its alert status was dropped and the division returned to training. Another alert on November 7 was also rescinded. Brigadier General Willard G. Wyman, a veteran of both the Pacific and European theaters of combat, assumed command of the division at the end of October.

On December 12, the entire division moved out to the field for joint maneuvers involving all three infantry regiments plus the artillery and attached combat-support units. Dean Joy, a former member of G Company, recalled that during the rest of December, with a brief respite for Christmas dinner, they must have walked a hundred miles, moved another hundred by truck, and dug foxholes in twenty different locations. For the first time, they experienced what it would be like to attack with the support of tanks and artillery (4).

Bound for Europe

On January 12, 1945, orders arrived to report to Camp Kilmer, New Jersey, a camp affiliated with the New York Port of Embarkation. This time it wasn't a false alarm. Men were recalled from furloughs, the new equipment was re-crated and warm clothing was issued.

The night before leaving, all bunks and mattresses were turned in and the men slept on the bare floors. Since their packs had been rolled, they used their jackets and overcoats for blankets. In the morning, after giving the barracks one last sweep and policing the ground around the buildings to the satisfaction of post inspectors, they marched down to the train.

When the troops detrained in New Jersey, the ground was covered with ice and snow. Many restrictions were imposed to prevent the revealing of information, including postal censorship and restricted phone calls. Twelve-hour passes were issued for a last quick taste of American life in New York or Philadelphia.

The next three days were devoted to lectures, movies, and clothing and equipment shakedowns. The medics administered typhus and typhoid shots as the troops stood in line for their final stateside physical exam. The day before departure, the sergeants chalked train seat numbers on each man's helmet. On the final day at Camp Kilmer, all belongings went back in the duffle bags and rifles were given another good cleaning.

The 5th Infantry departed Camp Kilmer by troop train on the evening of January 25 and arrived at about midnight at a Staten Island pier. There, to the accompaniment of a small army band, the five thousand men of the regiment and its attached units, along with General Wyman and some division headquarters personnel, boarded a large troop ship named the *U.S.S General Tasker H. Bliss*.

The *Tasker Bliss* was the leading ship in a fifty-two vessel convoy bound for the European Theater. The eleven-day crossing was uneventful except for a few u-boat alerts and a lot of seasickness. There were a couple of movies during the trip and nightly musical entertainment. A mimeographed newspaper was published daily with the news that the Russians were still ten miles from Berlin. If the Tasker Bliss turned on the steam, there still might be some war left.

Each morning the men readied their bunks for inspection and then went topside for calesthenics. Those woozy from mal de mer were excused. They would look for a place to sit down and watch the waves roll by or gaze at the convoy spread out on both sides of the ship.

On February 4, the coast of southwestern England appeared on the horizon. The convoy, destined for Le Havre, France, was forced to put in briefly at Portsmouth, England while waiting for the fog to clear on the French coast.

When they reached France, the once modern port city of Le

Havre was in ruins. Throughout the harbor the wrecks of transport and cargo ships poked out of the water. Nevertheless, the men of the 5th Infantry were delighted to go ashore shortly after midnight on February 7, 1945.

Ed Zebrowski, a former member of Headquarters Company, wrote:

> "We disembarked on floating docks and climbed directly into waiting two-and-a-half ton trucks, packed in like fish in a barrel of ice. Many of the trucks had been used for hauling supplies. They were topless and stripped of their side benches. The men sat on their packs and duffel bags.
>
> We roared off into the Normandy countryside, cold, tired, and hungry. We rolled along for an hour or so, through narrow, winding streets of darkened villages, the trucks nearly brushing up against the concrete walls and metal balconies of the shadowy buildings. Up hills, down hills, gears grinding, the lumbering vehicles slowed down to a near halt, engines whining and then speeded up again with a growl and finally stopped. We could hear some men talking in the distance, but couldn't make out the words. Truck doors slammed shut and we were off again into the blackness of the night, the trucks lurching around corners, the men groaning and complaining as we leaned against one another and tried to maintain our balance, our legs cold and numb.
>
> We finally reached our destination just as it started to get light, bone-weary after eight hours of rolling through the French countryside. It was later that we found out we were in St. Laurent en Caux, about ten miles from where we began our journey. We had been lost all night, going around in circles (5)."

Camp Old Gold

The regiment's new home was Camp Old Gold. It was located in the

Seine Inferieure in the northern half of Normandy which is split in two by the Seine River. The camp was a city of pyramidal tents. It was quickly re-named Mudville after the first hour of slipping and sliding in the muck of the company street.

A typical day began with an hour of calesthenics, followed by such duties as filling in old latrines and digging new ones. The hour before dusk was always spent cleaning weapons.

After a few days of settling in, the division began a series of company and platoon exercises to prepare for combat. When not engaged in marching and training there were the routine duties of guard and kitchen police. Kitchen duty was, by far, the preferred task. It was the soldier's one chance to get enough to eat. Guard duty meant two hours of trudging in the cold and rain.

Following the evening retreat ceremony, each tent sent out a patrol to round up eggs, bread and anything else edible. The French farmers were glad to swap their farm produce for cigarettes, candy and soap.

The G.I.'s also bartered for hard cider, since neither the soldiers nor the locals trusted the St. Laurent en Caux water system. Between the cider and a minimum of three canteen cups of coffee, there was a lot of nighttime foot traffic on the company streets between the pyramidals and the latrine.

Until the last week of the regiment's stay at Camp Old Gold, there were no showers and not enough coal to heat water on the tent stoves, so the troops shaved and sponge-bathed with a helmet full of cold water. Finally, at the end of February, word came that General Eisenhower was coming on March 1 to inspect the 71st Division. The engineer battalion got busy and rigged some cold water showers allowing the men to get rid of some of their grime and wash their clothes. Apparently Ike felt that the division was clean enough to go to work because orders were received on the 7th of March to depart for the front.

WITH THE 71ST DIVISION IN WORLD WAR II

Alsace-Lorraine

The following day, the regimental equipment and ordnance departed St. Laurent in a truck convoy. The personnel left from Yerville by train. Many of the men rode in boxcars, the 40 & 8s (built to transport forty men or eight horses) of World War I fame. Bales of straw were broken open to serve as bedding. In World War II, the 25-30 men who were crammed into the car wondered how 40 men of their father's generation could have survived in such a small space.

The train rumbled across France to Lenning in Alsace-Lorraine Province. Scheduled stops at Nancy and other points in the morning, noon and late afternoon were just long enough to heat C rations and coffee. From Lenning the men were trucked to outlying villages and assigned to quarters in houses and haylofts. During the night they could hear the rumble of artillery to the east.

On Saturday afternoon, March 10, the troops were ordered to turn in their duffel bags to the company supply sergeants and make ready for the last leg of their trip to the front. Their packs would have to contain all their necessary articles. They turned in their shelter halves and one of their two blankets and received the army's first sleeping bag, a tapered sack made of blanket material and a zipper that was inserted into a tapered, waterproof bag.

The 5th Infantry was to relieve the 398th Regiment of the 100th Infantry Division on a ridge in the Vosges Mountains, a few miles to the east. It was after dark when the transport trucks arrived, driven by men who had been hauling men and supplies until they could hardly keep their eyes open.

At 1017 hours on the warm sunny morning of March 11, 1945, Private Clarence Stevenson of Charlie Battery, 607th FAB, yanked the lanyard to fire the first projectile fired against an enemy by the 71st Infantry Division. The 71st was in combat. It was part of the XV Corps of General Alexander Patch's 7th Army.

The relief of the rifle battalions of the Century Division began on

March 12 at 1900 and was completed in less than two and a half hours. First and 2nd Battalions of the 5th Infantry took positions on the line near Lemburg and Goetzenbruck, France and 3rd Battalion was placed in reserve at St. Louis les Bitche.

That evening, 1st Battalion, 5th Infantry, occupying defensive positions on high ground two miles southeast of Lemberg, received heavy 88mm artillery fire from the German positions. SGT Milburn Rogers, a communications sergeant with Able Company, was the first man in the division to earn the Bronze Star. SGT Rogers, while under fire, laid and maintained a phone line from the company CP to forward observation posts enabling the placement of accurate mortar fire upon the German positions. At 2340 hours, another soldier in Company A was wounded, becoming the regiment's first WWII casualty. In 2nd Battalion, G Company's first casualty was SGT John Krumrine, who was shot by one of his own trigger-happy men when they were out on patrol some time before midnight on Tuesday, March 13.

The next few days were devoted to improving the defensive positions and to small reconnaissance patrols to determine the enemy positions and to locate the extensive minefields. Both front line battalions were under sporadic artillery and mortar fire. During the period from 12-18 March the 5th Infantry suffered five KIA and twenty-seven wounded, primarily from German schu mines and artillery fire (6). Defying artillery fire and unmarked minefields, PFC Lawrence Levandowski, a medic assigned to the regiment, exhibited such "personal bravery and zealous devotion to duty" on 15 March that he was awarded the Distinguished Service Cross.

Germany

On March 18, orders were issued to move by foot and by truck convoy to Roppeweiller to relieve the 399th Infantry in the vicinity of Roppeweiller and Liederscheidt. From there the regiment made its entrance into Germany and established positions overlooking the Siegfried Line. Donald Sitz, formerly a sergeant in C Company, wrote "Dragons teeth (for defense against tanks) and pill boxes dotted the terrain and German troops could be seen walking around their fortifications in a very self-assured manner. A few well placed rounds of artillery taught them more caution (7)."

All was quiet until March 19 when German mortar fire began falling in the 1st Battalion area. However, no casualties resulted and late that night the 5th Infantry was relieved by the 14th Infantry of the 71st Division. The regiment went into reserve at Walschbronn and awaited further orders.

The men of the 5th Infantry had a day of rest on March 21. They were issued clean clothing and had a chance to take a sponge bath. The following morning they were back on the road by 0600 with orders to make a quick dash of 74 kilometers to the north. They marched through the recently liberated French town of Bitche and, passing through a break in the Siegfried Line, seized Landau. Meeting little resistance, they passed through Landau and continued on to Altdor, Schwegenheim and Rickenbergershif. Many of the men rode atop tank destroyers. The following day, the 71st Division was shifted from the XV Corps to the XXI Corps.

During the twelve days that the 71st Division had been officially in combat, the U.S. First Army had put a full corps across the Rhine River on a captured railroad bridge at Remagen. Patton's Third Army and Patch's Seventh Army had breached the Siegfried Line at several places in the Saar region and were expected to cross the Rhine any day. The Russians were reported to be only two days march from Berlin.

On the 24th, orders were received to capture the bridges that crossed the Rhine at Germersheim. The 2nd and 3rd Battalions moved to an assembly area south of Schwegenheim. At 1000 hours word was received that Westheim, the next town to the east, had been seized by the 12th Armored Division. On the strength of that news, the 2nd and 3rd Battalions attacked the town of Lingenfeld.

According to 1st Sergeant Jesse Beckum's diary, the 3rd Battalion moved out at 1045 with his Company L on the right, Company I on the left and Company K in reserve (8). Love Company descended from a ridge about a thousand yards from the outskirts of the town and was half way across a flat open field when the Germans opened up with small arms and 88mm artillery fire. The company pushed on to the edge of town, re-organized, and moved down both sides of the main street, hugging the sides of the buildings to avoid persistent sniper fire. Machine gunner PFC Willis Priester was unable to take out the sniper with his MG, so he turned the weapon over to his assistant gunner and dashed into the building, armed with a carbine, to finish the job.

During the attack, five men were killed and sixteen were wounded. The medics were overwhelmed, so a rifleman, PFC Virgil Casto, risked his life to pull wounded men to safety and help stabilize them. When evening came, Casto volunteered for a patrol that was tasked with moving forward to a barn from which sniper fire was coming. The patrol reached the barn, killed its occupants, and remained there until the company moved up the following morning. Virgil Casto was killed during the capture of the barn. His efforts during his last day on earth resulted in his being awarded the Silver Star (9).

Sergeant Dean Joy recalls sitting on a sun-drenched hillside overlooking Lingenfeld, waiting for the order to move down the hill, when a squadron of P-47 Thunderbolts roared overhead, circled and then dove steeply in the direction of the town. After releasing their bombs, they made a series of shallow strafing runs and then flew off to the west leaving Lingenfeld covered with smoke. With that came the dreaded order "George Company, move out!(10)"

The 2nd Battalion reached the railroad between Westheim and Lingenfeld without any trouble. However, when the 3rd Battalion arrived in Lingenfeld, it received heavy artillery and sniper fire within the city limits. When the 2nd Battalion reached the woods south of Lingenfeld, it too came under fire. At this point, communications with the regimental command post were cut off and the situation became rather confused (11).

As the two battalions moved slowly toward a line just south of Lingenfeld, the Third lagged slightly behind the Second. In the early afternoon, having heard that the Germans had blown the Germersheim Bridge, Colonel Wooten relayed an order from division to "hold in place." At this time Companies G and E were out in the open. Company L, not being dressed on Company G, left a gap through which George Company received a lot of enemy fire from its left rear, causing numerous casualties.

Finally orders came to resume the attack in coordination with elements of the 12th Armored Division coming in from the east. At 1630, Fox Company started a sweep through the woods. Although the 12th Armored failed to attack in time, Fox Company's assault successfully cleared the woods and secured Germersheim. Numerous prisoners were taken and the company suffered no casualties. However, hundreds of retreating Germans had crossed the river before destroying the bridge.

When night fell, the 5th Infantry was ordered to hold in place and resume the attack in the morning. This was followed by word that they were to pull off the line and move to an assembly area in the vicinity of Neuhofen. The 71st Division, as it participated in this cleanup of the Saar-Moselle triangle and the drive to the Rhine, had traveled approximately 180 miles, in trucks and on foot, during its first twenty days of action.

During the engagement at Lingenfeld and Germersheim, four officers and sixty-five enlisted men were wounded; one officer and twenty-two enlisted men were KIA. The 5th Infantry captured one hundred and fifty enemy prisoners.

Sergeant William Randall of Company G scaled a wall on the outskirts of Germersheim and shot several Germans as they were trying to start their vehicles in the courtyard. Randall and his squad moved into the nearby house and held the place all night long against several German attempts to recapture it. Sergeant Randall received the Silver Star for his actions at Germersheim (12).

The temperature fell to below freezing during the night after the battles for Germensheim and Lingenfeld. The men had long since turned in their heavy overcoats and extra blankets. Their thin sleeping bags and raincoats did very little to keep them warm. When dawn came, someone passed the welcome word that they could build fires to heat water for coffee and heat their breakfast cans of hash or ham and scrambled eggs.

On March 25, the 5th Infantry was ordered to relieve the 399th Infantry on an outpost line due south of Ludwigschafen. The regimental CP remained at Neuhafen. The 1st and 3rd Battalions were placed on the line and the Second remained in reserve at Speyer some fifteen miles north of Germersheim on the west bank of the Rhine.

Donald Sitz wrote that on the 27th of March, "We took off for Rheingoheim on the Rhine...Rheingoheim had to be cleared of German Army personnel that had already donned civilian clothes and continued sniping. We patrolled the town. The third platoon set up a 'watch on the Rhine' capturing ten prisoners and keeping the enemy under constant observation (13)."

The 5th Infantry was relieved on the night of March 28 by the 410th Infantry, 103rd Division. The Fifth moved to Schifferstadt and Neustadt and was then convoyed to a new assembly area at Rockenhausen closing there by 0700 on March 30.

The arrival of truckloads of replacements brought many of the companies back to full strength. During the next forty-eight hour period, orders, changes and counter-orders seemed to fly at random. The confusion finally cleared at 0815 on March 30 with orders for the 5th Infantry to move across the Rhine to the town of Neu Isenberg, a suburb of Frankfurt.

At 0500 on Saturday, March 31, the four-mile-long convoy,

transporting the 5th Infantry, crossed the Rhine on a pontoon bridge near the city of Worms. Dean Joy wrote "All I can remember of the river crossing itself was the stink of diesel exhaust fumes and a smoke screen so thick we couldn't see more than a hundred yards in any direction. The smoke screen had been laid by artillery to obscure the bridge from German dive bombers, which were said to have made several attempts to knock it out (14)."

As tanks led the 2nd Battalion down the main street of Neu Isenberg, a single rifle shot rang out and the convoy of trucks came to a halt. Within minutes the entire battalion was off the trucks and conducting a house-to-house search for snipers. None were found but hundreds of civilians were turned out into the streets and searched. They were then told to find somewhere else to sleep that night as the regiment would be billeted in their houses and apartments. Sergeant Joy noted that there was no electricity or hot water, but they made do with candles and cold water sponge baths. They were especially happy to sleep on real beds under heavy German comforters.

At 1945 hours on April 1, Easter Sunday, the regiment was withdrawn from the VI Corps and attached to XII Corps. They were now part of General Patton's Third Army and were ordered to proceed to an assembly area in the vicinity of Ruchingen and prepare to protect the Third Army's flank.

The following morning, word came that the 5th Infantry's sister regiments, the 14th and the 66th, had trapped several hundred SS troops in a forest northeast of Hanau. The 5th Infantry was ordered to move there by truck and finish off the Germans. Second Battalion, with George Company on point, would lead the attack.

The G.I's formed a skirmish line and swept large areas of the forest but, by dusk, had flushed nothing but a few frightened deer. They returned to their trucks and were driven north to seize the town of Budingen. Sergeant Joy's diary for April 2 reads, "No SS troops. Mission snafu, wrong woods, 5 mi hike turns out to be 15 Miles."

On April 3, the regiment resumed its sweep of the area in the vicinity of Budingen. According to Sergeant Sitz, Charlie Company made contact with elements of the 6th SS Mountain Division Nord near Breitenbaum. Their first contact was at 1145, as they pushed the Germans through the woods and over the hills.

Early that afternoon, Dean Joy and five other men from George Company's mortar section, armed with two M-1s and four carbines, surprised an SS platoon as it emerged from the woods. At a range of three to four hundred yards, the carbines were useless, so those with the smaller arms, spotted for the two with the M-1s. The two shooters had killed or wounded at least a dozen of Hitler's elite when Fox Company arrived and captured the survivors.

By the end of the day, the men of the regiment had rounded up 554 enemy prisoners. They had killed forty-six and wounded fifteen. The 5th Infantry suffered 7 KIA and 4 WIA. The advance to the northeast continued on the following day, resulting in another one hundred prisoners (15).

On April 4, 2nd Battalion continued the fight with the 6th SS Mountain Division in the woods around Budingen. When darkness fell, it was moonless, cold and rainy. The G.I's dug in for the night.

When Charlie Company arrived at Salmunster they were warned that the place was crawling with snipers. Each house had to be searched from cellar to attic. Company C flushed the town and interrogated civilian captives, some of whom turned out to be SS troopers.

Sergeant Sitz continued, "Early the next morning (April 6) we passed through Fulda and relieved the 104th Infantry of the 26th Division. Our company was on outpost duty until the 7th when we received our first reinforcements and departed on motor convoy for a distance of sixth-three kilometers to Einhausen to clear the surrounding woods of enemy troops." Second Battalion, on the other hand, remained in Fulda, the site of division headquarters, until Sunday the 8th before joining a convoy to the outskirts of the large industrial city of Coburg.

With the 71ˢᵀ Division in World War II

On April 11, the entire 5ᵗʰ Infantry Regiment assembled in a large open field near the villages of Rodach and Rottenbach with orders to link up with the 11ᵗʰ Armored Division and advance to Coburg. The three rifle battalions dug in around the southeastern perimeter. There were plans to have the 5ᵗʰ Infantry attack Coburg on the morning of April 12 supported by a full battalion of tanks and nine battalions of field artillery. General Patton had insisted on a massive concentration of artillery.

While plans were being formulated for the attack, word came that the city authorities would like to negotiate a surrender. Colonel Wooten and the commander of the armored division met with the city representatives, arranged the terms, which involved surrendering all armaments, and moved their commands into the city. Sergeant Sitz recalled that, for the first time in many days, they were able to bathe, put on clean socks and enjoy a very welcome hot meal.

Compared with the other villages and towns through which the regiment had marched, Coburg was a metropolis and a happy hunting ground for GI's that were hoping to add to their war trophy collections. Many a citizen, enroute to the contraband collecting station, was relieved of his knife, ornamental saber, or pistol by a friendly young soldier, who presented the citizen of Coburg with a bogus receipt and promised to see that the weapon was placed in safe-keeping. A centrally located wine cellar experienced an astounding rush of business while the proprietor was nowhere on the premises.

While 1ˢᵗ Battalion established outposts ringing Coburg, the 2ⁿᵈ and 3ʳᵈ Battalions swept the woods to the east of the city. While doing so, a patrol from How Company was ambushed in the town of Sulzfeld. Consequently, artillery fire was brought to bear and Sulzfeld was leveled. The operation around Coburg had cost the regiment 6 KIA and 3 WIA. The 5ᵗʰ Infantry bagged 150 prisoners.

On April 12, the troops were saddened to learn of the death of President Franklin Roosevelt. Their commander-in-chief had passed away in Warm Springs, Georgia. Vice-President Harry S. Truman, one of Hunter Liggett's World War I artillery officers, took the oath of office and became the new president.

The 5th Infantry's sweep to the southeast continued. On the 14th, 1st Battalion was loaned to the 14th Infantry to assist in an attack on Bayreuth. First Battalion took the west half of the city leaving the east half for the 14th Infantry.

As they entered Bayreuth, Company A, which had the point, was pinned down by small arms fire. Company C outflanked the enemy position and knocked them out. Then the battalion, fearing a counterattack, double-timed through the streets and set up defensive positions on the edge of town.

Darkness fell before the entire battalion reached the center of the captured sector. With outposts manned, those men not on duty sought out billets and hurried about in preparation for a night's rest. The 1st Battalion CP was set up in a hotel and the others bedded down in adjacent buildings.

Some time later those still awake heard the silence of the night broken by the sound of sporadic anti-aircraft fire. A throbbing aircraft motor swelled and faded in the distance. The switchboard operation at the battalion CP listened to a phone conversation and learned that a German plane, strafing an outpost, had been driven off by defensive fire.

Quiet reigned again. The operator dozed at his switchboard until the silence was shattered by the sudden roaring of an engine, the clatter of machine guns, and the bursting of anti-personnel bombs. A missile exploded in the street outside the CP and shrapnel burst through the windows, wounding some and disturbing the sleep of many. Once the injuries were cared for and communications were restored, everybody went back to sleep.

The following morning two American fighters shot down a Junkers 88 that was preparing to strafe Company C. First Battalion was relieved of its part of town by the 14th Infantry, which took the entire credit for the capture of Bayreuth.

On 17 April, the 1st and 3rd Battalions of the 5th Infantry, augmented by 3rd Battalion, 14th Infantry, moved in the vicinity of Haag to help relieve the 14th Armored Division. When they entered the village of Greussen, the soldiers of Company L were welcomed by a group of Czech soldiers that had been sprung from a prison camp by the 14th Armored. They were armed with a variety of German weapons (16).

The following morning, a squad of Czechs asked to accompany 2nd Platoon of Love Company on a patrol. The former POWs proved very difficult to control. They were not the least bit interested in capturing German soldiers. They killed every SS trooper they could find. The following day the battalions moved on to Pegnitz, which was secured by 2nd Battalion on the 19th.

At this time the master strategy for smashing the German Army called for an advance by a wing of the 3rd Army in a southwestern direction toward Regensburg-Linz in order to make contact with the Russians advancing from Vienna. The division advanced with the three regiments abreast. The 14th Infantry was on the left, the 66th was on the right and the 5th Infantry was in the center.

As the 5th Infantry continued in its southeasterly sweep, it ran into pockets of stiff resistance on April 20th. Company C with two medium tanks, three tank destroyers and an anti-tank platoon were proceeding in the direction of Krotensee when it was reported that 200 German soldiers and several enemy tanks had been observed massing in the village.

Since artillery was unavailable from division, tankers and anti-tank gun crews were ordered to shell the town. Several hundred rounds were fired, causing the Germans to withdraw to a wooded draw south of town. While C Company was maneuvering for the assault, they received word that the Germans wanted to surrender. Lieutenant Tuxford, with two rifle squads and a tank, was given permission to round up the enemy troops.

As the G.I's approached the Germans, they were met with fire from machine guns and machine pistols. The firing persisted until they were able to withdraw to better positions. One of the tankers was hurt and the tank withdrew. Another tank advanced and was able to lay down a concentrated fire into the enemy positions. A concentration of nine machine guns, eight mortars and two antitank guns took care of the Germans. By the end of the day, the men of the 5th Infantry had captured four hundred enemy soldiers and had killed twenty at a cost to the regiment of two dead and four wounded.

On 21 April, as the regiment continued southeastward, it encountered scattered periods of fire from automatic weapons and self-propelled guns and occasional roadblocks. Six hundred and fifty Germans surrendered during the day and about the same number of Allied prisoners of war were liberated when the regiment seized the city of Sulzbach-Rosenberg following a two-and-a-half-hour fire fight.

Sulzbach had originally been the 14th Infantry's objective but, when the 5th Infantry discovered a good four-lane military road that wasn't on the map, and it became apparent that the 14th Infantry would not be able to get to Sulzbach by the time scheduled, the 5th Infantry was authorized to capture the town. By shuttling the troops forward using Anti-tank Company, Cannon Company and its own vehicles, the regiment advanced seventeen miles on the 21st of April. Second Battalion executed an encircling movement to the west and south to take the town of Rosenburg, thereby blocking the escape of enemy troops from Sulzbach.

By this time, a study of captured documents and interrogation of prisoners of war, had definitely established that the enemy was fighting a delaying action in an effort to gain time to rally its forces on the Danube River. There they hoped to make a determined stand. Instructions were received from Corps to accelerate the drive of the division and to by-pass small pockets of enemy troops. They would be mopped up by the Corps reserve.

The 5th Infantry was ordered to press forward and seize a crossing point on the Naab River at Schwandorf. Members of the 3rd Battalion rushed by truck convoy to an assembly area near the city. They found a damaged railroad bridge still standing, made some hurried repairs and jumped the Naab against light opposition. The battalion seized the city of Schwandorf and bagged five hundred German prisoners.

In the railroad yards west of the city they discovered several box cars loaded with political prisoners, primarily Russian. Many of them were dead and dying and all were emaciated. They had been badly treated by their SS guards. Those still alive were evacuated immediately to the hospitals in Schwandorf and the regiment pushed on, crossed the Naab River on a Treadway bridge and continued sweeping south toward the Danube. When the 5th Infantry reached the Regen River, there were no surviving vehicular crossing points. So, they swung left into the 14th Infantry's zone and crossed at Regenstauf.

The regiment reached the north bank of the Danube shortly after midnight on April 25th. At 0400 the men slid down the bank and clambered into assault boats, stowed their weapons, and grasped paddles in readiness for the dash to the opposite bank. Third Battalion led the assault. Sergeant Beckum wrote:

"At 0330 we moved out of the houses, called in check points and outposts and started to unload the boats for crossing. The boats were on trailers and were hard as hell to get off. After much struggle and silent cussing (no noise allowed), the boats were on the ground. Twelve men and two engineers made up the load for each boat ... The current was very fast. Boats were hard to control. My boat started out very well, but as we hit mid stream another boat rammed us on the rear side. Our boat started spinning and it took some time to get it straight again. Once under control we continued to cross and hit the other bank in good time. L and K Companies were pretty well mixed up when we left the boats, but were quickly brought under control and the companies moved out to their assigned sectors. It was a great feeling to get your feet on the ground, even though you knew it was full of Germans (17)."

Soon after crossing the Danube, Company L was pinned down by small arms and 20mm cannon fire. PFC Priester, who had taken out the sniper in Lingenfeld with his carbine, climbed to the top of the levee and spotted the 20mm anti-aircraft guns. Exposing himself to enemy fire, he placed his light machine gun on the crest of the levee and fired on the 20mm position to locate it for the 81mm mortar section. The guns were knocked out and Company L was able to resume its attack. Willis Priester received the Bronze Star for "heroic achievement in action against the enemy." The entire 3rd Battalion pushed on and destroyed thirteen more anti-aircraft guns after capturing their crews.

When Company C assembled behind a levee on the north shore of the river at 0700, they began receiving fire from 20mm guns, 88mm howitzers and mortars. Many men suffered shrapnel wounds and were evacuated by the medics. Sixty-millimeter mortar crews quickly set up behind the levee and soon provided enough counter-mortar fire to allow the company to cross. First Battalion attacked quickly and captured enemy positions at Altach and Eltheim.

The regimental CP was established at Altach by mid-afternoon. By the end of the day, the 5th Infantry had killed 45 enemy soldiers and had taken 750 prisoners. The regiment suffered one KIA and forty-five wounded during the assault across the Danube.

The attack had flanked the defenders of the city of Regensburg, placing them in an untenable position. On the morning of April 27, the German general responsible for the defense of Regensburg, came through the lines of the 14th Infantry in order to surrender to the 71st Division. He did so at 1020 when he met with General Wyman. Second Battalion, 14th Infantry moved to Regensburg to effect the city's capitulation.

WITH THE 71ST DIVISION IN WORLD WAR II

The weather was miserable for the next few days. Rain and snow fell as the division moved toward the Austrian border, gathering prisoners and laying claim to many small towns. The Isar River presented the next barrier in the path of the 71st Division.

On April 28, the 3rd Battalion, 5th Infantry sped to the city of Straubing, ten miles northwest of the Isar. There was no opposition. The city was captured as 1900 German soldiers surrendered. Cannon Company, 5th Infantry reached a railroad siding and found that the emaciated corpses of many Russian slave laborers had been pulled from train cars and piled in nearby burial pits. The G.I's had arrived before the SS troops could bury them.

The task of forcing bridgeheads on the Isar fell to the 14th and 66th Regiments. During the afternoon of April 30, heavy machine guns were moved into positions along the river. Late in the day, a heavy smoke screen was laid over enemy positions and the assault began. The three regiments met light and scattered enemy resistance after landing on the south bank.

When the 3rd Battalion, 5th Infantry reached the town of Mintraching, a local resident was told to find the burgermeister and tell him to surrender his town. Forty-five minutes later, enemy machine gun fire was received and the emissary returned. He had been intercepted by SS troops on his way into town. They had beaten him and had commandeered his shoes and socks.

The battalion commander, Major James Haley, made plans to attack the following morning. Third Battalion moved out at 0830, following a fifteen minute artillery preparation. There was minimal resistance when they entered Mintraching.

Meanwhile the 2nd Battalion took over the town of Pfatter, when the local burgermeister peacefully surrendered. After the troops moved into town, they encountered some gunfire from a copse of woods on the outskirts so they continued their sweep of the area.

Austria

When 2nd Battalion reached the Austrian border at Ering on May 2, Fox Company was leading the attack. It made contact with enemy forces defending a dam that crossed the Inn River.

Operating in broad daylight, with a flanking force assaulting in boats, the battalion fought its way across the dam and captured a demolition detail that had been ordered to destroy the structure. Some of their explosive charges were captured U.S. Air Force five hundred pound bombs. The 5th Infantry crossed the river and continued to round up prisoners and capture many small villages including the castle of Crown Prince Albert, heir to the Austrian throne.

Along with the grey-green uniforms of defeated German troops, there now appeared, in increasing numbers, Hungarian troops dressed in clothing the color of gunny sacking. These men had been stripped of most of their arms and equipment by the fast retreating German forces and were more than willing to quit. They passed along to the rear with weary delight and faint smiles.

The snow fell again and the day grew very cold. The weather left the countryside beautiful but made life miserable for the foot soldier. By evening the dam and nearby city of Mining were in the hands of the 2nd Battalion.

Late on May 3, the corps commander changed the direction of the attack to due east and assigned all units the mission of contacting the Russians at the Enns River. With the 5th Infantry now in reserve, and the 66th Infantry continuing its attack within its zone, the 14th Infantry drove east with the immediate task of attacking the city of Wels from the rear. The 14th forged rapidly ahead but then ran into a strongly defended enemy position near Horbach. This was just the first of a series of delaying actions that continued throughout the day.

When the 14th Infantry approached Lambach it came under hostile fire from that city. The 5th Infantry was directed to attack southwest from its reserve position. It did so, smashed the resistance in Lambach and captured the city.

On the following day, 1st Battalion was ordered to proceed to Friesman as quickly as possible. Company C was short of vehicles and it would have been impossible to complete the mission on foot, so they sent the few jeeps ahead to reconnoiter the route, while the rest of the company commandeered all of the wagons and horses that were along their route of advance. Soon fourteen wagons of horse drawn infantry moved toward Friesman (18). When they came to a town filled with former French POW's, new arrangements were made. The French knew the location of some abandoned German Army vehicles so the G.I's ditched the wagons and continued the journey in Wehrmacht trucks.

Gunskirchen Lager

On May 5, while Charlie Company was advancing on Friesman in various modes of transportation, 3rd Battalion, accompanied by Regimental I&R Platoon, was some six kilometers north of Lambach, Austria, when it stumbled upon Gunskirchen Lager, a concentration camp for 18,000 prisoners of the Nazis. The SS guards had abandoned the camp on May 2. Ed Zebrowski wrote,

"We came to a railroad crossing with hundreds of boxcars on a long siding. In front of each was a huge pile of corpses, ready to be hauled off to some mass grave. We had arrived too soon for the Waffen SS to conceal this horror ...We unloaded all of our K rations and water and those miserable, tortured souls reached out to touch us as if unable to comprehend that we were real and no mere figments of their imagination. Hands stretched out, tremulous, gaunt, blackened claws, grimy, crawling with insects, covered with scabrous sores; and as they reached out, we instinctively pulled back, unable to control our nausea and dread...There were three thousand starving and dying human beings crowded into each of a half-dozen log cabins designed to hold three hundred. The dirt floors had degenerated into foul muck. One twenty-hole latrine served the entire camp. Thousands suffered from dysentery and had been forced to stand in line for hours waiting to empty their bowels. Many were shot on the spot when they were unable to control themselves in other areas of the camp. In the buildings, there was so little room that they had to sleep on top of one another. When some of them died, the others were too weak to drag their corpses outside, so they continued to lie on their decomposing bodies (19)."

"Of all the horrors of the place," wrote Captain J.D. Pletcher of 71st Division Headquarters, "the smell, perhaps, was the most startling of all. It was a smell made up of all kinds of odors—human excreta, foul body odors, smoldering trash fires, German tobacco—which is a stink in itself—all mixed together in a heavy dank atmosphere, in a thick muddy woods, where little breeze could go (20)."

The inmates of Gunskirchen were a select group of prisoners, the intellectual class of Hungarian Jews, professional people, for the most part. Yet, these folks, who would normally be expected to maintain their sense of value, their human qualities, longer than others, had been reduced to animals by deliberate prolonged starvation, indiscriminate murder, on little or no provocation, and unbelievable living conditions. These pressures gradually brought about a change in even the strongest personalities.

The American troops soon organized things. Water was brought in German tank wagons and the G.I's found a German food warehouse three miles from Gunskirchen stocked with dried noodles, potatoes, soups, meats and other food. Austrian civilians took the contents of the warehouse to the camp under the supervision of American military government personnel, but before the soldiers could establish proper control, some of the prisoners had gorged themselves and died. Starving people had to learn to eat all over again.

As they left Gunskirchen, the infantrymen felt as though they had suddenly escaped from a prison of the damned but knew, in their hearts, that real escape was truly impossible. The terrible Gunskirchen smell had permeated their clothing and stayed with them. During the few hours that it took to drive through the surrounding pine forest, they were changed forever. The images that had been etched in their brains would never leave them. If any of them had had questions about the purpose of the war against the Nazis, they now had their answer.

Link-up with the Russians

The 5th Infantry, during its capture of Lambach, had seized two bridges beyond the city providing access to the area to the east. Their final objective was to link up with the Russians at the Enns River, some fifty miles east of the Inn River. They had approximately thirty-five more miles to cover.

On May 5, Colonel Wooten devised a bold plan that he hoped would enable the 5th Infantry to capture the city of Steyr and save the bridges crossing the Enns River (21). He organized a small task force of ten jeep loads of personnel including the Intelligence & Recon Platoon, an 81mm mortar crew from How Company, Major Keymont, the Regimental S-3, and Captain Adelbert Boggs, the Regimental S-1. The tiny group proceeded from Lambach to Steyr at a leisurely rate of thirty miles per hour.

At the town of Steiner, the German forces were so amazed at the audacity of the small column that they concluded the war was over and quickly surrendered. The enemy troops immediately cleared the road of their own vehicles and set up road guides to direct the 5th Infantry battalions that were following the task force by two hours.

As 1st Battalion advanced, Sergeant Sitz prayed "that the thousands of Germans behind us would not realize that we were cut off from the rest of the 71st Division." The G.I's hoped that somebody in the rear was disarming all those by-passed Germans.

The advance continued, passing through SS Panzer columns and Wehrmacht divisions. Steyr was captured without firing a shot.

Colonel Wooten's small task force then turned left along the river and was not stopped until it reached the town of Niederglink, two miles north of Steyr. At that point a German AAA battalion fired at them with 88mm dual purpose guns.

With further advance impossible, the small task force took defensive positions and requested reinforcements. Elements from the 2nd Battalion came forward and captured the enemy battery.

During the engagement, Company G shot down a German Storch observation plane. Although all had blazed away with their M-1 rifles, the men of George Company believed that it was probably the full magazine of .45 caliber tommy-gun slugs fired by their company commander, Captain Herbert Neal, that hit the plane's gas tank and sent it crashing into a large tree (22).

Colonel Wooten received the Distinguished Service Cross for his bold escapade on May 5. Captain Neal received a Silver Star for hustling to the aid of his regimental commander.

Germany Surrenders

Lieutenant General Lothar Von Rendulic, commander of the German Army Group South, sent an envoy to the 5th Infantry command post, with a message to the Commanding General of the Third Army, offering unconditional surrender. Soon another 20,000 German troops straggled in and surrendered to the 71st Division.

On May 6, the 3rd Battalion extended its positions north along the Enns. At the dam at Ernsthofen they encountered an SS Panzer Division that still had some fight left in it. Nevertheless the dam was taken intact and a bridgehead was established on the east bank of the river. The 5th Infantry had reached the end of its 775-mile push through Western Europe.

Reports were received that the armistice would be effective at midnight. The last shots fired against the German troops were by Item Company on the east side of the river. When the war ended at 0001 hours on May 7, Company I was farther east than any other Allied unit.

As the world celebrated the victory in Europe, weary men from Companies K and M, 5th Infantry, were still involved in the clean-up of Gunskirchen Lager. They spent several days sending the living to hospitals, supervising the burying of the dead, and trying to cover the stench coming from the barracks. As German prisoners dug mass graves, they disavowed any responsibility for the horrible concentration camp, calling it "just another SS mess." There is now a town of Gunskirchen near the site of the concentration camp. The Austrian government erected a monument to mark the location.

Other members of the 5th Infantry were now tasked with processing thousands of German prisoners through the repatriation center in Steyr. According to Ed Zebrowski, the former Wehrmacht troops were provided with new identification papers, deloused and sent on their way. Among the prisoners were ten generals, one being General von Rendulic.

On Tuesday afternoon, May 8, Sergeant Joy was sergeant of the guard on one of the bridges, when he spotted General von Rendulic's open staff car approaching with white flags flying. A young PFC named Donald Keefer raised his rifle with fixed bayonet and yelled for the car to stop. When the driver ignored him, Keefer shot out the vehicle's front tire.

Colonel Wooten and staff arrived shortly thereafter and told von Rendulic that his surrender would not be accepted until he went back, located and returned Captain Rafferty, the S-2 of 2nd Battalion. The previous day, Rafferty had led a patrol from the 71st Recon Company across the river to make contact with the Russians and hadn't returned.

As soon as the tire was changed, the German officers went back across the bridge and returned that evening with Captain Rafferty. General Wyman was there to meet them and the surrender of all troops in the German Army Group South was arranged. Thomas Rafferty received a Silver Star for his actions on May 7.

Ed Zebrowski's platoon was quartered in a house near a bridge that spanned the Enns. Before the Russians arrived, there was a constant stream of German soldiers and civilians crossing to the west bank of the river to escape the Russian troops. When the Red Army got there on May 9, the column of Germans stopped abruptly. Every night after that, the men in I&R Platoon would hear rifle and machine gun fire from the east side of the river. Being somewhat curious as to what kinds of games the Russians were playing, Zebrowski and his buddies went down to the river one morning to investigate. There were scattered bodies of German soldiers and civilians lying along the shore. People that had attempted to swim across were used for target practice by the Russian soldiers.

Army of Occupation

In February 1946, the 5th Infantry moved from Steyr, Austria to Augsburg, Bavaria to become part of the Army of Occupation in Germany. The regiment was responsible for a sector of a 225 square mile area assigned to the 71st Division. Along with routine road patrols and the operation of check points, they stood guard over a variety of military and civilian installations. There was a training program that emphasized tactics that were proving successful in the Pacific Theater (23).

Living conditions were similar to those of troops that were stationed stateside. The men were billeted in private homes and apartments or in barracks that once housed the German Army. The bulletin boards in front of the company orderly rooms were filled with weekly duty rosters, schedules of training and athletics, notices of USO shows and announcements of educational opportunities.

A point system was established in the European Theater to determine which of the several million American G.I's would be sent home for discharge and who would either stay in Europe as occupational troops or be sent to the Pacific, where war was still raging. The points formula involved marital status, number of children, length of service, time in the ETO, and time in actual combat.

One important item on each company bulletin board was an announcement of the next performance of the Fifth Infantry Soldier Chorus. This ensemble had been organized at Fort Benning by PFC Luther Onerheim and held its first rehearsal on September 1, 1944 in Sand Hill Chapel #5. Initial progress was slow because the forty-eight singers had difficulty making rehearsals. A plea for help was made to Colonel Wooten. He consented to giving the chorus a chance and had a meeting with all first sergeants. Attendance at rehearsals was no longer a problem (24).

As soldiers in an army of occupation, the choristers had many opportunities to perform. During the months following VE Day, the Fifth Infantry Soldier Chorus booked 110 major performances drawing from a repertoire of nearly one hundred memorized selections.

Sergeant Onerheim arranged for the 5th Infantry chorus to sing at the prestigious Salzburg Music Festival on September 2, 1945. Their set opened with *A Mighty Fortress Is Our God* and included Sibelius' *Thee, God, We Praise* and the F. Melius Christiansen arrangement of *Lost in the Night*, with solo by Richard Eichenberger.

On January 16, 1946, Sergeant Onerheim was driving to Saal, Germany to pick up props for a new tour. He met a six-ton engineering truck on an icy mountain road near Abendsburg. His jeep slid and struck the truck behind the cab. He suffered a severe basal skull fracture and died at 8:30 that evening without ever regaining consciousness (25). Colonel Wooten ordered all regimental and national colors lowered to half-mast on January 18 as a tribute to Onerheim. The colonel described Sergeant Onerheim as "The finest soldier and gentleman I have ever known." The chorus sang *Beautiful Savior* for the close of his memorial service at St. Paul's Lutheran Church in Augsburg.

Two Centuries of Valor

A final tour was made under the direction of chorus member Richard Eichenberger and, on February 3, the chorus gave its final performance in the 71st Division Chapel in Augsburg. Following that many of the singers rotated home or were called back to their companies.

Colonel Wooten requested a new series of programs but Eichenberger objected to singing inferior concerts to audiences who remembered the once first-rate chorus. Wooten responded by sending the remaining members of the chorus back to their respective companies.

Sidney Wooten turned the regiment over to Colonel Onslan Rolfe on March 1, 1946. The 71st Division was deactivated ten days later, but the 5th Infantry remained in Germany until it, in turn, was deactivated on November 15, 1946. Depending on their point totals, the men were either transferred to the 16th Infantry or shipped home to Fort Dix for discharge.

The 5th U.S. Infantry received World War II battle streamers for the American Theater, Rhineland, and Central Europe. The regiment had been in continuous combat from March 12 through May 8, 1945. Sixty-five members of the 5th Infantry were killed in action, three hundred and eight were wounded and fifteen were listed as missing. Members of the regiment were awarded two Distinguished Service Crosses, eight Silver Stars and seventeen Bronze Stars for gallantry during the waning days of the war. Prior to the cessation of hostilities, the 5th Infantry captured 14,750 German prisoners (26).

Following World War II, COL Sidney Wooten assumed command of the 17th Infantry Regiment of the 7th Infantry Division and led that unit in Korea. When he was relieved, he remained on in Korea to serve as chief advisor to the ROK Army. His last career assignment was that of Deputy Commander of the National War College. Major General Wooten died of pneumonia in Chevy Chase, Maryland, on December 26, 2003, at the grand old age of 96 (27).

WITH THE 71ST DIVISION IN WORLD WAR II

Reactivation

In September of 1945, while the men of the 5th Infantry and their Russian allies on the east bank of the River Enns maintained a somewhat prickly relationship, another group of American G.I's, the 7th Infantry Division in Korea, ran into the vanguard of the Soviet 25th Army at the 38th Parallel, near the village of Sond Do Kaijo. U. S. President Harry Truman and Russian Premier Joseph Stalin had previously agreed that the Russians would process and repatriate all Japanese prisoners north of the 38th Parallel and the Americans would be responsible for those captured south of the line.

The American negotiators understood that the 38th Parallel agreement was for the processing of prisoners. They never meant to divide Korea into two hostile camps. Stalin, on the other hand, seized the opportunity to drag North Korea behind the Iron Curtain of Communism. A group of Red Army advisors and a cadre of combat-hardened Koreans from the Chinese Peoples Liberation Army whipped the young North Korean Peoples Army into shape. The USSR provided the NKPA with tanks, heavy artillery and aircraft. On August 12, 1946, three soldiers from the 32nd Infantry Regiment were taken prisoner by Soviet troops occupying the northern part of Korea. The Americans were held for thirteen days before being released.

President Truman, intent on reducing the military budget, reluctantly ordered the U.S. Army to form a small defense force in South Korea, the Republic of Korea Constabulary. To prevent President Syngman Rhee from starting a war to unify the country, the Constabulary was denied armor, heavy artillery and aircraft. As North Korea's leader, Kim Il Sung, mobilized for war and North Korean soldiers began to replace Russian soldiers on the 38th Parallel. Wild fire fights broke out between the North Koreans and the Constabulary. The Truman Administration responded by slashing America's defense funding. Guaranteeing security for South Korea was not as high a national priority as was getting American troops out of the country.

The exit strategy involved leaving a token American garrison; a U.S. Army regimental combat team to train and assist the Republic of Korea Army. The American unit would be withdrawn when the ROK Army became operational.

The 5th Regimental Combat Team was activated in Seoul, Korea on January 1, 1949; twenty-five months after the 5th Infantry had folded its flag in Augsburg, Germany. The first personnel and equipment for the combat team were provided by the 7th Infantry Division. Most of the men serving in the 32nd Infantry Regiment, 48th Field Artillery Battalion, 7th Cavalry Reconnaissance Troop, and Company B, 13th Engineer (C) Battalion were transferred to the 5th RCT. The resulting composition of the combat team included the re-activated 5th Infantry, the 555th Field Artillery Battalion, the 72nd Engineer Company, the 58th Cavalry Reconnaissance Troop, Mechanized, and various combat support and service units. The 282nd Army Band was thrown in for ceremonial purposes. The combat team was under-strength. The rifle companies consisted of two rather than three rifle platoons and the weapons platoons had just a token number of crew-served machine guns and light mortars (27).

For the first two weeks, the 5th RCT's mission was to man defensive outposts on the 38th Parallel. When the Republic of Korea Army assumed that task in mid-January, the 5th RCT assisted the Korean Military Assistance Group by training members of the ROK Army in squad-to-battalion tactics. This partially involved running patrols near the 38th Parallel, where they were often shot at by NKPA troops. There were no casualties but it kept the G.I's on their guard.

Korea was not "good duty" from the perspective of most of the American soldiers. The natives were generally unfriendly. Korean men discouraged women from associating with the Americans. Those soldiers who frequented Seoul in the vicinity of the 32nd Street Circle were often robbed. If a Korean could hoist an item of Army property onto his back, it was gone, be it a generator or fifty-gallon drum of gas.

Understandably, morale soared in April, when the men learned that the 5th RCT was going to be transferred to Hawaii.

The combat team was severely under strength when it left Korea in June, 1949. The Eighth Army commander ordered the transfer of several hundred men to units in Japan. Those soldiers whose enlistments were expiring were sent stateside. Company C, for instance, arrived in Honolulu with thirty men. As the G.I's departed for the port of Inchon in truck convoys, Korean bystanders screamed insults, threw rotten fruit and spit at them.

As the men disembarked in Honolulu, young ladies from the Hawaiian Visitor's Bureau draped leis around their necks while beautiful hula dancers swayed to the music of an army band. An announcement in the June, 12th edition of the Honolulu Advertiser concluded with "All of Hawaii extends a warm greeting to the men of the 5th RCT and hopes to make their stay a pleasant one."

The combat team was assigned to quarters in the old concrete quadrangle barracks at Schofield Barracks. The scene was reminiscent of the regiment's two Panama deployments. The "Quads" had been vacant since the end of World War II and had been partially reclaimed by the jungle. There was a shortage of gardening tools so the men used their bayonets to hack their way into their new homes. Nevertheless, they were exceedingly happy to be there. They were issued a foot locker and a wall locker which, unlike Korea, did not have to be locked.

Colonel James Simpson devoted the next four months to preparing the 5th RCT to serve as the aggressor force in Exercise MIKI, a massive joint exercise in October of 1949 that would pit his command against the 2nd Infantry Division from Fort Lewis, Washington. Training areas were quite limited at Schofield Barracks. There were really no areas on Oahu for live-fire training, especially with artillery. The Triple Nickel (555th FAB) often trained near Ka'ena Point on Oahu's north shore. Their 105mm howitzers would pound away for hours at target barges towed by the navy.

Two Centuries of Valor

During Exercise MIKI, the 5th RCT earned many favorable comments from the army umpires. Colonel Simpson received accolades from several general officers for his unit's high level of professionalism, tactical prowess, and overall fine performance. However, as the "enemy", the combat team was scripted to lose the fight and they did so right on schedule. When the exercises were over, the men of the 5th RCT and the 2nd Infantry Division put on regulation khaki trousers, brown shoes and colorful Hawaiian aloha shirts and headed for a big evening at Waikiki.

On November 3, Mr. Beum Foo Yun, the First Secretary to the Republic of Korea Consul General in Honolulu, presented a silver plaque to the 5th RCT from the officers and men of the ROK Army. Official Korea was grateful for the excellent training provided them by members of the combat team.

The army looked forward to payday at the end of each month. Privates received $75 and generals earned approximately $800; not great pay even for 1950, but enough to buy a small sample of the good life in Honolulu. The beaches were free and four of them had been set aside for the army's exclusive use. Schofield Barracks offered a movie theater, a swimming pool, and an NCO and Enlisted Club where a soldier could enjoy a cold beer, hamburger and fries. For the more adventurous types, $75 would fund a modestly enjoyable weekend in Honolulu.

Several months prior to Colonel Simpson's retirement from the army in the spring of 1950, Colonel Godwin Ordway, Jr. took command of the 5th Regimental Combat Team. Colonel Ordway had served well during peace time in public relations assignments and had been able to impress General Ridgeway and Chief of Staff, General J. Lawton Collins. He would prove to be ill-suited to command an infantry regiment in combat.

CHAPTER ELEVEN

KOREA: THE FLUID WAR

On Saturday evening, June 24, 1950, military police and shore patrolmen interrupted the reveling in Honolulu bars, dance halls, theaters, and service clubs and relayed an order for all men in the 5th Regimental Combat Team to return to post. North Korea had invaded South Korea. Free transportation back to the base was provided by the Hawaiian Rapid Transit System. Taxis, buses, and even civilians offered rides to the soldiers. When they returned to Schofield Barracks, they were told to pack up their civilian clothes and turn them in at the supply room. They would have no need for "civvies" for awhile. President Truman had ordered General MacArthur to stop the North Korean invasion.

On July 1, Major General Charles Bolte, G-3, Department of the Army suggested that the 5th RCT be sent to Korea. There was some discussion as to whether the combat team should be deployed as a unit or broken up into separate battalions that would bring those outfits already in combat up to strength. It was subsequently decided to deploy the 5th RCT as a unit. On 13 July the Joint Chiefs of Staff ordered General Henry Aurand, CG of U.S. Army Pacific, to ship the 5th RCT back to Korea (1).

During the period of alert, the U.S. Army Pacific had bolstered the ranks of the 5th RCT with replacements. Many of them were Hawaiians, who had hoped to stay home with the combat team rather than being assigned to a unit in Japan. The 5th Provisional Training Company provided its latest batch of trainees and one hundred members of the 8292nd Post Engineers were told that they were joining the infantry. These new fillers had just enough time to zero-in their M-1 rifles and throw one practice grenade before boarding one of the four troop ships that would carry the 5th RCT to the Far East. When the combat team sailed from Honolulu on July 22, 178 officers and 3,319 enlisted men stood at the railing and waved goodbye to relatives and friends.

The Organization of the Combat Team

Most of the infantry regiments, already fighting in Korea, had gone into combat with two rather than three rifle battalions. One battalion in each regiment had been disbanded to save money. The two-battalion regiments were being asked to do what was normally expected of three battalions. Fortunately, that was not the case with the 5th RCT.

The 5th Infantry met the organizational standards of the day with three rifle battalions and a provisional battalion composed of Headquarters and Headquarters Company, Service Company, Tank Company, Heavy Mortar Company and Medical Company. "Head and Head" included a regimental headquarters section, a counter fire platoon, a communications platoon, an intelligence and reconnaissance platoon, and a security platoon to protect the regimental command post (2).

Service Company's soldiers handled personnel and graves registration tasks. They were also responsible for vehicle maintenance, shower facilities and keeping the combat team supplied with ammunition, food, clothing, equipment and fuel.

Medical Company consisted of a headquarters element, a collecting platoon and three medical platoons. The latter were usually attached to specific rifle battalions. For example, the medical aid men in 1st Platoon served the rifle companies in 1st Battalion. The medical platoon leader was both a surgeon and a sanitation adviser for his assigned battalion.

Heavy Mortar Company, composed of a headquarters section with a fire direction center (FDC) and three firing platoons provided long range, indirect supporting fires for the infantry. Four eight-man squads constituted a platoon. Their tubes fired a 4.2 inch, 25-pound mortar shell with a maximum range of 4400 yards. Each platoon was assigned to a different rifle battalion.

Tank Company operated with seventeen M-4A3E8 Sherman tanks or "Easy Eights." The tank was armed with a 76mm cannon, two .30 caliber machine guns and a .50 caliber anti-aircraft machine gun. Each tank had a crew of five men: commander, gunner, loader, driver and bow gunner. Company headquarters owned two tanks and a tank retriever and each of the three tank platoons was responsible for five Easy Eights.

Each of the three infantry battalions consisted of a headquarters company, three rifle companies and one heavy weapons company. The latter units, Companies D, H, and M, were armed with heavy machine guns, 81mm mortars and 75mm recoilless rifles.

The sections of the infantry battalion's headquarters company were similar to those of regimental headquarters company except that the battalions also had a pioneer and ammunition (P&A) platoon to lay and detect mines, set booby traps, string barbed wire, construct foot bridges, transport ammunition forward and provide security for the battalion command post.

The 72nd Engineer Company constructed and repaired bridges, improved roads, cleared and laid minefields, blasted tunnels and bunkers, and cleared areas for campsites, rifle ranges and parade grounds. As would be expected, this unit consisted of a headquarters unit and three platoons, in this case, of combat engineers. The 72nd was equipped with one road grader and three D-7 bulldozers. The engineers possessed small arms, rocket launchers, and vehicle-mounted .50 caliber machine guns. The unit was loaded with battle-hardened combat engineers and commanded by Captain Leslie P. Gayhart, who had received a direct commission in World War II.

The 555th Field Artillery Battalion was the standard army organization of three firing batteries, a headquarters battery and a service battery. Each firing battery, namely Batteries A, B, and C, operated four 105mm howitzers capable of dropping high explosives, smoke or white phosphorous ammunition on targets at a distance of up to 12,000 yards.

Lieutenant Colonel John Daly assumed command of the Triple Nickel in August of 1949. Daly, a graduate of the West Point class of 1936, served as an artillery officer throughout World War II. When the opportunity arose to command the 555th, he was serving as a regular army artillery instructor for the Hawaiian National Guard. From all reports, LTC Daly was a fine commander; a no-nonsense officer, who tolerated no slackness but trusted his people to get the job done.

Although President Truman had ordered an end to segregation in the armed forces in July of 1948, there were still some racially segregated army units at the beginning of the Korean War. Someone circulated a story that the Triple Nickel was an African-American battalion. That wasn't true. There were no Black soldiers in the 555th when the battalion went ashore in Korea. Second Lieutenant Clarence Jackson, a platoon leader in Company E, was the only Black soldier in the 5th RCT in July of 1950. Jackson was a product of the first racially integrated officer's training course at Fort Benning in 1949. He led his platoon from Chindong-ni to Kusong, received the Silver Star for gallantry, and rotated home in the spring of 1951 with the first group of veterans to leave Korea.

The four transports bearing the Fifth Regimental Combat Team entered the harbor of Pusan, Korea on the night of July 31, 1950. As the men went ashore the following morning, they chafed in the summer heat and got a good strong whiff of human waste and mounds of garbage. They formed up in a column of twos on the dock and set off for an assembly area where they were instructed to make a horseshoe pack with a change of socks and underwear and an extra set of fatigues. Theoretically, their belongings were to catch up with them later. They never did.

Korea: The Fluid War

The Pusan Perimeter

The Eighth Army's defensive perimeter began at Chindong-ni on the south coast of Korea and ran due north to Naktong-ni. From there it curved eastward to P'o-hang on the Sea of Japan. Holding this Pusan Perimeter was absolutely essential. All supplies and reinforcements came in through Pusan's port. Moreover, should it become necessary to evacuate Korea, Pusan would serve as the back door.

The 5th RCT was the first reinforcing unit to reach Korea from an area outside of Japan. They were most welcome. They would be followed, soon after, by the 1st Provisional Marine Brigade and the Second Infantry Division. The three under-strength infantry divisions that had been rushed from Japan had already suffered 6000 casualties.

An enemy drive on Pusan from the west along the Chinju-Masan corridor compelled Eighth Army Commander, General Walton Walker, to concentrate the newly arrived reinforcements in that area. This southern-most corridor became the strongest point in the Pusan Perimeter prompting General Walker to order the first American counterattack in the war (3).

On August 2, the 5th RCT traveled south to the coastal village of Chindong-ni by train and truck convoy. The North Korean Peoples Army's 6th Division was rapidly approaching Chindong-ni from the west in an effort to pierce the left flank of the Pusan Perimeter. Advanced elements of the North Korean division already controlled Hills 342 and 255, two key terrain features overlooking Chindong-ni and the road north to Masan. The combat team reached the village late on August 2 and dug in for the night.

The following morning, George Company attempted to wrest a high point named Yaban-san (Hill 342) from the North Koreans and was repulsed. The combat team had had its first taste of trying to deal with tough North Korean infantry on a morning when the thermometer was already exceeding 100 degrees.

Lieutenant Colonel John Throckmorton, commander of 2nd Battalion, decided not to mount a second attack in the merciless sun. He ordered Fox Company to attack after dark. When the G.I's reached the crest of the hill, the muzzles of numerous NKPA rifles and machine guns erupted in flame. Fox Company directed their own BAR and rifle fire at the muzzle flashes and called for mortar fire on the enemy positions. Confronted with an onslaught of grenades, the North Korean soldiers panicked and ran down the west side of the hill. Thanks to parachute flares, the men of Fox Company were able to pick off a few more enemy troops before the firing ceased. The survivors of the attack christened their objective Fox Hill.

Fox Company remained on Yaban-san until relieved by 1st Platoon, George Company, 5th Marines on the evening of August 8. During the previous five days, the soldiers had been subjected to constant NKPA small arms and mortar fire, 110° heat, and swarms of flies and mosquitos. They were running short of water and ammunition.

Corporal Jack Starkey spent much of his time on Fox Hill rendering first aid to his wounded comrades and evacuating those who could no longer fight. Whenever he returned to the crest of the hill, he brought back all the water and ammunition he could carry. On his last return trip, Starkey guided the Marines to the top of the hill. When the relief party became pinned down by an enemy machine gun, Starkey rose to his feet and took out the gun with a grenade. He was mortally wounded and received the Distinguished Service Cross posthumously (4).

On 5 August, General Walker visited the command post of General William Kean's 25th Infantry Division and outlined his plan for Task Force Kean. The task force's mission would be to launch a counterattack on the following day. The 5th RCT would seize a road junction a few miles west of Chindong-ni near the village of Tosan and then continue attacking to the northwest. The 5th RCT, the 35th Infantry and the 5th Marines were to link up at a mountain pass near Chinju.

Korea: The Fluid War

General Kean envisioned a pincer movement designed to surround and destroy the NKPA 6th Division.

Meanwhile, Easy Company had its hands full trying to hold the crest of Hill 255, due north of Chindong-ni. NKPA infantrymen, concealed by an early morning ground fog, attacked their positions, killing the three-man heavy machine gun crew and turning the gun on the members of Company E's first platoon. The platoon leader, Lieutenant Gordon Strong, was shot in the head when he tried to move from one position to another. Corporal Frank Valvo returned fire with his BAR, hitting several of the North Koreans and keeping the rest pinned down. PFC James Kawamura screamed "Come and get it" in Japanese as he emptied BAR magazines into the NKPA infantrymen, killing forty-one. As soon as there was a brief lull in the action, SFC Carl Dodd withdrew the remnants of the platoon. Private Kawamura covered their withdrawal. His courage and skill enabled the platoon to reoccupy the hill. He was awarded the Distinguished Service Cross (5).

The 1st Battalion crossed its line of departure at 0720 on the 6th. Although fog had prevented the air strike that was to precede the attack, they secured the Tosan road junction without any difficulty but then they got confused and proceeded south instead or north. As they tried to retrace their steps, North Korean resistance stiffened significantly.

The difficulties were compounded by a lack of wire communication. The combat team's phone lines had been carelessly laid by inexperienced troops in the path of an advancing platoon of tanks which promptly tore them to shreds. With phone communication down, the unreliable SCR-300 radios overheating and Colonel Ordway's unwillingness to lead from the front, the assault bogged down. General Kean was not happy.

Ordway could have advanced the 3rd Battalion up the right fork of the Tosan road to maintain the momentum but he chose to keep the Third at the rear of the road-bound column to protect the artillery. Meanwhile the main body of the 5th Marines, expecting to advance down the left fork of the Tosan road junction, stalled behind the 5th RCT's vehicles crowding the road at Chindong-ni. A number of Marine vehicles left the road only to become stuck in the mud (6).

Colonel Ordway, knowing his career was on the line, ordered LTC Throckmorton's 2nd Battalion to seize the ridge north of Tosan. Fox Company had been ordered to rest and reorganize after its ordeal on Hill 342, so Companies E and G moved out at 0930 on 8 August to attack the ridge. Heavy enemy fire, inability of the supporting artillery to adjust on target, and an absence of recoilless rifle ammunition caused Throckmorton's attack to bog down shortly before noon.

During the 2nd Battalion's attack, NKPA indirect fire weapons knocked out the 555th FAB's operations center and two of B Battery's howitzers. An enraged General Kean and an uncomfortable Colonel Ordway stopped by Throckmorton's CP that evening and General Kean gruffly demanded, "I want that hill tonight." John Throckmorton prepared an attack plan, using his two effective companies, George and Easy, supported by three tanks, the battalion's 81mm mortars and an attached platoon of 4.2 inch mortars (7).

At 2000 hours the two infantry companies crossed the LD, engaged in a sharply contested fire fight and routed the NKPA defenders with little loss of blood. The following morning, a smiling General Kean congratulated his WWII protégé, John Throckmorton.

From Tosan, the 5th RCT advanced in a northwest direction, astride a narrow country road, toward Much-on'ni. Despite the intense heat, many soldiers wore their gas masks to keep from choking on clouds of dust. Late afternoon rain showers brought welcome relief from the heat, but flies and mosquitos continued to plague the column. Men were beginning to go down with malaria, diarrhea and heat exhaustion. Sniper fire and small unit ambushes led to several casualties.

General Kean ordered the 5th RCT and the 5th Marines to

continue their advance throughout the night. Colonel Ordway placed the exhausted 2nd Battalion at the front of the advance rather than the un-blooded 3rd Battalion. Lieutenant Keith Whitham's 2nd Tank Platoon and Captain Alexander Kahapea's Fox Company formed the vanguard.

Bloody Gulch

Midway between Chindong-ni and Much'on-ni lie the villages of Pongam-ni and Taejon-ni. These twin villages sit at the eastern end of the Chinju Pass through the Sobuk-san Mountains. On the afternoon of 10 August, LTC John Jones' 1st Battalion was advancing on the north side of the road while LTC Throckmorton's 2nd Battalion was moving forward on the south side. The 1st Battalion seized Pongam-ni and began to consolidate on the high ground on the northern side of the pass. The 2nd Battalion dug in on the high ground south of the pass. Colonel Ordway ordered LTC Benjamin Heckmeyer's 3rd Battalion to punch through the pass and continue the march toward Much'on-ni.

The 3rd Battalion barreled through the pass, taking occasional small arms fire from the ridgelines. With the exception of two shot-out tires, the enemy inflicted either no casualties or light casualties depending on whose description of the attack one reads (8). Heckmeyer's battalion exited the pass and hunkered down for the night at the west end. This movement left regimental headquarters and Charlie Battery of the Triple Nickel without protecting infantry close at hand.

Colonel Ordway, apparently unaware of 3rd Battalion's remarkable progress, decided to delay moving the rest of the combat team through the pass until nightfall. General Kean, who was under pressure from General Walker to complete the mission so that he could relinquish one of his attacking units, was not happy but reluctantly concurred with Colonel Ordway's plan. Throckmorton's 2nd Battalion would be next to run the gauntlet.

Two Centuries of Valor

At 2100 on the night of 10-11 August, 2nd Battalion's P&A Platoon led the advance. When the platoon was approximately five hundred yards into the pass, NKPA fire opened up from both sides, wounding every man but the platoon leader, Lieutenant Norman Cooper. The wounded men were loaded on trucks and the column continued to fight its way through the pass. Second Battalion and Charlie Battery of the 555th FAB finally fought their way clear of the enemy fire and reached the west end of the pass at first light. An NKPA ambush bottled up elements of the convoy that were trailing Battery C.

As firing erupted, Albert Veenstra, veteran of a World War II ranger battalion and 1st Sergeant of George Company, bailed out of his stalled truck and called to those around to follow him (9). They had gone but a few yards when they heard North Koreans talking. Sergeant Veenstra tossed a couple of grenades into the middle of the conversation and the G.I's opened fire. Finding cover in a roadside ditch, they soon realized that they had bumped into more than they could handle.

Veenstra jumped up on a personnel carrier, upon which was mounted a .50 caliber machine gun, and began firing. He was totally exposed and his buddies in the ditch expected to see him cut down at any moment. In the light of the flames from the burning trucks, he was seen clearing the jammed gun while cursing it. Within a few minutes, he had expended the first box of ammunition with which the gun had been loaded. He called for another soldier to get him some more ammunition, all the time cursing the gun, the enemy and the fool who had set up the gun without stowing extra ammunition nearby. Like a mad man, SGT Veenstra went on raving, killing everything in front of him. When there was no more ammunition for the gun and the troops were running short of grenades and rifle cartridge clips, the first sergeant and other members of the 2nd Battalion withdrew down the ditch and back to the high ground south of the pass. While the North Koreans had been temporarily stunned by SGT Veenstra's ferocious

KOREA: THE FLUID WAR

fire, a wounded lieutenant had been able to load other wounded G.I's onto a jeep, make a U turn and head for safety.

At this point, Colonel Ordway received orders from General Kean to halt his advance. General Walker was insisting that General Kean break off a portion of his task force and shift it to another threatened portion of the Pusan Perimeter. The 5th RCT was nominated. Two of Ordway's infantry battalions and one artillery battery were west of the pass and the regimental trains were lined up, motionless, on the road. They would be sitting ducks when daylight arrived. The NKPA 6th Division was pressing the combat team hard, particularly from the north. Apparently, Colonel Ordway tried to explain his situation to General Kean, but radio communications with the 25th Division CP failed at the critical moment. Radio communications with division were still down at 0400, when Ordway finally decided to disregard General Kean's order and instructed the artillery and the supply trains to push through the pass.

At first light on the 11th, the men of the 555th FAB were awaiting orders to limber up their howitzers and move out when, suddenly, fire rained down from the ridgeline upon their exposed positions. Many of the artillerymen fell back to a stone wall that surrounded Taejon-ni. Some remained with their guns. They had no infantry support.

The 13th NKPA Regiment, supported by T-34 tanks and SU-76 self-propelled guns, struck the 555th and the 90th Field Artillery Battalions at Pongam-ni from three sides. The gun crews fought a courageous duel with the tanks, firing over open sights. The 105mm explosive rounds fired by the 555th had no effect on the T-34's and the 90th FAB couldn't depress the barrels of its 155mm howitzers sufficiently to hit the tanks. A couple of gun crews took direct hits from the tanks. The surviving cannoneers fought as infantry, often hand-to-hand as the NKPA rushed the gun positions with burp guns, grenades and bayonets.

Corporal Aubrey Gibson of A Battery, armed with a bazooka,

moved forward and took out three enemy machine gun emplacements before he ran out of ammunition. Dropping the rocket launcher, he sprang to a .50 caliber machine gun, mounted on a truck, and delivered accurate fire until he was wounded by an anti-tank shell. Gibson couldn't be found after the position was overrun. He was awarded the Distinguished Service Cross (10).

When LTC Daly, commander of the 555th, lost communication with A Battery, he and 1st Battalion's LTC John Jones, accompanied by some infantrymen, tried to reach the battery. Both battalion commanders were wounded; Jones, severely. Colonel Ordway sent LTC Roelofs, regimental S-2, to take over 1st Battalion.

When Colonel Ordway heard that his artillery units were being wiped out at the east end of the pass, he ordered the fatigued 2nd Battalion to retrace its steps, from its assembly area five miles to the west, and attack back into the pass.

This was not an easy task because the 2nd Battalion was under heavy attack at the time. After Throckmorton's soldiers repulsed the NKPA attack, they marched east to rescue the beleaguered artillery. At 1500, LTC Throckmorton observed a large NKPA force filtering through the hills to attack the 5th RCT command post. He broke off the eastbound attack and set up a perimeter defense around the regimental CP for the night.

For the next couple of days, the 1st and 2nd Battalions, in concert with the 24th Infantry Regiment, failed in an attempt to regain control of the pass. A secondary mission to recover the large number of abandoned vehicles and guns and bodies of soldiers listed as missing proved equally futile. Subsequent air strikes destroyed much of the equipment but did help many of the survivors escape from the pass alive. Most of the dead were recovered in September when the 25th Division broke out of the Pusan Perimeter. The 3rd Battalion avoided another trip through the Chinju Pass by returning to Chindong-ni by way of Haman.

Korea: The Fluid War

An Eighth Army directive reached General Kean at 1550 on August 16 dissolving Task Force Kean. The task force had not accomplished what General Walker had predicted would be a cakewalk—the winning and holding of the Chinju Pass. It did, however, produce certain beneficial results. The task force had chanced to meet head-on an attack by the NKPA 6th Division, stopping it and hurling it back. It also gave the 25th Infantry Division a psychological lift from finally going on the offensive.

The 555th FAB lost close to 100 soldiers killed and 80 wounded and all of its vehicles and six 105mm howitzers at, what became known as, the battle of Bloody Gulch. The bodies of fifty-five members of Headquarters, Service and Able Batteries were found bound with wire. They had been murdered by their captors. The 90th FAB also suffered heavy losses, losing 10 KIA, 60 WIA, 30 MIA and six 155mm howitzers.

The 1st Battalion was decimated. Charlie Company was reduced in a single night from 180 to 23 men. Throughout the night, the courageous actions of PVT William Vandervoort of Company C had been a big factor in the company's ability to repulse repeated North Korean attacks. The Distinguished Service Cross recipient was eventually killed by an enemy grenade (11).

Third Battalion, 5th RCT received a Distinguished Unit Citation for "extraordinary heroism" during the battle of Chinju Pass. The Eighth Army's description of the battalion's actions during the attack was qualitatively different than that described by LTC Roy Appleman in 1961. According to General Orders 239, Headquarters, Eighth United States Army, Korea, 6 May 1952:

"On 9 August, under cover of darkness, this battalion embarked upon its mission which was to seize high ground in the vicinity of Kogan-ni, then to continue the attack through Pansong-ni, and finally to make contact with the 35th Infantry Regiment and seize and hold the battalion's assigned sector of the divisional objective along the Nam

River. Moving rapidly over mined roads and through enemy-held terrain, the members of this battalion launched an attack against their initial intermediate objective. Advancing through intense automatic weapons and artillery fire, the personnel of the battalion displayed a matchless fighting spirit and, through their aggressiveness and singleness of purpose, they were able to rupture the numerically superior enemy's defense line, inflicting heavy casualties on the hostile troops.

As the battalion struck out for Pansong-ni, the desperate enemy subjected it to fire from almost every conceivable type of weapons, from small arms to artillery, but with dogged determination, its members pressed forward by forced marches, engaging and defeating the numerous hostile units which attempted to bar their way, regardless of size. Despite the constant harassment of large enemy patrols and individual snipers, an enemy fuel dump, ammunition stores and seven field guns were overrun and captured. After countless ambuscades, the members of this battalion, even though hampered by a lack of water and vital supplies, seized and held their objective on the Nam River until ordered to withdraw.

In this action, the friendly casualties were relatively light, despite the furious fighting, but an estimated 450 casualties were inflicted on the enemy. The 3rd Battalion, 5th Infantry, 25th Infantry Division, and attached units, displayed such superlative effectiveness in accomplishing its mission under extremely difficult and hazardous conditions as to set it apart and above other units participating in the campaign. The extraordinary heroism and esprit de corps exhibited by its members reflected great credit on themselves and are in keeping with the most esteemed traditions of the military service."

The citation was issued by order of the Secretary of the Army and signed by General J. Lawton Collins, Chief of Staff, U.S. Army. The "other units in the campaign", of course were the 1st and 2nd Battalions of the 5th Infantry and the 555th Field Artillery Battalion, the units that did most of the fighting and dying at Chinju Pass. It might be argued

Korea: The Fluid War

that 3rd Battalion was the only unit to accomplish its assigned mission. It did attack through the pass and link up with the 35th Infantry but there is a certainly a question of whether the battalion was "set apart and above other units participating in the campaign."

General Kean blamed Colonel Ordway for the losses at Bloody Gulch. He sent his assistant division commander, Brigadier General Vennard Wilson to deal with the hapless regimental commander. When General Wilson caught up with Colonel Ordway, the latter was establishing a new regimental CP some five miles behind the front lines. Wilson said "You know, since I've been in the army, normally there are two ways to do things, the right way and the wrong way... Now there's the Ordway, and that's no damn good. You're relieved." General Kean quickly appointed LTC John Throckmorton to replace Ordway as CO of the 5th RCT. LTC Albert Ward assumed command of the 2nd Battalion (12).

The 5th RCT, aided by John "The Rock" Throckmorton's assumption of command, quickly recovered from Bloody Gulch. The 25th Division's artillery commander, BG George Barth, intercepted guns, trucks and radios destined for the ROK Army and redirected them to the 555th FAB at Masan. A levy of army reservists arrived to replace most of the artillery personnel lost during Task Force Kean. General Barth selected LTC Clarence Stuart to succeed LTC Daly as commander of the 555th. Colonel Daly's wounds had necessitated his being flown to Tripler Army Hospital on Oahu.

The Triple Nickel acquired a number of self-propelled weapons, M-16 half-tracks armed with four .50 caliber machine guns (the Quad 50), older M-15 tracks equipped with a 37mm cannon and two .50 caliber machine guns on a revolving turret. There were either two M-16's or one M-16 plus one M-15 to support each battery. The new guns were used primarily as long-range automatic weapons to support infantry movements since very few North Korean planes flew over at this stage of the war.

Infantry replacements trickled in but the number was insufficient to bring the depleted rifle squads up to full strength. At times, the 72nd Engineer Company was the only regimental reserve.

Following the dissolution of Task Force Kean, the role of the 25th "Tropic Lightning" Division became a defensive one. The division's sector of the Pusan Perimeter ran for 25 miles from Chindong-ni on the south coast north to the confluence of the Nam and Naktong Rivers.

Sobuk-san

The 5th RCT was placed on a ridgeline to the left of the 25th Division and facing a higher ridgeline called Sobuk-san, which was in the hands of the NKPA. Battalion fronts averaged 8000 yards rather than the recommended 2000 yards, so the rifle companies formed strong points on select pieces of high ground and did their best to cover the gaps with intersecting fire. The 1st Battalion of the 5th RCT was on the right, a few miles south of Haman, the 2nd Battalion was in the center, and the 3rd Battalion was on the left, with K Company on the flank, a bit west of Chindong-ni.

There were no roads in the 5th RCT sector. Supplies had to be hauled up the steep trails on strong backs and the wounded and dead were evacuated the same way. The 25th Division authorized the combat team to hire local civilians to carry out these important tasks. The G.I's called these porters "chogi bearers."

The front opposite the combat team remained relatively quiet until August 20 when the 1st Battalion launched an attack to seize the crest of Sobuk-san. It was a crucial objective because the NKPA could see well into the American lines from that high point. The battalion, minus A Company, reached the crest after encountering light resistance. Later in the afternoon, the NKPA counter-attacked with two battalions and, despite a barrage of 1,093 rounds from the 555th FAB, the North Koreans regained the crest.

General Kean ordered LTC Throckmorton to try again. The Rock sent 1st Battalion back up the hill shortly after noon on the 21st. Once again, Able Company remained in reserve. An estimated one thousand defenders put up a terrific fight as the American troops clawed their way up the slopes.

After seizing the crest, the men of 1st Battalion piled stones to protect themselves from the inevitable counter-attacks. Digging foxholes in the rocky ground was impossible. Company B remained on the crest of the hill for 72 hours while being continually exposed to mortar and small arms fire. The company commander, LT Kermit Young, refused to be evacuated after he had been wounded. He was awarded the Distinguished Service Cross for his valorous leadership on Sobuk-san (13).

Incessant fighting for the mountain crest raged throughout August and into September. During one two-day period, August 23-24, that included a reconnaissance in force by Able Company, the 5th RCT reported the loss of 9 dead, 55 wounded and 11 missing.

Throughout 25 August, sporadic mortar and howitzer fire slammed into the 5th RCT's defensive positions. The newly arrived NKPA 7th Division was registering its weapons prior to launching an attack to push 1st Battalion off the hill top. The pounding intensified at 2130. When the fire was lifted two hours later, long lines of North Koreans advanced up the ridge.

Fifteen minutes before midnight, the attackers' main thrust hit Company C, throwing grenades and firing burp guns from the hip. M/SGT Melvin O. Handrich crawled out of his foxhole and stationed himself at the base of an outcropping of rocks where he began to radio firing directions for mortar and artillery support. He remained in that position for the next eight hours. When a squad of NKPA infantrymen came within fifty feet, he took them under fire with his carbine and dropped six of them.

Shortly after 0600 another enemy force of 150 men rushed C Company's sector. Handrich left what little cover he had and climbed atop a large boulder. From there he continued to call down salvo after salvo of deadly accurate artillery fire. When some North Koreans escaped the artillery bursts, Handrich stood calmly and cut them down with carbine fire.

When one group of attackers overran a portion of Charlie Company's battered perimeter, a group of G.I.'s panicked and broke for the rear. Handrich was on them in an instant. "Get back up there, dammit!" he exhorted. "This fight's not over yet."

Handrich got the rattled men back on the line, but as he did so, enemy bullets tore into his back and leg. Refusing treatment or evacuation, he went back to his previous position and continued calling in the artillery.

Shortly after 0700, the North Koreans succeeded in overwhelming Handrich. He went down firing his carbine into the mass of enemy soldiers rushing him. When the remnants of his company retook the position later that morning, seventy-one enemy dead lay in and around Handrich's position. His posthumous Medal of Honor was presented to his widow in April, 1951 (14).

On the morning of 28 August, an NKPA probe hit the 1st Battalion's positions on Sobuk-san and the attack was repulsed with numerous enemy casualties. The 5th RCT was gaining a reputation within the Pusan Perimeter as an outfit that held its ground. Nevertheless, elements of the NKPA 6th Division and the independent 83rd Mechanized Regiment continued to launch daily attacks around 0500. They were driven off by small arms fire and pre-planned defensive artillery concentrations. The NKPA was very effective with its mortar fire during this stage of the war. The combat team's losses for August total 101 killed, 494 wounded, 129 missing and 403 non-battle casualties.

The NKPA usually mounted two attacks every night against Able Company's perimeter. A young squad leader from Paragould, Arkansas, Corporal John Back, and another soldier manned one of eight machine guns that company commander Lieutenant Hank

Korea: The Fluid War

Emerson had demanded to defend his hard-pressed turf. When the North Koreans commenced their second attack of the night, Corporal Back and his buddy opened up with their machine gun, killing numerous enemy soldiers who were trying to maneuver through the barbed wire apron in front of the company perimeter. Unfortunately, one well thrown hand grenade landed in the hole shared by Back and his assistant gunner. The force of the explosion knocked Back out of the hole and killed his comrade.

Back quickly discovered that shrapnel had nearly severed one of his feet at the ankle. Hot fragments had punctured his body. In agony, he crawled back to the gun and, just as the North Koreans burst through the barbed wire, opened up with the machine gun, killing more than thirty enemy soldiers at point-blank range. He shattered the NKPA assault.

Lieutenant Hank Emerson, CO of Company A, recommended CPL John Back for the Distinguished Service Cross. Much later, the award was downgraded to the Silver Star by some rear-echelon staff officer. It was not until well after the war that LTG Hank Emerson learned that his squad leader was 17-years-old the night that he made his historic stand (15).

On 7 September, the 25th Division issued verbal orders for the 5th RCT to prepare for a relief in place. General Walker intended to pull the regiment off the line and place it in reserve near Taegu. However, what was left of the NKPA 6th Division wasn't going to let them depart easily. The North Koreans took advantage of an overcast sky on the night of 9 September to attack the 2nd Battalion. The G.I.'s, hampered by poor visibility, had difficulty seeing their targets.

Suddenly, the destroyer *U.S.S. Whiltsie*, steaming off the south coast of Korea, turned night into day by training her searchlights on the low clouds. Caught in the glare of reflected light, the NKPA troops were blasted off the hill. The 2nd Battalion was relieved the following day. For them, the battle of Sobuk-san was finally over.

One would think that 3rd Battalion, posted on the extreme left flank of the Pusan Perimeter near Chindong-ni, would have been the most embattled of the three rifle battalions of the regiment during the battle of Sobuk-san. That was not the case. The NKPA's concerted efforts to punch through the American defenses were focused farther to the north. The NKPA 83rd Mechanized did conduct a series of battalion-sized attacks on September 2 at the point where 3rd Battalion tied in with 2nd Battalion.

George Company's defensive fire, coupled with a cross fire from Fox Company's automatic weapons and 324 rounds delivered by the 60mm mortar section slowed the attack long enough for Air Force jets to swoop in and deliver the coup de grace. During the attack, one platoon from Love Company was pushed off its portion of the ridge but, following the air strike, was able to counterattack and regain its position. Private Earl Miller, a .50 caliber gunner from Company G received the Distinguished Service Cross posthumously for his role in this fight near Chindong-ni (16).

The 3rd Battalion did suffer losses as a result of patrol ambushes and indirect fire from Soviet manufactured 120mm mortars. They also suffered several casualties when a U.S. Navy destroyer mistakingly opened fire on a 3rd Battalion patrol. Communications with the Navy had to be routed through the 25th Division's Fire Support Control Center. The process was cumbersome and time-consuming.

Following their fight for Sobuk-san, the men of the 5th RCT moved to a small abandoned town near Taegu, surrounded by fruit orchards, vineyards, and corn fields. A rolling PX delivered chewing gum, beer, candy, cokes and milk. They got a chance to rest and prepare for the long awaited counteroffensive.

Waegwan

The 5th Regimental Combat Team was attached to the 1st Cavalry Division on 14 September. It went into an assembly area west of Taegu along the east bank of the Naktong River, six miles below Waegwan.

The following day, the Korean War entered a new phase when the 1st Marine Division and the 7th Infantry Division landed at Inchon, trapping the North Korean Army between them and the 8th Army on the Pusan Perimeter. The counter-offensive was on. The Eighth Army, under-strength and short of ammunition and bridge-building equipment, would have to strike fast to penetrate the NKPA's defensive line and join the race to Seoul. The 5th RCT was assigned the mission of spearheading the breakout from the Pusan Perimeter in the vicinity of Waegwan, a small town located on the Naktong River approximately fourteen miles northwest of Taegu.

The Naktong, which flowed north to south, was a natural barrier in this area of the front. A highway bridge and a railroad bridge spanning the river had been blown during earlier fighting but the North Koreans had repaired them enough to accommodate foot traffic. They had also created an underwater bridge of sandbags to the north of Waegwan. The bridges and the ford could be observed from Hill 268 to the south of the town. The hill would have to be taken before the infantry could cross the river.

Approximately one-third of the NKPA 3rd Division's troops had survived the summer's fighting. They were well protected in deep bunkers covered by logs and dirt. Their positions were connected by narrow trenches surrounded by barbed wire entanglements. Approximately 1200 North Korean soldiers defended the south approaches to Waegwan.

On the morning of September 16, the 1st Cavalry Division received word of the successful landing at Inchon. The 5th Cavalry and 5th RCT were immediately ordered to clear the high ground to their front in preparation for the main assault that would begin the following day. Overcast skies and intermittent rain prevented the use of close air support. The well-dug-in NKPA troops contested every inch of ground. The attack by the 5th Cavalry, reinforced by 2nd Battalion,

8th Cavalry, bogged down. Both units suffered heavy casualties.

Second Battalion, 5th Infantry, advanced against light resistance until it reached the vicinity of Hill 154, a small rise on the east bank of the river. At that point, the battalion came under heavy fire from automatic weapons and self-propelled guns. Field guns, located in caves on the west bank of the river, fired high explosive air bursts, showering the men of 2nd Battalion with shrapnel and wood splinters. The heavily forested ground near the river was a death trap for many of the men.

When 1st Platoon of Easy Company came upon a nest of four 45mm antitank guns, M/SGT John Jeal ordered the platoon into a defilade position while he charged the emplacement directly to draw fire. He was decapitated by an antitank round. Corporal Bobby Smith fired his BAR until he was out of clips and then took over a machine gun from a wounded crew. He delivered accurate fire that helped to protect the survivors of the pinned-down platoon until reinforcements arrived. When the platoon was once more able to advance, CPL Smith was wounded severely. Another member of Easy Company, SGT Benjamin Poinciano, was mortally wounded after taking out a machine gun nest that was slowing the advance of 2nd Battalion. Sergeants Jeal and Poinciano and CPL Smith became three more posthumous recipients of the Distinguished Service Cross.

John Throckmorton led from the front throughout the day, map in hand, as explosive shells burst around him. That evening he decided to revise his plan. In the morning, 3rd Battalion would take the right fork in the road and envelop Hill 268 from the east. The 2nd Battalion would continue its frontal assault toward Hill 140 and 1st Battalion would remain in reserve. Intermittent shellfire slammed into 2nd Battalion throughout the night killing and wounding more men.

The 2nd Battalion pushed off early in the morning of the 17th, determined to seize Hill 140's heavily defended crest. Easy Company advanced parallel to the river with George Company on its left flank.

KOREA: THE FLUID WAR

When Company G ran into a hornet's nest of mutually supporting machine guns, Corporal Arnold Ching hurled one grenade after another until all of the guns were silenced and 2nd Battalion was able to advance and overrun the smoking ruins of the NKPA bunkers on the crest of the hill.

Third Battalion set out early in the morning, accompanied by a platoon of three Sherman tanks. Three days of rain had turned the dirt road into deep muck and the tanks were soon mired. The infantry slogged forward and soon began receiving artillery and mortar fire. At that point, LTC Benjamin Heckmeyer received a radio message that his battalion had overshot a checkpoint and was in danger of missing Hill 268 altogether.

Once the battalion was reoriented, the forward elements discovered another piece of high ground between their column and Hill 268. This was Hill 160, a narrow E-shaped ridge running north to south with three fingers running downhill to the east. King Company was ordered to attack up the middle finger of Hill 160 and seize the crest. Love Company was to attack up the southern finger.

The NKPA opened up with automatic weapons fire as the King Company soldiers clambered up the hill. The company commander, CPT Joseph Lukitsch, requested artillery fire. King Company's weapons platoon began dropping 60mm mortar rounds on the crest while the three rifle platoons swept the area with automatic weapons fire.

Captain Lukitsch wanted to coordinate his assault with Love Company's attack and was alarmed to see that Love was pinned down over on his left by seemingly light enemy fire. Attempts to reach CPT Frank Hula, CO of Love Company, on his SCR-300 radio failed. Lukitsch ordered LT Randall Beirne, his weapons platoon leader, to go over to the left and get Love Company moving. He also told SGT William McCraine, his 3rd Platoon leader to swing left and attack through Love Company.

When Lieutenant Beirne reached Love Company, he saw groups of soldiers sitting on the ground. No one was moving or firing. One group was gathered around a dying Captain Hula, who had received a nasty head wound from a sniper's bullet. Beirne found 2nd LT James Young, Love Company's surviving senior officer and told him to get his men moving up the hill. As Beirne explained the tactical situation to Young, SGT McCraine's platoon barreled through the motionless men, weapons at the ready and closed for the kill on the North Korean troops. By the time Lieutenant Young got his men moving, McCraine's platoon was on top of the NKPA, hurling grenades into their foxholes and shooting the enemy who attempted to flee down the reverse slope toward Hill 268. The platoon didn't suffer a single casualty (18).

When Captain Lukitsch saw his 3rd Platoon hit the enemy position, he led the 1st and 2nd Platoons in an assault up the finger. There was no cover and they took a number of casualties. Once 1st Platoon reached the top of the hill, it swung right and rolled up the enemy dug in on the northern half of Hill 160. Lieutenant Beirne counted sixteen North Korean bodies on the crest of Hill 160. More enemy bodies lay farther down the slope. Love and King Companies split Hill 160 in half and dug in for the night, flooring their muddy fox holes with pine needles.

Toward sundown, Sergeant Frank Van Antwerp of Medical Company was advancing with an infantry platoon when they came under intense fire while out in the open. Van Antwerp crawled among the pinned down members of the platoon administering aid to the wounded. The arrival of darkness and heavy rain soon made his job more miserable and more difficult but he continued to care for and encourage the wounded men. When his medical supplies were exhausted, he crawled among the men to collect first aid packets and used them until they were all gone. Van Antwerp was crawling forward in an attempt to evacuate a wounded buddy when he fell victim to enemy fire. The fight for Waegwan had yielded another posthumous recipient of the Distinguished Service Cross (19).

Korea: The Fluid War

North Korean mortar and tank fire blasted Hill 160 throughout the hours of darkness leading to additional casualties. Between artillery barrages, the NKPA blew whistles to play on the frayed nerves of the G.I.'s. Ammunition and rations finally arrived at first light on 18 September along with orders to assault Hill 268.

The 5th RCT commenced its full regimental attack that morning. The 1st and 2nd Battalions attacked due north through the NKPA's defensive maze. Enemy machine guns were usually not discovered until they were firing point-blank into an advancing group of soldiers. Squad and platoon leaders used their automatic weapons to suppress each NKPA machine gun long enough for other riflemen to crawl forward and take out the gun crews with grenades.

The 1st Battalion ran into enemy T-34 tanks as it advanced on its objective, Hill 178. The tanks were apparently low on high explosive ammunition for their main guns and were firing armor piercing shells that had little effect on the advancing infantry. A man from Able Company, armed with one of the new 3.5-inch bazookas, crawled down a ditch toward a T-34 until he was within fifteen feet of the tank. His shot blew up the tank but he was too close to his target and was killed by the spray of shrapnel.

Meanwhile the North Koreans resisted 2nd Battalion's attack on Hill 121 with small arms and light machine guns coupled with flanking fire that was coming from antitank guns and T-34's located in caves on the western bank of the river. When the skies cleared, forty-two B-29 bombers appeared over Waegwan and dropped their loads of 500 pound bombs on the west bank in a tight, concentrated pattern, silencing the sources of the enfilade fire.

Third Battalion moved out at 0700 to attack Hill 268. King Company was halfway up the slope when they were met with automatic weapons fire. They went to ground and called for artillery support. Fire from the 555th FAB soon impacted the enemy emplacements that were scattered among five knob-like features on the hill.

Sergeant McCraine's platoon took ten casualties as it advanced up a draw that was covered by a Soviet Maxim heavy machine gun emplaced in a pillbox. McCraine and a squad leader, CPL Caen, worked around to the left of the pillbox and then crawled close enough to hurl a couple of grenades through the bunker's aperture. After the grenades and the ammunition stored within exploded in a tremendous blast, SGT McCraine and CPL Caen jumped into the enemy position and killed the handful of survivors. The 3rd Platoon then rushed forward and peeled off, left and right, to dispatch the NKPA defenders in nearby foxholes. Sergeant McCraine eventually received the Silver Star for his role in the fight for Waegwan.

Meanwhile, M/SGT Kermit Jackson and a squad-sized skirmish line were advancing up Knob Two toward a ring of foxholes when grenades began landing among the group, wounding three of its members. Jackson hurled three grenades at the foxholes, got the men to their feet and charged up the hill. They shot those North Koreans who had survived the exploding grenades, punching a hole in their defensive line. Then, concealing themselves behind a line of trees, they took the remaining defenders from the rear with grenades and small arms fire. Sergeant Jackson, a veteran of Anzio, had a problem with shooting men in the back. Each time he drew a bead, he would yell, "Turn around, you dirty S.O.B!" before eliminating them, one-by-one, with his M-1. The surviving enemy soldiers broke and ran towards Knobs Three, Four and Five.

The men of Item Company had been assigned the remaining three knobs. They quickly overran Knob Three but ran into very heavy automatic weapons fire and grenade explosions on Four and Five. They pulled back and called for artillery support and then resumed the attack after the last rounds had impacted. The NKPA defenders had survived the artillery barrage in deep bunkers. When Item Company came within twenty-five yards, the North Koreans opened up with machine guns, burp guns, rifles and grenades. The enemy fire killed ten G.I's and wounded many more.

Back on Knob Two, men from King Company's weapons platoon spotted a T-34 tank on the road next to the hill. It was out of bazooka range, but the second of two rounds from their 57mm recoilless rifle hit a soft spot and the tank swerved off the road and stopped. As the men were celebrating their lucky shot, they noticed that the survivors of Item Company were staggering back toward them. The company had been ordered to withdraw to a more defensible position. A few members of K Company along with able-bodied survivors of Item Company found some concealment behind the tree line as they returned to Knob 5 to gather up Item Company's wounded riflemen.

By nightfall, the 3rd Battalion had seized four of the five knobs on Hill 268. First Battalion was pinned down 500 yards short of its objective, Hill 178, while the men in 2nd Battalion were dug in on the crest of Hill 121 overlooking Waegwan.

Organic to the 24th Infantry Division

At 1800 hours on the 18th of September, the 5th RCT was detached from the 1st Cavalry Division in order to replace the 34th Infantry Regiment of the 24th Division. The 34th had gone into action in July with 2,000 men. Two months later, its 184 survivors were parceled out to the 24th's remaining regiments, the 19th and 21st.

By 19 September, news of the Inchon landing reached the ranks of the NKPA in the Waegwan area and their resistance began to soften. The 1st and 2nd Battalions seized Waegwan and overran an NKPA engineer unit attempting to lay a mine field in their path.

The 2nd Battalion continued its attack north of Waegwan toward Hill 303. Over 300 dead North Koreans were counted during the advance. Most of them had been victims of artillery and air strikes as they tried to flee northward on crowded roads. Much enemy equipment was captured, including an intact T-34 tank found by a patrol from 1st Battalion.

Item Company drew the short straw and moved up to the line of departure to lead the attack on Knob Five on Hill 268. Before they jumped off, a flight of P-51's hit the objective with rockets and napalm. When the planes departed, artillery blasted the hill with delay-fused shells. This was joined by the 2nd Battalion's 81mm mortars and 75mm recoilless rifles.

As the last 105mm and 81mm shells impacted Hill 268, Item Company moved out and met no resistance at Knob Three. When they reached Knob Four, however, they discovered that Knob Five was still defended by die-hard North Koreans who had survived the napalm and artillery fire. The G.I's were caught in the open and subjected to intense automatic weapons fire. The North Koreans, outmanned and outgunned, fought to the death. By noon, the hill was secured.

With the collapse of Hill 268, the NKPA line was flanked. The enemy soldiers pulled out of their positions, abandoning supplies and equipment that they could not physically carry. Ironically, they left 268 dead comrades on Hill 268.

On 20 September, the 5th RCT killed over a hundred North Koreans who attempted to escape from the trap by swimming across the Naktong. The 72nd Engineers cleared a path through a mine field and built bypasses at the blown bridges. As they worked, they were under continual enemy fire. The combat team captured nineteen prisoners, three SU-76 self-propelled guns and over a thousand rounds of tank ammunition. By nightfall, the 1st and 2nd Battalions were awaiting orders to cross the river.

As the men of the 5th RCT gathered on the banks of the Naktong that evening, morale was high, despite their heavy losses. They had punched a big hole in the NKPA's perimeter, liberated Waegwan and secured their river crossing. Although headlines back home would proclaim, "1st Cavalry Division Seizes Waegwan," John Throckmorton and his soldiers knew better. Third Battalion's receipt of a Distinguished Unit Citation for Bloody Gulch may have been questionable but its courageous effort at Waegwan demonstrated that it was, indeed, a distinguished unit.

Breakout from the Perimeter

The 1st Battalion crossed the river at 2035 on the evening of September 20th. The assault boats were manned by the 3rd Combat Engineer Battalion. First Battalion's initial objective was the high ground about one hundred yards south of the railroad bridge. Charlie Company led the assault. Able and Baker companies mistook a sandbar in the middle of the river for the west bank and exited their assault boats prematurely. They had to wade the rest of the way and, in the confusion, failed to link up with Charlie Company. They moved ahead and secured the high ground to their front. At daybreak, Charlie Company seized the high ground on the combat team's left flank. To help maintain the momentum of the advance, the 3rd Combat Engineers started ferrying the 5th RCT's vehicles across the Naktong.

On 22 September, the combat team was assigned the task of mopping up the by-passed NKPA units in the hills astride the main supply route. As they patrolled aggressively, they accepted the surrender of isolated groups of North Koreans.

That evening, LTC Throckmorton received orders to advance and capture Kumchon where remnants of the NKPA 105th Armored Division and the 1st Regiment, 9th Division had decided to make a stand. Their spirited defense had succeeded in holding up the 21st Infantry's advance.

The 1st Battalion passed through the 21st Infantry's lines at 2130. Baker Company was mounted on the decks of Tank Company's Shermans. When T-34's and antitank guns took the 5th RCT's tanks under fire, the men from Baker Company scrambled off and took positions on higher ground on both sides of the road. Losses began to mount and the advance slowed.

The crew of the lead Sherman was in a fight for its life and those tanks behind them couldn't deploy because of the steep banks on both sides of the road. The NKPA 849th Independent Antitank Regiment, situated on Hill 140, formed the backbone of the defense of Kumchon. Its T-34s and antitank guns fought a ferocious and skillful rearguard action that kept the 5th RCT from entering the town that night and all the next day.

When dawn broke on the 23rd, LTC Throckmorton was up front leading his rifle companies and tank platoons and coordinating the combat team's supporting arms. At one point, the Rock advanced 300 yards ahead of his lead rifle company to direct the fire of one of his tank platoons. Antitank fire struck two tanks as Throckmorton stood calmly in the open, pointing out targets to his tank commanders.

Supported by FEAF ground attack aircraft, the 5th RCT fought its way through successive enemy defensive lines. Eight T-34's attempted to bar the advance. Five were reduced to smoldering wreckage by napalm and rockets. Bazooka teams knocked out the other three. Nevertheless, Able and Baker Companies, attacking up the right and left sides of the road, continued to suffer heavy casualties to automatic weapons fire.

The 2nd Battalion came abreast of the 1st Battalion in the afternoon and attacked, through heavy fire, toward Hill 140. When George Company became pinned down by heavy automatic weapons fire, Fox Company attacked through them and gained a toehold on the hill. Before the remainder of Company F could join them, the company commander received orders to withdraw from Hill 140 and prepare for a night attack on a new objective.

Lieutenant James Johnson and his platoon of combat engineers were ordered to clear some mines that were holding up the advance. The engineers, supported by a few tanks, started to clear a lane through the minefield that straddled the road to Kumchon. Before they could complete the task, an expertly camouflaged NKPA machine gun crew, located on the left side of the road, opened up on the engineers. They

KOREA: THE FLUID WAR

took cover in a ditch on the right side of the road.

As LT Johnson threw a grenade, one tank crew closed the hatch and began firing blindly into the engineers. One of the bullets grazed Johnson's thigh and killed one of his men. Johnson limped over to the Easy Eight, grabbed the tank-infantry phone and yelled "You son of a bitch! If you fire one more round on that side of the road, I will personally blow you to kingdom come." The engineers were soon able to eliminate the machine gun and clear the road of mines.

The 3rd Battalion remained in reserve on 24 September as its rifle companies were far below their authorized strength. K Company, which began the assault on Waegwan with 160 soldiers, had dwindled to 78. An average of eighteen men remained in each rifle platoon.

The following morning the 5th RCT renewed its attack in conjunction with the 21st Infantry. While the 2nd Battalion destroyed an NKPA detachment that was dug in on the reverse slope of Hill 140, the 1st Battalion was heavily engaged with the remnants of an enemy battalion that barred its advance. The 3rd Battalion moved into Kumchon, fought house-to-house with NKPA defenders and had secured the town by 1445 hours.

Throughout the day, the 555th FAB had killed numerous North Koreans while the 72nd Engineer Company had cleared the road of mines. One of the engineers, SFC Charles Carroll, had actually walked ahead of the lead tank, during a combined infantry and tank attack, removing mines as the column proceeded. He stayed with the task until he was killed by machine gun fire (20). He was the one combat engineer in the 5th RCT to receive the Distinguished Service Cross. In 1959, Camp Carroll, a maintenance and supply storage base for all U.S. Army units currently in Korea, was constructed in Waegwan.

In two days of fighting the 5th RCT lost seventeen KIA and ninety-two wounded. Surgeon William Hedberg braved heavy fire to aid the wounded soldiers lying on the battlefield. He earned the undying admiration of the men and the Silver Star for gallantry.

The North Koreans suffered heavy losses at Kumchon. Several units, including the 849th Independent Antitank Regiment, fought to the last man. Their sacrifice enabled thousands of hardcore NKPA troops to escape north. Lieutenant Colonel Throckmorton received the Distinguished Service Cross for gallantry in action during the fighting at Waegwan and Kumchon (21).

While the 5th RCT continued to patrol and capture NKPA stragglers, Tank Company was temporarily attached to the 19th Infantry to spearhead its drive on Taejon. Tank Company's smaller Easy 8's were better suited than the 6th Tank Battalion's M-46 Pattons to lead a high speed chase over Korea's narrow roads and bridges. They engaged in numerous fights throughout the day, supported by flights of P-51 fighters manned by Australian and South African pilots. The tankers continued their advance during the early evening hours until they reached Okchon, seventy miles from their line of departure. At that point, having exhausted their fuel, they stopped and rested until the heavier Pattons and fuel trucks could catch up with them. The following morning the 6th Tank Battalion led the advance into Taejon while Tank Company circled the wagons to await the arrival of the 5th RCT.

During a lull in fighting, replacements began to arrive. The combat team received 232 replacements and 69 returned-to-duty personnel during September. The 5th Infantry was still some 1300 men below its authorized strength of 3792. The 555th FAB was in better shape with 670 of 678 authorized. The 72nd Engineers, with an authorized strength of 169 men, was down to 116 combat engineers. Seven hundred and forty-one KATUSA (Korean Augmentation to the U.S. Army) soldiers were serving in the 5th RCT at this time.

Invasion of North Korea

Failure of the United Nations forces to crush the North Korean Army, while it was south of the 38th Parallel, prompted General MacArthur and the UN Command to order an invasion of North Korea. Since a hammer and anvil maneuver had led to a successful landing at Inchon and breakout from the Pusan Perimeter, MacArthur built his plan for the invasion of North Korea around the same concept. Tenth Corps would conduct an amphibious landing on the east coast at Wonsan as the Eighth Army attacked up the west coast.

However, due to logistical problems, there was neither a hammer nor an anvil. Most of the Eighth Army's trucks and fuel were diverted to transport the 7th Infantry Division to Pusan where it would board amphibious assault ships bound for Wonsan. The port of Inchon was tied up by the 1st Marine Division which was heading in the same direction. The Eighth Army remained stalled south of the 38th Parallel until sufficient transportation was available.

On the 17th of October, the 5th RCT crossed into North Korea. The convoy proceeded north to Tongjang-ni, where the infantry dismounted and hiked, in the darkness and pouring rain, to Paekchon. One hundred and ninety-three bypassed NKPA stragglers surrendered during the advance.

The combat team moved north on deeply rutted, muddy roads along the west coast, alternating between traveling on foot and in the back of bouncing trucks. Along the way, they were greeted by North Korean civilians, who appeared very happy to see their liberators as they waved tiny American flags from the side of the road.

The nights had turned bitterly cold. When an issue of sleeping bags arrived, there were not enough to provide one for each man. LTC Throckmorton assigned the bags to the rifle companies. Everyone else would continue to rely on blankets and ponchos to stay warm. Throckmorton also demanded strict noise and light discipline from his soldiers. He forbade warming fires within the perimeter. The shivering men of the 5th RCT, glancing to their left and right, could see the warm campfires clearly marking the defensive positions of their neighbors; the 19th Infantry and 1st Cavalry Regiments. Many had mixed feelings about their tough regimental commander, whose brand of discipline would guide them through the coming months.

At 1730 on October 19, 1950, the first wave of the Chinese Peoples Volunteer Forces, who had removed all Chinese Army insignias from their uniforms, crossed the Yalu River and entered North Korea. This first group of 450,000 men, constituting eighteen infantry divisions, three artillery divisions and seven thousand support troops deployed in such a rapid and unexpected manner that it would be nearly a week before their presence came to the attention of the attacking U. N. troops.

Meanwhile, when the X Corps arrived off Wonsan, the navy discovered that the port was heavily mined and that their minesweeping units were insufficient to clear the necessary lanes to land the amphibious force on schedule. This resulted in a delayed capture of Wonsan by the ROK Army in an overland advance as the navy struggled to clear the mines.

The delay at Wonsan saved the NKPA from annihilation. The surviving North Korean soldiers found sanctuary in the rugged and frozen mountains adjacent to Manchuria and Siberia. The Wonsan operation had failed to act as a hammer to the Eighth Army's anvil and, more importantly, had served as a logistical drain on the Eighth Army's offensive. Advancing to the Yalu River would require fuel, ammunition and food; commodities that had been rendered scarce as a result of MacArthur's plan. On 21 October, LTC Throckmorton had to announce that rations would henceforth be restricted to "two meals per day or 3 meals per day at 2/3 quantity."

As the 5th RCT pushed deeper into North Korea, enemy troops surrendered in droves. In one week, 893 North Korean soldiers surrendered to the combat team. The 5th RCT reached Anjong-ni on 22 October, capturing 84 more NKPA stragglers without a fight. One soldier was wounded the next day during a brief firefight that resulted in the capture of 36 more North Korean troops. When the regiment reached Sinanju on 25 October, without encountering any resistance,

Korea: The Fluid War

the North Korean Army's disintegration appeared complete. Everyone thought the war was almost over. However, one of the North Korean troops that the 5th RCT captured on 25 October claimed to have seen 2500-3000 Chinese troops in Yongsan and another two to three hundred Chinese in the vicinity of Taechon.

Taechon fell to the 5th RCT on 29 October. Two of the 89 POW's taken during the day's advance were from the Chinese Peoples Volunteers. The combat team had captured the first Chinese troops to be taken prisoner in Korea. However, General MacArthur had staked his professional reputation on his firm belief that Red China would not come to North Korea's aid this late in the conflict. When the 5th RCT's Chinese prisoners were sent to the 24th Division S-2 for interrogation, nobody believed they were Chinese. At this stage of the war, reports that there were sizeable Chinese ground combat units in Korea were either ignored or interpreted in such a way that they agreed with MacArthur's strategic view.

Meanwhile, the remnants of the NKPA were making a remarkable recovery in their mountain strongholds. As the Eighth Army got closer to the Yalu, it encountered increasingly stiffer resistance from North Korean units.

From Taechon, the 5th RCT attacked northwest towards Kusong. The 3rd Battalion led the advance. When they bogged down amidst mortar and artillery fire, Throckmorton ordered the 1st Battalion to move up on the 3rd Battalion's left. The North Koreans gave ground reluctantly. Air Force B-26 bombers pounded the defenders and Kusong finally fell on Halloween Day.

On 1 November, the 1st Battalion attacked northward up a narrow valley into fierce enemy automatic weapons and mortar fire. A combined force of 5000 Chinese and NKPA soldiers had dug in to fight. Tank Company's 2nd Platoon supported the advance, firing high explosive shells into the enemy positions. Captain Hank Emerson's Able Company infiltrated the Chinese lines during the night and emerged at the rear of an enemy infantry company that was dug in on the forward slope of a ridgeline. As the Chinese fired down into the valley at other elements of the 1st Battalion, the men of Company A wiped out the surprised rifle company.

By sunset, the combat team had killed approximately four hundred NKPA and CCF soldiers, destroyed two self-propelled guns, eight 76mm field guns, eight mortars and six antitank guns. In one village, where all the huts were burning, the ammunition laboriously stored by the enemy had begun to cook off and explode.

Late that afternoon, a courier plane dropped a message to LTC Throckmorton ordering a halt to the combat team's northward advance. A few hours later, he was ordered to head south to Sinanju on the Chongchon River. After conducting a relatively unopposed advance to the Yalu River, the Eighth Army had entered a massive, carefully planned Chinese trap. One hundred and eighty thousand Chinese troops were poised to strike. Another 120,000 Chinese were preparing to annihilate the X Corps in the vicinity of the Changjin Reservoir.

When it reached the Chongchon River, the 5th RCT was hustled to the town of Kunu-ri which straddled an important road junction. Kunu-ri had to be held at all costs to back up the remnants of the ROK 7th Division.

The Chinese slammed into the ROK 7th Division the next morning and forced the ROK 5th Regiment off Hill 622, a key prominence overlooking the Kunu-ri crossroads. Company A of the 5th RCT halted and reorganized the fleeing ROK soldiers and ordered them to retake their former positions. The ROK's rallied and counterattacked, kicking the Chinese off the crest of the hill. The hill changed hands several times throughout the day, but, when the sun set, the battered and bloodied ROK's were back on top.

Meanwhile, overcast skies enabled the Chinese to hit other sections of the combat team's line without fear of UN air attacks. With bugles blaring and whistles shrilling, the Chinese infantry ran forward firing burp guns and rifles from the hip and hurling grenades.

The gun crews of the 555th set their 105mm howitzers for high angle fire and slammed hundreds of high explosive shells into the enemy ranks. The Chinese continued to attack, probing for a weak point in the 5th RCT's line.

A recoilless rifle squad in How Company had traded its recoilless rifle for another .50 caliber machine gun. Many of the Chinese that assaulted How Company's positions were soon lying in piles of bloody rags. PFC Gene McClure recalled "There were so many that you could not miss...But still they came on, and on, endless ranks of them (22)."

Within forty-five minutes to an hour, the CCF soldiers had increased their fire from positions they had taken on a hill three hundred yards to the front. When all other infantrymen had left the hill, PFC McClure's squad salvaged the barrel of the .50 caliber MG, placed a thermite grenade in the breech and withdrew.

Charlie Company drew considerable enemy fire as it defended a heavily wooded area. After 1st Platoon leader, LT Morgan Hansel and the company's first sergeant had been killed trying to silence a Chinese machine gun, Sergeant Hibbert Manley took command of 1st Platoon and had its survivors pull back a short distance and dig in. From there, they repulsed the Chinese. Many of the enemy soldiers were gunned down by Corporal Jake Kahaihipuna with a towel-wrapped machine gun in his massive arms. For his actions on that day, CPL Kahaihipuna was awarded the Silver Star.

Dog Company's 81mm mortar platoon fired as fast as the assistant gunners could drop rounds down their smoking tubes. Within an hour the mortar platoon had killed and wounded scores of Chinese. Service Company did a magnificent job throughout the day keeping the mortars supplied with ammunition.

The 5th RCT's stand at Kunu-ri temporarily stabilized the Eighth Army's hard-pressed lines but the combat team's casualties had soared since the active intervention of the Chinese. From 28 October to 4 November, the 5th RCT had suffered 97 battle losses, more casualties than during the first twenty-seven days of October.

Home by Christmas Offensive

Following the entrance of the Chinese into the war, and the near destruction of the 8th Cavalry at Unsan, General Walker concluded that he had neither the men, supplies, nor equipment to sustain an offensive toward the Yalu River. His infantry divisions now averaged thirty per cent of their authorized strength. Nonetheless, General MacArthur ordered Walton Walker to advance to the Yalu without delay.

General Walker had the choice of protesting his orders or remaining commanding general of the Eighth Army. He elected not to dispute MacArthur and to remain at his post. In private, he instructed his officers to exercise extreme caution in the forthcoming offensive and to break off attack in the event of stiff Chinese resistance. Three hundred thousand Chinese troops were poised to offer just that.

On 23 November, the combat team's soldiers enjoyed a traditional Thanksgiving Day turkey dinner. They were thankful to be alive, in relatively good health, and grateful that the weather had warmed up to a high of forty degrees. A number of men in K Company wore North Korean winter uniforms to dinner. U. S. Army cold winter gear had not arrived in sufficient quantities, so the soldiers had had to make do with the quilted over-garments that they had liberated from a North Korean warehouse.

The 5th RCT had been receiving the dirty end of the stick since it had been detached from the 25th Division in September. There was a marked disparity in manpower between the combat team and the 24th Division's two organic regiments; the 19th and the 21st. It would be returning to action with approximately five hundred fewer soldiers than either of the other two regiments but would be assigned missions equivalent to those of the 19th and 21st. Soldiers in the 5th RCT were proud of being part of a "bastard" outfit, one that seemed to be assigned wherever the situation was most desperate.

On 24 November, the 24th Infantry Division crossed the line of departure and advanced on the Eighth Army's extreme left flank. Chinese small arms and mortar fire increasingly annoyed the 5th RCT on its first day of the "Home by Christmas" offensive.

The Communist Chinese Forces launched their counteroffensive at dusk on November 25. Tens of thousands of lightly armed Chinese troops double-timed toward predetermined attack positions to the sound of bugles and the light of parachute flares. The Eighth Army had no time to call in artillery support before the battle was joined. The ROK II Corps, on the right of the line, was soon decimated and the U.S. 2nd Division, especially the 9th Infantry, incurred heavy losses. The 3rd Battalion, 9th Infantry was virtually wiped out, reduced to thirty-seven men after a couple of days of fierce combat.

MacArthur's spin on the "Home by Christmas Offensive" was that it was actually a reconnaissance in force and that it had successfully forced the Chinese to show their hand. He would go on to claim that the Eighth Army's 7337 casualties plus the 5638 suffered by X Corps were "about half the loss at Iwo Jima, less than one-fifth of that of Okinawa and even less in comparison with the Battle of the Bulge (23)." He omitted mentioning that the American victories on Iwo Jima and Okinawa, and in the Ardennes, were fought over a longer period than the few days it took for the CCF to defeat the Eighth Army and the X Corps. Within days of the Chinese counteroffensive, a battered Eighth Army commenced the longest retreat in the history of the United States Army.

The Chinese attack on 25 November did not strike the 24th Division in strength, so the 5th RCT was spared the dismal fate of many other American infantry units. On 26 November, the 24th Division was ordered to hold up until the deteriorating situation on other sectors of the front could be clarified. The combat team dug in on the division's right flank where it tied in with the ROK 1st Division.

At 2200 on 27 November, the offensive officially ended when I Corps issued orders to all commanders to commence a withdrawal the following morning. As these orders were disseminated, 3rd Battalion, 5th RCT occupied a perimeter defense on a low hill east of the main north-south supply route. The 2nd Battalion had dug in on another hill west of the MSR.

At 0255, King Company's position on the left side of the hill was hit by a rain of concussion grenades and machine gun fire. During the ensuing fight, the Chinese assault battalions suffered 150 casualties. A wounded SFC Charles Falk remained with his mortar crew adjusting the fire of an 81mm mortar on waves of attacking Chinese. His courage and skill were recognized with a Distinguished Service Cross (24).

When the 3rd Battalion commander ordered King and Love Companies off the hill, the exhausted CCF soldiers had no desire to pursue. King Company had suffered 29 casualties. When Company K's commanding officer, CPT Lukitsch, requested permission to counterattack and retrieve the bodies of the dead, permission was denied. The 3rd Battalion moved out at 0700 and headed for the combat team's assembly area north of Anju.

The 5th RCT was detached from the 24th Division and ordered to set up blocking positions to protect two bridges spanning the Chongchon River. It held the crossing sites as remnants of the Eight Army limped across the river. The soldiers of the combat team shivered in their foxholes as wind chill dropped the temperature to twenty-two degrees below zero.

When the 23rd Infantry, 2nd Division reached the Chongchon River, COL Paul Freeman inquired as to what outfit was securing the bridge. Upon hearing CPT Emerson's reply, he said, "Well, God bless A Company, 5th RCT!" The 23rd Infantry had made a narrow escape several hours earlier and was grateful to find a bridge securely held by friendly forces (25).

Korea: The Fluid War

When the 23rd Infantry had crossed the river, John Throckmorton, who had just received word of his promotion to Colonel, ordered Able Company to turn their trucks over to the 23rd Infantry and then to remain in position, on the south bank of the Chongchon, as long as possible to give the rest of the 5th RCT a head start. At 1915 hours the bridges were blown. Able Company crowded onto the engine decks of five tanks and moved out in pursuit of the combat team. Several cases of frostbite resulted from the exposed ride on the Easy-8's.

The 5th RCT served as rear guard throughout the retirement to Pyongyang. Losses during the week of 25 November to 2 December included 63 Battle and 37 non-battle casualties. On 2 December, the 5th RCT received the Combat Infantry Streamer in honor of its fine fighting performance.

Many of the soldiers, still in leather combat boots and cotton field jackets, would rather have skipped the battle streamer in favor of shoe-packs, parkas, and other winterized gear. Although the withdrawing army was not under significant enemy pressure, a panic developed among rear echelon supply personnel who set a torch to immense stocks of cold weather garments. At one point, members of the combat team witnessed new tanks being destroyed because there was no fuel to move them, and then, five miles further down the road, they saw someone blow up a fuel dump. On the plus side, the S-4 of 1st Battalion was able to rescue fourteen abandoned trucks, in good working order, more than replacing those that had been relinquished to the 23rd Infantry.

On 2 December, the 5th RCT was returned to the 24th Division and immediately set out for Yul-li to set up a blocking position. Colonel Throckmorton implemented a standard policy of having his battalions leapfrog from one point to another. The advance battalion would drive until it reached a piece of high ground along the route of withdrawal. Here, the rifle companies would dismount and dig in to form a perimeter defense. Once the main body and the rear guard battalion had passed through, the advance guard would assume the position of rear guard and the process would be repeated.

The 5th RCT occupied its blocking position at Yul-li from 4-7 December before rejoining the withdrawal in the direction of Uijongbu. On the evening of 13 December, 3rd Battalion's supply trains were overrun in a surprise attack conducted by North Korean guerrillas dressed in civilian clothes. Under heavy pressure, K Company retreated to the perimeter of Charlie Battery, 555th FAB. The gunners from Battery C fired point blank at the guerrillas throughout the night. The North Koreans attempted one final "manzai" attack the next morning but were repulsed with heavy casualties.

On 16 December, COL Throckmorton sent the 24th Infantry Division G-1 a request for 22 officers and 829 enlisted men to bring the 5th Infantry up to strength. The division artillery commander made a similar request on behalf of the Triple Nickel. The division commander finally agreed to replenish the 5th RCT's ranks with an infusion of replacements.

Two days later, Throckmorton requested re-authorization of the pentagon-shaped shoulder patch for his command. His proposal, a scarlet pentagon with a white scroll underneath containing the words "5th RCT" in infantry blue, was modified during the long approval process. The scarlet pentagon surrounded by a white border was finally authorized for wear on 14 March 1952.

Ridgeway's War

On the morning of December 23, the jeep carrying Eighth Army Commander Walton Walker was hit by an ROK weapons-carrier. The jeep rolled and General Walker died immediately as the windshield smashed into his skull.

Within minutes General MacArthur was informed of the accident. There was already agreement between MacArthur, President Truman, and the Pentagon that, if anything should happen to General Walker,

KOREA: THE FLUID WAR

he would be succeeded by Matthew Ridgeway, who had distinguished himself during World War II at the Battle of the Bulge.

When General Ridgeway arrived in Korea on 26 December, he was disappointed to find that the Eighth Army, as a whole, was a psychological wreck. He quickly relieved numerous exhausted senior commanders, blaming them for the Army's timidity about getting off the scanty roads, its reluctance to move without radio and telephone contact, and its lack of imagination in dealing with a foe whom they outmatched in firepower and dominated in the air and on the surrounding seas. He blamed the army leadership, not the G.I.'s for the debacle in Korea (26).

Ridgeway brought a fresh tactical perspective to Korea. He viewed the tank as a mobile, armored assault gun and demanded that his commanders commit their tanks and infantry into battle as teams. He also believed that too many artillery pieces had been disgracefully lost during the long withdrawal from North Korea. General Ridgeway preferred to let the CCF expend lives while he expended high explosive shells. He requested and received a lot of long-range self-propelled artillery battalions that dramatically increased Eighth Army's punch. Ridgeway's aim was to pummel the Communists until they sued for peace. Victory in the sense of overrunning North Korea and unifying the two countries was no longer Ridgeway's or President Truman's goal. General MacArthur still intended to unify Korea and that intention would eventually lead to his downfall.

Matt Ridgeway was also appalled to find that his soldiers still had insufficient winter clothing and were suffering from living in vermin-infested Korean buildings. He took immediate steps to increase supplies of tentage and cold weather clothing. Soon after the arrival of Ridgeway, the G.I.'s began to feel better about themselves. When "Old Iron Tits" (so named because of the ever-present grenades hanging on the front of his field jacket) insisted that they could beat the Chinese, the men believed him.

The Chinese welcomed Ridgeway by initiating their third offensive. They moved south across the 38th Parallel on New Year's Eve and directed their main effort toward the Eighth Army's left flank, where the army commanders had instituted a corset defense, interspersing ROK and American divisions. The CCF hurled their main efforts at the ROK units and the latter promptly withdrew, leaving wide gaps in the line. One of the gaps occurred in that sector defended by the 19th Infantry Regiment.

MacArthur had directed Ridgeway to not risk the destruction of the Eighth Army in a futile defense of Seoul. General Ridgeway would have preferred to continue the battle but the near total collapse of the ROK Army convinced him that Seoul was a lost cause. He ordered the army to move south across the Han River. The 1st and 3rd Battalions of the 5th RCT advanced northward to hold a blocking position long enough to cover the withdrawal of the 24th Division. At the same time, the 2nd Battalion was dispatched to help the hard-pressed 27th British Commonwealth Brigade.

The Chinese had a bit of bad luck on the morning of January 1. They had begun their campaign under overcast skies but, when the skies cleared suddenly on New Year's Day, waves of FEAF fighter bombers struck the exposed CCF infantry. The bombing, strafing and rocketing inflicted an estimated 8000 casualties on the Communist forces as the United Nations troops withdrew across the Han.

In accordance with COL Throckmorton's instructions, the 5th RCT's battalions leapfrogged as they moved south. The Triple Nickel lobbed white phosphorous shells at the Chinese whenever they pressed too close. The tired infantrymen slogged through the slush and the snow. Most would rather have been attacking north but there were just too many Chinese and not enough G.I's. Chinese pressure prevented the Eighth Army from holding the south bank of the Han and the withdrawal continued to Changhowan-ni where the 5th RCT dug in. Since 28 November, the combat team had retreated three hundred miles.

Recon patrols were dispatched around the clock to regain contact with the enemy, maintain communication with adjacent units, and screen the thousands of refugees flooding the area. Between 5 and 17 January, the combat team had no contact with the enemy.

On 17 January, division headquarters ordered the combat team to conduct platoon-sized patrols every other day to Ichon. The 27th Commonwealth Brigade covered the alternate days. On the 21st, G Company, reinforced by two squads from the 2nd Battalion I&R Platoon, upon reaching Ichon, captured two Chinese soldiers and participated in a fierce fire fight. They withdrew with seven wounded after expending all of their ammunition.

Replacements began to arrive in increasing numbers. On January 21 alone, 503 replacements and hospital returnees reported to the regiment. Colonel Throckmorton directed that all replacements receive a seven-day refresher course to give them a psychological boost before they were assigned to their units. Veteran platoon leaders and NCO's rotated to the rear for two-week intervals to train the new men.

Resume the Attack

On 29 January, division directed the 5th RCT to move to Ichon and prepare to attack northward toward Subuk-san, a series of ridges on the far side of a wide valley. As the combat team moved into place, John Throckmorton surveyed the snow-covered terrain from an L-5 Piper Cub. After seeing the lay of the land, he ordered the 1st Battalion to seize Objective Baker, Hill 256. Objective Able, Hills 407 and 471, were assigned to 2nd Battalion. The 3rd Battalion would remain in reserve.

The 2nd Battalion moved out at 0730. First Battalion commenced its attack one hour later. The battalions advanced slowly through a heavy morning fog which helped conceal the infantry but interfered with the adjustment of artillery fire and close air support. When the fog lifted at 1330, enemy resistance increased tremendously but coordination of artillery and air strikes became possible.

The 1st Battalion fought its way to the tops of Hills 475 and 476 by 1630 and killed many enemy soldiers during the ensuing mop up. A Chinese counterattack pushed Charlie Company out of its positions but the company reformed and regained its ground by 2110.

Second Battalion's Objective Able proved to be a greater challenge. George Company led the assault that morning and suffered considerable losses securing its objective on the lower part of a long ridgeline dominated by Hill 256. A flight of P-51's kept the enemy's head down as Easy Company moved through George Company and commenced its attack towards the summit.

Lieutenant Carl Dodd's 3rd Platoon of Company E ascended the ridge through heavy defensive fire. When a squad leader yelled at his men to take cover, LT Dodd yelled "Take cover, hell. Use marching fire and follow me!" When the squad stopped to help some men that had been hit, Lieutenant Dodd looked back and yelled "Come on. Follow me!"

Carl Dodd rushed up the slope armed with a .45 caliber pistol and seven grenades. When he used up his own grenades, he gathered more from the dead and wounded. One particularly persistent Chinese machine gun kept his soldiers pinned down. Lieutenant Dodd charged the gun, firing his pistol to keep the Chinese heads down. When he reached the bunker's opening, he hurled a grenade inside and killed the crew. At times, several CCF machine guns were firing at him. He kept advancing, knocking out a gun here, shooting a Chinese soldier there, as he continued his attack toward the summit of Hill 256. Whenever his soldiers bogged down, he continued the attack alone. His men followed, and many fell killed and wounded as they fought their way to the summit (27). They almost made it, but at 2110, COL Throckmorton ordered the 2nd Battalion to dig in for the night.

The 2nd Battalion's tactical aggressiveness and initiative stunned observers from corps and army headquarters who had witnessed the bitter, close-range infantry fighting. General Ridgeway was present the following morning when the 2nd Battalion rapidly cleared the remainder of Objective Able. He sent a telex to all American and South Korean corps and division commanders.

"The U. S. Fifth Infantry Regiment, COL Throckmorton commanding, attacked in daylight across a mile wide open plain and took a series of ridges up to 150 feet above the valley which dominated the ground this regiment had to cross. Chinese Communist forces had organized and defended these ridges tenaciously with individual foxholes and underground shelters…

In late afternoon I personally visited the 2nd Battalion, LTC Ward commanding, and went over the ground taken by E and F Companies. This operation achieved the true measure of tactical success—key terrain, a vital mountain pass—seized with heavy losses inflicted and only light losses sustained. The reason was due to proper appreciation and use of terrain and high leadership whereby high class infantry with supporting air and artillery worked its way along the ridges until all dominating ground was taken. This operation furnishes a fine example of how it ought to be done (28)."

President Truman subsequently awarded the Medal of Honor to 1st Lieutenant Carl H. Dodd in a ceremony held in the White House. On 23 January the 5th RCT was awarded another Combat Infantry Streamer.

In early February the 5th RCT continued to fight the Chinese near Subuk-san. The defenders delivered interlocking machine fire and mortar barrages from bunkers tunneled into both the forward and reverse slopes of the steep ridges. SFC Samuel Kealoha of Company M brought his 75mm recoilless rifle team forward and closing within a few yards, spotted the machine guns and directed his gun crew as they knocked out the machine gun nests with high explosive shells. Seriously wounded, he continued to direct fire until Love Company overran the Chinese position. The 5th RCT gained ground slowly, attacking during the day and digging in at night.

The unceasing strain of continuous close combat took a steady toll in battle casualties, sickness and sheer physical and mental exhaustion. Finally the combat team was pulled off the line and assigned to division reserve for a well-deserved rest. While they rested, COL Throckmorton insisted on strict discipline. Orders were issued pertaining to every aspect of the soldier's life from care of weapons, to saluting, and prevention of typhus and cold-weather injuries. Soldiers were required to wear their helmets during their waking hours.

The 5th Cavalry made a determined bid at this time to snag hospital returnees from the 5th RCT. Relations between the two regiments had not been rosy since an article in the Stars and Stripes had credited the 5th Cavalry with the capture of Waegwan. SFC Horace Anderson and SGT Charles Krone were standing in line at the I Corps Replacement Depot, after recovering from their wounds, when a second lieutenant from the 5th Cavalry attempted to pull rank and force the two veterans to report to his unit. SFC Anderson faced the officer down and replied "No, sir! We're either going to the 5th RCT or the stockade." They returned to the 5th RCT (29).

On 16 February, the 5th RCT was momentarily attached to the 25th Infantry Division and moved north to the Han River to block another massive attack by the CCF. When they reached the river, they found four to five hundred dead Chinese lying in demolished bunkers and foxholes, victims of an accurate and terribly destructive avalanche of high explosive artillery fire.

As the Chinese withdrew, General Ridgeway ordered a full-scale offensive against the center of the enemy line. The 5th RCT's assignment, during Operation KILLER, was to mop up along the south bank of the Han while conducting combat patrols along the north bank to keep the pressure on the CCF. When a senior State Department official complained about Ridgeway's use of KILLER as the code name, the Eighth Army commander replied that it was about time someone reminded the American people what war was all about.

KILLER was followed by RIPPER which commenced on 5 March with the mightiest artillery barrage of the war to date. The 5th RCT moved across the river and became heavily engaged on 6 March near Yangpyong.

Lieutenant John Bernotas and his platoon from Company L dug in on a key position and were waiting for the rest of Love Company to arrive when they were beset by a series of Chinese banzai attacks. At one point, LT Bernotas found it necessary to call in an artillery strike on their position. Though wounded twice, Bernotas held on until the rest of the company arrived. The Chinese attacks persisted.

One of the reinforcements was PFC Leonard Kravitz, an assistant machine gunner from Company M, who was on loan to Love Company. When his gunner was wounded, Kravitz took over the gun and delivered punishing fire on the Chinese. He then became the focus of their attack, enabling his comrades to withdraw. Later when his body was recovered, it was surrounded by many dead Chinese soldiers. Both Kravitz and LT Bernotas were awarded the Distinguished Service Cross (30).

Enemy resistance diminished rapidly and by March 10th the Eighth Army had outflanked Seoul. The 5th RCT went into reserve from the 9th to the 16th. On the 18th, the regiment returned to the task of chasing Chinese through the rugged hills.

The regiment attacked north near Ochon on March 22nd. M/SGT Robert Noneman of Company E, while directing his platoon into a perimeter defense, noticed an enemy force move into some nearby high ground that would have allowed them to deliver devastating fire on his men. Sergeant Noneman charged across open terrain and set up on an exposed knoll. He opened fire and inflicted many casualties even after he was seriously wounded. A Chinese sniper finally finished him. Robert Noneman received the Distinguished Service Cross posthumously (31).

The 5th RCT reached the 38th Parallel on 31 March. A tank and infantry patrol erected a red pentagon sign with the words "38th Parallel Courtesy of the 5th RCT" scrawled in toothpaste.

When April arrived, rumors of a rotation policy circulated throughout the combat team. In the event that it might be true, first sergeants were instructed to draw up lists of men who had deployed from Schofield Barracks in July. Of the 145 men who had deployed from Schofield in Easy Company, just fifty-nine remained and every one of the surviving soldiers had been wounded, several as often as four times. When General Ridgeway received a request for a combat officer to serve as senior aide for General J. Lawton Collins, Army Chief of Staff, he offered the job to John Throckmorton. The Rock accepted the transfer knowing that he would be going anyway when the rotation policy took effect.

Ridgeway selected LTC Harry Wilson to take over the 5th RCT. Wilson had been an airborne infantry officer in World War II during the liberation of the Philippines. His combat experience in Korea was limited to two daring, but brief, jumps in command of 1st Battalion, 187th Airborne RCT. Neither jump had encountered heavy enemy opposition. He had no experience leading "straight-legged" infantrymen. Anyone replacing Throckmorton was bound to have a tough act to follow. Most of the officers in the 5th RCT believed that their own 2nd Battalion commander, LTC Albert Ward, should have replaced Throckmorton. They felt somewhat reassured when Colonel Ward was appointed regimental executive officer.

The long awaited rotation policy became real when 190 members of the 5th RCT departed Korea on April 10, 1951. The reality of rotation was a definite morale boost for men who had had nothing to look forward to but endless combat until they became casualties. On the downside this policy led to a steady drain of leaders with combat experience and a corresponding increase of inexperienced replacements, many of whom were eighteen or nineteen-year-old draftees. Of the 532 replacements who reported to the 5th RCT, most were too young to vote for, or against, the government that had sent them to Korea.

On April 11, President Truman fired General Douglas MacArthur. General Ridgeway accepted the President's offer to replace MacArthur as commander-in-chief of the Far East Command and commander-in-chief of the United Nations Command. He would continue to oversee the war in Korea from his new office in Tokyo. General James Van Fleet left Second Army Headquarters at Fort Meade, Maryland to assume command of the Eighth U.S. Army.

The 5th Chinese Offensive

Following a few days in reserve, the 5th RCT relieved the 21st Infantry on Line Utah on April 20 and was preparing to attack north to Kumwha on the following day. The patrols that were sent forward encountered a lot of enemy activity from squads and platoons.

Lieutenant Charles Brannon and his platoon from Baker Company ran into a heavily fortified Chinese position. Brannon directed automatic weapons fire on one of two machine gun emplacements while he attacked a second emplacement and killed its occupants. When they reached the top of the ridge, Brannon determined that further progress was impossible. Though wounded, he provided covering fire while his men withdrew and requested an air strike on the objective.

Sergeant James Riddle, led another platoon from Company B up Hill 834. During the attack, he wiped out several enemy emplacements with grenades. He became wounded but refused medical attention and grabbed some more grenades and assaulted another enemy position. He led his men to the ridge and secured the hill before he bled to death. Lieutenant Brannon succumbed to his wounds on the 25th. Both Brannon and Riddle received the Distinguished Service Cross (32).

Enemy resistance solidified on 22 April bringing the Eighth

Army's offensive to a halt. Chinese rearguard actions had concealed the assembly of 337,000 CCF soldiers just itching to regain the initiative.

The 5th RCT dug in hastily, near nightfall, on a 6000 meter front in the vicinity of Unjimal. The MLR ran from east to west and straddled a narrow valley between rugged ridgelines upon which rested the combat team's flanks. First and 2nd Battalions defended the MLR but couldn't tie in because of the broken terrain. Each battalion was reinforced with one platoon of tanks and a 4.2 inch mortar platoon. The 3rd Battalion was in reserve on the valley floor. Visibility to the north was severely hampered by jumbled masses of boulders.

The regiment's left flank rested on the crest of Hill 795 where Easy Company tied in with K Company, 19th Infantry. The MLR ran west to east with the six rifle companies lined up as follows: Easy, Fox, George, Charlie, Baker, and Able. The rugged terrain prevented Able Company from tying in with the ROK 6th Division on its right. The members of Company A could maintain visual contact with the ROK's during daylight and could cover the gap with fire but it was still a source of concern given the South Koreans' repeated failures to stand their ground when assaulted by the Chinese. In theory, the 3rd Battalion would come up from the valley floor and plug the gap if there were a breakthrough but, in reality, that would require several hours of hard climbing.

Chinese 150mm artillery and 120mm mortar fires began to hit 1st Battalion at 1835. Then the enemy gunners shifted to 3rd Battalion and finally to 2nd Battalion. At 1920, an observer in a Piper Cub spotted Chinese infantry moving south along the ridgeline leading toward Hill 795. LTC Wilson alerted the 3rd Battalion for immediate deployment in support of either of its sister battalions. The 555th FAB caught a column of Chinese in the open. Its 105mm howitzers inflicted 200 casualties among the enemy soldiers but that was a drop in the bucket. There were soon too many targets. The entire Chinese 20th Army was

Korea: The Fluid War

on the move, intent on wiping out the U.S. 24th Division.

At 2120 the men of 2nd Battalion heard the shrill bugle calls and hunkered down in their fighting positions. Hundreds of Chinese soldiers, guided by the light of a full moon, struck the boundary between Easy and Fox Companies while another assault troop hit the boundary between Fox and George. When King of the 19th Infantry was overrun, the tactical situation for Easy of the 5th became perilous. When it became apparent that 2nd Battalion had been flanked on the left, LTC Wilson ordered them to withdraw. Easy Company's 2nd Platoon was ordered to stay and cover the very difficult nighttime withdrawal until it had expended its machine gun ammunition. Then it was to withdraw in small groups through the Chinese and link up with the company.

Lieutenant Leonard Warner and his How Company machine gun platoon held their positions during repeated attacks by hordes of Chinese. He was last seen on the morning of the 23rd engaged in hand-to-hand fighting with a group of enemy soldiers.

Private Hugh Sommer served in the last 2nd Platoon rifle squad to disengage. As they attempted to reach the Easy Company rally location, Sommer walked point for his squad. Mistaking an enemy soldier silhouetted to his front for an American, PVT Sommer called out that he was bringing his squad in and received an affirmative reply in English. As the squad approached, the Chinese soldier hurled several grenades in rapid succession. Sommer retrieved a couple of the grenades and hurled them away from his comrades before they exploded. He was in the process of tossing another when it exploded in his hands and killed him. The survivors, who finally killed the CCF grenadier, described Sommer's valiant behavior to their superiors. Hugh Sommer and Leonard Kalani Warner were both awarded the Distinguished Service Cross (33).

Meanwhile, across the valley, the ROK 6th Division lived up to its poor reputation. It quickly collapsed and left Able of the 5th RCT's right flank unprotected. The wholesale flight of the South Koreans was first reported at 0250 when 5th Infantry's I&R Platoon collared forty stragglers from the ROK 19th Infantry Regiment on the valley floor.

Shortly after 0100, two Chinese companies slammed into Able Company's forward most rifle platoon and virtually destroyed it. More than eighty members of the company were captured. The company commander, CPT Horace West, gathered the few survivors he could find in the darkness and led them off the ridge. They were able to evade the Chinese who swarmed around them in the darkness.

At one point during Able Company's harrowing descent, the battered riflemen were strafed by confused FEAF pilots. One of those wounded during the strafing was PFC James Scott Bumgarner.

PFC Bumgarner survived his wounds and would later become the much admired star of movies and television, James Garner. He had been in Oklahoma in 1950 when he received his draft notice. He served with the 5th RCT in Korea for fourteen months, receiving two purple hearts for wounds suffered in action. After his discharge in 1952, Jim Bumgarner enrolled at the University of Oklahoma for a semester. He dropped out of college and moved to Los Angeles to work with his father, a carpet layer (34).

Following the collapse of the ROK 6th Division on the combat team's right and the breakthrough along the boundary shared with the 19th Infantry on the left, the 5th RCT was in danger of a double envelopment. Since it didn't appear that the CCF were going to concentrate an attack on the valley floor, LTC Wilson ordered the 3rd Battalion's rifle companies to go up the hill and shore up the combat team's crumbling flanks. Love and King Companies were sent up to the left flank and Item Company was dispatched to occupy a blocking position south of Able Company. By 0300 all of the 3rd Battalion was in motion, scaling the ridges to fight the Chinese.

Stiff fighting continued on both ridgelines until 0915, when the 24th Infantry Division ordered the 5th RCT to withdraw through the

21st Infantry, the division reserve, and occupy an assembly area in the rear. King Company covered the combat team's withdrawal from its commanding perch on Hill 752, astride the western ridgeline (35).

On the eastern end of the line, elements from Able, Item and Charlie Companies fought a desperate, close range fire fight with a large CCF combat patrol during the disengagement. PFC Darrel Council, a machine gunner in Dog Company, remained at his gun to cover their withdrawal. He remained there firing into the attacking masses until his position was overrun and he became another posthumous Distinguished Service Cross recipient (36). Supporting fires from the 555th ringed King Company until the artillery battalion was told to pull out.

The 5th RCT pulled back to an assembly area at Ukkalgye, several kilometers behind the MLR. No one expected that they would remain there very long in view of the continuing deterioration up on the line which was still held by the 19th and 21st Infantry Regiments. Thanks to the disgraceful performance of the ROK 6th Division, there was now a 13,000 meter gap between the right flank of the 24th Division and the left flank of the nearest friendly unit, the 1st Marine Division. Shortly before midnight on 24 April, the Eighth Army's new commander, General James Van Fleet, concluded that the CCF penetrations were not going to be expelled by local counterattacks. He reluctantly ordered the army to fall back to Line Lincoln, a few miles north of Seoul.

The 24th Division's withdrawal called for the 19th and 21st Infantry Regiments to pass through the 5th RCT's lines. The combat team would then serve as rear guard for the trek south. The 2nd Battalion, with Tank Company and D Company, 6th Tank Battalion, moved a short distance north to set up a blocking position. The 3rd Battalion continued to hold a hilltop blocking position on the eastern flank. As the 1st Battalion ascended Gold Mine Trail to get into position, a strong force of Chinese infantry ambushed Able and Charlie Companies when they were just 600 yards shy of their objective. The Triple Nickel was running low on 105mm rounds, so the regimental tactical air controller directed air strikes against the columns of CCF troops moving through the hills.

The 19th and 21st Infantry Regiments disengaged from the MLR under heavy pressure and completed their passage through the 5th RCT's lines by 1100. LTC Wilson assigned the 2nd Battalion and both tank companies to rearguard. The 3rd Battalion would serve as advance guard and the 1st Battalion and the 555th FAB would follow the 3rd Battalion.

The simple plan fell apart before it could be implemented. LTC Wilson was unaware of the unit practice of leapfrogging during a retrograde movement, so he didn't designate an intermediate objective for the advance guard to occupy. To make matters worse, the 8th Ranger Company was still up on the MLR encircled by the Chinese and engaged in heavy fighting. Following the collapse of the ROK 6th Division, the rangers had been shifted to the 24th Division's right flank. By the evening of April 24th, they knew that they were surrounded and would have to fight their way out to join the withdrawal.

At daybreak on the 25th, the rangers moved out under fire and descended a steep ridgeline. They contacted the 3rd Battalion by radio using their code name "Old Rose." The combat team's signal people had never heard of Old Rose. Finally, a message reached 3rd Battalion from regimental headquarters to do what they could to extricate the rangers. Two platoons from Love Company were dispatched but were recalled when they ran into small arms fire (37).

Later that morning, a platoon from Company D, 6th Tank Battalion set out in their Patton tanks to find the ranger company. At 1155 the tankers reached a group of 65 mostly-wounded rangers (38).

Meanwhile, 3rd Battalion, 5th Infantry was long gone, leaving the combat team's left flank dangerously exposed. The 3rd Battalion's convoy, with most of Headquarters and Headquarters Company, soon reached the assembly area in the vicinity of Sopa after passing through the new MLR.

No effective enemy resistance was encountered during the 3rd Battalion's withdrawal. They had noticed the impact of a few mortar shells as they approached a narrow pass near the village of Pisi-gol but assumed that the 19th Infantry was probably registering its mortars. Actually, the mortar fire came from the CCF 60th Division which was dug in, on the high ground, on both sides of the pass.

By mid-day, members of the 2nd Battalion, from their blocking position on the valley floor could see columns of Chinese moving past them, heading south on the high ridgelines. However, company commanders were assured by regimental headquarters that there was no evidence that the combat team was being outflanked by Chinese troops. The survivors of 1st Battalion reached the valley floor around noon and crowded onto the Triple Nickel's trucks. They would serve as an infantry escort for the artillery battalion.

The survivors of the 8th Ranger Company did not reach the 2nd Battalion until 1630, giving the Chinese plenty of time to set up near Pisi-gol (39). The 2nd Battalion and Company D of the 6th Tank Battalion headed south. George Company, 5th RCT, was the last unit out.

When B Battery of the 555th neared the summit of the mountain pass southeast of Pisi-gol, the Chinese opened fire. A burst of automatic weapons fire killed the driver of a ¾ ton truck immediately behind the battalion commander's jeep. It caused the truck and its trailer to jack-knife and block the road. The battalion commander's jeep was the last 5th RCT vehicle to clear the pass that day.

Two Chinese battalions swept the motorized column with automatic weapons fire. Mortar fire added to the slaughter. A few of B Battery's trucks skidded out of control, turned over, caught fire and exploded. The remaining trucks halted as orders were passed from one end of the convoy to the other for C Company's soldiers to dismount, form up and assault the Chinese. A few cannoneers tried to unlimber their 105mm howitzers to return fire over open sights, but they never stood a chance and died next to their guns. Survivors leaped for the drainage ditches on both sides of the road.

Nick Tosques, a member of one of the Triple Nickel gun crews, remembers looking up and seeing a Chinese grenade coming at him and then was aware of nothing until he awoke in the darkness. He headed south, on foot, and soon came upon several soldiers who were huddled together along the road. One, who had been wounded in the arm, was crying. Tosques convinced the group to get on their feet and head south with him. They could hear Chinese talking all around them. Finally, Tosques suggested that they get rid of their rifles and lie down and pretend to be dead. Shortly thereafter, the Chinese moved among the reclining soldiers and prodded them with their bayonets to determine who were still alive (40).

Heavy and accurate Chinese fire decimated the infantrymen as they tried to deploy for combat. They had been crammed into the trucks with no regard for squad and platoon integrity and were unable to deploy and fight as a coordinated unit. Small groups of grimly determined soldiers fought their way up the ridgeline but, due to their uncoordinated actions and lack of fire support, they were unable to dislodge the entrenched Chinese.

Then a CCF assault struck the stalled column from the east, blowing bugles, throwing concussion grenades, and shooting burp guns from the hip. The G.I's, who were caught between the enemy and the burning trucks, were slaughtered.

Lieutenant Frank Athanason from A Battery could clearly see the Chinese on the ridgeline firing down at B Battery and Charlie Company. The range was about 1800 yards. He ordered his gun crews to commence direct fire at the Chinese. After firing a couple of volleys, Athanason was order to limber up his guns and join the convoy. He flagged down a tank that was heading south and instructed the tank commander to lead his battery down the road (41).

When A Battery reached the village of Kanggu-dong, they

came under heavy small arms fire from surrounding windows. Frank Athanason dismounted the jeep and ran abreast of the Easy Eight. There he stood pointing out targets for the tank commander. The point blank main gun and machine gun fire from the tank silenced the Chinese opposition and A Battery continued its journey south until it ran into the tail end of B Battery stalled on the road.

As they were being raked with automatic weapons fire, A Battery's gunners trained their weapons on the Chinese dug in on the ridgeline; a range of no more than 200 yards. They fired round after round of high explosive and managed to blast their tormentors off the face of the western ridge, but murderous fire continued from the eastern side of the road.

The battery had expended much of its basic load of ammunition while supporting 1st Battalion's dis-engagement on the Gold Mine Trail. When they ran out of high explosive rounds, they fired white phosphorous and, when that was gone, fired smoke rounds until they were gone. As the sun set, the men of Able Battery grabbed their personal weapons, some grenades and six bandoleers of ammunition per man and prepared to fight as infantry. LT Athanason formed the men into a ragged skirmish line and counterattacked up the ridge.

As A Battery was jumping off on its assault, LT Ed Crockett's platoon of three tanks came upon a road block, near the mouth of the pass, caused by flaming vehicles. The three Easy Eights left the congested road to bypass the wrecks and advanced as far as they could toward the mouth of the pass. When they could go no further, they stopped and were forced to beat off attacks from one Chinese squad after another. The CCF troops, armed with satchel charges and grenades, charged forward, scurrying over the bodies of their dead and dying comrades.

Farther north, Charlie Battery had received B Battery's appeal for fire support. They pulled off the road and quickly had their 105's firing high explosive rounds down range. Everyone not manning the howitzers set up a perimeter defense with the few surviving members of Able Company. They were soon receiving automatic fire and mortar rounds from both sides of the road. In the midst of this fight, Charlie Battery received orders to hook up their guns and continue south as fast as they could. They soon ran into the tail end of Able Battery and could go no further.

The cannoneers dismounted and laid their guns for direct fire as Captain Horace West and his Able Company prepared for the fight. West was hit several times but remained on his feet directing the fire of his soldiers until he was finally knocked to the ground by a burst of automatic fire. Several soldiers carried their company commander to a nearby tank and placed him on the engine deck. Horace West survived his wounds after a lengthy recovery period at various Army hospitals. He was awarded the Distinguished Service Cross for valor (42).

When Major Ward, at the 5th RCT command post in Sopa, received word of the ambush, he requested help from the 24th Division. The 21st Infantry was ordered to dispatch a company of tanks, reinforced with a company of infantry, and break through the pass from the south end. During its approach, the Chinese ambushed this task force, knocked out two M-46 Patton tanks and inflicted heavy losses on the infantry. The survivors retreated. Clearly, the 5th RCT was on its own.

Ed Crockett, head exposed from the turret of his tank, was searching a ridgeline to locate a machine gun that was engaging his tank when a 3.5 inch antitank rocket whizzed by his head. The Chinese had captured a 3.5 inch rocket launcher. Crockett was bent over, head inside, conferring with his gunner, when a second rocket slammed into the tank's frontal armor, slightly damaging the engine but fortunately hitting nowhere near the tank's fuel and ammunition supply. That time, a neighboring tanker observed the back blast from the rocket launcher and killed the Chinese gunners with a high explosive round.

Lieutenant Colonel Wilson, regimental commander, was in one hell of a fix. He had elected to send LTC Ward on ahead with regimental headquarters and stayed behind to travel with the 2nd Battalion. His operations officer was dead and the bulk of the combat team's command and control resources were in Sopa with LTC Ward. The 3rd Battalion was already in Sopa so was of no use to the main body that was being savaged in the vicinity of Pisi-gol. Major Claude Baker, the CO of 1st Battalion, was cut off from his command and his scattered rifle companies were pinned down along the length of a column of burning vehicles, disorganized and unable to fight in a coordinated fashion. The Triple Nickel was fighting hard but would soon exhaust its ammunition. Finally, LT Walter Fay, the Tactical Air Controller, was wounded which, disturbingly, left no one who knew how to request and direct air strikes. When Baker Company slid off its tanks, the company commander asked LTC Wilson where he wanted to commit the company. Wilson replied, "I don't know where to put them (43)."

Many of the soldiers who managed to escape from "Death Valley" owe their lives to LTC Clarence Stuart, CO of the 555th FAB. Stuart remembered that, earlier in April, the 72nd Engineers had improved a narrow mountain trail west of Pisi-gol that ran parallel to the MSR. It could accommodate trucks and tanks. LTC Stuart conducted a reconnaissance of the road and found it to be free of Chinese troops. He relayed this information to LTC Wilson. The regimental commander ordered the combat team to break contact and take the alternate route to the MLR (44).

Meanwhile LT Athanason's mixed force of cannoneers and infantrymen had overrun a couple of Chinese machine gun and mortar position as they counterattacked up the ridgeline. As he looked back he could see that the situation had changed in the valley below. Able Battery's vehicles had apparently turned around and escaped by the other route. So Athanason, now wounded, led his men back down the slope where they regrouped in a ditch before heading southwest across a rice paddy. They were soon pursued by Chinese who were blowing whistles and, fortunately, shooting high. As they crossed a small hill, a flight of Navy F4U Corsairs made three passes at the CCF troops, slowing them down.

At 0400 Athanason's group reached the MLR where they linked up with a platoon from the 6th Tank Battalion. The platoon leader was glad to see them because he had no infantry support. When LT Athanason asked for directions to the nearest aid station so that he could get attention for his wounds and those of several of his men, the tanker feigned ignorance of the aid station's location and advised the group to remain near the tanks until daybreak. So the exhausted and injured men stayed with the tanks. When the sun rose, Athanason discovered that the aid station was just a few hundred yards away, something the frightened tank platoon leader had known all along.

An early report suggested that the 5th Infantry Regiment lost an equivalent of one of its battalions during April's fighting. There were 20 KIA, 289 WIA and 243 MIA. The Triple Nickel reported 3 KIA, 50 WIA and 49 MIA.

Those missing in action included cannoneer Nick Tosques and his fellow captives. They remained in the pass for a couple of days undergoing interrogation by the Chinese and dodging incoming U.S. artillery. When the Chinese felt that they had gathered enough prisoners, they began the long march north, reaching a prison camp at Changson, North Korea around the end of June. Tosques was able to survive more than two years of interrogation, torture and starvation and was finally released during Operation Big Switch in August, 1953.

A handful of those missing in action did trickle in over time but a significant number of the men who were captured in the pass at Pisigol died in captivity from wounds, maltreatment and starvation. The remains of CPL Leslie R. Heath of Able Company, who was captured on the morning of April 23, 1951, were returned to the U.S. Army on July 16, 1993 by the Democratic Peoples Republic of Korea (45).

Lieutenant Crockett's crew had to abandon *Hawaii Calls* when her damaged engine overheated and stalled. They hitch-hiked out aboard the *Aloha* and the *Moana Loa*. Tank Company lost three Easy Eights and the 6th Tank Battalion lost nine Pattons. During the ambush, eighty-five 5th RCT vehicles, including thirty-two deuce-and-a-half trucks were destroyed.

Waiting for a few rangers was understandable but had been a serious tactical blunder as had the combat team's failure to position an advance guard on the next defensible hilltop during the withdrawal. The obvious southward movement of Chinese troops along the ridgelines had been ignored. LTC Wilson was entirely focused on dealing with a threat from the north. He had been elevated to a position of immense responsibility with little time to learn the ropes. Arthur H. Wilson was promoted to colonel shortly after the ambush but he was never promoted again.

Mao Tze Tung had placed unrealistic demands on his soldiers. Their morale cracked toward the end of April. It is estimated that 70,000 Chinese soldiers were killed or wounded during the spring 1951 offensive. There had been a horrifying loss of trained soldiers and commanders. They were being replaced by conscripts that lacked the skill and the morale of the original intervention forces. Human wave attacks could not overwhelm their enemy's firepower because that firepower was just too great. Mao ignored this information and ordered the CCF to launch another attack on the U. S. Eighth Army.

The 5th RCT moved forward on May 4 to establish a regiment-sized outpost line of resistance in the vicinity of Masogu-ri, the ruins of a village approximately 5000 yards forward of the 24th Division's sector of the MLR (46). The combat team's assignment was to "Seek out the enemy, attempt to determine his plan and deceive him as to the location of the division's MLR. Each infantry battalion set up a hilltop defense perimeter astride the Pukhan Valley. Eighth Army Commander, James Van Fleet, wanted to turn the Pukhan Valley into a death zone for any CCF elements that chose that route to Seoul. Tank-infantry patrols penetrated as much as six miles north of the outpost line for the next several days without a significant contact with the Chinese.

On the night of 12-13 May, Easy Company's perimeter was probed by a CCF patrol that threw grenades into the company positions. An ambush patrol from the 2nd Battalion caught this group of Chinese, as they withdrew, killing four and wounding six of them.

The following morning, Item and King Companies, reinforced with tanks and artillery, attacked an enemy concentration in the vicinity of Hyon-ni. This task force encountered a well-dug-in, stubborn opponent who lashed back with automatic weapons, 76mm field guns and mortars. Air strikes and artillery were called in on the Chinese but the task force was ordered home at 1530 before they had eradicated the enemy troops.

A prisoner captured on 15 May revealed that the CCF 191st Division, 64th CCF Army was massing for an offensive against the 5th RCT. The brief lull was over.

Given the news of the impending Chinese offensive, each battalion pulled back a few yards to higher ground. At dusk, listening posts were manned and ambush patrols left friendly lines to relay news of the enemy advance back to OPLR.

At 0015 on May 17, Love and Item Companies came under small arms fire from a platoon-strength patrol. Fifteen minutes later, King Company incurred four WIA's from 81mm mortar fire. Tank Company, concentrated between the 1st and 2nd Battalions, became heavily engaged, killing scores of Chinese with high-explosive rounds and machine gun fire. Love Company repulsed an assault by two CCF platoons.

By 0130 the Chinese attack had spread to 1st and 2nd Battalions but their main effort was still concentrated on 3rd Battalion. At 0145 Item Company came under heavy fire from approximately eighty Chinese soldiers who had infiltrated to the company's rear. Five minutes later

George Company reported, "Estimated enemy battalion coming down the road from west on horses. Engaging with fire now."

At 0150, LTC Wilson learned that one of Able Company's rifle platoons had been overrun and that the Chinese had forced a penetration between George and Easy Companies. Five minutes later, Wilson lost contact with Company G. He ordered all non-essential vehicles to withdraw to the MLR. At 0305 contact with George Company resumed. The company had withdrawn to a tighter 2nd Battalion defensive perimeter.

Tank Company fought a textbook delaying action. Ed Crockett's tank platoon covered the 2nd Battalion's withdrawal until he, too, was facing encirclement. Then he pulled his Easy Eights back three hundred yards while firing constantly at the advancing CCF squads and platoons.

At 0345 Colonel Wilson requested permission to pull back to the MLR (47). His request was bumped up to IX Corps G-3, Colonel Kunzig, who replied "Hold until daylight and further instructions will be issued." At that point 1st Battalion was being outflanked. Second Battalion pulled back some more and attempted to reorganize in the dark. A Chinese 81mm mortar barrage inflicted losses and added to the confusion. Second Tank Platoon shifted its front to face the growing threat from the northwest.

At 0435, Colonel Henry Mauz, 24th Division G-3, received notice that the combat team's 1st and 2nd Battalions had each been hit by estimated enemy battalions. Third battalion reported that it was battling with what appeared to be a reinforced battalion. Those in regimental headquarters felt that if they were hit again with the same strength, they would be unable to hold. The line was not stabilized. The corps commander, Major General William Hoge repeated "Move into perimeters and hold positions until daylight." Army doctrine discouraged night withdrawals since they had often led to disaster.

The stiffest fighting occurred at 0530. Enemy machine guns

lined the ridges and laid down a remarkable volume of fire. The night was illuminated by weapons flashes and flying tracers. At dawn, the crisis peaked. At 1000, 1st Battalion, supported by Able Company, 6th Tank Battalion, counterattacked and wrested its previous position on Hill 537 from the Chinese battalion that had overrun it during the early morning hours. The Chinese counterattacked on the night of May 19 but were driven off by Companies C and K.

Under the protection of the positions held by the 1st and 3rd Battalions, the 2nd Battalion advanced north along the west bank of the Pukhan River and secured Hill 388. Thereafter the Chinese resistance weakened as the 5th Infantry continued north over familiar hills west of the river. Coordinating with artillery and tank support, the 2nd and 3rd Battalions captured two more hills and sent a couple of enemy battalions scurrying to the northwest.

The entire Eighth Army began a counter-offensive named DETONATE on May 20. Members of the 5th RCT, carrying full packs, climbed up and down the steep ridgelines in a driving rain. They captured one deeply-entrenched hill after another, killing 176 Chinese and wounding 175 others.

Morale soared as the combat team pursued the fleeing CCF. A sense of despair gripped the starving, ill-equipped Chinese soldiers. Large numbers of them voluntarily laid down their arms. Incessant hunger had sapped the will of the survivors.

At dawn on May 27, as Fox Company ascended a trail on Hill 192, they came upon two Chinese soldiers who quickly laid down their weapons and surrendered to the company commander. Lieutenant John Henderson, the surprised CO, whipped out a pack of cigarettes and gave each of the prisoners a light. As soon as the two had taken a couple of puffs and smiled in gratitude, hundreds of heavily armed Chinese infantrymen emerged from behind the rocks above and surrendered. Fox Company quickly ran out of smokes. At 1430 that afternoon, 1141 CCF soldiers climbed down Hill 192, dropped their weapons and marched into captivity. They still possessed an ample supply of ammunition when they surrendered. The month of May ended with the 5th RCT in 24th Division reserve, patrolling behind the 19th and 21st Infantry Regiments north of Kapyong (48).

CHAPTER TWELVE

KOREA: THE BATTLE FOR THE RIDGES

During the first twenty-one days of June, 1951, the regiment had no contact with the enemy other than stragglers that were picked up by patrols. On June 22, the 5th RCT relieved the 32nd Infantry Regiment, 7th Division on Line Wyoming, near the 38th Parallel, and conducted normal close-in recon and security patrolling. Many replacements arrived in May and June and, by the end of June, more than half of the riflemen in the regiment had seen no combat action other than light patrolling (1). On 23 June, Soviet UN delegate, Jacob Malik, proposed that negotiations begin for a cease fire in Korea.

The men of the 5th RCT were not impressed by the defensive construction work that the 32nd Infantry had completed on Line Wyoming so they set about to improve the barbed wire entanglements, mine fields and overhead cover for bunkers. The 72nd Engineers were kept busy constructing access roads to the battalion sectors. They laid minefields, delivered barbed wire, axes, saws, and shovels to the rifle battalions and constructed a small air strip in the vicinity of the regimental command post.

The regiment experienced small enemy probes during the nights of 23-25 June and daytime security patrols identified enemy defensive positions within a thousand yards of the 2nd Battalion. On the 27th, the 19th Infantry established a patrol base 2000 yards to the northeast of 2nd Battalion and that put a stop to enemy contact at night along the 5th Infantry line. Their opponents to the north, the 20th CCF Army, had recently suffered heavy casualties and were content with conducting a rather passive defense.

However, on 8 July, word came of a possible enemy relief taking place by the 27th CCF Army and of a consequent danger to the 5th Infantry due to a change in enemy intentions. Thereafter patrolling was intensified in order to capture prisoners and identify units of the 27th Army. The enemy outpost line was one thousand yards north of Line Wyoming. Enemy patrols never ventured out during daylight and seldom did so at night so it became apparent, to those in command, that a raid would be necessary to secure prisoners.

First and 3rd Battalions participated in a division-level raid on 12 July intended to push back the Chinese outpost line and, hopefully, take some prisoners. The 3rd Battalion and two battalions of the 19th Infantry secured their objectives without enemy contact. Company A, on the other hand, drew heavy mortar and artillery fire and suffered thirty casualties. The company spent the night on its objective, on the western edge of a hill, some three hundred yards from a Chinese outpost. At noon on the 13th, Able Company assaulted the enemy outpost and ended joint ownership of the hill. Company B attacked north and secured its objective by 1800 hours. Thereafter all companies of the 5th Infantry held their positions. The Chinese did not counterattack but they did keep up an annoying artillery and mortar barrage until all friendly units were withdrawn to Line Wyoming on 15 July.

Given Able Company's high casualty rate, Colonel Wilson felt that smaller assault teams and better coordinated direct fire support would be a better approach. On 23 July, a patrol from Company E, led by a Lieutenant Crowlie, attempted to reach an enemy position, in broad daylight, by scaling the eastern slope of Hill 734. This assault ended in a grenade fight with a strong Chinese outpost on the north side of the ridge. The patrol, unable to gain the top, was forced to withdraw with two killed and five wounded members. Wilson attributed the failure of the assault to his having sent a small unit against an enemy outpost line without coordination with other units across a broad front.

So, the following day, 3rd Battalion with one platoon of tanks passed north through the 17th Regiment's line and probed the south face of Hill 734. Through great effort the tanks advanced over extremely uneven terraced valleys to a point on the last ridge south of the objective. From this point, the 3rd Battalion probed with tank fire and patrols but drew no hostile return action. No attempt was made to assault Hill 734 as tank support would have been impossible.

The accessibility of that sector of Line Wyoming defended by the 5th Infantry was less than optimum, particularly for 2nd Battalion. There were access roads to the rear of 1st and 3rd Battalions but, in the case of 2nd Battalion, wire, hot food and ammunition had to be carried in, over three thousand yards of rocky terrain, on the backs of Korean laborers. Litters had to be carried out the entire length of the trail, since there was no possibility of landing a helicopter close to the battalion's positions. The final approaches to 1st and 3rd Battalions were up steep, muddy footpaths. Colonel Wilson reported that it was difficult to recruit Koreans to serve as chogi bearers for 2nd Battalion.

Objective Yoke

On 30 July, the 5th RCT was ordered to conduct a limited attack north of Line Wyoming to deceive and destroy troops from the 243rd CCF Regiment. Third Battalion was assigned the task of assaulting and temporarily occupying Objective Yoke or "Million Dollar Hill" a 700-foot-high prominence to the north that allowed the Chinese to observe activity in the 5th Infantry's backyard. The hill was named not for its real estate value but for the cost of the tons of ordnance that had denuded its steep sides and narrow ridge (2).

Item and Love Companies assaulted and secured the hill on the morning of August 2nd. They were relieved by Company K at around midnight on the 3rd. During the changeover, an enemy company counterattacked but was unable to force a penetration and withdrew.

When the sun came up on August 4, King Company's commander, LT Robert Hight, organized his riflemen and machine gunners into a tight perimeter on the ridge line. He placed the company's three

60mm mortars on the highest part of the ridge but still within shouting distance of the company command post, which was located near the center of the perimeter. A reserve squad of eight men was stationed near the company CP. The riflemen surrounded their positions with trip flares and other warning devices.

At 2100 hours, as LT Hight was checking his positions, two of the flares were tripped and soon a group of Chinese came up the steep side of the ridge against the center of the company perimeter. Enemy soldiers pitched a shower of grenades in the direction of 2nd Platoon but the ridge was so narrow that most of them sailed over the defenders' heads and exploded harmlessly farther down the side of the hill. The fight lasted for about twenty minutes before the Chinese pulled back. The weapon noises had been joined by thunder claps followed by a steady falling rain, blown by a hard wind.

The Chinese made four more futile attempts during the night to regain the ridge. The first three were company-sized assaults and the last two involved smaller groups. Between attacks, enemy machine gun, mortar and small arms fire persisted from a distance. At this point many of the G.I's had their last clip of ammo in their rifles. Told that he would get no more ammunition until daylight, LT Hight called for artillery and heavy mortars to protect his positions.

The rain ended soon after dawn on the morning of 5 August. Several groups of Chinese attempted to retrieve some of their equipment but were met with machine gun and mortar fire. The men of Company K counted 39 enemy dead in front of their perimeter and suspected they had killed and wounded others. Five G.I's had been wounded during the action.

At 1500 hours an estimated enemy battalion was seen grouping on nearby Hill 461 as if preparing for another attack. Artillery and air strikes were placed right on the enemy assembly area and the counterattack never developed. One of the air strikes hit an ammunition dump on the north slope of the hill.

Late in the afternoon, LT Hight received orders to abandon Million Dollar Hill. The men set demolition charges all along the ridge and marched off just as it was beginning to get dark.

Fears that the previous spring's rotation of battle-tested veterans had weakened the 5th Infantry Regiment were groundless. The proud men of King Company were confident in their leaders and in each other. They had walked up Million Dollar Hill, stuck it to the Chinese, and were still alive to brag about it.

Two Months in Reserve

At 1300 on 8 August, 1951, the 5th RCT was relieved on Line Wyoming by the 31st Infantry Regiment and assigned to IX Corps reserve. Getting to the reserve bivouac area was made difficult by intermittent rains on the 8th and steady showers on the 9th rendering many of the roads impassable. By the 13th of the month, the roads had returned to normal, allowing the regiment to resume a number of activities.

The combat team moved to Soojihachon and was tasked with apprehending enemy stragglers, evacuating civilian personnel, protecting communications facilities and rehabilitating blocking positions and portions of Line Kansas. In their spare time, they were to participate in four weeks of training. In addition, the Special Services Section operated a full movie schedule and concluded the time in reserve with championship events in boxing, softball and volleyball. There were also concerts by the 24th Division Band.

Patrols during the month uncovered much evidence of previous battles. On the 21st of August, a 5th Infantry patrol found the bodies of 150 to 200 enemy troops. A starving Chinese soldier, who had been separated from his unit since June, gladly surrendered. The wreckage of a light aircraft was discovered. Both the plane and the pilot were burned beyond recognition. When elements of the 3rd Battalion were fired upon by a group of stragglers, the regiment set up a patrol base in the area. On 3 September, a patrol, on a screening mission, uncovered a cache of U.S. Army ammunition.

On 16 September, COL Alexander D. Surles relieved COL Arthur Wilson of command of the 5th Regimental Combat Team. In essence, an officer with a background in armored warfare relieved an airborne officer of the command of an infantry regiment. However, the timing was good. Colonel Surles took over the helm right in the middle of a training cycle, rather than in the midst of combat deployment, and participated in a regimental command post exercise and a division-wide training operation.

The Chuktae Valley Offensive

On October 3rd, all of the combat team's battalion and company commanders made a reconnaissance of the sector of Line Wyoming and the general outpost line occupied by the 31st Infantry Regiment and the Ethiopian Battalion. The relief was completed on the 7th.

On 13 October, the 5th RCT began its participation in a IX Corps offensive to seize the high ground south of Kumsong from an estimated five battalions of Chinese infantry (3). This first large scale coordinated action in three months would offer plenty of seasoning for the regiment's large number of new replacements. Thirty-one percent of the personnel had arrived since the last contact with the enemy.

First Battalion moved up to the line of departure under cover of darkness and began the attack at 0445. Company B experienced some delay when they ran into an enemy anti-personnel minefield. Once they breached that, they came under heavy machine gun and small arms fire from Chinese who were dug in atop Hill 633 near the village of Pandangdong-ni.

During the ascent of the hill, SGT Floyd Pelfrey, single-handedly destroyed three enemy gun positions with accurate automatic rifle fire. Several other members of Baker Company had made unsuccessful attempts to destroy a bunker position that was holding up the progress of the company. PFC Daniel Machinski charged the position head-on and killed its occupants with rifle fire and grenades. Then he continued the ascent but was killed when he attacked another bunker at the crest of the hill.

Company C was held up by fire from the same location as the enemy reinforced the hill through communication trenches on the reverse slope. When the company commander was hit, Corporal Rawland Otterstrom tried to rescue his wounded skipper but died in a hail of machine gun fire. This exposed the location of the gun and Otterstrom's buddies were able to take it out and extricate their captain. By 1300, when Able Company joined the fray, there was an entire enemy battalion on top of the hill.

The Chinese had made good use of the three prior months. The bunkers on Hill 633 had four feet of overhead cover and the hill was honey-combed with trenches and fighting compartments. Company C suffered heavy casualties and was ordered to pull back to an assembly area near the line of departure shortly after Able Company joined the attack.

Tank fire and all other supporting fires, including two air strikes, were brought to bear on the objective as Companies A and B inched forward. When night fell the two companies were short of the crest of Hill 633. They dug in where they were in order to hold the ground that they had gained and were under heavy mortar and artillery fire throughout the night.

Three members of 1st Battalion earned the Distinguished Service Cross on October 13th. Corporal Otterstrom and PFC Machinski were honored posthumously; Sergeant Pelfrey lived to receive his medal (4).

Second Battalion crossed the line of departure at 0530 on the 13th and Company F was on top of its objective by 1545. They were pushed off by a Chinese counterattack fifteen minutes later. By 1610 the rest of the battalion had taken its intermediate objectives and pushed on. Fox Company attacked again on the following morning and secured the hill.

Korea: The Battle for the Ridges

As Company A resumed its attack on the 14th, PFC Arthur Okamura discovered a minefield directly in the company's path. Although exposed to enemy fire, he devoted the next four hours to clearing mines until a booby trap exploded and mortally wounded him. PFC Okamura was the fourth member of 3rd Battalion to be awarded the DSC during this fall offensive (5).

The 2nd Battalion, 21st Infantry passed through the 1st Battalion, 5th Infantry early on the morning of the 14th and secured its next few objectives by 1400. The 3rd Battalion, 5th Infantry was then ordered to pass through 2nd/21st and they did so on the morning of the 15th. After fighting all day down a long ridge line to one crest and then onto the top of the next peak, the 3rd Battalion commander discovered that they were in the wrong neighborhood. The similarity of terrain features along the ridgeline and erroneous map reading had led them astray. The 3rd Battalion was ordered to hold in place and was attached to the 21st Infantry for operational control. The 5th Infantry, with thirty-one percent green replacements, was going to have to work harder to maintain the reputation of the regiment.

On October 16th, as the 2nd/21st continued attacking north, the 3rd/5th swung to the east. As it crossed a valley, it came under small arms and artillery fire from the forward slopes of its next objective. The advance continued slowly but ended successfully as the men of 3rd Battalion dislodged the enemy, just prior to darkness, with a bayonet charge.

With 3rd Battalion on the Chinese left flank, 2nd Battalion, 5th Infantry was instructed to keep pressure on the enemy troops to its front and to advance slowly but not force their adversaries to withdraw from the trap that was beginning to close. As they advanced, they met light resistance and spent a quiet night. Apparently, some of the Chinese were heading north and taking their mortars and artillery with them.

Pleased with the progress of the operation, the 24th Division staff decided to extend the operation as far north as a demarcation dubbed Line Polar. The 5th Infantry was instructed to continue the attack and then to organize and defend Line Polar, utilizing the most favorable terrain. Third Battalion was returned to control of the regiment.

The 3rd Engineers were finally able to bulldoze a supply route through to the 5th Infantry sector which greatly accelerated the arrival of supplies and evacuation of the wounded. Prior to that, the wounded had to be carried down the ridges to battalion aid stations that were consigned far to the rear because of the terrain.

On October 18th, 3rd Battalion was assigned an east-west ridge as its objective. Tanks and supporting weapons were moved into position in the valley under cover of the heavy early morning fog. As the fog lifted, K Company was met by a heavy volume of small arms and automatic weapons fire as it approached the base of the ridge. Company L and a platoon of tanks were sent around the eastern end of the ridge as K Company made its frontal assault. When the tanks appeared at the rear of the Chinese, all resistance crumbled.

The Columbian Battalion relieved the 2nd Battalion, 5th Infantry and the latter moved forward to an assembly area near the village of Chuktae-ri where it was soon joined by the 1st Battalion. Plans were made for the two battalions to resume the attack the next day while 3rd Battalion rested on its October 18 objective. Meanwhile the Chinese were reinforcing their defenses with two additional regiments from the 203rd Division, 68th CCF Army.

The attack on the 19th got off to a slow start due to heavy morning fog and drizzle. This persistent fog, usually lasting until 1000, hampered plans for tactical air support throughout the operation. Valuable daylight hours were wasted waiting for an air strike which might, or might not, happen. When the planes did arrive, they were late and were generally directed to targets of opportunity.

When the fog lifted, the 2nd Battalion was well up on its objective and took it by 1320 against light resistance. The 1st Battalion was having a more difficult time advancing against a well-emplaced and thoroughly prepared enemy. At 0940 Able and Charlie Companies were under heavy enemy mortar and artillery fire as well as increasing small arms and automatic fire.

At 1630 on the 19th, 2nd Battalion was ordered to have George Company attack 1st Battalion's objective from the west. Darkness prevented the completion of that attack and Company G, after suffering five killed, withdrew to 2nd Battalion's position. First Battalion withdrew slightly to break contact and dug in for the night. At 0245 a company-sized counterattack forced Charlie Company to withdraw through Baker Company. Company B repulsed the counterattack and restored C Company's previous position just prior to dawn. The bodies of seven members of Charlie Company were evacuated that morning.

All three battalions moved out on the morning of October 20th against moderate to heavy resistance. At 1030 on the morning of the 21st, the 5th Infantry closed up to Line Polar all across its sector. Second Battalion moved back to regimental reserve and the 1st and 3rd Battalions established an outpost line in front of their positions. Security patrols were sent out and reported no enemy contact.

Tank Company rolled forward to Kumsong on the 24th. The tankers shelled enemy positions along the route north of Kumsong and destroyed everything in the city that might have been of value to the Chinese. The patrol drew heavy small arms, automatic weapons, mortar and artillery fire as they neared the city and reported that there was an estimated enemy company on Hill 560 defending the heights north of Kumsong. This prompted the dispatch of a company-sized patrol from 2nd Battalion, which came under fire within one thousand meters of the hill. Small probing patrols then verified the enemy positions, strength and weapons before returning to Line Polar.

Throughout the ten-day offensive, Colonel Surles had maintained his command post in an M-39 personnel carrier, from which he and the artillery liaison officer, were able to maintain communications with division, battalions, tactical air and tanks. The M-39 was able to go places that would have been inaccessible to a jeep. It was certainly a natural habitat for a former armored commander.

The 555th Field Artillery, crowded into narrow ravines and small rice paddies, provided continuous and close support for the infantrymen. The gunners fired thousands of rounds in close support without a single short round.

In his command report, Colonel Surles concluded "Prior to this 10 day offensive, the regiment had engaged in no severe combat, as a regiment, since the end of May. During that period, rotation caused a tremendous loss in battle experienced junior officers and senior non-commissioned officers. The two month training period during August and September helped to alleviate this trouble. However the regiment was an inexperienced unit on 13 October. The 10 day offensive proved to be the perfect answer to this problem. The fighting was heavy, but casualties were moderate. The action was continuous and required quick and efficient movements by motor and foot, day and night. Supply and evacuation was difficult but not insuperable (6)."

Colonel Surles' report offered no details regarding the human cost of the October offensive other than to say that "casualties were moderate." Raymond Warner's list of those 5th RCT members killed during the war lists six officers and sixty-one enlisted men who died during the ten day fight in the Chuktae Valley. First Battalion, with twenty-six KIA, suffered the most losses as a result of running into heavier resistance on the 13th and 14th and the Chinese counterattack against Charlie Company on the night of the 19th.

Good Ground

The 5th Infantry Regiment occupied a four thousand meter chunk of Line Missouri (formerly Line Polar) and its outpost line of resistance as November began. The regimental sector, at this time, was occupied by 1st and 3rd Battalions plus two companies from the 2nd Battalion.

Korea: The Battle for the Ridges

The 24th Recon Company, attached to the regiment, was employed in the center of the outpost line. The 21st Infantry was on their left flank and the 19th Infantry on the right.

The terrain was an infantryman's dream. It consisted of low, rolling hills up to 400 meters in height, a small north-south valley on the left flank, through which the Kumsong River flows, and a wider valley near the right flank perpendicular to the MLR. Fields of fire for small arms, machine guns and recoilless rifles were excellent. The battalion mortars were emplaced in good positions behind the low hills and could reach far out to the front. The Heavy Mortar Company could cover the entire regimental front from a central location. The tanks and Quad 50's could be employed in the two valleys on the flanks and in another small valley in the center of the sector. Engineers had improved the existing road to facilitate supply and evacuation.

The positions were worked on daily as carefully planned wire and mines were laid by both of the forward battalions. Security patrols were conducted during the day and night while ambush and screening patrols were out from dark to dawn most every night. Strong combat patrols were dispatched regularly from the reserve battalion to feel out the enemy positions in more detail, to inflict casualties upon him, and keep him off balance.

On 1 November, Company E with Tank Company and with one platoon of 4.2 mortars in direct support was sent on patrol to the long ridge line running from the 3rd Battalion positions. Their objective was a knob 2500 meters to the front of the outpost line. The patrol approached from the valley to the west where the tanks could be used to the best advantage. The Chinese opened fire when Easy Company reached the base of the hill. In an hour's time, the patrol secured the objective. Nine enemy dead were left on top of the hill. Another squad of Chinese fled north. One tank had to be stripped and destroyed after being severely damaged in a mine field. This was the first tank lost to enemy action since the ambush in "Death Valley", the previous April.

Two Centuries of Valor

A security patrol ran into a platoon of Chinese at 2130 on the night of November 8-9. The patrol engaged the enemy but was forced back into Baker Company's perimeter. The enemy patrol was the lead element of an enemy company that would hit B Company from the right rear at 0025. At 0120 the 24th Recon Company, on the left of B Company, was attacked from the front and rear by another company of Chinese. These attacks were repulsed by 0200. Three prisoners were taken and, when the sun rose, thirty-nine enemy dead were found in front of friendly positions.

On 15 November, the 3rd Battalion, on the left, was relieved by 2nd Battalion, 21st Infantry and moved back into reserve. The 2nd Battalion, 5th Infantry moved from reserve and relieved the 2nd Battalion, 19th Infantry. This, in effect, shifted the regiment one battalion, or approximately 2000 meters to the east. By the end of the month, similar reliefs shifted the 5th Infantry so far east that it no longer occupied its easily defended position.

When a combat patrol confirmed reports that a ridge 2500 meters north of the 2nd Battalion was defended by two to three enemy companies, the regiment initiated a series of attacks by fire against that ridge. The attack by fire entailed focusing fires of all calibers on known enemy positions for a specified time interval. Beginning on 20 November, the 105's from the Triple Nickel, a battery of 155's from 24th Divarty, direct fire from the 5th Tank Company and assorted mortars, recoilless rifles and Quad 50's pounded the ridge each day for a period of ten to fifteen minutes. The gunners took time out for a great turkey dinner on November 22.

The use of the .50 caliber machine gun as a sniping weapon was introduced to the regiment during November. An 8X Marine Corps optical snipers sight was attached to the guns by Division Ordnance allowing very accurate sniping at a range of 2000 yards. In one instance, three Chinese were killed and three wounded at a range of 1600 yards.

Korea: The Battle for the Ridges

On the 27th of November, division headquarters ordered a discontinuance of attacks by fire in view of recent peace talk developments. Armistice talks had resumed at Panmunjom on October 25. The quiet days at the end of the month were spent winterizing positions and preparing for the colder weather to come. The first snow fell on the 22nd and continued throughout the following day.

By December, the regiment's gradual shift to the east placed it in terrain that was typical of Korea. The hills reached 700 meters in height and were steep and craggy. Digging in the rocky, now frozen, soil was difficult. The steep slopes restricted fields of fire and prohibited the defensive use of tanks and Quad 50's. Nevertheless the regiment's mission was to hold Line Missouri, at all costs, and conduct aggressive patrols.

Company D of the 3rd Engineers constructed two tramways to help re-supply those companies that were defending the highest positions. The regiment also employed over one thousand Korean chogi bearers to carry food and ammunition to the more remote points on the line.

Love Company's right flank was barely 200 meters from an enemy position on the same ridge. Members of the company were being wounded, on a daily basis, by mortar and small arms fire. On 3 December, the decision was made to ignore the recommended truce talk etiquette and clobber suspected mortar positions in that area. Thereafter, enemy fire on Company L was sporadic and ineffective and no further casualties, from this cause, were sustained.

On December 6, the 1st Battalion relieved the 3rd Battalion. Enemy artillery and mortar rounds welcomed the rested battalion. On the night of the 8th, an estimated 30 Chinese attacked the Baker Company outpost. They approached from the south, moving into a saddle which separated the outpost from the MLR, and cut the communication wires. They then slipped into the outpost by way of the opening in the wire used by the friendly troops for supply deliveries.

When the CCF patrol was discovered by the defenders, an intense small arms and grenade fight ensued. The Chinese patrol leader stood on top of the position and directed the fire of his men until he was taken out by machine gun fire. Subsequently the enemy soldiers were repulsed. They evacuated twelve wounded and left the bodies of four of their comrades behind. In the morning four more dead Chinese were found in the minefield near the outpost.

Fifth Infantry patrols had noted that the Chinese had established a bunkered position very close to the Charlie Company outpost. Early on the morning of December 10, a platoon-sized combat patrol assaulted the position and flushed the enemy, killing three and wounding five of the twelve occupants of the position. After blowing the bunkers, the friendly patrol started its withdrawal but received long range small arms fire from three sides. With the aid of smoke fired by the 24th Divarty, the patrol was able to make it back to the main line of resistance.

The 3rd Battalion relieved the 1st Battalion on 16 December. It became regimental policy to relieve the right battalion more frequently than the battalion on the left. In two of the company areas on the right, no hot meals could be served because of the enemy's unrestricted observation and his ability to place mortar and artillery fire on mess lines rendered the risk too great. Moreover, the extreme right flank company was located on very rocky ground and was unable to construct adequate shelters to counter the severe weather. A cold wave at the end of December included one night when the mercury dropped to minus 19° F.

When patrols reported that the Chinese had returned to the nearby position that had been blasted on December 3, a combat patrol from King Company moved on down the ridge on 19 December to clean house again. When they got within 150 yards of the objective, they were greeted by a heavily entrenched enemy platoon armed with automatic weapons and a .50 caliber machine gun. The patrol was withdrawn and 8-inch "bunker buster" shells were called in to destroy the objective.

Beginning the night of December 22, the Chinese initiated a Yuletide propaganda campaign. Enemy patrols came within hearing distance of the regimental positions and yelled phrases like "G.I's go home" and "What are you fighting for?" They left Christmas stockings filled with Christmas cards and propaganda leaflets hanging on trees and stakes. On Christmas Eve amplified phonographs blared Christmas carols across the valley. The 5th Infantry, somewhat lacking in Christmas spirit, searched for the source of the music with division artillery and mortar fire.

The 5th Infantry instituted its own audio equipment campaign in December when its patrols began placing small microphones and receiving sets in likely avenues of approach by enemy patrols. These listening devices were then registered in so that mortar concentrations could be placed on the spot when the sounds of approaching enemies were identified.

Another innovation before year's end was a reaction to the fact that there had been two instances of 4.2 mortar rounds exploding in their tubes. All firing of this weapon was suspended until a solution could be found. Heavy Mortar Company developed a system of having the crew lie behind a small revetment and fire the piece with a lanyard. Upon approval, they were allowed to resume using their big mortars. The new method reduced the rate of fire but didn't affect the overall effectiveness of the weapon to any great extent.

The fighting during December resulted in the deaths of thirteen enlisted men. Fifty were wounded in action. As the year ended, Colonel Surles was beginning to hear some grumbling. The cold weather and the relatively static conditions imposed by the reduction in allocated ammunition and by the territorial limitations agreed to in the armistice negotiations were making life unpleasant and monotonous for the men on the line. The ice covered slopes of the hills made patrolling difficult and increasingly dangerous.

The regiment was faced by 1300 members of the 103rd Regiment, 35th Division, 12th CCF Army. An equal number of reinforcements were within eight to twelve hours of the enemy positions. The Chinese had had two and a half months to fortify their line. Their bunkers were covered with four to six feet of dirt and several thicknesses of logs rendering them impervious to anything smaller than a direct hit by an 8-inch projectile or a tank shell right into the bunker opening.

Farewell to the Twenty-Fourth Division

On New Year's Day, the 5th Regimental Combat Team was still on Line Missouri with the 21st Infantry on the left and the 19th Infantry on the right. A new relief system was instigated which rotated the battalions in such a way that each would spend ten days on line followed by five days in reserve.

On January 8th, the combat team was released from the 24th Infantry Division and became an independent unit under IX Corps control. This was a major disappointment to many of the men because it had been rumored that, when the 24th's work was done, the combat team would return with them to Hawaii. The 19th and 21st Infantry Regiments and other elements of the 24th Division, the first division to fight in Korea, returned to Japan to become part of the Far East Command reserve.

On the night of 11 January, a platoon-sized combat patrol from Company F was dispatched to the northeast of the regiment's sector to take prisoners. There were covering fires as the patrol approached its objective, a cone-shaped hill, called Objective I. The Chinese held their fire until the patrol was within 25 yards of their position and they opened up with intense automatic weapon fire and a shower of grenades. Enemy machine guns firing from the north subjected the patrol to a cross fire. Friendly artillery and mortar was placed on the machine guns, silencing two but not all. At 0045 the patrol withdrew as heavy concentrations of artillery and mortar fire were called in to saturate the objective. At 1130 the following day, the Chinese defenders on the hill received further punishment from an air strike that employed 1000-pound bombs, rockets and machine gun fire.

Three nights later, Easy Company was given an opportunity to take Objective I. They ran into the same intense automatic weapons fire, hail of grenades, and machine gun fire that had stopped Fox Company. Easy Company suffered even more casualties than its predecessor. The steepness of the hill and the slippery snow covering the ground made a quick assault impossible. At 1155 hours the company was ordered to withdraw. The hill was apparently not worth the price.

Snow fell intermittently during the month and was seldom more than six to eight inches deep. The southern slopes of the hills were generally bare, since snow rarely remained in quantity for more than two or three days. The northern slopes, however, remained covered throughout the winter period. Night ambush patrols were seriously impacted by the weather since the men were unable to move through the snow without a crunching noise and remain in position for more than two hours without risking frostbite.

When a platoon from George Company launched a daytime attack against Hill 378 on 27 January, they were accompanied by a platoon of tanks. As the platoon ascended the hill, they were supported by overhead fire from the tanks. Two enemy squads, housed in bunkers, opened fire with automatic weapons and tossed grenades. Friendly casualties mounted rapidly and it soon became apparent that the attacking force was not of sufficient size to do the job. Following the withdrawal of the platoon, Hill 378 was subjected to a series of three artillery barrages and plans to hit it, the following day, with 8-inch shells were formulated.

At 0755 hours on 28 January, the 5th RCT passed to the operational control of the 40th Infantry Division, California National Guard. The "Sunshine Division" had been training in Japan since April of 1951

(7). At the 5th Infantry command post, the day was devoted to business as usual, planning for another raid on Hill 378.

At 0730 on the 29th, two platoons from Love Company, dressed in white snow suits and shod with climbing spikes, climbed the contested hill. They were supported by three platoons of tanks and one platoon of heavy mortars. The infantrymen found that Hill 378 had been vacated. Then they moved to the next objective, a hill mass further north, and found no one there as well. Demolition teams destroyed all bunkers. Some small arms fire was received from the north and the east until artillery fire silenced that threat. The patrol withdrew at mid-morning under a cover of artillery and mortar fire.

As February, 1952 began, the 5th RCT with the 160th Infantry on the right and the 223rd Infantry on the left, occupied the same 4000 meter section of Line Missouri in the vicinity of Kumsong. Conditions were quiet for the first week of the month.

On the 7th of February, the third regiment of the 40th Division, the 224th Infantry, began relieving the 5th Infantry Regiment on Line Missouri. Third Battalion pulled off first, then the First and finally the Second. The regiment reached its reserve area at Camp Kaiser, a tent city located a few miles south of Line Missouri, on the 10th of February. The regiment was then ordered to assume responsibility for security of the tungsten and coal mines, air strip and roads in the Sangdong area and to provide security for UN POW Camp #1 on Koje-do Island, off the southern coast of Korea.

Koje-do

By November of 1950, the United Nations forces found themselves with more than 130,000 prisoners of war on their hands. In January of 1951, it was decided that those prisoners housed near Pusan would be transported to Koje-do, a small island twenty miles southwest of the port city. Koje-do was mountainous, rocky and inhospitable. There was little flat ground for the dispersal of the compounds (8).

KOREA: THE BATTLE FOR THE RIDGES

As soon as POW Camp #1 was constructed, its four enclosures, each built to house 6000 prisoner, were soon swamped with 50,000 inmates. Conditions were soon beyond the control of the small contingent of guards. Hard-core POW groups began to seize control of the compounds. Riots and disturbances began and, in September, 1951, fifteen prisoners were murdered by "people's courts."

In October 1951, the 8137th Military Police Group was activated with three assigned battalions and four escort guard companies and was dispatched to the island. The following month, a battalion of the 23rd Infantry Regiment was sent to bolster security.

In February, 1952, 3rd Battalion of the 27th Infantry Regiment attempted to regain control of one of the compounds but was attacked by prisoners armed with clubs, axes, knives, barbed-wire flails, sharpened bamboo and shovels. The "Wolfhounds" were forced to withdraw. Fifty-five POW's were killed, 22 died of wounds and another 140 were injured. The story made headlines around the world. The United Nations Command responded by sending the 1st and 2nd Battalions of the 5th Infantry Regiment to help control the problem (9).

The 3rd Battalion was given the job at Sangdong. It was to secure the area and guard the tungsten ore shipments destined for Pusan. The battalion departed Camp Kaiser on 12 February and relieved the 35th Infantry the following afternoon. The battalion command post was located near Sangdong and the line companies were scattered over a wide area.

The remainder of the regiment left for Koje-do at 0200 hours on 19 February. The regimental trucks and tanks and Korean Service Corps members drove to Inchon to board LST's while the troops traveled by train from Chunchon to Inchon and boarded a troopship, the *U.S.S. Marine Phoenix*.

The troops disembarked at Koje-do on the afternoon of the 20th after an uneventful 30-hour cruise. However, one of the LST's loaded with vehicles rammed another and all four ships had to remain in Inchon harbor while repairs were made. Three of the LST's reached Koje on the 26th and the fourth, on the 27th. Without its full complement of crew served weapons, transportation, and communications equipment, the regiment was out of business from the 22nd until the 27th of February.

As previously mentioned, POW Camp #1 was operated by the 8137th Military Police Group. The 3rd Battalion, 27th Infantry remained on the island and was attached to the 5th RCT for an indefinite period. Since only two battalions were needed to secure the prison compound, 2nd Battalion of the 5th was placed in reserve. It provided guards for prisoner labor details and maintained a motorized force capable of quelling riots and other disturbances.

Colonel Surles insisted that the regiment maintain combat efficiency while on special assignment. The battalions were rotated so that in a three week period each battalion would do two weeks of security duty and spend one week in reserve. Part of the reserve period was spent on firing exercises. By mid-March, extensive known distance and transition firing ranges had been constructed using prison labor.

Frank Marcan, of Fox Company, recalled "During our stay on Koje-do, we encountered all types of disturbances in the compounds, especially the North Korean compounds. There were a number of times when our people had to go into the compounds and separate the prisoners. I guess they were putting North Koreans in with some Chinese, or some of the 'hard core' Chinese in with the more conservative Chinese, so we ended up separating those people. This caused many problems at the time, but normally the infantry guys were assigned duty, walking guard around the compounds. We were six hours on and eighteen hours off (10)."

During the first week of March there were disturbances in two of the hard core compounds. For their actions, the Communist activists in these two areas of the prison offered such excuses as food shortages or failure of the compound authorities to return some of their comrades who had been taken from the areas and placed in detention.

On 13 March, a work detail of anti-Communist POW's passed a Communist-dominated compound. The two groups began exchanging insults and then resorted to throwing rocks at each other. South Korean soldiers in the vicinity began shooting into the compound, wounding and killing several of the Communist prisoners. The 3rd Battalion, 5th Infantry Alert Platoon was dispatched immediately to the scene and quickly dealt with the disturbance.

The 3rd Battalion, 27th Infantry departed Koje-do on 16 March to rejoin its parent unit on the Korean mainland. Five days later, the combat team's 72nd Engineer (C) Company arrived on Koje-do and was billeted with the 453rd Engineer Battalion. Several Quad-50's arrived and were consigned to Tank Company. It was thought that the weapons would be a strong deterrent to rioting.

During the first week of April, conditions were calm on Koje-do. On April 8, a screening of all prisoners was initiated for the purpose of grouping prisoners with like political philosophies. The screening provoked many arguments and fights among the prisoners themselves and between the prisoners and the guards.

On April 10, a Korean guard accidentally shot and wounded a prisoner. The POW leaders refused to permit UN authorities to remove the injured man to administer medical treatment. At 1900 hours, one hundred Korean guards armed with clubs were sent into the compound to extract the wounded man. The POW's attacked the guards with sticks and barbed wire flails, forcing the guards to withdraw. The Korean guards, on the outside of the fence, opened fire on the prisoners, killing seven and wounding sixty-three. The reserve company and a machine gun section from the 2nd Battalion were immediately moved to the scene and quickly restored order. These men manned the gate, tower and compound perimeter for the remainder of the night.

Joe Love, who was then a young 1st lieutenant in G Company,

recalled that when the 2nd Battalion arrived at the compound, the POW leadership was directing a swirling mass of inmates to attack the main gate. Lieutenant Love and his battalion commander, LTC Wooley, went to the gate to parley and discovered about fifteen dead North Korean prisoners. Wooley told Love to have his platoon use live ammunition, if necessary. Love's men fired a few rounds down the outside lanes and every prisoner dropped to the ground, not wanting to incite a second massacre. It took no more than fifteen minutes to restore order (11).

One disturbance after another occurred between the 11th and 19th of April due to clashes between the factions within the compounds. Brutal beatings, frequently resulting in death, were common. The men of the 5th Infantry were often called upon to keep prisoners with conflicting views separated in the screening areas. Colonel Surles was generally pleased with the patience and firmness exhibited by the men of the regiment under such trying circumstances.

The Punch Bowl

The 38th Infantry Regiment relieved the 5th Infantry of its responsibilities on Koje-do on April 21. During the next three days, elements of the regiment boarded LST's and sailed to Sokcho-ri on the east coast near the 38th Parallel. From there they went by truck to Inje.

On 26 April, Colonel Lee Alfred relieved COL Alexander Surles of command of the 5th RCT. The regiment, now under the operational control of X Corps, assumed responsibility for occupying and defending two blocking positions between Inje and the front lines and providing security for three communications installations. The 555th FAB, that had been detached from the 5th RCT in March, was still absent. It was attached to X Corps. The 72nd Engineer Company was under operational control of the 2nd Logistics Command (12).

The regiment's mission was to eliminate any guerrilla or bandit activity encountered in its zone of responsibility and to keep all

Korea: The Battle for the Ridges

Korean civilians, except indigenous employees of the army, south of a line called the "Farm Line." This line followed the bed of the Soyang-gang River as it bisected the corps sector. Civilians were not permitted north of the Farm Line or to occupy the many villages and towns in the area.

During several days of patrolling and arresting some 381 violators, civilians virtually disappeared from the area north of the line. No evidence of guerrilla or bandit activity was encountered.

Throughout the month of May the regiment prepared for its eventual return to the MLR. The rotation program had stripped the unit of personnel with combat experience and the many new replacements needed physical conditioning and indoctrination in infantry problems that were unique to Korea. Following an inspection by the X Corps commander on May 4, the 5th Infantry was, once again, assigned to the 25th Infantry Division.

On 26 May, the commanding general of the 25th Division ordered an operation against guerrillas believed to be operating three relay stations for the purpose of forwarding and aiding line crossers and enemy agents. Information concerning these installations had been furnished by a guerrilla captured by the Korean National Police. Companies K and L were assigned this mission. The 3rd Battalion CO accompanied Love Company and the battalion S-3 accompanied King Company. The units spent the 27th and 28th screening the valleys and ridges north and south of the suspected locations. No evidence of recent habitation or activity was found in the area screened so, on the 28th, both companies returned to the base camp.

Lieutenant General Palmer, Commanding General of X Corps, reviewed the regiment on 8 June. He presented, at long last, the Distinguished Unit Citation to the 3rd Battalion and its supporting units for their role in the battle of the Chinju Pass in August 1950. Those units in support included the 3rd Tank Platoon, 3rd Medical Platoon, 2nd Heavy Mortar Platoon, 2nd Platoon of the 72nd Engineer Company and the liaison group from the 555th Field Artillery.

On 14 June, the 5th Infantry Regiment began preparations for the move to relieve the 14th Infantry Regiment, 25th Division on the northern lip of the Punch Bowl, a portion of Line Minnesota. The relief was carried out during the hours of darkness on three successive nights. The regiment was completely in place before dawn on the 19th. Its support elements were the 2nd Platoon, 92nd Searchlight Company, the 64th Field Artillery Battalion and Company A of the 65th Engineers.

The Punch Bowl is an ancient volcanic crater in Eastern Korea, some four to five miles in diameter and rimmed by hills ranging from one to two thousand feet in elevation. In the summer of 1951, it was occupied by elements of the II Corps, North Korean People's Army. The western edge of the crater was seized by the 2nd Infantry Division in July, 1951 following the battles of Bloody Ridge and Heartbreak Ridge. The ROK Eighth Division finally wrested the eastern edge from the North Koreans on August 27 and the 1st Marine Division attacked the north east rim on August 31. By a stroke of good luck they caught the NKPA III Corps in the process of relieving the NKPA II Corps and, in the resulting confusion, the Marines pressed home their attack and captured the entire northern lip of the crater on September 3, 1951 (13).

The 5th Infantry, all three battalions on line, minus B Company, defended an 8800 meter front on Line Minnesota. The regiment was on the right flank of the 25th Division. The Turkish Brigade was to its left and the 21st ROK Infantry, to its right. These UN forces faced elements of the 7th and 14th Regiments, 27th Division, II NKPA Corps as well as the 3rd and 14th Regiments, 1st Division, III NKPA Corps.

For the remainder of June, the regiment conducted a defense of its assigned sector of Line Minnesota by providing nightly patrols and daytime tank, mortar and artillery fire on enemy emplacements. At night, harassing and interdictory fires were placed on known enemy trails and possible avenues of approach.

Korea: The Battle for the Ridges

The positions that the regiment had inherited needed some help. The tactical wire forward of the line was strengthened and expanded. Wire was placed around the crew-served weapons and mortar positions. Foliage forward of the 1st and 3rd Battalion sectors was burned to improve observation and fields of fire. This was accomplished by using napalm land mines, portable flame throwers and a flame-throwing tank. The Regimental Anti-tank Platoon fashioned "hush flares" that were laid forward of the MLR. These were improvised illuminating devices activated by trip wires. The fighting bunkers, those facing the enemy, and the sleeping bunkers, on the defilade side of the ridge, were strengthened and improved.

Little could be done about the low hanging fog that reduced early morning visibility. On the plus side, it helped mask the regiment's morning construction activity but it greatly restricted observation of the enemy's situation, reduced the effectiveness of friendly artillery and permitted the North Koreans greater freedom of movement. The fog usually burned off by noon.

On June 20th, a letter arrived from division headquarters directing all units to conduct raids, company-sized or smaller, and furnish a prisoner to Division S-2 every three days. That evening, a platoon-sized patrol from Company C moved north under cover of preparatory fire. When they reached an enemy position, small arms and mortar fire soon made the area untenable and the patrol was ordered to disengage. Patrols were dispatched as soon as visibility permitted on the 21st to search for three members of the previous night's patrol that were missing. They returned with the bodies of SGT Carvin Wilson, CPL Harry Lucas and PVT Charles Koonce.

The raiding parties continued, but to no avail. Once discovered, the patrols would receive such heavy volumes of fire that the mission had to be aborted. Small security groups and ambush patrols proved more successful in gaining information and taking prisoners. These small groups were placed along routes used by enemy patrols.

On 6 July, a security group from Company I ambushed four North Koreans, killing one and wounding another. The dead soldier was searched and the wounded one evacuated to the MLR. The prisoner and the documents were then evacuated through intelligence channels.

Recon patrols were given the additional mission of capturing and killing the enemy. During July, friendly patrols were able to obtain documents from ten enemy soldiers who were killed in fire fights. Through interrogations and documents it was learned that the NKPA troops opposing the 5th Infantry were now with the 50th Regiment, 15th Division and the 90th Regiment, 1st Division. The regiment bagged three prisoners during July.

On 19 July, the 555th FAB returned to the fold; somewhat. It relieved the 64th FAB that had been providing general artillery support for the regiment but remained attached to X Corps. Stringent ammunition allocations were in place, restricting fire on small groups and inactive gun positions. However, there were no restrictions on the amount of ammunition available for defensive operations and for the protection of patrols working forward of the MLR.

During the last six days of July, the regiment's sector was deluged by sixteen inches of rain. The continuous downpour limited visibility for long range firing and hampered patrol action. Patrols working at great distance from the MLR had difficulty keeping in touch with their SCR-300 radios. Traffic on the dirt roads was restricted to supply and emergency use for a short period of time. The delivery of mail was temporarily interrupted. The fighting and sleeping bunkers were damaged and communication trenches were muddy and sometimes impassable.

The engineers worked hard to keep the roads open but repair of bunkers was impaired by a difficulty in obtaining sufficient quantities of sandbags and tar paper. Many of the empty sandbags that were available were found to be rotten and unserviceable.

Korea: The Battle for the Ridges

At the end of July, the regiment had been on the line for six weeks. Such long periods of time in the trenches led to the establishment of a small rest and recuperation area operated by Service Company for line personnel. The facility was equipped to process one hundred men daily. Those attending were relieved of duty in the morning and returned to their organization in the evening of the same day. During this break, they had the opportunity to shower, change clothes, watch a movie, attend a church service, drink coffee and write letters. There was a "mini-mart" version of the Post Exchange for the purchase of small items. An ordnance technician was available to check and repair personal weapons.

Before August began, the Turkish Brigade, on the regiment's left, had been relieved by the 27th Infantry Regiment. The 5th Infantry continued to tie into the 21st ROK Regiment on its eastern flank. Orders came from 25st Division to step up patrolling and make at least one enemy contact each 24-hour period in order to detect changes in enemy locations, capture prisoners, detect enemy build-ups, and prevent surprises. In response, Colonel Alfred inaugurated a policy of sending one combat patrol daily from each battalion, in addition to the normal ambush and recon patrols.

In late July, the regiment had received six dogs and their handlers from the 26th Infantry Scout Dog Platoon. When they arrived, the rainy weather had not been conducive to their use. In August the dogs were used on twenty-five patrols. The dog and his handler usually followed the point man. At times, when the wind was unfavorable or when the terrain was steep, the position of the dog was shifted to the rear of the patrol. In the case of ambushes, the animal was placed at the front of the ambush site. Usually, after about three hours on site, the dog either grew restless or dozed off and was moved to the rear of the patrol.

The scout dogs were most valuable when patrols were moving from and returning to the MLR. The dog's presence allowed the patrols to advance rapidly with less chance of being ambushed. Members of patrols that employed the scout dogs were favorably impressed and always expressed a desire to use them again. For some reason, the scout dog squad returned to the 26th Scout Dog Platoon on August 23. Colonel Alfred had recommended their continued use.

As September began, the 72nd Engineer (C) Company was released from attachment to the 2nd Logistics Command and returned to the combat team. They would serve as general support to the regiment under the control of the 65th Engineer Battalion.

On September 3, an enemy patrol of fifteen men moved up under cover of fog and haze through a small, wooded draw that ran into Item Company's position. At 1130, eleven members of the enemy group entered Company I's trenches through a drainage ditch and captured a machine gun bunker after killing the gunner with a grenade. After taking possession of the bunker, the infiltrators fired up and down the trenches on both sides of the bunker. Members of Item Company returned fire from both ends of the trench.

The company commander immediately organized a small group which moved over the crest of the hill and approached the bunker from the rear. He placed his men in positions where they were able to cover both entrances of the bunker with fire. An interpreter made an effort to persuade the enemy troops to surrender. However, the North Koreans continued to resist and, as they attempted to throw grenades and fire at the G.I.'s, they were picked off by small arms, automatic weapons and exploding grenades. Ten of the enemy soldiers were killed and one was wounded and captured.

Four days later, fifteen North Koreans paid Item Company another visit. Four of them were killed during a ten minute fire fight. Documents removed from the bodies identified them as members of 6th Company, 45th Regiment, 15th Division. Several days later, three enemy deserters surrendered to Company I and disclosed that they were also from 6th Company.

Colonel Alfred continued to hope that air support would improve as the enemy improved and strengthened his positions. He felt that more frequent and closer air strikes on North Korean artillery and mortar emplacements on Hill 795 were badly needed. He received seven of the fifty air strikes that he requested. Fortunately, allocations of howitzer rounds and .50 caliber ammunition were increased in September so that harassing and interdiction missions could be fired on enemy positions.

During September, the 5th Infantry received its first AN/PRC-10 radios to replace the old World War II SCR-300's. The new radios were not only lighter in weight but had better range and reception than the older models. Most of the communication load, however, continued to be by field phone. Far-ranging patrols used the PRC-10 but short ambush patrols and support elements for combat patrols were able to use the phone.

By the end of September, the 5th Infantry Regiment had been up on the line for 105 days without relief. During that period, seventeen members of the unit had been killed and seventy-seven wounded. The flow of replacements had not been sufficient to fill the vacancies created by casualties and normal rotation. Some soldiers, who had accrued their thirty-six rotation points, were retained until replaced. This coupled with a temporary freeze on enlisted promotions and revised requirements for promotion began to impact morale in the regiment. The freeze on promotions also made it impossible for the regimental staff to fill existing vacancies with experienced NCO's.

Finally Relieved

The 40th Infantry Division relieved the 25th Division on 22 October and the 5th RCT once more passed to operational control of the 40th. On October 30, the 223rd Infantry Regiment began to relieve the 5th RCT. Headquarters and Headquarters Company, Medical Company, Service Company, and the 72nd Engineer Company left during the day. First and 3rd battalions were relieved that night. First Battalion was assigned to the blocking area behind its former position and 3rd Battalion was sent to a reserve area. A disappointed 2nd Battalion remained in position on Line Minnesota.

While the U.S. Army struggled with the aftermath of budget cuts in Washington, Communist negotiators at Panmunjom continued to drag their feet. They opposed voluntary repatriation of prisoners of war, knowing that approximately half of their comrades preferred to remain in South Korea. Assaults on isolated positions, sieges of UN outposts, and especially heavy artillery bombardments characterized this phase. On a positive note, South Korean troops were finally demonstrating that, when properly trained and supported, they could go head to head with the Communist forces.

On 1 November, the 2nd Battalion was relieved on Line Minnesota by the 2nd Battalion, 223rd Infantry Regiment and headed down the hill. At 2150 on 3 November, the 3rd Battalion was alerted to move to the vicinity of Heartbreak Ridge, on the western edge of the Punch Bowl to deal with some heavy enemy action. Fortunately the situation eased and the 3rd Battalion was able to continue its trek to division reserve. The officers and men were billeted in tents. Tropical shells served as open-air mess halls.

Following a series of command inspections by COL Alfred, the regiment began a training program to restore the unit to maximum combat effectiveness. The regimental commander felt that a tune-up in the areas of leadership, military discipline, physical training and cold weather indoctrination was needed after weeks of confined trench duty. Patrolling and the construction of field fortifications were also reviewed. A regimental communications school conducted classes in message center procedures, wire laying and radio operation. Throughout November, several of the infantry companies departed the reserve area on practice alerts, in the event that they might be needed quickly to back-up the 223rd, 224th and 160th Regiments of the 40th Division. Companies C, E, K and L provided security for radio relay

Korea: The Battle for the Ridges

installations near the reserve area.

The temperature dropped during November. Highs ran around 55 degrees and there was one recorded low of 18. Supply sergeants scrambled to provide enough winter clothing, parkas with fox fur hoods and insulated rubber combat boots for the men. There was a shortage of the new boots, commonly called "Mickey Mouse" boots in medium sizes. The insulated boots were popular with the men despite their propensity to cause sweating and irritation. They significantly reduced the number of cold injuries to feet but doubled the incidence of fungus infections. There was also a critical shortage of gasoline, as well as anti-freeze, which created an additional problem as temperatures dropped below freezing.

On 16 December, 1st Battalion and 1st Platoon of Tank Company passed to the operational control of the 223rd Infantry. Able Company relieved the 40th Recon Company at a forward blocking position near the village of Chisong-ni. On the following day, the remainder of 1st Battalion assumed blocking positions for the 223rd. The tanks were delayed by ice and snow on the narrow dirt roads to the blocking positions and didn't arrive until 24 December. At one point in December, the temperature dropped to 9.5° Fahrenheit.

During December, 2nd and 3rd Battalions continued to train. The focus was on assault teams, platoon in attack, company in attack, company in defense and recon patrolling. Half of the training was conducted at night since much of the fighting, at this stage of the war, occurred shortly before dawn.

Since it had been over a year since there had been any major infantry attacks in Korea, there was some question as to whether the training and operations people had read a recent newspaper. The G.I's surmised that the army did not possess a field manual on trench warfare but, since it did have one devoted to the principles of armed assault, the training was focused on the attack rather than on the proper construction of bunkers, trenches and barbed wire obstacles.

Two Centuries of Valor

Back to the Rim

The year ended with the regiment making plans to return to the northern rim of the Punch Bowl to relieve the 223rd Infantry. Colonel Alfred claimed that the morale of the unit was "high" despite the fact that the shower unit had been inoperative for twelve days in December. Service Company was having difficulty obtaining replacement parts.

Throughout the first week in January, elements of the 5th RCT moved forward and once again assumed responsibility for the Punch Bowl sector of Line Minnesota. The narrow dirt road that wound to the northern rim was a string of cramped switch-backs that was suitable for jeep travel but very difficult for the deuce-and-a-half trucks carrying supplies and troops. Much stopping and backing was necessary to get the big trucks to the top of "Skyline Drive", 4079 feet above sea level (14).

After arriving, the men were immediately involved in improving their positions by repairing wire obstacles, planting napalm mines, deepening communication trenches, and redeploying automatic weapons to obtain better fields of fire. A Korean Service Corps battalion was attached to the combat team on 8 January to help with this rehabilitation of the regimental fortifications.

Trench walls in Korea sloped from the top of the trench toward the center line at the bottom. Completely vertical walls had a tendency to crumble from the impact of artillery ordnance and rain showers. They were generally six feet deep and three feet wide at the base. The trenches were purposely dug in a zig-zag fashion rather than perfectly straight. Shrapnel from a direct hit of an artillery or mortar shell would spread further in a straight trench (15).

The portion of Line Minnesota occupied by the regiment formed a shallow arc, defined by a ridgeline with generally uniform, though precipitous, slopes. Observation to the front was generally good except for a few close-in dead spaces in 2nd Battalion's area that were caused by the steepness of the forward slopes (16).

Korea: The Battle for the Ridges

Across the way, elements of the 50th and 45th Regiments of the 15th Division, III North Korean Corps occupied a series of hill masses which formed a rough horseshoe with the open end facing south. Numerous fingers extended downward from the hills to the valley floor. The enemy's MLR followed along wide, relatively level ridges that connected the hills. The many fingers leading south provided him with excellent sites for outpost positions. From his high ground, he looked down upon the 5th Infantry's fortifications.

One of the difficult challenges during the cold of winter was that of remaining alert at night. Soldiers on watch wore heavy clothing to keep from freezing. Shifts were shortened to two hours to allow frequent rests. The time and distance of patrols was shortened so that men would not be subject to sub-zero temperatures for long periods of time.

The men hewed resting niches in the forward wall of the trench near the fighting bunkers. These recesses were dug from two to three feet into the wall and were generally three feet high and six feet long. The bottom of the niche was two feet above the trench floor. The open side was often covered with a blanket or poncho.

Fox Company saw the first action during the January deployment. When an enemy platoon, supported by artillery and mortar fire, probed the company's positions at 0245 on 8 January, a Fox Company ambush patrol was caught in the open and subjected to 76mm artillery fire. Two G.I's were killed and nine were wounded. The enemy platoon, losing three KIA, was finally repulsed by artillery, mortar and small arms fire.

Patrols from King Company fought engagements on January 13 and 14. The first involved a small arms, automatic weapons and grenade fire fight which resulted in two enemy kills and the wounding of the friendly patrol leader. On the 14th, men from K Company collided with thirty North Koreans and a flurry of anti-tank grenades. As the K Company patrol withdrew, under heavy pressure, they directed mortar fire on the enemy troops. The following day, patrols from Companies A and I clashed with enemy squads.

On January 12, Colonel Harvey Fischer relieved Colonel Lee Alfred as regimental commander. One of his first actions was to issue a directive from regimental headquarters stating that carbines were not to be used on patrols because of their tendency to freeze-up during cold weather. The soldiers were instructed to limit small arms to the M-1 rifle and the Browning automatic rifle.

Falling snows made both visual and auditory observation of the draws leading to the 5th Infantry's positions very difficult during the hours of darkness. Throughout the night, short bursts from automatic weapons were fired down the draws to make them somewhat inhospitable.

The vulnerability caused by these draws was demonstrated at 0120 hours on 18 January when Fox Company was attacked by an enemy company. The main effort was directed toward the company outpost. Fifty NKPA troops attacked up the draw on the left side of the OP and another thirty came at it from the right. Fighting, sometimes hand-to-hand, continued until 0215 hours. Seven or eight enemy troops penetrated the MLR and a grenade fight ensued. Lt James Murphy led a 9-man squad in a counterattack and ejected the enemy troops.

At 0350, a George Company patrol located the enemy company's support platoon and directed artillery and mortar fire which killed ten North Koreans. Upon withdrawing, the enemy subjected 2nd Battalion's MLR to an intense artillery and mortar barrage. Fox Company lost three killed and twenty-one wounded during the action. It was estimated that the North Koreans lost 42 killed and 38 wounded. However, only three enemy bodies were left behind. Several screening parties departed the MLR prior to daylight but could find no trace of the North Koreans.

During the fire fight, all wire communication to Fox Company was cut by the incoming enemy artillery; some 800 rounds. The location of the attackers in proximity to the OP and MLR hindered supporting fires somewhat, but the 555th FAB was still able to fire 1375 rounds in support of Company F during the action.

On 24 January, three enemy squads started cutting the wire in front of Able Company's sector and detonated a napalm mine. They came under small arms and automatic weapons fire from Company A's troops on the MLR and on the company outpost. The North Koreans answered with burp gun fire but finally withdrew after suffering five KIA and ten WIA.

The following night an enemy squad tried to probe Easy Company's portion of the MLR but were discovered in the barbed wire. They withdrew after suffering one killed and four wounded. Later that evening a work party from Company E found a stockpile of grenades and a burp gun about three hundred yards to the company's front.

Early in the morning of 28 January, George Company began receiving heavy mortar and artillery concentrations. Ten minutes later, one hundred North Koreans attacked along a twenty-yard front. They focused their attack on CPL Leonard Atkins' .50 caliber machine gun position. Atkins fired his weapon until it was knocked out by a hand grenade and then defended his position with rifle fire until he was killed. Approximately thirty enemy soldiers spilled into Company G's trench. A thirty-minute counterattack with bayonets and grenades was required to dislodge them.

Corporal Bert Maudie, having just returned from a combat patrol, was in the George Company CP making his report when the North Koreans attacked the command post. Maudie grabbed his rifle and charged the enemy. He killed four of them and then fixed his bayonet and managed to keep the others away from the CP. The attackers withdrew (17).

Another George Company patrol, returning to the MLR, deployed near the combat outpost. As the enemy retreated, the patrol raked them with an intense flanking fire that inflicted twenty-five casualties. Many

North Koreans dropped their weapons and ran. One member of the G Company patrol was wounded.

Screening patrols removed weapons and documents from twenty enemy dead. The 625th and 555th Field Artillery Battalions had fired a total of 2460 rounds in support of the defense in addition to the 400 rounds of mixed mortar ammunition fired from the tubes of 2nd Battalion. Bert Maudie was awarded the Distinguished Service Cross for his valiant defense of the company command bunker.

During the night of 29 January, a machine gunner in Company B sensed movement out front and fired. He hit another member of Baker Company, who was occupying the company listening post, and knocked him reeling into the surrounding barbed wire area laced with anti-personnel and napalm mines. The severely wounded man pleaded for someone to help him. His cries could be heard throughout the battalion and probably by the North Koreans across the valley. However, any attempt to approach him during darkness would have been suicidal because he was surrounded by explosive devices. As the night wore on, his cries became weaker and weaker. He died just before daybreak.

At 0800 on 30 January, the 45th Infantry Division, Oklahoma National Guard, assumed control of the 40th Division's sector, so the 5th RCT was handed off to the 45th Division. During this exchange, the 19th Battalion Combat Team from the Philippines was attached to the 5th RCT and placed in reserve.

Throughout January, Tank Company deployed fourteen tanks in fixed positions on the MLR, where they could train direct fire on enemy fortifications. Their main guns proved to be very effective direct fire weapons against enemy machine gun emplacements and bunkers. Meanwhile the 72nd Combat Engineers exploded paths through mine fields to allow the erection of barbed wire aprons and concertina fences and used explosives to loosen frozen ground that was slowing efforts to deepen trenches. A lot of effort was directed to improving the roads leading to the 2nd Battalion's area.

On February 3, the 1st Battalion was relieved by the 19th Battalion Combat Team and pulled back to the floor of the Punch Bowl. Eight days later, 3rd Battalion was replaced by the 1st Battalion, 62nd ROK Infantry. Company K, however, remained on the MLR to augment 2nd Battalion, 5th Infantry.

In late February, General Maxwell Taylor, Eighth Army Commander, accompanied by LTG White, X Corps Commander and MG David Ruffner, 45th Division Commander, visited the 5th RCT. After lunch and a briefing by Colonel Fischer, General Taylor went up on the ridge to visit the 2nd Battalion Command Post and an observation post of the Triple Nickel.

On March 3, visibility was intermittently obscured by clouds and fog. Just as the fog was lifting, twenty enemy soldiers were sighted approaching between the right flank of Company K and the left flank of the 2nd Battalion, 62nd ROK Infantry. Another twenty were sighted moving from Hill 772 toward the MLR and an estimated squad was fast approaching the 1st Platoon of King Company. Through immediate employment of artillery, mortar and small arms the attack was stymied approximately 150 yards in front of the MLR. There were four enemy KIA and no friendly casualties.

That done, the men of King Company packed up and turned their position over to a company from the 62nd ROK. Second Battalion and Company K moved down to the reserve area. The Triple Nickel and Heavy Mortar Company remained in position to support the relieving units.

Two months on the line had taken their toll on the 5th U.S. Infantry. During the period, one officer and twenty enlisted men had been killed in action and seven officers and one hundred eighteen enlisted men had been evacuated with wounds. Two members of the K Company patrol that ran into a barrage of anti-tank grenades on 13 January were still missing. Cold weather, fatigue and other factors had resulted in the evacuation of two hundred twenty-two non-battle casualties.

Heavy snows fell during the few days that the regiment was in reserve. Unit training was suspended on 11 March during a 15-inch snow fall and the troops were employed to clear the roads. On Sunday, March 22nd, the 1st and 3rd Battalions began preparations to return to the line. Baker Company took over its new position on Line Minnesota at 2153 hours.

The remainder of 1st Battalion, augmented by Company L, returned to the Punch Bowl rim on 24 March and relieved the Filipino battalion. The 3rd Battalion moved into a blocking position behind Love Company. Both battalions devoted the next few days to restoring and improving the defensive positions on Line Minnesota as best they could, given a shortage of lumber, nails and other construction materials. Patrols were sent out nightly but there was relatively little contact with the enemy.

While the rifle battalions were in reserve, the 555th FAB had been busy firing 1087 missions that resulted in an estimated 145 dead and 139 wounded enemy soldiers. Heavy Mortar Company pounded enemy work details, patrols and automatic weapons with high explosive and white phosphorous rounds. Tank Company, with 14 tanks and crews on the MLR, had also delivered extremely accurate and effective fire on bunkers, gun positions, trenches and enemy troops.

When the 1st and 3rd Battalions returned to the MLR, Tank Company was relieved by Company B, 245th Tank Battalion and departed for the Estrada Tank Range to take the X Corps Tank Crew Proficiency Test. They scored an average of 90.4%, setting a record at the range. Back on the hill, the 245th Tank continued to prevent the NKPA from employing direct fire artillery against the regiment's positions and provided excellent supporting fires for patrols.

Following the big snowfall on March 15, the winter gave way to spring. Sunny skies during the latter half of the month dried the muddy roads and footpaths. Daytime temperatures rose into the 60's but the nights hovered around freezing. The winter had not been kind to the 72nd Engineers' dump trucks, ordnance vehicles and bulldozer blades. Replacement parts were virtually unobtainable. Five trucks were borrowed from the 45th Division to complete the shifting of the two battalions on line. Meanwhile the combat engineers worked constantly to clear drainage ditches and remove landslides caused by the thawing ground.

On 9 April, 2nd Battalion relieved 1st Battalion on Line Minnesota. The 1st Battalion moved into an assembly area at Tokkol-li in the Yang-gu Valley. The other two rifle battalions followed suit on the nights of the 15th and 16th. Finally, on the 18th, the 555th FAB was relieved and sent to the Tokkol-li assembly area; the artillery battalion's first respite since June of 1952. Thanks to the 700th Ordnance Maintenance Company, the transportation picture improved. The unit's mechanics had been able to patch together an additional forty-seven jeeps, ten 2 ½ ton trucks and four dump trucks for delivery to the 5th RCT.

West to the Iron Triangle

On April 19, the 5th RCT was released from operational control of the 45th Infantry Division and convoyed west for approximately 120 miles. By 0600 on the 20th all units had arrived at Chipo-ri, a new assembly area in the 3rd Infantry Division's sector. The combat team was placed under the operational control of the 3rd Division and the 555th FAB joined forces with the 3rd Division Artillery. The 5th RCT would now receive logistical support from the 3rd Infantry Division and the 8th Army. The afternoon of the 20th was devoted to preparation for an inspection by the 3rd Division brass.

On the night of 24 April, the 1st Battalion moved forward to the MLR, in this case, Line Missouri, and relieved the Greek Battalion attached to the 15th U.S. Infantry. One Greek officer was killed by enemy mortar fire during the relief. The following night, a battalion of Chinese attacked Outpost Harry, a critical terrain feature in front of the

15th Infantry sector. Heavy Mortar Company and the 555th FAB fired many high explosive and white phosphorous rounds in support of the OP. The 3rd Battalion remained in the assembly area for two more days and then moved to a new location where it remained in reserve.

Colonel Harvey Fischer relinquished command of the 5th RCT on 24 April to become Chief of Staff, IX Corps. LTC William Kasper filled in until the 28th, at which time, Colonel Lester Wheeler assumed command.

Line Missouri followed a low ridge that ran in a northwest direction. The ridge was higher in the west and declined gradually into the Kumwha Valley. The 1st Battalion, 5th RCT no longer faced a North Korean antagonist. It was now opposed by the 220th and 221st Regiments of the 74th Division, 24th Chinese People's Army. The Chinese were entrenched on higher ground, approximately 1500 meters from the regimental front. The elevation of their works allowed easy observation of the UN positions and favored defense of their own. The enemy trenches were shaped like a sickle, beginning on Hill 533, running directly north, then northwesterly down a finger, across a draw and northeasterly up the ridgeline to Hill 489.

As May began, 1st Battalion was in its battle position on Line Missouri. Companies E and F remained in a blocking position while the rest of 2nd Battalion carried out a training mission. The 3rd Battalion was in reserve, training for counterattack assignments. Following a few days of heavy rainfall the days became fair and unseasonably warm.

The men of 1st Battalion spent considerable time reorganizing and fortifying the line. Patrols were dispatched nightly. The battalion remained there until it was relieved by the 65th Infantry Regiment during the night of May 15-16.

First and 2nd Battalions withdrew to an assembly area in the Han-Tan-Chon Valley. Third Battalion had been placed on Line Wyoming, a secondary battle line that would serve as the MLR should the Chinese force a pull-back from Line Missouri. On the last day of May, 2nd and 3rd Battalions traded positions. The 72nd Engineers were engaged in the construction of roads into the regimental area and from there to Line Wyoming. The Triple Nickel remained in position to support 3rd Divarty. Heavy Mortar Company, however, returned to the reserve area to join the rifle battalions.

On 5 June, 1st and 3rd Battalions moved forward to assume the mission of a counterattack element for the 3rd Division. The 3rd Battalion moved into a blocking position known as "The Box". The 1st Battalion was located nearby in a 15th Infantry reserve area. Second Battalion remained on Line Wyoming. Two platoons of Heavy Mortar Company were loaned to the 65th Infantry and the remaining two platoons were attached to the 15th and 7th Infantry Regiments.

Outpost Harry

On June 11, the 1st Battalion was placed under the operational control of the 15th Infantry. The assignment for "Rotary Red" (radio code for 1st Battalion, 5th RCT) was to reinforce positions of the 15th Infantry on the MLR directly behind Outpost Harry.

Outpost Harry was located on a hill that was approximately four hundred meters in height. It lay four hundred and twenty-five yards northeast of the 15th Infantry's main battle position. The closest enemy held hills to the north and east, Hill 533 (Star Hill) and Hill 412 were somewhat higher in elevation than OP Harry.

A service road, that followed a stream bed, led to a bunker at the rear of the hill where a medical aid station and a supply point were located. A communication trench ran from the supply point some two hundred feet to the top of the hill where it merged with another trench that made a complete loop around the outpost. Within the perimeter were fighting bunkers, a command post and a forward observation bunker. The bunkers could accommodate a maximum of 150 infantrymen.

Outpost Harry was coveted by the Chinese. If they were able to wrest it from the 3rd Division, it would afford them the ability to observe into the division's rear area and provide a clear field of fire for direct fire weapons. Loss of the hill would probably force the U.N. units in that sector to withdraw ten kilometers to Line Wyoming. Throughout the first two weeks in June, aerial reconnaissance revealed that the Chinese were building for a major offensive.

These attacks began on the evening of June 10 as OP Harry was being defended by two under-strength platoons from K Company, 15th Infantry. At 1940 hours, a message came from the OP stating that an unknown number of Chinese had moved between North Star Hill and Star Hill and were headed their way. Within minutes the Chinese were pouring into the trench that looped the hilltop, killing those G.I's in the open as they rushed down the trench. The surviving members of K Company, along with midnight reinforcements from Easy Company, 15th infantry, fought throughout the night from bunker entrances as first, Chinese artillery and then defensive fires from the 3rd Divarty and 555th FAB plastered the hill. At 0500 Charlie Company/15th Infantry reached Harry and helped the tired remnants of King and Easy Companies kick the remaining Chinese off the hill.

At 2300 on June 11, Baker Company, 15th Infantry relieved Charlie Company. An hour later the outpost was hit from all directions. COL Akers, CO of the 15th Infantry, ordered Baker Company, 5th RCT to move from Hill 361 on the MLR to reinforce OP Harry. Charlie Company of the 5th RCT relieved Baker Company on Hill 361. Baker of the 5th RCT reached the OP at 0428.

Around 0400 on June 12, 1LT James Evans, CO of Company A, 5th RCT, was summoned for a briefing by the S-3 of 1st Battalion. He was ordered to take his company to Outpost Harry, get everyone except Company A and attachments off the hill, and restore the position as much as possible. He could expect another attack that night and was told that it would probably entail an entire Chinese regiment (18).

Korea: The Battle for the Ridges

Evans was provided no information as to the layout of Harry's trenches and gun emplacements or word of the enemy positions. He was not even told from what direction the Chinese had attacked on the previous night. So, he elected to make a reconnaissance of the hill before moving his company there. His recon team was composed of his radio operator, his company executive officer, LT Del Tolen, a rifle platoon leader, LT William Bradbury and LT Robert Cole, the weapons platoon leader. Those remaining behind were told to get the company ready for battle.

It was about 0430 and still dark as the recon team left the MLR, crossed a small road and picked up a trail leading to OP Harry's supply trench. They soon found the dirt road that served as supply route for the ammunition, water, and rations that were carried to the base of the hill. Eventually they found the mess/medical bunker at the bottom of the slope. The medical bunker was filled with wounded soldiers patiently waiting for an APC ride to the ambulance point.

The space on the top of the hill, where Company A was to prepare its defensive position was a lot smaller than Evans had expected. The Chinese were still lobbing an occasional artillery round but it didn't stop the lieutenant's review of the hill. It did, however, prevent him from standing on top of the hill for a good view of the fighting bunkers and trenches.

The condition of the trenches was a shock. Evans had been used to seeing trenches six to eight feet deep and three to five feet wide during his tenure on the rim of the Punch Bowl. These ditches were filled to the point that they were only two to four feet deep and two to three feet wide. There was barely enough room to carry a stretcher. In some places the trenches were completely filled with dead Chinese, pieces of wooden beams, dirt, rocks, and chunks of barbed wire and metal fence stakes.

The recon team made a quick inventory of items that were still usable for protection and what would have to be brought in to rebuild.

Sandbags were high on the list. It would not be possible to bring in replacement 12 X 12 timbers while the hill was continuing to receive Chinese artillery fire. They would just have to make do with the logs and timbers that were salvageable and small enough to move by hand. There appeared to be very little water or ammunition as far as the team could determine. Several radios were found but none worked.

Evans decided that he would deploy two rifle platoons and part of his weapons platoon on the OP. Weapons Platoon's .30 caliber machine guns and 60mm mortars would be appropriate for the defense. There was a good position for the 60's on the hill. He questioned whether there would be room to deploy the platoon's 57mm recoilless rifles since the weapons have a powerful back blast that might endanger the other infantrymen. He would depend on the weapons platoon leader to make that decision.

His plan would also include stationing 3rd Platoon, led by the Company XO, LT Del Tolen, at the mess/medical bunker at the base of the hill. It would serve as a counterattack team if needed. Members of 3rd Platoon could be at the top of the hill within 10 to 15 minutes after being summoned.

First Sergeant Clyde Shinault was directed to remain behind at the MLR. The former supply sergeant had the experience and ability to resupply the outpost. Plenty of ammunition and water would be critical during the night. There were no water, food, or medical supplies on the hill. Sergeant Shinault was going to be busy.

First and 2nd Platoons assembled at 0630 on the morning of June 12. The sun was shining brightly as they proceeded north along the service road to the outpost. LT Tolen and 3rd Platoon remained at the assembly area.

When the G.I's reached the top of the hill, the sight and smell of the outpost led to some gagging and vomiting but soon each squad had chosen one of the collapsed fighting bunkers and proceeded to rebuild it and clean out the trench with nothing more than their entrenching tools. They threw dead Chinese and body parts out of the trench and onto the surrounding barbed wire.

Evans selected a bunker a few yards from the one occupied by the artillery forward observer to serve as his command post. That way he would have quick access to fire control. The forward observer was in the process of setting up his radio net and placing his team in position.

At that point, Evans circled the hill to check out each bunker and gun position and to make sure that no one remained on the hill except members of A Company and its attached elements; the 555th FAB's forward observer team, a machine gun section from Company D, and a group from the 10th Combat Engineers that was still engaged in restoring the position.

As he made the rounds, he left orders that all bunkers would be sandbagged closed at dusk, leaving a small aperture for firing. He wanted to prepare for the possibility that he would have to call down variable time rounds right on top of the hill and wanted his men to be protected from flying shrapnel that would result.

As the day grew hotter, Sergeant Shinault kept the water, rations and ammunition coming up the hill. During the afternoon, the gunners from Company D reached the top of the hill and began setting up their weapons. They were followed by the engineers who lugged up napalm mines to place in front of the concertina wire. The Chinese continued to shoot as the engineers planted their mines.

Around 1815, as the sky began to darken, Evans received word that Colonel Wheeler was down at the mess/medical bunker and wanted to see him. As he descended the communication trench, he met the tall, lanky officer, who was already three quarters of the way up the hill. The regimental commander asked Evans how he was doing and if he needed anything. Evans replied that he had everything that he needed. Colonel Wheeler reminded him that he was to hold the hill at all costs. There would be no withdrawing or surrendering. He shook the lieutenant's hand, saluted him and then started back down the hill. According to Evans, Colonel Wheeler was probably the only senior officer in the U.S. Army to get that close to the top of OP Harry.

The Chinese had been attacking at around midnight on previous nights. On June 12, they launched their first assault at 2145. Enemy artillery and mortar rounds began exploding in front of the OP and then began walking in toward the front trench. The noise, dust and smoke prevented the outpost defenders from seeing more than a few feet from their positions. Large search lights beamed from the MLR to the path leading from Star Mass helped some.

Fifty yards from the front trench there was a depression in the ground. The Chinese, coming from Star Mass, ran down into this swale and then popped up right through their own artillery to the front of the hill. The artillery barrage destroyed much of the newly laid barbed wire.

When the enemy troops reached the front of the outpost, the machine gun section's guns began to chatter and the slaughter began. The artillery forward observer called in a request for artillery support and Company A's M-1 rifles began to speak. An assault force of approximately one hundred enemy soldiers divided at the front of the hill and one bunch began to ascend the steep incline on the outpost's left flank. Artillery was directed on the front and left flank of the hill. When the dust cleared the attackers were nowhere to be seen.

At 2200, Evans discovered that the telephone lines between his CP and other points on the outpost were no longer intact, so he moved from one area to another to visually determine what was happening. Ten minutes later, friendly VT ordnance began to burst around the outpost at an altitude of about twenty meters. The Chinese answered with a heavy dose of 120mm mortar and artillery fire. The rounds arrived too fast to be counted. At 2223, friendly artillery began falling short, impacting on the left front and rear of the outpost. The forward observer requested that friendly fires be lifted.

Korea: The Battle for the Ridges

Corporal John Ross of Company D took charge of two machine gun sections after their leaders had been wounded. He evacuated the wounded section leaders and led the rebuilding of three positions, including the digging out and repositioning of one crew.

At 2240 the second wave of enemy soldiers swarmed over the right flank of the outpost and entered the trenches. Evans could see the Chinese running on top of the bunkers. He yelled to the forward observer to request VT on the position and then called out to the defenders to take cover; VT was on the way.

The napalm mines had been exploded, the machine guns had fired constantly and still the hordes of Chinese came. The VT was helping but it hadn't killed all of them. Evans summoned LT Tolen and the 3rd Platoon.

The forward observer kept the VT coming until Tolen's group entered the communication trench. The platoon moved through the trench killing all of the Chinese in their way. Then they moved forward to the front of the outpost killing the rest of the enemy on the hill. After making sure that all of the enemy soldiers were dead, they returned to the mess/medical bunker while their buddies on the hill prepared for another attack, restocked ammunition, secured water and moved the wounded down to the mess/medical bunker. Evans requested more illumination. A flare ship had been dropping flares too far away from the hill. Around 2300 the outpost received a five-minute barrage of 76mm mortar fire followed by a brief lull.

At 2330 Outpost Harry was in complete darkness. A request was made to the 81mm and 60mm mortar crews to fire illumination flares. A forward observer in another OP made contact with the flare ship and was able to adjust the location of the flares. Two minutes before midnight, the Chinese were back with whistles blowing and burp guns popping. They came in waves, striving to enter the trenches but were turned back with small and automatic weapons fire after a twenty-five minute fight.

As the enemy troops withdrew, the Chinese concentrated more artillery fire on OP Harry. The smoke was so concentrated that observers on the MLR couldn't make out the outline of the outpost. Mortar illumination was increased but the defenders on Harry still reported that the lighting was insufficient. During the next two hours artillery support was requested to deal with small arms fire from the left rear, silence a machine gun firing from the left front and disperse a build-up of Chinese on the left flank.

The next attack, an entire Chinese battalion, came from the front at 0206. When the enemy soldiers were within a hundred yards of the outpost, all available supportive fires were focused on them. While that was happening, another contingent was attacking up the left slope and was soon in the trenches. Chinese were also observed on the right flank.

The defenders opened up with machine guns, rifles, carbines, and grenades. Once again, Evans called for VT and alerted Lieutenant Tolen. There was hand-to-hand fighting throughout the trenches. When the proximity-fused VT began exploding above the outpost teeming with Chinese, the shrapnel easily found its targets. All available artillery fires were being placed on OP Harry. At 0240, LT Tolen and 3rd Platoon swept through the trenches shooting, bayoneting and clubbing the surviving Chinese. PFC Joseph Gallo, who had remained at his post when the trench was breached, joined Tolen's counterattack and engaged in hand-to-hand fighting until the last enemy soldier was driven from the outpost.

Thanks to PFC David Gulbraa, Company D, many of the Chinese never reached the trenches on the left. Gulbraa, climbing to an exposed position, fired round after round from his recoilless rifle. He left his spot, momentarily, when his ammunition ws exhausted, made his way to the ammunition supply point and rushed back to resume firing.

There were many wounded G.I's. Those who could make it down to the medical bunker on their own were told to do so. An M-39 personnel carrier was dispatched from the MLR to pick up those who needed to get to a MASH unit. The company medics were busy.

At 0318, LT Evans got word that LT Bradbury had been killed. As he walked to Bradbury's sector, the going was difficult because the trench was getting so full of dead Chinese. He was relieved to find the young lieutenant leaning against a bunker eating a can of grapefruit while surrounded by twenty to twenty-five dead enemy soldiers. Bradbury said that he had been knocked down by the force of a nearby explosion and someone must have assumed that he was dead. Those present walked among the group of Chinese bodies and put .45 rounds in their heads to make sure that they were dead.

After that the men of Able Company began cleaning the trenches and throwing Chinese bodies and body parts over the side. Then they took bayonets and entrenching tools and commenced to dig out boulders and loose dirt. The incoming artillery continued.

At 0420 the surviving Chinese began to withdraw toward Star and Star Ridge. Artillery and mortar fire was shifted to try to kill them. At 0450 Evans reported that there were no more enemy troops on Harry. He requested medical supplies, litters and litter bearers and M-39's to transport the casualties. He let battalion headquarters know that the company had suffered heavy casualties, was out of ammunition for its burned-out weapons, and that, if the Chinese made one more attempt to wrest the hill away from his company, they would be unable to stop them.

At 0455, as daylight began, the Chinese opened up, for the last time, with heavy mortar and artillery fire. A company-sized unit appeared to be massing for one last try but a good pounding from the American artillery units changed their minds. A large Chinese machine gun was still firing from the left front. The artillery couldn't find the gunner but a 75mm recoilless rifleman from the MLR finally nailed him.

The forward observer from the 555th Field Artillery issued his cease fire request at 0505. Captain John Porter, CO of Charlie Company, 5th RCT, relieved LT James Evans at noon on the 13th. Evans walked back to the MLR, reported briefly to COL Wheeler and then sacked out for the first time in fifty-four hours.

The reader may wonder if the U. S. Army had a sufficient supply of Distinguished Service Crosses in the warehouse to recognize the heroic defenders of Outpost Harry. Apparently it didn't. Lieutenant James Evans received the Silver Star for his superb leadership during the siege of Outpost Harry and the Purple Heart for a shrapnel wound to his left leg. Other recipients of the Silver Star included: LT Delbert Tolen, leader of the counterattack team, CPL John Ross, machine gunner, PFC Joseph Gallo, rifleman, LT William Bradbury and SGT Arlie Hall. PFC David Gulbraa, the recoilless rifleman, received a Bronze Star with V Device.

In October, 1953, a Distinguished Unit Citation was awarded to Company A, 5th RCT; 1st Section, Machine Gun Platoon, Company D, 5th RCT; and the Forward Observer Team, 555th Field Artillery Battalion for "courageously withstanding five separate attacks by overwhelming enemy forces, while defending a vital outpost near Songnae-dong, Korea." They had defeated a reinforced Chinese regiment (19).

The one hundred and twenty-five defenders of Outpost Harry suffered 80% casualties on the night of June 12-13, 1953. Thirteen members of Company A and four members of Company D were killed in action.

The Chinese made two final attempts on the night of June 17-18 to capture Outpost Harry. This time they were met by the small arms, automatic weapons and bayonets of Company P, Greek Expeditionary Force. The attacking elements suffered one hundred twenty killed in action and four hundred and eighty wounded in a little more than an hour of mayhem.

Between June 10 and June 18, an estimated 4200 men from the CCF 74th Division were killed or wounded in an effort to wrest OP

Harry from the Americans and the Greeks. The UN forces suffered 550 casualties in their successful effort to deny their enemies access to the vitally important hill.

On the morning of June 14th, the 5th RCT was assigned responsibility for a sector of the MLR in the Chorwon Valley on the left flank of the 3rd Division. The 1st Battalion was released from the operational control of the 15th Infantry and moved to the new area. The battalion, augmented by one platoon from Heavy Mortar Company, 5th RCT and the 3rd Recon Company was given the additional responsibility of providing security for Outpost Tom.

On the night of June 16th, a platoon from Company A provided security for a group from the 10th Engineer (C) Battalion that was tasked with providing a mine-free path to an area north of the MLR known as Jackson Heights. This would allow tanks from the 64th Tank Battalion to provide direct fire at enemy artillery positions and some railroad guns on the reverse slope of Jackson Heights and the Star Mass (20).

When the infantrymen and the engineers returned, the tanks rolled north during daylight to conduct OPERATION RANGER. Approximately 800 yards north of the MLR, five tanks were disabled by enemy mines. Recovery work was hampered by enemy mortar fire. By the time the operation was terminated, seven tanks had been disabled and two destroyed by enemy mines.

The Kumsong Salient

The 23rd Infantry Regiment, 2nd Infantry Division relieved the 5th Infantry Regiment on Line Missouri on June 20. The Fifth was placed in Eighth Army reserve and moved into an assembly area near Chipo-ri. The 555th FAB and the 72nd Engineers remained in support of the 3rd Division. Heavy Mortar Company was placed under operational control of IX Corps and tasked with supporting the 2nd Division.

June had been a costly month for the 5th RCT. Two officers, twenty-eight enlisted men and nine KATUSA's had been killed in action. Five officers, 126 enlisted men and seven KATUSA's were wounded. One hundred and sixty-six men were evacuated because of illness. It was very likely that some had contracted Korean hemorrhagic fever, a mouse-borne virus that entered the respiratory system whenever dust was kicked up by wind and artillery explosions. Despite these losses, there had been enough replacements throughout the month to keep the regiment slightly over-strength at 251 officers and 4700 enlisted men.

On 1 July, the 5th Regimental Combat Team, minus the 555th FAB and Heavy Mortar Company moved east to the X Corps reserve area near Inje. The Triple Nickel remained in Central Korea to provide artillery support for the Capital ROK Division.

After a two-week review of platoon and company offensive tactics, the 5th Infantry returned to the control of the 45th Infantry Division. The rifle battalions moved forward by convoy to relieve elements of the 7th ROK Division. First Battalion relieved South Korean troops assigned to a blocking position. Second and 3rd Battalions relieved those 7th ROK Division battalions that were on the MLR. They went into position on the left flank of the 45th Division on a ridgeline east of the Puk-han Valley facing the 536th Regiment, 179th Division, 60th CCF Army.

On the night of the relief, an enemy platoon paid a welcoming visit to Easy Company. Following an hour-long fire fight, the Chinese withdrew, taking an estimated seven wounded comrades with them.

Meanwhile things became very unpleasant for the 555th Field Artillery. On July 12, the battalion had moved into position on the east central front in support of the ROK Capital Division. During the night of the 13th, two Chinese divisions penetrated a bulge in the Capital Division's sector of the MLR south of the town of Kumsong. The South Korean division fled, causing the ROK 3rd and 8th Divisions on their right to join them rather than face annihilation (21).

Korea: The Battle for the Ridges

By 0205, two battalions of Chinese infantry had reached the Triple Nickel's emplacements. A battery commander yelled, "Point blank! Fire at will! The Chinks are on us!" Gears spun as the howitzer barrels were lowered. The men sighted through the tubes and fire flashed in the faces of the enemy but the Chinese kept coming. They leaped into Charlie Battery's emplacements and grappled with the gun crews, then stormed the battery command post. The artillerymen could no longer fire their pieces. They threw magnesium grenades into the howitzers, rendering them inoperable and then engaged the enemy with small arms (22).

By 0250 Charlie Battery was out of business. At 0410 when Battery B could no longer fire its howitzers, the battalion commander issued the order to close station. As Battery A pulled out, its perimeter of defense was broken and fire fights erupted in the area. Chinese troops infiltrated to the rear of Headquarters Battery. When the artillerymen closed the battalion command post at 0430, they had to fight their way to the rear. Battery A had saved five of its guns. All other artillery pieces in the battalion had been lost.

The surviving artillerymen pulled back to Service Battery's area and a new command post was established. The five surviving guns were laid and fire was directed on the vacated positions in order to destroy any materials left behind. On the morning of July 14th, the air force bombed the vacated areas to add further destruction. Sadly, two weeks before guns became silent all across the Korean peninsula, the 555th Field Artillery had suffered 275 casualties, seventy-five of whom had perished.

The Chinese assault subsided after several days and the ROK II Corps, reinforced by the 3rd U.S. Infantry Division, drove forward to recapture the high ground along the Kumsong River. All objectives had been seized by Sunday, July 19th. There was no effort made to move all the way to the previous MLR because much of it had already been negotiated away during the truce deliberations.

Back at the main line of resistance, two reinforced CCF companies attacked King Company on 18 July using small arms, automatic weapons and artillery fire. After a thirty-minute skirmish, the Chinese troops withdrew, reorganized, and then repeated their assault on Company K. An hour later the enemy was forced to withdraw after losing approximately one hundred killed and a hundred wounded. Two G.I's were killed and eleven were wounded. Since the recovering 555th FAB had been ordered to reinforce the 2nd U.S. Division Artillery, the 5th Infantry was supported by the 158th Field Artillery Battalion of the 45th Infantry Division.

At 2030 hours on 27 July, the men of K Company sat in their bunkers calmly waiting for the armistice to go into effect at 2200. Suddenly thousands of Chinese mortar and artillery shells impacted along the line. SFC Harold Cross sat down at the field phone, near the entrance to his bunker, to relay reports of incoming rounds to the company command post. When a large caliber shell made a direct hit on the bunker, it collapsed trapping a badly-injured Sergeant Cross and his men under the debris. When the barrage subsided, Harold Cross and five other soldiers were pulled from the wreckage of the bunker. Cross was taken by ambulance to an aid station but the medics were unable to save him. He died four hours after the armistice took effect (23).

Homeward Bound

The morning after the shooting stopped, the 72nd Engineers began the process of constructing the 5th RCT's portion of the demilitarized zone. They bulldozed eight thousand yards of "safe lane" parallel to the DMZ, erected 8200 yards of double-strand fence and began the destruction of the bunkers.

On August 1, a mine-clearing detail was dispatched from the 72nd Engineers to rescue some men who had wandered into a minefield. The detail moved through 175 yards of known minefield to

Korea: The Battle for the Ridges

Korean Boys Town

In late 1952, COL Lee Alfred was approached by Hyun Dong Won, General Secretary of the Seoul YMCA, who told him of the need for a refuge for the many homeless boys who were roaming the crowded downtown area, living on what they could beg or steal, and sleeping in public buildings, railroad stations, or in the streets. They were part of the fifty thousand Korean children that had been orphaned by the war.

The 5th Regimental Combat Team began a campaign in early February, 1953 to build a facility for homeless Korean boys on the site of a former YMCA summer camp on Ram-ji-do, an island in the Han River near Seoul. All but one of the buildings on the island had been destroyed during the fighting. The plan was to build enough classrooms, workshops and housing units to accommodate two hundred boys. The combat team set a goal of $18,000 to carry the project through its first eighteen months of operation (24).

In the first week of the campaign, the Triple Nickel raised $2500 of its $2700 by holding a raffle. The 5th Infantry then conducted its own raffle. The raffle tickets were $10 each. The prizes included a seven-day trip to Japan, not chargeable to regular leave time, with $100 in spending money.

On March 10, 1953, LTC W. P. Knowles, representing COL Harvey Fischer, presented a check for $18,000 to Dr. Hyun of the YMCA. At that time the project was already in operation with two structures housing thirty-five boys. The ten additional buildings were completed by June. The facility was dedicated in memory of those members of the 5th Regimental Combat Team who had perished in Korea (25).

In the 1970's the Korean Boys Town was moved to another location and re-christened the San Dong Boys Town. The 5th RCT Association, which was formed in the 1990's, began a practice of annual contributions to the orphanage. The United States Korean Reconstruction Agency and the Third Army Headquarters at Fort MacPherson, Georgia have also made financial contributions to the project.

clear a path and recover one injured and one dead man.

On the afternoon of August 3, the 5th Regimental Combat Team was released from the control of the 45th Division. A week later, it returned to its old stomping grounds at Chipo-ri and began to immediately create a semi-permanent camp site. The infantry battalions were soon joined by the 72nd Engineers, the 555th FAB, and Heavy Weapons Company.

Bulldozer operators scraped and ditched 2100 yards of road and cleared six thousand square yards for a parade ground. The engineers then began a logging operation to provide space for a rifle range. On 10 September, Colonel Wheeler dedicated the 5th RCT parade ground to the memory of SFC Harold Cross of King Company.

Each company was issued two Quonset huts to serve as a mess hall and a combination supply-orderly room. Concrete floors were poured for each unit kitchen and the regiment's shower point. The bulldozer operators built an access road and taxi strip for the combat team's aviation section. Once these projects were completed, it was time to turn to winterization of the tents. The engineer's efforts were directed towards prefabrication of wooden tent floors.

A twenty-six week training program was initiated by all units except the Triple Nickel on 24 August. All personnel fired a qualification course with their individual weapons. There were frequent inspections and a review of crew-served weapons, mines and booby traps, map reading, combat training, physical training, bayonet training and troop information and education. On 27 August the combat team marched in review to music furnished by the 2nd Division Band.

Despite the truce, the Eighth Army remained alert during September. The men of the 5th RCT completed their weapons qualification. Company A was dispatched to IX Corps Headquarters to serve as command post security guard and the 555th FAB participated in a corps-wide alert on the 25th of the month.

Colonel Wheeler relinquished command of the 5th Regimental

Korea: The Battle for the Ridges

Combat Team to COL Ben Sternberg on November 1, 1953. However, it was COL E. H. Strickland, who replaced Sternberg on May 3, 1954, who would pack up the regiment and bring it home to a long-lost parent, the 71st Infantry Division.

Before shipping home, the regiment spent a period on Koje-do Island until space became available near the port of Pusan. It was a very pleasant interlude for most of the soldiers who had experienced at least one Korean winter near the 38th Parallel. Joe Stine remembers glorious days at the beach. The water temperature and mild, rolling surf were more inviting than that on California's coast. Joe and some other G.I's signed up for a Red Cross lifesaving course that was held just down the beach from the 600-bed Swedish Field Hospital. As the young men tried to attend to their instructor, they were distracted by topless Swedish nurses who were sunbathing on the hospital's section of beach, an area off-limits to U.S. Army personnel (26).

Between October and late December, 1954, the 5th RCT shipped home in segments. Most of the men exited the Far East in the same manner that they had entered. They were transported to Camp Drake, near Tokyo, for out-processing, then went by train to Yokohama to board a troopship for Ft. Lawton on the Seattle waterfront. From there they were bussed to North Fort Lewis, south of Tacoma.

CHAPTER THIRTEEN

THE COLD WAR

The 71st Infantry Division was re-activated at Ft. Richardson, Alaska on October 10, 1954 and the 5th Infantry rejoined its World War II parent organization as one of its three organic regiments. The relationship, however, would turn out to be a long-distance matter.

The 2nd Infantry Division, the unit that had suffered the most casualties of any division during the Korean War, had returned to Fort Lewis in the summer of 1954 and was quartered in the relatively new barracks on the main part of the post. The 5th Infantry, the 555th Field Artillery, Tank Company and the regimental aviation section were assigned to old 1917-era quarters at North Fort Lewis (1). The 71st Signal Company was attached to the regiment for additional communications support. The 72d Engineer (C) Company was inactivated on 17 November 1954 but re-activated at Ft. Benning in April 1956.

The barracks, orderly rooms and headquarters buildings were covered with that traditional yellow army paint that some early twentieth century quartermaster must have acquired at a bargain price. Being assigned to sub-standard quarters was nothing new to a regiment that had built Fort Snelling, had beaten back the jungle to get to neglected housing in the Canal Zone and Schofield Barracks and had worked so diligently to restore and improve bunkers on Line Minnesota. The men set to work to scrub the coal dust from the walls and windows and fill the ruts in the street. The "parade ground" of two-inch gravel would just have to wait. When evening arrived it was time to sit on one's bunk, with needle and thread and a pile of khaki shirts, and transfer the 5th RCT patch to the right shoulder and affix the red, white, and blue 71st Division patch to the left shoulder.

The Cold War

Many PFC's and corporals had completed their terms of enlistment and were gone from the regimental roster. Their replacements were arriving slowly and the Korean Service Corps was nine thousand miles away. There was a definite shortage of "chogi bearers" in November, 1954.

The author pulled KP duty on his first morning at Fort Lewis and was assigned to the position of "outside man" whose job it was to empty and scrub garbage cans and the tray washing tubs. As the sun rose, he was thrilled by his first view of snow-capped Mount Rainier. He remembers thinking that, despite being up to his elbows in greasy suds, Fort Lewis might just turn out to be a good place to soldier.

Major General James Collins assumed command of the 71st Division on December 7, 1954 and visited North Fort Lewis soon after the first of the year. The 5th U.S. Infantry crunched in review on the gravel parade ground. There was a celebration of the regiment's 147th anniversary on April 12 as the never-ending Northwest rain dripped on shiny helmets and boots.

On January 31, 1955, Congress declared an end to the Korean War "emergency" leaving the 5th Infantry with one mission at Fort Lewis, to fill its ranks and prepare for the next conflict, presumably with the Soviets (2). The post's 86,000 acres augmented by 324,000 more at the Yakima Firing Range offered plenty of elbow room for that purpose.

On April 18, 1955, the regiment convoyed to a camp site on the Columbia River within the boundaries of the Yakima Training Center in central Washington. There it participated in OPERATION APPLEJACK, serving as an aggressor force during six weeks of maneuvers with its opponent, the 2nd Infantry Division. The purpose of the exercise was to prepare the participating units for desert and mountain combat.

Many of the returning Korean War draftees completed their two-year terms of service in 1955. The army responded by shipping a sizeable group of Puerto Rican recruits to Ft. Lewis to replace them. The 5th Infantry was tasked with providing their basic and advanced infantry training. Personnel clerks scrambled to find Spanish-speaking soldiers in the regiment to serve as training cadre, while the Troop Information and Education Office coordinated classes in basic military English for the new recruits.

Operation Moose Horn

In February, 1956, 1st Battalion, 5th Infantry traveled to Alaska in a 45-mile-long convoy of some 212 vehicles to join with its sister regiments and with airborne infantry and armored units, in OPERATION MOOSE HORN. The convoy moved at an average speed of seventeen miles an hour over the snow-covered highways.

There, 1st Battalion, operating as a battalion combat team, attacked the aggressor forces defending Fort Greely. The 5th BCT maneuvered in a region where winds reached a velocity of 80 MPH and temperatures dropped to 65° below zero. The troops were fed four meals a day to provide enough carbohydrates to ward off the cold.

According to Jack Salyers, a member of Heavy Mortar Company, who went TDY with Charlie Company for Moose Horn, the timing of the exercise was a deliberate move, on the part of the army, to train soldiers for cold-weather combat. The soldiers were taught to systematically check each other for frost-bite. Those men on night-time guard duty were instructed to start the engines of all vehicles every hour and run them for five minutes to ensure that they would start when needed. The battalion returned to Ft. Lewis just in time to move out of the old World War I barracks (3).

In June of 1956, the 71st Division and the 2nd Division began a process of exchanging locations. As soon as the 9th Infantry Regiment departed for Alaska, the 5th Infantry moved into the newer quarters on the main post at Fort Lewis. The 555th Field Artillery Battalion was still attached and was under operational control of the 71st Division

The Cold War

Artillery. The regiment was now supported by the 271st Engineer (C) Battalion.

Operation Gyroscope—Germany

On August 25, 1956, the 5th Infantry Regiment was released from the 71st Division and the personnel and equipment at Fort Lewis were used to reactivate the 22nd Infantry Regiment, 4th Infantry Division. The orders further specified that the 61st Infantry Regiment at Fort Carson, Colorado (in training as part of the 8th Infantry Division) was to be re-designated the 5th Infantry Regiment. Only the regimental colors and trophies were sent to Fort Carson where they were presented to the new 5th Infantry on September 1, 1956. On January 16, 1957, the Triple Nickel was re-designated 1st Battalion, 79th Field Artillery Regiment (4).

Shortly after organizing at Fort Carson, increments of the 5th Infantry were on the way to Germany to exchange stations with the 39th Infantry Regiment of the 9th Infantry Division as part of OPERATION GYROSCOPE. All units of the regiment were positioned in new duty stations in Nuremburg, Germany on 9 October 1956.

The coming year was eventful for the regiment. Training was intensified for its new mission. The interest and enthusiasm of the veteran officers and NCO's was exemplary. The regiment proved that a high caliber training mission could be conducted concurrently with a program of athletics, entertainment and furloughs as the battalions scored high on the Army Training Tests. The test results and the continuing success of the athletic teams made the 5th Infantry a unit to be recognized.

Pentomic Reorganization

On September 21, 1956, the 101st Airborne Division became the army's first pentomic division. Designed for the nuclear battlefield, the pentomic division replaced the basic triangular organization of three infantry regiments with five battle groups, each slightly larger than a battalion and commanded by a bird colonel (5).

On August 1, 1957, the 5th Infantry Regiment was reorganized pentomically. Colonel Robert J. Rosa was appointed commander. Personnel from the 5th Infantry Regiment were assigned to the 1st Battle Group, 5th Infantry and the 2nd Battle Group, 8th Infantry. The excess personnel generated by this process were reassigned within the 8th Infantry Division. The 1st Battle Group, 5th Infantry was quartered at Monteith Barracks in Furth, Germany. It was composed of the nucleus of the former 1st Battalion, 5th Infantry and a company from the 2nd Battalion, 5th Infantry brought in from Johnson Barracks in Furth.

Pentomic reorganization turned out to be largely an exercise for the headquarters folks. When asked if it had changed the life of the ordinary soldier, Stuart Clayman, who served with Heavy Mortar Company, could recall no significant disruption in his life. He remembers exchanging his infantry blue fourragèr (shoulder cord) for one of artillery red but, other than that, it was the same barracks, same buddies, same duties and same chow until his two-year active-duty obligation had been met (6).

A Regimental Mascot

Throughout history, animals have played an important role in the life of the 5th Infantry Regiment. Captured Indian ponies transported the mounted infantry companies in Montana, mules hauled the regiment's baggage until 1923, and German Shepherds gave warning of approaching enemy troops in Korea and Vietnam. We can also assume that there were always non-working animals to share the regiment's rations and quarters.

When the 1st Battle Group, 5th Infantry was stationed at Monteith Barracks, the regimental baseball team played its home games on Bobcat Field and adopted the team name of the 5th Infantry Bobcats. At that time the name "Bobcat" did not extend to the non-ball player

The Cold War

members of the regiment.

There being no domesticated American lynx or bobcat available for adoption, Heavy Mortar Company acquired a 250-pound African lion named Charlie. Charlie's tour of duty with the regiment was uneventful until the night that he broke out of his cage and prowled the company streets. PFC Marvin Teel, while on night time radio duty, found Charlie sniffing around and brought him to 1st Battle Group Headquarters. There the large beast assisted with charge- of-quarters duty until his trainer, SPC Clarence Watson, came and retrieved him. The lion was soon housed in a more secure brick and wire pen (7).

In October, 1957, orders were received to initiate plans for a permanent change of station move to Lee Barracks in the vicinity of Mainz, Germany. This move was implemented on 15 November and the 1st Battle Group, 5th Infantry entered the second phase of its mission with NATO Forces in Europe.

Meanwhile, back at Fort Carson, the 2nd Battle Group, 5th Infantry was activated on December 1, 1957 and became part of the 9th Infantry Division. This reincarnation of the former 2nd Battalion, 5th Infantry remained with the 9th Division until it was inactivated in the fall of 1959.

The 1st Battle Group, 5th Infantry quickly adjusted to its new role with V Corps of the Seventh United States Army. In January of 1958, a levy of approximately 600 draftees was received to fill the gap left by a like number who departed for home after completing their two years of active duty. This led to a period of concentrated basic and advanced unit training. Approximately fifty percent of the time was spent in the field on training exercises and maneuvers.

Under the leadership of seasoned officers and NCO's the 5th Infantry was quickly crafted into a combat-ready force capable of performing any mission. This period of intensified training culminated with the 5th Infantry completing the Army Training Tests in August, 1958 with a rating of superior.

Members of the battle group exchanged their M-1 rifles, Browning automatic rifles and carbines for the M-14 rifle. The new rifle, capable of both semi-automatic and full automatic fire, used the standard NATO 7.62mm cartridge.

Rotation to Fort Riley

In September, 1958, the 1st Battle Group, 5th Infantry was alerted for rotation to Fort Riley, Kansas. It was released from the 8th Division in USAREUR and became part of the 1st Infantry Division, CONUS. The 1st Airborne Battle Group, 505th Infantry replaced the 5th Infantry at Mainz. The 5th Infantry replaced the 2nd Battle Group, 2nd Infantry Regiment at Fort Riley.

Advance parties were exchanged in October, 1958 and, with preparations complete, the battle group departed from Germany. It sailed from Bremerhaven on January 17, 1959 aboard the *U.S.S. Butner*. Upon arrival in New York, a week later, the majority of the soldiers availed themselves of a long-awaited leave.

Reassignment of personnel, coupled with losses prior to departure from Germany left the battle group at less than fifty percent of authorized strength. The officers and men once more began the task of rebuilding the 5th Infantry, now that it was part of the "Big Red One" at historic Fort Riley. COL Graham E. Schmidt assumed responsibility for that enterprise when he relieved COL W. R. Peers on January 26, 1959.

On March 2, 1959, the 1st Battle Group, 5th Infantry commenced a four-week training program in methods of instruction, weapons refresher training and general military subjects so that it would be ready to train the new recruits who would begin arriving in the middle of March. The battle group was given the mission of training approximately one thousand trainees in both basic and advanced individual training. The first cycle of basic training was completed by four hundred recruits on May 22, 1959.

The Cold War

Prior to completion of the basic training cycle, the 5th Infantry was given the added responsibility of supporting the tactical training of approximately two thousand senior ROTC cadets from throughout the 5th Army area. Between August, 1959 and January, 1960 the battle group trained over 2000 recruits in basic and advanced individual training (AIT).

During this period, the 5th Infantry participated in a celebration at Ft. Hayes, Kansas in commemoration of elements of the 5th Infantry that were stationed there following the Civil War. The 1st Battle Group also honored President Dwight D. Eisenhower, during a visit to his home in Abilene, Kansas. Throughout this ceremony, the massed colors of the 1st Infantry Division and its composite units were presented by an honor guard commanded by 5th Infantry officers.

In 1959, the U.S. Army shrank to 862,000 men, its lowest personnel total since 1950. In May, a 3rd Battle Group, 5th Infantry, with a D series TO&E, was activated as a reserve unit at Fort Devens, Massachusetts from personnel that had been assigned to the 301st Infantry. The D series configuration eliminated Heavy Mortar Company but added Company E as a fifth rifle company and a Combat Support Company to provide mortar support, assault weapons, and battlefield radar surveillance and reconnaissance capabilities. The 3rd Battle Group became part of the 94th Infantry Division, XIII U.S. Army Reserve. In the fall of 1959, the 2nd Battle Group, 5th Infantry was deactivated at Fort Carson, Colorado, leaving the 1st Battle Group as the only 5th Infantry unit on active duty.

In 1961, the 1st Battle Group, 5th Infantry needed another infusion of replacements and it was incumbent upon the unit to give many of these new men their basic combat training as well as AIT. Then the battle group went to Tarryall, Colorado to participate in the Army Training Tests. The training cadre had done its job. The 1st Battle Group earned a combined score of 95.4. Individual company scores ranged from 80 for Company E to 91.6 for Company A.

In April, 1962, the 1st Battle Group, 5th Infantry was still at Ft. Riley, Kansas, where its primary mission was support of the ROTC program at Camp Funston. When the ROTC mission was accomplished the battle group returned to the task of training infantry replacements. Once these recruits had completed basic and AIT with the 5th Infantry, they were assigned to units throughout the entire army.

The 25th "Tropic Lightning" Division

In the early 60's, as the army began to be drawn into the troubles in Vietnam, the pentomic organization was dropped in favor of returning to a modified triangular division of three brigades of three infantry battalions each. The 1st Battle Group, 5th Infantry was released from the 1st Infantry Division on February 1, 1963 and assigned to the 2nd Brigade, 25th Infantry Division as the 1st Battalion, 5th Infantry Regiment. This was accomplished by re-flagging the 2nd Battle Group, 21st Infantry. The battalion was quartered at Schofield Barracks, Hawaii, where it was brigaded with the 1st and 2nd Battalions of the 27th Infantry Wolfhounds (8). The men and assets at Ft. Riley became part of the 26th Infantry Regiment.

Due to budget restrictions, the division was composed of seven rather than nine infantry battalions. In addition to 1st of the 5th, there were two battalions each from the 14th, 27th and 35th Infantry Regiments, five battalions of artillery, the 69th Armored Regiment, the 65th Engineer Battalion, the 3rd Squadron, 4th Cavalry and several other support units. Companies E, D, and the Combat Support Company were dropped.

From the beginning of the new organization, according to Major General (Ret) Jerry Bethke, the men of 1st Battalion, 5th Infantry referred to themselves as "Bobcats (9)." Bethke commanded Charlie Company in 1963. There was no reference to the term "Bobcat" during the 1st Infantry Division period but, at some point between 1957 and 1963 the Bobcat name had generalized from the baseball team to all

The Cold War

members of the battalion.

In June and July of 1963, the 5th Infantry, commanded by Colonel Keneth Johnson, participated with the rest of the division in Exercise Dhanarajata, a training mission in Thailand (10). Jerry Bethke remembers that Dhanarajata was intended as a show of force to counter an imminent communist threat from Laos.

Following the maneuvers, the battalion participated in a Southeast Asia Treaty Organization (SEATO) parade in Bangkok. They were reviewed by the King of Thailand before packing up and returning to Schofield Barracks.

At the time of reorganization, the 5th Infantry had received sixty-eight M-113 armored personnel carriers from the motor pool. The new "mechanized" battalion was comprised of three rifle companies, A, B, and C, and a Headquarters Company that included a headquarters contingent plus reconnaissance and medical platoons.

During the fall of 1963, Companies B and C moved by water to the Pohakoloa Training Area on the island of Hawaii to support the Fourth Cavalry and the Sixty-ninth Armored Division as the latter units completed their annual Army Training Tests. The 5th Infantry companies were joined by the remainder of the battalion on November 3.

During the next thirty days, the 1st Battalion conducted its own tests and engaged in small arms and crew-served weapons firing. It cooperated with elements of the 65th Engineers, the Fourth Cavalry Regiment, and the 25th Aviation Group.

In January of 1964 the battalion received sixty replacements straight from eight weeks of basic training. The 5th Infantry provided them with their advanced individual training. The battalion was also directed to instruct its sister battalions in the deployment of the mechanized unit. The personnel carrier crews demonstrated company-sized movements over the rough and hazardous terrain at the Kahuku Training Area, completing this task in mid-March (11).

Company A had the opportunity to demonstrate its prowess as a mechanized unit to a larger audience in February, 1964 during Exercise Quick Release on Okinawa. They flew to Okinawa from Hickam Field while their armored personnel carriers traveled by water. Following the four-day mock battle on the northern part of the island, the company was given superior ratings by all observers.

On August 2, 1964, all U.S. forces were placed on alert after North Vietnamese gunboats were reported to have attacked the Navy destroyer, *U.S.S. Maddox*, in the Gulf of Tonkin. On 17 September, Companies A and B underwent three days of jungle training at Kahuku.

In 1965, the battalion returned to the "Big Island" to undergo annual proficiency testing and to support other units that were doing the same. While at the Pohakoloa Training Area in March, Recon Platoon, assisted by the 65th Engineers, worked on the construction of "Bobcat" Trail #2. This was the first official reference that the author could find that was related to the current regimental nickname (12).

On August 12, 1965, 1st Battalion (Mechanized), 5th Infantry held an Organization Day parade to celebrate the battalion's second anniversary. Whether anyone, at the time, reminded the unit of its 157 year heritage is unclear. Two days later, Lieutenant Colonel Thomas Greer replaced Lieutenant Colonel Thomas Tarpley as battalion commander. "Tug" Greer, as his peers called him, was a 1950 West Point graduate and veteran of the Korean War.

After completing its annual tests in September, the battalion continued to train at Kahuku. The subjects included; code of conduct, jungle survival training, rappelling cliffs, ambush and counter-ambush training, land navigation, river crossing techniques and firing the .50 caliber machine gun, mounted on M-113 armored personnel carriers, while the vehicle was moving. The preparation for combat in Vietnam was becoming more focused.

The Kahuku Mountains are steep mounds of volcanic rock with little top soil. According to Lance Wickman, who was a platoon leader

The Cold War

in Charlie Company at the time, the men had been struggling up and down the rocky slopes for five days and were looking forward to returning home, turning in their equipment and heading for the beach (13).

On the final day of the exercise, LTC Greer dropped by Charlie Company's position and told the company commander that he would like the company to establish defensive positions. That meant digging foxholes in volcanic rock with entrenching tools. The company commander pulled the platoon leaders together and gave them orders for establishing defensive positions. He said "Since we want to get this over quickly, we won't actually dig foxholes. Instead we will simply do 'simulated foxholes.' We will just mark out on the ground where we would put the foxholes."

When Tug Greer came around to inspect the defensive positions, he was told that the markings on the ground were simulated foxholes. "Simulated foxholes" roared Greer. "I ordered this company to prepare defensive positions and that means digging foxholes! This company is going to stay out here and dig until it learns how to dig foxholes that look like they came out of the training manual."

While the rest of the battalion packed up weapons and equipment and headed back to the base and an afternoon at the beach, Charlie Company remained on that hillside struggling to penetrate the hard rocky surface. LTC Greer didn't win any popularity contest that afternoon but, by evening, they had foxholes that did look like they had come out of a training manual.

Greer was privy to information that he could not share with the men on that beautiful Hawaiian afternoon. He knew that they were involved in their last training exercise before the battalion would ship to Vietnam. He had vivid memories of his classmates who had died on the rugged slopes of Korea and was determined to do all that he could to save the lives of those men now entrusted to his care.

CHAPTER FOURTEEN

VIETNAM

American troops were involved in the Vietnam struggle as early as 1954 when a few of them assisted the French withdraw after suffering their defeat at Dien Bien Phu. Several hundred U.S. advisors then began helping the South Vietnamese in 1959. On July 8 of that year, the Viet Cong killed Major Dale Buis and Master Sergeant Chester Ovnard, usually considered the first Americans to lose their lives in the Vietnam War. By the end of 1961, more than 3000 U.S. military personnel were in South Vietnam. On February 6, 1962, the U.S. Army established the Military Assistance Command Vietnam (MACV) in Saigon (1).

In April of 1963, the 25th Infantry Division began sending a few men at a time to Vietnam for temporary duty as machine gunners aboard Army H-21 helicopters. These door gunners included at least two Bobcats, CPL Horace Collins of Company C and PFC Jerry W. Osborn of Headquarters, 1st Battalion. At the start of 1964, nearly 15,000 U.S. "advisors" were in South Vietnam, many of them participating in combat while ostensibly serving only to give advice. Collins and Osborn were killed in action in 1965 before the 5th Infantry was deployed to the battle zone (2).

In August, 1964, when the *U.S.S Maddox* encountered three North Vietnamese patrol boats, President Lyndon Johnson claimed that the encounter was an unprovoked attack on U.S. ships. He was able to persuade Congress to pass the Gulf of Tonkin Resolution, a blank check for a wider and deeper U.S. involvement.

The initial campaign plan for U.S. forces in Vietnam was prepared in 1965 by General William C. Westmoreland, Commander of the U.S. Military Assistance Command. It consisted of three general phases:

VIETNAM

Phase One—commit those American and allied forces necessary "to halt the losing trend" by the end of 1965; Phase Two—"during the first half of 1966" take the offensive with American and allied forces in "high priority areas" to destroy enemy forces and reinstitute pacification programs; and Phase Three—if the enemy persists, he might be defeated and his forces and base areas destroyed during a period of a year to a year and a half following Phase Two. In other words, General Westmoreland planned to wrap things up by the end of 1968.

South Vietnam was divided into four tactical zones. Each zone was the responsibility of a separate corps of the Army of the Republic of Viet Nam. The South Vietnamese III Corps was responsible for the III Corps Tactical Zone or, more specifically, defending the approaches to Saigon.

The 173rd Airborne Brigade was the first U.S. Army unit to arrive in the III Corps Zone. The paratroopers were deployed to the Bien Hoa Air Base in May, 1965. They were followed by the 1st U.S. Infantry Division in October, 1965.

On 27 December 1965, the 25th Infantry Division was alerted to deploy to the III Corps Tactical Zone. The division's 2nd Brigade, consisting mainly of the 1st and 2nd Battalions, 27th Infantry and the 1st Battalion, 5th Infantry, arrived at Vung Tau, South Vietnam on 18 January 1966 aboard the *USMTS General Gordon* (3). Vung Tau is a seaport on the South China Sea.

The brigade's orders were to deploy in the Cu Chi District between Saigon and the Cambodian border. The men were flown to Tan Son Nhut Air Force Base and trucked to Cu Chi. The deployment was completed late in the afternoon on January 29.

This time when Colonel Greer told the troops to establish a defensive position, they knew what to do. They were in Tug Greer's battalion. A neighboring battalion that arrived about the same time as the 5th, scooped out some shallow cavities—planning to dig real foxholes the following day. That night the Viet Cong launched a massive mortar barrage upon the green troops. The men of 1st Battalion, 5th Infantry were secure in their foxholes but their neighbors were not so fortunate. When the sun came up on January 30, Tug Greer's name was again on everybody's lips—but this time with reverence and respect (4).

That morning, two rifle companies of the 5th Infantry passed through the lines of the 27th Infantry and attacked outward to expand and clear the base camp perimeter. They were followed by 2nd Battalion, 27th Infantry and Bravo Company of the 65th Engineers. During a five day operation, twenty tunnel complexes were located and destroyed.

On January 31st, a booby trap was detonated killing SPC Armando Tesillo and SGT Dan Shearin of Company B. Their deaths were a wake-up call for the 5th Infantry Bobcats. Vietnam was the real thing; not a training exercise on the Big Island (5).

Valentines Day, 1966, was a tough day for Alpha Company. At 0630 the company left the base camp on foot and crossed the Ben Muong River to conduct a reconnaissance in force. Security for their river crossing and route of withdrawal was provided by platoons from Companies B and C. Throughout the morning Company A swept the area, destroying houses and rice caches. By 1100, ten soldiers had suffered wounds.

Suddenly two Chinese Communist claymore mines (round-shaped, command-detonated mines filled with chunks of steel connecting rods) were detonated by the Viet Cong killing Captain William Hoos of A Company, three of his soldiers, two forward observers from the 8th Artillery, and two non-combatant photographers. Three other Alpha Company soldiers were wounded. The surviving members of the party reached the relative safety of the camp perimeter at 1630 hours.

Shortly after midnight on February 18, 1st Platoon of Charlie Company slipped across the Ben Muong on a raiding mission. They moved through dry rice paddies and stopped about twenty-five meters short of the wood line of a rubber plantation. SP4 Daniel Fernandez and his squad leader moved about three hundred meters into the trees and then returned to the platoon and reported seeing no available target. The platoon then moved back about 100 meters and set up a perimeter defense near a graveyard. They planned to wait until mid-morning before returning to the base camp.

At about 0700, the left flank of the raiding party was attacked by a group of Viet Cong. The M-60 machine gunner on the left, SP4 Joseph Benton, killed three of the enemy before he was killed. The Viet Cong reacted with intense small arms and automatic weapons and grenade fire. The G.I's on the left fell back about twenty yards, leaving Benton's body. Hernandez and a medic dashed forward to retrieve the dead soldier. Three other men advanced to help them. When the man carrying the gunner was hit in the leg, the group dropped to the ground and returned fire. Suddenly Daniel Fernandez spied a grenade that had dropped among the group. He accidentally kicked the grenade as he attempted to get away from it and it rolled near the wounded man who had been carrying the dead gunner. Yelling a warning, Fernandez dropped on the grenade and absorbed the blast with his body.

As artillery, mortar and air strikes hit the enemy positions, the surviving members of Company C pulled back to the rice paddy. The body of Joseph Benton, the mortally wounded Hernandez and the wounded man that he had saved were dusted-off to the hospital. The remaining members of the platoon reached the base camp perimeter at 0935 hours. Specialist Daniel Hernandez was posthumously awarded the Congressional Medal of Honor for his sacrifice (6).

First Battalion, 5th Infantry began a two-day search and clear effort, OPERATION CLEAN SWEEP, on February 22. The mission involved clearing a wooded area some 1500 meters southeast of the Cu Chi base camp. Companies A and B crossed the line of departure at 0830. They were eventually followed, on the right, by the 1st Battalion of the 49th ARVN Regiment. The South Vietnamese troops reached their line of departure seventeen minutes late. The assault was supported by Bravo Company of the 65th Engineers and 1st Battalion, 8th Artillery. The task force located and destroyed many Viet Cong tunnel complexes and bunkers. They uncovered three food caches, including eight hundred pounds of rice, and numerous documents and articles of clothing (7).

Clean Sweep was the 5th Infantry's first real combat experience using armored personnel carriers during a battalion-sized assault. In Korea, tracked vehicles had been largely reserved for transporting supplies to and wounded from a dangerous zone, like an outpost. The M-113 armored personnel carriers proved to be difficult to coordinate through heavily wooded areas but were invaluable when crossing large open areas like rice paddies. Air observation helped with the coordination problem; that of maintaining a straight battle line.

The APC's or "tracks", as they were called by the troops, were designed to transport an eleven-man infantry squad, in a tight squeeze. Entry was made through a hydraulic ramp on the rear of the vehicle. There was a four foot square cargo hatch in the ceiling of the carrier and a smaller machine gun hatch right behind the engine wall and to the right of center. Alfred Hohman, a soldier in Headquarters Company, 5th Infantry in 1965-66, designed and welded a three-piece metal shield on all of the battalion's tracks to protect the .50 caliber machine gunner. The shield could be rotated so that the gunner could fire in any direction.

Four years later, SP5 Donald Bissonette created another safety measure for the M-113. He added extension bars to the two steering levers enabling the driver to steer while sitting atop the driver's hatch. He was exposed to small arms fire but safer from exploding mines and booby traps (8).

Operation Clean Sweep continued until the 24th of February. Most of the Viet Cong had fled the area but there was confirmation that eleven enemy soldiers had been killed and estimates of thirteen additional KIA. The 5th Infantry lost two soldiers from Headquarters Company and three from Bravo Company. Eighteen members of the company were wounded; ten requiring hospitalization. The men who died during Operation Clean Sweep brought the battalion death toll for February, 1966 to thirteen.

As the days went by the soldiers of the 5th Infantry experienced some harsh lessons. They were learning a lot about the booby traps employed by the Viet Cong. Hand grenades, unexploded cluster bomblets and Chinese claymores were detonated by trip wires that varied in their distance from the ground. They would appear on trails and in tunnels (9).

In late March it was reported that a main force battalion of VC had been operating in the 5th Infantry's sector of responsibility. Whenever these forces learned that a major U.S. attack was underway, they would withdraw to safety in areas known as the Ho Bo Woods and the Iron Triangle. OPERATION CIRCLE PINES, an eight-day search and destroy operation was devised to deal with the problem. The 1st of the 5th was to seal off all routes of escape while the 7th ARVN Regiment conducted a search and destroy operation in the village of Phu Hoa Dong (10).

On 29 March, the first day of the operation, enemy contact was light. Two Bobcats were wounded. By evening the task force had killed ten VC, captured three others and located three rice caches. On the following day, Recon Platoon and A Company found large stores of ammunition and medical supplies. Ten night ambush sites were established but they spent a quiet night.

It was on April 4, the seventh day of Circle Pines, that the most significant action took place. At 0819, Recon Platoon discovered several large rice caches in a well concealed and fortified area. A half hour later, the battalion, engaged in a northern sweep, came under heavy rifle grenade fire. Artillery and gun ships were called in and the VC were engaged by small arms fire. During the day, 23 Viet Cong were killed. The sweep netted over four tons of rice and a large amount of military equipment, munitions and arms. Nineteen members of the battalion were wounded and eleven were killed during Circle Pines.

As in previous operations, it was becoming more apparent that working side-by-side with the Army of the Republic of Viet Nam was very difficult. During attacks the ARVN troops neglected to stay in line. After the first day, the South Vietnamese soldiers had stopped following the operational plan and failed to adequately clear Phu Hoa Dong.

On April 13, 1st Battalion, 5th Infantry, accompanied by tanks from C Company of the 69th Armored Battalion and a platoon from the 65th Engineers, began a two-day operation in an area known as the Filhol near the Ho Bo Woods. The terrain was primarily dense areas of rubber trees and rice paddies. The 305th Viet Cong Battalion was known to have established bases in the neighborhood.

As search and destroy teams moved through the jungle, seven armored personnel carriers, three tanks and one tracked vehicle retriever hit mines. One of the tanks was penetrated by a rocket propelled grenade round that slightly injured one of its crew.

At 0950 Company B ran into sniper and RPG fire from an area combed with tunnels and spider holes and lost five men killed and seven wounded. When evening came, Companies A and C and Recon Platoon closed into a battalion base camp. Company B established a perimeter around three tanks that had become mired and remained there until the tanks were extracted at 2300.

The following afternoon, three men from Company A discovered a rice cache. As they were examining it, a booby trap was detonated killing PFC Lewis Thomas and injuring the other two. A dust-off helicopter tried to get in to retrieve the three men but came under automatic weapons fire. It was able to touch down successfully after gunships and artillery blasted the enemy fighters. All elements were back within the Cu Chi Base Camp perimeter by 1900 hours after a

VIETNAM

costly two days in an area laced with mines.

Elements of the 2nd Brigade moved into the area around Ap Binh Tay, ten miles west of Cu Chi, on April 20. As the 27th Infantry sealed off the west and south, the 5th Infantry moved in with its armored personnel carriers to block the east. At the same time, B Troop, 3rd Squadron, 4th Cavalry sealed off the north completing the noose. Minutes later the 69th Armor joined the Wolfhounds. More than 111 suspects were rounded up during the resulting sweep. Interrogation and screening revealed that twenty-two were confirmed Viet Cong. The captured VC's were turned over to South Vietnamese officials for "further processing." In addition to the 22 prisoners, 54 were killed and 15 individual weapons, 19 mines and one 81mm mortar were seized.

On April 23, a sergeant from Company B was conducting a class on the use of the Claymore anti-personnel mine in the battalion motor pool. He and his pupils were inside an APC, with the rear ramp down, when the Claymore, which has a lethal range of fifty meters, accidentally detonated. PFC Francisco Correa-Morales and PFC John Isaacs died immediately and four others were rushed to the hospital. The four wounded men died during the course of the following five weeks (11). The Cu Chi area was proving to be a tough assignment. The entire 25th Infantry Division lost 91 men killed in action between January and the first of May, 1966. Forty-one of the casualties were members of 1st Battalion, 5th Infantry.

When the people of Hawaii heard of the wide-spread poverty in the Vietnamese villages, they donated soap, toothpaste, toothbrushes, clothing, toys and many other items to assist the men of the 25th Division in their campaign to befriend the villagers. During the first week in May, the battalion helped distribute and show the locals how to use the items. At the same time, members of the battalion's medical platoon participated in a MEDCAP (Medical Civic Action Program) to the outlying villages (12).

On June 3, the 5th Infantry joined three other battalions in OPERATION MAKIKI, a search and destroy mission in the Bao Trai area. As soon as the battalion reached its assigned area of operations, Recon Platoon observed several VC fleeing through tall grass. They shot two and ran over two more. A detailed search of the area turned up many VC hiding underwater in a rice paddy (13).

Fragmentation grenades were found to be ineffective under water. The submerged guerrillas had to be hunted down and killed with small arms and automatic weapons fire. The platoon members killed twelve and captured nineteen of the enemy. Large caches of rice and ammunition were found on the 6th and the 7th of June. On two occasions snakes fell from bamboo hedgerows into the open cargo hatches of APC's and inflicted snake bite injuries which required medical evacuation of the victims.

The 5th Infantry returned to the vicinity of Boi Loi and the Ho Bo Woods for a separate six-day battalion operation on June 25. It was code-named OPERATION COCO PALMS. The area was honeycombed with well-constructed bunkers and tunnels. During the next five days, the battalion destroyed 155 bunkers and 78 tunnels. It was suspected that only a small percentage of the tunnels and bunkers were destroyed. The Viet Cong inhabitants fought from inside the tunnels and died when explosive charges, set by the 65th Engineers demolition team, were detonated near them, collapsing the tunnels. Flame throwers mounted on tracks proved to be very useful during this operation because of the existence of so many bunkers.

At this point in the war, a technique to adequately destroy a complex tunnel system had not really been developed. Shallow tunnels, less than 6 feet in depth, could be filled with acetylene gas and then detonated. However, most of the tunnels in the Boi Loi-Ho Bo Woods area were much deeper. Such tunnel systems required the setting of several explosive charges placed at key levels and wired in parallel with a detonating cord. When detonated, there was a simultaneous explosion of all charges resulting in a complete cave-in. This method required a large amount of explosives and involved crawling through the tunnel and possibly encountering some inhospitable residents (14).

On the morning of June 28, PFC Gerald Rolf of Company B was the first to enter a tunnel. The man following him said "We got to a corner in the tunnel. It turned 90 degrees to the right. He (Rolf) moved part way around a corner and said, 'Oh,no' and then some shots were fired and he was dead." The men who went into the tunnel to retrieve his body came under fire and had to use their dead buddy's body as a shield as they exited. PFC Rolf was one of six Bobcats to die during Operation Coco Palms.

Many of the tunnels around Cu Chi had been constructed early in the 20th Century to be used for food storage. In the 1950's, the Viet Minh began using the tunnels for military operations in their fight against the French. During the Vietnam War, the Viet Cong improved and enlarged them. They sealed off sections to guard against grenades and tear gas and were actually able to employ rabbits and moles to dig ventilator holes rather than betray the location of their tunnel with a vent pipe.

Division command had requested a B-52 air strike in the Boi Loi/Ho Bo Woods area for an hour preceding the ground attack, since the Viet Cong bunkers were capable of withstanding direct hits by artillery rounds. The ground attack was delayed for nearly an hour because the Air Force didn't respond to the request in a timely fashion. Finally, when the request was denied, the 1st Battalion and its supporting elements moved into the Ho Bo Woods. The 7th Air Force did provide some satisfactory close air support during the operation.

Counteroffensive — Phase II — July, 1966

Following Operation Coco Palms, the 25th Division Chemical Section provided technical supervision as the troops dispersed 2,4-D defoliant around the perimeter of the Cu Chi Base Camp. A mixture of the defoliant and diesel was loaded into tear gas dispensers and sprayed from trucks or from back-pack dispensers. Additional applications were needed to keep up with new growth.

During a three-hour period on July 19, four platoons from Alpha Company, 27th Infantry were gradually inserted into an area by helicopter. Soon after digging in, they became heavily engaged with a Viet Cong battalion. At 1504 hours, Company B of the 5th Infantry was alerted as a possible reaction force and mounted its vehicles. They could hear the sound of constant firing from artillery and helicopter gunships as they waited impatiently for their orders. People were in trouble and the Bobcats were ready to go to help extract the besieged Wolfhounds. Suddenly the artillery fire stopped because the forward observer and his radioman had been killed and no one was calling in fire. (15) The Viet Cong blew through Alpha Company's perimeter, shooting and bayoneting the Americans in their fighting positions. Meanwhile, the men of Company B, 5th Infantry were told to stand down.

At 0630 on July 20, Companies A and B and Recon Platoon, 5th Infantry, left the base camp to search the area of the previous day's battle. Three hours later they came upon the bodies of sixteen members of the 27th Infantry and four VC soldiers. The G.I's were lying side by side in a straight row. They were fully clothed but had been stripped of their weapons and equipment (16). Since the Wolfhounds had not been reinforced, the Viet Cong had had plenty of time to walk around and tidy things up after wiping them out. As they were returning to base camp, Company A and Recon Platoon apprehended eighteen enemy suspects.

The planting season in Hau Nghia Province stretched from June through August. In areas controlled by the VC, the local guerrillas needed to stack their weapons and sow their fields during daylight hours. Document checks of these farmers turned up quite a few VC suspects and proved to be a relatively safe way to neutralize these unarmed enemy soldiers.

During the first half of August, the elements of the battalion were scattered throughout the area. The battalion was shifted from the 2nd Brigade, 25th ID to the division's 1st Brigade. While 3rd Platoon of Company A was attached to 1st Battalion, 27th Infantry, the remaining platoons provided security for an artillery battery at Go Dau Ha. Company B provided support for 4th Battalion, 9th Infantry and Company C was tasked with search and destroy missions to the northeast of Go Dau Ha.

LTC Victor Diaz, who had just relieved LTC Thomas Greer as battalion commander, expressed his displeasure with this fragmented arrangement. In his view, using a mechanized unit to provide security for an artillery battery failed to make use of the battalion's mobility and shock action. Furthermore, splintering the battalion led to an overall reduction in firepower and flexibility (17). One could conjecture, that Colonel Diaz, an older officer, wanted to apply Korean War tactics to an insurgency war. The 5th Infantry's war in Vietnam, however, was more akin to the regiment's earlier fights with the Comanches or the Filipino Insurrectos.

It would be late September before all units of the battalion would be reunited. During the month, antitank mines had extracted a heavy toll. Sixteen members of the battalion, including ten from Company A, died when their vehicles exploded. A seventeenth man died and three others were seriously wounded when Company B received 15 rounds of friendly 105mm artillery fire. LTC Diaz concluded that the mines were becoming larger, causing greater physical damage to the APC's. On September 23, the MACV admitted what had been publicly known for several years—that the United States was using chemical defoliants, including Agent Orange, to destroy the jungle canopy in Vietnam (18).

The following month, President Johnson met, in the Philippines, with heads of six Asian nations but was able to persuade only South Korea to send a meaningful number of troops to support the U.S. effort. By the end of 1966, U.S. troop strength in Vietnam was 385,000, about 100,000 more than Defense Secretary Robert McNamara had promised a few months earlier. Statements from Washington and the daily MACV press briefing were beamed home on the evening television news. These broadcasts were nicknamed "The Five o'clock Follies" by the growing number of war detractors.

During October, thunderstorms were often encountered in the afternoons and evenings. Ground fog, prevalent along the streams, persisted until mid-morning. The rain hampered the use of command and control helicopters on several occasions and one air strike was cancelled because of a low ceiling. Nevertheless, the battalion continued daily search and destroy operations in the surrounding area. These sweeps were frequently guided by former Communist soldiers or Chieu Hoi's (the Vietnamese phrase for "I surrender.")

Tom Forsythe, who was commander of A Battery, 3rd Battalion, 13th Artillery at the time, still feels grateful that the 5th Infantry was in his neighborhood (19). Forsythe recalled "We were on our way to the ARVN Training Compound in Trung Lap to establish a firing position in support of some infantry units operating in the Iron Triangle. The rice paddies and roads were flooded from monsoon rains. We got to a bridge just outside of the compound when we discovered that the bridge could not support our tracks and ammunition trucks loaded with tons of 155mm projectiles. We were forced to turn back to Cu Chi. On the way back one of my howitzers and a projectile laden ammo truck became mired in the mud. My jeep sunk up to its windshield. I noticed an eerie silence in Trung Lap due to the total absence of villagers. I decided to unload the projectiles from the ammo truck so that we could pull the vehicle out. It was about 1700 hours."

Battery A immediately came under automatic weapons fire from the wood line. An RPG went whizzing by one of its howitzers. After a

VIETNAM

fairly intense but short fire fight, the artillerymen continued to receive sporadic periods of automatic weapons and sniper fire. Captain Forsythe chuckled to himself as he checked his artillerymen, whom he had deployed in a perimeter in the rice paddies. They looked really worried and were reluctant to fire for fear of revealing their positions.

After several hours of alternating between trying to unload the truck and dropping into the mud to avoid getting shot, Forsythe swallowed his pride and called for help. Two platoons from Bravo Company, 5th Infantry arrived on the scene at 2300 hours. The infantrymen turned their tracks in the direction of the enemy muzzle flashes and placed suppressing fire on them until the Viet Cong decided to call it a night. Then the troops from Bravo Company chained several of their tracks together and began pulling Alpha Battery's vehicles out of the mud. In an hour's time the artillerymen were back on the road for Cu Chi.

Forsythe concluded, "The infantrymen were superb in applying their craft. This rescue was a walk in the park for them. As we were about to depart the village of Trung Lap, the Mech platoon leader, West Point '64, an underclassman of mine, said 'Tom, enjoy the trip home, compliments of the Bobcats.' Darn ego of mine took a beating."

To underscore Tom Forsythe's observation that this incident had been just another ho hum assignment for 1/5, the battalion journal simply reveals that two platoons from Company B closed base camp at 0110 hours after conducting a night road runner operation to and from Trung Lap to escort one battery of the 3/13 Artillery back to Cu Chi. Now you know the rest of the story.

From the 12th until the 25th of November, the battalion continued to participate in OPERATION ATTLEBORO, reconnoitering the area between Nui Ba Den (The Black Virgin Mountain) and Katum, near the Cambodian border. Attleboro was a massive operation involving the 25th and 1st Infantry Divisions. Although enemy contact was scattered, there were some brief intense encounters.

Two Centuries of Valor

On the 19th Of November, Sergeant Richard Hale's squad from Company A bumped into an entrenched Viet Cong force and began receiving heavy automatic weapons and mortar fire. Sergeant Hale moved his APC into the center of the action, had his squad dismount and led them in an assault on the enemy positions. When one of his men was hit by grenade fragments, Hale sent his squad back with the wounded man and, armed with a bowie knife and a pistol, charged the bunker alone. He ran the last thirty yards through intense fire, leaped into the emplacement and killed its two occupants. Sergeant Hale then reorganized his squad and continued to search the area until he was shot in the chest by a sniper. Painfully wounded and weak from the loss of blood, Hale crawled to the enemy position and killed two more Viet Cong soldiers with his pistol.

During the same action, PFC Johnny Owens sighted a bunker from which an automatic rifle was being fired. Owens leaped from his track and dashed 75 meters through heavy fire to kill the enemy soldier with grenades and rifle fire. When he entered the bunker, he found wires leading to a command detonated mine. He disarmed the mine and promptly rejoined his platoon as it overran another Viet Cong position and killed ten more insurgents.

Following the fight, the company policed up the bodies of the Viet Cong warriors and their weapons, including an old Browning Automatic Rifle and an M-1 Garand. Sergeant Hale survived his chest wound and received a Distinguished Service Cross. PFC Owens was awarded the Silver Star for his courageous conduct [20].

The battalion civil affairs team was busy, during the fall of 1966, in the neighborhood of Tan Phu Trang. During the day, they helped provide medical care for the villagers, taught English classes and assisted with the construction of a dispensary, a school house, and some tactical defensive structures. When night came, they formed ambushes, killing at least five VC.

VIETNAM

Tay Ninh

In January, 1967, LTC Richard Rogers relieved LTC Victor Diaz. On the first of February, the battalion shifted from Cu Chi to Tay Ninh Province, some 48 kilometers to the northwest. First Battalion, 5th Infantry came under the operational control of the 196th Light Infantry Brigade.

Tay Ninh, a transition area between the gooey muck of the Mekong Delta to the south and the thick jungle of Cambodia to the north, was an exit point for the Ho Chi Minh Trail which was used to transport troops, weapons and military equipment from North Vietnam through Laos and Cambodia and from there to points further south. The area had a dense jungle canopy that could conceal a buildup of forces. The 25th Division had been placed there to plug the hole.

Just outside the camp lay Tay Ninh City with a population of around 65,000 people—one of the largest towns in South Vietnam. The downtown area had paved streets and fluorescent lighting. It was quite a change from the dust and ruts of Cu Chi.

Now that they were stationed sixteen kilometers from Cambodia, elements of the battalion attacked along the Tonle Roti River which marked the Cambodian border. Small arms fire was frequently exchanged from both sides of the river. Eleven Bobcats died conducting search and destroy operations in this area.

On 5 February, Alpha Company was conducting an operation near Tapang Son. When the lead elements of the company came under extremely intense fire, 3rd Platoon moved forward to flank the enemy position. SSGT James Bostock and PFC Henry Lopez were killed. One of the platoon's APC's was struck by an enemy recoilless rifle round and burst into flames, seriously wounding all of its occupants.

PFC Joseph Brady, exposing himself to withering enemy fire, dismounted his own track and rushed to the aid of his comrades. Upon arriving at the flaming personnel carrier, he entered the vehicle and assisted one of the wounded soldiers to the relative safety of Brady's own vehicle. Then he returned to the burning vehicle and helped another wounded comrade to safety.

Once he was assured that all of the wounded were safely evacuated, Brady returned to the disabled APC and attempted to extinguish the fire. Realizing that the flames were spreading too rapidly, PFC Brady crawled into the driver's compartment and shut off the master switch, completely disregarding the intense heat. Then he climbed into the cupola of the vehicle and began to place .50 caliber fire into the enemy positions, attempting to suppress the enemy fire and allow the other members of the platoon to flank the enemy positions. He quickly found his target, eliminated the enemy automatic weapons by killing three Viet Cong gunners but continued to receive sniper fire. He searched for the snipers until he was mortally wounded by one of them. Because of his courageous actions, the wounded men in the armored personnel carrier were quickly evacuated, the enemy automatic weapons were silenced, the flames were controlled, the vehicle was salvaged and his comrades were able to disperse the enemy without sustaining further friendly casualties. Joseph Brady's Distinguished Service Cross was presented to his family in October, 1967 (21).

Throughout the remainder of February, the battalion remained in War Zone C between Tay Ninh City and the Cambodian border. The area was a dense forest riddled with enemy bunkers, tunnels and base camps inhabited by members of the 272nd Viet Cong Regiment. The Bobcats cleared areas to establish two fire bases; Pershing and Foche. Eleven soldiers in the battalion died during this effort.

Seven kilometers north of Nui Ba Den lay the "French Fort", a relic of the French colonial period of Vietnam. The battalion moved to that location on March 14 and set about clearing the nearby roads and escorting convoys.

During much of April, 1967, the entire 2nd Brigade participated in an operation in Gia Dinh Province for the purpose of interdicting Viet Cong supply routes running to and from Saigon. On April 22, the

VIETNAM

5th Infantry returned to the Ho Bo and Boi Loi Woods, north of Cu Chi, for more of the same. Apparently the VC had been forewarned because they had methodically evacuated the area after setting a number of mines and booby traps. Seven more Bobcats died during the month, primarily as a result of antitank mines.

On April 25th, the Department of the Army awarded the Valorous Unit Citation to the 1st Battalion (M) 5th Infantry and the rest of the 2nd Brigade Task Force, 25th Infantry Division for its role in securing the real estate for the base of operations at Cu Chi. The text of the citation offers a good summary of the 5th Infantry's first four months in Vietnam.

"Ordered to secure a base of operations for itself and he remainder of the 25th Infantry Division in the vicinity of Tan An Hoi in the Cu Chi District of Viet Nam, the Brigade Task Force embarked on 66 days of continuous combat operations in a completely Viet Cong dominated, heavily entrenched and fiercely defended area."

The citation went on to say "In January, 1966, combat operations began to seize, clear and secure the area selected for the base of operations. For the initial four days, brigade combat elements moved forward against devastating automatic weapons and never-ending harassing sniper fire, well established mine fields and vast underground systems of tunnels, trenches, spider holes and fortifications unrivaled in Vietnam… .During the period 30 January to 5 April, the brigade conducted eleven major operations against the Viet Cong with battalion or larger sized forces engaged in a fierce battle against a hostile enemy."

The writers of the citation concluded that body counts revealed that a total of 449 Viet Cong had been killed, that Viet Cong activity throughout the Cu Chi district was severely disrupted and that the Viet Cong had been greatly discredited in the eyes of the local populace (22).

Two Centuries of Valor

Counteroffensive—Phase III

Lieutenant Colonel Chandler Goodnow relieved LTC Rogers as battalion commander in May, 1967. On the 3rd and 4th of the month, the battalion conducted a sweep of the Ho Bo Woods. Four men from Company B were killed when their APC hit a mine. The following day, six more Bobcats succumbed to mine and booby trap explosions. Contacts with enemy troops were intermittent throughout the two-day operation and slacked off during the rest of the month but antitank mines continued to plague the battalion, killing a total of fourteen men.

Early in the month of May, actor James Garner, a former rifleman with A Company, 5th RCT in Korea, spent thirty-six hours at the Cu Chi base camp. Garner, a Purple Heart recipient, spent much of the time at the 12th Evacuation Hospital chatting with wounded Bobcats.

During the summer, the battalion conducted many airmobile assaults and continued to provide security for engineering projects. Enemy contact was light. PFC Guillermo Munoz was the only fatality during July. He died when a man walking near him stepped on an anti-personnel mine.

In early August, 5th Infantry patrols uncovered some very large weapons caches and grenade manufacturing sites. On the 4th, Charlie Company conducted a search along the banks of the winding Oriental River.

"We were probing through hedgerows with sharp poles when I noticed a piece of ground that didn't fit in with the rest of the area" said PFC Joe Duncan. "The grass was different and most of it was dead." Digging with the pole he unearthed the cover of a small tunnel. Inside was a large roll of thick steel wire. Searching further around the area he found several other small holes filled with rifle grenades (23).

The find touched off a large scale search with every man available on his hands and knees probing the wet earth with bayonets and bamboo sticks. By mid-afternoon, Charlie Company had unearthed

VIETNAM

a drill press, a stamping machine for turning out grenade handles, thirty pounds of empty cartridges, forty pounds of gunpowder and several boxes of tools for making grenades and reloading cartridges. Afternoon patrols on the 6th and 7th found another munitions factory and a large ammo cache near the banks of the Oriental River.

There were no fatalities in August. Four of the eleven men injured during the month were victims of an angry water buffalo.

Captain Albert Amos, civil affairs officer for the battalion, published and air-dropped leaflets during August asking Vietnamese civilians to provide information about the location of mines and weapons caches. On the day following distribution of the leaflets, a villager approached CPT Amos' APC waving one of the leaflets. The officer was thrilled that the leaflet had worked so quickly. An interpreter spoke to the man while the captain waited. "First we learned that the man had had too much to drink" said Amos, "secondly, he had seen the helicopter fly over and the leaflets fall out and he was just returning the lost paper we had dropped (24)."

In late September, men from Company B provided support for Rome plow operations that took place between Highways 1 and 7A just north of Cu Chi. Rome plows were large tractors with a specially configured dozer-type blade developed for brush clearing. They were made by the Rome Caterpillar Company in Rome, Georgia. The blade was more curved than the usual bulldozer blade with a sharply honed bottom edge that could cut through tree trunks up to three feet in diameter. Bars were added to the top of the blade to force trees away from the tractor. There was a "headache bar" installed over the operator's position to protect him from falling debris.

As the year progressed, casualties resulting from search and destroy and security duties led to a steady drain of non-commissioned officers. About 50% of the authorized slots, in the 25th Division, for men in pay grades E-5 and E-6 remained unfilled. Thanks to the Selective Service System, there was no shortage of E-2's and E-3's.

Those arriving at Cu Chi would have a week of orientation before stepping into the "boonies." The orientation addressed such topics as patrolling, booby traps, and how to treat the Vietnamese civilians.

On September 30, 1st Battalion, 5th Infantry returned to the division base camp at Cu Chi after 142 days in the field. They were given a week to pull maintenance on vehicles and equipment before returning to the fight.

By this time, Cu Chi had grown to the size of a small town. It was surrounded by machine gun bunkers that were protected by strands of razor wire. Within the compound was an airstrip, a helicopter pad, medical facilities and a prisoner pen. Each unit had an assigned area that contained the unit headquarters, motor pool, and mess hall. The men slept in above-ground hootches but could take shelter in nearby bunkers during enemy mortar attacks.

The hootches were constructed on wooden platforms that stood about a foot above the ground. The lower half of the wall was wood and the upper half was canvas that could be rolled up to allow ventilation. There was a low wall of sandbags surrounding the hootch that offered some protection from mortar shrapnel for those lying down on their bunks (25).

Charlie Company fashioned a shower from an old airplane wing which they filled with water. During the day the sun would heat the water. When the infantrymen returned from the field in the late afternoon, there was usually enough hot water for the first twenty-five men, unless it had been used up by rear-echelon soldiers during the day.

Battalion supply sergeant Floyd Young took Headquarters Company's laundry into the village of Cu Chi. During one of these weekly visits, he conversed in broken Vietnamese-English with 12-year-old Ngyuen Van Day and learned that the boy had been forced to quit school and shine army boots to support himself and his sick mother. His father had been killed by the Viet Cong. Young promised to help financially if the boy would return to school. It took several visits to convince the proud adolescent to do so (26).

Sergeant Young and his two clerks, Specialists John Collins and James Johnson, pitched in to buy Day school supplies, clothes and food. They even bought a bicycle and gave him money to support his mother. The excited young student dropped by the supply room every afternoon to tell the men about all the things he was learning. Floyd Young wanted to adopt Day and take him back to the United States but the boy decided that he should stay with his mother. Inspired by their success with Day, the three supply room men encouraged four other boys and one little girl to return to school. They paid for their school expenses and board.

LTC Chandler Goodnow left the battalion in October. He had led the 1st Battalion, 5th Infantry for five months, the average tenure for a battalion commander in Vietnam. During the four-month period between October, 1967 and February, 1968, the battalion was commanded by LTC Fremont Hodson, Major Ralph Hook, and LTC Henry Murphy. Hodson, who had served with the 7th Infantry Division during the Korean War, was with the 1st Battalion, 27th Infantry before being transferred to the 5th Infantry (27).

As 1967 came to a close, the elements of the battalion were scattered throughout the countryside. Company A provided security for engineering and Rome plow activities. Company B left one platoon at Cu Chi for a base camp reaction force, sent another to provide security for Fire Support Base Janet, on the northeastern edge of the Filhol, and deployed the remainder of the company at a ferry crossing on the Saigon River. Company C experienced daily combat as it teamed with the 24th ARVN, a Vietnamese ranger outfit. During one of these clashes, on December 1, Marvin Rex Young was wounded by shrapnel and received the first of three Purple Hearts.

By the end of 1967, regular nocturnal enemy mortar and rocket-propelled grenade attacks had prompted the construction of more substantial sleeping positions within nighttime perimeters. The new SOP required that the soldiers be entirely underground with a sandbag cover. The men dug the holes three feet deep and ringed them with two layers of sand bags, allowing space for firing ports that faced outward. They then placed several strips of perforated steel landing-strip plating across the top of the sand bag walls and piled two layers of sand bags on top of the steel plate. This became the required sleeping arrangement for all men who were not out on ambush patrols or manning listening posts.

As Christmas was fast approaching, Protestant Chaplain Thomas McInnes of the 25th Division and Father Robert Falabella of the 1st Battalion, 5th Infantry decided to leave the Cu Chi Base Camp and conduct services for men of the battalion who were deployed deep in the Boi Loi Woods (28). When they arrived at the forward base camp, they discovered that Bravo Company was preparing to sweep through a Viet Cong base camp that had been discovered the previous evening. The two clerics joined the expedition.

When they reached the VC camp's outer perimeter, the chaplains went separate ways. Father Falabella stayed with the platoon searching the first line of bunkers. At one point, they found a well that had footholds cut into its side. The platoon leader probed the well with a long bamboo pole. When the pole struck a metallic object at the botton, Fallabella, realizing that he was the smallest man in the group, offered to descend. He slid down the bamboo pole and waded around in two feet of water, but found nothing. Meanwhile Chaplain McInnes had been crawling through tunnels and bunkers. He found a lot of rice but little else. At the end of the day, the two mud-covered and somewhat disappointed chaplains returned to the battalion base camp. They waited until morning to conduct their church services.

On January 1, those companies in the bush received word that they would be celebrating New Year's Day with a turkey dinner. The roasted birds and pumpkin pies were being trucked out to them from

VIETNAM

Cu Chi. Roger Hayes wrote "I could see the truck working its way through our perimeter's entrance and maneuvering inside, past a garden plot that belonged to a local resident, to the vicinity of our chow line. Suddenly the truck lurched and black dust and smoke enveloped the vehicle as the sound and concussion of an explosion spread across the perimeter. Our chow truck had hit a mine. Inspection of the damage revealed that our turkey dinner had been riddled with shrapnel and was unsafe to eat. With that explosion, the holiday became just another in a long string of days without distinction."

In early January, 1968, the 5th Infantry received new armored personnel carriers that ran on diesel rather than gasoline. Fuel tanks filled with diesel were less apt to explode immediately when hit by a mine or a rocket-propelled grenade. Diesel powered vehicles would burn for a few minutes, allowing time to evacuate the wounded and dead, before the ammunition on board began to cook off. The diesel track, model M113A1, had a larger fuel tank and provided a cruising range of 300 miles, a hundred miles more than its predecessor.

Tet Counteroffensive, 1968

The Viet Cong, whose 1967 activities had been largely limited to delay and harassment, increased offensive operations in early 1968. They began to focus attacks on the U.S. and ARVN base camps, apparently to keep the allied troops from reinforcing operations "outside the wire" and to cover the movement of VC forces to the Saigon area (29).

At the end of January, Viet Cong and North Vietnamese regulars celebrated the Tet holiday by launching major offensives in thirty-three of the forty-four provincial capitals in South Vietnam, including storming the U.S. Embassy in Saigon. However, mounting a large scale attack is not an effective tactic for an insurgent army that faces a foe possessing superior fire power. There were so many Viet Cong casualties during the Tet offensive that the Viet Cong would never again be a major fighting force. Nevertheless, the Americans at home were shocked by the audacity of the offensive and deemed the battle a Communist victory. It was, in a psychological sense, because of its impact on the American public.

At 0655 hours on February 2, the Cu Chi Base Camp came under a mortar attack. When an ammunition dump was hit, the secondary explosions destroyed the Headquarters and B Company areas of the battalion, wounding two Bobcats. The mess halls for Companies A and C were damaged as well. Fortunately, at the time, most of the battalion was at a new base location two kilometers northeast of Tay Ninh conducting search and destroy operations and providing security for supply convoys and two bridge repair projects.

A Real Bobcat

When the smoke had cleared, rear echelon troops rushed to check on the condition of Tito, the live bobcat that was in the custody of Company A. Tito (short for gatito or little cat) was "drafted" in June of 1967. First Sergeant Ignacio Medina had written to the mayor of El Paso requesting that the city provide a mascot for the battalion. Roberto Cisneros of Juarez, Mexico had seen a story about the unusual request in a local newspaper. He offered to donate Tito, a family pet that had grown too large to keep.

After a trip to the El Paso Zoo, where Tito received inoculations and a medical checkup, he was caged in a special shipping box. Employees of Pan American Airways sponsored his twenty-hour jet flight to Saigon where the cranky, growling feline was met by a detail led by LT Richard Ward, Executive Officer of Headquarters Company.

When Tito and his escort reached Cu Chi, he was assigned to a small cage constructed of cyclone fencing. Responsibility for the bobcat was passed from one rear-echelon soldier to another as the men completed their 12-month tours. Tito apparently survived subsequent mortar and rocket attacks because he was still alive in April of 1971 when the 5th Infantry finished its operational mission in Vietnam. He returned with the battalion to Hawaii and died there sometime later (30).

Charlie Company was responsible for guarding the twenty-five kilometer stretch of road between Tay Ninh and Dau Tieng. According to Roger Hayes, road security was the company's favorite duty. He wrote "We left the rock crusher each morning shortly after dawn. One platoon cleared the road, with one squad walking down the middle—operating a mine detector or two and checking for other signs of enemy activity. Two other squads provided flank security, one on either side of the road, slightly ahead of the team on the roadway. The remainder of the company followed behind on their tracks. The APC in the rear peeled off and set up facing into the woods and rubber plantations, with the road at its rear. The next APC did the same a little farther along on the opposite side of the road, and so on... .Once we were in place...We posted one man on guard, then spent the rest of the day resting in the shade, writing letters, cleaning our weapons, sleeping, or socializing with the numerous Vietnamese civilians who came out in hopes of selling us their wares."

The battalion, under another new commander, LTC Thomas Lodge, remained in the area of Tay Ninh until the 10th of February until it was ordered to a new blocking position approximately three kilometers northwest of Tan Son Nhut Air Force Base. There had been earlier reports that two battalions of VC were lurking in the neighborhood. The battalion stopped by Cu Chi that evening for showers and a change of clothing and then proceeded to Tan Son Nhut, its APC's filled halfway to the top with gear and ammunition. The following day the battalion moved forward to a new position at Hoc Mon and set up listening posts and night ambushes.

Setting up a new position, even if just for the night, involved unloading the tracks, surrounding the perimeter with concertina wire and digging positions for ground-mounted .50 caliber and M-60 machine guns. Trip flares and claymores were placed outside the wire and the men could not bed down until they had dug their regulation sleeping holes.

In regard to clean clothing, each soldier was issued four sets of jungle fatigues made of lightweight, rip-proof material. Shirts were worn outside the pants to promote circulation and cooling. Most of the time a soldier preferred to dispense with underwear in order to keep his crotch drier and free of fungus and bacterial infections (31). Like their elders in the Korean War, the troops wore their steel helmets during daytime operations and soft headgear for night-time patrols. By the Vietnam War, the jungle hat had replaced the pile cap.

In the bush, each Bobcat had to carry everything that he would need during the day. He wore a web belt to which were attached a canteen, bayonet and a couple of ammo pouches. A butt pack was attached to the rear of the belt. The weight of this gear was supported by the web suspenders that soldiers have worn during much of the 20th century. Field dressings, a compass, and several grenades were attached to the front of the suspenders.

The week of February 10-17, 1968 was the bloodiest week of the war for U.S forces in Vietnam. Five hundred forty-three soldiers and marines were killed in action and 2,547 were wounded. Seven of those killed and eighteen of the wounded were members of the 1st Battalion, 5th Infantry. The carnage was compounded by a misdirected B-52 strike on Ap Binh D, a small hamlet due north of the battalion's position. Fifty-one civilians died and ninety-three were injured.

On February 14, Charlie Company was conducting a reconnaissance-in-force two kilometers northeast of Hoc Mon, a village ten miles north of Saigon, when it came under fire from heavily fortified North Vietnamese Army positions. Platoon Leader Ralph Williams rushed forward to organize his men and evacuate casualties. While running to a farm house to assist a wounded platoon member, he was struck in the knee by enemy fire. He quickly treated his wound and began moving toward cover when he noticed that one of his machine gunners had been hit by tracer bullets, causing the soldier's clothing to burst into flames. Ignoring the raking curtain of hostile fire, LT Williams crawled to the wounded gunner and removed his burning garments. Then, as he rose up to throw a smoke grenade at the North Vietnamese to screen the withdrawal of his troops, he was mortally wounded. Lieutenant Williams was honored with a posthumous award of the Distinguished Service Cross (32). Second Lieutenant David Isbell and five other men from C Company also died during the day's fighting.

On February 19, at 0748, Recon Platoon departed the night base at Hoc Mon to conduct a RIF to the northwest, following the Cau Sang River. Upon hearing that Recon Platoon had encountered a North Vietnamese battalion in well fortified positions, Charlie Company and three tanks from Company A, 2/34th Armor converged on the area of the contact. At 1134 hours, one APC from Recon was hit by a RPG round and the platoon began receiving small arms fire from its front and rear.

At 1539, Company C requested a dust-off for seven wounded. An hour later, they requested lifts for four more. PFC Thomas Loback, a medic with Headquarters Company, was busy with a platoon that was pinned down by intense small arms, automatic weapons and rocket fire coming from an enemy force positioned in a hedgerow. Hearing a call for help, Loback crawled through a withering fusillade and administered first aid to five wounded men and then helped them reach a position of relative safety. Spotting another wounded comrade, PFC Loback raced across an open rice paddy and treated the soldier. The wounded man was wounded a second time as he moved toward cover. Loback rushed back to the soldier and treated him again. As he began to pull his seriously injured patient to safety, Thomas Loback was killed instantly by automatic weapons fire. Three months later, PFC Thomas J. Loback was posthumously awarded the Distinguished

Service Cross (33). A second medic, SP4 Joseph Zale, was also killed during the fight along with two soldiers from Charlie Company.

By the end of the day on 19 February, one platoon of Charlie Company had been reduced to five men who were combat effective. Those men who had been wounded were loaded on a dust-off chopper and flown to the 12th Evacuation Hospital at Cu Chi for x-rays and surgical treatment. Those with minor wounds would return to the field and those with moderate wounds would recuperate in the battalion area in the northeast corner of the base camp.

While on another reconnaissance mission on February 23, Company C ran into a deadly barrage of fire from a well-entrenched enemy force. Sergeant George Bowling was directing the men into strategic position when he noticed that a track commander had been wounded and was unable to fire his 50-caliber machine gun. Bowling raced, through intense fire, to reach the wounded man and replaced him behind the gun.

As he placed withering fire on the enemy troops, he ordered his men to withdraw to allow supporting fire to engage the enemy. Finding that he was unable to break contact, SGT Bowling grabbed several grenades and advanced on the enemy emplacements, destroying one bunker with an accurate toss. After the artillery was lifted, he led an assault on the enemy positions. Several months later, Bowling received the Silver Star for his valorous action.

Companies A and B, Recon Platoon, and Company A, 34th Armor conducted a sweep northeast of Hoc Mon on March 6. At 1604 they ran into heavy contact. Company A, 5th Infantry was advancing with men walking in front of the APC's. Upon receiving sniper fire, they turned on line and advanced toward the fire. Suddenly, small arms, automatic weapons and anti-tank rocket fire erupted from a dense wood line. Third Platoon was in the middle and took the brunt of the fire. Medic Kendall Fortney was killed and five members of the platoon were seriously wounded by the initial fusillade. Medic John Haines raced forward to help his comrades. With bullets striking all around him, he moved from one wounded man to another administering first aid. SP4 Haines was hit while attending to one of his platoon members but disregarded his wound and rushed to help the platoon sergeant who was lying in an open area raked by machine gun fire. As Haines was applying a bandage to the sergeant, he was killed instantly by machine gun fire. The survivors were ordered to pull back and air strikes with napalm were called in during the night.

At 0755 hours on March 7, the body of John Haines was recovered. During the battle on March 6, Company A suffered eight wounded and three killed. Company B lost five wounded and two killed. One APC was destroyed and one tank and one APC were damaged. At 1720 all personnel were accounted for and the units closed back to the battalion forward base. SP4 John Haines received the Distinguished Service Cross posthumously for his extraordinary courage and devotion to duty (34).

On March 13 the battalion moved briefly to the Cu Chi base camp and then north to the area known as the Filhol. Around noon on the following day, Alpha Company was engaged in a reconnaissance-in-force (RIF). As men on foot preceded the APC's, one was hit in the chest by sniper fire and died before a dust-off could reach the site. The others were ordered to take cover while artillery was requested. The artillery rounds landed right on Company A, killing two Bobcats and wounding twenty-three others.

In defense of the artillerymen, effective artillery support was difficult to provide in the Boi Loi, Ho Bo Woods and Filhol Plantation area because of the jungle canopy and the canopy of the rubber trees. Projectiles would hit the tall trees and pre-detonate. Occasionally short range targets could be hit by direct fire with shells armed with concrete-piercing fuses that could penetrate the wood line and explode deep in the forested area (35).

On the 19th, the battalion moved forward to the Saigon River on the north fringe of the Filhol where Alpha and Bravo Companies and Recon Platoon discovered a large cache site consisting of nearly a hundred bunkers and tunnels. Their find, including mines, mortar, RPG, and small arms rounds, twenty-eight tons of rice and a thousand pounds of canned food was loaded on ten 5-ton trucks and the battalion and truck convoy returned to Cu Chi for a well-deserved four days of rest, if one can consider dodging enemy mortar rounds on an almost nightly schedule restful. Enemy mortar and rocket attacks had increased significantly during the Tet offensive.

Counteroffensive—Spring, 1968

On March 26, 1968, the battalion, minus Charlie Company, left Cu Chi and set up a forward base half way between Tan Son Nhut and Duc Hoa. Conmpany C remained attached to the 2nd Battalion, 34th Armored Brigade and conducted reconnaissance operations in the vicinity of Trang Bang, northwest of Cu Chi. The company maintained contact for three days of intense fighting during which they claimed to have killed 240 of the enemy.

On April 16, while Company B provided security for two artillery batteries that were being moved from Hoc Mon to the battalion forward base at Vinh Loc, a round of canister exploded killing SP4 James Young. He was the battalion's only fatality during April, 1968.

Company C ventured out from its base camp on a soccer field near Trang Bang to conduct company sweeps during the day and platoon ambushes each night. On May 1 they took over the perimeter of another company that had received mortar fire nightly for the preceding two weeks. That night Charlie Company was subjected to more than fifty incoming rounds. Three men were seriously wounded. The company made contact with the Viet Cong on the following day, resulting in a fire fight that lasted all day and into the night.

On the morning of May 12, the battalion left the area near Saigon and moved back to the northwest corner of the Filhol Plantation near the Saigon River. The following day, as it proceeded north along Highway 7A, southwest of Trung Lap, the lead APC for Company A hit an antitank mine. During the ensuing fire fight, Captain Robert Hoop, the company commander, dismounted from his track and was killed by a sniper's bullet. That evening, northwest of Trung Lap, another Company A track hit a mine. One soldier was killed and three were wounded in that mishap.

Before darkness fell the battalion established a night position. Shortly before 2300, on May 15, the night base was rocked by incoming 82mm mortar rounds. Six men were wounded and dusted off. Anticipating an attack, a half dozen ambush patrols were established within four hundred meters of the base perimeter. Minutes later there was an eruption of enemy small arms and RPG fire. One of Company B's patrols radioed that it was returning to the perimeter with three casualties. As it did so, one of B Company's APC's was hit by a rocket propelled grenade round and was set on fire.

Alpha and Bravo Companies called in air strikes and returned fire with small arms and mortars. Six men from Company A and eight men from Company B were wounded. Then word came that six more men from Company B had been killed at their ambush site. There would be no way to retrieve their bodies while the night base was under fire.

When daylight came, a search of the area, aided by a tracker dog team, revealed the bodies of Viet Cong soldiers, weapons, ammunition and equipment. There were numerous blood trails. The bodies of the six men in the ambush patrol were retrieved. Word came that their throats had been cut.

On May 18, the battalion shifted to a new base area close to Highway 6A, four miles south of its junction with Highway 238. Ambush patrols were sent out shortly after 1900 hours. One patrol ran into an unknown size enemy force and returned to base after expending most of its ammunition.

Early on the 19th, the battalion base began receiving mortar and

Two Centuries of Valor

RPG fire. When the ambush patrol from Company A spotted a large enemy assault force, the patrol members set off their Claymores and opened fire. Artillery and air strikes responded as well. Four Bobcats were killed and several others were wounded. Others fought their way back to the battalion perimeter. Many dead Viet Cong were found in front of the ambush site.

The battalion moved again on May 21 and established a forward base in the area north of Trang Bang. Shortly after midnight, enemy gunners unleashed a one hundred round mortar barrage on the battalion base. They followed the mortar attack with a barrage of RPG's but failed to score direct hits on the battalion's hastily dug bunkers or its tracked vehicles. Then two battalions of North Vietnamese attacked the perimeter. One Bobcat ambush patrol engaged an enemy company that was moving to the attack killing at least ten enemy soldiers.

When the first enemy assault came, men of the 5th Infantry opened fire with .50 caliber machine guns, automatic weapons, grenade launchers and mortars. Air Force AC-47 flare-ships illuminated the open rice paddies around the battalion's position making easy targets of the ten-man enemy assault groups. After more than an hour of small arms, artillery and helicopter fire teams, the attack was suppressed.

At daylight, a sweep of the battlefield revealed thirty-four dead enemy troops and heavy blood trails indicating that many more had been wounded during the attack. Three men from Company A and two from Recon Platoon died during the fighting.

On May 23, all elements of 1st Battalion, 5th Infantry were reunited. The battalion returned to Cu Chi and was able to spend the next seven days at the base camp. Roger Hayes wrote "On May 23, we went back to Cu Chi for the first time in 170 days, a division record for time spent in the field. A mile or so out, we pulled over in an open area near the main roadway and tied purple pennants to the radio antennas on our tracks to identify ourselves as the 1st of the 5th (Mech)

Infantry…We entered the gates of Cu Chi proudly and felt as though we were in a parade. It was great to be back. The rear-echelon troops had heard of our exploits in the field, and for a day or two we enjoyed celebrity status in the huge base camp."

The next day was spent removing everything from the APC's and cleaning the interiors. The treads and engines were given a thorough going-over and weapons were cleaned. When the work was completed, there was time for the men to relax and begin to grieve for their twenty-nine brothers who died during the month of May.

On Wednesday, May 29, the stand down ended and the battalion left base camp to resume one of its favorite duties, road security. Company A secured a battalion forward base while Company C went on to Tay Ninh. Recon Platoon moved to Dau Tieng to provide convoy security between Tay Ninh, Bau Co, and Dau Tieng. Throughout the early summer, the battalion kept Highway 1 clear from Tay Ninh to the Hoc Mon Bridge for twice-daily supply convoys. The battalion was now under the command of LTC Andrew H. Anderson, who had served with the 1st Cavalry Division during the Korean War.

The work day began at 0600 with morning mine sweeps. A portion of each platoon would provide flank guard for the others who were checking the road for mines. The flank guards would check each clump of vegetation, or other likely ambush spots, by lobbing rounds from M79 grenade launchers in the direction of the suspected site. It took about three hours for each unit to complete this morning task (36).

After the mine sweeping was complete, the infantry companies would keep watch over the roadways until the final convoy of the day had passed. Then they would return to their forward base for the night.

Battle of Ben Cui

General Westmoreland left Viet Nam in July, 1968. He was replaced by General Creighton Abrams, Jr. Abrams had the difficult task of implementing the so-called Vietnamization policy instituted by the Johnson administration. It required the gradual reduction of American forces in Vietnam while keeping the North Vietnamese Army at bay.

By its very nature, the challenge of keeping the North Vietnamese at bay was serving to implement Johnson's policy of gradual reduction. Between May 1 and July 31, 345 members of the 25th Infantry Division were killed in action; some 1424 had been wounded. Slots for infantry captains and high-ranking NCO's remained vacant. It was not uncommon to see lieutenants serving as company commanders and to expect infantry squads of six or seven men to do the work of twelve.

At the beginning of August, the entire 1st Brigade, 25th Infantry Division assembled in the Tay Ninh–Dau Tieng area near the Saigon River. A base camp was established on part of an abandoned rubber plantation. The former superintendent's house and an above-ground swimming pool stood in the middle of the brigade's perimeter.

The base camp received sporadic small arms harassment during the first half of the month. This increased to mortar and rocket fire on the 17th. These attacks were conducted by the 5th and 9th VC/NVA Divisions. Their objective was apparently to expose Saigon by drawing allied forces north.

On August 19, the battalion left the base camp to sweep the area northwest of the airstrip on the Ben Cui Plantation. Bravo and Charlie Companies drove west on Highway 239, for a mile or two, toward Tay Ninh. Charlie Company dropped off at a large circular clearing while Bravo Company continued a little further west. Suddenly AK-47 fire erupted from the tree line. Charlie Company had to fight its way west to link up with Bravo Company and Recon Platoon. Artillery, air strikes and gun ships were called in for support. The G.I's made two assaults against the enemy position before they were able to punch through it and convince the Viet Cong fighters to break contact. After sweeping the area, the three units returned to Dau Tieng stung by the loss of nine dead and sixty-three wounded comrades.

On August 21, at 0640, the men of Charlie Company departed Dau Tieng to, once more, reconnoiter the Ben Cui Rubber Plantation. The enemy had been using the plantation to infiltrate men and supplies from War Zone C in the north to Saigon in the south (37).

The Bobcats took a scout dog with them. Their mission was to sweep in a northeasterly direction from Dau Tieng, staying about one thousand meters south of Highway 239. Recon Platoon, plus the 3rd Brigade CRIP (Combined Reconnaissance and Intelligence) Platoon, and the crew of one twin 40mm self-propelled anti-aircraft weapon left a few minutes later. They were to move parallel to Company C along the highway.

Charlie Company advanced with two rifle teams abreast. The 1st Platoon, on the left, was led by SSG Mainor Lang and the 3rd Platoon, on the right, was led by 1LT Arthur Cook. The platoons were followed by their personnel carriers and 2nd Platoon. 1st LT John Snodgrass, the company commander, moved on foot, alternating his position between the lead platoons.

At 0831 hours, the scout dog sensed trouble. His handler suspected that there might be an enemy concentration to the southwest. The battalion S-3, observing the operation in a helicopter, swooped low over the area of concern but could see nothing unusual. The rubber trees were 25-30 feet in height and the underbrush had been cleared in most sections of the plantation. Lieutenant Snodgrass directed 81mm mortar fire into the area but nothing stirred. Recon Platoon conducted a search of three buildings on the southern edge of a village that had been used by the enemy for billets and classrooms and found nothing significant.

Following the dog handler's hunch, Charlie Company shifted to the southwest and moved out of the open into the rubber trees. At 1110 hours, the company began receiving sniper fire from the west and southwest. One Bobcat was killed and another was wounded. The sniper fire was soon followed by automatic weapons and rocket propelled grenade fire. Gunship support was requested and the lead elements of Charlie Company increased their volume of fire. Lieutenant Snodgrass had 2nd Platoon advance to the right flank of 1st Platoon to increase the fire power up front.

Company C had run into the 5th NVA and 9th VC Divisions. The enemy, dressed in green and camouflaged uniforms, advanced, rushing from tree to tree. Some were attempting to move along the south flank of Charlie Company. The volume of fire soon reached an extremely high rate and Sergeant Lang, leader of 1st Platoon, was killed.

SP4 Michael Mangan maneuvered his armored personnel carrier into a position from which he could deliver the most effective fire and began firing his light anti-tank weapon at the charging enemy. At this point, LT Snodgrass, realizing that he could not effectively employ the APC-mounted .50 caliber machine guns over his dismounted troops, ordered the three forward platoons to pull back and form a perimeter around 4th Platoon. As they did, incoming RPG rounds and automatic fire reached a crescendo. As they withdrew, Snodgrass ordered the mortar squads to pull back out of the trees so that they could get overhead clearance. Charlie Company opened up with all available weapons, including M-72 LAW's (light anti-tank weapons) in an effort to suppress the enemy attack.

As Specialist Mangan backed his vehicle into the defensive position, it was struck by an enemy rocket which caused it to burst into flames. Mangan, exposing himself to the enemy barrage, was able to extinguish the fire but was wounded in the arm. The APC was then struck by a mortar round.

Finding his carrier inoperative, Mangan ran to another assault vehicle to assist its machine gunner. When the latter had expended his ammunition, Mangan ran through a hail of bullets to obtain a re-supply from his demobilized track. As he climbed into the vehicle, it was struck by a rocket, knocking him to the ground. Struggling to his feet, he picked up the vital ammunition and carried it to the machine gunner's position. He was mortally wounded as he delivered the ammo to his comrade.

When Snodgrass's headquarters group came within 50 to 75 yards of 4th Platoon's position, an RPG round exploded nearby wounding the company commander, one of his radio operators, the heavy mortar forward observer, and the artillery forward observer. A second radio operator was killed. Three nearby APC's were knocked out. The wounded men were placed in an undamaged track and LT Arthur Cook, 3rd Platoon's leader, assumed command of the company.

Following Sergeant Lang's death, Sergeant Marvin Young had taken charge of 1st Platoon. Young deployed his men into better positions and directed their fire. Since their communications had been knocked out, they didn't know that the rest of the company was pulling back.

When Sergeant Young finally realized that they were alone, he ordered the platoon to withdraw. He remained behind to provide covering fire. Then noticing six men still fighting on the right front flank, he ran to their location. As he ran he was shot through the side of his face, completely losing one eye. He reached the six men and laid down a base of fire to cover their withdrawal.

Young had trouble moving, as a result of his wound, and one of the men dropped back to help him. As they resumed their withdrawal, a group of North Vietnamese over took them and shot SGT Young in the upper arm. He went down. The other soldier remained with Young to help him hold off the enemy. Young suffered another wound in his leg and his companion got hit in the foot. Sergeant Young, knowing that he would be unable to go any further, thanked his helper and ordered him to leave.

At 1135 the battalion S-3 urgently asked for the air strikes and gunships that had been previously requested but had not arrived. Twenty minutes later, the forward air controller stated that it would be twenty to twenty-five minutes before the arrival of the first air strike but that a helicopter light fire team (one observation helicopter and two helicopter gunships) was on the way. The light fire team arrived at 1201 and was immediately employed along the south flank of Charlie Company.

"At this point," recalled LT Arthur Cook, "the company was totally disorganized. They were in a rough perimeter, the tracks were still firing toward the front and the fire was still coming at us from the right flank; a little from the left flank, but mostly from the front and the right...I had several men killed; a lot of them were wounded.

... There were so many killed and wounded at that point, that I just started getting everybody in the tracks. I started yelling at everybody 'get in the tracks and get the tracks moving.' It took me about ten minutes before I could get everybody I could get; the dead I just had to leave there. The wounded people, everybody I could get my hands on or everybody else could get their hands on we started throwing in the tracks. Those that were still outside the tracks, we yelled at them to get on the tracks and, to my knowledge, everybody that was still alive and moving, at that time, got on the tracks."

When all wounded had been loaded onto personnel carriers, Company C retraced the same route that it had used that morning. It exited the rubber plantation at a clearing and established a perimeter to accommodate the dust-off helicopters. They were soon joined by Recon Platoon and the 3rd Brigade CRIP that had been participating in the fight from their vantage point on the road. The dust-offs of the wounded were completed at 1254 hours. Twenty minutes later, the survivors of the fight at Ben Cui were back at the Dau Tieng Base Camp.

Seventeen Bobcats died during the 30-minute fire fight at Ben Cui. A preliminary battalion report listed twenty-one wounded. Interviews with the platoons involved yielded an estimated enemy body count of 207. These estimates did not include those VC killed by air, artillery or helicopter gunships. The 1st Battalion, 5th Infantry received a Presidential Unit Citation for "Extraordinary Heroism in Military Operations" for the period 18 August through 20 September, 1968. LT Arthur Cook received the Silver Star for "exposing himself to withering Communist fire until he was sure that all wounded were ready for evacuation" and Sergeant Marvin Rex Young was posthumously awarded the Congressional Medal of Honor for "conspicuous gallantry and intrepidity in action" at Ben Cui (38). SP4 Michael Mangan was posthumously awarded the Distinguished Service Cross (39).

On the 22nd, the battalion was placed under operational control of the 27th Infantry Regiment in order to resume the hunt at Ben Cui. At 0640, Company B and a detachment from the 3rd Squadron, 4th Cavalry departed Dau Tieng and headed west into the plantation along Highway 239. Recon Platoon proceeded west along 239 and then turned south paralleling Highway 19 and then west into the Ben Cui. Company C entered the plantation about 500 meters south of Company B. Elements of 2nd Battalion, 27th Infantry followed Company C.

At 0928, Company B ran into heavy automatic weapons and RPG fire west of the intersection of Highways 239 and 19. Artillery fire, air strikes and helicopter light fire teams were called in on the enemy positions. More than two hours elapsed and the enemy fire persisted. Recon Platoon and Charlie Company moved north and linked up with Company B at 1200 hours. Company B was ordered to pull back and regroup on line with the reinforcing units. The line was jagged and, in the midst of the confusion, two M-60 machine gunners, SGT Humberto Acosta-Rosario and PFC Philip DeLorenzo, were left out front.

At 1455, the fighting had subsided to the point that it was possible to search for the two missing men from B Company. Searchers found the body of PFC DeLorenzo and his M-60. They located SGT Acosta-Rosario's machine gun but there was no sign of its owner. After searching the area with negative results, all units left the contact area and moved to the abandoned Ben Cui airstrip to establish a night perimeter. Four ambush patrols were set.

Humberto Acosta-Rosario's body was never found. There were unconfirmed reports that he'd been captured but that was repeatedly denied by the North Vietnamese government. Acosta-Rosario was the only member of the 1st Battalion, 5th Infantry who was left behind in Vietnam, a fact that continues to be a source of frustration and pain for those men who served with him.

On the morning of August 23, Company C located approximately one hundred bunkers that showed signs of recent use. An hour later they located the first body of the seventeen soldiers who were missing in action from the fight on the 21st. By 1430 hours they had located and removed all seventeen bodies that had been left on the battlefield some forty-eight hours earlier. They returned to the night perimeter at the air strip.

The 1st Brigade, 25th Infantry Division assumed responsibility for the Dau Tieng area on August 29. The 2nd Brigade, minus the 1st Battalion, 5th Infantry, returned to Cu Chi. The Bobcats had unfinished work in the area and would lose nineteen more of their brothers-in-arms as they continued to sweep the Ben Cui and Michelin Plantations until mid-November.

Early on the morning of September 11, Company A began receiving mortar, RPG and small arms fire within its night perimeter, about three hundred meters from the Ben Cui airstrip. The barrage was quickly followed by an enemy ground assault by an estimated Viet Cong battalion. A number of Bobcats sustained wounds from the initial contact. Captain Akos Szekely, SP4 Thomas Roberts and PFC Albert Lazzarotto were killed.

SP5 Ronald Soppe, a medic assigned to Alpha Company, moved quickly among his wounded buddies to stabilize them. When he noticed that a personnel carrier had been set afire by an RPG, he rushed to the burning track and quickly extinguished the fire. As he attempted to reach a wounded comrade, he was severely wounded in the arm by RPG fragments.

Disregarding his own welfare, he continued on to the wounded man, treated him and carried him to a safe position. Then, ignoring his own wound and constantly exposed to hostile fire, he went to the aid of six other soldiers. When the firing ceased, he helped load the wounded on a helicopter and remained behind in case of a second assault. On 24 March 1969, General Abrams presented Soppe with the Distinguished Service Cross in recognition of the young medic's extraordinary heroism and devotion to duty (40).

In October, a rocket propelled grenade hit LTC Anderson's vehicle, severely wounding the battalion commander. Anderson was not an "eye-in-the-sky" type of combat leader, flying overhead while his troops maneuvered on the ground. When action was imminent, he wanted to be on the ground with his men. Following Andy Anderson's medical evacuation, LTC William Klein assumed command of the battalion.

Counter-offensive, Phase VI, November, 1968

As Phase VI of the counter-offensive began on November 2, it was apparent that "Vietnamization" would not be an easy policy to enforce. The number of American fighting men in Vietnam had not declined during General Abrams first five months in command. In fact, American troop strength had increased by ten percent to 636,100. In August, anti-war protests and riots had taken place in Chicago during the Democratic Party's August convention. On the 31st of October, President Johnson declared an end to the bombing of North Vietnamese targets. Since 1965, Operation Rolling Thunder had dropped 643,000 tons of bombs on ammunition dumps, oil storage facilities, factories, power plants and airfields in the north. Nine hundred and twenty-two allied aircraft had been lost to North Vietnamese defensive action (41).

Meanwhile, back on the ground, the 5th Infantry continued

its operations out of Dau Tieng. On November 14, Company A, accompanied by a scout dog team and an ARVN unit, was sweeping Highway 14 in a southerly direction when a command-detonated claymore mine was exploded in the vicinity of the company's point element. Three Bobcats, two members of the scout dog team and one dog were killed.

On November 15, 1968, the 1st Battalion, 5th Infantry moved its operations to the Boi Loi Woods area, where its units spent the rest of the year securing supply routes and Rome Plow operations west of Cu Chi. These missions were relentlessly plagued by booby traps and anti-tank mines. During the last six weeks of the year, booby traps killed three Bobcats and injured twenty. Anti-tank mines accounted for three deaths and twenty-eight wounded. Twenty-six men from the battalion died as a result of small-arms, RPG and mortar fire during that time period.

November 29 was a rough day for Recon Platoon. While clearing Highway 7A, one of their tracks hit an anti-tank mine about two kilometers north of the Highway 1 Junction. One Bobcat died in the explosion and the APC was totaled. Twenty minutes after resuming their mission, another APC was damaged by a command-detonated Claymore mine and its occupants began receiving sniper fire. Two wounded were evacuated. Twenty minutes later the platoon was hit by a command-detonated mortar round. One man was killed and three others were wounded. When a dust-off helicopter landed to evacuate the four men, it landed on, what was believed to be, a mine. The explosion killed another soldier and wounded four more.

On the morning of December 6, Company B was sweeping an area two kilometers southwest of Trung Lap when they discovered a cache of RPG and mortar rounds. The following evening, Company A joined Company C in the Trung Lap area and set up a night defensive perimeter. At 1855, they were hit with a mortar barrage, wounding ten Bobcats.

VIETNAM

Lieutenant Dennis Hunsley of Charlie Company spotted an RPG crew preparing to destroy several vehicles. Hunsley grabbed a 90mm recoilless rifle and wiped out the insurgents. He then dodged incoming mortar shells to aid in the evacuation of his wounded men. He was recommended for the Silver Star for his heroic actions.

The fighting around Trung Lap persisted through December. Trung Lap was basically a Viet Cong garrison. In the evening the women and children could be seen leaving the village to go into the jungle to spend the night with their husbands and fathers.

Companies A and C remained in that area while Bravo Company and the Recon Platoon operated several kilometers south, near the intersection of Highways 1 and 7A. On December 13, when Companies A and B of the 5th began taking heavy enemy fire, Companies A and B of the 12th Infantry were airlifted to reinforce the battalion's effort and linked up to form a blocking force. The Viet Cong finally broke contact, leaving bodies, weapons and equipment. By 1750 hours, five dead and fourteen wounded Bobcats had been removed from the site of the battle.

Company C set an ambush patrol near the junction of Highways 1 and 7A on the evening of December 19. At 2005, ten VC walked into the kill zone and were wiped out by Charlie Company's patrol. The carnage for December ended on the 29th when one of Bravo Company's tracks hit a booby-trapped 155mm artillery round, killing five soldiers and wounding eleven.

Bob Hope and his entourage made their fifth trip to Vietnam in 1968 to entertain the troops during the Christmas holidays. They were scheduled to visit Cu Chi on December 18. Bill Adler, from Alpha Company, recounted "I drove in from Dau Tieng, going on R & R, and the other guys were going back to Cu Chi for other reasons. So we loaded up and made the run and when we arrived, dusty and dirty, they told us that the Bob Hope show had already started. Well, I told the other guys to see if they could make it and I would take care of the track and other things…The guys came back and were all in a good mood. They arrived late but they were escorted right down to the front row. The guys said that the cameras were on them. Of course, I said "Sure they were!' … Two years later or so, I'm sitting at home, like a lot of us, watching a rerun of a Bob Hope special when it came to Cu Chi. There they were! Still brings a smile on a hard year forty years ago (42)."

In late 1968, D Company, 5th Infantry was activated by diverting several squads from Headquarters Company. Company D was armed with the new mounted M132 flame thrower. Their flame tracks carried two hundred gallons of flame fuel allowing a firing time of 32 seconds at a range of 200 meters.

On January 20, 1969, Richard M. Nixon replaced a tired Lyndon Johnson as president of the United States. He vowed to strengthen the Vietnamization policy by implementing the "Nixon Doctrine". He insisted that U.S. allies in Asia supply the manpower for their own defense. He announced that he was going to pull 25,000 of the 535,000 troops out of Vietnam and reduce the U.S. presence in Korea.

Despite the Nixon Doctrine, things didn't change much back at Trung Lap. Daily encounters with anti-tank mines and booby traps racked up more dead and wounded as the Bobcats swept the area and provided Rome plow security. During the three months between November 1, 1968 and January 31, 1969, thirty-eight members of the 1st Battalion, 5th Infantry perished in Vietnam. The numbers for the entire 25th Division were 236 KIA and 3,955 WIA. Allied operations during the same period killed more than 25,000 Viet Cong and North Vietnamese soldiers.

On the morning of February 22, Companies B and C departed the forward base to conduct a RIF operation. Company B ran into an ambush about seven kilometers north of Trung Lap. Following artillery and air strikes, the company swept the area and found the bodies of two NVA soldiers with weapons. This led to the first mention, in battalion reports, that North Vietnamese regulars were operating in the battalion's area of responsibility.

The following morning at 0930, Company C moved out to conduct another search and clear mission near Xom Moi. At 1453 they requested a dust-off for one dead and three wounded comrades. The company had moved within very close range of an entrenched, well-concealed North Vietnamese unit.

Lieutenant Peter Bernardo, seeing that the intense hostile fire was preventing his platoon members from returning fire, quickly assaulted and silenced one of the enemy's automatic weapons positions. He provided suppressive fire so that his unit could withdraw and call in supporting fire.

During a second assault, LT Bernardo rushed two more enemy fortifications and destroyed them with hand grenades. Once more, he enabled Company C to withdraw by placing devastating suppressive fire on the NVA positions. As they withdrew, air strikes pounded the area.

On the third and final assault of the three-hour fire fight, LT Bernardo was seriously wounded. He and six other casualties were dusted off at 1830 hours. A half hour later, as more air strikes and artillery support were being placed in the area, Company C moved to Fire Support Base Patton. Peter Bernardo survived to receive his Distinguished Service Cross (43).

The Tet 1969 Counter-offensive

The fighting around Trung Lap became even more intense in March of 1969. On the 3rd of the month, Company C established a night perimeter beside Highway 237, four kilometers northwest of the town. The company began receiving small arms and RPG fire at 0535. It responded with company weapons and helicopter gunships. Fortunately there were no friendly casualties.

Two hours later, Companies C and D of the 12th Infantry were air-lifted into an area several kilometers northwest of Charlie of the 5th Infantry's night perimeter. The 12th Infantry immediately established heavy contact and Companies A and C of the 5th were dispatched to reinforce them. Alpha and Charlie Companies, having to fight their way through to the 12th, arrived there at 1327 hours. An hour later, as the fighting subsided, D of the 12th pulled out and the Bobcats began a sweep of the contact area. Shortly after 2100, Companies B and C of the 5th were back within their night perimeters. During the day two members of Company C had been killed and Companies A and C suffered a total of 38 wounded. The following morning, Companies A and C and Recon Platoon policed up the enemy bodies and weapons in the contact area.

On March 14, the battalion was ordered to conduct a nighttime patrol east of Cu Chi. Companies B and C departed their perimeters shortly after midnight on the 15th. At 0122 hours, there was a report from Company C that its two lead APC's, from Lieutenant Hunsley's platoon, had been hit. They requested a helicopter light fire team.

A few minutes later, as they were receiving fire from the front and both flanks, they began backing out of the contact. Meanwhile Company B moved toward the Company C position. Dennis Hunsley dismounted his armored personnel carrier, which had been hit by a RPG round, and carried two wounded men to safety. Returning to his vehicle, he found that the APC beside it had received a direct hit and he made a third and fourth trip through intense fire to carry two more men back to the medic. Suddenly there was a burst of automatic weapons fire from the flank as he was trying to organize the withdrawal. Hunsley led an attack that silenced the fire from the emplacement and then carried another casualty to the medic track. Remaining behind until his men had withdrawn, LT Hunsley climbed into a damaged APC and was driving it from the battle area when he was fatally wounded by an enemy RPG. He was posthumously awarded the Distinguished Service Cross for his heroism and devotion to his men (44).

VIETNAM

At daybreak on March 24, a dismounted patrol from Charlie Company moved forward to check on the occupants of the damaged APC's. They reached the downed vehicles at 0402 hours and found no one alive. The patrol swept the area of contact. Five men from C Company had been killed and nineteen wounded during the ill-fated night mission. The two companies returned to their perimeters and spent the next few days securing Rome plow operations and securing Highway 7A for convoy use.

Bravo Company ran into trouble on the 25th while guarding Rome plows that were working north of Trung Lap. At 0955, they began receiving a cross fire of RPG and AK-47 rounds from three enemy bunkers. One Bobcat was immediately wounded and two others took cover in a nearby house that had been partially destroyed. The rest of the company pulled back and concentrated its fire on the enemy positions. Several attempts were made to retrieve the wounded soldier and those in the house, but the volume of enemy fire was too fierce.

Finally, LT Stephen Doane, leader of Second Platoon, was able to crawl close to two enemy bunkers that were located about thirty meters apart. When he reached the first bunker, he threw in several grenades and sprayed it with his M-16. Unaware that a grenade had been tossed from the second bunker, LT Doan was hit by shrapnel. Members of his platoon, seeing that he was wounded, pleaded with him to pull back. Ignoring them, he crawled to the second bunker, where he was immediately met with a burst of AK -47 fire. He pulled the pin of a grenade and threw himself into the bunker, taking out its occupants. With two of the three bunkers out of action, the platoon was able to move forward and retrieve the three men in the area of the old house

At 1112 hours, Bravo Company requested the assistance of a helicopter light fire team from brigade but were told that none was available. However, thirty minutes later, a gun ship did arrive. Despite the increase in suppressing fire, the enemy fire persisted for the next four hours, culminating with the unwelcome arrival of ten incoming 82mm mortar rounds. Two more hours would pass before Companies B and A could sweep the area and make their count of enemy bodies, ammunition, and miscellaneous equipment. LT Stephen Doane was posthumously awarded the Congressional Medal of Honor for his heroic actions on March 25 (45).

Earlier in the spring, the death of a young girl in the village of Trung Lap had raised fear that there might be an outbreak of bubonic plague. Fifth Infantry medics assisted by members of the battalion civil affairs section administered 3600 plague prevention inoculations. Twenty plague cases were discovered and treated and all of the patients recovered.

Three months later there were three deaths in the hamlet of Ap Dong indicating that the plague had reappeared. Members of the battalion dusted 950 homes with DDT to kill the plague-carrying fleas and provided another 3800 inoculations to civilians and 400 to ARVN soldiers.

Following the second plague eradication, the village chief of Trung Lap feted the battalion surgeon, Captain Roy Hodge, and his staff at an elaborate thank-you dinner. During the event, the Bobcats distributed school kits containing paper, ink, crayons, rulers, pens and pencils that had been donated by 2nd Brigade soldiers. Recently captured Viet Cong rice was also distributed to the villagers. One might wonder whether the men of the 5th Infantry were beginning to win the hearts of a few of the citizens of Trung Lap, a Viet Cong stronghold.

In April, 1969, U.S. troop strength in Vietnam reached its peak at 543,400. On the 14th of May, President Nixon proposed an eight-point peace plan that would provide for mutual withdrawal. A month later, he announced the withdrawal of 25,000 troops.

The G-2 Section of the 25th Infantry Division sensed that the strategy and expectations of the enemy were changing somewhat. The campaign plans for the NVA and the Viet Cong no longer called for total victory. The Communists still expected to be victorious but in an indirect way. Military activity would be conducted to gain political and psychological advantage over the United States and South Vietnam. It would focus on weakening the resolve of the U.S. forces and hastening their departure.

On April 10, a "Spooky" gunship was flying, in darkness, near the B Company night perimeter, approximately eight kilometers northwest of Trung Lap. Stray rounds from the Spooky killed one member of the company and wounded two others. At this point in the war, the Spooky was a modified AC-47 Gooneybird, a cargo plane with three rapid-firing Gatling guns. Such guns were capable of firing 6000 rounds a minute. Once modified, the Gooneybirds were given the more elegant name of "Dragonship." Therefore, the ground soldiers referred to them as "Puffs." These planes also carried enough parachute flares to turn night into day, so accidents like this one involving the Bravo Company position were quite rare (46).

The following morning, at 0320 hours, Company B was attacked by an estimated company-sized VC force. The Viet Cong were met by intense small arms fire, artillery, helicopter gunships, and Spookies. At daybreak, Bravo Company gathered up many dead enemies and their weapons and equipment. No U.S. casualties resulted from this fight.

During the early afternoon of April 11, the CRIP element from Headquarters Company was on a reconnaissance mission southeast of Trung Lap when the point man detected an enemy ambush in time to warn his comrades. A fire fight erupted and the Viet Cong were routed. The recon platoon pressed forward after the fleeing enemy.

Upon entering a wooded area, the Bobcats ran into a cross fire from automatic weapons, rifle grenades and mortar rounds. Spotting a source of fire on the left flank, Specialist Gonzalo Villaseñor and PFC Martin Lechuga turned toward the emplacement. Villaseñor was hit in the leg but both men continued advancing, crawling toward the bunker and alternately firing their rifles and tossing grenades. Just as they succeeded in silencing their target, they came under fire from another enemy fortification, wounding SP4 Villaseñor a second time. Nevertheless, they persisted, firing a hail of rifle fire until a fatal head wound ended Villaseñor's advance.

Knowing that his comrade was severely wounded and that he would be unable to pull him through the fusillade to safety, Lechuga placed himself in front of Villaseñor to protect him from further wounds. PFC Lechuga then returned fire until he was fatally wounded. Both men received the Distinguished Service Cross posthumously for their extraordinary heroism (47).

More than thirty fire support bases were spread throughout the III Corps area of operations. One of them, Fire Support Base Patton, home of the Bobcat's 4.2 inch mortar section, was located on the northern outskirts of Trung Lap. On 27 April, FSB Patton came under mortar attack. The mortar men and their security detachment, the battalion's Recon Platoon, returned fire. During the fracas, one man from the mortar platoon was killed and three others were wounded. One Bobcat from Recon Platoon suffered wounds.

While the mortar shells fell on FSB Patton, Captain Hodge, the battalion surgeon, left the safety of his APC to search for casualties and treat their wounds. Throughout the attack he continued to administer to the men and evacuate them to a safe place. Roy Hodge received the Silver Star for his actions on 27 April. A short time later, he was relieved by Captain Thomas McMillan.

On May 21, Company B, with one platoon from Company C and the 132nd Regional Force Company, conducted a search operation at Giong Viec hamlet between Phuoc My and Cu Chi. The lightly armed Regional Forces, called "Ruff Puffs" by their American allies, were roughly akin to the American militia in colonial times. They were brave, seasoned soldiers with 20-30 years of combat experience beginning with their war with the French. In 1964, they were integrated into the

VIETNAM

South Vietnamese Army and placed under the command of the Joint General Staff. During the Vietnam War they fought on their home turf so they knew every inch of the terrain (48).

As they neared the hamlet, the Bobcats and the Ruff Puffs, captured a Viet Cong soldier armed with an AK-47. He admitted that he was a squad leader and that there were twenty other VC in the village. An amplified announcement was made and one other VC surrendered.

The Regional Forces Company and two platoons from Company B swept the hamlet and found that a dozen of the Viet Cong had been killed by the preparatory artillery fire placed on the site. Six more surrendered, along with their weapons, ammunition and equipment.

Among the prisoners of war was a nurse who had previously worked for the 554th Engineer Battalion at the Cu Chi Base Camp. She revealed information that led to the capture of three other female employees at Cu Chi who had been involved in the mining of the 554th's mess hall on January 3, 1969.

The number of combat deaths in the 25th Division began to drop significantly as spring rolled on. This was also true of the 5th Infantry where twenty-two men died in March, eleven in April and four in May.

Summer-Fall 1969

The Vietnam Summer-Fall 1969 Campaign commenced on June 9. The date made little difference to the ground soldiers around Trung Lap, where it was business as usual. On June 10, LTC Robert Kurek relieved LTC Klein as battalion commander.

Five days earlier, Companies A and C of the 5th had joined forces with Companies B and C of the 12th Infantry, Company A of 34th Armor and elements of the ARVN 49th Infantry to participate in a five day RIF northwest of Trung Lap. At 1248 hours, the Bobcat units ran into heavy small arms, automatic weapons and RPG fire. During the firefight a helicopter gunship was downed, killing the four man crew and three APC's were destroyed by enemy fire. Six Bobcats, including medic Charles Ramsey, were killed during the encounter. Fourteen men were wounded.

On the fourth day of the reconnaissance, while Company A of the 5th and A of the 12th checked the site of an air strike north of Trung Lap, they ran into an enemy force and called in artillery and gunship support. Following the encounter, they found documents indicating that the enemy unit was an element of the 268th VC/NVA Regiment.

On the evening of June 13, S/SGT Bobby Brock of Company A was in command of an ambush patrol just north of Phuoc My. At 2120 they were engaged by an enemy squad. Sergeant Brock moved among his men directing fire and providing first aid. He continued to do so after he became wounded.

Captain Ron Chatelain, an artillery forward observer, witnessed the ambush from his helicopter and directed supportive fire on the enemy troops. He then directed the helicopter pilot to land and pick up any casualties. Sergeant Brock assisted with the loading of casualties. When the chopper was hit and began to burn while lifting off, Sergeant Brock and a wounded Captain Chatelain pulled the more seriously wounded crew and passengers to safety. Brock was wounded a second time by RPG shrapnel but returned to his men and directed them back into a defensive perimeter as Chatelain called in and adjusted gun ship fire to cover the approach of another dust-off helicopter. Sergeant Brock remained on the ground until all casualties had been loaded. Both men received the Distinguished Service Cross for their heroism on the evening of June 13 (49).

Bobby Brock may be the 5th Infantry's most decorated Vietnam veteran. In addition to the Distinguished Service Cross, he was awarded four silver stars, two Army Commendation Medals, four Bronze Stars, three air medals and four Purple Hearts. He completed three tours in Vietnam, serving with the 35th Infantry Regiment in 66-67, Company

VIETNAM

A of the 5th in 68-69 and finally with C Company, 1/5, in 69-70.

On June 15, Bravo Company rushed east to Trang Bang to assist Troop A of the 4th Cavalry, which was engaged with a large, fortified enemy force north of the city. The usual plastering from artillery, air strikes, and helicopter gunships suppressed the enemy fire. Many enemy bodies littered the area of contact. Company B relived the experience two weeks later when they shifted east to help Charlie Company of the 14th Infantry deal with a Viet Cong force near the Saigon River, east of Cu Chi. When the VC broke contact, they left the bodies of many comrades. The recent increase in large force confrontations by the North Vietnamese Army and the Viet Cong did not seem to be "weakening the resolve" of the 1st Battalion, 5th Infantry Regiment.

In early June, 1969, the new battalion surgeon, CPT Thomas McMillan, decided that the usual medical civic action program (MEDCAP) was not reaching all the people who needed medical care. McMillan put a big sign in front of Fire Support Base Devins, five miles northwest of Cu Chi, advising the locals that he would be conducting office hours from 8 to 9 A.M. six days a week (50).

The response was overwhelming. A genuine cross section of Vietnamese folks, young and old, came to see the "bac si" seeking a cure for their discomforts. Dr. McMillan soon realized that he couldn't have sixty or more patients at a time inside the perimeter of the FSB so he loaded a truck with supplies and set up a mobile drug store and aid station just outside the perimeter wire. An ARVN interpreter-medic assisted him.

An hour was insufficient time to see all of the patients but it was all that McMillan could spare. After being "in the office", he and his aides had to reload the truck and head off to one of the local aid stations where more Vietnamese were waiting for treatment.

On July 29, Recon Platoon and a squad of Ruff Puffs were sweeping Highway 7A, southwest of Thai My, when they noticed a Viet Cong soldier exiting a bunker entrance. When he was fired upon, he dove back under cover and refused to respond to calls to surrender. This led to the firing of several LAW's at the bunker. Two VC emerged from the entrance and were captured. They were interrogated by Regional Force members and one of the prisoners admitted that there were more Viet Cong troops in the bunker. Another surrender appeal was made and, there being no response, a shape charge was detonated on top of the bunker, killing its remaining occupants.

During the summer, the battalion maintained a forward base at Fire Support Base Devins. Around noon on August 21, Recon Platoon, accompanied by one of Company D's track-mounted flame throwers, discovered four tunnels beside a hedgerow about two kilometers north west of the FSB. There was evidence of recent use around the entrances to the tunnels.

As they approached the next hedgerow, a Viet Cong soldier was observed running from some tall grass toward the hedgerow. The flame thrower zapped the hedgerow, flushing the enemy soldier and he was shot. Another Viet Cong had been killed by the flame thrower.

Suddenly, another VC made a break from the tall grass into the hedgerow. Recon Platoon dropped back and sprayed the hedgerow with automatic weapons fire. An air strike and artillery barrage were requested and Company C, with two additional flame tracks, arrived from FSB Devins.

As soon as the air strike was over and the artillery was lifted, soldiers from Charlie Company approached the hedgerow on foot. They were met with bursts of automatic weapons fire from several positions. An RPG round hit one of the company's APC's just as a soldier on the track had stood to throw a hand grenade. The blast knocked him from the track and his grenade rolled and wounded two of his buddies. At that point, the 5th Infantry force withdrew to allow a helicopter light fire team to expend its load on the hedgerow. The three flame tracks then sprayed the hedgerow and the patch of tall grass to its right. This time, when the Bobcats advanced on the hedgerow, they met no resistance.

The daily contacts were drawing closer to Cu Chi. On September 19, helicopter gunships received heavy ground fire while flying about two kilometers east of Phuoc My. Companies A and B along with Recon Platoon, the 132nd Regional Forces and elements of the 12th Infantry were dispatched to the area of the threatening ground fire. They took positions on the east, west and south sides of the contact area and waited until air strikes and artillery fire were lifted. Then they swept the area. The only resistance came from two NVA soldiers in spider holes, who were quickly apprehended. There were no American or South Vietnamese casualties.

The battalion death toll dropped from four men in August to three in September and then to no one killed in action in October. A stepped-up program of defoliation along the enemy's infiltration routes contributed to this welcome trend. He could no longer move south along the Saigon River, during daylight hours, without being observed from the air.

LTC Frederick Delisle became battalion commander in October. Delisle had previously served as Cu Chi Base Camp Defense Coordinator. LTC Robert Kurek left to become Chief of Staff for 25th Infantry Division Operations.

In early January, Lieutenant Colonel DeLisle, Major Ron Baker, Battalion S-3, and Command Sergeant Major Ignacio Medina were returning to Cu Chi from Fire Support Base Devins. Their headquarters track was being escorted by two personnel carriers from Recon Platoon. Upon hearing that Company B was attacking a nearby hamlet, the headquarters staff headed in that direction. As they approached the fire fight, they directed their vehicle through an opening in a bamboo thicket and then dismounted. Suddenly Medina straddled and detonated what may have been a booby trap or a Chinese claymore mine. The shrapnel flew in all directions, wounding DeLisle, Baker and Medina.

Ron Baker recalls that the sergeant major's injuries were the most serious, so he was evacuated in the first available helicopter, a light observation craft. Baker, who had just ten days left in his second tour in Vietnam, said "Fred and I sat on a paddy dike and waited for the dust-off ship from Cu Chi. I can remember singing Peter, Paul and Mary's I'm Leaving on a Jet Plane over and over until Fred told me to shut the &#@% up."

The incident was observed by B Company Commander Ralph Laubacher who was flying overhead in a light observation helicopter. Laubacher recalls "There were a lot of enemy running around as my 3rd Platoon broke through the bamboo...I directed the platoon to where the enemy was trying to run and hide. My 2nd Platoon followed the 3rd Platoon while my 1st Platoon remained in a blocking position. It was a great operation. We had no casualties in Company B and we killed and captured quite a few bad guys, including a tax collector who had a lot of documents and money. The only ones hurt were DeLisle, Baker and Medina."

It was painful to witness. "Any line track driver knew not to drive through obvious openings in thickets," continued Laubacher. "But they were in a hurry and wanted to get to the action. Our battalion, its officers and men were at their best when DeLisle and Baker led the Bobcats. CSM Medina was a great soldier with a great reputation (51)."

LTC DeLisle, had received abdominal wounds. Once stabilized, he was flown to Japan and then home to recuperate. He was replaced by LTC Ted Westerman. Major Sheridan replaced Major Baker as battalion S-3.

On January 25, 1970, the responsibility for the defense of the Cu Chi Base Camp passed from the 2nd Brigade to the 3rd Brigade. The 2nd Brigade, composed of 1st Battalion, 5th Infantry, 2nd Battalion, 12th Infantry, and 3rd Squadron, 4th Cavalry was tasked with promoting small unit combined operations in the central portion of the III Corps area. The aim was to upgrade the abilities of the ARVN Regional Forces and Popular Forces with a stress on night operations.

The 1st Battalion, 5th Infantry was placed under operational control of the 1st Air Cavalry Division on April 2, 1970. On the 10th, Company C's defensive perimeter was attacked. SFC Leroy Davis had just begun to return the fire when his bunker was struck by an enemy rocket. He was seriously wounded. Nearly blinded, he returned to his gun and continued to direct suppressive fire toward the attacking enemy soldiers. When a second enemy rocket hit the bunker, he was wounded again. Ignoring the pain, he placed fire on the enemy until he collapsed. His determined actions helped prevent the enemy from overrunning the company's position. Sergeant Davis lived to receive his Distinguished Service Cross (52).

Sanctuary Counter-Offensive

North Vietnamese and Viet Cong units had maintained base areas in eastern Cambodia, a self-proclaimed neutral country, since the mid-1960's and had been using the port of Sihanoukville (Kompong Som) to move war supplies into position. On March 18, 1969, President Nixon ordered "secret" bombing of these Cambodian base areas to put pressure on the North Vietnamese to enter serious negotiations and to interdict the supplies flowing through the port.

Although elaborate measures were taken to keep the bombings secret, lest their revelation fuel anti-war protests, the New York Times published a story about the bombings in May. The news leak infuriated Nixon and the telephones of several journalists and government officials were wire-tapped. When the bombings were officially acknowledged in 1973, they stirred the demand in Congress for Richard Nixon's impeachment.

On April 29, 1970, Nixon approved a limited incursion into Cambodia. News of the incursion set off a wave of anti-war demonstrations, including one at Kent State University that resulted in the deaths of four students, at the hands of National Guard troops.

Elements of the South Vietnamese Army crossed into eastern Cambodia on April 28. They were followed three days later by units from the 1st Air Cavalry Division. On May 4 and 5, the 1st Battalion, 5th Infantry and 2nd and 3rd Battalions, 22nd Infantry moved to the vicinity of Thien Ngon to relieve the 1st Air Cav and prepare for their attack into Cambodia.

At 0710 on May 6, OPERATION BOLD LANCER began when the 3rd Battalion of the 22nd made an air combat assault into Cambodia near the village of Tasuos. One company secured a bridgehead on the western bank of the river. The 2nd Battalion, 22nd Infantry concurrently attacked and seized a bridgehead on the opposite bank. Company E, 65th Engineer Battalion then commenced the construction of a pontoon bridge at that location. The bridge was completed and operational by 2315 hours. Two platoons from the 5th Infantry crossed the bridge and assisted with night security on the Cambodian side of the river.

The remainder of 1st Battalion, 5th Infantry and the 2nd Battalion, 22nd Infantry crossed the river at 0715 hours on the 7th. The 5th Infantry attacked west briefly before turning south toward Tasuos. The 2nd of the 22nd immediately turned south along the river bank. Battery B of the 11th Artillery crossed at noon and moved west behind the Fifth.

Due to political upheaval at home, these U.S. Army units were instructed not to venture more than thirty kilometers from the Vietnam border. This directive by President Nixon did not apply to the six ARVN battalions under the operational control of the 1st Cavalry Division.

At 1300 hours, Company A made contact with an enemy force about six kilometers northeast of Kampong Trach. During the ten-minute fire fight, one Bobcat was killed and another was wounded. Several enemy soldiers died. Several hours later, Recon Platoon got into a scrap in the same neighborhood, losing one killed and one wounded. When a platoon from Company B arrived on the scene, the Communists withdrew.

Vietnam

On the morning of May 9, Charlie Company located a large base camp with mess halls and bunkers. The complex was approximately four hundred meters square. Later that afternoon, they began receiving automatic weapons and RPG fire. Helicopter light fire teams, artillery and air strikes were called in to suppress the fire. The battalion continued its detailed search of Base Area 354, northeast of Kampong Trach for the next six days.

Company C began receiving the usual mix of direct and indirect fire in the early morning of May 12. SP4 Ardie Ray Copas jumped to the .50 caliber machine gun on his track and opened fire. A RPG round hit the track wounding four soldiers standing next to the vehicle and knocking Specialist Copas to the ground. Ignoring his own wounds, Copas remounted the vehicle and recommenced firing his weapon, despite the potential cook-off of the mortar rounds within the track. He continued to place devastating fire on the North Vietnamese troops until the other wounded Americans had been safely evacuated. Before he could vacate the burning track, another RPG hit the vehicle and ended Copas' life.

Five members of the battalion died and six APC's were destroyed during the fight. One Kit Carson Scout (former Viet Cong soldier) died when he went to assist Ardie Ray Copas. Forty-four members of Charlie Company were wounded but thirty of them had minor injuries that didn't require a dust-off. Company C was sent back across the river to the Tay Ninh Base Camp. Copas was awarded the Distinguished Service Cross posthumously (53).

On May 15, the 1st Brigade, including 1st Battalion, 5th Infantry minus C Company, moved north to the Katum area. The following afternoon, Bravo Company ran into an enemy force about three kilometers northwest of Katum. Artillery and air strikes were called in to assist in suppressing the enemy fire. Two Bobcats from Company B were killed and six were wounded during the fight.

On the evening of May 16, members of Company C were

attending a stage show at Tay Ninh, when SP4 James Paul of the 125th Signal Battalion attempted to gain entry to the show. Paul was turned away. He returned soon after with an M-16 rifle and opened fire on those soldiers waiting for the show to begin. Two members of Company C died and ten were wounded during Specialist Paul's attack. Paul was subsequently convicted of two counts of voluntary manslaughter and ten counts of assault to commit voluntary manslaughter. He spent five years in a disciplinary barracks before being paroled.

During the last half of May, the brigade continued to cross back and forth between Tay Ninh, South Vietnam and Kampong Province, Cambodia. Company A and Recon Platoon found caches of communications equipment and rice. Company A also discovered a large hospital, four miles west of Sotey. It was a complex of 130 bunkers, fifty houses and three kitchens.

The thirty-day incursion into Cambodia resulted in the killing of 11,349 Communist troops and significant damage to their supply infrastructure. Allied forces captured 600 supply caches. Time spent in the Cambodian sanctuary had also been costly for the 5th Infantry, especially Alpha Company. The battalion suffered nineteen combat deaths in addition to the two Bobcats murdered at Tay Ninh. Ninety-three members of the battalion were wounded. The 25th Division reported 114 KIA and 1259 WIA for May 1 through July 31, 1970.

Counter-Offensive, Phase VII, July 1970

On July 1, 1970, the 2nd Brigade, 25th Infantry Division moved east to a new operations area in Long Khanh Province. A forward brigade command post was established at Operations Base Lynch, twelve kilometers south of Xuan Loc, the province capital.

The 1st Battalion, 5th Infantry moved to the Xuan Loc area on July 6. LTC Oliver Combs replaced LTC Westerman as battalion commander. Battalion casualties during July were limited to wounds suffered by four members of Charlie Company during an early evening fire fight west of Xuan Loc on July 28.

During the remainder of summer and well into the fall, the battalion continued to operate in the vicinity of Xuan Loc. Contact with enemy units was infrequent. Between August 1 and November 1, there were four deaths in the battalion; one attributed to malaria.

On October 12, 1970, the 25th Division was notified that it would soon re-deploy. Its service in Vietnam was coming to a close. Units were ordered to stand down at either Cu Chi or Camp Frenzell-Jones near Long Binh. The 25th Infantry Division held its farewell ceremony at Cu Chi Base Camp on November 25, 1970.

The 2nd Brigade, being the last element of the division to arrive in Vietnam, would stay on for several more months as an independent brigade. The restructured unit included: 2/12 Infantry, 3/22 Infantry, 1/27 Infantry, 1/5 Infantry, 1/8 Artillery; B Company, 65th Engineer Battalion; D Troop, 3/4 Cavalry, 125th Signal Company, 25th Combat Support Battalion, 38th Scout Dog Platoon, 66th Combat Tracker Team, F Company, 75th Rangers, 18th Military History Detachment, 25th Military Intelligence Company, 25th Military Police Company, 20th Public Information Office Detachment and the 9th Chemical Detachment. The 2nd Brigade was placed under the operational control of the II Field Force Vietnam. LTC Patrick Moore led the 1st Battalion, 5th Mechanized Infantry Regiment during its final days in Vietnam.

Field Force was the term used during most of the Vietnam War to designate U.S. military corps-level control. U.S. corps numbers were not used to avoid confusing them with the South Vietnamese corps zone designation. As mentioned earlier, the III Corps area, in which the 5th Infantry spent much of its deployment, was the III Corps of the Army of the Republic of Vietnam, not the U.S. Army.

On December 20, the 2nd Brigade was notified of its impending redeployment. It was to complete its stand down at Camp Frenzell-Jones no later than April 28, 1971. Following one more month in the field, 2nd Brigade transferred some of its responsibilities to the 1st

Australian Task Force and the 1st Cavalry Division. The brigade would no longer receive replacements. The surrounding fire support bases began to shut down.

On March 15, SGT Phillip Monson of A Company died of fragmentation wounds that he had received earlier in the year. He was the last Bobcat to die in Vietnam.

The 1st Battalion, 5th Infantry Regiment completed its operational mission requirement in Vietnam on April 5, 1971. It had been deployed for 1900 days. The soldiers at Camp Frenzell-Jones, anxious to return to "the world," were treated to frequent stage shows, cook outs, sports activities, an expanded PX, and movies. There was an early shipment of excess personnel to eliminate a large number of people who would otherwise have had nothing to do. On April 30, the 2nd Brigade Color Guard departed Tan Son Nhut Air Base for Hawaii.

The Vietnam War continued for four years after the 1st Battalion, 5th Infantry returned to Hawaii. As the conflict dragged on, support from the American people and the soldiers in Vietnam declined even further. Racial tensions and other disciplinary infractions multiplied throughout the armed forces even as President Nixon was able to convince the North Vietnamese to conclude a peace settlement and the South Vietnamese to accept it. This agreement was commonly called the Paris Peace Accords. In late January, 1973, Nixon announced an end to hostilities in Vietnam. During the next two months, prisoners of war were exchanged and the American combat units in Vietnam withdrew.

Over the next two years, the North Vietnamese thumbed their noses at the Paris Peace Accords and prepared to resume offensive operations. In the spring of 1975, the Communists launched a massive offensive that quickly destroyed South Vietnam's will to resist. Lacking support for U.S. intervention, President Gerald Ford was forced to watch as America's former ally collapsed. The Communist victory ended the Vietnam War.

CHAPTER FIFTEEN

GUARDIAN OF THE PACIFIC

During the Vietnam War, the United States had maintained a strategic reaction force for contingencies, other than Vietnam, in the Pacific area. Originally the 29th Infantry Brigade of the Hawaii National Guard had been federalized to serve in that capacity. On December 6, 1969, a 4th Brigade, 25th Infantry Division was activated for that mission. One element in the 4th Brigade was the 2nd Battalion, 5th Infantry. The 4th Brigade was dissolved on 15 December 1970 when the 25th Division, minus its 2nd Brigade, returned to Hawaii from Vietnam. Second Battalion, 5th Infantry, its personnel and equipment were used to bring the 1st Brigade, 25th Infantry Division up to strength (1).

Third Battalion, Panama

On 26 June, 1968, while the 1st Battalion, 5th Infantry was battling with Communist forces near Tay Ninh, Vietnam, an interesting reincarnation of 3rd Battalion, 5th Infantry Regiment was organized at Fort Kobbe in the Panama Canal Zone. It replaced the 3rd Battalion, 508th ABN Infantry, 193rd Infantry Brigade. An element of the 5th Infantry would be providing security for the Canal Zone for the third time since World War I.

Third Battalion, 5th Infantry was created by collapsing 3rd Battalion of the 508th into one company of airborne infantry, Company A, and adding two regular rifle companies, B and C, and a combat support company to provide heavy weapons fire support (2). The battalion was brigaded with the 2nd Battalion, 187th Infantry as part of the 82nd Airborne Division.

The soldiers in 3rd Battalion, 5th Infantry did not refer to themselves as "Bobcats." According to Mark Beattie, who served with Company C in the late 70's, the paratroopers in Company A shared the brigade nickname "Moatengators" with the 2nd Battalion of the 187th (3). Members of Company B were the "Bandidos" and the Combat Support Company "Cobras" kept a python in a cage outside company headquarters. The brigade surrounded a pond with a cyclone fence and stocked it with live alligator mascots.

Recent efforts to learn more about the commanders and activities of 3rd Battalion during its first nine years at Fort Kobbe were disappointing (4). Nevertheless, when Mark Beattie joined the battalion in October, 1977, the battalion commander was LTC Virgil Fernandez. He was relieved by LTC William Hartzog in mid-1978. When Hartzog was given a brigade in April, 1979, MAJ James Woods served as acting battalion commander until the arrival of LTC James Mace. Mace commanded the 3rd Battalion from January, 1980 until November, 1981 when he left to take over the 2nd Ranger Battalion at Fort Lewis, Washington.

Given the terrain and political situation in Central America, much of the battalion's program was devoted to counter-insurgency training in the jungles of the Canal Zone. Company A's Mortar Platoon broke numerous firing records and set high Army Training and Evaluation (ARTEP) standards for indirect fire exercises.

During LTC Mace's tenure with the 3rd Battalion, LT John F. Mulholland served in the unit as a rifle platoon leader, weapons platoon leader and as executive officer for Company C. His company commander was CPT Geoff Lambert, a former Green Beret.

Eventually, several of the battalion officers of 3/5, achieved star rank. Major General Hartzog commanded the 1st Infantry Division and then the U.S. Army's Training and Doctrine Command (TRADOC) during the latter part of his career. Major General Geoff Lambert led Special Forces Command at Fort Bragg prior to his retirement. BG John Mulholland is currently Counter-Terrorism Coordinator for

Central Command and Brigadier General James Mace retired as Chief of Staff of Fourth U.S. Army at Fort Sheridan, Illinois. He returned to his alma mater, the Citadel, to serve as Commandant from 1997-2005.

Enlisted members of the battalion were also among those men who went on to distinguished army careers. CSM Frank Leota, recently retired Command Sergeant Major of the 25th Infantry Division and, previously CSM of the 2nd Battalion, 5th Infantry in Afghanistan, began his army career in 1980 as an A Company "Moatengator."

When the 1st Battalion, 508th Infantry was re-activated in Panama in 1987, the 3rd Battalion, 5th Infantry, once more, folded its flag. First Battalion of the 508th, as part of the 193rd Infantry Brigade participated in Operation Just Cause, the invasion of Panama in December 1989.

The Army's Low Ebb

Following the Vietnam War, the Secretary of the Army directed that the 25th Division's two brigades be brought up to full strength to increase its capability as a strategic reserve for the Pacific area. In the event that the division would require a third brigade, the Hawaii National Guard's 29th Infantry Brigade could again be placed on active duty. The 1st Battalion, 5th Infantry was now part of the 1st Brigade along with the 1st Battalions of the 19th Infantry and the 27th Infantry.

However, simple bureaucratic juggling couldn't rebuild the army. Seven years of fighting an unpopular, divisive war combined with the social upheaval of the 1960's had led to a steady erosion of morale, fighting power, readiness and quality among America's soldiers. In a 1973 Harris poll, Americans were asked to rank occupations from most to least respected. The military finished very close to the bottom, just above garbage men. The Vietnam War had eroded public support for the draft. The Selective Service Act expired on June 30, 1973 and Congress refused to extend it (5).

Army Chief of Staff, General Creighton W. Abrams, Jr., believed that the army was better off without the draft. In his view, draftees were a burden and believed that their absence would allow him to build a modern, well-trained, all volunteer force of quality soldiers armed with superior weapons. Prior to his death from cancer in 1974, Abrams devised a total-force concept to make sure that the army would never again be committed to combat without a call-up of the reserves and the National Guard.

First time soldiers enlisting in the new all-volunteer force were offered a 61% pay raise and better conditions of service. These reforms failed to attract sufficient qualified enlistees. As a result the army accepted thousands of recruits who had failed to complete their high school educations. Congress compounded the problem by cutting recruiting budgets and letting the G.I. Bill for Education, an important recruiting tool, expire. As the quality of recruits declined, problems with discipline and drug abuse increased. In 1979, the army fell 17,000 men short of its recruiting goal. The all-volunteer force was in trouble.

Memories of that period in the life of the 1st Battalion, 5th Infantry among former enlisted members are mixed. While some report memories of "nonsense, waste and apathy", James "Hawk" Halloway, felt that his positive experience with the Bobcats convinced him to become a career soldier (6).

By the time these young men became soldiers, the American public was demanding an end to the demoralizing gloom that had settled over the country after the Vietnam War. In 1980 Ronald Reagan was elected President, in part, because the voters believed that he would rebuild the military. Creighton Abrams' vision of a well-prepared army as a deterrence to war had ignited his successors, including Generals Fred Weyand, Norman Schwarzkopf and Colin Powell.

During the Reagan administration, defense spending more than doubled from $140 billion in 1980 to $300 billion in 1989. The G.I. Bill was renewed and, in January, 1981, the new recruiting campaign

"Be All You Can Be" was adequately funded. During the next ten years, the educational level of recruits increased significantly, AWOL's declined by 80%, courts-martial dropped by 64% and drug use fell to negligible levels (7).

An important aspect of the army's rebirth was the restoration of unit pride. LTC Michael Ferguson, commander of 1st Battalion, 5th Infantry from 1972-75, revived the tradition of celebrating the anniversary of the regiment's 1808 organization. Part of the Organization Day was devoted to athletic contests. A two-mile relay team from Company C was victorious on April 14, 1975. The members of that same relay team, led by SP4 Kenneth Kruger, burned off some more calories the following November by climbing 13,754 feet to the summit of Mauna Kea while training at the Pohakoloa Training Area. They chose the precipitous northeast slope for their route (8).

At this point in time, there were approximately five hundred officers and men assigned to the 1st Battalion, 5th Infantry. The battalion was composed of Headquarters and Headquarters Company, three rifle companies, A, B, and C, and Combat Support Company.

Operation New Life

By April of 1975, over 100,000 refugees had fled South Vietnam as the Communist takeover became more imminent. The 5th Infantry and other army logistical and medical units were sent from Hawaii to Guam to join forces with Navy Seabees and erect and operate a refugee reception camp at Orote Point on an abandoned World War II Japanese air base (9). The 1st Battalion arrived on April 27. During its sixty days on Guam, the task force erected 3200 tents, 191 wooden toilets and 300 showers. Other duties ranged from providing camp security, cooking, administering immunizations, and guiding refugees through the process and making sure that they got back on the right bus to return to their temporary quarters.

The first load of refugees arrived on April 23, 1975 and from then on, five thousand a day arrived at Anderson Air Force Base and Naval Air Station. On May 7, fifteen thousand more refugees arrived by ship. From the airbase and the port, they were transported by bus to the Orote Point site and sixteen smaller reception centers on the island.

At the beginning of the mission, days were long. Those units providing security often had to endure 36 to 48 hour periods without sleep. However, as the number of newly-arrived refugees declined, free time became more available. First Battalion, 5th Infantry returned to Hawaii on June 20th, leaving the 1st Battalion, 27th Infantry and other elements of the 25th Division to wrap things up. At year's end, the army closed the Guam center after having processed 112,000 refugees (10).

Training Exercises

At Schofield Barracks the battalion staff prepared the following mission statement: "The mission of the 1st Battalion, 5th Infantry is to maintain the highest possible level of combat readiness for contingency operations. These contingencies include possible deployment anywhere in the Pacific, on short notice, and employment in ground combat. Readiness is maintained by a continuous training program which involves field problems, off-island deployments, individual and unit testing and frequent inspections (11)."

Beginning in 1976 and annually thereafter, the 1st Battalion, 5th Infantry participated in OPERATION TEAM SPIRIT, a U.S armed forces exercise to test the capability of quickly reinforcing South Korea. Hawk Holloway, formerly of Alpha Company, recalled that Team Spirit 1979, which took place from February 1 to March 31, was a valuable exercise and outstanding experience. He didn't feel the same way about Team Spirit in 1981, when the battalion spent nine and half days of the eleven-day exercise in Corps reserve. During that exercise, five divisions maneuvered against each other as they practiced defending against chemical warfare, electronic jamming, live fire in air-to-ground and air-to-air maneuvers and amphibious operations.

During the intervening year, 1980, the battalion traveled to New Zealand. In 1985, U.S. forces were not allowed to return to New Zealand because our warships were allegedly carrying nuclear weapons.

In 1982, the battalion, under the command of LTC Charles Rothlisberger, went to the Philippines to participate in Balikatan Flash, a live-fire exercise in support of the Philippine Army. Like the annual Operation Team Spirit in Korea, the Balikatan (Tagalog dialect for shoulder to shoulder) would become an annual joint training exercise.

In August of that year, LTC Eugene Bernhardt assumed command of the 1st Battalion and remained in that position for the next two years. Bernhardt, who had first shipped to Vietnam as a non-com, had been awarded a direct commission during that conflict. He rose to the rank of captain by the time of his third and final tour (12).

In February 1983, it was time once again for Team Spirit in Korea. The entire 1st Brigade participated in that year's exercise. As previously mentioned, the 5th Infantry's sister battalions were elements of the 27th Infantry Wolfhounds and the 19th Infantry "Rock of Chickamauga," the regiment that had fought side-by-side with the 5th RCT in Korea as part of the 24th Division (13).

During Team Spirit '83, 1st Brigade was bivouacked in a tent city at Camp Page on the outskirts of Chunchon, approximately twenty-five miles south of the Demilitarized Zone. Prior to the training exercise, the brigade, led by 1st Battalion, 5th Infantry, marched in a welcoming parade sponsored by the city of Chunchon. Thousands of South Korean citizens lined the streets. The city's children, who had been released from school for the day, held banners with greetings for the American soldiers.

During the exercise, the 5th Infantry was assigned to a mountainous sector that was impassable to anything larger than a jeep. On the opening day of Team Spirit, snow fell on the exercise area and the temperatures dropped to below zero at night. The battalion was treated to a dose of the same weather that had plagued the 5th Regimental Combat Team thirty years earlier.

The high point of Team Spirit came when the battalion, minus Company A, conducted an airmobile raid deep behind "enemy" lines. They caught their adversary by surprise and destroyed one of his cavalry troops with TOW anti-tank fire. Meanwhile, Company A, attached to 1st Battalion, 27th Infantry, crossed the Han River on rafts and linked up with the main body of the battalion.

During the 1983 exercise, Albert Chang, who had served as regimental photographer for the 5th RCT, took members of the battalion on a tour of some of the combat team's battle positions south of the Han River. Chang, who was still a photographer with the army, was thirty years older than most of the men on the tour, but could still hump the steep Korean hills (14).

The battalion deployment to the Republic of Korea provided major logistical challenges. The battalion maintenance section, led by 1LT Tom Person, succeeded in keeping the battalion vehicles running during the fast-paced exercise. Employing a practice developed during the previous September's training exercise on the Big Island, a maintenance rally point, set up just behind the main line of resistance, returned damaged vehicles to service in record time.

As the battalion command group prepared to depart for Fort Leavenworth, Kansas, in November, 1983, to participate in a computerized command post training exercise, Hurricane Iwa struck the Hawaiian Islands causing extensive damage. The Kansas trip was cancelled so that clean-up work could take place. Working over the Thanksgiving weekend, men from the battalion cut up and hauled away tons of fallen trees and branches and provided water and ice to areas that had lost access to water and electricity.

Before 1983 was over, Bravo Company, commanded by Captain Joey MacDonald, was sent to Australia for a month of desert conditioning. The company landed in Brisbane and moved out into the desert. The purpose of the brutally demanding exercise was to practice a quick reaction to trouble in Oceania (15).

The entire battalion went to Australia in 1984 for an exercise called PAC BOND '84 and trained with the First Royal Australian Regiment and a complement of officers from, as the Aussies say it "Two Battalion, Four RAR" at Lavarack Barracks near Townsville on Australia's east coast.

The 25th Division conducted two more major training exercises during 1984 at the Pohakoloa Training Area and the Parker Sheep Station on the island of Hawaii. The maneuvers at PTA were code-named Opportune Journey 84. A company of Ghurka soldiers from 2 Ghurka Battalion, Hong Kong, trained with the 5th Infantry for thirty days during Opportune Journey. Colonel Bernhardt observed that the Ghurkas were "exceedingly good soldiers." Many members of 2 Ghurka Battalion had fought in the 1982 Falklands War.

The 5th Infantry Bobcats distinguished themselves in many ways during 1983-84. SP4 Joseph Castro of C Company was selected as 25th Division Soldier of the Year for 1983, the second year in the row that a man from the battalion had been so honored. Over sixty battalion members competed in the Honolulu Marathon in December, more than any two other battalions combined. Combat Support Company won the USASCH Flag Football Championship in January and Bravo Company won the 25th Division Combat Football Championship in August.

During the 1980's, 1st Battalion, 5th Infantry sponsored Bobcats Lair, an educational program for some of Hawaii's children with handicaps. The soldiers provided transportation, maintained the Lair's building and landscaping and assisted with retreats and field trips. In

July, Company C provided tents and personnel for a summer camp for special needs children at Camp Ho'omaluhia.

On 17 August 1984, LTC George F. Close assumed command of the 1st Battalion, 5th Infantry. Like his immediate predecessor, George Close was a graduate of both the Airborne and Ranger Schools. Trained in rotary winged flight as well, he had served as a platoon leader and company operations officer with the 121st Combat Assault Aviation Company in Vietnam. He subsequently completed several assignments with the 9th Infantry Division before reporting to Schofield Barracks and relieving LTC Bernhardt (16).

In the mid 1980's, the 5th Infantry adopted another mascot named Charlie. Company C attempted to raise a black Labrador puppy named Charlie but the animal's behavior was more reminiscent of the downtrodden Army of the 1970's. For the better part of a year, Charlie lived in a little blue dog house outside of the company barracks in Quad A. He was a favorite of the children of the soldiers in Company C and was frequently fed "bootleg" snacks from the mess hall and their homes. He soon came to prefer these delicacies and turned up his nose at the puppy chow that he should have been eating.

Charlie's unhealthy diet caused him to leave messes in the hand-to-hand training area and he was soon in trouble with the command sergeant major. According to Alex Von Plinsky, who was company commander, concerted counseling failed to modify Charlie's bathroom behavior and he was eventually granted a "rehab transfer" and was shipped to CONUS with one of the soldiers who was separating from the army and returning home to the farm (17).

When the battalion returned to Korea for Team Spirit 1985, it was once more quartered at Camp Page. While there, the mayor of Chunchon asked the soldiers to join in a commemoration of the liberation of his city during the Korean War. Because of its proximity to the North Korean border, the town had changed hands several times. The battalion participated in a victory parade and a memorial service.

Guardian of the Pacific

On October 17, 1985, Vice President George H. W. Bush, enroute to meetings in China, stopped off at Honolulu to visit the 25th Division. Accompanied by Division Commander MG Claude Kicklighter and ADM Ronald J. Hays, CINCPAC, the Vice-President reviewed the troops. Then he spent almost three hours with the 5th Infantry. Bush joined Charlie Company for lunch and dined on a MRE (Meals, Ready to Eat or, as the troops call them,"Meals Refused by Ethiopians") packet of diced turkey. He then visited the bayonet assault course, where he was briefed by Captain Von Plinsky and 1st Sergeant Edward Naylor and walked through the course as C Company executed a bayonet assault (18).

Combat Support Changes

Throughout the last half of the twentieth century, the army deactivated, reflagged, shifted and reconfigured its units in the name of coping with changing conditions. Nowhere were these constant changes more evident than in the process of providing support to the rifle companies. The provisional battalion and attached artillery and engineer elements of World War II and Korea gave way, in the late 50's, to five-company battle groups served by a combat support company. With the return to the brigade format in the 1960's, much support came from the specialty platoons of the battalion headquarters company and other brigade elements.

When Captain John De Fede joined the 1st Battalion, 5th Infantry in 1984, he assumed command of the battalion's resurrected Combat Support Company. His company had three anti-tank platoons equipped with three "gun jeeps", armed with mounted TOW wire-guided missiles, and three ammo jeeps carrying three rockets each. There was a 4.2 inch mortar section, a scout platoon and a communications section. The company had a TO&E strength of 148 officers and men (19).

Many of Combat Support Company's vehicles, consisting of jeeps, deuce-and-a-half trucks and M-561 Gamma Goats were older than the men driving them. The Goats, introduced to the army in 1970, were noisy, difficult to enter and had poor traction in sandy areas. By 1985 there was some difficulty finding spare parts and operator's manuals (20). They were phased out in the mid 1980's and most drivers and motor pool sergeants were not sorry to see them go. In 1986, when the "light infantry divisions" were formed, the combat support companies were discontinued.

De-activation

Between 1985 and 1987 the army sought to achieve balance among all its forces, including the National Guard and Reserves. The 6th Infantry, 10th Mountain, and 25th Infantry Divisions were designated "light infantry divisions." Being designated "light" at this point was a mere formality, since the battalion had long since relinquished its armored personnel carriers. As a consequence of the changes, the 1st Battalion, 5th Infantry became 3rd Battalion, 21st Infantry on 16 January 1986 (21).

As might have been predicted, the abrupt change from that of a snarling 5th Infantry "Bobcat" to that of a 21st Infantry "Gimlet" (a small drill for boring holes) did not sit well with the members of the battalion, from Colonel Close on down through the ranks. The officers and men were all familiar with the rich history and traditions of the 5th Infantry and felt a sense of being demoted, in spite of the impressive record that had been established by the 21st Infantry since its inception in 1861.

Several Korean War veterans, living on Oahu, expressed the opinion that the Department of the Army folded the 5th Infantry's flag because there were no living Medal of Honor recipients to lobby on behalf of the regiment (22). It was true that 20th century warriors Melvin Handrich, Daniel Fernandez, Marvin Rex Young, and Stephen Doane had all received the award posthumously but, in 1986, Carl Dodd, who earned the CMH near Subuk, Korea was still very much alive in

Laurel County, Kentucky. Dodd died ten years later, on October 13, 1996, at the age of seventy-one.

While a younger generation of the 5th Infantry stood guard in the Pacific, one of the regiment's finest commanders during the Korean War was buried at Arlington. General John Lathrop "The Rock" Throckmorton died on February 13, 1986 at the age of 73. His ascent to four star rank, following Korea, had included attendance at the National War College, Commandant of West Point, command of the 82nd Airborne Division, Commanding General, Third Army and Commander-in-Chief, U.S. Strike Command.

With the 2nd Division in Korea

When the Korean War truce was ratified in 1953, a de-militarized zone was established that runs for 151 miles across the peninsula and serves as a buffer zone between North and South Korea. The zone is 2.5 miles wide on either side of the Military Demarcation Line, a six-foot wide barbed wire corridor. Until the late 1950's, there was no fence along the MDL, making it easy for North Koreans to slip across.

In 1965, the Republic of Korea sent its best division, the Capitol Division, and a marine brigade to fight alongside U.S. forces in Vietnam. In 1966, the ROK 9th Division followed. That year, the two U.S. infantry divisions in Korea, 2nd and 7th, dropped well below authorized strength as the army's priority shifted to Vietnam. North Korea's dictator, Kim Il Sung, always probing for an opportunity to topple the ROK government, escalated the number of cross-border incidents.

During the two deadliest years in Vietnam, 1967-68, contacts between North Korean troops and patrols from the 2nd and 7th U.S Infantry Divisions increased markedly near the Demilitarized Zone. These hostilities began on February 12, 1967 when North Koreans ambushed a patrol from the 23rd Infantry, killing one American. Three months later, North Korean raiders blew up an army barracks at Camp

Greaves, just south of the DMZ. Several Americans died in the blast. In August, 1967, a work party from the 13th Engineers was attacked by North Koreans resulting in three more American deaths and, in October, a small boat from the 2nd Infantry Division was attacked as it patrolled the Imjin River.

On March 27, 1968, a patrol from the 2nd Division surprised a group of North Korean infiltrators and killed three of them. A month later, a company from the 31st Infantry, 7th Division engaged in a fire fight with a North Korean company while patrolling the DMZ. During that summer and fall, patrols from both the 2nd and 7th Infantry Divisions fought in several actions with North Korean infiltrators killing a number of Communist troops.

Between 1966 and 1969, North Korean attacks along the DMZ killed 44 Americans and wounded 111. Three hundred twenty-six ROK troops were killed and 600 were wounded. The North Koreans lost 715 killed and an unknown number were wounded. Following a March, 1969 attack on a U.S. Army fence-repair detail, these DMZ incidents subsided.

On three occasions during the 1970's, U.S. and South Korean soldiers discovered tunnels running under the DMZ. One of these, located near Panmunjom, was two meters high and two meters wide. Then, on 14 July 1977, a CH-47 helicopter was downed by anti-aircraft fire when it strayed over North Korea. Three dead and one wounded soldier were returned three days later at Panmunjom. It was also at the Panmunjom Peace Compound on 23 November 1984, that a North Korean Army defector made a break for the south side of the line. Attempts by the North Korean guards to shoot him brought a quick response from the U.S. and South Korean guards and a sharp fire fight ensued. One American soldier was wounded. By 1987, ninety U.S. soldiers had died in combat in Korea since the implementation of the 1953 truce accord (23).

These continuing tensions on the Korean Peninsula were at

their apex when the 5th Infantry was revived after sixteen months of inactivity. On 24 April 1987, the 1st Battalion, 5th Infantry reappeared when the 1st Battalion, 31st Infantry was re-flagged and the 31st Infantry Polar Bears became Bobcats. LTC Rick Holmes remained in command of the battalion. The colors of 1st Battalion, 31st Infantry were transferred to Ft. Sill, Oklahoma (24).

The battalion was initially garrisoned at Camp Howze, near the city of Tongduchon about forty-one miles north of Seoul. It was part of the 3rd Brigade, 2nd Infantry Division. The new Bobcats, already equipped with M-113A armored personnel carriers were, once again, the 1st Battalion (Mechanized) Infantry. The battalion was composed of Headquarters Company, four rifle companies (A, B, C and D) and Echo Company, to provide heavy weapons support.

Holmes led the battalion during the spring 1988 Team Spirit Exercise and during one of many periods of political unrest in South Korea. President Chun Doo-hwan had kept the country in an authoritarian grip since the assassination of his predecessor, Park Chung-hee in 1979.

When political demonstrations erupted in June of 1987, the Korean National Assembly, siding with those who wanted democratization of their country and fearful that political unrest might taint the forthcoming Summer Olympics in Seoul, forced Chun to resign. South Korea's first direct elections were scheduled for December. Roh Tae-woo took over as transitional president.

From summer until early fall 1988, U.S. Army units deployed near the DMZ to prevent infiltrators from coming south to stir up trouble. South Korea very much wanted to impress the international community with its stability and newly industrialized economy. During that period, the 1st Battalion, 5th Infantry, commanded by LTC David W. Hunt, relieved the 5th Battalion, 20th Infantry on the DMZ and was, in turn, relieved by the 1st Battalion of the 503rd Infantry.

Prior to undertaking DMZ duty, the battalion trained for the job.

Two Centuries of Valor

Echo Company went to a nearby firing range to test the skills of its Mobil Acquisition Counter-infiltration Element (MACE) (25). MACE patrols traveled in Humvees in order to be able to move quickly to the aid of an embattled foot patrol or to intercept North Korean infiltrators. While participating in the DMZ mission, the battalion provided daytime and nighttime combat patrols and occupied two platoon-sized outposts overlooking the line. At the time, these were the only U.S. Army combat patrols being conducted in a hostile area (26).

From January 9 until January 14, 1989, the 1st Battalion, 5th Infantry participated in "Winter Haze", a division-level command post/field training exercise. The day before the exercise ended, the Bobcats cooperated with the 2nd Engineer Battalion at the Rodriguez Range to blast paths through a series of wire and mine field obstacles. Another generation of riflemen learned how valuable combat engineers can be when obstacles stand between the rifle companies and their objectives (27).

On August 25, 1989, a congressional delegation consisting of Representatives John P. Murtha (PA), Barbara Kennelly (CT) and Robert Livingston (LA), all members of the House Appropriations Subcommittee on Defense, came to the DMZ for a quick visit with LTC Hunt and members of the battalion (28). They were briefed on the mission and visited with the young Bobcats who were manning Guardpost Oullette. From there they could view activity at Panmunjom in North Korea. The soldiers at Oullette were visited, a few days later, by Vice President Dan Quayle during his 11-day Asian tour (29). When the battalion returned to Camp Hovey, the men were rewarded with free tickets to the Olympic Games.

The 1989 staging of Operation Team Spirit also occurred during LTC Hunt's tenure with the battalion. This annual exercise, which never failed to make the North Korean authorities nervous and even more belligerent, probably reached its peak, in terms of visible activity, that spring.

Dan Baggio, who was commander of Charlie Company at the time, has vivid recollections of Team Spirit 89. "1-5 really kicked butt!" he said. "We were doing so well that the controllers held us back so not to embarrass our opponents." Baggio's company was in the vanguard of a major attack (30).

In 1990, it was decided that the 2nd Division would turn over Camp Howze to the ROK Army and consolidate further north on the Korean Peninsula. That summer, the battalion, commanded by LTC John Mitchell, departed the 3rd Brigade at Camp Howze and moved north to Camp Hovey and formed the 2nd Brigade with the 1st Battalions of the 503rd and 506th Air Assault Infantry Regiments.

The next battalion commander, LTC George Higgins, was present when the battalion turned in its M113A3 personnel carriers for Bradley Fighting Vehicles (31). This change was not without its drawbacks. Upgrading to the smaller vehicle necessitated dropping three riflemen from each squad. Echo Company, the support unit, remained equipped with a variant of the older M113 tracks that carried the TOW anti-tank missile launcher (32).

The Bradley crews of Company C were the first to receive their new vehicles in early August of 1991. Charlie Company took their Bradleys out on the Rodriquez Range Complex and learned to fire the 25mm guns. They were impressed. They now had a fast, mobile fighting vehicle that they felt could keep up with any tank (33).

In 1992, the 3rd Brigade, 2nd Infantry Division was inactivated in response to the U.S. Congress' mandate to reduce troop strength in Korea. Division Commander Creighton Abrams, Jr., then moved to rebalance his two remaining brigade combat teams (34). First Battalion, 506th Infantry was shifted to the 1st Brigade and 1st Battalion, 72nd Armored Regiment came to Camp Hovey to team with the 1st Battalion, 503rd Air Assault Infantry and the 1st Battalion, 5th Infantry. The latter was commanded by LTC Richard Rowe. General Abrams now had two triple-threat units; sometimes called "light/heavy" brigades.

Operation Team Spirit eventually fell victim to nuclear proliferation talks that were ongoing between the two Koreas and the United States. The North Koreans signed on to a non-proliferation treaty, that they had no intention of honoring, when President George H. W. Bush unilaterally withdrew all U.S. nuclear weapons outside of the territorial United States.

The maneuvers were cancelled in the spring of 1994 as further inducement. They were replaced, the following year, by a less visible annual exercise entitled Reception, Staging, Onward Movement and Integration (RSOI)(35). It is primarily a command post exercise that takes place every March for a week and involves South Korean and U.S. units from South Korea and a few other U.S. troops from Japan, Guam and the United States.

LTC Phil Pope, a Desert Storm veteran who had entered the army as a private in 1971, relived Richard Rowe in July, 1994 and was commanding the battalion in August of 1995 when the 1st Battalion, 9th Infantry at Ft. Lewis and the 1st Battalion, 5th Infantry at Camp Howze exchanged flags (36). Once again there would be a Manchu presence in Korea and a Bobcat unit at the Infantry Center of the Pacific Northwest. The 9th Infantry had been the only surviving element of the 7th Infantry Division following the closure of Fort Ord, California.

The 9th infantry colors and battle streamers were welcomed back to the 2nd Division by division commander, Major General Tommy R. Franks (37). During his remarks, General Franks reviewed the noble history of the 9th Infantry Regiment, a participant in all of America's wars. The reflagging was a fair exchange. One hundred and eighty years earlier, on May 17, 1815, men from a deactivated 9th Regiment had swelled the ranks of Colonel James Miller's 5th Infantry.

Back to the 25th Division

The 2nd Battalion, 5th Infantry was re-activated at Schofield Barracks on 16 August 1995. Eight days later, the 1st Battalion, 5th Infantry received its colors at Ft. Lewis. The two battalions of the 5th Infantry had returned to the 25th Infantry Division. First Battalion was assigned to the 1st Brigade at Fort Lewis and 2nd Battalion became part of the 3rd Brigade at the division's home base, Schofield Barracks.

It had been nearly forty years since there was a 5th Infantry presence at Ft. Lewis. Lieutenant Colonels Elliot Rosner, James Harris III, Michael Rounds and Todd McCaffrey led the 1st Battalion during this chapter of the battalion's history. In the wake of Hurricane Mitch in 1999, Colonel Rosner commanded Joint Task Force Bravo, a relief mission to Honduras that was one of the largest combined humanitarian efforts of the U.S. Army and the Marine Corps in history (38).

Analog vs. Digital Warfare

When Colonel Surles set up the 5th RCT command post in an armored personnel carrier close to the shooting during the Chuktae Valley offensive in Korea in October, 1951, he gave us a glimpse of the future of war fighting. In his forward mobile Tactical Operations Center (TOC) he was able to increase the accuracy and volume of needed information while maintaining communications with division, battalion, tactical air and tanks. The information that he received by radio, and used for making his command decisions, was a stream of sound. It was analog data. We humans perceive the world in analog. Everything we see and hear is a continuous transmission of information to our senses. However, digital data, an electronic estimate of analog data, is easier to manipulate and preserve. More importantly, computers can handle only digital data.

Forty-six years after the Chuktae Valley offensive, LTC James Harris III, commander of 1st Battalion, 5th Infantry, had an opportunity to lead his Bobcats in training exercises that allowed them to contrast digital and analog communications (39). In March of 1997, the 1st Battalion joined the 1st Brigade, 4th Infantry Division and "fought" as a digitized force in the Army Warfighting Experiment at the National Training Center at Fort Irwin, California. Six months later the 5th Infantry participated in maneuvers at Fort Polk, Louisiana as a strictly analog force.

At Fort Irwin, different software programs provided data to the battalion commander, S-3, S-2, and the fire support officer and aided their decision making. All staff elements were linked to subordinates and superiors through the internet. Every unit in the battalion could see the battle situation on their digital screens allowing them to reposition quickly to target the enemy.

At Fort Polk, however, communicating by radio and FAX slowed the battalion's ability to plan and execute. The digitized force also boasted a wide array of cutting-edge night vision devices as well as 120mm mortars and a mortar fire control system with a level of precision, range and explosive power superior to the 81mm mortars and 105mm howitzers used by the analog forces.

Six years later, the high-tech equipment tested by the 1st Battalion, 5th Infantry at Fort Irwin was operational in Iraq. The battalion received the Army Superior Unit Award for its contribution to the modernization of light infantry capabilities.

Sinai Peacekeepers

When Egypt and Israel signed a peace agreement known as the Camp David Accords on March 26, 1979, they agreed that international peacekeepers would be essential for the Sinai Peninsula, site of five wars between the two nations since 1948. In 1981, further negotiations between the two former adversaries resulted in a body known as the Multinational Force and Observers (MFO). International troops assigned temporarily to the MFO man a network of 35 watchtowers, checkpoints, and observation posts along a narrow strip of desert running the length of the eastern Sinai (40).

The United States contributes an infantry battalion to the MFO's southern sector, as well as 235 support personnel, including doctors and specialists in land mine disposal. In January 2000, the 1st Battalion, 5th Infantry, commanded by LTC Michael Rounds, pulled a 6-month deployment with the Sinai peace-keeping mission. They returned to Fort Lewis in June of that year (41). Brigadier General (Ret.) Michael Rounds currently serves as the director of the Human Performance Resource Center at the Uniformed Services University of the Health Services in Bethesda, Maryland.

The Stryker

In February, 2002, a new armored vehicle was named the Stryker to honor two Medal of Honor recipients, PFC Stuart Stryker of WWII and Specialist Robert Stryker, Vietnam. It currently serves as the primary weapons platform for the army's newly structured Stryker Brigade Combat Teams.

The Stryker, built by Michigan-based General Dynamics Land Systems, is a wheeled vehicle, designed to move troops quickly into battle. It can turn more quickly and in a smaller area than a tracked vehicle. It is faster and, because it has no tracks, doesn't tear up the streets and curbs - - avoiding inconvenience and expense to local residents. Thanks to the work of units like the 1st Battalion, 5th Infantry, the Stryker contains a digitized sensor suite that results in much better access to intelligence information than was possible in older combat vehicles. A newly added steel cage looks ungainly but grenades generally bounce off it before they explode.

Starting in the spring of 2002, the 1st Brigade, 25th Infantry at Fort Lewis began to reorganize from a light infantry brigade, with no armored vehicles, to a Stryker configuration. On 17 December 2003, Secretary of Defense Rumsfeld gave final approval to converting the 2nd and 3rd Brigades at Schofield Barracks to Stryker brigades. The 1st and 2nd Battalions of the 5th Infantry Regiment were preparing for a new level of mechanized warfare.

CHAPTER SIXTEEN

THE GLOBAL WAR ON TERRORISM

On September 11, 2001, Saudi terrorists, linked to Osama bin Laden's al Qaeda terrorist network, hijacked four American airliners, crashing two into the World Trade Center towers in New York City and another into the Pentagon in Arlington, Virginia. A fourth airliner crashed in rural Pennsylvania after passengers fought to regain control of the aircraft. More than three thousand people were killed in the attacks, most of them in the World Trade Center.

General Tommy Franks, who was traveling to Pakistan, returned immediately to his Central Command Headquarters. Al Qaeda and its Taliban allies were based in Afghanistan, part of Frank's area of responsibility.

Operation Enduring Freedom

On the 7th of October, OPERATION ENDURING FREEDOM began with the intent to destroy terrorist camps and infrastructure within Afghanistan, capture al Qaeda leaders, and overthrow the Taliban regime. While the early military operations consisted largely of air strikes, army special operations troops were deployed to Afghanistan to advise Northern Alliance forces fighting the Taliban and to coordinate bombing missions. A thousand soldiers from the 10th Mountain Division were deployed to Uzbekistan to protect an airfield used by U.S. forces for search and rescue operations. On 28 November, the soldiers of the 10th Mountain Division moved from Uzbekistan to Mazar-e Sharif, Afghanistan. Theirs was the first deployment of conventional American troops to Afghanistan (1).

During early March, 2002, troops from 1st Battalion, 87th Infantry, 10th Mountain Division; the 3rd Brigade, 101st Airborne Division, and

The Global War on Terrorism

the 1st Battalion, 75th Rangers battled Taliban and al Qaeda fighters in eastern Afghanistan. In just over a week of intense action, coalition forces killed an estimated five hundred enemy personnel at a cost of eight American servicemen KIA and another forty wounded.

Meanwhile the active battalions of the 5th Infantry at Fort Lewis and Schofield prepared for deployment. One of the innovations introduced during this period of training was the Javelin Anti-tank weapons system, a portable missile system with a very precise day/night sighting device and 2500 meter range that can be operated by one dismounted infantryman. The 1st Battalion received its Javelins in December 2002 and the 2nd Battalion was so armed a month later. At the time there was some speculation that the U.S. Army would soon be facing Iraqi armor. The Javelin would also prove useful against bunkers and other ground fighting positions.

In July 2003, the commanding general of the 25th Infantry Division was notified that eight thousand Tropic Lightning soldiers would be sent to Afghanistan for a six month tour of duty to relieve those soldiers who were currently battling the "anti-coalition forces." The orders stated that the 2nd Brigade would deploy in February of 2004 and the 3rd Brigade, including the 2nd Battalion, 5th Infantry, would replace the 2nd Brigade in the summer (2). However, on November 6, 2003, the orders were changed. The 3rd Brigade's shipping date was accelerated to April and the two units would be facing one-year tours of duty.

The achievements of the 10th Mountain Division in Ghazni Province paved the way for their successors from the 2nd Battalion, 5th Infantry who arrived in April, 2004. The 2/5th Infantry and the rest of the 3rd Brigade Combat Team were given the mission to deny sanctuary to the terrorists and to create the conditions for security, stability and reconstruction in the war-torn land.

The Battalion in a Stryker Brigade

The 2nd Battalion, 5th Infantry and attachments, commanded by

LTC Terry Sellers, was comprised of Headquarters Company, three rifle companies, a medical platoon, Battery A of the 7th Field Artillery, a platoon of combat engineers and C Company of the 125th Military Intelligence Battalion.

Headquarters Company had S-1 and S-4 sections to handle administration and logistics, as well as a scout platoon, communications platoon, anti-tank platoon and an 81mm mortar platoon. There were four mechanics to maintain the battalion's one hundred vehicles and a seventeen-man food service team to deliver a hot breakfast and a hot dinner to the forward operating bases.

While in Ghazni Province the 2/5th was attached to the 6th Marine Regiment. In June the battalion moved to Tirin Kot in Oruzgan Province and reverted to the control of the 3rd Brigade, 25th Division.

As in Vietnam, the components of the battalion were usually deployed in a dispersed fashion. In July, a rear command post was maintained in Kandahar. Company A (TM Quick Strike) provided security to Forward Operating Base (FOB) Anaconda. It shared the responsibility with Scout Platoon. First Platoon, Company C (TM Cobra) drew a security detail in Kabul.

The rest of Company C was involved in a mission to increase voter registrations in a nearby district. Company B (TM Bushmaster) and Battery A of the 7th FAB (Wardogs) were engaged in an operation in Zabol Province to find and kill Taliban insurgents and address medical, educational, and other quality of life issues with the local villagers (3).

Operation Lightning Resolve

The first major task assigned to this Task Force Bobcat was to curtail efforts by the Taliban and other anti-coalition militia (ACM) to disrupt the Afghan presidential elections scheduled for October 9, 2004. The battalion's effort was code-named OPERATION LIGHTNING RESOLVE.

The Global War on Terrorism

By July, the working conditions had improved for those soldiers at battalion headquarters. Two morale phones were installed and a PX stocked with comfort items like snacks, tobacco and reading materials was opened. The construction of tents with wooden floors and air conditioning was underway. There were showers and sufficient water so that a soldier could bathe every three days. On July 21, the mid-tour leave policy began for all soldiers in the battalion. Priority went to those men who had become new fathers since the deployment (4).

In August the days became uncomfortably hot and dusty, but Task Force Bobcat continued to help with voter registration in preparation for the presidential election. Company A completed a mission requiring them to air assault into a Taliban-held area to recover eleven kidnapped and massacred Pashtuns and Hazarans. They located and unearthed the remains and returned them to their families. The mission came off without an incident.

While that was happening, Company B moved into an unmapped area in Gizab District to befriend the locals and help with voter registration. On the return trip they recovered a substantial cache of heavy weapons and munitions as well as forty pounds of marijuana and two kilos of opium.

Scout Platoon and Company A worked out of FOB Anaconda, 8000 feet above sea level in Oruzgan Province. They trudged through boiling hot days and slept in dusty holes covered with shelter halves. They were often limited to one hot meal a day. They went two months without a shower but were able to rinse themselves off with water from a water truck. Until the troops were able to acclimate to the heat and elevation, many had chronic nosebleeds.

The heat and very fine Afghan dust dictated constant care and cleaning of equipment. Returning from patrols, the soldiers focused first on the cleaning of weapons, night vision goggles and radios, then on repairing equipment and restocking supplies. There was little time during operations to attend to these details and to check magazine springs and discard dented rounds (5).

The Afghan national election took place on October 9, 2004. The day went relatively smoothly according to messages received from each of the battalion's six outposts. Company B, in cooperation with Afghan soldiers, found and destroyed several IED's during the voting period.

When the voting was over in Deh Rawoud, Captain Richard Ducote, Charlie Company CO, and nine of his soldiers came under heavy fire while they were escorting some Afghan citizens to Kandahar along with some ballots to be counted (6).

"The insurgents didn't want those ballots to be counted" said Ducote. "The ambush was at very close range with a lot of gunmen surrounding us. One of their RPG's hit the front vehicle in our convoy, which ended up severely injuring a lieutenant riding in the vehicle. We were trying to treat the officer, 1LT Andrew Sloan, who was slipping in and out of consciousness while we were returning fire."

With one vehicle disabled and no possibility of communication with headquarters because of their location, the nine soldiers, with their wounded officer, piled into their remaining Humvee and the elections convoy sped for higher ground. There they were able to radio headquarters and request medical evacuation for LT Sloan (7).

Luck ran out for Company C on October 14 when one of its Humvees, on a routine patrol, was destroyed by a remote-control IED in the town of Miam Do, northwest of Deh Rawoud. Specialist Kyle Fernandez, of Company C, and Staff Sergeant Brian Hobbs of Headquarters Company were killed in the blast (8). An army helicopter gunner, hovering above the destroyed vehicle, spotted the suspected bomber on a motorbike and killed him.

The election went somewhat smoother for Alpha Company as its three platoons protected fifteen polling sites in the Khas Uruzgan and Chora districts. With the exception of a small skirmish in the village of Margunday, a missing bridge, destroyed to hinder voter turnout, and

The Global War on Terrorism

a light snow fall, the Afghans turned out in droves to elect their new president.

When the men of C Company weren't busy patrolling the polling places, they were teaching children in the local primary school to brush their teeth and organizing a soccer and volleyball league for the older. It was a dark day in the history of 5th Infantry athletics when the volleyball team from Shazaman High School defeated A Company's team by 15 to 3 and 15 to 6.

There was further heartbreak for Company C in November when Specialists Jacob Fleischer and Dale Fracker were killed by an IED near Deh Rawoud. Fracker's brother, Herman was a marine. At the time of Dale's death, Herman had just completed back-to-back tours in Iraq and was facing the possibility of a third trip. Much to his parents' relief, Herman exercised his right as a lone surviving sibling to avoid returning to the war zone.

As Company B patrolled its polling sites, they discovered and destroyed an IED and a 107mm rocket that were primed to disrupt the election. During the late afternoon of Election Day, some voters were driving home on a tractor when they hit a mine buried in the road. Two Afghans were killed and one was wounded by the blast.

Fourteen thousand Afghan men and a thousand women voted in Bravo Company's area. Throughout the night of October 9th, two howitzer sections of the artillery battery fired illumination shells to help the patrols. Try as they might, the Taliban had failed in their efforts to keep eight and half million Afghans away from the voting booth (9).

Two weeks later, the cooking crew worked well into the night preparing for Thanksgiving Day, 2004. There was turkey, ham, Cornish hens, seafood and all of the usual side dishes. The cooking staff, both battalion and National Guard, were motivated by the promise that General John Abizaid, CENTCOM Commander, would be joining them. However, the general was unable to make it because of unforeseeable bad weather (10). At this point in the battalion's tour, all forward operating bases had satellite dishes, so there was plenty of traditional football viewing for Thanksgiving.

Operation Lightning Freedom

Once the election was over, the operational emphasis was shifted to furnishing support for Afghan reconstruction and the training of Afghan security forces. The winter was approaching and, with it, there would be some decline in combat actions against anti-coalition militia (ACM) forces.

By early December, the men of Task Force Bobcat were beginning to experience the Afghan winter. Nighttime temperatures, at the lower-level facilities, were in the low 30's and the days never got beyond the mid-50's. Up at FOB Anaconda, daytime temperatures were in the thirties and dropped below zero at night.

Fortunately, by this time, there were wooden-floored tents with heat in the forward operating bases in addition to morale phones, internet access, satellite television and hot water for showers and laundry. There was also a general feeling that patrol missions and relations with the Afghan people were going well. The latter were feeling comfortable enough to come forward and offer information that helped the Afghan Government and Coalition forces rid their towns and villages of anti-coalition militia members. Frequently, this information came at a price.

Prior to going home on leave in December, SGT Enrique Elizalde and his sniper section from Scout Platoon were told to implement an aerial reaction force (ARF) to capture an anti-coalition militia commander who was holed up in a high mountain village. According to Elizalde, the army had learned of the commander's location in the same way that they learned much of their information.

"Some of the Afghanis want to make money so they can go to Pakistan" said the sergeant. "It's like people who want to migrate from

The Global War on Terrorism

Mexico into the U.S. To Afghanis, Pakistan is their U.S. They all want to go to Pakistan. If you have enough money to pay your way into Pakistan, you can go through the border, no problem. So what people do is they tell the army, 'I know where an ACM commander stays, but I want money for it.' Another section of the military will do research and confirm or deny the commander's presence there. If he's there, they put up a mission and send us (11)."

Elizalde's sniper section was airlifted to the target village. As the helicopter hovered, they watched the houses to see if anyone tried to bug out. The snipers called such a suspect a "squirter." If the fleeing suspect is armed, they can usually take him out from the helicopter. If he isn't armed, then the standing orders are to land and capture him.

The sergeant continued "On the third day of our ARF, the ACM commander tried to flee across the river on a raft. He had his 8-year-old kid with him. The helicopter gunner fired some warning shots and the enemy commander stopped in the middle of the river. He surrendered and left his kid on the raft. But the kid fell off into the water, where it is about 40°, and this kid is freezing."

Sergeant Elizalde dropped his gear and swam across the river to help the boy. When he reached the raft, he signaled for the child to come to him. However, Elizalde did not know that, in that part of Afghanistan, signaling with your fingers pointing up means, "Come here, I'm going to hurt you." To signal "come here" one turns his fingers down.

The boy, not knowing what was going to happen to him, clung to the raft and cried. Elizalde, perplexed by the boy's outburst, said that he just picked him up by the back of his shirt, slammed him on the raft and took him back to shore. When asked why he went after the child, the sergeant shrugged. "I guess it's just good to do one good thing when you have to do fifty bad things every day."

During December, the dispersed elements of 2/5th continued their operations in unseasonably wet weather. The command post at

Kandahar continued to receive and push forward every necessity from new helmets and cold weather boots to Christmas dinner. Company B was all together at FOB Ripley for the first time since departing Ghazni in June 2004. First Platoon of Company A had drawn the security duty in Kabul. Company C remained at FOB Cobra and was able to eliminate many more Taliban fighters during the month. Their medical team set up a health clinic where they were able to treat 180 Afghans per day. The scout, anti-tank and mortar platoons were kept busy supporting operations by Alpha and Charlie Companies.

On December 12, Bravo Company at FOB Ripley hosted the Afganistan branch of the Honolulu marathon. Around 200 soldiers traveled to the forward operating base to participate in the 26.2 mile run. LT Mike Baskin, executive officer of Alpha Company, turned in the best time, but all soldiers who finished the distance got a prize. One of the consolation prizes was a trip to Kandahar to see a USO show featuring comedian Robin Williams (12).

During January, Bravo Company distributed sacks of wheat seed throughout the district of Nesh hoping that the farmers would choose to cultivate wheat rather than opium poppies. Company C patrolled the villages checking on its civil affairs projects. Multiple wells were being dug and a large school was being built in the town outside of FOB Cobra.

In early February, it was already time to begin planning for the battalion's redeployment to Hawaii. When the battalion leadership met on February 10, local civilian officials such as Provincial Governor Jan Mohammed Khan and Police Chief Rozi Khan were included in some of the deliberations. The group set the conditions for provincial elections in the spring and for the battalion's relief in place by 2nd Battalion, 504th Parachute Infantry Regiment.

While the brass discussed redeployment, B Company took part in an air and ground assault into Mirabad to go after some bad guys who had been working with the locals to plant several IED's along two of the company's patrol routes in Tirin Kot. The villagers reported all of the IED's to the local police who then relayed the information to the battalion. Men from Company B were able to disarm and destroy all of the devices before anyone was injured. They gathered up a few suspects for further questioning.

Later in the month, a village in the Bahguchar Valley, hard hit by snow storms, became inaccessible by road. The footpaths in and out of the valley had been snowed in since October. Word came that several villagers had lost their lives due to the cold weather and untreated illnesses. Governor Khan, Battalion Commander LTC Sellers, Battalion Surgeon, Major Barnett Gibbs, soldiers from B Company, Afghan National Army troops and several medics formed a relief party and flew in with cooking oil, heating fuel, food, water and medical supplies (13). Soldiers lowered to check the snow depth before landing the big Chinook helicopters, frequently sank up to their chests in white powder. Major Gibbs and his medics treated numerous villagers. The Bobcats were really looking forward to getting back to the warm beaches of Waikiki.

On 29 March, while returning to FOB Cobra from a patrol in the Cehar Cine/Osay District, two men from C Company were seriously injured when their vehicle hit an IED. Specialists Dennet Oregon and John Short were medevac'd to FOB Ripley. The 2nd Field Surgical Team, assisted by Task Force Surgeon Gibbs and battalion medics stabilized the two soldiers before shipping them to Kandahar on a UH-60. At Kandahar, John Short underwent six hours of surgery but, due to arterial damage, lost his leg just below the knee. SPC Oregon spent some time in the Landsthul Regional Medical Center in Germany before going home to Tripler Army Hospital on Oahu. SPC Short was sent to Walter Reed Medical Center (14).

As everyone's mind was on going home to Hawaii, there was still plenty of natural disaster to keep the troops busy. Two days of heavy rain began melting the snow in B Company's area causing the

Helmand River to flood. Soldiers from the battalion, making use of the task force's Chinook helicopters, plucked more than four hundred locals from the water and from islands caused by the flooding. The families were flown to locations where food, water, tents and blankets were distributed. Those rescued reciprocated by bringing out trays of bread, turkey, and mutton and pots of tea to share with the soldiers (15).

In March, advance parties from the 504th Parachute Regiment, 173rd Airborne Brigade from Vicenza, Italy arrived at Kandahar to begin the relief in place. The 2nd Battalion, 5th Infantry's productive year in Afghanistan was coming to a close.

All elements of the 25th Infantry Division were back at Schofield Barracks by June, 2005. On June 26, LTC Malcolm Frost relieved Terry Sellers as commander of the 2nd Battalion. The battalion folded its flag on 16 November 2005 when it became 3rd Squadron, 4th Cavalry, a reconnaissance unit (16).

In March, 2007, the army awarded the Meritorious Unit Commendation to the 2nd Battalion, 5th Infantry for its service in Afghanistan in 2004-2005. This award is given to units that have rendered outstanding service for at least six months of military operations against an armed enemy. The unit must display such outstanding devotion to duty and superior performance of exceptionally difficult tasks as to set it apart from and above other organizations with similar missions. The degree of achievement required is the same as that which would warrant award of the Legion of Merit to an individual soldier.

Operation Iraqi Freedom

Between January and mid March of 2003, the U.S. Army deployed 57,500 troops in the Persian Gulf region. The build-up in Kuwait involved two divisions, the 3rd Infantry and the 101st Airborne and elements of the 2nd Brigade, 82nd Airborne Division. The 4th

The Global War on Terrorism

(Mechanized) Division arrived last after being diverted from Turkey.

On 20 March 2003, U.S. Army and Marine forces invaded Iraq to remove Saddam Hussein and find and destroy his alleged "weapons of mass destruction." Fourteen months later, the country was returned to a new Iraqi government which was unable to provide security for its people, so the American troops and a few other coalition forces remained.

In October, 2004, six months before the 2nd Battalion, 5th Infantry returned from Afghanistan, the 1st Battalion, 5th Infantry arrived in Iraq. Prior to the battalion's departure from Fort Lewis, Washington, Battalion Commander LTC Todd McCaffrey wrote the following letter to Fred Deverse, then president of the 5th Infantry Chapter, 25th Infantry Division, an organization composed of veterans and active duty members of the 5th U.S. Infantry Regiment (17).

Fred,

> Greetings to you and the rest of the 5th Infantry Association. I know CSM Vic Mercado has passed along much of our final pre-deployment news, but I thought it appropriate to send a short Commander's update on 1st Battalion's readiness and final deployment activities and a few personal comments on these men—America's most recent Greatest Generation.
>
> We're ready to begin deploying 1-5 IN soldiers to combat for the first time since Vietnam. Our initial flow of advance personnel will depart Fort Lewis within the next several weeks and be joined by the remainder of the Bobcats in northern Iraq by mid October. Our soldiers are trained and ready. They take pride in the accomplishments of their battalion ancestors from Lundy's Lane, Mexico, the western frontier, to the jungles and hilltops of Vietnam. They watch news of their Second Battalion brothers in Afghanistan fighting on America's initial front on terrorism and stand ready to take their place as proud veterans as we write the newest chapter of our regiment's combat history

in Iraq.

I spend a lot of time watching, training, and talking with these soldiers. As you'd expect, and probably remember from your own service, each has his own views on this war. However, as United States soldiers throughout our heritage, they follow orders and are prepared to do their duty not because of individual political beliefs but because of a common bond of brotherhood and immense pride in this unit, the army, and this nation. I am deeply humbled to serve and lead them.

Like soldiers from other units, today's Bobcats come from across this nation. Their names and faces would remind our (5th Infantry Chapter) members of their own service: Rivera from New York, Torres from Puerto Rico, Nelson from Minnesota, Davis from Georgia, Bachl from South Carolina and every state in between. In this season of political campaigns, these men remind me daily that our service is not to a party or administration; it's to a constitution and a nation. I believe with absolute certainty that the U.S. Army has never put a more trained and ready outfit into harm's way. These men will serve with courage, compassion, intelligence and a knowledge that their sacrifice will help the Iraqi people to a true freedom and, in that effort, make us all more secure.

Our equipment (what little we'll take as we're falling-in on another Stryker battalion's vehicles) has already shipped. Our soldiers took advantage of a well deserved leave to visit with family and friends before our most-interesting-year. Just this past week we completed our final block of platoon level collective training and are now focused on final personnel preparations and turning our barracks over to the installation. In sum, all we can do here has been done and we're ready to get going with what lies ahead.

As I said before, we're undoubtedly the best trained army in our history. With certainty, we'll be the most well-connected with family and friends. Troops will have access to e-mail, phones and a myriad of services to keep them tied to the goings-on on the home front. They'll receive mail and packages from loved ones and neighbors. We hope to offer frequent updates to the Association newsletter to keep the membership tied into today's warriors. The Association has been and continues to be a great friend of this battalion. I thank each member in advance for their thoughts and prayers for today's Bobcats, both those currently in Afghanistan and those of us soon to be in Iraq.

Commanding soldiers is the highest privilege. Commanding Bobcats is both a privilege and an honor. Thanks again for all your support and prayers.
Respectfully,
Todd McCaffrey
Lieutenant Colonel, Infantry
Commanding

The Battle for Fallujah

The 1st Battalion, 5th Infantry reached Iraq on the 11th and 12th of October where they relieved the 1st Battalion, 23rd Infantry at Camp Taji, northwest of Baghdad, and scrambled to get ready for combat operations. They had arrived just in time to participate in the second battle for Fallujah (18).

The battalion's first assignment involved security operations between Fallujah, Abu Ghraib and Baghdad to prepare for the assault. It was placed temporarily under operational control of the 10th Mountain Division and was ordered to deploy a portion of the battalion to Camp Striker, adjacent to the Baghdad International Airport, from where it would be conducting patrols. Alpha and Bravo Companies remained at Taji. Charlie Company was about to shift to Camp Striker when new orders came returning the entire battalion to the Fallujah operation. The battalion was placed under the tactical control of the 2nd Brigade

Combat Team, 1st Cavalry Division.

Brigade headquarters in Northern Iraq requested that the battalion send one of its infantry companies to work with the 2nd Squadron, 14th Cavalry. Alpha Company was given that assignment. In exchange, Alpha Troop of the 14th Cavalry was sent south to help the Bobcats. On 29 October, key personnel from the battalion flew to Camp Victory at the Baghdad Airport to meet with the folks from 1st Cav and discuss plans for the upcoming assault on Fallujah. The battalion arrived at Camp Fallujah on the morning of 4 November.

Bravo Company moved from Camp Fallujah to a former Iraqi National Guard compound in the vicinity of Karmah, east of Fallujah. Karmah was believed to be a safe haven for insurgent leaders. The company sealed off two bridges along the main route from Fallujah to Karmah.

Alpha Troop's area of operations extended north from Camp Fallujah to Bravo Company's southern boundary. It set up blocking positions at two major road intersections leading into the city. Charlie Company's boundaries extended west from Bravo's and joined with 1st Battalion, 5th Cavalry's flank, where they blocked the three bridges. Headquarters Company controlled the Battalion Quick Reaction Force in addition to its responsibilities for vehicle recovery and medical support.

The battalion's role was to participate in a cordon around the city to prevent insurgents from leaving and others from reinforcing those who were bottled up within Fallujah. The fight within the city was the responsibility of the 1st and 7th Marines and two U.S. Army mechanized infantry battalions. Ground operations began on the night of 7 November.

Two days later, the battalion shifted its focus by keeping smaller crews at the blocking positions and using the remaining forces to conduct dismounted patrols in the populated areas. This was done in an effort to prevent the Anti-Iraqi Forces (AIF) from using the smaller east-west routes coming in and out of the battalion's sector and to disrupt their efforts to target friendly troops with direct and indirect fire.

North to Mosul

On 11 November, in the midst of an ongoing fight in Karmah, the Bobcats received word from brigade that they must be prepared to move the entire battalion north to Mosul within six hours of notification. They were to rejoin the 1st Brigade, 25th Division and help deal with increased insurgent activity in that northern city. Shortly thereafter, the notification came and the battalion began to withdraw to Camp Fallujah. Charlie, A/14th Cavalry, and Headquarters Companies were back at Taji before the sun came up on the 12th, but Bravo Company was stuck at the Delta Compound until 1/5th Cavalry could affect a relief in place, somewhat tricky since both units were in contact with the enemy (19).

Mosul, 396 kilometers north of Baghdad, is Iraq's second largest city. It is the north's major center for trade, industry and communications. The city of nearly 600,000 inhabitants has been populated since Biblical times. It is situated on the west bank of the Tigris River (Nahr Dijilah) across the river from the ancient ruins of Ninevah.

While traveling north, word was received over the satellite radio that LTC McCaffrey must break off one of his companies south of Mosul at Hammam al Alil and have it secure FOB Aggies, where it would remain until further notice. Charlie Company drew that assignment.

The first elements of 1/5th arrived at FOB Marez in Mosul on the afternoon of 13 November and the final serials moved in late that evening. Brigade operations were to begin the following morning and 3rd Battalion, 21st Infantry needed an infantry company to assist them. Bravo Company was tapped for that purpose. They set up traffic control points on the two southern-most bridges across the Tigris River to support 3/21st Infantry and 1/24th Infantry operations in the city. They returned to 5th Infantry control just as the battalion finished setting up its new command post.

The 1st Battalion, 5th Infantry's 850 soldiers became part of Task Force Olympia, an eight thousand man contingent that assumed responsibility for Northern Iraq, relieving the 101st Airborne Division. The 101st had maintained 32,000 troops in the area but there had been an assumption that conditions had become more stable and that security could be maintained with a smaller force.

The Bobcats took over an area in Mosul that extended to the outlying villages and hamlets to the south and west of the city, including Hammam al Alil and FOB Aggies in the Tigris River Valley, that portion supervised by Charlie Company. Alpha Troop assumed control of the area west of Route Tampa (Highway 1) as well as the small towns and routes west of Mosul. Bravo took control of the area that was bordered by Mosul to the north, the Tigris to the east, Charlie Company's area to the south and Route Tampa to the west. The companies began establishing random traffic control points along the major routes.

On 17 November, Bravo Company was tasked with clearing Station 4 West, a former Iraqi police station that had been seized earlier by insurgents. They found that the post was deserted and virtually destroyed. They remained there until it was determined that it was not worthwhile to secure a pile of rubble.

The 10th Iraqi Regular Army Battalion had just recently finished basic training and had a dearth of leadership in its ranks. The new soldiers were thrown together in a unit and told to move to Mosul. Headquarters Company initiated contact with these soldiers and began the task of finding them some place to stay on the FOB and working them into company operations. Each IRA company was assigned to a 5th Infantry company to be trained and integrated into patrols and traffic control points. The Iraqi soldiers were eager to learn, but language and training gaps made it difficult to deploy them without direct U.S. Army supervision.

When Thanksgiving Day rolled around, the enlisted men at Battalion Headquarters, FOB Marez, were treated to turkey and pie served, as army tradition dictates, by officers and senior NCO's. There was access to phones and the internet and the television showed replays of the Ron Artest fight during a recent Indiana Pacers basketball game. However, at Company C's outpost, where there were very limited shower facilities, little access to the outside world, and no chow hall, there was an air of loneliness (20).

Mess Sergeant Edmund Savedra was less than ten minutes away from Charlie Company's remote post with a load of turkey dinners when an explosion shattered the windshield of his truck and showered the sergeant and his two passengers with glass. It looked, for a moment, like it was going to be a replay of New Years Day, 1968 for Charlie Company. Savedra floored the gas pedal and flew over the country roads without looking back to see who was shooting at them. He knew how much the isolated company wanted its Thanksgiving dinner and he was determined to get it there.

A subsequent inspection of the blast area revealed a crater, two feet deep, and the burning hull of a Toyota truck. Army investigators surmised that insurgents had buried artillery shells under the truck and then had detonated them as the lightly armored dinner wagon rolled by.

During the battalion's first month in Mosul, more than 160 bodies, many of them the mutilated remains of U.S trained members of the Iraqi National Guard, were discovered in and around the city. The Iraqi National Guard battalion stationed in nearby Hammam al-Alil had dissolved in the face of a November 10 attack.

The search for information about the local insurgents became LTC McCaffrey's most crucial task leading up to the January 30 elections. To gather such information, the battalion had to rely upon mass arrests, hit-and-miss traffic stops, and a few frightened Iraqis who snitched; often to avenge the murder of a family member. While being interviewed by a reporter from the Washington Post, MAJ Omar Jones, Battalion S-3, said "I'm beginning to think this is the Mayberry of Iraq—not a bad guy around. No one knows any of them (21)."

A typical round-up of the usual suspects in the village of Qabr Abd took place in the numbingly cold hours before dawn in early December. More than two hundred young Iraqis were collected and were lined up, hands pressed against a wall, as attack helicopters circled overhead and ground troops kept them under surveillance. Troop A set up blocking positions on the major routes into town and Charlie Company set a cordon around the town and executed the searches within the city limits.

For the next four hours, each man of military age was photographed. His name was checked against a laminated list held by another soldier. Then he was escorted to a place in front of the headlights of a humvee where an informant, concealed in the darkness of the humvee cab, identified some of the men as insurgents. Back at headquarters, other informants confirmed that thirty-four of the men were involved in the insurgency, seven of whom were on the brigade's wanted lists.

While Charlie Company and Alpha Troop were conducting these round-ups in the Bobcat AO, Bravo Company moved out to FOB Sykes for approximately a week. While there, they operated in the city of Tal A'far in conjunction with Alpha Company, 5th Infantry and 2nd Squadron, 14th Cavalry. The combined force was extremely effective in striking planned targets and disrupting the enemy's planning. Bravo Company returned to 5th Infantry control on 6 December, but Alpha Company remained in the northern city.

While on mounted patrol in Tal A'far, SGT Darrell Griffin of Company A described an incident when his vehicle was hit by an IED.

The Global War on Terrorism

He recounted "As we were taking heavy small arms fire, Doc and I were pulling out our 1st Sergeant, whose leg had been broken by the powerful blast. As soon as we handed him down, we began to treat SGT Gordon by applying a tourniquet to his nearly severed leg. When I climbed down from the vehicle to assess PFC Rosenthal, I noticed that his face had been severely burned, so I thought, but it was merely soot from the blast. As soon as I knelt down to cut his pants off to assess his wounds, asphalt began chipping all around us due to the small arms fire getting closer. Once at the front of the vehicle, we began taking heavy fire from a mosque off to our east and there was just nowhere else to take cover. Luckily our commander's vehicle approached the wreckage and we immediately loaded all the casualties and they were brought back to FOB Sykes (22)."

Non-lethal activities were also an important part of the battalion's operations. They were largely confined to information operations and civil affairs projects. The Information Operations Team's job was to capitalize on successes of the battalion and brigade, to emphasize the damage created by the terrorists and to mitigate any damage that Coalition Forces might have wrought in any given area. The main mode of passing information was through the use of pamphlets and flyers printed in Arabic. Most of the villagers in the Bobcats' AO did not own a telephone or listen to the radio and the television channels they watched provided a biased and jaded view of the fight in the greater Mosul area.

The Civil Affairs Team went from village to village talking to the tribal and religious leaders, determining their major needs and drafting projects to be completed with U.S. funds. They were able to show that the Bobcats were not only in the neighborhood to destroy the enemy but to rebuild the infrastructure and assist the local population in putting the community back on its feet. Winning the local trust, especially to the point where they were willing to help the battalion find, fix and destroy the enemy, was a constant challenge, but Civil

Affairs' efforts proved very effective.

Hammam al Alil, the most populated small town in the Bobcats' area of operations, was crucial to the security of the entire area. All neighboring villages were tied to Hammam al Alil for support of some kind. Ridding Hammam of insurgents would have far reaching effects. LTC McCaffrey met with mayoral candidates on several occasions and, on 15 December appointed Khalif Kadir Muhammed as the city's mayor. Khalif had been a general in the Iraqi Special Forces, had a clean record and voiced his support of the Iraqi interim government. On 20 December, Khalif gathered the town leadership to meet with LTC McCaffrey and they all pledged to establish security in the area and to work together to rebuild some of the systems that were dysfunctional.

Earlier in December, elements of the 10th Iraqi Army Battalion moved, with an Alpha Troop escort, to Al Kisik and the 11th IRA Battalion returned with Alpha Troop to FOB Marez. As the ultimate success of the U.S. mission in Iraq depended on the Iraqi security forces taking control of their country, the Bobcats devoted significant time and resources to making the 11th IRA Battalion successful.

Mortar Platoon took on the task of giving the Iraqis advanced training for the real world missions they would soon face. The sessions focused on weapons safety, room/building clearing techniques, traffic control and searching vehicles and personnel.

One company of the 11th IRA Battalion went south to FOB Aggies to work with Charlie Company in the Hammam al Alil area. They conducted foot patrols in the local area and provided security for the Hammam Iraqi Security Forces Compound to prevent further looting of the facility. The IRA developed a rotation plan whereby the company at Hammam would switch out with a different IRA company from FOB Marez every seven days.

The Iraqi soldiers conducted several cordon-and-knock operations, one in Buwayr with Bravo Company and one in Salaam

The Global War on Terrorism

Village with Alpha Troop. Having the Iraqi soldiers conduct the searches of buildings put an Iraqi face on the mission. They were able to search sensitive sites, such as mosques, that U.S forces would not be able to search. The platoon leaders from the Bobcat units noted substantial improvement in the leadership of the IRA battalion and in the general discipline of the soldiers over the course of the month.

As four hundred task force members gathered for lunch in the crowded dining facility at FOB Marez on December 21, a suicide bomber entered the canvas-covered structure and detonated an explosive device. Small metal pellets, the size of BB's sprayed in every direction, killing twenty-two people and wounding sixty-six. The concussion shook the entire base, lifting people from their seats in barracks as far as a quarter mile away. Among the dead were three Bobcats: S/SGT Julian Melo, HHC, 5th Infantry, S/SGT Darren VanKommen, A Troop, 14th Cavalry and 1/SGT Paul Karpowich, an advisor working with the Iraqi 98th Division Training Brigade (23).

The bomber was apparently a member of the Ansar al-Sunnah Army, a Sunni group that was determined to turn Iraq into an Islamic state like Afghanistan under the Taliban regime. He was dressed as an Iraqi National Guardsman. Since there was an Iraqi National Guard contingent within the perimeter of the forward operating base, his presence in the mess hall would not have seemed unusual.

As December grew to a close, the battalion conducted ceremonies to honor their lost comrades and to award its members their Combat Infantryman Badges, Combat Medical Badges and 25th Division Combat Patches. These small pieces of embroidered cloth were symbols for each soldier of his sacrifice to his nation, to his unit and to the brother at his side. Darrel Griffin received the Bronze Star with V Device for his life-saving actions in Tal Afar.

Election Preparations

The pace of combat picked up in January as the battalion prepared for the Iraqi national elections that would be held at the end of the month. Company A remained detached from the battalion and under the command of the 14th Cavalry at FOB Sykes. Company B and A/14th Cavalry, stationed at FOB Marez, continued to interdict enemy movement into and from Mosul, covering an extremely large area west and south of the city. Charlie Company still occupied FOB Aggies. Its focus was on engaging with the local leaders, interdicting enemy movement and working a number of civil affairs projects. Back at FOB Marez, the platoons of Headquarters and Headquarters Company guarded detainees and provided security for the battalion command post, an assignment that had been brought sharply into focus by the dining facility bombing.

On January 3, SGT Griffin's squad moved out from its base in an old castle in Tal A'far to recover the body of an Iraqi policeman's son, who had been beheaded. Griffin wrote:

> "We took some Iraqi cops to the scene and did in fact see a headless body with the head carefully stacked on top of the chest with the body lying flat on the ground. The three police officers went up to the body to identify it while security was maintained for them by us. Before they got within 8 feet of the body, the body exploded and killed one while severely injuring the others…We took the torso back to the castle where we have been for awhile, and had to unzip the body bag so that other family members could identify the lower half by the shoes he was wearing.
>
> "Later in the day, some Iraqi police, who were family members of the destroyed body, began to drink heavily and one of them started shooting randomly into the crowded traffic circle below the castle. We watched as he killed a 17-year-old girl, a 7-year-old girl and a 28-year-old male. We could not intervene, as this was happening, for very complex reasons. This has been one of the most horrific days of my entire 34 years of living on this earth…I

am stupefied and stand in tragic awe in the face of this carnage, what could I possibly say? Where was God today?" (24)

Fourteen months later, while serving his second tour in Iraq, Darrell Griffin was shot by a sniper while standing in the hatch of his armored vehicle. He died enroute to the military hospital at Balad Air Base. There will be no more poignant letters and vividly descriptive journal entries coming home from that young soldier.

In the days leading up to the elections, it was important to demonstrate the battalion's maneuver and firepower capabilities in the Hammam Al Alil and Qabr Abd region. The combined operation involved dismounted infantrymen, mortar fire, AH-64 Apache close-combat attack, Stryker vehicles and a company air assault in UH-60 Blackhawk helicopters. Alpha Troop set up traffic control points along Routes Tampa and Toyota North, Bravo Company set its own TCP's at a bridge over the Tigris and along Route Santa Fe to support a brigade surge in the city, and Charlie Company targeted two houses in Hammam that were serving as homes for suspected insurgents. Recon Platoon drew the task of screening the east side of the city along the west bank of the Tigris.

Additional elements were attached to the battalion for the duration of this OPERATION OCTOPUS SQUEEZE. These groups included Bravo Company/14th Infantry, an air assault company from the 25th ID, HQ/151st AV, an attack weapons team from South Carolina, and A/106th AV, an air lift platoon from the Midwest. B/14th provided a company to make an air assault from Mosul Airfield to raid a suspected enemy cache site on an island in the Tigris, just east of Hammam. The 106th AV provided the transportation for the assault, while the 151st was responsible for reconnaissance and air strike support.

The air assault was delayed for approximately 45 minutes due to poor weather and a lingering fog. When the helicopters did draw close to the landing zone on the island, the water had risen too high to make a safe insertion of more than one aircraft at a time. Given the inability to mass combat power on the island, LTC McCaffrey decided to scratch the air assault mission completely. The rest of the operation went as planned and without incident. The infantry companies made successful searches of their targets and were able to detain several suspected insurgents.

The next task in preparation for the elections was to identify buildings to be used for polling stations. School buildings were sought for the majority of the sites because they were generally within walled compounds that would be relatively easy to defend. The battalion operations sergeant major, accompanied by the civil affairs team, traveled to all the schools in the Bobcats' AO, overtly passing out supplies and interacting with the headmasters but covertly making assessments as to whether or not the site would be suitable for polling.

Following the school assessments, the civil affairs team identified several bogus polling sites in addition to the two actual sites. During the week prior to the election, soldiers from Charlie Company and engineers made movements and placed obstacles in and around the deception sites, hoping that the insurgents would focus their planning on those locations.

It wasn't until after the brigade imposed a city-wide "no roll" policy, on 27 January, prohibiting the use of non-military vehicles, that the soldiers tipped their hand about the actual polling sites. The engineers proceeded to bulldoze earthen berms around the polling sites, erect wire, picket and "hedgehog" obstacles and place concrete barriers. The polling sites were made virtually impregnable to a vehicle-borne threat and made any individual suicide bomber attempt highly unlikely.

Charlie Company occupied both polling sites until the arrival of the Iraqi 11th Battalion. On January 28th, the 2nd and 4th Companies of the 11th Battalion moved out to the polling sites. Alpha Troop cleared their route. Bravo Company and a Scout Weapons Team provided a surface and aerial escort and Charlie Company relieved them of their

The Global War on Terrorism

previous assignment providing security at the schools in Hammam al Alil. The 3rd IRA Company assumed a traffic control position along Route Tampa and the 1st IRA Company moved to Arij to patrol and protect critical infrastructure in that area.

Throughout the remainder of the day on the 28th and into the 29th, the men from the Iraqi 11th Battalion emplaced obstacles, improved their fighting positions, and developed traffic patterns for the voters on Election Day. Late in the afternoon of the 29th, Bravo Company escorted the Iraqi election officials and the official ballots to each of the polling sites. Meanwhile Charlie Company and Alpha Troop continued to man traffic control points and to patrol actively in the area surrounding the polling sites.

Early in the morning on Election Day, the last American soldiers, the Advisor Support Team imbedded with the IRA, departed the polling sites and withdrew to FOB Rock for the duration of the polling sites' hours of operation. At 0700 on January 30, 2005, the 11th IRA Battalion opened the doors and allowed the Iraqi people of Hammam al Alil and the surrounding villages to democratically select their leaders for the first time in fifty years. Approximately eight hundred locals voted at the Hammam al Alil polling sites and Election Day ended without any major incident. The 11th IRA Battalion and their Bobcat mentors returned to FOB Marez with a deep sense of accomplishment.

Training the Iraqis

Following the election, there was a deliberate shift in focus. The U.S. forces dedicated the bulk of their time to making the Iraqi security forces more successful. This could only be accomplished by increased training but, given the high degree of enemy threat in Mosul, most of this training would be on-the-job; conducted during combat patrols.

Powerful IED attacks soon after the elections reminded the battalion that the enemy was not ready to fade away. On 3 February, SGT Stephen Sherman of C Company was killed by a roadside bomb, while riding in a Stryker vehicle near Hammam al Alil. SGT Sherman, a University of Oregon graduate, was a chemical operations specialist. He was the battalion's fourth combat death in Iraq (25).

In February, the battalion sector was expanded when it was given responsibility for a significant portion of southeast Mosul, as well as the villages along the eastern side of the Tigris River extending to the Za'ab River. The battalion had to make some shifts in company boundaries to accommodate the change. Alpha Troop gained the southernmost neighborhoods of Mosul west of the Tigris while Bravo Company ceded the north and west of Mosul to 1st Battalion, 24th Infantry and picked up the rather tough assignment of the iniquitous neighborhoods of Palestine, Somer and Domis. It would also conduct patrols south along the Tigris River Valley into the villages of Salamiyah and Humera.

Thanks largely to the successful elections, the men of 1st Battalion, 5th Infantry began to see a shift in the local sentiment. The Iraqi civilians began to show increased support for the Coalition forces and their disdain for the fear and destruction perpetrated by the insurgents.

An increased number of citizens began pointing out the homes and safe houses of enemy combatants. Some volunteered to identify the faces of insurgents, risking their lives and the lives of their families. This increase in intelligence created additional targets and actions on those targets. All of the companies made significant headway in their towns and villages rounding up insurgents and sending the message that the enemy needed to fear not only the Americans, but also the Iraqi locals around them who were fed up with their agenda of abuse and terror. The battalion information operations team worked with Iraqis to reinforce the change in public sentiment by assisting with the distribution of a newly minted newspaper, *Mosul Today*.

Route Minneapolis, along the northern border of the Palestine neighborhood, had become quite a problem for the Bobcats, as they

The Global War on Terrorism

had taken sniper fire, RPG's, small arms fire, and IED's from those neighborhoods on the periphery since taking over the area at the beginning of the month. This prompted LTC McCaffrey to direct a battalion level sweep of the entire area on February 25. The operation included Alpha Troop, Bravo Company and 1st Company, 1st Iraqi Intervention Forces Battalion. The tangible results included the discovery of one large weapons cache, one IED and one dead enemy sniper. However, the intangible effect of massing combat power and shutting down the Palestine neighborhood, at will, left a more lasting impression on the minds of the insurgents. Brigade assigned a Naval Special Warfare Team of snipers and a Long Range Surveillance Team to provide further help for counter-sniper operations and with the prevention of IED emplacements.

During February the battalion discovered large weapons caches and many types of IED's. Aggressive patrols, combined with the sharp eyes and instincts of seasoned soldiers, allowed these discoveries to become a regular occurrence.

In March, the men of Company A continued to earn their combat pay in Tal A'far, west of Mosul. Their efforts were not without cost as three members of the company had been shipped stateside to recover from wounds suffered in a large IED explosion.

B Company shifted to southeastern Mosul. Its immediate impact there included killing several insurgents, recovering a significant cache of weapons and munitions and conducting frequent raids to capture suspected terrorists. Charlie Company happily moved from its outpost, FOB Aggies, to FOB Marez. The men had long since earned an opportunity for better living conditions.

As in Afghanistan, each company in the battalion had given itself a nickname. The men of A Company were the Apaches, B Company, the Deathmasters, and C Company was Charlie Rock. Headquarters Company initially honored the older brothers from the Vietnam War by calling themselves the Hobos, stemming from the 1st Battalion, 5th

Infantry's operations in the Ho Bo Woods, north of Saigon.

In the interest of continuity and tradition throughout this history of the 5th Infantry Regiment, the author has chosen to emphasize the usual army alphabet company designations rather than the newer company nicknames or code names. Bravo Company, for instance, is more easily recognized than Deathmasters by readers who served with Baker Company of the 5th in World War II and Korea and Bravo of the 5th in Vietnam. Charlie Company has been around for several wars.

In March, Captain Chris Bachl, the commander of Headquarters Company, submitted a request to rename his unit the "Hawks." The company's scouts, snipers, and mortar men were undertaking the widest range of missions in the battalion. The medics and the clerks were saving lives, keeping the supplies flowing and maintaining a clear operational picture of the battlefield. The hawk seemed to be a better symbol for the company's fast, aggressive tactics.

Captain Bachl moved aggressively to establish relationships with civic leaders in Albu Sayf and Sairamon. Working with the Civil Affairs Team, Headquarters Company developed a model jobs program in Albu Sayf, employing hundreds of out-of-work citizens. The Mukhtar of Albu Sayf managed the program and distributed the wages to the local workers.

In addition, the battalion began efforts to rebuild key infrastructure throughout the area, utilizing local contractors and leaders, infusing much needed money into the local economy and increasing confidence in local governmental institutions. Headquarters Company initiated several projects in Albu Sayf including a new bridge on Route Toyota, a much needed medical clinic, and some heating and air conditioning upgrades. Charlie Company improved the facilities for force protection at the Qabr and Hammam al Alil police stations and the mayor's house. They opened negotiations with the local leadership to build a fire station, hospital and a new community meeting hall with the local leadership.

The Global War on Terrorism

There was a pleasant surprise in March when members of the Iraqi Police began to reappear in Qabr Abd and Hammam al Alil. For the first time since November, policemen were manning old checkpoints in the city of Mosul.

The battalion sought to quickly determine the level of fortitude brought to the fight by the re-emerging policemen. Charlie Company, working with Mayor Kalif of Hammam, was able to develop a strong relationship with both the Hammam and Qabr Abd policemen. Two operations with the police during March netted a number of AIF operatives and helped to turn the sentiment in Qabr Abd from anti-Coalition forces to one of pro-Coalition forces or, at least, neutral.

Early in the deployment the Bobcats learned that operational borders did not necessarily coincide with tribal boundaries. Recognizing that there were close ties between the residents on the east and west sides of the Tigris River Valley and those communities directly to the battalion's south in 2nd Battalion, 8th Field Artillery's battle space, OPERATION ANVIL was executed. ANVIL, at the time of the operation, was the largest one-day operation of the deployment, integrating a field artillery battalion, an infantry battalion, a special forces detachment, and two Iraqi battalions. The Iraqis took the lead as U.S. forces remained in supporting roles.

The 112th Iraqi Army Battalion, a predominantly Kurdish unit from 2/8 FAB's AO, conducted a cordon and search in the town of Salamiyah in the east Tigris Valley. Bravo Company was posted in the Palestine/Somer/Domiz neighborhood to disrupt a mass exodus from the south into Mosul. The 102nd Iraqi Battalion, another unit from the 8th Field Artillery's area, accompanied by Charlie and Headquarters Company, conducted a cordon and search in Hammam al Alil in the west valley, while a company of Albanian infantry conducted dismounted patrols with Headquarters Company in Albu Sayf, to the north of Hammam. It was truly a multi-national operation.

The following week, Task Force Bobcat conducted OPERATION

CUTLASS on the 15th of March. The 103rd Iraqi Army Battalion from Irbil conducted a cordon and search in the village of Shamsyat on the east side of the river in search of a large cell of Anti-Iraqi Forces. Bravo Company, 5th Infantry, isolated the village while the 24th Company, 6th Iraqi Intervention Force patrolled the Palestine neighborhood. The 103rd Iraqi Battalion was able to search the village unimpeded.

To the west, the 11th Iraqi Battalion and Charlie Company conducted dismounted patrols and traffic control points to inhibit the ability of the AIF to move freely from east to west across the river and south to north into Mosul proper. Headquarters Company and the Albanians swept Albu Sayf and their partnership produced two small weapons caches and a carload of insurgents with false ID cards.

As pleasant weather arrived in April, CSM Victor Mercado noticed an improvement, as well, in the political climate in Mosul. In his letter to *Paw Prints*, the battalion's monthly newsletter, he stated that the local citizenry was stepping forward to accept government positions, the Iraqi police were receiving new recruits daily and the Iraqi Army was displaying more confidence and willingness to take charge of their country.

Unfortunately, the nice weather didn't diminish the resolve of the insurgents and the battalion continued to receive attacks. Each day the Bobcats captured insurgents and located caches of weapons and ammunition. Some of the detainees led them to other insurgents and weapons caches. The men of the battalion were becoming very good at recognizing the bad guys and sensing when something was amiss.

In March, the 24th Battalion, 6th Iraqi Intervention Force (Sidewinders) replaced the 1st Battalion, 1st IIF (Vipers) and quickly demonstrated an ability to operate independently. On the morning of the 30th, the newcomers agitated the local insurgency and contact was made. The situation immediately intensified and elements of Bravo Company were sent in for support.

Identifying the origin of contact, the Sidewinders quickly

The Global War on Terrorism

consolidated and conducted a cordon and search. A terrorist tried to engage the Iraqi troops with a grenade but the device detonated and injured the thrower. The unskilled insurgent was detained and the Sidewinders continued their search. They located a large IED in the fronds of a palm tree and then searched a nearby house which turned out to be an IED production facility. They were able to remove a large amount of unexploded ordnance and electronic devices, including cell phones and other potential IED detonators.

As the Iraqi and American soldiers reorganized, an IED was detonated, wounding a member of Bravo Company and seriously injuring and killing innocent bystanders. Though the day ended tragically for innocent civilians, the Sidewinders demonstrated their bravery and fortitude in the face of enemy fire and their timely and effective counter attack, resulting in the elimination of one more AIF safe house.

On April 2, S/SGT Ioasa Tava'e Jr., a squad leader in A Company, was killed by small arms fire as he led his squad down a narrow street in Tal A'far. Junior Tava'e, a third generation soldier, was the fifth soldier from the tiny country of American Samoa to die in Iraq (26).

Brigadier General Khalif, the mayor of Hammam al Alil, continued to work closely with Charlie Company, despite being targeted for assassination by the terrorists. At one point, insurgents attacked his residence and killed several of his bodyguards. Still, his commitment to creating a better home and a peaceful country for his family remained undaunted.

The Task Force PSYOPS began employing a loudspeaker vehicle to broadcast pro-Coalition forces and pro-Iraq messages. The loudspeaker was also used as a means to make important announcements to the locals, such as a change in curfew hours. Distribution of the Mosul Times and production of a semi-weekly radio show at the Iraqi Media Network were also responsibilities of the team. During the battalion's assigned air time, a leader from the 1st/5th and an Iraqi leader from the Bobcat AO would speak to the citizens of Mosul and address any concerns or question that callers would raise.

At 1700 hours on 28 April, two Alpha Company soldiers, SGT Eric Morris of Sparks, Nevada and 1LT Will Edens of Columbia, Missouri, died when an IED exploded near their Stryker just outside of Tal A'far (27). It was the most lethal attack on a Stryker since the vehicles had started arriving in Iraq in December, 2003. The insurgents had found it necessary to significantly increase the size of IED's to take out the heavily armored vehicles.

Two other soldiers, SPC Ricky Rockholt and PFC Robert Murray, from the 2nd Squadron, 3rd Armored Cavalry died in the blast. Lieutenant Edens and Sergeant Morris were taking the recent arrivals from Fort Carson on a patrol to familiarize them with Tal A'far before turning over their responsibilities to them. It was Sergeant Morris' second tour in Iraq (28).

In May the long, hot summer began. Troop A returned to the 14th cavalry enabling Alpha Company, 5th Infantry to rejoin the battalion at FOB Marez. For seven months, the Apaches had provided most of the dismounted forces within Tal A'far, a city that was fractured by tribal disputes and heavy insurgent activity, and had borne the brunt of the brutal fighting within the city.

One week after its return to the battalion, Alpha Company and the 3rd Battalion, 3rd Brigade IIF conducted OPERATION KILLINGTON, a joint effort to clear the Al Wahda neighborhood of Mosul. It provided a good opportunity for the company to become intimately acquainted with its new AO. Traffic control points were established and information pamphlets were distributed. The Iraqi soldiers performed well and strengthened their relationships with the Al Wahda community.

Four days later, the entire battalion conducted a sweep that was code-named OPERATION SNOWSHOE. Bravo Company moved through its sector in the southeastern quarter of Mosul. Alpha Company swept just to the northeast of Bravo. As the two companies advanced, Charlie Company set up a screen on the west side of the Tigris in order to interdict any AIF that were flushed out of their hiding places by Companies A and B. A platoon from 2/8th Field Artillery screened to the south of the Za'ab River.

Bravo Company seemed to be getting a handle on the very nasty southeastern quarter of Mosul to the point that civil affairs projects like soccer fields and a playground became possible. Charlie Company would periodically check in at their previous home, FOB Aggies, when they were out on a mission. They provided security for the construction of a new Iraqi Army facility and police station. The men were hoping that the summer would fly by and were beginning to count the days until early October when they would redeploy to Fort Lewis.

Following its return to Mosul in early May, Company A had made a huge impact on the eastern portion of the city. In an area that was once a site of daily attacks, the company's constant pressure had neutralized much of the threat there and had had a great impact on the local citizenry. Time and again, as LTC McCaffrey talked to the people, he was told that his soldiers were wanted in their neighborhoods to provide security. On Alpha Company's eastern flank, Bravo Company's aggressive patrolling, interaction with the locals and ruthless pursuit of the enemy had brought relative calm to the Palestine area of Mosul.

To fill the gap left by the departure of Alpha Troop in the southwest of the city, Charlie Company expanded its area of responsibility to the north. The company was now spread from the southern hamlet of Hammam al Alil to just north of the Baghdad Traffic Circle. Extending some twenty kilometers for north to south and twelve kilometers west to east, the company executed a wide range of operations, thanks to the Stryker vehicles exceptional mobility. The expanded area of responsibility became even more workable when Charlie Company regained its 2nd Platoon. That platoon had been attached to Alpha Troop to augment its limited dismounted force.

Two Centuries of Valor

During May the Bobcats and the Qabr Abd police located ten weapons caches. The haul included sizeable numbers of 60mm and 82mm mortar rounds, RPG rounds, hundreds of sticks of TNT and, most importantly, 32 anti-tank mines and 2 tons of artillery propellant. The Bobcats also located and detonated nine IED's. Several soldiers from the battalion testified at the Criminal Court of Iraq in Baghdad to assist in the indictment of insurgents detained earlier in the year.

Mosul is frequently called Um Al-Rabi'ain (The City of Two Springs) because autumn and spring are very much alike but, by the middle of June, the daytime highs were reaching 110° and more. More than one soldier swore that he would never again complain about the drizzly weather in the Pacific Northwest.

On 14 June, U.S. Special Forces dealt a staggering blow to Al Qaeda in Iraq by capturing Shakara, the Emir of Mosul, a powerful Al Qaeda leader. As the Al Qaeda command worked to reconsolidate and reorganize, hostile contact picked up in the battalion's area of operations.

On 19 June there was a long-anticipated shift in the relationship between the Coalition forces and the Iraqi Army. Henceforth, Military Transition Teams, similar to the Korean Military Advisory Group of a half century earlier, would teach and coach the Iraqis. Battalion and brigade staffs of the primary war fighting units were relieved of that responsibility.

The security in Mosul was further improved in June by the return of the 2nd Squadron, 14th Cavalry "Rattlesnakes" to the Lancer Brigade Combat Team. The Rattlesnakes were assigned the task of keeping an eye on the insurgent "rat lines" running in and out of the city. All land east of Route Minneapolis, in the Bravo Company AO, was relinquished to the Rattlesnakes allowing B Company to focus its combat power inside the greater Palestine area.

The Global War on Terrorism

Regards to Broadway

Over the course of the year, Bobcats had found thirty-four IED's, either detonated or prior to detonation, on Broadway, the main street running east and west. Broadway was within Bravo Company's AO and they were determined to neutralize the threat.

On the evening of 27 June, an Air Force EC-130, electronic warfare aircraft, flew over Broadway to study traffic patterns. Immediately following the fly-over, Bravo Company snipers moved into pre-determined over-watch positions. They observed Broadway on the nights of the 27th and 28th in preparation for a physical search of the route by sappers from the 73rd Engineer Company. When those engineers had completed their work, the heavy engineers of the 94th Battalion, brought in their equipment and reduced the berms of dirt and debris lining both sides of Broadway. The berms were a popular hiding site for the IED emplacers (29).

On the morning of June 29, Department of Defense civilians flew over Broadway in a UH-60 Blackhawk and used a high resolution imagery device to take an "after shot" of the route. Over the course of the next three nights, high elevation imagery shots were taken to identify any decrease in traffic patterns during suspected IED emplacement time periods.

In the weeks that followed, a zero incidence of IED detonation and discovery of unexploded IED's attested to the success of the operation. There was one small IED explosion in July that inflicted little damage but, for the remainder of the battalion's deployment, Broadway was IED Free.

August was a milestone for the 1st Battalion, 5th Infantry. It was the last full month of combat operations in its support of Operation Iraqi Freedom. The advance party from the 172nd Stryker Brigade Combat Team, the "Arctic Wolves", had arrived and the advance party of the Lancer Brigade had departed for Fort Lewis. With forty days of combat operations left to execute, the Bobcats needed to establish the conditions for the forthcoming referendum vote on the new Iraqi constitution and integrate their replacements, the 4th Battalion, 23rd Infantry "Tomahawks."

The Bobcats and the 3rd Battalion, 12th Infantry created quite a stir back home, in mid-August, when they raided a warehouse in Mosul that was apparently being used as a chemical weapons laboratory. The warehouse contained 1500 gallons of chemicals, many of them dangerous, that were believed to be destined for attacks on Coalition and Iraqi forces and civilians. U.S. military photos revealed a bare concrete-walled room filled with stacks of plastic containers, coiled tubing, hoses and a large metal contraption that looked like a still. The lab was new, dating from some time after the U.S. invasion of Iraq in 2003. Alpha Company spent a good deal of the month securing the building as chemical experts from Baghdad and the United States studied the stockpile and equipment (30).

In early August, the Iraqi agency in charge of elections began its efforts to register the citizens of Ninevah Province. Joint organizational meetings were held with the district election officials and battalion officers from the Lancer Brigade. The site locations were identified within the battalion's area in the communities of Al Karama, Al Wahda, Palestine, Arij, and Hammam al Alil. By the middle of the month, the sites were open and registering voters.

A strong military presence was crucial to grease the skids for October's election. Lancer Brigade crafted OPERATION FINAL FURY to focus brigade assets on some predetermined hot spots. During the four day surge, there were multiple recon missions resulting in the detainment of many persons of interest. Nine quick raids led to the seizure of seventeen suspects and a stash of weapons and equipment.

Redeployment

In his final contribution to the battalion newsletter, *Paw Prints*, in September, 2005, LTC McCaffrey described the forthcoming

The Global War on Terrorism

redeployment to Fort Lewis:

> "The battalion is preparing to complete its mission within weeks. Our replacement unit, the 4th Battalion, 23rd Infantry Regiment from Alaska has begun to arrive and we're well into our out-load tasks of packing containers, preparing equipment, and attending pre-redeployment briefings. By the time this edition reaches you, I expect us to be very close to transferring authority to the Tomahawk Battalion and getting ready for flights home.
>
> "The battalion will return in at least two large groups. The bulk of the unit (approximately 75%) will redeploy directly from FOB Marez, stop briefly in Kuwait (1-2 days) and then fly to McChord Air Force Base near Fort Lewis. The other 25% of the battalion will spend about a week in Kuwait preparing vehicles for ship movement to the U.S. Those soldiers will return approximately one week following the first group. Commanders and first sergeants are creating redeployment manifests now and your soldier should know whether he will return directly from FOB Marez to Fort Lewis or if he will stay the extra week in Kuwait assisting with the ship loading process. The Rear Detachment Commander will notify the Family Readiness Group."

As the vans were being packed and vehicles uploaded onto flatbeds for the drive south, the Bobcats still had a lethal fight on their hands. During the first week of September, the men of Recon Platoon were conducting a routine raid on a suspected AIF safe house, when their suspicions were verified. The platoon received a barrage of small arms fire. Sergeant Nick Malich, the sniper section leader, received a severe shoulder wound. A soldier from 4th Battalion, 23rd Infantry, who went along to get the lay of the land, acted quickly in the face of the oncoming fire, and with the help of Headquarters Company snipers, shielded Sergeant Malich with a burst of return fire and rushed him to safety. S/SGT Malich was evacuated to the Combat Surgical Hospital and then onward to Germany and the United States. The incident was a sobering reminder that the job was not yet complete.

By the evening of September 11, the Bobcats had yielded control of their entire area of operations to the Tomahawks. Three days later, as the two battalions gathered in the hot afternoon sun behind the command post, the colors of the 1/5th were cased and the colors of the 4/23rd were unfurled.

There would be no more combat for the battalion. Now the focus would be on logistics. Platoons from Alpha and Bravo Companies began escort duties for convoys heading south. The Kuwait out-load crew boarded C-130's on the 15th and 16th of September and flew to the western desert of Kuwait to prepare for the arrival of the main body.

The Bobcats now encountered the longest week of their deployment as they tried to fill the hours until flights became available for the first leg home. They put on skits, played football, watched movies and engaged in hours of conversation in the Marez chow hall. Finally, on 19 September, the flights began arriving.

From the 20th through the 22nd, the battalion was air-lifted to Kuwait where the weather was hot and the sun unrelenting. For the next five days they lounged in the USO tent, drinking iced coffee and avoiding the sub-par chow hall as much as possible.

On 23 September, they boarded wide-body aircraft at the Kuwait City International Airport for a 72-hour journey that took them to Eastern Europe, Ireland, Maine and finally McChord AFB, Washington. The Bobcats arrived home, in the shadow of Mt. Rainier, to 50° temperatures and blue skies.

After deplaning, busing to Fort Lewis and signing for barracks rooms, the Bobcats had one more stop to make. At Soldiers' Field House, just down the road from the barracks, hundreds of screaming family members and friends anxiously stood by to greet their men. After a short welcome home speech, the men were released to their families, issued a forty-eight hour pass and placed on a half-day

The Global War on Terrorism

work schedule for the coming month. Their real leave would come in December.

The Battalion Welcome Home Ball was held on 21 October and the brigade held a redeployment ceremony on the 27th. On October 31, LTC Dan Barnett relieved LTC Todd McCaffrey as battalion commander. The 1st Brigade, 25th Infantry Division, including 1st Battalion, 5th Infantry received the Valorous Unit Award for its fight to secure Mosul during January and February, 2005.

On June 1, 2006, on a drizzly day at Gray Army Airfield, Fort Lewis, Washington, the men of 1st Battalion, 5th Infantry stood parade as the 1st Brigade, 25th Infantry Division was deactivated and re-flagged as the 2nd Cavalry Regiment, 4th Brigade, 2nd Infantry Division. The 1st Battalion, 5th Infantry became the 1st Squadron, 2nd Cavalry. At the time of the ceremony, the advance party from the battalion, now cavalry squadron, had already arrived in Velseck, Germany (31).

Reactivation at Fort Wainwright

During 2006, the U.S. Army began transitioning from a division-centered force to a group of more mobile, essentially independent, brigade combat teams. These units, each composed of about 3700 soldiers, can, within 96 hours, deploy to major war theaters or to global hot spots or areas in need of humanitarian assistance. Three-quarters of each brigade is composed of three mechanized infantry battalions and a reconnaissance, intelligence, surveillance and target acquisition squadron (RSTA). The intelligence capability of these units, from their military intelligence company down to the rifle company level is more robust than any in history. Despite the inherent chaos of combat these brigade combat teams should not experience having to find a fight by bumping into it.

The 172nd Stryker Brigade, that had relieved the 1st Brigade, 25th Division in Mosul, Iraq in September, 2005 was due to return to Fort Wainwright near Fairbanks, Alaska in August 2006. However, on

July 27, 2006, the 172nd's tour in Iraq was extended for four months to help restore order in Baghdad. When it finally exited Iraq on 3 December 2006, the brigade had served the longest combat tour of any unit since Vietnam. During its deployment the brigade sustained 353 casualties, including 21 Soldiers killed in action. The 172nd Stryker Brigade received a Valorous Unit Award for its role in Operation Iraqi Freedom.

On December 14, 2006, 1st Battalion, 17th Infantry, 172nd Stryker Brigade became the 1st Battalion, 5th Infantry, 1st Stryker Brigade, 25th Infantry Division. It is brigaded with the 3rd Battalion, 21st Infantry; 1st Battalion, 24th Infantry; and 2nd Squadron, 14th Cavalry. The brigade's supporting units include Company D (Anti-tank), 52nd Infantry; 2nd Battalion, 8th Artillery, 73rd Engineer Company, 184th Military Intelligence Company and the 176th Signal Company. Lieutenant Colonel Shawn Reed assumed command of the battalion. CSM Jim Herbert became the battalion's "first soldier."

The Infantry Company

Since Korea, when rifle companies acquired recoilless rifles and horse-traded for additional .50 caliber machine guns, company commanders have striven to increase the fire power under their immediate control. Over a half century, while company manpower has been trimmed by 10%, the lethal capability of the unit has sky-rocketed (no pun intended.)

Each rifle company in the 1st Battalion, 5th Infantry has a ten man mortar section. The section travels in two Stryker mortar carriers equipped with a mounted 120mm mortar and dismountable 81mm and 60mm tubes. According to LTC Reed, the weapons are incredibly responsive and accurate and, in the case of the large mortars, place serious indirect fire at the fingertips of the company commander, a capability that used to be relegated to battalion commanders and above (32).

The Global War on Terrorism

The twelve men in the company's Anti-tank Platoon move in a Stryker variant armed with a 105mm main gun and a 7.62mm medium machine gun. The 105 is self-loading, so no more than three soldiers are required to operate the vehicle; a driver, gunner and vehicle commander.

Each rifle platoon is made up of three nine-man rifle squads and a seven-man weapons squad. The rifle squad employs a mix of weapons, including five M4 carbines (5.56mm), two grenade launchers, and two M249 (5.56mm) light machine guns. Each company's three-man sniper team is armed with a semi-automatic M107 50-caliber long range sniper rifle, one older M24 (7.62mm) sniper rifle and an M203 grenade launcher. The weapons squad employs five 37mm automatic guns (M4) and two 7.62mm (M240) machine guns.

The Stryker's chassis design allows a wide range of variants and each company in the battalion employs at least five configurations of the vehicle. The company commander and executive officer ride in Infantry Carrier Vehicles (ICV) armed with .50 caliber machine guns. Company headquarters security is provided by the four man crew in a Fire Support Vehicle (FSV). The two company medics travel in an unarmed Medical Evacuation Vehicle (MEV) and the riflemen move about in Infantry Carrier Vehicles, some armed with machine guns and others with 40mm grenade launchers.

In addition to the company commander, executive officer and first sergeant, each company has an armorer and sergeants in charge of supply, communications, and nuclear, biological, chemical warfare. The companies are supported, at the battalion level, by a mortar platoon, a recon platoon, a medical platoon and a sniper section. The mobile battalion operations center is entirely digital and utilizes FM communications equipment.

Preparing for Another Deployment

One of the first tasks faced by the reactivated 1st Battalion, 5th Infantry involved the overhaul and retrofit of 289 Stryker vehicles that had experienced sixteen months of combat in Iraq. Once completed, there was a necessity to train the new soldiers and retrain the veterans to use the improved vehicles.

In June of 2007, Company A flew to Australia to train with Australian armored forces at the Shoalwater Bay Military Training Area. The company, which has retained its Iraq War nickname "Apache", included about fifty percent new recruits. This was its first training exercise and gave the soldiers some deployment experience, an opportunity to see the full capabilities of the Stryker vehicle and a chance to get away from Alaska's snowy terrain and train in a jungle and desert environment. The Bobcats and Aussies launched joint maneuvers. They were opposed by U.S. Marines posing as civilians and insurgents.

During late July soldiers from throughout the brigade vied for their Expert Infantryman Badges by taking a land navigation course and demonstrating their prowess on 38 individual tasks covered in the EIB testing. To even qualify for testing, the soldier had to hit 36 out of 40 targets with his M-4 carbine.

One hundred members of 1st Battalion went to the Philippines in February to participate in Balikatan 2008. The joint exercise focused on humanitarian projects on Luzon, Central and Western Mindanao, the Sulu Archipelago and Palawan (33). Approximately 14,000 local residents received medical and dental care. Veterinary services were provided to more than six hundred animals. U.S. and Filipino engineers rebuilt classrooms at Maragondon National High School that had been destroyed by fire a year before. Additional community infrastructure projects were completed in more than ten local communities.

Early publicity for Balikatan had elicited demonstrations by the Moro Islamic Liberation Front who complained that the exercises might result in human rights violations. American Ambassador Kristie Kenney responded that there would be no military exercises. The

The Global War on Terrorism

operation's main focus would be on humanitarian assistance.

Ambassador Kenney's information was essentially correct, but there was some time devoted to familiarizing the Filipino troops with several new weapons, a course in marksmanship with the M-16 rifle and M-4 carbine and some training in squad-level patrolling. At Fort Ramon Magsaysay, soldiers from the 5th Infantry demonstrated their unit's heavier fire arms including the M-107 and M-24 sniper rifles and the AT-4 anti-armor rocket launcher. U.S. soldiers continued to be impressed with the discipline, eagerness to learn and commitment of the Filipino soldier. This mutual respect between the two armies is probably the most important product of the Balikatan program.

The Baqubah Bobcats

In May of 2008, the Department of the Army confirmed that seven brigade combat teams would be rotating to Iraq in the fall of the year in support of Operation Iraqi Freedom. These units included the 1st Stryker Brigade, 25th Infantry Division from Fort Wainwright, Alaska (34).

The 1st Battalion, 5th Infantry's return journey to the Middle East began with a deployment ceremony at Fort Wainwright on 11 September 2008. This time the battalion would be replacing a cavalry squadron so it would not be inheriting the vehicles of the unit being relieved. The battalion's Strykers were trucked to Anchorage and shipped to San Diego. They were off-loaded briefly at San Diego so that the troops could use them for a short period of training at the National Training Center at Ft. Irwin (35).

As in the previous deployment, the Bobcats were first sent to Kuwait for a period of target practice and adjustment to the heat and the dust. From there they made the 360-mile trip from Kuwait to Diyala Province, Iraq by helicopter, truck and cargo plane. By October 15, the 1st Stryker Brigade had completely relieved a very grateful 2nd Cavalry Regiment. The latter had been in Baghdad for ten months and Diyala for another five.

Two Centuries of Valor

Diyala Province is a farming area about the size of Maryland, extending to the Iranian border. It is renown for its production of oranges and dates but is facing the worst drought in fifty years. Prior to the brigade's arrival, there were two recent suicide bombings targeting Iraqi soldiers. These attacks resulted in fifty deaths and a like number of injuries.

Brigade Headquarters and five of the seven infantry battalions, including 1st Battalion, 5th Infantry, were located at Forward Operating Base Warhorse near the provincial capital of Baqubah, a city of 500,000 Arabs, Turkomen and Kurds. Third Battalion, 21st Infantry and 5th Squadron, 1st Cavalry were located at two other forward operating bases. From these strongholds, companies and batteries were placed at combat outposts all over Diyala Province. From there they supported some five thousand partners in the Iraqi Army and police force, assisted with the installation of irrigation systems and other government projects and provided security for the 2009 elections.

First Battalion, 5th Infantry was tasked with clearing and stabilizing the volatile provincial capital. The battalion discovered many caches of arms and munitions, eliminated a significant number of insurgents, and accomplished its objectives during the first forty-five days of the operation (36).

During the first four months of the battalion's deployment, platoon-sized patrols were ambushed on several occasions by Al Qaeda insurgents. During these fire fights most of the insurgents were able to die for their cause.

On October 16, 2008, SPC Heath Pickard of Charlie Company became the first Bobcat to die during the 5th Infantry's second deployment in Iraq. Pickard and ten of his comrades were wounded during a rocket attack on FOB Warhorse. The Palestine, Texas native succumbed to his wounds in the hospital at Balad Air Base. He left a wife and four-month-old son (37).

Eight days later, Heath Pickard's best friend, PFC Cody Eggleston, who was wounded in the same attack, died at Bethesda Naval Medical Center in Maryland. The young Oregonian, who turned twenty-one on his way to Iraq, left a young wife and six-year-old stepdaughter. Pickard and Eggleston were posthumously awarded the Bronze Star, Purple Heart, Good Conduct Medal, and Combat Infantryman's Badge for their service in Iraq (38).

Following four months in Diyala Province, the Company A, "Daggers," were shifted north to the 1st Battalion/5th Infantry's former area of operations, the city of Mosul, where some of the heaviest action was taking place. Attached to the 3rd Squadron, 8th Cavalry, the Daggers were immediately involved in clearing operations, patrols and raids. Veterans of the previous deployment in Mosul found that their local partners, the National Police and other Iraqi security forces had improved significantly (39).

As the rest of the young Bobcats soldiered on in Diyala, the 2nd Battalion, 5th Infantry was reactivated at Fort Bliss, Texas. On August 16, 2009, the 2nd Battalion became part of the 3rd Infantry Brigade Combat Team, 1st Armored Division. The newest pack of Bobcats is commanded by LTC Howard C. Kirk, assisted by Command Sergeant Major Stanley Varner. The battalion's long range training plan projects that it will be combat ready by August 16, 2010 (40). The mountainous terrain in New Mexico and West Texas, complete with winter snow, is providing a training venue similar to Afghanistan for the new battalion.

In early September, the 1st Stryker Brigade, 25th Infantry Division relinquished Diyala Province to the 3rd Stryker Brigade, 2nd Infantry Division and a vastly improved Iraqi Army. The 1st Brigade returned home to Fort Wainwright to prepare for its next deployment.

Recent events in the life of the 5th U.S. Infantry have filled the author's heart with conflicting feelings of sadness and pride. The unit, blessed with a rich history, continues to accomplish its missions with distinction as it continues to pay the price in young lives. A third century of valor has begun.

Appendix A

COLONELS OF THE 5TH INFANTRY

COL Alexander Parker ....May 3, 1808–December 31, 1809
COL John Whiting .... December 31, 1809–September 3, 1810
COL Josiah Constant .... September 3, 1810–April 4, 1812
COL W. D. Beall ....April 24, 1812–August 15, 1812
COL Daniel Bissell ....August 15, 1812–March 9, 1814
COL John Bowyer .... March 13, 1814–May 17, 1815
COL James Miller... May 17, 1815–June 1, 1819
COL Josiah Snelling ....June 1, 1819–August 20, 1828
  (LTC Henry Leavenworth in command, 1819-1821)
COL William Lawrence ....August 20, 1828–July 15, 1831
COL George M. Brooke..................................July 15, 1831–August 1, 1844
LTC James McIntosh .... August 2, 1844–May 1846
                August 2, 1846–August 20, 1846
MAJ Martin Scott ....May 1846–August 1, 1846
              August 20, 1846–September 7, 1846
MAJ Dixon S. Miles .... September 7, 1846–March 1848
COL William G. Belknap...................................March 1848–March 8, 1851
COL Gustavus Loomis....................................... March 9, 1851–June 1, 1863
COL John F. Reynolds ....June 1, 1863–July 1, 1863
LTC T. L. Alexander .... July 1, 1863–October 16, 1863
BVT LTC Bankhead ....Fort Wallace, 1868
COL Daniel Butterfield...........................October 16, 1863–March 12, 1869
  (No record of Butterfield having reported to the regiment)
COL Nelson A. Miles........................... March 13, 1869–December 15, 1880
COL Pickney Lugenbeel .... December 15, 1880–February 6, 1882
                (Lugenbeel never reported.
    LTC Joseph N.G. Whistler commanded regiment.)
COL Daniel Huston ....February 6, 1882
  (Huston never reported. LTC Whistler continued as interim Cdr.)
COL J. D. Wilkins...June 22, 1882–August 2, 1886
COL George Gibson ....August 2, 1886–August 5, 1888
COL Nathan W. Osborne ....August 5, 1888–January 30, 1895

COLONELS OF THE 5TH INFANTRY

COL William L. Kellogg .... January 30, 1895–April 17, 1897
COL H. C. Cook .... April 17, 1897–June 30, 1898
COL Richard Comba .... June 30, 1898–March 1901
MAJ William C. H. Bowen .... March 1901–July 10, 1901
COL C. L. Davis .... July 11, 1901–February 10, 1903
LTC George P. Borden (Cdr in Philippines) ... February 11, 1903–June 1903
COL H. H. Adams (Cdr in USA) .... Feb 10, 1903–April 11, 1905
COL Calvin P. Cowles .... April 11, 1905–June 26, 1913
COL Charles G. Morton .... June 26, 1913–September 29, 1916
COL Evan M. Johnson .... September 29, 1916–May 5, 1918
COL B. S. Morse .... May 5, 1918–July 16, 1918
COL Harold L. Jackson .... July 16, 1918–April 22, 1919
July 25, 1919–August 29, 1919
LTC Robert E. Spence .... April 22, 1919–April 27, 1919
June 14, 1919–June 29, 1919; August 29, 1919–September 7, 1919
COL William F. Clemry .... April 27, 1919–June 14, 1919
COL James A. Lynch .... June 29, 1919–July 25, 1919
COL Edgar A. Fry .... September 7, 1919–May 29, 1920
September 15, 1923–September 6, 1925
LTC Allen J. Greer .... May 29, 1920–December 12, 1921
COL Harry E. Knight .... December 12, 1921–Sept 15, 1923
COL John W. Wright............................ September 7, 1925–August 23, 1929
COL Lucius C. Bennett .... August 24, 1929–July 31, 1932
COL Joseph W. Beacham, Jr. .... August 1, 1932–August 1, 1934
COL Frederick F. Black .... August 2, 1934–July 4, 1936
COL Wilson B. Burtt .... July 5, 1936–January 19, 1938
LTC Robert J. Halpin .... January 20, 1938–May 17, 1938
COL Charles A. Hunt .... May 18, 1938–Dec 6, 1939
COL Louis P. Ford .... December 7, 1919–May 28, 1941
COL B. F. Delamater, Jr. .... May 29, 1941–unknown
COL John V. Ayott .... Unknown–March 10, 1943
COL William H. Bigelow .... March 11, 1943–June 24, 1944
COL Sidney C. Wooten .... June 25, 1944–February 28, 1946
COL Onslan S. Rolfe .... March 1, 1946–November 14, 1946
(Regiment inactive from November 15, 1946 to January 1, 1949)
COL James R. Simpson .... January 2, 1949–January 1, 1950
COL Godwin Ordway, Jr. .... January 2, 1950–August 15, 1950

Two Centuries of Valor

COL John L. Throckmorton, Jr. ....Aug 16, 1950–April 20, 1951
COL Arthur H. Wilson, Jr. .... April 21, 1951–Sept 15, 1951
COL Alexander D. Surles, Jr........................... Sept 16, 1951–April 25, 1952
COL Lee L. Alfred ....April 26, 1952–January 9, 1953
COL Harvey H. Fischer ....January 10, 1953–April 29, 1953
COL Lester L. Wheeler...............................April 30, 1953–October 31, 1953
COL Ben Sternberg......................................November 1, 1953–May 2, 1954
COL E. H. Strickland ....May 3, 1954–August 30, 1956
COL Robert J. Rosa ....September 1, 1956–June 30, 1957
LTC John W. Jackson ....July 1, 1957–July 31, 1957
COL W. R. Peers ....August 1, 1957–January 25, 1959
COL Graham E. Schmidt ....January 26, 1959–April 14, 1960
COL Alpo K. Marttinen ....April 15, 1960–January 2, 1961
LTC Joseph A. DeSantis ....January 2, 1961–January 11, 1961
COL Russell R. Reed ....January 11, 1961–January 30, 1963
COL Keneth Johnson, 1/5,.................................February 1, 1963–unknown
LTC Thomas Tarpley, 1/5, ... unknown–August 14, 1965
LTC Thomas U. Greer, 1/5,........................... August 14, 1965–August 1966
LTC Victor Diaz, 1/5, ...August 1966-January 1967
LTC Richard C. Rogers,.. January 1967–May 1967
LTC Chandler Goodnow, 1/5, ...May 1967–October 1967
LTC Fremont B. Hodson, 1/5, ...October 1967–December 1967
MAJ Ralph K. Hook, 1/5, ...December 1967–January 1968
LTC Henry B. Murphy, 1/5,....................................... January–February 1968
LTC Thomas C. Lodge, 1/5, ... February–June 1968
LTC Andrew H. Anderson, 1/5, ...June–October 1968
LTC William E. Klein, 1/5, ...October 1968–June 1969
LTC Robert A. Kurek, 1/5, ...June–October 1969
LTC Frederick C. Delisle, 1/5, ...October 1969–January 1970
_____, 2/5, ...Dec 6, 1969–Dec 15, 1970
LTC Ted G. Westerman, 1/5, ...January–July 1970
LTC Oliver B. Combs, 1/5, ... July–November 1970
LTC Patrick J. Moore, 1/5, ...Nov 1971–April 1971
_____, 1/5, ... April 1971–June 1972
LTC Michael L. Ferguson, 1/5, ...1972–1975
LTC Phillip G. Gibbs, 1/5, ...1975–June 28, 1977
LTC Virgil Fernandez, 3/5, ... 1977- mid -1978

COLONELS OF THE 5TH INFANTRY

LTC Craig H. Boice, 1/5, ...June 29, 1977–Dec 15, 1978
LTC Edward M. McDonald, 1/5, ...December 15, 1978–1980
LTC William W. Hartzog, 3/5, ...mid-1978–April 1979
MAJ James Woods, 3/5, ...April 1979–January 1980
LTC James Emory Mace, 3/5, ...Jan 1980–November 1981
__(Panama)_____, 3/5, ...November 1981 - 1987
LTC Charles Rothlisberger, 1/5, ... 1980–August 1982
LTC Eugene Bernhardt, 1/5, ...August 1982–August 17, 1984
LTC George F. Close, 1/5, ...August 17, 1984–January 1986

(1st Battalion inactive January 1986–April 1987)

(3rd Battalion inactivated in Panama, 1987)

LTC Richard Holmes, 1/5,................................... April 1987–1988
LTC David W. Hunt, 1/5, ... 1988-June 1990
LTC John M. Mitchell, 1/5, ...June 1990–July 1991
LTC George Higgins, 1/5, ...July 1991-July 1992
LTC Richard Rowe, 1/5, ...July 1992-July 1994
LTC Phillip Pope, 1/5, ...July 1994–August 1995
LTC Elliot Rosner, 1/5, ...Ft. Lewis, Aug 1995-1996
LTC John Campbell, 2/5, ... Schofield, August 1995 - ?
LTC James E. Harris III, 1/5, ...1996-1998
LTC Michael Rounds, 1/5, ...1998–2000
LTC Phillips, 2/5, ...1998–May 2000
LTC Thomas Barth, 2/5, ...June 2000–July 1, 2002
LTC Barry Tyree, 1/5 ....2000–May 2002
LTC Terry L. Sellers, 2/5, ...July 1, 2002–June 26, 2005
LTC Malcolm Frost, 2/5, ...June 26, 2005–November 16, 2005

(2nd Battalion de-activated November 16, 2005)

LTC Todd McCaffrey, 1/5, ...May 2002–October 31, 2005
LTC Dan Barnett, 1/5, ...October 31, 2005–June 1, 2006

(1st Battalion deactivated June 1, 2006)

(1st Battalion reactivated December 14, 2006)

LTC Shawn Reed, 1/5, ...Dec 14, 2006–Dec 16, 2009

(2nd Battalion reactivated July 2, 2009)

LTC H. Clint Kirk, 2/5, ...July 2, 2009–April 4, 2011
LTC Brian A. Payne, 1/5, ...December 16, 2009 - July 11, 2012

Appendix B

5th Infantry Medal of Honor Recipients

BAIRD, 1st LT George W., Regimental Adjutant, Bear Paw Mountain, 30 September 1877. Issued 27 November 1894. "Most distinguished gallantry in action with the Nez Perce Indians." Born: Connecticut.

BAKER, John, Musician, Company D, Cedar Creek, MT, October 1876 to January 1877. Issued 27 April 1877. "Gallantry in engagements." Born: Germany.

BALDWIN, 1st LT Frank D. (1st Award) Peach Tree Creek, GA, 20 Jul 1864, as CPT, Co D, 19th Michigan Infantry, "Led his company in a counter charge, under a galling fire, ahead of his own men, and singly entered the enemy's lines, capturing and bringing back two Confederate officers, fully armed, besides a guidon of a Georgia regiment.

(2nd Award) "As 1st LT, 5th U.S. infantry, rescued with two companies, two white girls by a voluntary attack upon Indians whose superior numbers and strong position would have warranted delay for reinforcements, but which delay would have permitted the Indians to escape and kill their captives."

BURKE, PVT Richard, Company G, Cedar Creek campaign. Issued 27 April 1877. "Gallantry in engagements." Born: Ireland.

BUTLER, CPT Edmond, Wolf Mountain, MT, 8 January 1877. Issued 27 Nov 1894. "Most distinguished gallantry in action with hostile Indians." Born: Ireland.

BYRNE, SGT Denis, Company G, Cedar Creek campaign. Issued 27 Nov 1894. "Gallantry in engagements." Born: Ireland.

CABLE, PVT Joseph A., Cedar Creek campaign. Issued 27 April 1877. "Gallantry in action." Born: Missouri.

CALVERT, PVT James S., Company G, Cedar Creek Campaign. Issued 27 April 1877. "Gallantry in action." Born: Ohio.

5ᵀᴴ Infantry Medal of Honor Recipients

CARTER, 1ˢᵗ LT Mason, Bear Paw Mountain, MT. 30 Sep 1877. Issued 27 November 1894. "Led a charge under galling fire, in which he inflicted great loss upon the enemy." Born: Georgia.

CASEY, CPT James, Wolf Mountain, MT, 8 January 1877. Issued 27 November 1894. "Led his command in a successful charge against superior numbers of the enemy strongly posted." Born: Pennsylvania.

COONROD, SGT Aquilla, Company D, Cedar Creek campaign. Issued 27 April 1877. "Gallantry in action." Born: Ohio

COPAS, SP4 Ardie R. Upgrade of Vietnam War DSC in 2014.

DE ARMOND, SGT William, Company I, Upper Wichita River, TX, 9-11 Sep 1874. Issued posthumously 12 April 1875. "Gallantry in action." Born: Pennsylvania.

DOANE, 1ˢᵗ LT Stephen H., Company B, Hau Nghia Province, Republic of Vietnam, 25 March 1969. "Extraordinary courage and selflessness as he destroyed enemy bunkers and protected the men of his platoon" Issued posthumously. Born: New York.

DODD, 1ˢᵗ LT Carl H, Company E, Subuk, Korea, 30-31 January 1951. Issued 4 June 1951. "Led his platoon forward under hostile fire, inspiring them with his courage, eliminated all enemy defenders of Hill 256" Born: Kentucky.

DONELLY, PVT John S., Company G, Cedar Creek campaign. Issued 27 April 1877. "Gallantry in action." Born: Ireland.

FERNANDEZ, SP4 Daniel, Cu Chi, Vietnam, 18 February 1966, issued 26 April 1967. "For conspicuous gallantry beyond the call of duty." Born: New Mexico.

FREEMAN, LTC Henry B, "Gallantry in Action" at Battle of Stones River, 31 Dec 1862. Served with 5ᵗʰ Infantry from 1895-1898.

FREEMEYER, PVT Christopher, Company D, Cedar Creek campaign. Issued 27 April 1877. "Gallantry in action." Born: Germany.

GREER, 2LT Allen J., 4ᵗʰ Infantry, Majada, Laguna Province, Philippines, 2

July 1901. Issued 10 March 1902. "Charged alone an insurgent outpost with his pistol, killing one, wounding two, and capturing three insurgents with their rifles and equipment." (LTC Allen Greer went on to command the 5th Infantry from 29 May 1920 until 12 December 1921.) Born: Tennessee.

HADOO, CPL John, Company B, (1) Cedar Creek campaign. Issued 27 April 1877. "Gallantry in action." Born: Massachusetts.

HANDRICH, SFC Melvin O., Company C. Sobuk-San Mountains, Republic of Korea, 25-26 August 1950. Issued posthumously on 2 August 1951. "Led his company in repelling 150 attacking North Koreans, accounting for 70 of the dead himself." Born: Wisconsin.

HAY, SGT Fred S., Company I, Upper Wichita River, TX, 9 Sep 1874. Issued 23 April 1975. "Gallantry in action." Born: Scotland.

HOGAN, 1ST SGT Henry, Company G. (1st Award) Cedar Creek campaign, "gallantry in action" Issued 26 June 1894 (2nd Award) Bear Paw Mountain, 30 Sept 1877 "rescuing LT Henry Romeyn." Born: Ireland.

HOLLAND, CPL David, Company A. Cedar Creek campaign, Issued 27 April 1877 for "gallantry in action" Born: Michigan.

HUNT, PVT Fred O., Company A, Cedar Creek campaign, Issued 27 April 1877 for "gallantry in actions." Born: Louisiana.

JAMES, CPL John, Upper Wichita River, TX, 9-11 September 1874. Issued 23 April 1875 for "gallantry in action." Born: England.

JOHNSTON, CPL Edward, Company C, Cedar Creek campaign. Issued 27 April 1877 for "gallantry in action." Born: New York.

KELLY, CPL John J. H., Company I, Upper Wichita River, TX, 9 September 1874. Issued 23 April 1875 for "gallantry in action." Born: Illinois.

KELLY, PVT Thomas, Company I, Upper Wichita River, TX, 9 September 1874. Issued 23 April 1875 for "gallantry in action." Born: Ireland

KENNEDY, PVT Philip, Company C, Cedar Creek campaign. Issued 27 April 1877 for "gallantry in action." Born: Ireland.

5ᵀᴴ Infantry Medal of Honor Recipients

KNOX, CPL John W., Company I, Upper Wichita River, TX, 9 September 1874. Issued 23 April 1875 for "gallantry in action." Born: Iowa.

KOELPIN, SGT William, Company I, Upper Wichita River, TX 9 September 1874. Issued 23 April 1875 for "gallantry in action." Born: Prussia.

KRAVITZ, Leonard M. Upgrade of Korean War DSC in 2014.

KREHER, 1ˢᵀ SGT Wendelin, Company C, Cedar Creek campaign, Issued 27 April 1877 for "gallantry in action." Born: Prussia.

LONG, 2LT Oscar F., Bear Paw Mountain, 30 September 1877. "Having been directed to order a troop of cavalry to advance, and finding both its officers killed, he voluntarily assumed command, and under heavy fire from the Indians advanced the troop to its proper position." Born: New York.

MC CORMICK, PVT Michael, Company G, Cedar Creek campaign. Issued 27 April 1877 for "gallantry in action." Born: Vermont.

MC DONALD, 1ˢᵀ LT Robert, Wolf Mountain, MT, 8 January 1877. Issued 27 November 1894 for leading "his command in a successful charge against superior numbers of hostile Indians." Born: New York.

MC GAR, PVT Owen, Company C, Cedar Creek campaign. Issued 27 April 1877 for "gallantry in action." Born: Massachusetts.

MC HUGH, PVT John, Company A, Cedar Creek campaign. Issued 27 April 1877 for "gallantry in action." Born: New York.

MC LOUGHLIN, SGT Michael, Company A, Cedar Creek campaign. Issued 27 April 1877 for "gallantry in action." Born: Ireland.

MC PHELAN, SGT Robert, Company D, Cedar Creek campaign. Issued 27 April 1877 for "gallantry in action." Born: Ireland.

MILES, COL Nelson A, 61ˢᵗ NY Infantry, Chancellorsville, VA, 2-3 May 1863. Issued 23 July 1892 for "Distinguished gallantry while holding his command at an advanced position against repeated assaults by a strong enemy force; was severely wounded." Born: Massachusetts.

MILLER, CPL George, Company H, Cedar Creek campaign. Issued 27 April 1877 for "gallantry in action." Born: New York.

MITCHELL, 1ST SGT John, Company I, Upper Wichita River, TX, 9-11 September 1874. Issued 23 April 1875 for "gallantry in engagement with Indians." Born: Ireland.

MONTROSE, PVT Charles H., Company I, Cedar Creek campaign. Issued 27 April 1877 for "gallantry in action." Born: Minnesota.

ROCHE, 1ST SGT David, Company A, Cedar Creek campaign. Issued 27 April 1877 for "gallantry in action." Born: Ireland.

RODENBURG, PVT Henry, Company A, Cedar Creek campaign. Issued 27 April 1877 for "gallantry in action." Born: Germany

ROMEYN, 1ST LT Henry, Bear Paw Mountain, 30 September 1877. Issued 27 November 1894. "Led his command into close range of the enemy, there maintained his position and vigorously prosecuted the fight until he was severely wounded." Born: New York.

ROONEY, PVT Edward, Company D, Cedar Creek campaign. Issued 27 April 1877 for "gallantry in action." Born: New York.

RYAN, PVT David, Company G, Cedar Creek campaign. Issued 27 April 1877 for "gallantry in action." Born: Ireland.

SHEPPARD, PVT Charles, Company A, Cedar Creek campaign. Issued 27 April 1877 for "bravery in action with Sioux." Born Missouri.

TILTON, MAJ Henry R., Regimental Surgeon, Bear Paw Mountain, 30 September 1877. Issued 22 March 1895 for "fearlessly risking his life and displaying great gallantry in rescuing and protecting the wounded men." Born: New Jersey.

WALLACE, SGT William, Company C, Cedar Creek campaign. Issued 27 April 1877 for "gallantry in action." Born: Ireland.

WHITEHEAD, PVT Patton G., Company C, Cedar Creek campaign. Issued 27 April 1877 for "gallantry in action." Born: Virginia.

5TH INFANTRY MEDAL OF HONOR RECIPIENTS

WILSON, CPL Charles, Company H, Cedar Creek campaign. Issued 27 April 1877 for "gallantry in action." Born: Illinois.

YOUNG, SGT Marvin R., Company C, Ben Cui, Republic of Vietnam. 21 August 1968. "…after assuming command of his platoon, he went to the aid of a small element of the point squad. He died while providing protective covering fire so that they could withdraw. ." Born: Texas.

Appendix C

Mexican War Roll of Honor
5th Infantry Regiment

ALBERTSON, PVT Abraham, Company B, DOW Resaca De La Palma, 11 May 1846, age 33, occ. soldier, born Salem, New Jersey.

BOSTWICK, PVT Samuel, Company E, Resaca De La Palma, 9 May 1846, age 23, occ. clerk, born Webster, New York.

BROOKE, PVT James H., Company H, DOW Molino del Rey, 10 September 1847.

BROWN, PVT Edward, Company G, DOW Molino del Rey, 11 September 1847.

BURWELL, 2 LT William T., Aide-de-Camp, Molino del Rey, 7 September 1847.

CALHOUN, PVT Samuel, Company E, Molino del Rey, 7 September 1847.

CARR, CPL Samuel, Company E, Molino del Rey, 7 September 1847.

CARTWRIGHT, PVT Jonas, Company F, DOW Molino del Rey, 14 September 1847.

CLARK, PVT William, Company B, Resaca De La Palma, 9 May 1846, age 28, occ. laborer, born Painesville, Ohio.

COGLAN, PVT John, Company F, DOW Molino del Rey, 8 October 1847.

CONNOR, PVT John, Company H, Molino del Rey, 7 September 1847.

CRAWFORD, PVT Robert, Company E, Molino del Rey, 7 September 1847.

DOORLEY, SGT John B., Company A. Resaca De La Palma, 9 May 1846, age 26, occ. tailor, born Baltimore, MD.

Mexican War Roll of Honor
5th Infantry Regiment

ERNST, PVT George, DOW Chapultapec, September 1847.

FARMER, SGT Henry, DOW Chapultapec, September 1847.

FOSTER, PVT Thomas, Company K, Molino del Rey, 7 September 1847.

FRASER, PVT Hugh, Company A, DOW Molino del Rey, 25 September 1847.

GILLESPIE, PVT John, Company E, MIA and presumed dead, Molino del Rey, 7 September 1847.

GOODING, PVT Thomas W., Company E, Molino del Rey, 7 September 1847.

GOTTINGER (GOLLINGER), SGT John, Company A, Molino del Rey, 7 September 1847.

GREEN, CPL Peter, Company B, Resaca De La Palma, 9 May 1846, age 23, occ. laborer, born Stokestown, Ireland.

HARDY, PVT Thomas, Company E, MIA and presumed dead, Molino del Rey, 7 September 1847.

HENDRICKSON, PVT Isaac, Company A. Resaca De La Palma, 9 May 1846, age 21, occ. carpenter, born Butler, Ohio.

HENRY, PVT Daniel, Company A, DOW Molino del Rey, 29 September 1847.

HAWLEY (HOWBY), PVT Timothy, Company A, Molino del Rey, 7 September 1847.

HOBBER, PVT Frederick, Company B, Molino del Rey, 7 September 1847.

HOGG, PVT Thomas, Company F, DOW Molino del Rey, 22 September 1847.

HONER (HOFFER), PVT John B., Company F, Molino del Rey, 7 September 1847.

INGALLS, PVT, Company I, DOW Monterrey, September 1846.

JAMES, CPL T., Company E, Churubusco, 20 August 1847.

KINGSMAN, PVT George, Company A, DOW Molino del Rey, 21 September 1847.

KOARSTAUPFADS (KIEPATENFADT), PVT John, Company G, Molino del Rey, 7 September 1847.

LANDRADGE (SANDRIDGE), SGT Alfred, Company A, DOW Molino del Rey, 25 September 1847.

LIEMAN, PVT B., Company I, Churubusco, 20 August 1847.

MACKENZIE, PVT Alexander, Company H, Churubusco, 20 August 1847.

MAYHEW, PVT John, Company A. Resaca De La Palma, 9 May 1846, age 21, occ. soldier, born Canada.

MC CLELLAN, SGT Alexander, Company G, DOW Molino del Rey, 5 October 1847.

MC CLUSKY (MC CLOSKY), PVT William., Company K, Molino del Rey, 7 September 1847.

MC CUE, PVT Patrick, Company G, DOW Molino del Rey, 30 September 1847.

MC ELROY, PVT Thomas, Company F, DOW Molino del Rey, 12 October 1847.

MC EVERSTEIN, SGT James, Company K, DOW Molino del Rey, 13 September 1847.

MC INTOSH, BVT COL James S., DOW Molino del Rey, 27 September 1847.

MC KAY, PVT Francis, Company B, Molino del Rey, 7 September 1847.

MC KINNEY, PVT J. C., Company A, Churubusco, 20 August, 1847.

MC LOY, PVT James, Company K, Chapultapec, 13 September 1847

Mexican War Roll of Honor
5th Infantry Regiment

MERRILL, CPT Moses E., Company K, Molino del Rey, 7 September 1847.

MIENICK, PVT HYRAM, Company B, Molino del Rey, 7 September 1847.

MINOT, SGT Stanislaus, Company I, Molino del Rey, 7 September 1847.

MOELLER, PVT Henry, Company K, MIA and presumed dead, Molino del Rey, 7 September 1847.

MOORE, PVT Peter, Company I, Molino del Rey, 7 September 1847.

MURRAY, PVT Owen, Company E, Molino del Rey, 7 September 1847.

NIXON, PVT John, Company D, Resaca De La Palma, 9 May 1846, age 28, occ. soldier, born Cavan, Ireland.

OWENS, PVT Griffith, Company E, Molino del Rey, 7 September 1847.

PENTZ, PVT Peter, Company E, Molino del Rey, 7 September 1847.

PETERS, PVT Jacob, Company F, Resaca De La Palma, 9 May 1846, age 32, occ. farmer, born Prussia.

PLACE, PVT William A., Company E, DOW Molino del Rey, 9 September 1847.

POLE, PVT Thomas S., Company B, Molino del Rey, 7 September 1847.

QUITMAN, SGT Augustus, Company B, Molino del Rey, 7 September 1847.

REED, PVT W. E., Company I, Chapultapec, 13 September 1847

REILY, PVT Bernard, Company F, DOW Molino del Rey, 24 September 1847.

REYNOLDS, PVT William, Company E, MIA and presumed dead, Molino del Rey, 7 September 1847.

ROBERTS, ASST. SURG. William, DOW Molino del Rey, 13 October 1847.

Two Centuries of Valor

RONNER, PVT John P., Company B, Molino del Rey, 7 September 1847.

SAYERS, PVT Horace, Company A, DOW Molino del Rey, 10 September 1847.

SCANLAN, PVT Patrick, Company G, DOW Molino del Rey, 25 September 1847.

SCHUMAKER, PVT Nicholas, Company H, DOW Resaca, 27 May 1846, age 32, occ. laborer, born Belgium.

SCOTT, BVT LTC Martin, Molino del Rey, 7 September 1847.

SHARP, PVT David, Company E, Molino del Rey, 7 September 1847.

SHERIDAN, PVT John, Company H, Churubusco, 20 August 1847.

SHIPLEY, PVT Joseph, Company G, DOW Molino del Rey, 21 September 1847.

SMITH, CPT Ephraim Kirby, Company H, Dow Molino del Rey, 11 September 1847.

SMITH, 2ND LT J. P., Chapultapec, 13 September 1847.

SMITH, PVT James C., Company I, Molino del Rey, 7 September 1847.

SMITH, PVT James G., Company I, Molino del Rey, 7 September 1847.

STEWARD, PVT Charles, Company B, Molino del Rey, 7 September 1847.

STOKELY (STOCKLEY), CPL Benjamin, Company H, DOW Resaca, 10 May 1846, age 23, occ. soldier, born Franklin, Pennsylvania.

STRONG, 2 LT Erastus B., Company K, Molino del Rey, 7 September 1847.

VAN ALSTYNE, PVT A., Company E, Churubusco, 20 August 1847.

WEIDMAN, PVT Thomas, Company A, Molino del Rey, 7 September 1847.

WHITE, PVT Patrick, Company F, Resaca De La Palma, 9 May 1846, age 35, occ. soldier, born Ireland.

Mexican War Roll of Honor
5th Infantry Regiment

WILSON, PVT Samuel, Company E, Churubusco, 20 August 1847.

WRICK, PVT John, Company G, DOW Molino del Rey, 29 September 1847.

YOUNG, PVT Conrad, Company K, MIA and presumed dead, Molino del Rey, 7 September 1847.

Appendix D

World War II Roll of Honor
5th Infantry Regiment

Name	Hometown /County	Date of Death	Burial
Alexander, 2LT David L. Jr. (Vosges) France	Aiken County, SC	3/13/45	Epinal
Allen, PVT Floyd W.	Winnebago County, IL	4/11/45	No Listing
Asay, SGT David W.	Utah County, UT	4/12/45	No Listing
Babich, T5 Frederick J.	Gogebic County, MI	3/25/45	No Listing
Bargdill, PFC Charles C.	Delaware County, OH	3/18/45	No Listing
Baumgard, PVT Leonhard A.	Nobles County, MN	3/25/45	No Listing
Bontecou, 1LT Pierre	Prince County, VA	4/5/45	No Listing
Books, PVT Everett W.	Elkhart, IN	4/3/45	No Listing
Box, 2 LT Maury D.	Alcorn County, MS	4/3/45	No Listing
Broderson, PVT George F.	Kings County, NY	4/20/45	No Listing
Campbell, SGT John M.	Maryland	4/20/45	St. Avold, France
Castillo, PVT Jose L. (Silver Star)	Los Angeles, CA	4/3/45	No Listing
Casto, PFC Virgil P. (Silver Star)	Kanawaha County, WV	3/25/45	St. Avold
Chow, PFC Wesley Y.	Fresno, CA	5/6/45	No Listing
Currier, T5 James J.	San Francisco, CA	4/4/45	No Listing
Eddington, PVT Edward H.	Marion County, IN	4/26/45	No Listing
Enfield, PFC Robert L.	St. Louis, MO	5/6/45	No Listing
Faulkner, PVT Ralph H.	Knox County, TN	4/26/45	St. Avold, France

Feltman, T/SGT Alfred T.	Bronx, NY	3/25/45	No Listing
Ficke, PFC Martyn A. (Silver Star)	Fairfield County, CT	4/21/45	No Listing
Foster, PVT Edward J.	Santa Rosa County, FL	4/8/45	No Listing
Freeman, PFC Lester L.	Pershing County, NV	4/20/45	St. Avold, France
Gaines, 1LT Thomas C. Jr.	Somerset County, PA	4/11/45	Margraten, Netherlands
Goff, PVT Kenneth W.	Susquahanna County, PA	4/22/45	St. Avold, France
Gosney, S/SGT Maurice E.	Effingham, IL	4/11/45	Margraten, Netherlands
Gouse, PFC Frederick F.	Philadelphia, PA	5/3/45	No Listing
Grubb, PVT William T.	San Francisco, CA	4/3/45	Margraten, Netherlands
Hargrove, PVT Elvin	Allen Parish, LA	Not listed	No Listing
Harshbarger, PFC Calvin W.	Augusta County, VA	3/25/45	No Listing
Head, PFC Austin P.	Davidson County, TN	Not listed	No Listing
Hill, PFC Boyd C.	Marshville, NC	Not listed	No Listing
Hill, PFC Jack	Jefferson County, TN	4/20/45	No Listing
Krumrine, SGT John V.	Carroll County, MD	3/14/45	St. Avold, France
Lamb, PFC Russell A.	Fayette County, IL	3/25/45	No Listing
Louie, PFC Tew M.	San Francisco, CA	Not listed	No Listing
Lozano, PFC Jesus	Hidalgo County, TX	3/25/45	No Listing
McHugh, PFC Richard A. (Silver Star)	Multnomah County, OR	Not listed	No Listing
McVay, PFC Walter R.	Hancock County, OH	4/11/45	No Listing
Miller, PFC Noel L.	Franklin County, OH	Not listed	No Listing
Miller, PVT William G.	Madison County, IL	Not listed	No Listing

Two Centuries of Valor

Mitchum, PFC Troy Jr.	Wise County, TX	4/14/45	Neupre, Belgium
Monterio, PFC Francis T.	Norfolk County, MA	4/11/45	Margraten, Netherlands
Nagem, CPL Anthony J.	San Diego, CA	Not listed	No Listing
Neill, PVT Grover W.	Hardin County, TN	Not listed	No Listing
Pandel, 1LT James P.	Los Angeles, CA	5/12/45	No Listing
Pettigrew, S/SGT Carl E.	Sullivan County, TN	4/11/45	Margraten, Netherlands
Quinn, PVT Gerald J.	Queens County, NY	3/25/45	No Listing
Revilock, S/SGT Steven	Cuyahoga County, OH	4/4/45	Margraten, Netherlands
Ricketts, S/SGT Forrest D.	Decatur County, IN	Not listed	No Listing
Roberts, PFC Thomas H.	Juneau County, WI	3/25/45	No Listing
Rubens, PVT Arthur T.	Clastop County, OR	3/25/45	St. Avold, France
Sacco, PFC Frank	Indiana County, PA	3/17/45	St. Avold, France
Savely, S/SGT Fred W.	Franklin County, OH	Not listed	No Listing
Sidell, PFC Stanley	Los Angeles, CA	3/25/45	St. Avold, France
Silverman, 2LT Bernard	Kings County, NY	3/25/45	St. Avold, France
Smith, SGT Harold B.	Harrison County, WV	5/6/45	St. Avold, France
Stone, PFC James E.	Greenville County, SC	Not listed	No Listing
Taylor, PFC Albert H. Jr.	Lee County, AR	3/25/45	No Listing
Toles, PFC George M.	Madison County, IN	3/24/45	No Listing
Viadell, SGT Wayne H.	Newton County, IN	3/17/45	No Listing

World War II Roll of Honor
5th Infantry Regiment

Viele, SGT James F.	Hudson County, NJ	3/25/45	St. Avold, France
Wagers, T/SGT Louie	Dorchester County, SC	4/3/45	NL (Silver Star)
Watson, PVT Vance A.	Clark County, NV	3/25/45	No Listing
Weaver, PFC Carl E. (Silver Star)	Sullivan County, TN	5/6/45	St. Avold
Woodburn, PFC George R.	Bowie County, TX	4/7/45	No Listing

NOTE: In the interest of saving space, lists of the approximately 1500 members of the 5th Infantry who died in Korea and Vietnam were not appended to this book. The Korean War list maintained by Raymond Warner, a survivor of the ambush near Pisi-gol, was published in Michael Slater's *Hills of Sacrifice: The 5th RCT in Korea*. Denis McDonough, who served in Vietnam in 1967, has developed a KIA list for that conflict. Anyone wishing a reasonably accurate Vietnam Roll of Honor may contact the author at samkier@montereybay.com for an attachment. Combat casualties from other campaigns are frequently mentioned in the narrative of this book.

NOTES

I. The War of 1812

1. COL Raymond K. Bluhm, Ed. *U.S. Army: A Complete History*. Arlington, VA: The Army Historical Association, 2005. P.164.
2. Military Service Institution. *The Fifth Regiment of Infantry*. 1894. 3.www.history.mil/books/R&H/R&H-5IN.htm. P.1.
4. First Battle Group, 5th Infantry Regiment. *History of the Fifth United States Infantry*. Ft. Riley, KS. June, 1962. Annex C.
5. Malcolm Muir, Jr. David S Heidler & Jeanne T. Heidler, (eds) "James Wilkinson," *Encyclopedia of the War of 1812*. Annapolis, MD: Naval Institute Press, 1997. pp. 553-555.
6. Eric Jarvis, "Battle of Lundy's Lane" Heidler & Heidler, pp. 307-309.
7. *The Niagara Campaign of 1814: The Battle of Lundy's Lane*. http//www.galafilm.com/1812/e/events/lundy-amer.html.
8. John M. Keefe, "Battle of Plattsburgh." Heidler & Heidler. pp. 419-420.
9. John C. Fredriksen, "Battle of Cook's Mills." Heidler & Heidler, pp. 127-128.
10. Nichols, Jennifer, US Army Center of Military History. E-mail correspondence with author, April 2013.
11. Heflin, Kirk and MAJ Thomas E. Hanson. "3rd United States Infantry Regiment (The Old Guard)" *On Point*. Summer 2007. p. 31.

II. Taming the Northwest

1. Marcus L. Hansen. *Old Fort Snelling: 1819-1858*. Cedar Rapids, IA: The Torch Press, 1918. p.8.
2. First Battle Group, 5th Infantry Regiment, *History of the Fifth United States Infantry,* Ft. Riley, KS, June, 1962. pp. 5-8.
3. Minnesota (Fort Snelling area) Weather for the year 1820. http://home.att.net/~station_climo/YR1820.htm.
4. *Old Fort Snelling*. pp. 27-31.
5. Thomas W. Cutrer, "George Mercer Brooke" *The Handbook*

of Texas Online www.tsha.utexas.edu/handbook/online/articles/BB/fbr.html (accessed December 30, 2007)
6. First Battle Group, *History of the Fifth United States Infantry*, p.6.
7. First Battle Group, *op cit*, pp. 7-8.
8. Koehs, Michael, "Fort Wilkins: Copper Harbor, MI," Fort Wilkins Natural History Assn., 1995.

III. War with Mexico

1. Robert F. Dorr, *Alpha Bravo Delta Guide to the U.S. Army*. New York: Alpha Books, 2003. P.66.
2. Raymond K. Bluhm (Ed), *U.S. Army: A Complete History*, p.288.
3. John S.D. Eisenhower, *So Far from God: The U.S. War with Mexico, 1846-48*. New York: Random House, 1989. p.81.
4. Francis B. Heitman, *Historical Register and Dictionary of the United States Army from Its Organization, September 29, 1789 to March 2, 1903*. Washington: Government Printing Office, 1903. Vol. II, pp. 391-474.
5. William Hugh Robarts, *Mexican War Veterans*. Washington D.C: Brentano's, 1887. www.dmwv.org/honoring/chucon.htm. p. 3 of 7. (Accessed 12/18/2007)
6. Michael Hogan, *The Irish Soldiers of Mexico*. Guadalajara: Fondo Editorial Universitario, 1997. p. 19.
7. Military Service Institution, *The Fifth Regiment of Infantry*. p.4.
8. Z. Boylston Adams, Surgeon, US Medical Corps, *Assistant Surgeon William Roberts, Medical Corps*. http://ameddregiment.amedd.army.mil/Leadership_Courage.asp (Accessed 12/20/2007)

IV. Return to the Frontier

1. Laredo Community College, *Historic Fort McIntosh*. www.laredo.cc.tx.us/campus/campus_history.htm p.1 of 2. (Accessed 12/31/2007)
2. Grant Foreman, *Fort Gibson: A Brief History*. http://freepages.rootsweb.com/~texlance/misc/fortgibsonappendix.htm (Accessed 12/20/2007)

3. First Battle Group, 5th Infantry, *History of the Fifth United States Infantry*. p. 15.
4. *U. S. Army: A Complete History*. p. 334.
5. Randolph B. Marcy, Excerpts of report from CPT Randolph Marcy to Secretary of War describing explorations in the Southwest in 1849. U.S. Army Military History Institute, Carlisle Barracks, PA.
6. W.B. Morrison, *Fort Arbuckle*. www.chickasawhistory.com/FTA1.htm. pp 1-6. (Accessed 11/9/2007)
7. Legends of America, *Texas Legends: The Ghosts of Fort Phantom*. www.legendsofamerica.com/TX-FortPhantom.html. pp. 1-3. (Accessed 6/15/2008)
8. Thomas Cutrer, *Randolph Barnes Marcy*. www.tshaonline.org /handbook/online/articles/MM/fma43.html pp. 1-3. (Accessed 5/17/2009)
9. Military Service Institution, *The Fifth Regiment of Infantry*. p.5.
10. First Battle Group, 5th Infantry. p. 16.
11. *U.S. Army: A Complete History*. p. 364.
12. Heitman, *Historical Register and Dictionary. . .* pp. 391-474.
13. Bailey,Lynn, *The Long Walk: A History of the Navajo Wars, 1846-68*. Tucson:Westernlore Press, 1988. pp. 131-147.
14. "The Bascom Affair, Apache Pass, February 4, 1861" *MilitaryHistoryOnline.com*. Accessed 1/15/2110.

V. The Civil War in New Mexico

1. Heitman, *Historical Register and Dictionary. . .*Vol. II, p. 181-185.
2. Alvin Josephy, Jr. *The Civil War in the American West*. New York: Alfred A. Knopf, 1991. P.24.
3. First Battle Group, 5th Infantry. p.17.
4. *The Civil War in the American West*. pp. 61-74.
5. M.S.I, *The Fifth Regiment of Infantry*. p.6.
6. *The Civil War in the American West*. p.89.
7. First Battle Group, 5th Infantry. p.18.
8. George Hand, *The Civil War in Apacheland*. Silver City, New Mexico: High-Lonesome Books, 1996. pp. 26-66.
9. James Abarr, *Monument to Frontier Duty*.

NOTES

      www.abqjournal.com/venue/day/heritage_selden.htm pp.1-4 (Accessed 12/12/2007)
10. M.S.I, *The Fifth Regiment of Infantry.* p.6.
11. Heitman, Register and Dictionary . . . Vol I, p. 156.

VI. The Red River War

1. Jerome Greene, *Indian War Veterans: Memories of Life and Campaigns in the West, 1864-1898.* New York: Savas Beattie LLC, 2007. p. 230.
2. M.S.I, *The Fifth Regiment of Infantry.* p.7.
3. *The Red River War of 1874.* www.texasbeyondhistory.net /redriver/index.html. pp. 1-4 (Accessed 8/19/2009) See also www.tshaonline.org/handbook/online/articles/ RR/qdr2.html. pp. 1-4 (Accessed 5/19/2009)
4. Robert Wooster, *Nelson A. Miles and the Twilight of the Frontier Army.* Lincoln: University of Nebraska Press, 1993. pp. 66-67.
5. Frank D. Baldwin, Letter to Mrs. Alice Baldwin written at Fort Dodge, KS on September 17, 1874. USAMHI, Carlisle Barracks, PA.
6. SPC Ross A. McGinnis, *Medal of Honor: Full-text Citations, Indian War Campaigns.* www.army.mil/medal Ofhonor/mcginnis/medal/citations (Accessed 8/19/2009)
7. First Battle Group, 5th Infantry. p.24.
8. PFC James Townsend. Author's e-mail correspondence with PFC Townsend, custodian of regimental artifacts and documents at Fort Wainwright, AK. January, 2008.
9. Charles M. Robinson III, *Kiowa Chief Satanta.* The History Net. www.TheHistoryNet+%7C+Wild. p.4. (Accessed 3/20/2007)
10. "Odd Bills and Reports by Congressional Committees" *New York Times,* January 14, 1896.

VII. Fort Keogh, Montana

1. Josef James Warhank, *Fort Keogh: Cutting Edge of a Culture.* M.A. Thesis, CSU Long Beach, December 1983. p.8.
2. Robert Wooster, p. 83.
3. Robert Wooster, p. 83.

4. Warhank, p. 14.
5. Frank D. Baldwin, CPT Baldwin's diary entries for November 6 – December 21, 1876. USAMHI, Carlisle Barracks, PA. pp. 16-29.
6. MSI – Fifth Regiment of Infantry – p. 476.
7. Greene, *Indian War Veterans*. p. 158.
8. Jeffrey V. Pearson, "Nelson Miles, Crazy Horse, and the Battle of Wolf Mountains" *Montana; The Magazine of Western History,* 51 (Winter, 2001) p. 53.
9. Pearson, p. 67.
10. Jerome Greene, p. 161.
11. First Battle Group, 5th Infantry, p. 28.
12. Warhank, p. 8.
13. Alice B. Baldwin, *An Army Wife on the Frontier.* Salt Lake City: University of Utah, 1975.
14. Jerome Greene, p. 54.
15. Robert Wooster, p. 93.
16. Merrill D. Beal, *I Will Fight No More Forever: Chief Joseph and the Nez Perce War.* Seattle: University of Washington Press, 1963. p. 210.
17. Merrill D. Beal, p. 217.
18. Merrill D. Beal, p. 229.
19. "Thirteen Indians killed and thirty-seven captured – Loss of troops, Capt. A. S. Bennett and one private." *New York Times,* September 13, 1878.
20. Lieutenant General Hunter Liggett (1857-1937) www.arcent.army.mil/bios/biograph.htm, p.1.
21. Warhank, p. 53.
22. First Battle Group, 5th Infantry, p.31.

VIII. The Cuban Occupation and Philippine Insurrection

1. First Battle Group, 5th Infantry. p. 32.
2. "Col. Osborne Seriously Ill" *The New York Times,* April 19, 1897.
3. "Capt. Romeyn is Favored" *The New York Times,* July 13, 1896.
4. "Atlanta's Military Row" *The New York Times,* April 19, 1897.

Notes

5. First Battle Group, 5th Infantry. p.32.
6. "Lieut. Bradley Fever Victim" *The New York Times,* August 31, 1898.
7. First Battle Group, 5th Infantry. p. 33.
8. Robert D. Ramsey, *Savage Wars of Peace: Case Studies of Pacification in the Philippines, 1900-1902.* Ft. Leavenworth, KS: Combat Studies Institute Press, 2007. p. 44.
9. Heitman, pp. 391-474.
10. Ramsey, p. 52.
11. First Battle Group, 5th Infantry. p. 34.
12. Sid Thurston, "A Brief History of the 5th U.S. Infantry, Company M" www.spanamwar.com/5thUS.htm p. 1 (Accessed 3/17/2008)
13. Ramsey, p. 60.
14. "Charles Lukens Davis, Brigadier General, United States Army" Arlington National Cemetery Website (Accessed 4/21/2008)
15. First Battle Group, 5th Infantry. p. 34.
16. First Battle Group, 5th Infantry. p. 34.
17. "Mark Twain, The Greatest American Humorist, Returning Home" *The New York World,* October 6, 1900. (Internet archive accessed 1/16/2008)
18. "Brings 302 Dead Soldiers. . .Nearly Four Hundred Happy Men of the Fifth Infantry Also Arrive from the Philippines" *The New York Times,* September 13, 1903.
19. Bluhm, *U. S. Army: A Complete History,* pp. 518-520.
20. "Calvin Duvall Cowles" Arlington National Cemetery Website. (Accessed 4/21/2008)
21. "War Department Wipes Out Fake Rifle Scores. Two Companies of 5th Infantry Must Repay Prize Money" *The New York Times,* February 3, 1907.

IX. World War I and the Great Depression

1. First Battle Group, 5th Infantry. p. 36.
2. Edward G. Lengel, *To Conquer Hell: The Meuse-Argonne, 1918.* New York: Henry Holt & Co., 2008 pp. 359-387.
3. Lieutenant General Hunter Liggett (1857-1937) www.arcent.army.mil/bios/biograph.htm pp. 1-3.

4. First Battle Group, 5th Infantry. p. 38.
5. Edwin L. James, "Germans Mourn as Americans Go" *The New York Times*. August 19, 1919.
6. First Battle Group, 5th Infantry. p. 39.
7. Bluhm, *U. S. Army: A Complete History*, p. 611.

X. With the 71st Division in World War II

1. First Battle Group, 5th Infantry, p. 42.
2. 1-158 Infantry Battalion, Bushmasters, Arizona National Guard Webpage www.azguard.gov/1-158/1-158%20History.htm
3. Fred Clinger and Arthur Johnson, *The History of the 71st Infantry Division*. Augsburg, Germany: 71st ID Public Relations Office, 1946. pp 1-9.
4. Dean P. Joy, *Sixty Days in Combat: An Infantryman's Memoir of World War II in Europe*. New York: Random House, 2004. pp. 45-46.
5. Edward Zebrowski, *My Brother, Hail and Farewell*. Tampa, FL: Woodstock Books, 1994. p. 18.
6. First Battle Group, 5th Infantry, p. 46.
7. Donald H. Sitz, "History of Company C, Fifth Infantry, World War II" www.bobcat.ws/ww2history.htm p.2.
8. Leo T. Kissell, "Combat Diary of 1st Sergeant Jesse W. Beckum, Co. L, 5th Infantry" *Red Circle News*. July 2005. p. 12.
9. Kissell, Beckum's Diary. p. 12.
10. Dean Joy, p. 36.
11. First Battle Group, 5th Infantry. p. 47.
12. Dean Joy, p. 152.
13. Donald Sitz, p. 2.
14. Dean Joy, p. 165.
15. First Battle Group, 5th Infantry. p. 48.
16. Kissell, Beckum's Diary. p. 12.
17. Kissell, Beckum's Diary. p. 13.
18. Donald Sitz, p. 4.
19. Edward Zebrowski, p. 140.
20. CPT J. D. Pletcher, "The Americans Have Come – At Last" www.remember.org/mooney/Section1.html pp. 1-6.
21. First Battle Group, 5th Infantry. p. 51.

NOTES

22. Dean Joy, p. 257.
23. Clinger and Johnson, *History of the 71st Infantry Division*. pp. 103-104.
24. Allin Sorinson, Webpage devoted to the 5th Infantry Soldiers Chorus http://music.drury.edu/chorus/chorus.htm pp. 1-5.
25. "Popular Director of Fifth Chorus Killed in Accident" *Red Circle News*. January 26, 1946.
26. First Battle Group, 5th Infantry. pp 50-51.
27. www.arlingtoncemetery.net/scwooten.htm. Accessed 1/30/2008.
28. Michael Slater, *Hills of Sacrifice: The 5th RCT in Korea*. Paducah, KY: Turner Publishing Company, 2000. P.16.

XI. Korea: The Fluid War

1. James F. Schnabel, *U.S. Army in the Korean War: Policy and Direction: The First Year*. Washington, D.C: Office of the Chief of Military History, DOA, 1971. pp. 45-46.
2. Michael Slater, *Hills of Sacrifice*. pp. 33-38.
3. LTC Roy E. Appleman, *South to the Naktong, North to the Yalu*. Washington, D.C: Office of the Chief of Military History, DOA, 1961. p. 267.
4. Headquarters, Eighth U.S. Army, General Orders No. 20 (January 13, 1951) NARA, College Park, MD.
5. HQS, 8th U.S. Army, G.O. No. 89 (October 1, 1950)
6. Appleman, p. 272.
7. Appleman, p. 275.
8. Appleman's description differs from the language of 3rd Battalion's Distinguished Unit Citation. According to the latter source, the battalion "advanced through intense automatic weapons and artillery fire." See DOA, Washington, D.C, General Orders No. 69 (July 11, 1952)
9. Gene McClure, "One Helluva Soldier" in *Faces of War: Korean Vignettes*. Arthur Wilson and Norman Strickbine, editors. Portland, OR: Artwork Publications, 1996. p. 17.
10. HQS, 8th U.S. Army, G.O. No. 68 (September 15, 1950)
11. HQS, 8th U.S. Army, G.O. No. 49 (June 9, 1953)
12. Michael Slater, *Hills of Sacrifice*. p. 67.
13. HQS, 8th U.S. Army, G.O. No. 89 (October 1, 1950)

14. Edward F. Murphy, *Korean War Heroes*. Novato, CA: Presidio Press, 1992. p. 29.
15. Michael Slater, *Hills of Sacrifice*. p. 83.
16. HQS, 8th U.S. Army, G.O. No. 151 (November 1, 1950)
17. HQS, 8th U.S. Army, G.O. No. 189 (Smith) and No. 37 (Jeal)(December 5, 1950 and January 22, 1951) SGT Poinciano's citation, apparently not available on-line, is included in a brief, unpublished unit history released on 9 January 1951. Available from NARA.
18. Michael Slater, *Hills of Sacrifice*. pp. 97-98.
19. HQS. 8th U.S. Army, G.O. No. 37 (January 22, 1951)
20. David R. Zimmerman, "Break-out at Waegwan and Sgt. Charles Carroll" *Battle Stars*. 5th RCT Assn. January-February, 2005.
21. HQS, 8th U.S. Army, G.O. No. 79 (February 17, 1951)
22. Michael Slater, *Hills of Sacrifice*. p. 134.
23. General Douglas MacArthur, *Reminiscences*. New York: McGraw-Hill, 1964. p.374.
24. HQS, 8th U.S. Army, G.O. No. 20 (January 13, 1951)
25. Michael Slater, *Hills of Sacrifice*. p. 157.
26. Matthew B. Ridgeway, *The Korean War*. New York: Doubleday & Co. Inc, 1967. pp. 86-88.
27. Edward Murphy, *Korean War Heroes*. pp. 139-140.
28. Clay Blair, *The Forgotten War: America in Korea, 1950-53*. New York: Time Books, 1987. pp. 663-664.
29. Michael Slater, *Hills of Sacrifice*. p. 175.
30. HQS, 8th U.S. Army, G.O. No. 5 (Kravitz) and No. 46 (Bernotas)(January 15, 1952 and June 25, 1951)
31. HQS, 8th U.S. Army, G.O. No. 1034 (December 30, 1951)
32. HQS, 8th U.S. Army, G.O. No. 453 (Brannon) and No. 650 (Riddle) (August 14, 1952 and August 18, 1951)
33. HQS, 8th U.S. Army, G.O. No. 18 (Sommer) and No. 714 (Warner)(February 18, 1953 and September 21, 1951)
34. Billy Smith, "Actor James Garner is a Bobcat," *The Bobcat Bulletin*, Summer 2007, p. 11.
35. 5th RCT Command Report, April 1951. NARA. p.5.
36. HQS, 8th U.S. Army, G.O. No. 64 (June 30, 1952)
37. Robert W. Black, *Rangers in Korea*. New York: Ballantine Books, 1989. pp. 145-149.

Notes

38. 5th RCT Command Report, April 1951. p. 7.
39. Robert W. Black, *Rangers in Korea*. p. 153.
40. Sam Harvey, "Former POW hopes vets will talk things out" *Coastal Point*, March 11, 2005.
 www.coastalpoint.com (Accessed Aug 29, 2009)
41. Michael Slater, *Hills of Sacrifice*. p. 211.
42. HQS, 8th U.S. Army, G.O. No. 955 (December 1, 1951)
43. Michael Slater, p. 218.
44. 5th RCT Command Report, April 1951. p. 8.
45. "Korean War MIA Serviceman Identified – CPL Leslie R. Heath of Bridgeport, Illinois. DPMO Press release www.kwva/pow_mia/P_050721-heath-remains_identified.htm
46. 5th RCT Command Report, May 1951, p.1.
47. G-3, HQS 24th ID Journal Entry, 17 May 1951
48. Michael Slater, p. 231.

XII. Korea: The Battle for the Ridges

1. 5th RCT Command Report, June 1951, p.1.
2. Russell A. Gugeler, *Combat Actions in Korea*. CMH Publication 30-2, 1954. Chapter 15.
3. 5th RCT Command Report, October 1951, pp. 1-6.
4. HQS, 8th U.S. Army, G.O. No. 192 (Otterstrom) and No. 954 (Pelfrey) (April 12, 1952 and December 1, 1951) PFC Daniel Machinski is listed as a recipient of the DSC but no citation was available on line.
5. HQS, 8th U.S. Army, G.O. No. 986 (December 12, 1951)
6. 5th RCT Command Report, October 1951, p. 14.
7. William Berebitsky, *A Very Long Weekend: The Army National Guard in Korea, 1950-1953*. Shippensburg, PA: White Mane Publishing Co., 1996. pp. 197-211.
8. Donald Knox, *The Korean War: Uncertain Victory*. New York: Harcourt Brace, 1988. pp. 417-430.
9. 5th RCT Command Report, February 1952. p. 2.
10. Frank O. Pruitt, *Delayed Letters from Korea*. 1st Books Library, 2002. pp. 43-48.
11. COL RET Joseph Love. Interview with author on May 19, 2007 and subsequent e-mail correspondence.
12. 5th RCT Command Report, April 1952, pp. 2-3.

13. Harry G. Summers, Jr. *Korean War Almanac.* New York: Facts on File, Inc., 1990. p. 219.
14. James Evans, *A Morning in June: Defending Outpost Harry.* Tuscaloosa:University of Alabama Press, 2010, p. 19.
15. James Evans, p. 29.
16. 5th RCT Command Report, January 1953. p. 9.
17. HQS, 8th U.S. Army, G.O. No. 522 (May 20, 1953)
18. James Evans, p. 115.
19. HQS, 8th U.S. Army, G.O. No. 923 (October 11, 1953)
20. HQS, 64th Tank Battalion Command Report, June 1953, NARA, pp. 3-8.
21. 5th RCT Command Report, July 1953, pp. 3-5.
22. "Survivors Tell How Chinese Overran American Artillery" *Savannah Morning News,* July 17, 1953.
23. Michael Slater, *Hills of Sacrifice,* p. 232.
24. PFC Jim Morrissey, "Yanks Drive for Korean Boys' Town," *Pacific Stars and Stripes,* February 15, 1953.
25. PFC Jim Morrissey, "Korea Boys' Town Opens Through 5th RCT's Gift," *Pacific Stars and Stripes,* March 27, 1953.
26. Joe Stine, Interview with author and subsequent e-mail correspondence. September 17, 2007.

XIII. The Cold War

1. This area is currently labeled "D Block" by Ft. Lewis authorities. www.globalsecurity.org/military/Facility/fort-lewis.htm
2. Korean War Statistics (Republished from VA Web Site) www.veteransinfo.net/links/korean_war_statistics.htm
3. Jack Salyers, interview with author and subsequent e-mail correspondence and news clippings (July through October, 2007.
4. First Battle Group, 5th Infantry. p. 56.
5. Bluhm, *U.S. Army: A Complete History.* p. 793.
6. Stuart Clayman, phone interview. July, 2007.
7. Articles, "Charlie Makes the Movies" and "Alert GI Apprehends Experienced Prowler" provided to the *Bobcat Bulletin* by William Mawhinney, Jr., formerly of HQ Co, 1/5, 1956-58.

NOTES

8. Unit History, 25th Infantry Division, www.25thida.com/division.html p. 5.
9. MG RET G.H. Bethke, E-mail correspondence, July, 2007.
10. COL Keneth L. Johnson, "Historical Events of the First Battle Group, 5th Infantry Prior to Reorganization (1963), NARA, p.1.
11. LTC Thomas Tarpley, "Annual Historical Summary, HQ, 1st Battalion (Mech) 5th Infantry" 1 January 1964 thru 31 December 1964. p. 1.
12. LTC Thomas U. Greer, "Annual Supplement to Unit History" 1 January 1965 – 31 December 1965. p. 2.
13. Don Sparhawk, "Elder Lance B. Wickman Encourages Students to Seize the Day" Rexburg, ID: BYU-Idaho Media Relations, October 23, 2003.

XIV. Vietnam

1. Harry G. Summers, Jr., *The Vietnam War Almanac*. New York: Ballantine Books, 1985. pp. 29-31.
2. www.thewall-usa.com/search.asp
3. Larry Hadzima, *The First Battalion (Mechanized) Fifth Infantry, Twenty-fifth Infantry Division in the Vietnam War, 1966-1971*. Compiled by 1st Bn (M) 5th Infantry Society of Vietnam Combat Veterans, Inc., January, 2000. p.1.
4. Don Sparhawk, "Elder Lance B. Wickman. . ."
5. Hadzima, p. 3.
6. HQS, U.S. Army, Vietnam, G.O. No. 21 (April 26, 1967)
7. HQS, 1st Bn (Mech) 5th Infantry, After Action Report, 25 February 1966. pp. 1-6.
8. "Safety Innovation," *Tropic Lightning News*, January 5, 1970.
9. Hadzima, p.7.
10. HQS, 1/5 (M), After Action Report, 10 April 1966, pp. 1-9.
11. Hadzima, p. 12.
12. "Tropic Lightning Here to Help" *Tropic Lightning News*, May 13, 1966.
13. HQS, 1/5 (M), After Action Report, 12 June 1966, pp. 1-10.
14. HQS, 1/5 (M), After Action Report, 13 July 1966, p. 15.
15. COL (Ret) Thomas K. Forsythe, Interview with author,

January 2009.
16. Larry Hadzima, p. 17.
17. HQS, 1/5 (M), After Action Report, 14 September 1966, p. 17.
18. Summers, *The Vietnam War Almanac*, pp. 39, 66-68.
19. Forsythe, *Ibid*.
20. (Hale) HQS, U.S. Army, Vietnam, G.O. No. 181 (January 13, 1967) (Owens) G.O. No. 1852 (December 14, 1966).
21. HQS, U.S. Army, Vietnam, G.O. No. 46 (October 26, 1967.
22. Department of the Army, G.O. No. 20 (April 25, 1967)
23. "VC Cache Camouflage Under Par" *Tropic Lightning News*, August 28, 1967.
24. "Viet Excites U.S. Officer" *Tropic Lightning News*, August 28, 1967.
25. Roger Hayes, *On Point: A Rifleman's Year in the Boonies, 1967-1968*. New York: St. Martin's Press, 2000. p. 152.
26. "25th G.I's Help Children" *Tropic Lightning News*, October 16, 1967.
27. "LTC Hodson Mech XO" *Tropic Lightning News*, November 6, 1967.
28. "Two Chaplains Go Below; Earth's Surface, That Is" Tropic Lightning News, January 1, 1968.
29. Larry Hadzima, "Bobcats 1968", op. cit., p.3.
30. Conversations with MG RET Andrew Anderson and CSM RET Ignacio Medina (2008).
31. Roger Hayes, *On Point*, pp. 106-107.
32. HQS, U.S. Army, Vietnam, G.O. No. 1800 (April 18, 1968).
33. HQS, U.S. Army, Vietnam, G.O. No. 1820 (April 19, 1968.
34. HQS, U.S. Army, Vietnam, G.O. No. 1839 (May 22, 1969).
35. Thomas Forsythe, ibid.
36. Roger Hayes, p. 46-47.
37. MAJ Richard Baun, 18th Military History Detachment, September 1, 1968. "Small Unit After Action Report" (Interview with John Snodgrass, Harold Metzger, Arthur Cook, Ronald Grim and A.G. McSwain following the battle of Ben Cui, 21 Aug 1968).
38. HQS, U.S. Army, Vietnam, G.O. No. 27 (April 23, 1970)
39. HQS, U.S. Army, Vietnam, G.O. No. 5006 (October 29, 1968).
40. HQS, U.S. Army, Vietnam, G.O. No. 5845 (December 26,

1968).
41. Summers, *The Vietnam War Almanac*, pp. 297-298.
42. Bill Adler, Interview and e-mail correspondence with author, October 2008.
43. HQS, U.S. Army, Vietnam, G.O. No. 4392 (December 6, 1969).
44. HQS, U.S. Army, Vietnam, G.O. No. 1553 (May 2, 1969).
45. HQS, U.S. Army, Vietnam, G.O. No. 7 (March 9, 1971).
46. Summers, *The Vietnam Almanac*, p. 182.
47. (Villaseñor) G.O. No. 2024, (Lechuga) G.O. No. 2025 (June 9, 1969).
48. Summers, p. 334.
49. (Brock) G.O. No. 3309, (Chatelain) G.O. No. 3311 (August 29, 1969).
50. SP4 Dennis Dibb, "Medcap With New Twist" *Tropic Lightning News*, September 8, 1969.
51. The author corresponded with Ron Baker, Bn S-3, Tom Ward, Bn Adj, Bill Correia, Bn S-2 and Ralph Laubacher, Cdr,B Co. regarding this incident. This is an attempt to merge their memories of 40 years ago.
52. HQS, U.S. Army, Vietnam, G.O. No. 4684 (October 3, 1970)
53. HQS, U.S. Army, Vietnam, G.O. No. 119 (January 13, 1971)

XV. Guardian of the Pacific

1. 25th Infantry Division Assn, "A Brief History of the 25th Infantry Division" www.25thida.org/division.html p.6 (Accessed 4/10/2007).
2. BG (Ret) James E. Mace, Correspondence with author, July, 2008.
3. Beattie, Mark (3-5, 1977-78) E-mail correspondence with author, December 2009.
4. Efforts to obtain information from the 82nd Airborne Division were unsuccessful despite assistance from the Army Public Affairs Office.
5. John C. McManus, *The 7th Infantry Regiment: Combat in an Age of Terror*. New York: Tom Doherty Associates, 2008. pp. 167-168.

6. Hawk Halloway (Co. A and CSC, 1978-81) E-mail correspondence, July 2007.
7. Matthew Seelinger in Bluhm, *U.S. Army: A Complete History,* p. 873.
8. Kenneth W. Krueger (Co. C, 1974-77) E-mail correspondence, July-August, 2008.
9. HQS, 25th Infantry Division, LETTER ORDERS NUMBER 4-120, 25 April 1975(Courtesy of Keith Beauchamp)
10. "Bobcat Soldiers Back from Guam" *Tropic Lightning News,* June 27, 1975.
11. HQS, 1st Battalion, 5th Infantry, Extract from a document used to orient replacements to the battalion. Courtesy of Alex Von Plinsky.
12. Gene D. Bernhardt, E-mail correspondence, August-October, 2007.
13. HQS, 1st Battalion, 5th Infantry, "Annual Historical Summary for Fiscal Year 1983, (March 13, 1984).
14. Tom Person (Bn S-4, 1981-84) E-mail correspondence, July 2007.
15. Tom Person, *Ibid*.
16. HQS, 1st Battalion, 5th Infantry, "Change of Command Ceremony," 17 August 1984. Courtesy of Alex Von Plinsky.
17. Alexander Von Plinsky III, (CO of Co. C, 1984- 85) E-mail and postal correspondence with author, August, 2007.
18. "A White House Visitor" *Central Military Sun Press,* October 17, 1985.
19. John De Fede (CO of CSC Co., 1984-85) E-mail correspondence, October, 2007.
20. Northeast Forest Fire Supervisors, "M-561 Gamma Goat: An Analysis of the Vehicle for Wildfire Use," May 1988. pp. 2-7.
21. HQS, Department of Army, G.O. No. 2, 5 January 1987.
22. Alexander Von Plinsky III, *Ibid*.
23. COL (Ret) Karl H. Lowe, *America's Foreign Legion: The 31st Infantry Regiment at War and Peace* (A book in progress), 31st Infantry Website, Chapter 15.
24. SP4 M. Torres-Charon, "1/31st takes 1/5th title at ceremony" *Indianhead,* May 22, 1987.
25. SPC Tim Herfendal, "Infantrymen Test 'MACE' Team's

Notes

   Skills," *Indianhead*, June, 1988.
26. COL David Hunt, E-mail correspondence, September 2008.

27. SPC M. Adams, "2ID Deploys for Winter Haze" *Indianhead*. January 20, 1989.
28. SPC Peter Bliley, "U.S. Representatives tour DMZ Guardpost" *Indianhead*, /September 8, 1989.
29. SPC Wayne Hall, "VP Quayle Visits DMZ During 11-day Asian Tour, *Indianhead*, October 6, 1989.
30. COL Dan Baggio, Director of Public Affairs, Fort McNair PAO, E-mail correspondence, September 2008.
31. MG Richard Rowe (CO of 1/5, July 1992-July 1994) E-mail correspondence, September 2008.
32. COL David Hunt (CO of 1/5, 1988-1990) E-mail correspondence, September 2007.
33. PVT John Paramore, "1st Bn, 5th Infantry first to fire MPRC" *Indianhead*, November 2, 1991.
34. MG Richard Rowe, *Ibid*.
35. MG Richard Rowe, *Ibid*.
36. "Pope Assumes Controls of 1/5 In." *Indianhead*, July 21, 1994.
37. "Infantry Units Reflagged as Manchu Regiment Returns" *Indianhead*. September 13, 1995.
38. SPC Larry Lang, "Clinton Thanks U.S. Troops in Central America Relief Effort" *American Forces Press Service*, March 11, 1999.
39. LTC James E. Harris III, "To Fight Digitized or Analog" *Military Review*. November/December 1999. pp. 12-17.
40. McKeeby, David, "Sinai Peacekeepers are the Quiet Success of camp david accords," *America.gov*, December 19, 2007.
41. Niles, Daryl, CSM Ret., E-mail correspondence with author, March 2010.

XVI. The Global War on Terrorism

1. Bluhm, *U.S. Army: A Complete History*, p. 925.
2. Gregg Kakesako, "Deployment for 25th likened to Vietnam" *Honolulu Star-Bulletin Hawaii News*. November 9, 2003.
3. LTC Terry Sellers, "Memorandum for Bobcat Families" July 13, 2004. pp. 1-2.

4. Sellers, *op cit,* p. 2.
5. SGT Frank Magni, "Soldiers Stay Ready in Afghanistan", *Defend America.* September 24, 2004.
6. Kristin Fitzsimmons, "Military Hero," *Hawaii Army Weekly,* March 11, 2005.
7. Sharee Moore, "After the Firefight Ended" *Hawaii Army Weekly,* March 11, 2005.
8. "Two Schofield Barracks Soldiers Killed in Afghanistan" 25th ID Media Release, October 22, 2004.
9. Battle Base, *Bobcat's Newsletter,* November 2004.
10. Viper Base, *Bobcat's Newsletter,* December 2004.
11. Katie Worth, "Sniper Shares Experiences in Afghanistan" *Pacific Daily News* (Guam), December 27, 2004.
12. Mary Vorsino, "Army Marathoners Race through a Danger Zone" *Honolulu Star-Bulletin,* December 13, 2004.
13. Task Force Bobcat, *Bobcat's Newsletter,* March 2005.
14. Task Force Bobcat, *Bobcat's Newsletter,* April 2005.
15. SPC Claudia Bullard, "U.S. Forces Aid Afghan Flood Victims" *American Forces Press Service,* March 25, 2005.
16. SPC Leslie Alberts, "Bobcats Bid Goodnight as Night Raiders Mount Up" *Hawaii Army Weekly,* November 10, 2005.
17. LTC Todd McCaffrey, *The Bobcat Bulletin,* Fall 2004.
18. HQS, 1/5, *Unit History, 1st Battalion, 5th Infantry Regiment, TF Bobcat,* 15 Sept 2004 – 30 Nov 2004. p. 1.
19. HQS, 1/5, *Unit History, op cit,* p. 6.
20. C. Mark Brinkley, Army Times, "Soldiers Dodge Car Bomb to Deliver Dinner, *USA Today,* November 25, 2004.
21. Scott Wilson, "Fear Hamstrings Quest for Intelligence in N. Iraq" *Washington Post,* December 11, 2004.
22. Alex Kingsbury, "E-mails Reveal a Fallen Soldier's Story" *U.S. News and World Report,* May 13, 2007.
23. Bill Nemitz, "Carnage in Mosul" *Maine Press Herald,* December 22, 2004 and *Unit History, op cit,* 1 December – 31 December, 2004. p. 7.
24. Darrell Griffin, Sr. and Darrell "Skip" Griffin, Jr., *Last Journey: A Father and Son in Wartime,* New York: Atlas & Company, 2009. pp. 133-134.
25. A. Scott Ferguson and Dan Kaplan, "Neptune Soldier Killed

in Iraq" *Asbury Park Press,* February 4, 2005.
26. Daniel Thigpen, "Fort Lewis Soldier Dies in Mosul Attack" *Tacoma News Tribune,* April 5, 2005.
27. HQS, 1/5, *Unit History, 1-30 April, 2005.* p. 8.
28. Michael Gilbert, "Bomb Kills Four Stryker Soldiers" *Tacoma News Tribune,* May 3, 2005.
29. HQS, 1/5, *Unit History, 1-30 June, 2005.* p. 4.
30. Ellen Knickmeyer, "Iraqi Chemical Stash Uncovered" *Washington Post,* August 14, 2005.
31. Don Kramer, "Two Historic Units Reflag During Ceremony" *Northwest Guardian,* June 1, 2006 and
David Rising, "Fort Lewis Strykers Arrive in Germany, *Army Times,* July 28, 2006.
32. LTC Shawn Reed, E-mail correspondence and TO&E attachments, October 2007.
33. Public Affairs Office, USARAK, "U.S., Philippine Forces Kick Off Balikatan with a Bang" *Alaska e-Post Online,* February 29, 2008.
34. Army Public Affairs, "Army Prepares for Fall 2008 Active-duty Rotations in Iraq" *Global Security.org,* May 19, 2008.
35. COL Burdett Thompson (CDR, 1/25 SBCT) "Diyala Province, Iraq: FOB Warhorse" (Letter to friends and families of the Arctic Wolves, October 30, 2008)
36. COL Thompson, Briefing delivered to 25th Infantry Division Assn. reunion, Fairbanks, AK, September 19, 2009.
37. "East Texas Soldier Killed in Iraq" *Associated Press – Texas News,* October 21, 2008.
38. Mike Francis, "The Death of Cody Eggleston" *The Oregonian,* October 29, 2008.
39. SPC Anthony Jones, "Dagger/1-5 Reunites with Arctic Wolves Brigade" *Alaska Post,* August 7, 2009.
40. LTC H. Clint Kirk IV, Letter to *The Bobcat Bulletin,* Fall, 2009.

SELECT BIBLIOGRAPHY

Archives and Manuscript Collections
1. Camp Red Cloud, Korea. 2nd Infantry Division Museum
2. Carlisle, PA. United States Army Military History Institute
3. College Park, MD. National Archives and Records Admin.
4. Schofield Barracks, HI. 25th Infantry Division Museum
5. Washington, D.C. U.S. Army Center of Military History

Dissertations and Theses
Warhank, Joseph J., *Fort Keogh: Cutting Edge of a Culture*. M.A. Thesis, CSU Long Beach, December, 1983.

Journals, Magazines and Pamphlets
1. *The First Battalion (Mechanized) Fifth Infantry, 25th Division in the Vietnam War, 1966-71*.
2. First Battle Group, 5th Infantry Regiment, *History of the Fifth United States Infantry*, Ft. Riley, KS. June, 1962.
3. *The Magazine of Western History*
4. *Military Review*
5. *On Point: Journal of Army History*
6. *Unit History: 1st Battalion, 5th Infantry Regiment*, TF Bobcat, 15 Sept 2004 – 31 Aug 2005.

Newspapers and Newsletters
1. *Alaska Post*
2. *American Forces Press Service*
3. *Army Times*
4. *Asbury Park Press*
5. *Associated Press – Texas News*
6. *Battle Stars – 5th RCT Assn.*
7. *The Bobcat Bulletin – 5th Inf Regt Assn.*
8. *Bobcat's Newsletter – 2nd Bn, 5th Infantry*
9. *Central Military Sun Press*
10. *Defend America*
11. *Hawaii Army Weekly*

Select Bibliography

12. *Honolulu Star-Bulletin*
13. *Indianhead – 2nd Infantry Division*
14. *New York Times*
15. *New York World*
16. *Northwest Guardian – Ft. Lewis*
17. *The Oregonian*
18. *Pacific Stars and Stripes*
19. *Paw Prints – 1st Bn, 5th Infantry*
20. *Red Circle News – 71st Infantry Division*
21. *Tacoma News Tribune*
22. *Tropic Lightning News – 25th Infantry Division*
23. *USA Today*
24. *U.S. News and World Report*
25. *Washington Post*

Books

1. Appleman, LTC Roy E., *South to the Naktong, North to the Yalu*. Washington, D.C: Office of the Chief of Military History, DOA, 1961.
2. Baldwin, Alice B., *An Army Wife on the Frontier*. Salt Lake City: University of Utah, 1975.
3. Beal, Merrill D., *I Will Fight No More Forever: Chief Joseph and the Nez Perce War*. Seattle: University of Washington Press, 1963.
4. Berebitsky, William, *A Very Long Weekend: The Army National Guard in Korea, 1950-1953*. Shippensburg, PA: White Mane Publishing Company, 1996.
5. Black, Robert W., *Rangers in Korea*. New York: Ballantine Books, 1989.
6. Blair, Clay, *The Forgotten War: America in Korea, 1950-53*. New York: Time Books, 1987.
7. Bluhm, COL Raymond K. (Ed) *U.S. Army: A Complete History*. Arlington, VA: The Army Historical Association, 2005.
8. Clinger, Fred and Arthur Johnson, *The History of the 71st Infantry Division*. Augsburg, Germany: 71st ID Public Relations Office, 1946.
9. Dorr, Robert F. *Alpha Bravo Delta Guide to the U.S. Army*.

New York: Alpha Books, 2003
10. Eisenhower, John S.D. *So Far From God: The U.S. War with Mexico, 1846-48*. New York: Random House, 1989.
11. Evans, James, *A Morning in June: Defending Outpost Harry*. University of Alabama Press, 2110.
12. Greene, Jerome, *Indian War Veterans: Memories of Life and Campaigns in the West, 1864-1898*. New York: Savas Beattie LLC, 2007.
13. Griffin, Darrell, Sr. and Darrell "Skip" Griffin, Jr., *Last Journey: A Father and Son in Wartime*. New York: Atlas & Company, 2009.
14. Gugeler, Russell A., *Combat Actions in Korea*. Center for Military History Publication 30-2, 1954.
15. Hand, George, *The Civil War in Apacheland*. Silver City, New Mexico: High-Lonesome Books, 1996.
16. Hansen, Marcus L., *Old Fort Snelling: 1819-1858*. Cedar Rapids, IA: The Torch Press, 1918.
17. Hayes, Roger, *On Point: A Rifleman's Year in the Boonies, 1967-68*. New York: St. Martin's Press, 2000.
18. Heidler, David S. and Jeanne T. Heidler (Eds) *Encyclopedia of the War of 1812*. Annapolis, MD: Naval Institute Press, 1997.
19. Heitman, Francis B., *Historical Register and Dictionary of the United States Army from Its Organization, September 29, 1789 to March 2, 1903*. Washington: Government Printing Office, 1903.
20. Hogan, Michael, *The Irish Soldiers of Mexico*. Guadalajara: Fondo Editorial Universitario, 1997.
21. Josephy, Alvin Jr., *The Civil War in the American West*. New York: Alfred A. Knopf, 1991.
22. Joy, Dean P., *Sixty Days in Combat: An Infantryman's Memoir of World War II in Europe*. New York: Random House, 2004.
23. Knox, Donald, *The Korean War: Uncertain Victory*. New York: Harcourt Brace, 1988.
24. Lengel, Edward G., *To Conquer Hell: The Meuse-Argonne, 1918*. New York: Henry Holt & Co, 2008.
25. Lowe, COL Karl H., *America's Foreign Legion: The 31st Infantry Regiment at War and Peace*. (A book in progress)

Select Bibliography

      31st Infantry Website, Chapter 15.
26. MacArthur, GEN Douglas, *Reminiscences*. New York: McGraw-Hill, 1964.
27. McManus, John C., *The 7th Infantry Regiment: Combat in an Age of Terror*. New York: Tom Doherty Associates, 2008.
28. Murphy, Edward F., *Korean War Heroes*. Novato, CA: Presidio Press, 1992.
29. Pruitt, Frank O., *Delayed Letters from Korea*. 1st Books Library, 2002.
30. Ramsey, Robert D., *Savage Wars of Peace: Case Studies of Pacification in the Philippines, 1900-1902*. Ft. Leavenworth, KS: Combat Studies Institute Press, 2007.
31. Ridgeway, Matthew B., *The Korean War*. New York: Doubleday & Co. Inc, 1967.
32. Schnabel, James F., *U.S. Army in the Korean War: Policy and Direction: The First Year*. Washington, D.C: Office of the Chief of Military History, DOA, 1971.
33. Slater, Michael, *Hills of Sacrifice: The 5th RCT in Korea*. Paducah, KY: Turner Publishing Company, 2000.
34. Summers, Harry G., Jr., *The Vietnam War Almanac*. New York: Ballantine Books, 1985.
35. Wilson, Arthur and Norman Strickbine (eds) *Faces of War: Korean Vignettes*. Portland, OR: Artwork Publications, 1996.
36. Wooster, Robert, *Nelson A. Miles and the Twilight of the Frontier Army*. Lincoln: University of Nebraska Press, 1993.
37. Zebrowski, Edward, *My Brother, Hail and Farewell*. Tampa, FL: Woodstock Books, 1994.

Index of Persons

Abarr, James, 465
Abercrombie, John, 55-6
Abizaid, John, 403
Abrams, Creighton Jr., 348, 355, 393
Acosta-Rosario, Humberto, 353
Adams, H.H., 125, 445
Adams, M., 478
Adams, Z. Boylston, 464
Adler, Bill xxvi, 357, 476
Aguinaldo, Emilio, 120
Akers, Colonel, 286
Alberts, Leslie, 479
Alexander, Thomas L., 71
Alfred, Lee, 266, 271-2, 276, 278
Amos, Albert, 333
Ampudia, Pedro, 35-6, 39-40
Anaya, Pedro, 57
Anderson, Andrew H., 347, 355, 446
Anderson, Horace, 224
Appleman, Roy, 189, 470, 482
Archer, Captain, 70
Arista, Mariano, 36-8
Armstrong, John, 10, 17
Aspinwall, Thomas, 12
Athanason, Frank, 234, 237
Atkins, Leonard, 279
Atkinson, Henry, 31
Aurand, Henry, 177
Bachl, Chris, 426
Back, John, 195-6
Baggio, Dan, vii, 393, 478
Bailey, Lynn, 475
Baird, George, 117
Baker, Ron, 369-70, 476

Baldwin, Alice B., 100, 467, 482
Baldwin, Frank D., xv, 75-9, 86-92, 97-8, 109, 119, 124, 137, 448
Baltzell, G. F., 122
Bamford, Lieutenant, 118
Bankhead, Brevet LTC, 74
Barker, Luther, 93, 98
Barnett, Dan, 437, 447
Barron, James, 3
Barth, George, 191
Bascom, George, 61, 71
Baskin, Mike, 406
Baun, Richard, 475
Beacham, Joseph W., 131, 138, 445
Beal, Merrill, 467
Beattie, Mark, 378
Beauchamp, Keith, 477
Beckum, Jesse, 152, 161
Beirne, Randall, 199-200
Belknap, William G, 52-53, 56
Bell, J. Franklin, 123
Bennett, Andrew S., 80, 88, 108, 467
Bennett, Lucius, 131, 445
Benton, Joseph, 317
Berebitsky, William, 472
Bernardo, Peter, 359
Bernhardt, Eugene, 383-5, 447
Bernotas, John, 225, 471
Bethke, Jerry, 310, 473
Beum Foo Yun, 176
Biddle, Jonathan, 106
Big Crow, 94, 96-7
Bigelow, William, 142
Big Foot, 115

• 486 •

Index of Persons

Big Horse, 93
Bissell, Daniel, 18, 444
Bissonette, Donald, 318
Black, Robert W., 471
Black Hawk, 30-31
Black Horse, 79
Bliley, Peter, 478
Bluhm, Raymond K, 463
Bolte, Charles, 177
Borden, George P., 81, 123, 127
Bostock, James, 329
Bowen, William C. H., 123, 445
Bowling, George, 342
Bowyer, John, 17-18, 20, 444
Bradbury, William, 287, 293-4
Bradley, John, 119
Brady, Joseph, 329
Brannon, Charles, 227
Bravo, Nicolas, 50
Brinkley, C. Mark, 479
Bristol, Henry, 70-1
Brock, Bobby, 366
Bronson, Byron, 97
Brooke, George M., 4, 12, 16, 30, 33, 444, 463
Brotherton, David, 65
Brown, Jacob, 13-16, 18
Brughiere, John, 90, 110
Buffalo Horn, 108
Buffalo Hump, 59
Bullard, Claudia, 479
Bumgarner, James S., 230, 332, 471
Burnham, Captain, 122
Burns, Danny, 97
Burtt, Wilson B., 131,445
Bush, George H. W., 387
Butler, Edmund, 97- 99
Butterfield, Daniel, 71, 444

Cadwalader, George, 45
Caen, Corporal, 202
Cahill, Luke, 72
Canby, Edward, 60, 63-7, 69-70
Capron, Allyn, 117
Carleton, James, 69-70
Carroll, Charles, 207
Carson, Kit, 64-5
Carter, Charles, 116
Carter, Mason, 81, 94
Casey, James, 94, 96, 98
Cass, Lewis, 27
Casto, Virgil, 152, 459
Castro, Joseph, 385
Chaffee, Adna, 76, 123
Chandler, John, 9
Chang, Albert, 384
Chapman, William, 49, 53
Chatelain, Ron, 366
Chaves, Manuel, 68
Ching, Arnold, 199
Chivington, John, 67-69
Churchill, Sir Winston, 18
Cisneros, Roberto, 338
Clark, Charlotte Ouisconsin, 24
Clark, Nathan, 24
Clary, R.E., 33
Clay, Henry, 34
Clayman, Stuart, 306, 473
Clinger, Fred, 469, 482
Close, George F., 386, 388, 447
Cochise, 61, 66
Cole, Robert, 287
Collins, Horace, 314
Collins, J. Lawton, 176, 190, 226
Collins, James, 303
Collins, John, 335,
Comba, Richard, 121, 145
Combs, Oliver, 374

Cook, Arthur, 349, 351-52
Cooper, Norman, 186
Copas, Ardie Ray, 373
Correa-Morales, Francisco, 321
Correia, Bill, 476
Council, Darrel, 231
Cowles, Calvin Duvall, 127-129, 468
Crawford, William H., 22
Crazy Horse, 83, 92-95, 97, 102, 467
Crockett, Ed, 235-6, 238, 241
Crook, George, 83, 112
Cross, Harold, 298, 300
Crowlie, Lieutenant, 245
Custer, George, 83-84, 102, 112
Cutrer, Thomas W., 463
Daly, John, 180, 188, 191
Davis, Charles Lukens, 123, 125, 468
Davis, Leroy, 371
Davis, William D., 141
Davison, Lorenzo, 122
Dearborn, Henry, 4, 8, and 9
De Fede, John, 387
De la Vega, Romolo Diaz, 48
DeLorenzo, Philip, 353
DeArmond, William, 77, 459
Delisle, Frederick, 369
Dent, Frederick, 47
Deverse, Fred, vii, 409,
Diaz, Victor, 325, 329, 446
Dibb, Dennis, 476
Dixon, Private, 29
Doane, Stephen   361-2, 449
Dodd, Carl, 183, 222-23, 388
Doo-hwan, Chun, 391
Dorr, Robert F., 464
Drummond, Gordon, 14-15

Ducote, Richard, 402
Duncan, Joe, 332
Duncan, Thomas, 65
Edens, Will, 430
Eggleston, Cody, 442
Eichenberger, Richard, 171-172
Eisenhower, Dwight, 138, 148, 309, 464
Elizalde, Enrique, 404
Emerson, Hank, 194-195, 211, 216
Emmerson, John, 32
Evans, James, 286-294, 472-473
Ewers, Ezra, 94-95, 111
Falabella, Robert, 336
Falk, Charles, 216
Fay, Walter, 237
Ferguson, Michael, 381
Ferguson, Scott, 479
Fernandez, Daniel, 317
Fernandez, Kyle, 402
Fernandez, Michael, 381
Fernandez, Virgil, 378, 446
Fischer, Harvey, 278, 284, 299
Fitzsimmons, Kristin, 478
Fleischer, Jacob, 403
Fleming, Private, 122
Ford, Louis P., 140
Forsyth, Thomas, 24
Forsythe, G. A., 73
Forsythe, Tom, 326-327, 474
Fortney, Kendall, 342
Four Legs, 24
Fowle, John, 27
Fracker, Dale, 403
Francis, Mike, 480
Franks, Tommy, 394, 398
Fredriksen, John C., 463
Freeman, Edmund, 57

Index of Persons

Freeman, Paul, 216
Frost, Malcolm, 408, 447
Fry, Edgar A., 133
Gaebler, Fritz, 138
Galas, Bob, xxv
Gallo, Joseph, 292, 294
Garner, James, 230, 332, 471
Gatewood, Charles, 112-113
Gatlin, Richard, 62
Gayhart, Leslie P., 179
Giacobbe, Wadie, 139
Gibbs, Barnett, 407
Gibson, Aubrey, 187
Gibson, George, 74, 114, 444
Gilbert, Michael, 479
Goodnow, Chandler, 332
Gordon, Sergeant, 417
Gracie, Archibald, 62
Grant, Ulysses S., 47
Gray, Thomas, 98
Green, Tom, 64
Greene, Jerome, 466-467, 483
Greer, Allen, 134
Greer, Thomas U., 312-313, 315-316
Grey Beard, 78
Griffin, Darrell Jr., 416, 420-21, 479
Griffin, Darrell Sr., 479
Gugeler, Russell A, 472
Gulbraa, David, 292, 294
Haddoo, John, 104
Hadzima, Larry, 474-475
Haines, John, 342-343
Hale, Owen, 104, 106
Hale, Richard, 328
Haley, James, 163
Hall, Arlie, 294
Hall, Wayne, 478

Halloway, James, 380, 382, 476
Hampton, Wade, 3, 10-11
Hand, George, 465
Handrich, Melvin O., 193-4, 388, 450
Hansel, Morgan, 213
Hansen, Marcus, 463
Hanson, Thomas E., 463
Hardy, Sir Thomas, 16
Hargous, Charles, 95
Harris, James III, 395, 447-48
Harrison, William H., 5
Hartzog, William, 378
Harvey, Sam, 471
Hathaway, F. H., 81
Hay, Fred S., 77
Hayes, Roger, 337, 339, 346, 475
Hays, Ronald J., 387
Heath, Leslie R., 238, 472
Heckmeyer, Benjamin, 185, 199
Hedberg, William, 207
Heflin, Kirk, 473
Heidler, David S., 463
Heintzelman, Charles, 99-100
Heitman, Francis, 71, 464-466, 468, 483
Henderson, John, 242
Herbert, Jim, 438
Herfendal, Tim, 477
Hernandes, Colonel, 124
Higgins, George, 393, 447
Hight, Robert, 246-248
Hill, Robert, 62
Hobbs, Brian, 402
Hodge, Roy, 362-364
Hodson, Fremont, 335
Hogan, Henry, 117
Hogan, Michael, 464

Hoge, William, 241
Hohman, Alfred, 318
Holloway, James (Hawk), 380, 382, 476
Holmes, Rick, 391
Hook, Ralph, 335
Hope, Bob, 357-358
Hoos, William, 316
Howard, Oliver, 105-108
Hula, Frank, 199-200
Hull, William, 6-7
Hunsley, Dennis, 357, 360
Hunt, Charles A., 131, 140, 141, 445
Hunt, T. F., 31
Hunt, David W., xxix, 391-92, 447, 477-78
Huston, Daniel, 113, 444
Hyun, Dong Won, 298-299
Ilges, Guido, 110
Isaacs, John, 321
Isbell, David, 341
Izard, George, 17-19
Jackson, Clarence, 180
Jackson, Harold L., 445
Jackson, John W., 446
Jackson, Kermit, 202
James, Edwin, 468
James, John, 77
Jarvis, Eric, 463
Jeal, John, 208
Jefferson, Thomas, 3-4
Jenkins, Lloyd, 139
Jerome, Lovell, 106
Johnson, Arthur, 469, 482
Johnson, Evan, 131, 445, 474
Johnson, Gary, vii
Johnson, James, LT, 206-7
Johnson, James, SPC, 335
Johnson, Keneth, 310, 446
Johnson, Lyndon, 314, 325, 348, 355, 358
Johnston, Albert Sydney, 58
Johnston, Edward, 460
Jones, Anthony, 480
Jones, John, 185, 188
Jones, Omar, 416
Joseph, Chief, 103, 105-108, 117, 467, 482
Josephy, Alvin Jr., 465
Joy, Dean, 145, 152, 155-56, 169, 469
Kahaihipuna, Jake, 213
Kahapea, Alexander, 185
Kakesako, Gregg, 478
Kasper, William, 284
Kawamura, James, 183
Kealoha, Samuel, 223
Kean, William B., 183-185, 187, 189, 191-192
Keefe, John, 463
Kellogg, William, 117
Kelly, John, 77
Kelly, Luther (Yellowstone), 94
Kelly, Thomas, 77
Kennelly, Barbara, 392
Kenny, Kristie, 440
Keogh, Myles W., 101
Ker, Croghan, 36
Khalif, Mayor, 418, 429
Khan, Jan Mohamed, 407, 416
Khan, Rozi, 406
Kicklighter, Claude, 387
Kicking Bear, 115
Kingsbury, Alex, 479
Kirk, Howard C., 443, 480
Kisik, Al, 418
Kissell, Leo T., 469

Index of Persons

Klein, William, 355, 365
Knickmeyer, Ellen, 480
Knight, Harry E., 135
Knowles, W. P. 299
Knox, Donald, 472
Knox, Henry, ix
Knox, John A., 77
Koeplin, William, 77
Koonce, Charles, 269
Kramer, Don, 480
Kravitz, Leonard, 225
Krone, Charles, 224
Kruger, Kenneth W., 381, 477
Krumrine, John, 150
Kumzig, Colonel, 241
Kurek, Robert, 365, 369
Laden, Osama bin, 398
Lambert, Geoff, 378
Lame Deer, 102
Landero, J. J., 43
Lang, Larry, 478
Lang, Mainor, 349-51
Laubacher, Ralph, 370, 476
Lawrence, William, 30, 444
Lazzarotto, Albert, 354
Lear, Clinton, 56
Leavenworth, Henry, 22-26, 444
Lechuga, Martin, 363-64, 476
Lengel, Edward G., 468
Leota, Frank, 379
Levandowski, Lawrence, 150
Lewis, Granville, 77
Liggett, Hunter, xvii, 109, 116-17, 131-34, 142-43, 158, 467-68
Little Assiniboine, 90
Livingston, Robert, 392
Loback, Thomas, 341
Lodge, Thomas, 339
Long, Oscar, xxx, 117
Looking Glass, 106
Loomis, Gustavus, 55, 71, 444
Lopez, Henry, 329
Love, Joe, 265-266
Lowe, Karl H., 477
Lucas, Harry, 269
Lugenbeel, Pickney, 444
Lukitsch, Arnold, 199-200, 216
Luykx, Kirk, xxii
Lyman, Wyllys, 77
Lyons, Eugene R., 122
MacArthur, Arthur, 121
MacArthur, Douglas, 121, 177, 208-211, 214-15, 218-219, 227, 471
MacDonald, Joey, 385
Macdonough, Thomas, 17-18
Mace, James E., 378
Machinski, Daniel, 249, 472
Mackenzie, Ranald, 78
Macomb, Alexander, 17, 22
Madison, James, 17, 22
Magni, Frank, 478
Malich, Nick, 435
Mangan, Michael, 350, 353
Manley, Hibbert, 213
Marcan, Frank, 264
Marcy, Randolph, 54, 58, 62, 465
Marshall, George C., 132
Martin, W. F., 122
Maudie, Bert, 279-80
Maus, Marion, 104
Mauz, Henry, 241
Mawhinney, William Jr., 473
McCaffrey, Todd, 395, 409, 411-15, 418, 421, 425, 434, 437, 447, 479

McCann, Bernard, 98
McClellan, George B., 56
McClernand, Edward, 104
McClure, Gene, 213, 470
McCraine, William, 199-200, 202
McDonald, Robert, 96-99
McDowell, Winchester, 129
McGinnis, Ross A., 466
McInnes, Thomas, 336
McIntosh, James S., 33-34, 38, 51, 444
McKinley, William, 118-120
McManus, John C., 476
McMillan, Thomas, 364, 367
McMullen, Alexander, 14
McNamara, Robert, 326
Medicine Bear, 91, 94-96
Medina, Ignacio, 338, 369
Melo, Julian, 429
Mercado, Vic, 409
Merrill, Moses, 53
Merritt, Wesley, 120
Miles, Dixon, 51-52
Miles, Mary Hoyt Sherman, 74
Miles, Nelson A., xv, 74-79, 81, 83, 86-87, 89-92, 94, 99, 102-103, 105-106, 109-110, 112-115, 120-121, 125-126, 136-137, 444, 451, 466-467, 484
Miller, Earl, 196
Miller, James, 6-7, 14, 16, 20, 23, 54, 394, 444
Miller, John, 21
Miller, S. W., 109
Miner, Charles, 85
Mitchell, John, 1st/SGT, 77
Mitchell, John, LTC, 393

Moncrief, Corporal, 132
Monson, Phillipp, 376
Moore, Patrick, 375
Moore, Sharee, 478
Morales, Juan, 43
Moreno, Francisco, 40
Morris, Eric, 430
Morrison, W. B., 465
Morrissey, Jim, 473
Morton, Charles, 129-130
Muhammed, Khalif Kadir, 418
Muir, Malcolm, 463
Mulholland, John F., 378
Munoz, Guillermo, 332
Murphy, Edward F., 470-471
Murphy, Henry, 335
Murray, James, 278
Murray, Robert, 430
Murtha, John P., xxix, 392
Myers, Christopher, 19
Naylor, Edward, 387
Neal, Herbert, 168
Nemitz, Bill, 479
Newbold, Charles, 71
Niles, Daryl, 478
Nixon, John, 456
Nixon, Richard, 358, 362, 371-72, 376
Noneman, Robert, 225
Noonan, Patrick, 80
Nowlan, H. J., 102
O'Brien, Lieutenant, 116-118
O'Brien, James, PVT, 122
O'Brien, Pat, 143
Okamura, Arthur, 251
Oliver, Lieutenant, 25
O'Malley, Dominick, 100
Onerheim, Luther, 171
Ordway, Godwin Jr., 176, 183-5,

Index of Persons

187-8, 191
Oregon, Dennet, 407
Osborn, Jerry W., 314
Osborn, Nathan, 115-117
Otis, Elwell, 84-85, 121
Otterstrom, Rawland, 250
Ovenshine, Samuel, 81
Owens, Johnny, 328
Palmer, LTG, 267
Paramore, John, 478
Parker, Alexander, 4, 444
Patch, Alexander, 149
Patton, George, 155, 157
Paul, Gabriel, 77
Paul, James, 374
Pearson, Irving, xxiii
Pearson, Jeffrey V., 467
Peers, W. R., 308, 446
Pelfrey, Floyd, 249
Pershing, John, 131-32
Person, Tom 384, 477
Pickard, Heath, 442
Pierce, Franklin, 45
Pilkington, Andrew, 16
Pillow, Gideon, 45
Pike, Zebulon, 8
Pinkney, Ninian, 19
Pletcher, J. D., 166, 469
Plympton, Joseph, 31
Poinciano, Benjamin, 198
Polk, James K., 34-35, 41, 52
Poor Buffalo, 77
Pope, James W., 88, 95
Pope, John, 76
Pope, Phil, 394
Porter, John, 294
Prevost, George, 17-18
Priester, Willis, 152, 162
Pruitt, Frank O., 472
Purcell, Edward, 25
Putnam, MAJ Purley, 16
Pyron, Charles, 68
Quayle, Dan, 392
Quitman, Augustus, 456
Quitman, John A., 45
Rains, Gabriel, 62
Ramsey, Charles, 366
Ramsey, Robert D., 468, 484
Randall, William, 153-54
Rathman, August, 98
Reagan, Ronald, 380
Red Bird, 27-29
Rehbease, Otto, 126
Reynolds, John F., 70
Rhee, Syngman, 173
Riall, Phineas, 12-14
Rich, Lucius, 62
Riddle, James, 227
Ridgeway, Matthew, 176, 219-220, 223-4, 226-7
Riley, John, 47-48
Ripley, Eleazar, 12, 14-15
Roberts, Benjamin, 64
Roberts, Thomas, 354
Roberts, Dr. William, 51
Robinson, Charles M. III, 466
Rockholt, Ricky, 430
Roelofs, Thomas B., 188
Rogers, Richard, 329, 332
Rogers, Milburn, 150
Roh Tae-woo, 391
Rolf, Gerald, 323
Rolfe, Onslan, 172, 445
Roman Nose, 73
Romeyn, Henry, 106-107, 117-119, 450, 452, 467
Roosevelt, Franklin D., 157
Roosevelt, Theodore, 124, 127

Rosa, Robert J., 306, 446
Rosenthal, PFC, 417
Rosner, Elliott, 395, 447
Ross, John, 291
Rothlisberger, Charles, 383, 447
Rounds, Michael, 395, 447
Rowe, Richard, 393, 447, 478
Ruffner, David, 281
Ruggles, Daniel, 62
Rumsfeld, Donald, 397
Sage, William H., 133
Salyers, Jack, xxii, 304, 473
Santa Anna, Antonio, 42, 46
Savedra, Edmund, 415
Schmidt, Graham E., 308, 446
Schnabel, James F., 470
Scott, Dred, 32
Scott, Martin, 39-40, 47-49
Scott, Winfield, 12-17, 27, 41-44, 50-51
Seelinger, Matthew, 477
Selden, Henry, 65, 70
Sellers, Terry, 400, 407-408, 447, 478
Shakara, Emir, 432
Shambow, Louis, 104
Sheaff, Roger, 18
Shearin, Dan, 316
Sherbrooke, John, 16
Sheridan, Philip, 75
Sheridan, Major, 370
Sherman, Stephen, 423
Sherman, William T., 74-75, 85, 99
Shinault, Clyde, 288-289
Short, John, 407
Sibley, Henry H., 63, 66, 69
Simpson, COL James, 175-176
Simpson, LT James H., 64

Sitting Bull, 83, 85-87, 90-92, 103, 105, 108-111, 115
Sitz, Donald, 151, 154, 156-7, 167, 469
Slater, Michael, 462, 470-473
Sloan, Andrew, 402
Slough, John P., 67
Smith, Billy, 471
Smith, Bobby, 198
Smith, Harold B., 461
Smith, James C., 457
Smith, James G., 457
Smith, J. P., 457
Smith, Persifor F., 34
Snelling, Josiah, 5, 7, 23, 26-27, 29-30, 444
Snodgrass, John, 349-350
Snyder, Simon, 86, 104
Sommer, Hugh, 229
Soppe, Ronald, 354
Sorenson, Allin, 470
Sparhawk, Don, 474
Spence, Robert, 133, 445
Spragins, Robert L., 142
Stalin, Joseph, 173
Staniford, Thomas, 38
Starkey, Jack, 182
Sternberg, Ben, 301, 446
Stevenson, Carter, 57, 62
Stevenson, Clarence, 149
Stine, Joe, 301, 473
Strickbine, Norman, 470, 484
Strickland, E. H., 301, 446
Strong, Gordon, 183
Stuart, Clarence, 191, 237
Stumon, Lon, 122
Sturgis, Samuel, 105
Summers, Harry G., 472, 474-76, 484

Index of Persons

Sung, Kim Il, 173, 389
Surles, Alexander D., 249, 253-54, 259, 264, 266, 395, 446
Szekely, Akos, 354
Tarpley, Thomas, 312, 446
Tava'e, Ioasa, 439
Taylor, Maxwell, 281
Taylor, Zachary, 4, 34, 42, 133
Tecumseh, 3-7
Teel, Marvin, 307
Terry, Alfred, 83
Tesillo, Armando, 316
Thigpen, Daniel, 479
Thomas, Bryan, 62
Thomas, Lewis, 320
Thompson, Burdett, 480
Thornton, Seth B., 36
Throckmorton, John, xx, 182, 184-5, 188, 191-2, 198, 204-206, 209-210, 212, 217, 221, 226
Thurston, Sid, 468
Tilton, Henry, 107
Tolen, Del, 287-88, 291-2
Tosques, Nick, 234, 238
Townsend, James, 466
Truman, Harry S., 158
Tung, Mao Tze, 239
Tuxford, Lieutenant, 159
Twain, Mark, 125-126, 468
Twiggs, David E., 45, 63
Tyree, Barry, 396, 447
Valvo, Frank, 183
Van Antwerp, Frank, 200
Van Day, Ngyuen, 334
Van Dorn, Earl, 59
Van Fleet, James, 227, 231
Van Horne, Thomas, 6
Van Kommen, Darren, 429
Van Vliet, Stewart, 81
Vandervoort, William, 189
Varner, Stanley, 443
Veenstra, Albert, 186
Villamor, Juan, 123
Villaseñor, Gonzalo
Vincent, John, 9
Von Plinsky, Alexander III, 386-7, 477
Von Rendulic, Lothar, 168-69
Vorsino, Mary, 479
Wahl, Lutz, 116
Walker, Walton, 181-2, 185, 187, 189, 195, 214, 218
Ward, Albert, xx, 191, 223, 226, 236-7
Ward, Richard, 338
Ward, Tom, 476
Warhank, Josef J., 466-467, 481
Warner, Leonard K., 229
Warner, Private, 122
Washington, George, ix, x
Watson, Clarence, 307
Watson, Samuel E., 55
Watson, Vance A., 472
Wayne, Anthony, x
Weeks, N. G., 43
Weld, Lewis, 66
Wellington, Duke of, 16, 19
West, Horace, 230, 236-7
Westerman, Ted, 370
Westmoreland, William C., 314
Wheeler, Lester, 284, 289-90, 300-301
Whistler, Captain, 23
Whistler, Joseph N. G., 83-4, 110, 113, 444
White, Lieutenant General, 281
Wickman, Lance, 312, 474

Wilcox, Captain, 37
Wilkins, John D., 113-114, 444
Wilkinson, James, 4
Williams, Lieutenant, 122
Williams, Ralph, 340-41
Wilson, Arthur H. (Harry), 226, 228-230, 232, 236-37, 239, 241, 245-46, 446
Wilson, Carvin, 269
Wilson, Charles, 452
Wilson, Samuel, 458
Wilson, Scott, 479
Wilson, Vennard, 191
Wilson, Woodrow, 113
Winder, William, 9, 21
Wingate, Benjamin, 70
Witham, Keith, 195
Wood, C. E., 106
Wooden Leg, 96
Woodruff, Thomas M., 120
Woods, C. R., 74
Woods, James, 378, 447
Wool, John, 18
Wooley, Lieutenant Colonel, 266
Wooster, Robert, 466-67
Wooten, Sidney C., xix, 142, 144, 153, 157, 167-69, 171-72, 445
Worth, William, 34, 39-46, 48-50
Worth, Katie, 479
Wyman, Willard G., 145-46, 162, 169
Young, Floyd, 334-35
Young, 2LT James, 200
Young, SP4 James, 344
Young, Kermit, 193
Young, Marvin Rex, 335, 351, 353, 388
Young, Samuel, 121

Zebrowski, Edward, 147, 165, 169-70, 469
Zedillo, Ernesto, 48
Zimmerman, David R., 471

INDEX OF SUBJECTS

Abra Province, 121, 123
Abu Ghraib, 411
AC-47 flare ship, 346
AC-47 Gooneybird, 363
Adobe Walls, TX, 75
Aerial reaction force (ARF), 404
Afghan National Army, 407
Afghan national election, 402
Air Force EC-130, 433
Al Karama, 434
Al Qaeda, 398-99, 432, 442
Al Wahda, 430, 434
Albu Sayf, 426-28
Albuquerque, NM, 63
Aloha, Sherman tank, 239
Alsace-Lorraine, 149
Altach, 162
Altdor, 151
American Expeditionary Force, 132
AN/PRC radio, 273
Andernach-on-the-Rhine, 133
Anderson Air Force Base, 382
Anjong-ni, 210
Ansar al-Sunnah Army, 419
Antelope Hills, 77
Anti-coalition forces, Afghan (ACF), 399
Anti-coalition militia (ACM), 400
Anti-Iraqi Forces (AIF), 412
Antwerp, 135
Ap Binh D, 340
Ap Binh Tay, 321
Apache Canyon, 61, 68
Arickaree Creek, 73
Arij, 423, 434

Arizona, Dept of, 112
Arkansas Territory, 23
Army Superior Unit Award, 396
Army Training Tests, 305, 307, 309, 311
Augsburg, 170
Australia, 141, 385, 440
Austria, 164-5, 170
Bad Axe River, 31
Bagambang, 125
Baghdad International Airport, 411
Bagupan, 125
Bahguchar Valley, xxx, 407
Balad Air Base, 421, 442
Balikatan 2008, 440
Balikatan Flash, 383
Bannock Indians, 108
Bao Trai, 322
Baqubah, xxxi, 442
Bark Creek, MT, 91
Barrio Quiom, 122
Batac, 122
Battle Butte, 94-5, 98
Bau Co, 347
Bayreuth, 158-59
Bear Paw Mountains, 103
Bear Springs, NM, 59
Belem Causeway, 50
Ben Cui, vii, xxiv, 347-349, 352-354, 452, 475
Ben Muong River, 316
Bernal Springs, NM, 67
Beum Foo Yun, 176
Bismarck, ND, 114
Bitche, xviii, 150-51
Black Buttes, MT, 87

Black Hills, 83
Black Rock, NM, 59
Bloody Gulch, 185 – 191, 204
Bloody Ridge, 268
Bobcats Lair, 385
Boi Loi, 322-23, 331, 336, 343, 356
Boys Town, Korean, 298-99, 473
Bowleg's Town, FL, 57
Bradley fighting vehicle, 393
Brazos River, 55-56
Breitenbaum, 156
Brest, 133
Broadway, Mosul, 432-33
Brownstown, MI, 6
Bubonic plague, 362
Bucay, 122
Budingen, 155-56
Buena Vista, 42
Bulalo, Cabanatuan, 124
Burlington Heights, ONT, 9
California column, 69
Camas Prairie, ID
Cambodia, 329, 371-374
Camp Beauregard, LA, 132
Camp Carroll, 207
Camp Cold Water, 26
Camp Cottonwood Creek, KS, 73
Camp David Accords, 396
Camp Davidson, KS, 73
Camp Detroit, 6
Camp Devens, 136, 309
Camp Drake, 301
Camp Fallujah, 412-13
Camp Fremont, CA, 131
Camp Frenzell-Jones, 375-76
Camp Funston, 309
Camp Greaves, 389-90
Camp Gregg, 125
Camp Ho'omaluhia, 386
Camp Hovey, 391-393
Camp Howze, 393-94
Camp Jackson, 141
Camp Kaiser, 262-63
Camp Kilmer, NJ, 145
Camp Meade, MD, 133
Camp Old Gold, 147-48
Camp Page, 383, 386
Camp Roberts, CA, 144
Camp Robinson, NE, 101
Camp Striker, 411
Camp Supply, 76-77
Camp Taji, 411
Camp Van Dorn, MS, 141
Camp Victory, 412
Camp Weld, 67
Camp Zachary Taylor, KY, 133
campaign plan, U.S. forces in Vietnam, 314-15
Campaña Mountain, 141
Canadian River, 55, 77
Cantigny, army transport, 135
Canyon de Chelly, NM, 39
Capitan, NM, 59
Carroll, MT, 89
Casa Mata, 49
Cau Sang, 341
Cedar Creek campaign, 85, 104, 448-452
Cehar Cine/Osay District, 407
Central Command, 379, 398
Cerralvo, 39
Cerro Gordo, 33, 44, 48
CH-47 helicopter, 390
Changjin Reservoir, 212
Changson, 238
Chapultapec, 49-50, 454-457

Index of Subjects

Charlie, mascot lion, xxiii, 306-307
Charlie, black Labrador, 386
Chateauguay River, 10
chemical weapons laboratory, 434
Chesapeake, USN frigate, 3
Chicago, 30, 113, 116-17, 126, 355
Chieu Hoi, 326
Chindong-ni, 180-85, 188, 192, 196
claymore mine, Chinese, 369
Chingu-Masan Corridor, 181
Chinju Pass, 182, 185, 188-90, 267
Chinook helicopter, 407-408
Chipo-ri, 283, 295, 300
Chippewa River, 12-15, 19-20, 23, 26
Chiricahua Apaches, 61, 69
Chisong-ni, 275
chogi bearers, 192, 246, 257, 303
Chongchon River, 212, 216
Chora, 402
Chorrera, 141
Chorwon Valley, 295
Chrysler's Farm, ONT, 12
Chuktae Valley, 249, 254, 395
Chunchon, 263, 383, 386
Churubusco, 45-48, 71, 114, 455, 457-58
Chusca Valley, NM, 60
Citizen's Military Training Camp, 136
Ciudad Camargo, 39
Civil Affairs Team, 328, 417, 422, 426
Civilian Conservation Corps, 138

Clark's Fork, MT,
Clear Creek,, 85
Clear Fork Valley, 56
Coblenz arms competition, 134
Coburg, 156-7
Columbia, The Dept of, 105, 110
Columbus, GA, 144-5
Combat Support Company, 309-10, 377-78, 381, 385, 387
Constabulary, South Korea, 173
Convento de Churubusco, 47
Cornwall, ONT, 11
Corpus Christi, TX, 34
C-rations, 141
Criminal Court of Iraq, 432
Cross Timbers, OK, 31
Crow Indians, 94, 96-7, 108, 110, 112
Cuban Occupation, Army of, 128
Cu Chi, 315, 317, 320-324, 326-7, 329, 3442-47, 354, 356-8, 360, 364-65, 367, 369-70, 375, 449
Czech soldiers, 159
Dagat, 122
Danube River, 160-162
Datu of Binadayan, 124
Dau Tieng, xxiv, 339, 347-49, 352-54, 356-57
Deadwood, 112
Death Valley, vi, 237, 255
Defoliant, 323-24
Deh Rahwoud, 402
Demilitarized Zone, Korea, 299, 389-392, 478
Detroit, MI, 6, 22
digital warefare, 395-96
Dilia, NM, 59
Dining facility explosion, 419

Distinguished Unit Citation, 189, 204, 267, 294, 470
Diyala Province, 441-43, 480
Dodge City, KS, 75
Domis, 424
Einhausen, 156
Elk River, 101
Elm Creek, 56
Eltheim, 162,
Empire, Panama, 130
Engers, 135
Enns River, 164, 167
Enterprise, steamship
Ering, 164
Ernsthofen, 168
Estrada Tank Range, 282
Exercise Dhanarajata, 310
Exercise MIKI, 175-76
Exercise Quick Release, 311
Expert Infantryman Badge, 440
Fallujah, 411-13
Farm Line, 267
Farnsworth Trophy, 139
Federacion Ridge, 40
Fifth Infantry Soldier Chorus, 171
Filhol, 320, 335, 343-44
Fire Base Foche, 330
Fire Base Pershing, 330
Fire Support Base Devins, 367-9
Fire Support Base Janet, 335
Fire Support Base Patton, 359, 364
Five o'clock Follies, 326
FOB Aggies, 413-14, 418, 420, 425, 431
FOB Anaconda, xxx, 400-401, 404
FOB Cobra, 406-7

FOB Marez, 413, 415, 418-20, 423, 425, 430, 435
FOB Ripley, 406-407
FOB Sykes, 416-7, 420
FOB Warhorse, 442, 480
Fort Arbuckle, 55, 57, 465
" Armstrong, 22
" Assinniboine, 112
" Barrancas, FL, 112
" Bascom, 72
" Belknap, xvi, 56, 59
" Benning, 144, 302
" Benton, MT, 103
" Bliss, 63, 69, 114, 443
" Brady, 30-31
" Bridger, 58
" Brown, 114
" Buchanan, 60-61
" Buford, 84, 90, 111-12
" Carson, CO, 142, 305, 309
" Craig, xvi, 63-64, 69-70
" Crawford, 23-24, 27-28, 31
" Custer, 112
" Davis, 114-15, 131
" Dearborn, 30-31
" Defiance, 60
" Devens, 136, 309
" Dix, 172
" Dodge, 75, 466
" Ellis, 112
" Erie, 12, 15-16, 18-20
" Ethan Allen, 137-38
" Fauntleroy, 59-60
" George, 9-10
" Gibson, 53, 55-56, 464
" Greely, 304
" Hancock, 114
" Harker, 74
" Hays, 74

Index of Subjects

" Howard, 23, 27, 30-31
" Irwin, 396
" Keogh, iii, xiv, 83-109, 115, 466, 481
" Kobbe, 377-78
" Lawton, 301
" Leavenworth, 31, 79-81, 116-117, 128, 384
" Lewis, v, 175, 301-305, 378, 395-399, 409, 431-437, 479-480
" Lincoln, 107
" Lyon, 73
" Mackinac, 30
" Malden, 7
" Marion, 79
" Massachusetts, NM, 58
" McIntosh, 53, 57, 114, 464
" McKinley, 136
" McPherson, 117
" Meigs, 22
" Merrill, 53
" Moreau, 17
" Peck, 86
" Phantom Hill, 56
" Pitt, ix
" Point, Galveston, 119
" Polk, 396
" Preble, xviii, 136, 138, 244-6
" Quitman, 70
" Ramon Magsaysay, 441
" Reynolds, 73
" Richardson, 302
" Riley, 73, 308-309
" Ringgold, 114
" Sam Houston, 116-117
" Schlosser, 13
" Scott, 17
" Shaw, 112
" Sheridan, 120, 379
" Sill, 79
" Smith, 53-55
" Snelling, xiii, 23, 27, 29-32, 302, 463, 483
" St. Philip, 119
" Stanton, 59
" Sullivan, 116
" Sumner, 70-72
" Thorn, 69
" Towson, 53
" Vincennes, 6
" Wainwright, 441
" Wallace, 73
" Washita, 56
" Wayne, 22
" Wilkins, 33
" Williams, 136
" Wingate, 70
" Winnebago, 30-31
" Wise, 67
Fortress Sherenbreitstein, 135
Fox Hill, 182
Fox Indians, 30
Fox River, 23
French Fort, 330
Friesman, 165
Fulda, 156
Furth, 306
Garand rifle, 141
Gatling gun, 75, 363
General Terry, 114
Germaine incident, 78-79
Germersheim, 151, 153-54
Ghazni Province, 399-400
Ghent, Treaty of, 17, 20
Gia Dinh Province, 330
Gimlets, 21st Inf, 388
Giong Viec, 364

• 501 •

Gizab District, 401
Glendive Creek, 84-5
Glengarry Fencibles, 19
Go Dau Ha, 325
Goetzenbruck, 150
Gold Mine Trail, 231, 235
Gray Army Airfield, 437
Green Bay, WI, 20, 23
Greussen, 159
Guam, 120, 381-82, 394, 477, 479
Guardpost Oullette, 392
Gunskirchen Lager, 165-67, 169
Haag, 159
Haman, 188, 192
Hammam al Alil, 413-14, 418, 421-23, 426-7, 429, 431, 434
Hampton Roads, VA, 3
Han River, 220, 224, 299, 384
Hanau, 155
Han-Tan-Chon Valley, 284
Hastings, MN, 26
Hatch's Ranch, 59
Hau Nghia Province, 324, 449
Hawaii Calls, Sherman tank, 238
Hazarans, 401
Heartbreak Ridge, 268, 274
Helena, MT, 112
Helena, steamboat, 114
Helmand River, 407
hemorrhagic fever, 296
Henry, repeating rifle, 85
Hill 121, 201, 203
Hill 140, 198, 206-207
Hill 154, 198
Hill 160, 199-201
Hill 178, 201, 203
Hill 192, 242
Hill 255, 183
Hill 256, xx
Hill 268, 197-201, 203-204
Hill 303, 203
Hill 342, 181, 184
Hill 378, 261-262
Hill 412, 285
Hill 475, 221
Hill 476, 221
Hill 489, 284
Hill 533, 284-85
Hill 622, 212
Hill 633, 249-50
Hill 734, 245-246
Hill 752, 231
Hill 772, 281
Hill 795, 228, 273
HMS Confiance, 18
HMS Leopard, 3
Ho Chi Minh Trail, 329
Hoboken, NJ, 133
Ho Bo Woods, 319-20, 322-3, 332, 343, 425
Hoc Mon, 339-342, 344, 347
Honolulu Marathon, 385, 406
Hootches, 334
Horbach, 164
Hotchkiss gun, 111
Humera, 424
Hunkpapa Sioux, 83
Hunter Liggett Military Reservation, 134, 142
Huntsville Prison, 78
Hurricane Iwa, 384
IED, 402-403, 406-7, 416, 423-25, 429-30, 432-33
III Corps Tactical Zone, 315
Ichon, 221
Inchon, 175, 197, 203, 209, 263-264

Index of Subjects

Independencia Hill, 40
Indian Territory, 31, 53, 55, 75-6, 107
Information Operations Team, 417, 424
Inje, 266, 296
Inn River, 164, 167
Insurrection, Philippine, 116-131, 467
Isar River, 163
Jackson Heights, 295
Jalapa, 44-45, 48, 52
Javelin Anti-tank weapon, 399
Jeep, 141, 167, 171, 187, 218, 233, 235, 254, 276, 326, 384
Jefferson Barracks, 27
Johnson Administration, 348
Johnson Barracks, 306
Kabul, 400, 406
Kahuku Training Area, 311-12
Kampong Province, 374
Kampong Trach, 372-73
Kandahar, 400, 402, 405-408
Kanggu-dong, 234
Kapyong, 243
Karmah, 412-13
Katum, 327, 373
Khas Uruzgan, 402
Kilpatrick, Army troopship, xvii, 125
Kiowa Indians, 59
Kit Carson Scout, 373
Knickerbocker, troopship, 119
Kogan-ni, 189
Koje-do, 262-266, 301
Korean National Assembly, 391
Korean Service Corps, 263, 276, 303
Krag-Jorgensen rifle, 119
Krotensee, 159
Kumchon, 205-208
Kumsong River, 255, 297
Kumsong Salient, 295
Kumwha Valley, 227, 284
Kunu-ri, 212-13
Kusong, 180, 211
Kuwait, 408, 435-36, 441
La Colle Mill, 11-12
Lafayette, IN, 4
Laguna Province, 123-24, 449
Lake Champlain, 10, 17-18, 129
Lake Erie, 12
Lake Huron, 23
Lake Lanao, 124, 137
Lake Michigan, 23
Lake Ontario, 12
Lake Shore Docks, 126-127
Lake Winnebago, 23
Lakota Sioux, 93, 95, 97
Lambach, 164-65, 167
Land's End, SC, 119
Landau, 151
Lapwai Reservation, 107
Las Calitas, NM, 60
Las Guasimas, Cuba, 117
Lavarack Barracks, Australia, 385
Le Havre, France, 146
Lee Barracks, 307
Legion of the U.S., x
Lemburg, 150
Lenning, 149
Liederscheidt, 150
Line Lincoln, 231
Line Minnesota, 268, 274, 276, 282-83, 302
Line Missouri, 254, 257, 260, 262, 283-85, 295

Line Polar, 252-254
Line Utah, 227
Line Wyoming, 244-46, 248-49, 284-86
Lingenfeld, 151-54, 162
Little Big Horn River, 83
Lobos Island, 43
Long Binh, 375
Long Khanh Province, 374
Ludwigschafen, 154
Lundy's Lane, 13-14, 34, 136, 409, 463
Lyons Creek, ONT, 18-19
M-132 flame thrower, 358
M-14 rifle, 307
M-561 Gamma Goat, 387
M-72 LAW, anti-tank weapons, 350
M-79 grenade launcher, 347
M-119, Personnel Carrier, xli
Maguage, 6-7
Maine Stein Song, 137
Mainz, 307
Manila, 121-22, 125
Margunday, 402
Masan, 181, 191
Masogu-ri, 239
Matamoros, 35-36, 39, 47
Mayen, 135
McClellan Creek, TX, 78
Meals, Ready to Eat (MRE), 387
Mechanized battalion, origin of, 311
MEDCAP, 321, 367, 476
Menominee Indians, 22
Meritorious Unit Commendation, 408
Meuse-Argonne, 131, 468, 483
Mexican Revolution, 116
Mexico City, 44-45, 48-52

Miles City, MT, 101
Military Demarcation Line, Korea, 389
Military District 1, Luzon, 121
Military Transition Teams, 432
Milk River, 90, 109
Million Dollar Hill, 246-248
Mining, Austria, 164
Minneconjous Indians, 85
Minnesota River, 25
Mintraching, 163
Mirabad, 406
Missouri, Dept of, 83, 113, 115
Missouri River, 22, 31, 87, 90, 107, 110
Moana Loa, Sherman tank, 239
Moatengators, 378
Mobil Acquisition Counter-infiltration Element (MACE), 392
Mobile Force Maneuvers (1940), 140
Modoc Indians, 73
Molino del Rey, 48, 50-51, 53, 453-8
Monteith Barracks, 306
Monterrey, 39-42, 47, 51, 454
Montpelier flood, 138
Montreal, Quebec, 10
Mormons, 57-8
Moro, 124, 440
Mosul, 413-15, 417, 420-21, 423-25, 427-32, 434, 437, 443, 479
Mosul Times, 429
Mosul Today, 424
Mt. Maquiling, 124
Mt. Vernon Barracks, 116
Much'on-ni, 185
Muddy Creek, MT, 102

Index of Subjects

Naab River, 161
Naktong River, 196-97, 204-5, 470, 482
Naktong-ni, 181
Nam River, 190
Nancy, France, 149
Napoleon cannon, 84, 98
Narvacan, 122
Navajo Indians, 71
Niederglink, 168
Nash District, 406
Neu Isenberg, 154-55
Neuhafen, 154
Neustadt, 154
New Hope Cantonment, 25
New Zealand, 383
Nez Perce Indians, 103-108, 448
Niagara River, 9, 12-14, 16-18
Ninevah, 413, 434
Nixon Doctrine, 358
North Fort Lewis, 301-303
North Star Hill, 286
Northern Alliance forces, 398
Northern Pacific Railroad, 111
Nueces River, 36, 53
Nuevo Leon, 42
Nui Ba Dinh, 327
Nuremburg, 305
Objective Yoke, 246
Ochon, 225
Oglala Sioux, 83
O. H. Perry, keelboat, 27
Okchon, 208
Olympic Games, Korea, 392
Omaha, NE, 114
Operation Anvil, 427
" Applejack, 303
" Attleboro, 327
" Bold Lancer, 372
" Circle Pines, 319-20
" Clean Sweep, 317-19
" Coco Palms, 322-23
" Cutlass, 427
" Detonate, 242
" Enduring Freedom, 398
" Final Fury, 434
" Gyroscope, 305
" Iraqi Freedom, 408, 433, 438, 441
" Killer, 224
" Killington, 430
" Lightning Freedom, 404
" Lightning Resolve, 400
" Makiki, 322
" Moosehorn, 304
" New Life, 381
" Octopus Squeeze, 421
" Ranger, 295
" Ripper, 225
" Rolling Thunder, 355
" Snowshoe, 430
" Team Spirit, xxix, 382-83, 386, 391-394
Operations Base Lynch, 374
Opportune Journey "84, 385
Oriental River, 332-33
Outpost Harry, vi, xxi, 283, 285-87, 290-94, 472, 483
P'o-hang, 181
PAC BOND xxviii, 4, 385
Pacora, 141
Paekchon, 209
Paiute Indians, 73
Palestine neighborhood, 424-25, 427-28, 431-32, 434, 442
Palo Alto, TX, 36-38, 54
Pampa, TX, 78
Panama, xxvii, 130-32, 139-41, 175, 377-79, 447
Pandangdong-ni, 249

Panmunjom, 257, 274, 390, 392
Pansong-ni, 189-90
Paraiso, 140-41
Parañaque, 122
Paris Peace Accords, 376
Park Chung-hee, 391
Parrott gun, 75
Pashtuns, 401
Paso de Ovejas, 45
Paw Prints, 428, 434, 482
Pedregal, 46
Pegnitz, 159
Pentomic reorganization, 305-306
Perote, 44
Pfatter, 163
Phenix City, AL, 144-45
Phu Hoa Dong, 319-20
Phuoc My, 364, 366, 369
Picacho Peak, AZ, 69
Picnic Island, FL, 119
Pidigan, 122
Piña, Panama, 141
Piña Station, TX, 114
Pine Ridge Reservation, 115
Pisi-gol, 233-238, 462
Plattsburgh Barracks, 126, 129
Pohakoloa Training Area, xxviii, 311-12, 381, 385
Point system, WWII rotation, 170-71
Pongam-ni, 185, 187
Poplar River, 109-10
Porcupine Creek, 109
Porcupine River, 90-91
Portage, WI, 30
Portland, ME, 135-138, 140
Prairie du Chien, WI, 22-23, 25, 29
Prairie Traveler, 59

Presidential Unit Citation, Ben Cui, 353
Prophet's Town, 4
PSYOPS, 429
Puebla, 44-45
Puente Nacional, 45, 48
Puerto Rican recruits, 303
Pukhan River, 242
Pukhan Valley, 239
Punch Bowl, xxi, 266, 268, 274, 276, 281-82, 287
Pusan Perimeter, 181, 187-88, 192, 194, 196-97, 209
Qabr Abd, 416, 421, 427, 431
Queenstown Heights, NY, 13
Ram-ji-do, 299
Red River, 56-7
Red River War, 72-73, 75, 77, 79, 81, 466
Redwater Creek, MT, 92
Redwater, MT, 110
Regen River, 161
Regensburg, 162
Regenstauf, 161
Regimental crest, 136
Republican River, 73
Resaca de la Palma, 37, 54, 62, 453-7
Rheingoheim, 154
Rhine, 133, 135, 151, 153-55
Rickenbergershif, 151
Rifle range scandal, 128
Rinconada Pass, 41
Rio Grande, 35-37, 39, 42-43, 45, 53, 64, 69, 116
Rio Hato, 141
Rock Island, IL, 24
Rodach, 157
Rodman gun, 98
Rodriquez Range, 393

INDEX OF SUBJECTS

Rome plow, 333, 335, 356, 358, 361
Roppeweiller, 150
Rosebud Creek, 109
Rosebud River, 83
Rotary Red, 285
Rottenbach, 157
Route Minneapolis, 424, 432
Route Santa Fe, 421
Route Tampa (Hwy 1), 414
Route Toyota North, 426
RSOI exercise, 394
Ruchingen, 155
Ruff Puffs, 364-65, 367
Rumbold Trophy Shoot, 139
Rush Springs, OK
Saar-Moselle Triangle, 153
Sac Indians, 22, 30-31
Sacket's Harbor, NY, 8-9
Saigon, 314-15, 330, 335, 337-38, 340, 343-45, 348-9, 367, 369, 425
Saigon River, 335, 343, 345, 348, 367, 369
Sairamon, 426
Salaam Village, 418
Salamiyah, 424, 427
Saline Valley, KS, 73
Salmunster, 156
Saltillo, 40-42
Salzburg Music Festival, 171
San Cosme Road, 50
San Dong Boys Town, 299
San Juan River, 40
San Luis Potosí, 42
Sanctuary Counter-Offensive, 371
Sandwich, ONT, 6
Sangdong, 262-63
Sangre de Cristo Mountains, 67

Sans Arc Indians, 85
Santa Catarina River, 41
Santa Fe, NM, 66, 69
Santa Fe, Tlaxcala, 51
Santa Fe Trail, 31, 63
Santa Lucia Mountains, 143
Santiago, Cuba, 119-20
Saranac River, 17
Saratoga, frigate, 17
Saratoga, troop transport, 119
Sault Ste. Marie, MI, 30
Schifferstadt, 154
Schofield Barracks, vi-vii, 175-77, 226, 302, 310-11, 382, 386, 394-95, 397, 408, 479, 481
Schu mines, 150
Schwandorf, 161
Schwegenheim, 151
SCR-300 radio, 199
Sea Girt, NJ, 128
Seminole War, 57
Seoul, 174, 197, 220, 225, 231, 239, 298-99, 391
Shamsyat, 428
Sharps, repeating rifle, 98
Shawnee Indians, 3
Shazaman High School, 403
Shoalwater Bay, Australia, 440
Shoshone Indians, 108
Sibley tent, 84
Siegfried Line, 151
Sierra Madre Mountains, 112
Sihanoukville, 371
Silesian Brigade, 133
Silver City, ID, 108
Sinai Peninsula, 396
Sinanju, 210, 212
Skyline Drive, 276
Snake Creek, 103, 105

Sobuk-san, 185, 192-96, 450
Sokcho-ri, 266
Solomon Valley, KS, 73
Somer, 424
Songnae-dong, 294
Soojihachon, 248
Sopa, 232, 236-37
Sotey, 374
Soyang-gang River, 267
Spanish American War, 113
Spanish influenza, 132
Spencer carbine, 76
Springfield rifle, M-1903, 127
St. Anthony, Falls of, 23, 26
St. Augustine, FL, 116
St. Francis Barraccks, 116
St. Laurent en Caux, 147-48
St. Louis les Bitche, 150
St. Patrick's Battalion, See San Patricio's Battalion
Standing Rock Reservation, 115
Star Hill, 285-86,
Star Mass, 290, 295
Star Ridge, 293
Station 4 West, 414
Steiner, 167
Steyr, xix, 167-170
Stoney Creek, ONT, 9
Storch observation plane, 168
Straits of Mackinac, 23
Straubing, 163
Stryker variants, 439
Stryker vehicle, 423, 440
Subuk-san, 221, 223
Suez Canal, 126
Sultan of Bayan, 124
Sulzbach-Rosenberg, 160
Sulzfeld, 157
Tactical Operations Center, 395
Tacubaya, 48, 51

Taechon, 211
Taegu, 195-97
Taejon-ni, 185, 187
Taji, 411, 413
Tal A'far, 416, 420, 425, 429-430
Taliban, 398-400, 403, 406, 419
Tan Phu Trang, 328
Tan Son Nhut Air Force Base, 315, 339
Tapang Son, 329
Task Force Kean, 182, 189, 191-92
Task Force Olympia, 414
Tasuos, 372
Tay Ninh City, 329-30
Tay Ninh Province, 329
Tayum, 122
Texas Panhandle, 75, 80
Thien Ngon, 372
Tigris River, 413-14, 421, 424, 427, 431
Tippecanoe Creek, 4
Tirin Kot, 400, 406
Tito, the bobcat, xxvi, 338-39
Tokkol-li, 283
Tongduchon, 391
Tongjang-ni, 209
Tongue River Cantonment, xiii, 84-86, 92, 101
Tongue River Valley, 94
Tonkin, Gulf of, 312, 314
Tonle Roti River, 329
Tortugas Island, 119
Tosan, 182-84
TO&E, D Series, 309
TOW anti-tank missile, 393
Traffic control point (TCP), xxxi, 414
Trang Bang, 344, 346, 367
Treadway bridge, 161

Index of Subjects

Treaty of Guadalupe Hidalgo, 52
Treaty of Medicine Lodge, 75
Trinidad, CO, 72
Trung Lap, 326-327, 345, 356-359, 361-366
Tub Town, 100
Tule Canyon, 56
Turner, Cheyenne talisman, 95
Tybee Island, 119
UH-60 Blackhawk helicopter, 407, 421
Uijongbu, vii, 218
Ukkalgye, 231
Um al-Rabi'ain (Mosul), 432
Unjimal, 228
USMTS General Gordon, 315
USS *Butner*, 308
USS *Chesapeake*, 3
USS *Eagle*, 17
USS *General Tasker H. Bliss*, 146
USS *Huron*, 43
USS *Maddox*, 312
USS *Maine*, 118
USS *Marine Phoenix*, 263
USS *Preble*, 17
USS *Saratoga*, 17
USS *Ticonderoga*, 17
USS *Whiltsie*, 195
USS *Yarmouth*, 141
Ute Indians, 72
Valorous Unit Award, 437-38
Valorous Unit Citation, 331
Valverde, 64, 67, 70
Vancouver Barracks, 110
Veracruz, 43-45, 48, 51-52
Vietnamization policy, 348, 355, 358
Vinh Loc, 344
Vosges Mountains, 149

Vung Tau, 315
Wabash River, 4-5
Waegwan, vi, 196-97, 200-208, 224, 471
Wall Creek, MT, 94
Walla Walla, WA, 111
Walschbronn, 151
War Zone C, 330, 349
Washita River, 55, 77
Wels, 164
Westheim, 151-52
Whigs, 34
Willow Creek, 109
Winchester, repeating rifle, 98
Winnebago Indians, 22
Winter Haze, exercise, 392, 478
Wolf Mountain, xiv, 92, 99, 101, 448-49, 451
Wonsan, 209-10
World Trade Center, 398
Worms, 155
Wounded Knee Creek, MT, 115
Xom Moi, 359
Xuan Loc, 374-375
Yakima Firing Range, 303
Yalu River, 210-212, 214, 470, 482
Yang-gu Valley, 283
Yangpyong, 225
Yellowstone River, 83-84, 86, 101, 103, 110
Yerville, 149
Yongsan, 211
York, ONT, 8
Yul-li, 217-218
Za'ab River, 424, 431
Zabol Province, 400

Index of Military Units

1st Air Cavalry Division, 371-372
1st Army Corps, 131, 216, 224
1st Australian Task Force, 375-76
1st Battle Group, 5th Infantry, 306-310
1st Cavalry Division, 196-197, 203-2-4, 347, 372, 376, 411
1st Colorado Volunteer Infantry, 67
1st Infantry Division, 131, 308-310, 378
1st Infantry Regiment, x, 53
1st Iraqi Intervention Forces Bn, 425
1st Marine Division, 197, 209, 231, 268
1st Marine Regiment, 412
1st New Mexico Volunteer Infantry, 64
1st Provisional Marine Brigade, 181
2nd Battalion, 504th PIR, 406
2nd Battle Group, 5th Infantry, 307-309
2nd BCT, 1st Cav, 411
2nd Cavalry Regiment, 58-60, 102, 104, 109, 111, 437, 441
2nd Division Band, 300
2nd Field Surgical Team, 407
2nd Infantry Division, 175-176, 181, 268, 295, 302-303, 390-391, 393, 437, 443, 481
2nd Squadron, 14th Cavalry, 412, 416, 432, 438

II NKPA Corps, 268
II ROK Corps, 215, 297
3rd US Army, 151, 155, 168, 299, 389
3rd Bn, 5th Infantry, Panama, 377
3rd Cavalry Regt, 59-60
3rd Engineer (C) Bn, 205
3rd Divarty, 285-86
3rd Infantry Div, 197, 283, 285-86, 295
3rd Infantry Regt, 132
III NKPA Corps, 268
III NKPA Div, 197
4th Bgde, 25th ID, 377
4th Cavalry Regt, 78, 310, 321, 353, 367, 370, 408
4th Infantry Div, 305, 395, 449
4th Infantry Regt, 5-7, 10, 17-18, 21, 128
4th New Mexico Vol Inf, 67
V Army Corps, 131, 307
5th Cavalry Regt, 197, 224, 412-13
5th Marine Regt, 182, 184
5th Provisional Training Co, 177
5th ROK Regiment, 133-5, 212
VI Army Corps, 155
6th Cavalry Regt, 112
6th Infantry Regt, 115, 123, 388
6th Iraqi Intervention Force, 428
6th Marine Regt, 400
6th NKPA Div, 181, 183, 187, 189, 194-95
6th ROK Div, 228-233, 238-39

Index of Military Units

6th SS Mountain Div, 228-233, 238-39
7th US Army, 149
7th ARVN Regt, 319
7th Cavalry Regt, 84, 101
7th Field Artillery Bn, 400
7th Infantry Div, 172-74, 197, 209, 335, 394
7th Infantry Regt, 61, 476, 484
7th Marine Regt, 412
7th Military Dept, 55
7th NKPA Div, 193
7th ROK Div, 212
VIII Army Corps, 120
8th US Army, 197, 283
8th Cavalry Regt, 197, 214, 443
8th FAB, 316, 318, 438
8th Infantry Div, 305-306, 308
8th Infantry Regt, 34, 38-9, 43, 113-114
8th Ranger Co, 232-233
8th ROK Div, 268
IX Army Corps, 133, 241, 248-49, 260, 284, 295, 301
9th Infantry Div, 305, 307, 386
9th Infantry Regt, 12-13, 304-305, 394
X Army Corps, 210, 212, 215, 266-7, 270, 281-82, 296
10th Cavalry Regt, 55, 74, 78
10th Iraqi Battalion, 418, 422-23
10th Mountain Div, 398-99, 411
"11th Cavalry", 102-111
11th Iraqi Battalion, 418, 422-23
XII Army Corps, 155

12th Armored Div, 151-53
12th Evacuation Hospital, 332, 342
13th FAB, 326
13th Infantry Regt, 9
13th NKPA Regt, 187
14th Armored Div, 159
14th Infantry Regt, 9
XV Army Corps, 149, 151
15th Cavalry Regt, 124
15th Infantry Regt, 113-114, 284-286, 295
15th NKPA Div, 272
16th Infantry Regt, 172
17th Infantry Regt, 172
18th Infantry Bgde, 136
19th BCT, Philippines, 280-81
19th Infantry Regt, 208-09, 220, 228-230, 233, 244-256, 260, 379, 383
19th ROK Regt, 230
20th CCF Army, 228
XXI Army Corps, 151
21st Infantry Regt, 13-16, 205-207, 227, 231-232, 236, 243, 251, 255-56, 260, 310, 388, 413-14, 438, 442
21st ROK Regt, 268
22nd Infantry Regt, 84, 92, 102, 305, 372
23rd Infantry Regt, 12, 16, 127, 216-17, 263, 295, 389, 411, 435
24th ARVN Regt, 335
24th Divarty, 256, 258
24th Division Band, 248
24th Infantry Div, 151, 203, 211, 214-218, 220, 229-232, 236, 239, 241, 243,

248, 251, 253, 255-56, 258, 260, 284, 318, 335, 383, 414, 424, 428, 438, 472
24th Infantry Regt, 188
24th Recon Company, 255-56
25th Infantry Div, 182, 187-92, 195-96, 214, 224, 267-68, 271, 273, 310, 314-15, 321, 331-33, 336, 348, 354, 362, 365, 374-75, 377, 379, 382, 385, 387, 394-95, 399, 400, 408-9, 413, 419, 437-438, 441, 443, 473, 476-77, 480-482
25th Infantry Regt, 14
26th Infantry Regt, 310
26th Infantry Scout Dog Platoon, 271
27th British Commonwealth Bgde, 220-221
27th Infantry Regt, 310, 316, 321, 324-5, 353
29th Infantry Regt, 132
31st Infantry Regt, 248-49, 391, 477, 483
32nd Infantry Regt, 173-4, 244
33rd Infantry Regt, 131, 173-4, 244
34th Armored Bgde, 341-344, 365
34th Infantry Regt, 142, 203, 341-2, 344, 365
35th Infantry Regt, 182, 189, 191, 263, 310, 366
37th Infantry Regt, 74
40th Infantry Div, 261, 273

40th Infantry Regt, 20
40th Recon Co, 275
41st Infantry Div, 131

45th Infantry Div, 280, 283, 296, 298
48th US Volunteers, 123
49th ARVN Regt, 317
50th Infantry Regt, 133-5
50th NKPA Regt, 270
61st Infantry Regt, 305
62nd ROK Regt, 281
64th FAB, 268
65th Engineers, 268, 311-312, 316, 318, 320, 322
65th Infantry Regt, 284
66th Combat Tracker Team, 375
66th Infantry Regt, 142, 155, 159, 163-164
69th Armored Bn, 320-21
71st Infantry Div, iii, 140-143, 145, 147-49, 151, 153, 155, 157, 159, 161-163, 165-173, 175, 302-305, 469
71st Recon Company, 169
71st Signal Company, 302
72nd Engineer (C) Company, 174, 179, 192, 207, 266-67, 273, 302
73rd Engineer (C) Co. 433, 438
77th Infantry Div, 131
79th Field Artillery Regt, 305
83rd Mechanized NKPA Regt, 196
89th Infantry Div, 142-43
90th FAB, 187, 189
90th NKPA Regt, 270
91st Infantry Div, 131
92nd Searchlight Co, 268
100th Infantry Division, 149
101st Airborne Division, 305, 398, 414
102nd Iraqi Battalion, 427

Index of Military Units

103rd CCF Regt, 260
103rd Infantry Div, 154
103rd Iraqi Battalion, 428
104th Infantry, 156
105th NKPA Armored Div, 205
125th Military Intelligence Bn, 400
132nd Regional Forces Company, 364, 369
158th FAB, 298
158th Infantry Regt, 141
160th Infantry Regt, 262
172nd Stryker BCT, 433
191st CCF Regt, 240
196th Light Infantry Bgde, 329
220th CCF Regt, 284
221st CCF Regt, 284
223rd Infantry Regt, 262, 273-76
224th Infantry, 262
271st Engineer (C) Bn,
410th Infantry Regt, 154
453rd Engineer Bn, 265
503rd Air Assault Infantry, 393
506th Air Assault Infantry, 393
536th CCF Regiment, 296
554th Engineer Bn, 365
555th Field Artillery Bn, 174-5, 179-80, 184, 186-92, 207-208, 213, 218, 228, 231-33, 237, 266, 268, 279-80, 282-284, 286, 289, 293-298, 300-302, 304
564th FAB, 144
581st Anti-tank Battery, 144
849th NKPA Independent AT Regt, 206
8137th Military Police Group, 263-4

8292nd Post Engineers, 177
Capital ROK Div, 296
Clarke's Brigade, 46
Columbian Battalion, 252
Ethiopian Battalion, 249
Greek Expeditionary Force, 283, 294, 295
Imperial German Army, 132
Iraqi National Guard, 412, 415, 419
May's Dragoons, 38
Multinational Force, Sinai
Phu Loi VC Regt, 350
Ringgold's Battery, 35
San Patricio Battalion, 46-48
Turkish Brigade, 268, 271

www.ingramcontent.com/pod-product-compliance
Lightning Source LLC
Chambersburg PA
CBHW071552080526
44588CB00010B/876